ROUTLEDGE LIBRARY EDITIONS: LACAN

Volume 5

JACQUES LACAN

JACQUES LACAN
An Annotated Bibliography
Vol. I

MICHAEL CLARK

Routledge
Taylor & Francis Group

LONDON AND NEW YORK

First published in 1988

This edition first published in 2014
by Routledge
2 Park Square, Milton Park, Abingdon, Oxfordshire OX14 4RN

and by Routledge
711 Third Avenue, New York, NY 10017

First issued in paperback 2015

Routledge is an imprint of the Taylor & Francis Group, an informa business

British Library Cataloguing in Publication Data
A catalogue record for this book is available from the British Library

ISBN: 978-0-415-72851-5 (Set)
ISBN 13: 978-1-138-97348-0 (pbk)
ISBN 13: 978-0-415-73238-3 (hbk)

Publisher's Note
The publisher has gone to great lengths to ensure the quality of this book but
points out that some imperfections from the original may be apparent.

Disclaimer
The publisher has made every effort to trace copyright holders and would
welcome correspondence from those they have been unable to trace.

JACQUES LACAN

An Annotated Bibliography

Vol. I

Michael Clark

GARLAND PUBLISHING, INC.
NEW YORK & LONDON
1988

Library of Congress Cataloging-in-Publication Data

Clark, Michael, 1950-
Jacques Lacan–an annotated bibliography/Michael Clark.
p. cm.–(Garland reference library of the humanities; vol. 526)
Includes indexes.
ISBN 0-8240-8848-4 (alk. paper)
1. Lacan, Jacques, 1901- –Bibliography.   2. Psychoanalysis-
-Bibliography.   I. Title.   II. Series
Z8469.39.C58 1988
[BF109.L28]
016.15019'--dc19   87-30454

Printed on 250-year-life, acid-free paper
Manufactured in the United States of America

GENERAL EDITOR'S INTRODUCTION

The Garland Bibliographies of Modern Critics and Critical Schools series is intended to provide bibliographic treatment of major critics and critical schools of the twentieth century. Each volume includes an introduction that surveys the critic's life, career, influence, and achievement, or, in the case of the volumes devoted to a critical school, presents an account of its central figures, origins, relation to other critical movements and trends, and the like.

Each volume is fully annotated and contains listings for both primary and secondary materials. The annotations are meant to be ample and detailed, in order to explain clearly, especially for a reader coming to a critic or critical school for the first time, the point and purpose of a book or essay. In this sense, the bibliographies are also designed to be critical guides. We hope that the volumes will inform and stimulate the reader even as they give basic information about what material exists and where it may be located.

We have tried to include as many of the most important critics and critical schools in this series as possible, but some have been omitted. Some critics and critical schools have already received (or are in the process of receiving) adequate treatment, and we see no need to duplicate the efforts of others.

WILLIAM E. CAIN
Wellesley College

Table of Contents

Indexes

Preface

This bibliography lists and describes works by and about Jacques Lacan published in French, English, and seven other languages including Japanese and Russian. It incorporates and corrects where necessary all information from all earlier published bibliographies of Lacan's work, including Joël Dor's *Bibliographie des travaux de Jacques Lacan* (Paris: InterEditions, 1983, 207 pages); and it includes all information about Lacan's published work on record in the Bibliothèque de l'Ecole de la Cause freudienne. Also included as background works are books and essays that discuss Lacan in the course of a more general study, as well as all relevant items in various bibliographic sources from many fields. (The sources most useful for this bibliography are listed after the preface.)

Works by Lacan are listed as Primary Works and arranged chronologically. Works about Lacan are listed as Secondary Works and arranged alphabetically by the author's name. Background Works are also arranged alphabetically. There are four indexes: name, article, book and journal title, and topic. Alphabetical lists of Lacan's works (including titles of all translations) appear at the beginning of the indexes for books and for articles. A list of Lacan's works that have been translated into English appears in the Index of Topics under "Lacan."

The following account of works by and about Lacan in French and English may therefore be considered fully comprehensive, though current methods of indexing and the rapidly increasing number of publications on Lacan's work make inadvertent omissions inevitable. In addition, over 2,500 other items tangentially related to Lacan's work in French, English, and other languages were identified during the course of research for this book. While their relevance to the bibliography is obvious, including them all would have expanded the volume to an unmanageable length, so the listings of works in other languages and the sections on background works are selective and note only the more influential and representative items in those categories.

The work of Jacques Lacan presents special problems for the bibliographer. A great deal of material has been published under Lacan's name, but very little of it was actually written by Lacan for publication. Apart from his thesis and a few articles, many of the items included in this bibliography as "Primary Works" are in fact transcripts from recordings, shorthand records, or notes of oral presentations delivered by Lacan at conferences or in the seminars he conducted from 1953 to 1980. Some of these transcribed texts were authorized by Lacan and some not, and it is not always clear how closely Lacan reviewed those texts that he authorized. Other items, such as the descriptions of his early case reports or the abstracts of the seminars that have not been published, are even further removed from Lacan's hand. I have identified the source of each item as precisely as possible, but readers should beware that even this most fundamental category of "works by Lacan" is problematic to some extent and should be treated as an interpretation rather than a direct reflection of some self-evident group of texts.

The material presented below as "Secondary Works" is even more heterogeneous. It includes books and articles that are about Lacan or that discuss him at some length, but it does not include all of the books and articles that use concepts, terms, formulas, and topological figures introduced by Lacan. Such a list might very well include every work about psychoanalysis published in France since the 1950s, for Lacan's influence has been so pervasive that even works which seem to ignore him completely are, necessarily, engaged in a tacit polemic by that very silence. Nor does the list of secondary works include every article that mentions Lacan's name or that has been published in a journal sponsored by a group associated with Lacan. I have identified and described most of these journals in the section titled "Books About," but I have listed only items *by* Lacan that appeared in those journals and articles that focus exclusively on some aspect of Lacan's work. Furthermore, classifications into "secondary" and "background" works were not always obvious, so readers should check both sections (as well as the title indexes) when looking for a particular article.

Another kind of material related to Lacan's work has also been excluded from this bibliography. As of 1987, six of the 27 seminars have been published in book form by Editions du Seuil. The editor of these seminars, Jacques-Alain Miller, has published preliminary texts of several other seminars in the journal *Ornicar?*. Texts of the remaining seminars do exist, usually in the form of bound photocopies of typescripts that circulate privately (though widely) or that are sold through informal arrangements with bookstores. Of these texts that I have seen, none of them include information about the source of the text or about the editor and publisher, and few even note a place and date of printing. Consequently, their authority cannot be determined, and I have not listed them in the bibliography. For a description of these texts, their possible sources, and an account of the issues involved in their publication, see F358.

As these caveats suggest, the most elementary decisions regarding this presentation of Lacan's work have involved a considerable number of judgments beyond the usual problems of inclusion and exclusion inherent in any bibliography. To present Lacan's work in any form is to represent it within the terms of a specific reading that must take its own place within the rapidly evolving field of Lacanian studies. The authority of any bibliographical reading, including this one, therefore must be earned through the tests of utility and insight to which any reading should be subjected, and it should not be offered or accepted under the guise of a specious empiricism that would disguise interpretation as simple description or disinterested enumeration.

To admit the interpretive dimension of these tasks is not, of course, to abdicate responsibility for accuracy and precision. I have noted as fully as possible the first place of publication for each text printed under Lacan's name, including the date, place, and occasion of its original presentation in the case of texts transcribed from oral sources. When the information was available, I have also reported the name of the person responsible for establishing the printed text, and I have provided a list of all translations and reprints. I have not, however, separately noted translations and reprints of articles included in *Ecrits* and translated and/or reprinted in various editions of that collection. For translations and reprints of these items, see the list of subsequent editions of A2. If these items have been translated and/or reprinted somewhere other than in an edition of *Ecrits,* that information is noted as usual in the annotations.

The annotations that describe the items listed in this bibliography attempt to render the central points of Lacan's remarks as accurately as is feasible in such brief sketches. The annotations themselves are only a general description of the items and are intended to direct readers to the original texts. (I have quoted from published translations where available; other translations are my own.) Some selection and distortion is inevitable in any description, of course, and this problem is especially acute with Lacan's work. Even in most of his written texts Lacan deliberately avoided ordinary expository argument in favor of an elliptical, paronomastic style that resembles the associative structure of extemporaneous speech and the vagaries of informal diction and phrasing. The annotations do attempt to replicate the general structure of Lacan's presentations, but I have noted and explained Lacan's puns and unusual phrasing only where they make a point that Lacan does not make elsewhere in the text in a more straightforward form.

The difficulties of Lacan's discourse become especially acute in works produced during the last two decades of his career, which are frequently based on "mathemes" and topological figures such as the Klein bottle and the Borromean knot. While Lacan was always careful to point out that such devices cannot function without the discourse in which they are embedded, the opposite is true as well, and his remarks about these figures do not simply paraphrase the diagrams. Consequently, even so modest a goal as identifying the salient points in one of these essays not only generalizes Lacan's highly specific vocabulary but also introduces the rhetoric of expository argument in conjunction with texts that are deliberately conceived as foreign, if not hostile, to that discourse. Special figures such as these topological forms, occasional typographical oddities, and the various graphs and diagrams Lacan used throughout his career have not been reproduced in the annotations, though they are described and their importance noted. Readers should beware that one of the most common terms, designated by Lacan as "l'objet petit *a*" or more simply "l'objet *a*," appears in this bibliography as "*l'objet a*" because foreign words are underlined and so cannot be distinguished from the "*a*" in Lacan's printed text.

In addition to the major categories of "Primary Works," "Secondary Works," and "Background Works," this bibliography is divided further into the following sections. The section headings are generally self-explanatory, but note the following special policies:

Primary Works

Section A. Includes Lacan's thesis (the only book-length work he published) and collections of his essays, conference papers, and interviews. The essays in these collections are listed and annotated separately in the appropriate sections. Seminars published in book form are listed in Section B. The items in this section are arranged chronologically by date of publication.

Section B. Includes Lacan's seminars from 1953 to 1980, with titles and places of publication for any part of the seminar or abstract of the whole that was published for public distribution. When several abstracts by different authors have appeared in various journals, all of these items are listed and significant differences among them noted. Xeroxed typescripts and other records of unpublished seminars are not listed. The items in this section are arranged chronologically by date of presentation or composition.

Section C. Includes essays Lacan wrote for publication and transcripts of conference papers published for public distribution. These items are arranged chronologically by date of presentation or composition.

Section D. Includes translations, reviews, and prefaces by Lacan for texts by other authors, as well as prefaces and afterwords for collections of his own work. The exception to this rule is the apparatus for *Ecrits,* which is listed and annotated in Section A for reasons I explain in that note. The items in this section are arranged chronologically by date of composition.

Section E. Includes case reports, interviews, discussions at conferences, and letters that were printed for public distribution. The annotations for this section describe only what Lacan said in an interview or discussion, except where noted. These items are arranged chronologically by date of presentation or composition.

Section F. Includes books and collections of essays about Lacan and special issues of general journals. I have also listed and described journals that regularly publish articles related to Lacan, such as those associated with psychoanalytic groups influenced by his work. These items are arranged alphabetically by the author's or editor's name except for special issues of journals, which are listed under the title of the journal.

Section G. Includes essays about Lacan. These items are arranged alphabetically by author's name.

Section H. Includes reviews of Lacan's work, grouped by the work being reviewed and arranged alphabetically within these groups by title of the journal in which the review appeared. If a review deals with more than one book, it is listed, numbered, and annotated under the book that is its main focus; it is listed without a number under the other books it discusses, with a cross-reference to the annotated entry. Unless otherwise noted, reviews are about editions in the language in which the review is written.

Section I. Includes dissertations that are about Lacan or that are based explicitly on Lacanian concepts and terms. These items are arranged alphabetically by author's name.

Section J. Includes miscellaneous items about Lacan such as comments and observations in newspapers, etc., arranged alphabetically by author's name or by title if published anonymously. Brief collections of comments by several people, such as obituary notices, are listed under the title of the journals in which they appear.

Section K. Includes books in which Lacan is discussed but is not the main topic, arranged alphabetically by author's name. I have not listed anthologies if they just reprint a single essay about Lacan; these anthologies are cited with full bibliographical information in the annotation to the essay that is reprinted in them.

Section L. Includes essays that mention Lacan in passing as well as many that discuss him at greater length. The annotations are intended to describe what an essay says about Lacan, not the essay as a whole. These items are arranged alphabetically by author's name.

Items are numbered continuously throughout, but each number is preceded by a capital letter locating the item in its appropriate section. No item is numbered twice; reprints are noted at the end of each annotation. However, items often associated with a section other than the one in which they are classified do appear twice: once with their number and annotation in the appropriate section, and again without a number or annotation in the section where readers might expect to find them. For example, Lacan's seminar sessions are numbered and annotated in Section B. However, many of them have appeared as articles, and I have listed them, without a number, in Section C, with a reference to their place in Section B. There are only two exceptions to the practice:

(1) Major collections of essays by and about Lacan are numbered as books, even when the essays themselves were originally published elsewhere and are listed and numbered separately. Annotations for such collections describe introductory essays and any other editorial apparatus, and they usually include a table of contents with cross-references to the essays themselves.

Occasionally, abstracts of seminars have been collected, translated, and published in the form of short monographs, and other collections of miscellaneous reprinted items have appeared in similar forms. These collections usually are not numbered separately in this bibliography, but they do appear without a number in the appropriate sections, with cross-references directing the reader to the items collected in the pamphlet or book in question. Conversely, the annotations of those items note their appearance in the collection.

(2) Items noted in other bibliographies but which could not be verified have been listed in the appropriate section without a number, and the source of the reference noted.

Unnumbered items are marked in the margin with asterisks, such as H***. All unnumbered items have been indexed and cross-referenced using split numbers that indicate their place in the bibliography. For example, A5/6 indicates the item that is listed and annotated between items A5 and A6.

Bibliographic Sources

Bibliographies of Works by Jacques Lacan

(The following items include selective bibliographies as well as those that aspire to a complete listing of Lacan's works. They are listed in chronological order. Except for Joël Dor's *Bibliographie,* the bibliographical portions of these items are not numbered or listed separately in this bibliography. Brief lists of works accompanying essays, sections of books, etc. are generally omitted unless they were the source of a reference I could not verify and are cited as such in this bibliography.)

Wilden, Anthony. "Jacques Lacan: A Partial Bibliography." *Yale French Studies,* no. 36/37 (1966): 263-68.

Palmier, Jean-Michel. *Lacan: le symbolique et l'imaginaire.* Paris: Editions Universitaires, 1969.

Ehrmann, Jacques, ed. *Structuralism.* Garden City: Anchor Books, 1970.

Harari, Josué. *Structuralists and Structuralisms: A Selected Bibliography of French Contemporary Thought (1960-1970).* Baltimore: Diacritics, Inc., 1971. 82 pages.

De Wolf, Michel. "Essai de bibliographie complète." *Magazine littéraire,* no. 121 (1977): 28-36.

Lemaire, Anika. *Jacques Lacan.* Translated by David Macey. London: Routledge and Kegan Paul, 1977. Pages 254-60.

Heinrich, Hans-Jürgen. "Bibliographie der Schriften von Jacques Lacan." *Psyche* 34 (1980): 958-73.

Miller, Joan M. *French Structuralism: A Multidisciplinary Bibliography.* New York: Garland, 1981. 553 pages.

Lacan Study Notes 1, no. 1 and no. 2 (1982-1983).

Mitchell, Juliet, and Jacqueline Rose. *Feminine Sexuality: Jacques Lacan and the Ecole freudienne.* New York: Norton, 1982. Pages 174-76.

Muller, John, and William Richardson. *Lacan and Language: A Reader's Guide to Ecrits.* New York: International Universities Press, 1982.

Clément, Catherine. *The Lives and Legends of Jacques Lacan.* Translated by Arthur Goldhammer. New York: Columbia University Press, 1983. Pages 215-20.

Davis, R.C., and R. Macksey. Selective Bibliography. *M[odern] L[anguage] N[otes]* 98 (1983): 1054-63.

Dor, Joël. *Bibliographie des travaux de Jacques Lacan.* Collection L'analyse
au singulier. Paris: InterEditions, 1983. 207 pages.

General Bibliographic Sources

(This list is restricted to sources that were particularly useful for the topic of this
bibliography and/or that contain references that could not be verified. It omits
general reference sources such as the *National Union Catalog,* the *British
National Bibliography,* indexes to book reviews and major newspapers, etc.)

Arts and Humanities Citation Index
Biblio: catalogue des ouvrages parus en langue française dans le mode entier
Bibliographie de la philosophie
Bulletin signalétique: histoire et sciences de la littérature
Bulletin signalétique: philosophie
Bulletin signalétique: sciences du langage
Deutsche bibliographie
Dissertation Abstracts International
France-actualité: index de la presse écrits français
MLA Bibliography
*Point de repère: index analytique d'articles de périodiques québéçois et
        étrangers*
Répertoire bibliographique de la philosophie
Social Sciences Citation Index
The Philosopher's Index
The Index of Psychoanalytic Writings

Acknowledgements

I am grateful for the support of the National Endowment for the Humanities and
of the University of California, Irvine, which funded much of the research for
this bibliography. I would also like to thank the research assistants who helped
me in various ways: Guiseppina Bencivenga, Judith Pike, Anne Tomiche,
Krista Walter, and especially Theron Britt. Jean-Louis Gault furnished
information about many of the items published in Japanese. My wife, Kate
Clark, assumed most of the proofreading duties, cross-checked the indexes,
and helped me to prepare the final copy of the manuscript. Warren Montag and
Tobin Siebers reviewed several aspects of the manuscript and offered valuable
advice along the way. Patrick Colm Hogan, Françoise Meltzer, Ellie Ragland-

Sullivan, and many others whose works are listed in this bibliography generously responded to my inquiries about items that are out of print or published in journals that are virtually inaccessible, and I would like to thank them as well.

Jacques Adam, librarian of the Ecole de la Cause freudienne, was kind enough to make available the remarkable collection of books and journals held by the ECF in Paris. Jacques-Alain Miller also provided invaluable assistance and advice, including an early skepticism that made me rethink the place of my project in a field that continues to resonate with the vitality of Lacan's presence years after his death. A special thanks is due to John P. Muller, Diplomate in Clinical Psychology, Senior Researcher at the Austen Riggs Center in Stockbridge, Massachusetts, and co-author with William J. Richardson of *Lacan and Language: A Reader's Guide to the Ecrits*. He generously agreed to review the manuscript with an eye toward my representation of the clinical dimension of Lacan's work. I owe much of the precision and accuracy of those annotations to his advice; any distortions that remain are, of course, my own responsibility.

Biography

Jacques Marie Emile Lacan was born on 13 April 1901 to Alfred and Emilée Baudry Lacan, an upper-middle class Parisian couple who arranged for their son to be educated by the Jesuits at the prestigious Collège Stanislas in Paris.[1] After completing his studies at the Faculté de médecine de Paris, Lacan began his residence at the Hôpital Saint-Anne in Paris. There he specialized in psychiatry under the direction of Gaétan Gatian de Clérambault, a specialist in "mental automatism" whom Lacan later described as his "sole master in psychiatry" (A2, page 65).[2] From 1928-1929, Lacan studied at the Infirmerie Spéciale près de la Préfecture de Police and received a *Diplôme de médecine légiste* (specialist in legal medicine) after working at the Hôpital Henri Rousselle from 1929 to 1931.[3] In 1932, after a second year at Saint Anne's Clinique de Maladies Mentales et de l'Encéphale, Lacan received the *Doctorat d'état* in psychiatry and published his thesis, *De la psychose paranoïaque dans ses rapports avec la personnalité* (A1).

Lacan's thesis testifies to the growing interest in psychoanalysis among French psychiatrists as well as among lay people such as Marie Bonaparte and Madame Solkonika, who helped found the Société psychanalytique de Paris in 1926. All but two members of the original SPP were physicians, and these doctors started a new psychiatric society at the same time, l'Evolution psychiatrique. The purpose of this group was to present psychoanalysis to the

French medical profession in a form that would be more respectable than the suspiciously poetic version popularized by the surrealists. This tension between the artistic and medical dimensions of psychoanalysis is reflected in Lacan's own career; Lacan worked with his colleague Henri Ey in l'Evolution psychiatrique, but he also retained his friendship with André Breton and others associated with the surrealist movement. At the same time as his psychiatric papers were appearing in *Annales médico-psychologiques,* Lacan was publishing articles in the surrealist journal *Le minotaure* in 1933; he even published a poem clearly influenced by surrealist themes and imagery (E117).[4]

Lacan joined the SPP in 1934 after a training analysis with Rudolf Lowenstein, who had come to Paris from Berlin to help Bonaparte in her early years with the organization. Two years later Lacan presented his first formal paper in psychoanalytic theory to the Fourteenth Congress of the International Psychoanalytic Association at Marienbad, "Le stade du miroir: théorie d'un moment structurant et génétique de la constitution de la réalité, conçu en relation avec l'expérience et la doctrine psychanalytique" (C44). This paper was never published, but Lacan did elaborate on his theory of the mirror stage four years later in a pair of essays on the family published in the *Encyclopédie française* (C45 and C46). With the onset of World War II, however, the SPP drastically reduced its activities, and Lacan himself published nothing else until 1945, when he wrote the first of two articles on logic that were printed in *Cahiers d'art.*

After the war, the SPP was reduced to eleven members, the size of its founding group. But with an enthusiastic recruitment program and a renewed interest in the training of new analysts, it grew rapidly. By 1951, seventy analysts were in training, and they were analyzing another hundred people. The training of new analysts was one of the most controversial issues in the post-war society because it focused the tension between two groups competing for power within the organization. Most of the medically trained analysts favored a strict and closely supervised training program similar to preparation of medical doctors. A more liberal group, which consisted of lay analysts, intellectuals, artists and only a few doctors, emphasized the need for a more creative and less systematic practice that allowed for more individuality in the preparation and certification of candidates.[5]

Lacan was associated with the second group. He was appointed to the SPP's Committee on Teaching in 1948, and in 1949 he wrote the Society's training statutes, which opened the training to non-medical candidates and granted them the full right to practice psychoanalysis (see E149). When the SPP moved to form its own training institute in the summer of 1952, however, Sacha Nacht was appointed director. Nacht, outgoing President of the SPP, was the leader of the group that wanted to restrict the Institute's certification to physicians. His appointment therefore generated considerable controversy, and when Lacan gained the support of Marie Bonaparte—who was responsible for most of the society's funds and who lacked the medical degree Nacht would require for analytic practice—Nacht resigned. Lacan replaced him as Director briefly, and on 20 January 1953 Lacan was elected President of the SPP. Curiously, at that time Nacht and his group were once again given control of the training institute (perhaps because Bonaparte had shifted her allegiance back to Nacht), and they continued their effort to medicalize psychoanalytic training as a sub-discipline of neurobiology.

By the time the new Institute officially opened in March 1953, the conflict between Lacan and Nacht had escalated considerably. The most specific issue separating them was Lacan's advocacy of the "short session," which discarded the standard analytic hour in favor of sessions of variable lengths that could be as short as five minutes. The theoretical principles behind this practice have been debated at length, but the very possibility of such variation threatened the "professional" character of analytic practice as conceived by Nacht, and it may have cost Lacan the presidency (see F412, page 107). In January of 1953, Lacan did promise to follow the rule of the standard session, but some members of the SPP felt that he did not keep the promise. More importantly, the new rules for analytic training that Nacht and his group instituted in 1953 required a training analysis of at least three 45-minute sessions each week for 12 months; since those who had trained with Lacan had undergone variable sessions that were usually shorter than that, the new rule effectively disenfranchised all of Lacan's students as well as discrediting Lacan's own practice.

Under pressure from a student revolt that Lacan was accused of instigating, the SPP returned a vote of no confidence in Lacan on 16 June 1953, and he resigned from the presidency (see F379, page 110, and F412, page 258 no. 24). Lacan then formed a new group, the Société française de psychanalyse, with Daniel Lagache, Juliette Favez-Boutonier, Françoise Dolto, and Blanche Reverchon-Jouve. The two groups quickly diverged along the usual lines: the SPP sided with the medical and scientific community, and the SFP with the more humanistic community of non-medical intellectuals.

Both groups desired recognition by the International Psychoanalytic Association and that desire intensified the hostility between them. Many members of the IPA were outraged at Lacan's short sessions and his more informal training analyses, and they insisted that his resignation from the SPP implied his withdrawal from the IPA as well. Lacan responded that he had simply been resisting the authoritarian principles of the SPP because it contradicted the very nature of psychoanalysis. The IPA remained adamant, however, and in a meeting attended by Nacht's group (but which was closed to

Lacan and Lagache), a special committee was appointed to investigate the situation. Two years later, the committee recommended that the SFP be denied membership in the IPA simply because it lacked proper training facilities, though many interpreted the decision more as a personal victory for Anna Freud and Heinz Hartmann, then President of the IPA, who had moved to exclude the group associated with Lacan and Lagache in the first place.[6]

In September 1953, the SFP convened for the first time at Rome, and Lacan threw down a gauntlet before the international psychoanalytic community with his paper "Fonction et champ de la parole et du langage en psychanalyse," which became known as the "Discours de Rome " (C58). Distributed in written form and accompanied by an oral presentation, "Fonction et champ" is a long and complex essay that challenged the prevailing theory and practice of psychoanalysis on a number of fronts. Most importantly, Lacan insisted on the centrality of speech to the analytic context and to any theoretical conclusions that might be drawn from it. This emphasis on speech and language turned psychoanalysis away from biology and neurology and reoriented it radically toward Saussurean linguistics and certain traditions in European philosophy. In addition, Lacan's bitter and sardonic attack on the concept of the ego as a unifying force and stable foundation for psychic integration simply rejected most of the "innovations" in psychoanalytic theory proposed since Freud's death and generally supported by the IPA. (The political implications of such a drastic departure from the official doctrine are obvious, but they take on a sharper point when Hartmann's role in the exclusion of Lacan's group is considered: Hartmann's *Ego Psychology and the Problem of Adaptation* [1939] was a basic text of the ego psychology that Lacan ridiculed in his paper. Consequently, the *Discours de Rome* not only served as Lacan's declaration of independence from the IPA but also exacerbated the already antagonistic relations between that group and the SFP.)[7]

In the years following the *Discours de Rome,* Lacan emerged as the most important single figure in French psychoanalysis. He presented a number of theoretical papers at conferences, and he continued to train new analysts. In the fall of 1953, he also began a series of seminars at Hôpital Saint-Anne in which he developed a detailed reading of Freud's texts that began to attract a large number of followers. Nevertheless, by 1959, some members of the SFP began to tire of their status as outsiders to the psychoanalytic community at large, and the society decided to petition once again for membership in the IPA. Another committee was appointed by the IPA to review the new petition, and two years later in 1961 it submitted its report to the Twenty-second Congress of the International Psychoanalytic Association at Edinburgh.

The IPA once again refused to recognize the SFP, but it did propose that the SFP become a study group under the supervision of the international organization. However, to accede even to this modest—and, some felt, deliberately insulting—offer, the SFP would have to meet a list of 19 requirements that quickly became known as the Edinburgh demands (see F380, pages 19-22). The delegation from the SFP recognized that several of the requirements were implicitly aimed directly at Lacan, but they returned to Paris anyway to report the IPA's decision. After the delegation left, the IPA inserted another demand as number 13: Jacques Lacan and Françoise Dolto were to be gradually phased out of training new analysts for the society.

This demand created tremendous dissension within the SFP, and a group was appointed to mediate between the French society and the IPA. When representatives of the IPA visited Paris in January of 1963, however, they found Lacan still entrenched at the center of a devoted following, so the IPA declared flatly that Lacan had to be removed from the list of training analysts by 31 October 1963. If he were not, the IPA would never recognize the SFP as an official psychoanalytic society. (For a record of the discussion of Lacan's case by the IPA, see J1062 and J1063). This ultimatum forced a confrontation between pro- and anti-Lacanian groups within the SFP itself, and on 13 October 1963 the Society's Committee on Teaching refused Lacan permission to train analysts.[8] The general body of the society voted to support that decision a month later, and the next day Lacan proclaimed the end of the seminars (see E172).[9]

During these two years of controversy, Lacan apparently wrote little and published nothing except two essays in literary and cultural journals: one on Merleau-Ponty in *Les temps modernes* (C82) and another on Kant and Sade in *Critique* (C83). After Lacan suspended his seminar, he even lacked a forum for his teaching. A short time later, however, Fernand Braudel invited him to continue the seminars under the aegis of l'Ecole Pratique des Hautes Etudes. Louis Althusser and Claude Lévi-Strauss also intervened on Lacan's behalf, and on 15 January 1964 Lacan began what has become the best-known of all the seminars, *Les quatre concepts fondamentaux de la psychanalyse* (B22). In the first session he referred to the pronouncements of the IPA as his "excommunication" and noted the comic dimension of being "the object of what is called *a deal* " within the religious order of that organization. "There was nothing particularly exceptional, then, about my situation," Lacan added, "except that being traded by those whom I referred to just now as colleagues, and even pupils, is sometimes, if seen from the outside, called by a different name" (B22b, page 5).

Addressed to a broader audience than the seminars at Hôpital Saint-Anne, *Les quatre concepts* ranges beyond the commentary on technical writings of Freud that had occupied Lacan during the first ten years of the seminars. While still taking Freud's texts as his point of departure, over the course of the next ten years Lacan began developing concepts such as the "*objet a*," the barred subject (usually represented as $\$$), and the *Autre* (Other) that had occasionally appeared in the earlier seminars in less systematic forms. Such topics were still scarcely accessible to a general audience, but Lacan's seminars nevertheless began drawing huge crowds and were largely responsible for the surge of interest in psychoanalysis within an intellectual community that had never gotten over its initial resistance to Freud's ideas. Even before he published a collection of his writings in 1966, Lacan had emerged as one of the most prominent figures among the heterogeneous group that came to be labelled "structuralists," and he had established psychoanalysis as a primary mode of inquiry into the broad range of philosophical issues that occupied most of the writers associated with that movement.[10]

The SFP's decision to accept the demands imposed by the IPA created an intolerable antagonism between Lacan's supporters and the rest of the society. By the end of 1964, the members who opposed Lacan had formed their own group, the **Association psychanalytique de France**, which was admitted to the IPA in July 1965.[11] In the meantime, Lacan had joined with Françoise Dolto, Serge Leclaire, Guy Rosolato and others to form the Ecole française de psychanalyse, which quickly became known as the Ecole freudienne de Paris. In the "Acte de fondation" (E178), Lacan declared that the new school would return to the "original praxis" that Freud had instituted under the name of psychoanalysis and would guard against deviations from that practice. The school was to have three divisions: a section of "pure psychoanalysis," which would be responsible for the training of new analysts; a clinical section; and, most significantly in the light of past controversies, a section devoted to the "*rencensement du champ freudien*" (an homage to the Freudian field), which would explore connections between psychoanalysis and other disciplines. Lacan also promised to do away with the rigid, vertical hierarchy that had ossified the IPA and replace it with a "circular organization" of small groups that would support valuable work of any sort. Thus, Lacan says in a note, the new Ecole would be a "school" in the antique sense, a refuge from the "malaise of civilization" and a base of operations for forays against it.[12]

The EFP was born in polemical opposition to the psychoanalytic establishment represented by the IPA, and the antagonism between the two groups quickly worsened over the issue of authorizing new analysts. There were no fixed requirements for membership in the EFP; there was no set curriculum of courses for analysts in training; and in the EFP there was no distinction between analysts certified to train other analysts and those who were not. The decision to become a practicing analyst was entirely left up to the individual, who simply notified the School's secretary that he or she was ready to see patients. This policy constituted the "self-authorization" of the analyst, and Lacan considered it an accurate and inevitable consequence of the most fundamental principles of psychoanalysis itself.

The self-authorization of analysts in the EFP outraged psychoanalysts in most other organizations, who saw the policy as irresponsible and "unprofessional" and as a threat to the tenuous scientific respectability that had developed around psychoanalysis governed by the IPA. The lack of clear administrative guidelines also generated conflict within the EFP as some members began to feel that Lacan was exercising an autocratic and arbitrary power at odds with the school's professed mission.[13] In 1967 this internal dissent culminated in an organized resistance to Lacan's proposal of "*la passe,*" a procedure that would distinguish between the A.M.E. ("*Analyste membre de l'Ecole,*" or general member of the School), and the A.E. ("*Analyste de l'Ecole,*" or "School Analyst").[14]

La passe was a means of determining an analyst's ability to do innovative, theoretical work in psychoanalysis based on a presentation by three "passers" to whom the analyst had described his own training analysis. The passers—chosen from the candidate's own analysands—would report what they had heard to a committee composed of senior analysts in the school (which always included Lacan), and that committee would then decide whether or not to appoint the candidate as an A.E. Lacan considered this method useful because it dramatized the distinction between the subject of speech as represented by the passers and the actual individual who speaks, a theoretical distinction crucial to Lacan's analytic practice. But *la passe* contained obvious opportunities for abuse at every stage, and the very designation of *Analyste de l'Ecole* carried with it a value judgment about the superiority of theoretical work that reinstituted a sense of vertical hierarchy within the school in direct contradiction to Lacan's professed aims.

Lacan responded immediately to criticism of his proposal, denying charges that *la passe* was designed to reinforce his authoritarian isolation from other members of the EFP. Solitude was the very thing that he had renounced by forming the school, Lacan said (E190). Nevertheless, resentment among some of the members over Lacan's domination of the school continued and increased when the EFP decided that all of the articles in its new journal, *Scilicet,* would be published anonymously—except those by Lacan himself, which would appear under his name. It was not until January of 1969 that the EFP finally voted to approve Lacan's proposition of 9 October 1967, and at that time ten of Lacan's closest followers—among them Piera Castoriadis-Aulagnier, François Perrier, and Jean-Paul Valabrega—left the EFP to form Le Quatrième Groupe, which became known as "Lacanians without Lacan."[15]

While the controversy over *la passe* occupied the EFP, Lacan's status as a public figure was increasing steadily. The publication of his collected essays in *Ecrits* (A2) in 1966 elevated him into a circle of intellectual superstars that had become the unlikely center of media attention; popular magazines carried his picture alongside those of Roland Barthes, Michel Foucault, and Jacques Derrida. *Ecrits* sold over 5,000 copies only three days after it appeared in the bookstores, and translations followed in English, Japanese, and virtually all European languages. Lacan's seminars at the Ecole normale became a premier social event with standing room only in the large hall where he lectured, and arcane theoretical debates on psychoanalytic issues previously confined to internal newsletters and conference papers suddenly began appearing in *La quinzaine littéraire, Le nouvel observateur,* and *Le monde.* The difficulty of Lacan's writing and the idiosyncratic, highly theatrical nature of his spoken lectures generated a controversy that reached far beyond the small circle of those who had actually read his work, and Lacan was castigated in the popular press for offenses ranging from cultural elitism and hermetic perversity to social subversion. By May 1968 Lacan's notoriety had reached the point where one of the Directors of the ENS could actually accuse him of starting the student-worker riots of that year, even as those students and many analysts were attacking Lacan as a representative of the dogmatic authority imposed by the Parisian intellectual establishment.[16]

Contradictory public response to a prominent figure is not unusual, especially when the subject of such attention clearly enjoys and encourages the confusion and outrage as Lacan did. There was, however, some basis for the charges from both sides. One of the principal tenets of the student revolt was a general disaffection with intellectual discourse expressed by the popular slogan *"les structures ne descendent pas dans la rue, "* and Lacan's learned, often aloof and mystifying presentations were ill-suited to the populist thrust of revolutionary rhetoric. When Lacan appeared at the newly formed campus of the University of Paris at Vincennes, the uneasy relation between him and the newly radicalized university students was apparent. Amidst frequent heckling from the audience, Lacan mocked the students' ambition to escape the discourse of the university and argued that the only escape from discourse was aphasia. "Revolutionaries such as yourselves aspire only to the discourse of the master," Lacan retorted to the students who challenged him. "You want a Master, and you will have one."[17]

Lacan's experience at Vincennes exemplifies the complex role of institutional identification in French psychoanalysis during the 1960s, and Lacan himself seemed ambivalent about his position as the leader of one of the most influential psychoanalytic groups in France. Despite Lacan's belief that psychoanalysis could not be taught or transmitted systematically, a Department of Psychoanalysis was started at Vincennes in January 1969 under the leadership of Serge Leclaire, who directed it until the end of 1971. The courses offered in the department generally focused on Lacan's work, and earlier Leclaire had been instrumental in winning acceptance for Lacan's ideas when he had been President of the Société française de psychanalytique. At first, Lacan had no official connection with the university; but in the summer of 1974 he declared himself "Scientific Director" of the department and appointed his son-in-law, Jacques-Alain Miller, as chairman.[18] Lacan renamed the department Le Champ freudienne (the "Freudian Field"), cancelled the scheduled classes, and required formal course proposals of anyone who wanted to teach in the department. Lacan's intervention restored order to what most of the faculty perceived as a rapidly deteriorating situation at the new campus, and in January of 1975 Lacan expressed his hope that, "perhaps at Vincennes," linguistics, logic, and, most importantly, topology could lend a scientific rigor to the study of psychoanalysis (E257). The institutionalization of Lacanian psychoanalysis then proceeded another step in 1976 when a program of clinical psychoanalysis was organized that certified its graduates after only two years of coursework.[19]

As Lacan's control of the department at Vincennes tightened, his relations with the general membership of the EFP grew tense. French psychoanalysis had become increasingly heterogeneous since the formation of the Ecole, and that pluralism had found a popular forum in the "intergroup" Confrontation, which was founded by two members of the SPP and which published the collection *Cahiers Confrontation*. A variety of perspectives also appeared in the pages of *La nouvelle revue de psychanalyse,* which had begun as the official journal of the SPP and under the direction of Jean-Bertrand Pontalis had published work inspired by analysts little known in France at the time, such as Melanie Klein and D.W. Winnicott.[20] This diversity challenged Lacan's predominance over the psychoanalytic scene at large, and within the EFP tensions increased over internal differences in theoretical principles and over renewed complaints about what some felt to be Lacan's arbitrary and repressive conduct as President. A large portion of the school protested after Lacan fired the Vice-President without explanation (see no. 20). Finally, when Miller was elected to the board of directors in September 1979 under what was interpreted as a violation of the group's by-laws, a formal letter of protest was filed by the disgruntled members of the EFP.

On 5 January 1980 Lacan responded to the protest with the "Lettre de dissolution," which was addressed to members of the EFP but quickly published in *Le monde* (B38a). In the letter, Lacan noted the dissension within the EFP and the growing disagreement about fundamental tenets of psychoanalytic theory and practice, and he declared that the School had ceased to serve its purpose and was now defunct. Two weeks later he wrote another letter to members of the School (also published in *Le monde*) in which he challenged those who wanted to follow him to put their allegiance in writing

(B38b). More than 1,000 did so (though the membership of the EFP numbered only about 600), and shortly after that Lacan announced the formation of a new group that would follow him "pour le Cause freudienne," which became known as the Ecole de la Cause freudienne. Lacan's unilateral decision to dissolve the EFP was challenged by some members in court, and the EFP was able to retain its official status for a few more months. On 27 September 1980, however, the General Assembly voted to support dissolution, and the EFP ceased to exist. Almost eighty when he formed the ECF, Lacan continued his psychoanalytic practice but offered no seminar that fall for the first time in thirty years. Lacan retained at least nominal control over the ECF even as his health deteriorated during the next year, but he had largely ceded authority to his son-in-law by 9 September 1981 when Lacan died following an operation to remove an abdominal tumor.[21]

Notes

[1]Lacan's brother, Marc-François Lacan, became a Benedictine priest, and Lacan dedicated his thesis to him in 1932.

[2]Clérambault is best known today for the Clérambault-Kandinsky complex, a syndrome associated with any psychosis in which the patient believes that his mind is controlled by a person or power outside himself. Lacan was especially influenced by Clérambault's work on this phenomenon, which was more generally termed "*l'automatisme mental* " and which Clérambault associated with the separate phenomenon of the persecution complex. Many of Lacan's early case reports deal with automatism, and in "*De nos antécédents* " (A2, page 65), Lacan wrote that although Clérambault's concept of mental automatism must be criticized for its "mechanistic ideology of metaphor," nevertheless Clérambault's understanding of the "subjective text" comes closer to a structural analysis than any other clinical effort of French psychiatry.

For a complete account of Clérambault's career and his influence on Lacan, see the second volume of Elisabeth Roudinesco's *La bataille de cent ans: histoire de la psychanalyse en France* (F393). In the light of Lacan's later work on the mirror stage, it is interesting to note that Clérambault committed suicide in front of a mirror in 1934 (see F316, page 55).

[3]See Lacan's discussion of criminal cases in his thesis (A1) and in his comments on the notorious case of the Papin sisters (C42). For more general

comments on the importance of psychoanalysis to the issue of criminality, see C54.

⁴Lacan's link with surrealism is complicated. He shared with the surrealist artists an interest in the phenomenon of automatism, especially in relation to speech and automatic writing, and he compared the writings of schizophrenics to surrealist imagery and poetic theory (C41). Salvador Dali seems to have been directly influenced by Lacan's work on paranoia, and scholars have debated less direct associations between Lacan's pre-war writings and other poets and painters of the period. For comments on Dali's relation to Lacan, see G873, L1526, L1707, and L2233.

⁵Much of my account of the controversy surrounding Lacan's association with the SPP and the subsequent formation of the SFP is based on the documents and various communications collected in two volumes published as supplements to the journal *Ornicar?: La scission de 1953* (F379) and *L'excommunication* (F380). The most detailed narrative of Lacan's career in the context of French psychoanalysis in general may be found in the second volume of Elisabeth Roudinesco's *La bataille de cent ans: histoire de la psychanalyse en France* (F393). In English, see Sherry Turkle's excellent history of Lacan's impact on French psychoanalysis, *Psychoanalytic Politics: Freud's French Revolution* (F412). For shorter histories of these events see G451 and G853.

⁶The documents surrounding Lacan's resignation from the SPP and his petitions for recognition from the IPA have been collected and published by Jacques-Alain Miller in F379.

⁷Readers familiar with the history of psychoanalysis in the United States will notice a similarity between this controversy among French analysts and the split between "Freudians" and "culturalists" in the American analytic community at this time. In 1941, three prominent members of the New York group of the American Psychoanalytic Association—Karen Horney, Clara Thompson, and William Silverburg—split off to form their own group, the Association for the Advancement of Psychoanalysis. The specific motivation for the split was the feeling that the APA had become too authoritarian in its administration of psychoanalytic research and training, but this charge stemmed from a much more fundamental disagreement about the importance of culture in the formation of an individual's psychic organization. Horney and the other dissidents felt that cultural influences were more important than biological factors, whereas the APA insisted on what it called the more properly "Freudian" emphasis on

biology as the determining ground of psychoanalysis. Horney actually resigned her place in the APA, and the split continued to widen until the culturalists formed their own umbrella organization in 1956: the American Academy of Psychoanalysis, which had its own training institute and journal. Despite these parallels between the controversies in France and the United States at this time, however, Lacan explicitly argued that his emphasis on man's relation to the signifier has nothing to do with the culturalist position proposed by Horney. For Lacan's rejection of any similarity between his position and that of the culturalists, see C73, rpt. A2, page 689; tr. A2j, page 284.

[8]The motion to remove Lacan's name was instigated by Wladimir Granoff and signed by Juliette Favez-Boutonier, Daniel Lagache, and Georges Favez. Lacan mentions the motion in a letter to Serge Leclaire of 10 November 1963 in which he apologizes for missing the plenary session of "notre Société" and explains that his very presence would have required the society to disavow the motion that it eventually supported. See E171.

[9]For a brief chronological summary of these events and for the complete texts of the various proceedings, see F380.

[10]Lacan's relations with the other major figures usually called structuralists were ambivalent. He shared with other members of that group an interest in Saussure's distinction between signifier and signified and in the critique of traditional humanistic emphases on the individual subject as an autonomous cogito. Lacan spoke of himself at times as a structuralist because of his interest in linguistics as a methodological approach to psychoanalysis, and in a widely publicized interview, Jean-Paul Sartre named Lacan as a primary offender in what he considered structuralism's failure to recognize the importance of history in human experience (see L2343; for Lacan's response, see E183).

Lacan occasionally cited the work of Claude Lévi-Strauss as an important influence on his work during the 1960s, though he insisted that their respective understandings of "structure" were quite different (see E187). Lacan's attitude towards the work of Michel Foucault is less clear. He once mentioned Foucault's *Historie de la folie* as a useful study of madness, and Lacan attended a meeting of the Société française de philosophie at which Foucault presented his essay "What is an Author?" When called upon to comment on the essay, however, Lacan managed to avoid even mentioning Foucault's paper. See E202. (Lacan did devote a session of Seminar XVI to a discussion of Foucault's essay; see B27a.) Lévi-Strauss and Michel Foucault attended at least one of Lacan's seminars, though both men later professed to have understood little of what he said. Louis Althusser was perhaps his strongest ally. In addition to supporting Lacan's move to the ENS, Althusser also insisted on the importance of Lacan's work to Marxism at a time when Marxism and psychoanalysis were considered unrelated and often antithetical to each other (see G433). A decade later, however, Althusser bitterly criticized Lacan as a "magnificent and pitiful harlequin"; see G432 and G508. Lacan's most substantial and celebrated dispute with a member of this group took place with Jacques Derrida over Lacan's reading of Poe's "The Purloined Letter"; see C69 and G544. For a description of the ongoing debate over this exchange, see F374/375. For further comments on Lacan's relation to structuralism, see the Introduction to this bibliography.

[11]For an account of the IPA's decision to recognize this new group, see *The International Journal of Psychoanalysis* 47, part 1 (1966): 88-90. Among the members of the newly-formed AFP were Lagache, Anzieu, Wladimir Granoff, Jean Laplanche, and Jean-Bertrand Pontalis.

[12]The "Acte de fondation" was first printed for public distribution in F380 and has been reprinted with an adjoining note in A9.

[13]Turkle describes the troubled history of the EFP in Chapter 5 of F412. Many of the complaints reported there, however, and other published accounts of conflict during the early years of the EFP described below in Section G were expressed many years after the fact, and undoubtedly reflect the often bitter antagonisms among competing Lacanian factions that have formed since the 1960s.

[14]For a more detailed description of *la passe* and its theoretical justification, see C88.

[15]The letter of withdrawal submitted when these members resigned has been published as J1018. Turkle provides a useful description of the basic policies of Le Quatrième Groupe and its differences with the EFP in F412, page 260, no. 12. This group began its own journal, *Topique*, published in Paris by l'Epi.

Just before the vote on 25 January 1969, Lacan wrote a letter to the general assembly of the school explaining once again the proposals set forth in October 1967 and justifying the distinction between the A.E. and the A.M.E.; see E202.

[16]It is always difficult to gauge just how far the fame of such media sensation penetrates into the general public, but a survey taken in 1980 reported that 80 percent of those polled had never even heard of Lacan. Perhaps even more significantly, 65 percent said they would refuse a psychoanalysis even if it were offered to them free of charge. See J1114.

[17]For Lacan's remarks at Vincennes, see E204. In remarks to the Société française de philosophie, Lacan also claimed that if the events of this time signified anything, it was precisely just such a descent of structures into the street (see E203).

There are many histories of the uprisings in May 1968; for a discussion of that movement in the context of the period's intellectual history see K1295. On Lacan's eviction from the ENS see F396, page 29, and E203/204.

[18]Miller's presence at Vincennes lends some credence to the otherwise implausible charges of cultural subversion directed at Lacan by the ENS. Miller was part of a group of philosophy students known as a "cartel" who were influenced by the work of Louis Althusser. David-Menard has characterized this group as "Maoist activists" in 1968, and they entered the ENS together and began publishing their work in *Cahiers pour l'analyse*. See G528.

Miller had married Judith Lacan, the youngest of Lacan's three daughters, and had been teaching at a *lycée* in Besançon before returning to Paris in 1973.

[19]The events surrounding the formation and subsequent reorganization of the Department of Psychoanalysis at Vincennes are complex and cannot easily be separated from the personal conflicts and bitter antagonisms expressed by most of the people involved. A description of the goals for the newly reformed department was published in the first issue of *Ornicar?*, the official journal of the Champ freudien (1975, pages 12-15). For Lacan's description of the goals for the new program, see E257. Three years later Lacan reaffirmed his support for the program at Vincennes but admitted that analytic discourse has nothing to teach. How can one teach something that even Freud believed cannot be taught, Lacan asked. Instead, the goal must be to "*corriger l'objet*" (see E287).

The call for course proposals generated its own controversy, since they were all to be judged by Lacan, Miller, Jean Clavreul, and Charles Melman, who had just come to Vincennes. This "Scientific Committee" was immediately accused of censorship by applicants whose proposals were refused. Perhaps the most celebrated case was that of Luce Irigaray, who had been teaching at Vincennes part-time and whose recent book *Speculum* (K1220) had been critical of certain tenets of Lacanian psychoanalysis from a feminist perspective. For Irigaray's course proposal, which was rejected, see J1064.

The proposal for a program in clinical psychoanalysis drew fire from a number of groups, but none were more vociferous in their criticism than Le Quatrième Groupe. See G491, where the proposal itself is reprinted.

During these years, Lacan also opened relations briefly with universities in the United States when he spoke at several campuses on the East Coast; see E270.

[20]Confrontation was founded by René Major and Dominique Geahchan in 1974, and its debates attracted an audience that often numbered in the hundreds. Although proclaiming itself open to the full range of psychoanalytic discourses in France, Confrontation was seen by many members of the EFP as an anti-Lacanian organization. When the Vice-President of the EFP, Denis Vasse, decided to speak before the group, Lacan abruptly removed him from office.

[21]A detailed though polemical account of the personal, institutional, and theoretical issues involved in the dissolution of the EFP is available in English: see G528. Various documents by Lacan relating to the dissolution and to the formation of the Ecole de la Cause freudienne have been collected and reprinted in *Acte de fondation, et autres textes* (A9). The Cartels constituants de l'analyse freudienne, an umbrella organization made up of many psychoanalytic groups in Paris, is publishing an extensive history of the dissolution and the various groups that grew out of it in the journal *Tribune* (see F411). Item F324 reprints—with a running commentary—many of the texts associated with this controversy that were not included in A9. It is the most detailed history of these events.

Following Lacan's death, groups influenced by his work have continued to proliferate. The Ecole de la Cause freudienne received Lacan's personal sanction in two letters published in the school's newsletter, where Lacan claims the ECF is the sole group responsible for carrying on his teaching and describes it as *"l'Ecole de mes élèves, ceux qui m'aiment encore "* (see E298 and E299). A group from the Ecole freudienne de Paris who resisted Lacan's ultimatum and opposed the Ecole de la Cause freudienne (Claude Rabant, Marianne Monnet, and others) formed Entre temps in March 1980 and published a bulletin of that name. Rabant and several other members of Entre temps then formed the Cercle freudien in September 1981, and others founded the Ateliers de psychanalyse in January of 1983. Another group that emerged after the dissolution of the EFP was the College de psychanalyse, which was founded on 3 November 1980 and is open to members of any psychoanalytic organization.

One of the best known groups that evolved from the ECF was CERF (Le Centre d'études et de recherches freudiennes), which was founded on 7 March 1981 by several members of the ECF who had become disillusioned with Miller's handling of that group: Jean Clavreul, Solange Falade, and Charles Melman. Melman had done his training analysis with Miller and was one of the original directors of the Cause freudienne. Three members of the CERF (Melman, Claude Landman, and Contardo Calligaris) began the journal *Le discourse psychanalytique* in September of 1981, but dissension quickly set in. By the publication of the issue for January-April 1982, the journal split with CERF and that organization disintegrated. Its members regrouped in four different organizations: Melman left to form the Association freudienne on 26 June 1982, and others from CERF formed the Ecole freudienne on 18 February 1983; the CFRP in July 1982; the Conventions psychanalytique on 27 May 1983; and the Cout freudien on 20 June 1983.

Detailed descriptions of these organizations and even newer ones, their histories and the psychoanalytic journals associated with them may be found in the first three issues of *Tribune* (F411). For a full list of items related to Lacanian organizations, see the Index of Topics under Lacan, organizational controversies.

INTRODUCTION

"C'est à vous d'être lacaniens, si vous voulez;
moi, je suis freudien."
["It is up to you to be Lacanians, if you wish;
me, I am a Freudian."]
(C98, page 30)

Lacan's career may be divided into four stages that correspond to shifts in the conceptual focus of his work and that are usually marked by changes in his affiliations with professional organizations:[1]

1926-1953—These years include Lacan's early psychiatric training and his initial work in psychoanalysis, and they conclude with his break with the International Psychoanalytic Association, which was codified in the "Rome Discourse" (C58).

1953-1963—In this period Lacan began his annual seminars on Freud's texts and established the centrality of language and speech to psychoanalysis. Despite the unusual emphasis on the symbolic dimension of human experience, however, Lacan claimed that his work was simply a "return to Freud" that promised to protect Freud's original discovery from the distortions of subsequent psychoanalytic speculations such as American ego psychology or the "culturalists" associated with Karen Horney.

1963-1974—These years begin with Lacan's final "excommunication" from the IPA, his resignation from the Société française de psychanalyse, and the formation of the Ecole freudienne de Paris under Lacan's leadership. This period is characterized by an elaboration of terms and concepts he had introduced earlier such as the Other, the *objet a,* and other issues not explicit in Freud's own work. As Jacques-Alain Miller says of the shift in Lacan's interests at this stage, such terms come to the center of Lacan's elaboration of Freud's texts and "the problems posed by their articulation were superimposed upon and sometimes substituted for the initial problematic" (G738, tr. page 619).

1974-1981—In 1974 Lacan conducted a seminar on the fundamental triad of Lacanian psychoanalysis: "R.S.I.," the real, the symbolic, and the imaginary. These categories had been introduced much earlier, but in this seminar Lacan mapped their interrelations with the figure of the Borromean knot, and from this point his discourse drew upon the mathematical fields of topology, set theory, and symbolic logic rather than linguistics and semiotics (see note 1).

Miller claims that during these years Lacan "plunged into a form of 'meta-theory,' of pure signifying dimension, in which the familiar meanings of psychoanalysis wither away little by little" (G738, tr. page 620). Others have claimed that Lacan simply abandoned any intention of communicating with his audience, withdrew into the hermetic circle of his own notoriety, and began manipulating meaningless "mathemes" in a theater of pure self-indulgence. Regardless of Lacan's motives, however, the "mathematicization" of psychoanalysis that occurred during this period continues to influence psychoanalysis in France, especially the branch associated with Miller, the Department of Psychoanalysis at Vincennes-Saint Denis, and the Ecole de la Cause freudienne, the group formed by Lacan just before his death.

Such schematic divisions are always misleading, of course, and especially in the case of Lacan's career. As early as 1953 he claimed that he was offering language as an example of structuration simply because most of his audience would probably be incapable of understanding mathematical examples, and as his own commentary in A2 makes clear, most of the central themes in his later work are evident, at least in retrospect, in some of his earliest writings.[2] Yet Lacan himself resisted such retrospective discovery and claimed that efforts to find his later ideas "already there" in his earlier works were nothing more than his students' delusions (A2, page 67). Consequently, relations among the stages sketched here and the relative importance of any one stage to the full extent of Lacan's work are problematic, and questions of continuity or breaks in the evolution of Lacan's *oeuvre* will remain beyond the scope of this introduction. The chronological sequence of items described in this bibliography should provide readers with a guide to the works that will enable them to make up their own minds on this issue.

Readers who are unfamiliar with the whole range of Lacan's writings may, however, be somewhat confused by the great number of works included here, most of which have not been translated and many of which are available only in the private newsletters and limited journals of Parisian psychoanalytic organizations. For such readers the following synopsis of Lacan's career should be of some use, though as more experienced readers will quickly recognize this sketch is highly selective, deals with only the most influential aspects of his work, and reflects the exigencies of coherent exposition rather than the myriad and complex array of Lacan's thought. Furthermore, this introduction focuses on those aspects of Lacan's work that have influenced the widest range of readers, including philosophers, literary critics, film theorists, and feminists as well as psychoanalysts. Such a focus reflects the diversity of Lacan's own interests, but it also tends to abstract concepts and terms from the context in which they evolved. As Lacan insisted throughout his career, his theoretical claims were derived directly from the clinical experience of his analytic practice, and despite the variety of people who attended his seminars Lacan was always careful to identify his primary audience as practicing analysts. The obvious relevance of Lacan's work to other fields notwithstanding, readers should keep in mind the concrete and highly specific context in which that work was originally conceived and communicated. For despite his preeminence in the contemporary intellectual scene since the publication of the *Ecrits* in 1966, Lacan maintained that he aspired to nothing other than a fidelity to the texts that had opened up not only a new field of medical knowledge but a new understanding of human subjectivity. As he said in one of his last public performances, "It is up to you to be Lacanians, if you wish; me, I am a Freudian" (C98, page 30).

Section One: 1926-1953

From his earliest medical training in the 1920s to the famous "Rome Discourse" of 1953, Lacan concentrated on what he eventually called the "imaginary" register of human experience. Lacan's interest in the imaginary structure of human relations grew out of his early clinical experience with *délires à deux* and "automatism," forms of disturbances that involved the patient's identification with some "other," real or imagined, who took over the patient's identity and was blamed for various kinds of aberrant behavior.[3] In his thesis (A1), however, Lacan's theoretical explanation for such phenomena went beyond the traditional categories of psychiatric medicine to include Freud's concepts of narcissism and paranoia, and by 1936 (see C44) Lacan's account of the imaginary was indebted more directly to his theoretical elaboration of the "mirror stage" of human development identified by the French psychologist Wallon.[4] The psychiatric paradigms of Lacan's medical training had been largely supplanted by the concepts and categories of psychoanalysis, and the initial phase of Lacan's analytic work had begun.

Lacan's elaboration on prior understandings of the mirror stage established the themes that would dominate his work of this period. Wallon, for example, had situated this stage of human development between the ages of six and eighteen months, and he characterized it by the child's sudden recognition of its "self" in the image reflected in the mirror. For Lacan, following Freud's own account of narcissistic identification in the child, this image was simply the most obvious instance of a whole series of "others" with whom the child identified, and he argued that the imaginary or "specular" structure of the mirror stage characterized the more general process through which the individual forms a sense of self. Lacan also argued that the "fictional direction" in which that sense is oriented toward an other necessarily alienates the individual from the "self" and instills a hostility or "aggressivity" within the very structure of the ego.[5]

In Lacan's work, the imaginary thus takes on a far greater importance than the developmental role Wallon ascribed to the mirror stage. It constitutes the elementary structure of human identity as an "intersubjectivity" that substitutes a relation between self and other for the more popular notion of a coherent, autonomous ego. It also posits alienation and aggressivity as endemic to human subjectivity rather than as aberrations from a more stable norm. Furthermore, Lacan insisted that the imaginary realm of intersubjectivity was the sole domain of psychoanalysis (see C49), and any attempt to reinforce a patient's "ego" could only mask the symptoms and exacerbate the illusory identifications in which the patient was trapped. So while Lacan's first contributions to psychoanalysis grew out of his earlier interests in strictly conventional topics of medical psychiatry, his importation of psychoanalytic concepts into that field challenged the positivistic and heavily somatic bases of traditional psychiatric knowledge and practice, and his theoretical speculation quickly put him at odds with the ego-centered practice of the psychoanalytic establishment.[6]

The theoretical implications of the mirror-stage would occupy Lacan's attention for 20 years. The narcissistic object-relations formed within the imaginary register inevitably led to what Lacan called the "paranoic knowledge" that constituted the human perception of reality. This emphasis on the fundamentally "subjective" basis of knowledge yielded an epistemological skepticism that undermined the positivistic tendencies inherent in the biological dimension of Freud's work and its subsequent medicalization by many later analysts (see C51). More importantly, the "fictional" direction of imaginary identification with an "other" situated rivalry and dissension within the ego itself, which led Lacan to portray the ego as merely an illusion of coherence and mastery that covered up the fundamental lack and alterity that persisted beneath this *méconnaissance* or "misrecognition" of the self.[7] Within this "alienating function of the *I*, " Lacan says, there lies the "function of *méconnaissance* that characterizes the ego in all its structures," and in a direct attack on the therapeutic pretensions of ego psychology, he goes on to trace the debilitating effects of that function in the social as well as personal sphere. At one point Lacan described the ego as "a superstructure engaged in social alienation" (E151), and writing just after World War II Lacan said:

> We can thus understand the inertia characteristic of the formations of the *I*, and find there the most extensive definition of neurosis—just as the captation of the subject by the [imaginary] situation gives us the most general formula for madness, not only the madness that lies behind the walls of asylums, but also the madness that deafens the world with its sound and fury.
>
> The sufferings of neurosis and psychosis are for us a schooling in the passions of the soul. . . . (C53, rpt. A1, page 99; tr. page 7)

In 1953, the theoretical differences between Lacan and the International Psychoanalytic Association exploded into open conflict when the IPA refused to recognize officially the Société psychanalytique de Paris with which Lacan was associated. Although fraught with the usual personal antagonisms and ambitions endemic to institutional rivalries, the debate settled on Lacan's advocacy of the "short session" and its threat to the professional status of psychoanalysis in the eyes of the public and medical community (see the biographical sketch above). It is unclear, however, if Lacan himself saw this as a crucial issue, since in January 1953 he promised to conform to the usual "analytic hour" adopted by the IPA as its standard. (Whether or not he kept that promise is debatable; see F412, page 107.) When he did split with the IPA later that year in the famous *"scission"* of 1953, Lacan did denouce these authoritarian training practices, but he took his stand on a more fundamental theoretical issue. He called it the "Function and Field of Speech and Language in Psychoanalysis" (C58), and he summed up his position in the claim that "psychoanalysis has only a single medium: the patient's speech" (C58, rpt. A2, page 247; tr. A2j, page 40).

The issues raised in this long and complicated manifesto occupied Lacan for the following decade, but its polemical thrust was immediately obvious. "This ego," Lacan said, "whose strength our theorists now define by its capacity to bear frustration, is frustration in its essence. Not frustration of a desire of the subject, but frustration by an object in which his desire is alienated" (A2, page 250; tr. page 42). Consequently, rather than strengthening the patient's sense of ego, Lacan argued that the analyst must "suspend the subject's certainties until their last mirages have been consumed" and the subject can assume his history "in so far as it is constituted by the speech addressed to the other" (A2, pages 251, 257; tr. pages 42, 48). Unlike the imaginary other of the mirror stage, however, which threatened to capture the subject within the fictional direction of the ego, this new "other"—which Lacan began to designate as the Other (*Autre*) with a capital "O" ("*A* ")—was situated in what Freud called *die andere Platz* or "other scene": the unconscious. The relation of this Other to the subject, Lacan said, is constituted not through the "drives" or "regression" so familiar to ego psychology but as a language. This conclusion brought Lacan to one of his most famous proclamations, "the unconscious of the subject is the discourse of the other" (A2, page 265; tr. page 55). [8]

This emphasis on language, discourse, or what Lacan began calling more generally the "symbolic" reflects what Lacan claimed was the centrality of language to Freud's own work. Lacan argued that Freud showed in the *Traumdeutung* that the dream "has the structure of a sentence," and Lacan insisted that the elaboration of the dream must be understood as a rhetoric, governed by rhetorical tropes such as "Ellipsis and pleonasm, hyperbaton or syllepsis . . . metaphor, catachresis, autonomasis, allegory, metonymy, and synecdoche . . . . The symptom is itself structured like a language," Lacan adds, and "resolves itself entirely in an analysis of language" (A2, pages 267-69; tr. pages 57-59, *passim*). Despite the fashion for adaptational therapies and behaviorist conditioning, he says, things do not begin with the act. "It was certainly the Word (*verbe*) that was in the beginning, and we live in its creation . . . . It is the world of words that creates the world of things . . . . Man speaks, then, but it is because the symbol has made him man" (A2, pages 271, 276; tr. pages 61, 65).

> The psychoanalytic experience has rediscovered in man the imperative of the Word as the law that has formed him in its image. It manipulates the poetic function of language to give to his desire its symbolic mediation. May that experience enable you to understand at last that it is in the gift of speech that all the reality of its effects resides; for it is by way of this gift that all reality has come to man and it is by his continued act that he maintains it. (A2, page 322; tr. page 106)

Freud was well aware of the centrality of speech to psychoanalysis, Lacan argues. That is why he suggested that the ideal faculty of psychoanalysis would include alongside psychiatry the history of civilization, mythology, and other fields of the humanities, to which Lacan adds rhetoric, grammar, and "that supreme pinnacle of the aesthetics of language, poetics." If such topoi sound archaic, Lacan says, so much the better, "For psychoanalysis in its early development [is] intimately linked to the discovery and study of symbols," and this emphasis on the symbolic in psychoanalysis "expresses in fact nothing less than the re-creation of human meaning in an arid period of scientism" (A2, pages 288, 289; tr. page 76).

Lacan's understanding of the importance of the symbolic and its role in human experience derived from two specific sources beyond Freud's work. One was Saussurean linguistics, from which he borrowed the distinction between the signifier and the signified and between speech (*parole*) and language (*langue*). The other was the structural anthropology developed by Claude Lévi-Strauss, from which Lacan derived his understanding of combinatorial functions and their role in organizing kinship structures. Much has been written about Lacan's self-acknowledged debt to structuralism and his claim that Saussure simply recast Freud's discovery in linguistic terms.[9] Yet Lacan carefully distinguishes between semiotic approaches that treat "language as a sign" conveying meaning—"*le malentendu du langage-signe* "—and his own psychoanalytic interest in language and its relation to the subject (see A2, page 296; tr. pages 83-84). Lévi-Strauss showed, Lacan argues, that the network of symbols is not subordinate to the signifying intentions of an individual; rather, the symbolic governs social relations as a whole, precedes the individual's arrival into that society, and persists after his death. In fact, the symbolic would overwhelm and annihilate the individual entirely "if desire did not preserve its part in the interferences and pulsations that the cycles of language cause to converge on him." Rather than meaning or communication, Lacan says "What is at stake in an analysis is the advent in the subject of that little reality that this desire sustains in him with respect to the symbolic conflicts and imaginary fixations as the means of their agreement, and our path is the intersubjective experience where this desire makes itself recognized (A2, page 279; tr. page 68).

This emphasis on the place of desire in the intersubjective ground of speech and language distinguishes Lacan's psychoanalytic understanding of language from that of structural linguistics and structural anthropology, which (at least for Lacan) tend to reduce language to a code and speech to communication. "The function of language is not to inform but to evoke," Lacan says; "What I seek in speech is the response of the other. What constitutes me as subject is my question . . . . I identify myself in language, but only by losing myself in it like an object" (A2, page 299; tr. page 86). Thus there emerges a distinction between the subject's "ego" understood as an autonomous *cogito* and the "I" of his discourse (A2, page 304; tr. page 90), and Lacan claims that it is the job of analysis to distinguish between them and to provide the occasion for the subject's own recognition of that distinction—what Lacan will later call the "radical ex-centricity" of the subject understood as an "effect" of the signifier. "We always come back, then to our double reference to speech and to language. In order to free the subject's speech, we introduce him into the language of his desire, that is to say, into the *primary language* in which, beyond what he tells us of himself, he is already talking to us unknown to himself, and, in the first place, in the symbols of the symptom" (A2, page 293; tr. page 81). [10]

Lacan's distinction between these two kinds of discourse, which he designates in this essay as "empty" and "full" speech, forms a theoretical ground in support of his two most radical innovations in psychoanalytic technique: the short session, and what Lacan calls the "analyst's abstention" (A2, page 309; tr. page 95). Both of these technical strategies are designed to frustrate the *méconnaissance* through which the subject tends to attribute an ideal subjectivity to the analyst and an autonomous objectivity to the reality that he perceives through the lens of his imaginary identification with that idealized subject. (What Lacan describes here as illusions are, of course, the implicit goals behind the therapeutic practice of ego psychology and adaptationalist analysis respectively.) Lacan agrees with more conventional analysts that this tendency is essential to the transference at the heart of analysis (see A2, page 308; tr. page 94). He contradicts traditional practice, however, when he insists that the analyst must undermine those imaginary relations because they make up the empty speech that masks the subject's place in the order of signifiers that comprises the symbolic order.

The short session constitutes an obstacle to these illusions because it prevents the subject from using the session to map his speech—and his sense of himself—onto the preordained coordinates of the analytic hour. "The fixing of a termination [to the analytic session]," Lacan says, "is equivalent to a spatializing projection in which he [the subject] finds himself already alienated from himself at the very beginning." To conform to the subject's expectation, in other words, is to "re-establish in the subject his original mirage insofar as he places his truth in us" (A2, page 310; tr. page 96). Cutting off the session abruptly thus "punctuates" the subject's speech and reveals the "dialectical" character of its intersubjective context, in which all speech is a request directed towards an "other" who is different from the subject and not in his power—in this case, the analyst. Terminating the session at unpredictable moments thus underscores the "otherness" of the analyst and "plays the part of a metric beat which has the full value of an actual intervention" (A2, page 252; tr. page 44).

These abrupt and apparently arbitrary terminations could, however, easily lead to an even more exaggerated sense of the analyst as an ideal or "strong" ego if he gives in to that flattering attribution of power. That is why

Lacan also insists that the analyst's role is a corollary "abstention" or "non-action." "What, then, lies behind the analyst's attitude?" Lacan had asked five years earlier: "The concern to provide the dialogue with a participant who is as devoid as possible of individual characteristics; we efface ourselves, we deprive the speaker of those expressions of interest, sympathy, and reaction that he expects to find . . . . We wish to avoid the trap that already lies concealed in the appeal, marked by the eternal pathos of faith, that the patient addresses to us" (C51, rpt. A2, page 106; tr. page 13).

The inevitable resentment that this attitude evokes in the patient is just an indication that "at a deeper level of emotional demand, it is participation in his illness that the patient expects from us" (A2, page 106; tr. page 13). The demand for a response, in other words, is motivated by the narcissistic identification with an other that has trapped the patient within the imaginary, and the fury unleashed by the Lacanian analyst is a manifestation of the aggressivity inherent in such identifications (see C51, C53). Meeting that demand with silence "suspends the mirage" that motivates it, forcing the subject to recognize the split between the "I" that speaks the demand to an auditor and the image of an ideal ego that the patient projects onto the analyst as a reflection of his own narcissistic desire for omnipotence.[11] Thus the analyst's technique must hinge on the distinction between these two positions of the subject:

> It is therefore always in the relation between the subject's ego
> (*moi*) and the "I" (*je*) of his discourse that you must understand
> the meaning of the discourse if you are to achieve the
> dealienation of the subject.
>
> But you cannot possibly achieve this if you cling to the
> idea that the ego of the subject is identical with the presence that
> is speaking to you. (C58, rpt. A2, page 304; tr. page 90)

The subject's sense of self is not, however, strictly limited to an imaginary projection onto the image of the analyst. As Lacan had demonstrated in his thesis, it is also implicated in the way that the subject represents the world to himself and his place in it, which Lacan simply calls the "reality" of the subject's experience. By making visible the complex web of imaginary identification and symbolic relations that support this reality, the analyst's abstention also marks the juncture between the symbolic order and what Lacan calls the "Real," which is experienced here as pure negativity, that which is *not* "there" in the subject's speech and which frustrates the imaginary identification with the analyst as an idealized image of the self. The analyst's refusal to reply, along with the corollary "dialectical punctuation" that occurs when the session is abruptly terminated, serve to reveal and to clarify the intricate relations among the three "elementary registers" of human experience that Lacan claims have never been distinguished before in psychoanalysis: the symbolic, the imaginary, and the real (see A2, page 309; tr. page 95).

Section Two: 1953-1963

Lacan's address to the conference in Rome thus declared his independence from the International Psychoanalytic Association on technical and theoretical grounds just as it snubbed the institutional hierarchy that had condemned him. His radical critique of therapeutic intervention and the attack on ego psychology, his rejection of a standard length for the analytic session, and his insistence on the centrality of language to analytic theory and practice challenged the traditional aims and methods of psychoanalysis as a discipline and reoriented the field towards what Lacan designated as the real, symbolic, and imaginary registers of human experience. These topics continued to occupy Lacan throughout the next decade and, in somewhat different forms, for the rest of his career.

Immediately following the "Discours de Rome," Lacan cast his theoretical innovations in a "return to Freud" that proceeded through detailed commentaries on several of Freud's texts. Lacan presented his remarks in a series of seminars at Saint Anne's Hospital, and this series was attended primarily by the analysts who had followed him after his break with the SPP. Following several years of smaller, less formal meetings, the seminars began in November of 1953 with a close reading of the "technical writings" of Freud and continued in this format through July of 1963. Each seminar was devoted to a specific topic of Freud's work and usually to one or two texts, and they were organized around regular oral presentations by Lacan and by members of the audience (see Section B for a complete description of these seminars).[12] Focussing on concepts such as the ego, transference, psychosis, the death drive, and repression, Lacan reoriented Freud's texts towards issues of language and signification which, Lacan said, Freud had recognized but had not been able to articulate because he lacked the Saussurean vocabulary necessary to describe them.

A striking example of this reorientation of Freud's work is Lacan's commentary on the case of Schreber, which Freud had studied in detail in "Psycho-Analytic Notes on an Autobiographical Account of a Case of Paranoia (Dementia Paranoides)" (1911). Freud claimed that Schreber's psychotic delusions were a defense against latent homosexual desires, but Lacan claims instead that they are the consequence of a "foreclosure" (*Verwerfung*) of a "primordial signifier," the name-of-the-father. It is Schreber's inability to assume a place in the symbolic order of language, Lacan says, that results in his fantasies about becoming the wife of God. "What is refused in the symbolic order re-emerges in the real," Lacan adds, and he goes on to argue that the auditory hallucinations Schreber hears murmuring ceaselessly around him are nothing other than imaginary manifestations of the symbolic functions that he lacks (see B14).

Lacan's critique of Freud's explanation of psychosis in this specific case derives from his more general revision of Freud's theory of the Oedipus complex. Lacan had been interested in the Oedipus complex since the 1930s, and he had traced its function in the formation of the subject's sense of self through narcissistic identifications within the family (see C45 and C46). By the time he began his seminars, though, Lacan conceived the Oedipal basis of subjectivity, sexual identity, and even the unconscious entirely within what he called the "order of the signifier." In the third section of Seminar III, for example, Lacan claims that the Saussurean distinction between the signifier and the signified is essential to the structure of the unconscious, which he describes here as being structured "like a language" (B14, page 187). The signifier operates according to its own laws, Lacan says, independently of any signified. It is "a sign which returns to another sign, which is as such structured to signify the absence of another sign" (B14, page 188). Disturbances in this chain of signifiers actually *produce* the delusions described by Schreber. There is no autonomous realm of repressed desires lurking somewhere "beyond speech" that can "break through" the chain simply because it is the signifiers themselves that generate the "absence" or "other scene" identified by psychoanalysis as the unconscious.

Even more importantly in terms of Freud's own account of the Oedipal conflict, Lacan argues that the subject's relation to the order of signifiers is what determines sexual identity, not some "innate" or biological predisposition. Prior to the subject's entry into the symbolic, Lacan says, there is a stage at which the subject can either accept (*Bejahung*) or reject (*Verwerfung*) the signifier in place of the object or the imaginary other. This is what Freud characterized as the Oedipal phase, and it occasions the passage of the subject from an imaginary identification with the father as "other" to a symbolic relation with the signifier of the father. That signifier Lacan calls the "name-of-the-father"; in cultural terms, it is the "Law," or, in Freudian terms, the phallus. Accepting one's relation to the phallus replaces the imaginary identification between self and other with a symbolic recognition of the place of the Other as the locus of speech and as the ground of one's being as subject in and to language.

Conceived in this way, Freud's notion of the Oedipus complex shows us that "the subject finds his place in a preformed symbolic apparatus which installs the law in sexuality" (page 191). Sexual identity thus derives from the symbolic resolution of an imaginary conflict, and Lacan claims that Freud identified this situation as "castration." Instead of wanting to *be* the phallus—that is, to be what the mother wants, the imaginary object of desire—the subject wants to *have* the phallus, to possess the symbolic attributes of subjectivity that come about through the subject's relation to the phallus as a signifier or, as Lacan says, as the primary signifier, the signifier of a lack. It is just this possibility of something "missing" or "lacking" that underlies the role of the phallus as a signifier, and it is the function of the phallus that it "literally rips out [the relation between man and woman] from the imaginary to situate it in the domain of the symbolic" (page 200). [13]

To assume their positions as subjects in the symbolic order, both men and women must undergo this "castration." Lacan goes on to say, however, that the positions occupied by men and women in the symbolic are not symmetrical, and he describes the feminine sex as possessing the character of absence or emptiness, or that of a "hole" around which her being oscillates. Despite his rejection of the biological determination of sexual identity, then, Lacan reinforces Freud's account of women as "lacking" something that men "possess," at least in the symbolic sense, and this position eventually became a point of bitter controversy when Lacan returned to it years later in response to the challenge of feminism (see Seminar XX [B31]).

In the 1950s, however, such judgments generally went unchallenged, and the semiotic dimension of Lacan's work seemed most radical. During this period, Lacan produced two of his most influential works: the seminar sessions in April 1955 on Poe's "The Purloined Letter," which were later published as C69, and other sessions on metaphor and metonymy from May 1956, which Lacan eventually presented as the paper "L'instance de la lettre" (C71). In both of these works, Lacan portrays the subject's sense of self and its relations to others as determined by the operation of the signifier. What Freud teaches us in *Beyond the Pleasure Principle,* Lacan says, is that "the subject must pass through the channels of the symbolic." Poe's story, however, shows that "not only the subject, but the subjects, grasped in their intersubjectivity . . . model their very being on the moment of the signifying chain which traverses them. If what Freud discovered and rediscovers with a perpetually increasing sense of shock has a meaning, it is that the displacement of the signifier determines the subjects in their acts" (C69, rpt. A2, page 30; tr. *YFS,* page 60).

This "displacement" of the signifier is made possible by its autonomy from the signified, and Lacan shows how Poe's story demonstrates that it is the letter itself, not its "message," that determines how the characters relate to each other. Even more importantly, Lacan says, the circulation of the letter among various characters proves that the position occupied by a particular individual vis-à-vis others in the story is not based on any inherent "character traits" or "personality" but instead depends entirely on the location of the letter at a particular moment. What Poe's story shows us is that our sense of self, of power, of Law, and even of "femininity" is merely an effect of the signifier and is a product of our inextricable subjection in and to what Lacan calls here the "insistence of the signifying chain."[14]

In "The Insistence of the Letter in the Unconscious, or Reason since Freud" (C71), Lacan goes on to specify the functions by which the signifier produces those effects. He notes that the relation between the signifier and the signified may be "arbitrary," as Saussure claimed, but nevertheless it is precisely determined by the interaction between what Roman Jakobson identified as the two poles of language, metaphor, and metonymy.[15] Lacan discusses these tropes in detail and offers his most systematic explanation of the connection between Freud's account of the unconscious and Saussure's distinction between the signifier and signified. Reminding his audience that language exists long before the entry of any individual subject, Lacan attacks the notion of an integrated self as represented in Descartes's *Cogito ergo sum* and claims instead that Freud discovered "the self's radical ex-centricity to itself" in relation to language (A2, pages 495, 524; tr. pages 148, 171). Freud identified a "radical heteronomy . . . gaping within man," Lacan says, a split that results from the subject's relation to the signifier or "the 'letter,'" which Lacan defines here as "the essentially localized structure of the signifier" (A2, page 501; tr. page 153).

Lacan represents the function of the signifier with the "algorithm" S/s, which he uses to represent Saussure's theory of what Lacan calls "the primordial position of the signifier [S] and the signified [s] as being distinct orders separated initially by a barrier resisting signification" (A2, page 497; tr. page 149). What is important about Saussure's discovery, Lacan says, is not the celebrated arbitrariness of the connection between signifier and signified. Rather, it is the notion of a barrier between them. The signifier does not immediately refer us to some signified as its fixed meaning; instead, the chain of signifiers operates according to "the laws of a closed order" in which the signifier never crosses over to the realm of the signified but "always anticipates meaning by unfolding its dimension before it." As a result, Lacan says that meaning "insists" (*insiste*) in the chain of signifiers but that it never "consists" in any one of them. Consequently, we must accept the idea of an "incessant sliding [*glissement incessant*] of the signified under the signifier" (A2, pages 501-02; tr. pages 152-54).

Lacan's emphasis on the barrier that separates the signifier from the signified leads him to distinguish metaphor from metonymy as the two sides or "slopes" (*les versants*) of the field of the signifier. Saussure stressed the horizontal linearity of the chain of discourse, Lacan argues, and that chain is constituted through the metonymic combination of one signifier after another. But there is in fact a "polyphony" of discourse that also aligns each signifier vertically along the several staves of a musical score at any point, and that dimension is constituted through the metaphorical substitution of one signifier for another (A2, page 503; tr. page 154).

In a detailed analysis of what he calls the "creative spark" of metaphorical substitution, Lacan rejects the usual arguments that metaphor allows the simultaneous presentation of two signifiers or, even worse, the possibility of presenting two signifieds within the discursive realm of the signifier. Instead, metaphor "flashes between two signifiers one of which has taken the place of the other in the signifying chain, the occulted signifier remaining present through its (metonymic) connection with the rest of the chain" (A2, page 507; tr. page 157). In other words, as one signifier replaces another, it drives the first "beneath the bar" where it occupies the place originally occupied by the signified—in short, where the earlier signifier functions as the "meaning" of the current signifier. Lacan says this is how the *effect* of meaning or signification is achieved, even though we can never actually cross over from the realm of the signifier into that of the signified. He therefore endorses an inverted version of Saussure's formulation of the sign—S/s—but qualifies it by substituting another signifier in the position of the signified: S'/S.[16]

Lacan's modification of Saussure's formula has extensive implications for his understanding of subjectivity as well. Lacan claims that man has traditionally deluded himself into believing that he occupies the axis joining the signifier and the signified; or, in other words, that subjectivity is situated on the bar in Saussure's formula s/S as it marks the site of signification and the juncture between words and things. According to Lacan, however, signification possesses a *"valeur de renvoi "* because it is constituted within a retrospective relation between two signifiers, and this relation installs a *"manque de l'être "* or "lack-of-being" in the subject's relation to the object. The axis between the signifier and the signified is nowhere, Lacan asserts, or at least always was nowhere until Freud discovered it in the unconscious (tr. page 166). Lacan claims that Freud's discovery proved the Cartesian *cogito* to be a "mirage," and he argues that Descartes's "I think therefore I am" should actually read "I think where I am not, therefore I am where I do not think" (A2, page 518; tr. page 166). The solution, Lacan says, was also defined by Freud: *Wo es war, soll Ich werden,* which Lacan translates as *"Là où fut ça, il me faut advenir "* ("There where it [i.e., the id] was, I must come to be" [A2, page 524, my translation]). This phrase marks what Lacan calls the "radical ex-centricity" of the subject's relation to its "self," the "radical heteronomy that Freud's discovery shows gaping within man" (A2, page 524; tr. page 172), which results from the "signifying game" between metonymy and metaphor insofar as it includes "the active edge that splits my desire between a refusal of the signifier and a lack of being" (A2, page 517; tr. page 166). Language thus poses the question of being to the subject or, more accurately, "in place of the subject," and Lacan claims that man is caught "in the rails of metonymy," "eternally stretching forth towards the *desire for something else [le désir d'autre chose]*" (A2, page 518; tr. page 167).

Lacan's detailed accounts of the semiotic properties of the signifying chain rewrote Freud's works in the terms of Saussurean linguistics, and it insured his reception as part of the "structuralist" movement that dominated the French intellectual scene during the 1960s and 1970s. Lacan himself recognized that affiliation, though at times uneasily (see E183). Read in conjunction with structuralist analyses in literature or anthropology, however, Lacan's specifically psychoanalytic interests become apparent. Lévi-Strauss's analysis of myth or the syntactic analyses of plot and character exemplified by Propp or Todorov tend to abstract structural properties from their specific, concrete contexts and treat them as universal combinatory laws. Lacan, conversely, insisted on the "materiality" of the signifier. He argued that the subject's relation to the signifying chain was based on a desire that originated in the concrete, lived experience of the subject's individual past and that was oriented towards the real.[17] Moreover, although the position of the subject described by Lacan was informed by the order of the signifier and sustained by its rhetorical functions, that position also bore within it a loss and yearning that registered its link with the imaginary, as well as a sense of dread and despair that exposed its inevitable complicity with the death that marked the limit of the symbolic:

> Thus the symbol manifests itself first of all as the murder of the thing, and this death constitutes in the subject the eternalization of his desire.
>
> The first symbol in which we recognize humanity in its vestigial traces is the sepulture, and the intermediary of death can be recognized in every relation in which man comes to the life of his history . . . .
>
> So when we wish to attain in the subject what was before the serial articulations of speech [*parole*], and what is primordial to the birth of symbols, we find it in death, from which his existence takes on all the meaning it has. It is in effect

as a desire for death that he affirms himself for others; if he identifies himself with the other, it is by fixing him solidly in the metamorphosis of his essential image, and no being is ever evoked by him except among the shadows of death.

To say that his mortal meaning reveals in speech [*parole*] a center exterior to language is more than a metaphor; it manifests a structure. (A2, pages 319-20; tr. pages 104-05)

This inevitable imbrication of speech, desire, and death occasioned by the subject's relation to the symbolic occupied much of Lacan's attention in Seminar VI (1958-1959), which focuses on an extended reading of *Hamlet*. In the course of that reading, Lacan portrays Hamlet suspended between an imaginary identification with his mother and a symbolic subjection to the Dead Father (represented literally by the Ghost). He also presents an extended commentary on what he calls "*le petit objet a*" (also referred to as the "*objet a*"), which might be defined simply as the object of desire as such, i.e., that which is missing and is experienced as an imaginary fantasm. In addition, Lacan elaborates on the role of the "Other," introduced in C58 in distinction to the imaginary "other" of the mirror stage, and argues that *Hamlet* illustrates the inevitable subordination of imaginary identification to the law of the symbolic. In doing so, Lacan says, Shakespeare's play demonstrates that "the desire of man is the desire of the Other" in the sense that the desire is both "for" the Other and also modeled on what the subject experiences as the Other's desire.

Relations among the subject, the Other, and the "*objet a*" were articulated further in Seminar IX (1961-1962), where Lacan describes them as an effect of the "splitting" of the subject endemic to the alienating direction of imaginary identification and its resolution in symbolic representation. The psychoanalytic discovery of the unconscious, Lacan says, means that the subject is constituted by what it cannot know and in relation to an object that it can never possess. The result is what Freud identified as the *Ichspaltung*, the "splitting" of the subject which underlies the psychoanalytic understanding of identification. (Lacan's terms for this splitting are "*le refente*" and "*le clivage*," which he generally uses interchangeably.) The "*objet a*" is an effect of that division, a remainder ("*un reste*") that designates the cause of desire. "*Dissimulé dans l'Autre*," this "*objet a*" thus orients the movement of identification at the same time that it serves as its goal, the "*point d'arrêt*" of metonymic deferral.

The exact nature of the "*objet a*" and the "Other" cannot be specified in Lacan's work because the terms indicate functions or principles rather than single entities or concepts, as suggested by Lacan's substitution of the letter "a" for what he earlier called the imaginary "other." As a corollary, Jacques-Alain Miller has suggested that the Other be thought of simply as a letter, an "O" (or

"A" for *Autre*) that serves algebraically to designate any number of concepts—death, the symbolic father, the role of the analyst, the locus of speech, the unconscious, etc.—linked only "by their dimension of exteriority and by their determinant function in relation to the subject" (G738, tr. page 623). This tendency toward algebraic formulations becomes pronounced in Lacan's published work from this period. He tends to reprise many of the topics introduced in C58 and the earlier seminars—psychosis, transference, the symbolic basis of sexual identification—but he now rewrites them in diagrams that map increasingly complicated relations among a collection of terms and figures that proliferate at a surprising and often confusing rate (see, for example, C72 and C80).

Unlike the Borromean knots and other topological figures that appear in Lacan's later work, however, where the figures serve as the basis for Lacan's theoretical speculation, the graphs and diagrams from this period tend rather to supplement the more or less expository argument embodied in Lacan's recourse to Freudian terms and formulations. The works published during this time often dwell on this connection, attributing to Freud, for example, a distinction between the male organ and the phallus understood as a signifier that occasions the splitting of the subject, the "privileged signifier of that mark in which the role of the logos is joined with the advent of desire" (C73, rpt. A2, page 692; tr. page 287). Similarly, Lacan dismisses the usual psychoanalytic formulation of feminine sexuality in terms of passivity, masochism, and frigidity as a biologistic distortion of Freud's own concepts (C77). The "phallocentrism" of Freud's model, Lacan says, is "entirely conditioned by the intrusion of the signifier in man's psyche" and is "strictly impossible to deduce from any pre-established harmony of this psyche with the [biological] nature that it [purportedly] expresses" (C72, rpt. A2, pages 554-55, tr. 198). Thus despite the much-publicized neologisms, the quasi-algebraic formulas, and extended permutations of diagrams that at times attained almost comic proportions (a fact that did not escape Lacan's own wry notice), Lacan remained rather narrowly faithful to what he called his "return to Freud" throughout the period framed by his split with the Société psychanalytique de Paris and the formation of the Ecole freudienne de Paris in 1964.

Section Three: 1964-1973

Lacan's "excommunication" from the Société française de psychanalyse brought about a number of changes. Most visibly, the site of his seminars moved from Saint Anne's Hospital to the Ecole Normale Superieur, and his audience suddenly broadened to include a much wider range of intellectuals and academics than had previously heard him speak. Changes in the direction of Lacan's work were not, however, so apparent at first. During the years leading up to this break and immediately following the formation of the EFP, Lacan published almost nothing outside of three brief essays on philosophical and literary figures (see C82, C83, and C84) and even briefer abstracts of his seminars for the *Annuaire de l'Ecole practique des hautes études*. With the notable exception of B18, B22, and B31, only partial texts of some of the seminars from 1959-1974 have been published, and little reliable information about the unpublished seminars is available to the public.

The most extended written texts by Lacan that appeared during the second decade following his declaration of war with the international psychoanalytic community were in fact internal communications regarding the structure and policies of the Ecole freudienne de Paris (C88-C92). Published in *Scilicet,* the journal of the EFP, the policies advocated in these papers are intended to institutionalize some of the most radical implications of the theoretical innovations proposed by Lacan in the preceding decade, such as the "self-authorization" of the analyst and the elevation of theoretical work over the practice of psychoanalysis which was suggested by the procedure of *la passe.* But while Lacan's proposals were certainly controversial and marked significant changes in the organizational practices and policies governing the transmission of psychoanalysis along Lacanian lines, they clearly were derived from the theoretical principles established during the years 1953-1963 and suggest that Lacan's attention had turned for the moment to institutionalizing his return to Freud rather than extending its conceptual implications.

Given the lack of new and speculative publications during this period, it is ironic that Lacan's current reputation as one of the most influential thinkers in post-war France derives almost entirely from these years. The basis for that reputation is, of course, the *Ecrits* (A2), a monumental collection of 924 closely printed pages edited by Lacan himself, with an elaborate apparatus designed to guide the reader through the 28 essays reprinted there. In *Ecrits,* Lacan points out and sometimes corrects earlier mistakes, contextualizing and expanding some essays while dismissing others as mere historical curiosities. In short, Lacan seized the occasion of his collection to offer the reader a guided tour through the intellectual biography that had made Lacan what he was in 1966: the most prominent and controversial psychoanalyst in France. A work whose difficult and idiosyncratic style immediately became the subject of controversy, awe, scorn, and emulation, *Ecrits* suddenly extended Lacan's influence far beyond the audience capable of following his arguments or even interested in them. Projecting a public persona that dramatized the obscurity of his writing and reinforced it with a wryly self-conscious attitude of haughty disdain and outrageous mystery, Lacan quickly came to personify the best and worst aspects of that peculiarly Parisian phenomenon, the intellectual superstar.[18]

It is impossible to tell how seriously Lacan took the public interest in his work. He clearly delighted in flaunting his idiosyncrasies—at one point, Lacan freely admitted to being a little psychotic, though he averred that being even more psychotic might make him a better analyst (E280)—and he was prone to brutal and gratuitously humiliating public attacks on what he considered obtuse or foolish responses to his arguments. Nevertheless, Lacan also repeatedly and painstakingly described the principal tenets of his approach to psychoanalysis for interviewers from magazines and newspapers, and the clarity of his remarks in many of these interviews belies the charges of deliberate obfuscation so often levied against him by reviewers and by rival figures such as Foucault, Derrida, and eventually Althusser. Time and again, Lacan answered questions about his intellectual heritage, explaining how Freud's work was related to broader philosophical issues and recognizing his debt to, as well as differences from, the work of Jean-Paul Sartre, who was still an intellectual touchstone for the French public in the 1960s and whose career Lacan claimed to have watched with interest from its beginning (see E183 and E187). (It is difficult to keep in mind that Lacan was 65 when the *Ecrits* was published, considerably older than Sartre and later writers such as Barthes, Foucault, Derrida and others who suddenly emerged into the limelight at this time.) Even when challenged by students at Vincennes as a reactionary spokesman for the State, Lacan responded seriously and tried to explain how the revolutionary rhetoric of their accusations simply reinforced the demand for a Master that their—and his own—politics rebuked. So while some of his justifications for the undeniably difficult character of his written and spoken style may have been proposed with tongue in cheek, Lacan clearly seems to have been interested during these years in conveying an accurate and precise sense of his work to a wide audience, a pedagogical goal that inevitably reduced the time for theoretical innovation.

That goal was pursued largely in the seminars, where Lacan set about consolidating his work, clarifying and elaborating the speculative insights of the preceding decade. During this time, a more specifically Lacanian discourse gradually supplanted the traditional Freudian terms and formulations that characterized his earlier work, and issues and topics began to appear that derived more from Lacan's own interests than from the traditional concerns of psychoanalysis. A significant portion of Seminar XI, for example, which is entitled *The Four Fundamental Concepts of Psychoanalysis,* is devoted to the topic of *le regard,* or the gaze, and is inspired not by Freud's work so much as that of Merleau-Ponty and especially Sartre.[19] Rather than associating the gaze with the instinctual drive of the *Schaulust,* Lacan describes it as a function of the *objet a,* a product of the subject's splitting in relation to the signifier, and he claims that the function of the gaze is inherent in the *méconnaissance* of narcissistic identification that characterizes what Lacan calls the "scopic field" of the imaginary.[20]

Even when Lacan does turn to more conventional Freudian topics, such as the four concepts "fundamental" to psychoanalysis—the unconscious, repetition, transference, and the drive—he conceives them entirely within the parameters developed in the earlier seminars. The unconscious is merely "a play of the signifier" (B22b, page 130), a gap in the signifying chain. Repetition is derived not from instinctual need but from the subject's conjunction with the inevitable lack that marks the signifier's relation to the real. Transference is a repetition of the "missed encounter" inherent in symbolic relations and the subject's inevitably ex-centric position in relation to his own subjectivity. And the drive is more like a "montage" than an organic need, a montage whose "partial" character arises because the sexuality of the subject must pass through the "networks of the signifier" (B22, pages 154, 161; tr. B22b, pages 169, 177). As he had for forty years, of course, Lacan insisted that such definitions are simply based on a close reading of Freud's work. Unlike Lacan's earlier revisions of Freud's theories of psychosis, though, and unlike his extended commentary on the concept of the ego that tended to translate the issues of Freudian discourse into semiotic terms, the seminars for the years 1964-1973 take their point of departure from a problematic derived from the elaboration of concepts and terms peculiar to Lacan's own work, such as the *objet a,* the barred subject ($), the Other, and, increasingly, *jouissance.*

Most of these terms had been introduced earlier, and relations among them had been explored to account for phenomena that psychoanalysts had traditionally attributed to biological drives or some essential psychic realm that language merely reflected or "expressed." Now, however, Lacan began identifying effects that he claimed were either confused or entirely invisible from more traditional perspectives. For example, Lacan increasingly emphasized the importance of the "fading" of the subject before the object of his desire. He identified this effect within Jones's account of "aphanisis" (see B22, page 191ff; tr. page 210ff), but its precise function emerges as such only within the conceptual framework of Lacan's increasingly complicated graphs and formulas. Most importantly, however, it was during these years that Lacan began focussing on the phenomena of "*jouissance,* " an experience of pleasure ordinarily conflated with sexuality but that in Lacan's work problematizes the entire character of sexual relations, desire, and the subordination of the body to the law of the signifier.

In Seminar XI, for example, Lacan observes that his comparison of the drive to a "montage" is necessitated by the way "sexuality participates in the psychical life, in a way that must conform to the gap-like structure that is the structure of the unconscious" (B22, page 160; tr. page 176). There is nothing whatsoever in the psyche by which the subject may situate itself as male or female, Lacan says. Gender identity is entirely dependent on the scenario situated in the field of the Other, the Oedipus complex. Consequently, sexuality is represented in the psyche by something other than sexuality itself, and is established through the overlap of two different "lacks": one inherent in the subject's dependence on a signifier that can be found only in the field of the Other; and the second, the "real lack," derived from what the living being loses in reproduction: "namely, that the living being, by being subject to sex, has fallen under the blow of individual death" (B22, page 186; tr. page 205).

Lacan's point here seems to be that the reproduction of the body through sex implies the death of the parent in the life of the child, something like the presence of the signifier depends on the "death" of the thing that it represents. Consequently, the body of the subject is related to its progeny across the insurmountable barrier of death, just as the thing is related to the signifier that "represents" it across the insurmountable barrier between the signifier and the signified. In both cases, the subject is separated from its point of reference by an absolute "otherness" and so experiences that relation as a "lack." This is why the subject's relation to the Other is constituted through a dialectical combination of "joining" and "separation" that Lacan identifies as "fading" or, in Jones's terms, "aphanisis." There simply cannot be a subject without this aphanisis occurring somewhere, and it is in the alienation inherent in this "fading" that the "dialectic of the subject" is born in the "central lack in which the subject experiences himself as desire" (B22, pages 201, 239; tr. pages 221, 265). The subject is thus inevitably barred from discourse, a situation Lacan designates as the barred subject ($), and the objects of its desire are always the same: they are all the "lost" object, designated by the *objet a*.

The fading of the subject before the object of its desire would preclude the consummation of the more specific form of desire that motivates sexual relations in most traditional accounts, and Lacan in fact claimed repeatedly that there is no such thing as sexual relations. Most of the seminars from this period take up this surprising claim, and it forms a central focus of Lacan's attention throughout the decade. Idiosyncratic as it sounds, however, Lacan's rejection of the existence of sexual relations led to an even more controversial claim that eventually split his feminist followers into antagonistic camps. One of the reasons sexual relations are impossible, Lacan asserted, is that women can only function as a "*pas-tout*," literally a "not-all" in the symbolic realm of social intercourse that defines human relations (see C94).

All of these claims rely on the constitutive role of the symbolic in human experience. In Seminar XIV, for example, Lacan claims that the great secret of psychoanalysis is that there is no such thing as the sexual act, and he defends that claim by exploring the semiotic basis of the act itself. Lacan defines "act" as a doubling of the signifier that will permit the subject to be inserted in a signifying chain where it is inscribed. He then argues that the sexual act is impossible because there is always a third object between man and woman whose substitutive function creates a slippage that prohibits them from being related in an essentially fixed opposition. This third object is the phallus, the "sign of a lack" (see B25, page 248). Relations between men and women always take place in reference to this "third" that grants the relation its significance and lifts their pleasure from mere satisfaction to *jouissance* (B25, page 66).

Jouissance is thus based on reference to something other than what is immediately present in the relation between two individuals, and it is this reference beyond the couple that differentiates *jouissance* from pleasure. Lacan describes *jouissance* as suspended between the two bodies, always dependent on the body of the other, so that the *jouissance* of this other remains adrift ("*reste à la dérive* " [B25, page 94]). *Jouissance* therefore functions as the limit of pleasure and is associated with the *objet a* as that which always remains beyond that limit, instituting the principle of repetition and always eluding the pleasure principle. Lacan claims that the *objet a* is that part of the body where *jouissance* can take refuge, and he says that the (barred) subject's conjunction with the *objet a* is "engendered" there, at the disjunction in the field of the Other between the body and *jouissance* (B25, page 107).

The most extended discussion of this issue in Lacan's work occurs in Seminar XX (B31), which is one of Lacan's best-known works. Lacan argues that sexual relations are impossible: "*il n'y a pas de rapport sexuel,* " Lacan remarks several times (see B31, pages 35, 53, etc.). They are impossible because the very notion of two individuals joining together to make a "One"— the aim of love, *l'amour* —ignores the fundamental gap (*la béance*) that is the cause of the subject's desire in the first place and that is the origin of its demand for love (B31, page 16). Man's desire is the desire of the Other, Lacan says; that is why the unconscious was invented. But love ignores that; it is "*une passion qui peut être l'ignorance du désir.* " As a result, love always demands more love, "again" ("*encore* "). In fact, Lacan observes, "*encore* " "is the proper name of the fault line [*la faille*] in the Other from which the demand for love originates" (B31, page 11).

The most controversial passages in Seminar XX deal with the issue of sexual differentiation and focus on two closely related topics: the site of sexual difference, and the origin of femininity. Lacan recognizes that "*l'être du corps* " (the "being of the body") is sexed, but he claims that this is "secondary." Experience teaches us that the *jouissance* of the body cannot be attributed to these sexual traces because that *jouissance* "symbolizes the Other" (B31, page 12). One of those sexed beings, man, is marked as "male" only because he is "provided with" the organ "*dit phallique.* " I say "called phallic," Lacan adds, just as the other being is marked by the possession of "*le sexe corporel, le sexe de la femme.* " "*De la femme,* " he stresses, for the same reason the male is only "called" phallic: there is no transcendent identity that underlies the implicit division between the sexes. Their "sexuality" derives from signifying attributes conferred on people by their relation to the symbolic.

In short, Lacan stresses these phrases to emphasize that sexual indentity has its origin in language, not the body. This is true for both sexes, but in this seminar Lacan focuses on the discursive constitution of femininity, which he characterized earlier as incomplete, "*pas-tout*" or "not-all": "The sexed being of *ces femmes pas-toutes* does not derive from the body but results from the logical exigency of speech [*parole*]" (B31, page 15). Any time a speaking being ("*un être parlant* ") of any sort, male or female, assumes a role under the banner of women, Lacan says, that being is situated within the phallic function as "*pas-tout*" (B31, page 68). He goes on to argue that "Woman" as a general category exists only as excluded by the nature of things, which is in fact the nature of words. Thus the very notion of making One of these "two" sexes is misleading, since they are not "two" at all but are only situated as oppositions within the logic of speech. Conversely, it is not possible to transcend their division in speech, since they exist only in relation to each other, a "difference" constituted entirely within the symbolic order—and in relation to the *objet a.* Lacan concludes that this sexual being, like any form of being that would be posed as absolute, "is ever only the fracture, the break, the interruption of the formula 'sexed being' insofar as the sexed being is interested in *jouissance* " (B31, page 16).

Feminists have vehemently criticized such claims as sexist recapitulations of the tired phallocentricism of Freud's own works, which define woman as lacking something that man has, a penis. Lacan argues, of course, that any subject, male or female, is constituted about a lack, a "*manque à être* " inherent in its relation to the symbolic; but he does say that men and women relate to this lack differently. A woman seeks a man under the title of signifier ("*au titre de signifiant* "), but a man treats a woman as the missing *objet a* or, in other words, as a fantasm of wholeness or totality—which is, as we have seen, excluded by the nature of things, or words. This missing part is signified by—and in fact "is"—the phallus, so Lacan describes the *jouissance* inherent in this relation as "phallic." There is a type of *jouissance* associated with the feminine, however, one "beyond the phallus" that is derived from the very "*pas-tout*" character of femininity (B31, page 68). Lacan claims that the silence and mystery surrounding this supplementary *jouissance* is the same mystic ecstasy experienced by saints and represented in Bernini's statue of Saint Theresa (which serves as the cover illustration for this seminar). This is the "*jouissance* of the Other," Lacan says, the Other that woman might be if she existed (B31, page 77).

Lacan claims that what really polarizes people on the issue of femininity and its relation to *jouissance* is the question of just what woman knows about the place of the Other "*dont elle jouit* " (B31, page 82): "There is a *jouissance* proper to her (i.e., the woman), to this 'her' which does not exist and which signifies nothing. There is a *jouissance* proper to her and of which she herself may know nothing, except that she experiences it—that much she does know" (B31, page 69; tr. F370, page 145). Because she experiences this feminine *jouissance* without knowing it, the woman is suspended between two points in Lacan's system: between the S(Ø) that marks the place of the Other (unattainable by definition and hence barred), and the place of the phallus that marks the position of man in the symbolic and that is supported by *phallic jouissance,* the "*jouissance de l'idiot* " (B31, page 75).

Lacan's account of the feminine is obviously an attempt to explain the idealist images of Woman, and it is also a deliberately polemical attack on the essentializing tendency of some feminist movements to treat the feminine as a privileged realm of being that is autonomous from not only the masculine culture but from cultural determination in general.[21] Feminists sympathetic to Lacan argue that he has simply exposed the cultural (symbolic) mechanisms through which woman is constituted as "lacking" in Western culture and so provides at least the grounds on which that subordination can be contested (see F333 and F334). Feminists hostile to Lacan argue that he presents this account not only as a universal scheme—and hence inevitable—but also as a prescriptive program designed to keep women in their place, which is no place (see K1219, K1220). Whatever Lacan's intentions, however, his contentious and condescending address to women practicing psychoanalysis and his characterization of woman as "*pas-tout*" and ignorant of her own *jouissance* recalled the very worst sexist elements in traditional psychoanalysis and insured that this seminar would remain one of the most controversial texts published under Lacan's name.[22]

Lacan's remarks about knowledge and truth in the eighth section of Seminar XX shift the focus of the seminar from the definition of sexuality to the role of *jouissance* as a link among the three registers of experience that he designates as the real, the symbolic, and the imaginary. Lacan distinguishes between the "truth of being" ("*la verité* ") and a knowledge supported entirely by the signifier as such that has *jouissance* as its limit, and he claims that the question of knowledge is one of love, not being (B31, pages 85, 84). Oriented towards *jouissance,* this knowledge obtains a power far beyond the illusory fantasm of a "whole truth," and Lacan emphasizes the difference between truth and knowledge by labeling the domain of knowledge a *"mi-dire, "* a "half-saying" that recognizes its limit as the cause of desire rather than the fantasy of being. That limit is marked with the *objet a,* the cause of desire, which Lacan here defines as the *"semblant "* of being. A trace of the imaginary form in which the ego "envelopes" the object and situates it as the object of desire, Lacan claims that the *objet a* constitutes reality for the subject. Lacan is careful, however, to distinguish between this reality and the real, which he says is inscribed only as an *"impasse de la formalisation, "* an opening between the *semblant,* constituted by the symbolic, and the reality that is supported by the concrete experience of human life (B31, pages 85, 87).

The issue of knowledge thus turns on a relation between being and saying for Lacan, and he claims that for him being is just *"un fait de dit, "* a fact or product of speech (B31, page 207). The symbolic must not be confused with being but instead only supports the "ex-sistence" of saying (*"dire"*), which undermines the imaginary relation of the individual to his body and constitutes the subject simply as *"un supposé à ce qui parle, "* a supposition of that which speaks, or, more simply, the "I." Earlier, in C71, Lacan had explored the "ex-centric" position of the subject in speech at length and traced it through the algebraic formulas that marked the relation between metonymy and metaphor as a property of the signifier. In this seminar, Lacan diagrams the relation between being and saying with the figure of the Borromean knot, a figure of three interwoven loops borrowed from the field of topology and used by Lacan to suggest the inextricable interdependence of the real, the symbolic, and the imaginary. Proposing several variations of this figure and other "little loops of thread" as the bases of his remarks, Lacan goes on to praise "mathematical language" in general for its adequacy to the "exigencies of pure demonstration" (page 116), and he concludes this penultimate section of the seminar by asserting *"La mathématisation seule atteint à un réel. "*[23]

Section Four: 1974-1981

This turn towards mathematics marks the final phase of Lacan's career, when relations among the real, symbolic, and imaginary registers of human experience occupy most of Lacan's attention, and when he began relying on mathematics and topology rather than his version of Saussurean linguistics as the paradigmatic discourse of psychoanalytic theory. Many issues are conceived in reference to permutations on the Borromean knot, and Lacan's remarks refer as much to his own diagrams and three-dimensional figures as to readings of Freud and the complex network of cultural and philosophical references that support Lacan's earlier work. Dismissed by some as senile wanderings and praised by others as a step toward scientific rigor, these knots and mathemes generated yet another controversy among Lacanian psychoanalysts that persists today. It has divided current Lacanian work between those oriented towards the increasing "mathematicization" of psychoanalysis and others who see such efforts as a futile and misleading attempt to found a "meta-theory" of psychoanalysis, preferring instead the more discursive and concrete style of Lacan's earlier work.[24]

Much of Lacan's work from this period is inaccessible or obscure. Nothing from Seminars XXI and XXVI has been published, and the texts for the other seminars that have appeared in *Ornicar?* are quite brief and do not always render the many diagrams from these seminars clearly, despite some imaginative graphics. Nevertheless, these final seminars do address a number of issues raised earlier in Lacan's work and at times propose rather drastic reevaluations or at least extensions of previous positions. Perhaps the most important of these issues is raised by Lacan's extended comments on the real, which is considered here in relation to *jouissance* and meaning ("*sens*") in addition to being considered as part of the Lacanian triad made up of the real, the symbolic, and the imaginary, or "RSI" as Lacan begins calling it.

Proceeding from relations suggested by yet another version of the Borromean knot, Lacan claims that intersections among the three loops of the knot—which stand for the real, symbolic, and imaginary dimensions of human experience—help situate three other phenomena: the *jouissance* of the Other, which arises in the area shared by the imaginary and the real; phallic *jouissance,* situated within the common space of the symbolic and the real; and meaning, which lies at the junction of the imaginary and the symbolic. In addition, each of these areas is associated with yet another set of terms or effects: meaning with "consistency"; phallic *jouissance* with "ex-sistence"; and the *jouissance* of the Other with the effect of a hole ("*trou* ") in the real. The importance of the real to all of these relations is established unequivocally by Lacan in Seminar XXIII, where he claims flatly that the real is what holds together the imaginary and the symbolic (B34d).

Despite its centrality to human experience, Lacan insists that the real cannot be experienced directly because it is, like the unconscious, "*troué,* " literally "holed" (B33d, page 50), and orients our experience by serving as its limit. Lacan says that this limit appears in Freud's work as death, and he claims that the death drive described by Freud *is* the real in so far as it can be thought only as an impossibility (B34). The connection between the real and the unconscious occurs in the speaking being ("*le parlêtre* ") because that being is "incarnated" within the symbolic and so subject to the only thing that can make a hole in the real, i.e., the signifier. In Seminar XXIII Lacan claims that language itself can be understood only if we treat it as something that makes a hole in the real rather than something that carries a message or meaning (B34a), and he adds that in fact the orientation of the real forecloses meaning entirely because the real is *"toujours un bout, "* an end or limit that circumscribes the hole around which the effect of meaning arises. The rim of this "hole" is where the effect of ex-sistence emerges, Lacan says, and it is associated with *jouissance* insofar as it concerns the Other of the body or, more simply, the Other of the opposite sex (B33).

Lacan moves through these remarks very quickly, but the later sessions of Seminar XXII focus these new terms rather closely on the topic of femininity and its relation to the real and to the unconscious. Despite the phallocentric nature of the symbolic, Lacan says, women do not have to try to integrate themselves into the categories of man because they have a special relation to the unconscious. They treat the unconscious with *"une sauvagerie, "* with *"une liberté d'allure tout à fait saisissante. "* If I had to embody the idea of freedom, Lacan says, I would choose a woman (B33, page 95). Returning to this topic in a later session, Lacan also claims that "women are real, and terribly so," and he contrasts their mode of existence to that implicated in the symbolic and its relation to the unconscious:

> *Elles sont réelles, et même terriblement. Elles ne sont même que ça. Elles ne consistent qu'en tant que le symbolique ex-sistent , c'est à dire l'inconscient. C'est bien en quoi elles ex-sistent comme symptôme dont cet inconscient provoque la consistance, ceci apparemment dans le champ mis à plat du réel.* [25] (B33d, page 25)

The feminine thus comes to elude the discrete categories of the Lacanian triad even while it remains caught up in their relations. Rather than being situated in the symbolic or the imaginary as competing feminists have argued, woman emerges in Lacan's later work as a particular kind of relation among all three registers, participating in each of them yet altering their status by the very difference that constitutes the feminine as "opposite" to the phallic subject. Thus Lacan argues that woman is subjected to castration just as man is, but he admits that psychoanalysis has not yet determined her relation to the *objet a* and *"cette ex-sistence de réel qu'est le phallus "* (B33b, page 109). Five years later Lacan returned to this point in Seminar XXVII and insisted that "the" woman is not deprived of phallic *jouissance*; she simply experiences it from another place. This does not mean I think women are men, Lacan says, even though some have accused me of that. Instead, it simply means that "*la satisfaction véritable-phallique* " is something different for women. It is a "*satisfaction qui se situe de leur ventre. Mais comme répondant à parole de l'homme,* " which means roughly that it is "a satisfaction situated in their womb, but answering to the word of man" (B38c, page 16).

As this remark suggests, Lacan lost none of his contentious, controversial manner in his last works, nor did he abandon the speculative vision and the energetic impatience with which he cast off outworn practices and ideas at the beginning of his career. In the last years of his life, he dissolved the school he had founded and began another, and in this last group of seminars, he continued to propose courses of study and fields of investigations that he must have known he would never be able to pursue. At the age of 75, Lacan began a series of readings of Joyce's works that joins a rather conventional interest in the author's biography to an ambitious effort to read the texts of *Ulysses* and *Finnegans Wake* as an embodiment of the "symptom" he considered the proper object of psychoanalytic intervention (see B34 and C95). The next year in Seminar XXIV, Lacan expanded his remarks about Joyce to suggest a more general theory of poetic language as "*imaginairement symbolique*," a "pure knot" supported not only by writing but by "*la résonance du corps*" (the "resonance of the body"), the materiality of the signifier that dramatizes our tenuous being as "*L'homme parle être* " (B35a).

It is entirely appropriate, then, that Lacan concluded his last full seminar by proposing the possibility of a new kind of signifier, one free from the domain of memory that imposes the symbolic on us all as the mark of our subjection. Why don't they invent a new signifier, Lacan asked, one that would be free of all species of meaning and that would open the way to what I have called the real? If I ever reconvene the seminar regarding this signifier, Lacan tells his audience, I'll post a notice. "*Ce serait un bon signe,* " he observes, and "since I am only relatively debilitated mentally—that is to say just like the rest of the world—it may happen yet that a little light will come to me" (B35e, page 23). The continued impact of Lacan's work suggests that he was, indeed, able to invent a new signifier, if not exactly the one he hoped for. And in doing so, he opened up psychoanalysis to a wide range of intellectual inquiry and established the "return to Freud" as a primary point of departure in contemporary thought.

Notes

[1]The following divisions reflect the "*scissions* " that are usually cited as turning points in Lacan's career. The only exception is the designation of a

fourth stage beginning in 1974 with Lacan's extensive elaboration of the figure of the Borromean knot and other topological figures in Seminar XXII (1974-1975). Lacan claims to have introduced the knot as early as Seminar XIX (1971-1972), and he does discuss it briefly in Seminar XX (1972-1973) (see B31, page 112). In Seminar XXII, however, Lacan's discourse undergoes a radical paradigmatic shift towards the topological models that occupied him for the next five years, and I have followed Jacques-Alain Miller in treating this shift as a significant turn in the course of Lacan's work (see G738). For similar reasons, I have ignored the last *"scission, "* Lacan's dissolution of the Ecole freudienne de Paris in 1980 (see B38a), because it had little effect on the direction of his work since Seminar XXII. For an account of the political and institutional significance of this last controversy, see the biographical sketch above.

²In C58 Lacan suggested "the experience of number association" as an explanatory model "To those who have not studied the nature of language in any depth," and he claims that Boolean logic and set theory will add a necessary rigor to psychoanalysis (A2, pages 269, 281; tr. pages 59, 75). Lacan had published two essays on mathematic and symbolic logic prior to this address; see C47 and C48.
Despite his resistance to those who found such echoes indicative of a deeper continuity linking the various stages of his career, Lacan wryly noted the connections between his early and later writings when he collected some of them in *Ecrits*. Commenting on a group of early essays that he refers to as *"nos antécédents, "* Lacan places them in the *"futur antérieur "* and says of the pieces "they will have anticipated our insertion of the unconscious into language" (A2, page 71).

³Most of Lacan's earliest writings appeared in medical journals such as *L'encéphale* and *Revue neurologique* and consist of case histories usually presented with one or more colleagues. The cases generally fall into the category of paranoid psychosis, but many of them testify to Lacan's interest in disturbances directly related to language and what he will later discuss in terms of narcissistic identification. See for example his account of the relation among language, writing, and certain forms of schizophrenia in C40, C41, and E124, and his analysis of *"folies simultanées "* or *"délires à deux "* in E121, E122, the famous case of the Papin sisters in C42, and the case of Aimée to which he devoted his thesis, A1. During this time, Lacan also treated a number of cases of "automatism," a disturbance identified by his mentor Gaétan Gatian de Clérambault. (For an account of Clérambault's work see the preceding biography of Lacan, no. 2).

There is nothing remarkable about a young psychiatrist's interest in such topics, but in retrospect these phenomena constitute a bridge between Lacan's psychiatric training and the most radical aspects of his subsequent interest in psychoanalysis. Automatism, for example, especially in the form of the Clérambault-Kandinsky complex, describes the psychotic syndrome experienced by a patient who believes his mind is controlled by some person or power other than himself. This control is usually manifest in the form of voices dictating the patient's behavior and in many cases speaking through the patient's own lips. Clérambault also argued that automatism was closely related to the persecution complex, and that association brought the psychiatric understanding of automatism in line with Freud's psychoanalytic concept of paranoia.

Unlike more traditional psychiatric explanations, however, Freud did not rely on organic etiology. Instead, he portrayed paranoia in conjunction with narcissism as a projection of the individual's own resentment or aggression onto an "object" or other person with whom the individual unconsciously identified. Lacan was quite interested in this theory—his first publication in a psychoanalytic journal was a translation of Freud's essay on paranoia (D99)—and his exploration of *délires à deux* had provided him with dramatic and concrete examples of how influential such identifications can be in determining one's sense of self and relation to others. Such cases thus provided Lacan with a perfect opportunity for merging his psychiatric training with the more speculative insights of psychoanalysis, and he devoted his thesis to just that task (see A1). (The importance of language in such cases also looks forward to Lacan's emphasis on the role of the signifier—or, more generally, the symbolic—in the constitution of human subjectivity.)

[4]Lacan derives this concept from several sources. In K1239, Laplanche and Pontalis cite the French psychologist H. Wallon as a source for Lacan's concept of the mirror stage (see Wallon, "Comment se développe chez l'enfant la notion du corps propre," *Journal de psychologie* [1931]: 705-48, and *Les origines du caractère chez l'enfant: les préludes du sentiment de personnalité* [Paris, 1934]). Lacan himself alludes (in C53) to the work of the American J.M. Baldwin and (in C51) to Wallon and the Charlotte Bühler's study of transitivism *Soziologische und psychologische Studien über das erste Lebensjahr* (Jena: Fischer, 1927). In C55, Lacan also notes the work of Otto Rank on the importance of "mirror-reversals" and "phantom doubles" in suicide (*Der Doppelgänger: eine psychoanalytische Studie* [Leipzig: Internationaler Psychoanalytischer, 1925]).

In addition to these psychological sources, Lacan notes the relevance of biological studies of imprinting and mimicry in animals (see C53), though as he says in C55, most of this material had not yet been published when he first introduced the concept of the mirror stage in 1936.

More important than the biological parallels, however, was the philosophical tradition associated with Hegel's analysis of the relation between Master and Slave in *The Phenomenology of Spirit*. In the 1930s Lacan attended the lectures in which Alexandre Kojève discussed this aspect of Hegel's work, and most of Lacan's comments about Hegel are indebted to Kojève's reading. For an account of Lacan's use of Kojève and Hegel's work in general, see F374, pages 64ff., and F420, pages 193ff. Kojève's lectures were published as *Introduction à la lecture de Hegel* (Paris: Gallimard, 2nd edition 1947).

[5]Lacan's account of the mirror stage is not incompatible with the developmental schema described by Freud, but it certainly resulted in a new set of emphases and implications when Lacan set out to describe the Oedipal structure of familial complexes in C45 and C46. Originally written for the *Encylopédie française* in 1938, these essays contain Lacan's first published account outside his thesis of the importance of imaginary identification in the formation of human subjectivity and are among the more important works published during this period. Virtually inaccessible since World War II, the essays have now been published in book form and are being translated into English.

[6]What became known as "ego psychology" effectively began with Heinz Hartmann's book *Ego Psychology and the Problem of Adaptation* (New York: International Universities Press, 1939). Ernst Kris and Rudolf Loewenstein were important collaborators with Hartmann, and Lacan cited all three as sources for this "American way" of thinking about the ego (see C74). Lacan did his training analysis with Loewenstein, but Hartmann, Kris, and Loewenstein all emigrated to New York before the war. For Lacan's remarks on Hartmann, see E179. During the controversy of 1953, Lacan wrote to both Hartmann and Loewenstein appealing for support; see E157 and E159.

Lacan's concept of the ego as an "alienating function" was especially controversial because it directly contradicted the theory of the ego as an adaptational function that is autonomous from the instinctual drives and so capable of serving as an integrative foundation for personal identity. Associated most closely with the work of Hartmann and non-analytic psychologists working in the United States, "ego psychology" had become doctrine within the International Psychoanalytic Association by the early 1950s. Its practitioners emphasized the adaptation of the individual to the environment and the integration of psychic functions into a non-conflictual "whole" personality, and they stressed the therapeutic, "practical" powers of psychoanalysis as a companion to, if not a servant of, the field of psychology. Lacan's portrayal of the ego as an illusion or, even worse, as a neurotic symptom of narcissistic fixation thus contradicted the prevailing wisdom of the time and undercut the therapeutic applications that had begun to win psychoanalysis a broader acceptance at least in Germany and the United States.

Lacan summarized his objections against the therapeutic ends of ego psychology two years later in C63, where he attacked the "naive objectification" behind the concept of the ego as a synthetic function. Lacan claimed that the ego cannot integrate anything because it is based on a narcissistic relation that gives rise to an aggressivity inherent in the "splitting [*déchirement*] of the subject against himself, a splitting that he knew from the primordial moment in which he saw the image of the other" (A2, pages 344-45).

⁷In C49, Lacan discusses the *méconnaissance* at the heart of the phenomenon of automatism, since there the patient fails to recognize his productions of speech or writing as his own (cf. E115 and E122). Arguing against Henri Ey's contention that delusional belief depends on an "error" or mistake, Lacan says that such misperceptions have nothing to do with belief attached to sensible impressions. Rather, they stem from the fact that the phenomena perceived by the patient seem to address him personally. "They double him, respond to him" as he questions them, Lacan says; the truly remarkable thing about automatism is that the patient can understand the phenomena without recognizing himself in them.

Lacan goes on in this essay to link such phenomena to the issue of signification and its relevance to "being in general, that is to say, of language for man" (C49, rpt. A2, page 166), and he situates *méconnaissance* within the "dialectic of being" that informs other kinds of paranoid delusion as well. Citing Hegel and Merleau-Ponty as his sources, he insists on the centrality of this dialectic to the formation of the self and its position in the world, and then he links the dialectic to what psychologist Charlotte Bühler called "transitivism," in which the ego is "captured" by the image of the other (C49, rpt. A2, page 180). So, Lacan concludes (echoing Hegel), "the very desire of man is constituted . . . under the sign of mediation, it is the desire to have his desire recognized. It has for its object a desire, that of the other."

The exact nature of the "lack" Lacan discusses in this context is not identified so consistently in his work. In these early essays, Lacan claims that the lack stems from the biological prematuration of the human infant, which is born without fully developed nervous and perceptual systems and so lacks the physiological mastery of its body that would allow it to experience its movements as the product of a coherent and controlled "self" (see C53). Lacan says that this state is experienced as a sense of fragmentation that yields fantasies of a dismembered body, a *"corps morcelé. "* These images of detached body parts and contorted figures are perceived as part of the real, but in fact they are the negative counterpart of the (equally fantastic) imago of a coherent ego. See E139.

Lacan's biological explanation of lack is thus accompanied by his psychological emphasis on the role of the "other" in the initial recognition of the self in an image or "imago," which inscribes a lack within the alterity at the heart of the identification. A third explanation of lack that is increasingly important in Lacan's later work is his ontological concept of the lack as lack-of-being, a *"manque-à-être"* that owes a great deal to Hegel's notion of internal mediation and the "labor of the negative" described in the *Phenomenology of Spirit* but which is attributed by Lacan to the operation of the signifier.

[8]Some years later after he had begun consistently distinguishing between the other and the Other in his texts, Lacan explained that "My reason for using a capital 'O' in stating that the unconscious is the discourse of the Other is to indicate the 'beyond' [*l'au delà*], wherein recognition of desire and the desire for recognition are joined" (A2, page 524).

[9]Two of the earliest book-length studies of Lacan's work, F348 and F932, debate the merits of that work largely in terms of its application of Saussure to psychoanalytic concerns. For a more detailed discussion of Lacan's relation to the structuralist movement, see the biographical sketch above, no. 10. For Lacan's discussion of a paper by Lévi-Strauss, see E164.

[10]Lacan's emphasis on the intersubjective character of speech and his rejection of both communication and denotation (or reference) as the end of language is even more evident in the discussion that followed his presentation of this paper. Language is neither "signal, nor sign, nor even sign of the thing insofar as the thing is an exterior reality," Lacan says; "the relation between the signifier and signified is entirely enclosed in the order of Language itself, which completely conditions its two terms." No doubt discourse is concerned with things, he adds, but those things are words, signifiers, which have replaced things in the symbolic order. See E160.

[11]Much of Lacan's defense of this analytic technique here is based on his critique of Freud's methods in the cases of Dora, the Wolf Man, and the Rat Man. (For a more extended analysis of the imaginary doubling behind the obsessive relationship described by the Rat Man, see C60.)

[12]These seminars were as controversial as Lacan's analytic practice, since among the "Edinburgh demands" issued by the IPA was a stipulation that students could not attend seminars presented by their analysts without special permission from the international organization. Furthermore, students from outside France were also forbidden to attend according to another stipulation that forbade the French group from training foreigners without approval from the psychoanalytic institute in the student's home country. Such demands obviously contradicted Freud's own practice and were largely ignored, but they do indicate the extent to which the IPA felt that Lacan's theoretical ideas were as threatening as his technical innovations. For a full account of this controversy see the biographical sketch above and F412, page 113.

[13]This emphasis on the function of a "lack" or "absence" in the operation of the signifier derives most immediately from Saussure, though Saussure does not emphasize its importance as much as Lacan does. The idea that the signifier actually depends on absence or lack for its existence reflects Lacan's debt to Alexandre Kojève, who argues that the sign necessarily implies the "murder of the thing" because it supplants the thing to which it refers and actually comes into being only in the absence of the thing. See Kojève's *Introduction à la lecture de Hegel,* pages 372-74. For Lacan's interest in "lack" as a psychic and biological phenomenon, see no. 7, above.

[14]Derrida complains (in G544) that Lacan does assume a fixed point outside the frame of the story from which the signifier's circuit can be traced and measured in absolute terms: the place of the analyst. Lacan had already rejected that role for the analyst, however, and Derrida's criticism initiated a long series of defenses and counter-charges by a number of authors. See F374/375 for an account of this controversy and a collection of the relevant texts.

[15]The connection between Lacan's use of these terms in this essay and Jakobson's distinction between them in Jakobson's and Morris Halle's *Fundamentals of Language* (1956) is not as obvious as it seems. Although Lacan and Jakobson both treat metaphor and metonymy as polar tendencies in the subject's use of language, Lacan's semiotic account of the signifier's role in both tropes is unlike Jakobson's analysis, which treats the poles as "linguistic predilections" rather than as constitutive categories of subjectivity. Lacan himself disclaimed any debt to Jakobson and said that he mentioned Jakobson only to acknowledge the apparent similarity pointed out by many of his followers, who then blamed him for not being faithful to Jakobson's work (D105). Lacan addressed a brief portion of Seminar XX to Jakobson (B31,

pages 19-28), and this section of the seminar has been translated into English; see B31a.

Lacan seldom voiced such reservations regarding his use of Saussure. Nevertheless, some of Lacan's "modifications" of Saussure's concept of the sign and the distinction between *langue* and *parole* extend those terms considerably, and F348 criticizes Lacan for distorting Saussure's work beyond recognition. See E211 for Lacan's comments on his use of Saussure and Jakobson as supplements to Freud's work; see also no. 16, below.

[16]Lacan modified Saussure's work in other ways as well, perhaps most importantly in his disagreement with Saussure's claim that the relation between the signifier and the signified is "arbitrary." Lacan argued that, in fact, there is no relation between them at all. If signifiers refer to anything, it is to other signifiers or to discourse itself. *"Le mot référence en l'occasion ne peut se situer que de ce que constitue comme lien le discours. Le signifiant comme tel ne réfère à rien si ce n'est à un discours . . . à une utilisation du langage comme lien "* (B31, page 32).

[17]I never said the unconscious was structured like "Language," Lacan often reminded his seminars; I said it was structured like *a* language (see E269d). In C86, he also denied the existence of any such "meta-language," insisting that there is only "concrete language," the kind people speak (page 188). This emphasis on the specificity of actual languages served to ground Lacan's notion of the "unconscious" in concrete social and historical contexts (see E131), and in C45 and C46 he even went so far as to suggest that the very possibility of a psychoanalytic concept of the unconscious was based on Freud's experience as part of a bourgeois family in turn-of-the-century Vienna. It also distinguishes Lacan's treatment of language from that of most structuralists, who usually follow Saussure in conceiving of language as an abstract structure that is embodied in a necessary but separable concrete utterance. In response to a question from an audience at MIT, Lacan claimed to owe Lévi-Strauss a great deal but insisted that their notions of structure were quite different. I conform only to the work of Freud, Lacan added (E270e, page 53).

In Seminar VI (B17), Lacan raised this point again to argue for the corporeal, though not biological, bases for psychoanalysis. Although our experience is structured by the signifier, Lacan says, *we* are the ones who furnish the material for the signifiers themselves. It is with our own members–in their imaginary forms–that we fashion the alphabet of this discourse which is the unconscious, just as an actor lends his body as the support of the characters he plays (page 18).

This focus on the lived experience of specific individuals characterizes most of Lacan's work before the war, but after the war his public discourse became increasingly abstract, despite his occasional warnings to the contrary. So, by the 1970s, feminists could convincingly accuse Lacan of generalizing the phallocentric schema of psychoanalysis into a universal model of human nature, and his increasing use of mathematical topology further distanced his theoretical work from the concrete arena in which it was practiced.

[18]A considerable portion of Lacan's notoriety stemmed from his obscure style of speaking and writing. As early as 1933, a reviewer of A1 complained in the *Annales médico-psychologiques* about the "artistic" and philosophical quality of Lacan's writing, which was probably an indirect complaint against the link between psychoanalysis and surrealism but which would be echoed for the next 50 years. On the whole, French commentators have tended to be more tolerant of Lacan's stylistic eccentricities, though Alain de Benoist has denounced Lacan's work as impenetrable nonsense that is "unfalsifiable" only because it makes no verifiable claims (see H974), and François George has excoriated what he calls the "Lacan-effect" and its attraction to weak minds (see F335 and G612).

Virtually all British and American reviewers have denounced Lacan's writing as needlessly difficult, even when praising various translations for their accuracy and fidelity to Lacan's text. Some of these complaints stem from a silly Franco-phobia (see for example Anthony Clare's characterization of Lacan's style as "that tipsy, euphoric prose-poetry which is one of the more tiresome manifestations of the French spirit" [H985]), but even the most serious and sympathetic of these reviews note the formidable difficulty of Lacan's presentations. For two of the more important reviews of Lacan's work in English, see G934 and G885; also see the responses inspired by these reviews, which are listed in the notes to these items. A more extended defense of Lacan's style can be found in F334.

Lacan himself was fully aware of the difficulty of his writing and at one point called himself the "Gongora" of psychoanalysis after the seventeenth-century Spanish poet who was famous for his neologisms and exaggerated obscurity. Lacan also recognized that it was well known that the *Ecrits* could not be read easily, and in one of his seminars he made a "little autobiographical confession": he had never thought that they would be read (B31, page 29). In Lacan's opinion, writing (*un écrit*) was never made to be read in the first place (B22, page 251), and he claimed that the difficulty of his work was a deliberate strategy designed to elicit a certain kind of response from the reader: "Writing is distinguished by a prevalence of the *text* . . . that makes possible the kind of tightening up that I like in order to leave the reader no other way out than the way in, which I prefer to be difficult" (C71, rpt. A2, page 493; tr. A2j, page 146).

Lacan also defended the complexity of his writing on the basis of necessity. People don't grind their teeth when a mathematician uses a formal apparatus, he observed in an interview, and they should be equally tolerant of a psychoanalyst who aspires to a similar rigor (E187). Nevertheless, even sympathetic followers suffered under the burden of Lacan's style. At a conference sponsored by the EFP, Lacan noted that he usually rewrote an essay a good twelve times, but the preface to the German translation of *Ecrits* was a first draft. That's a good thing, one of the audience responded; if you had rewritten it, I couldn't have understood anything at all (E244, page 71).

[19]Freud was interested in this topic, of course, as his work on voyeurism and scopophilia shows. Freud attributed the pleasure associated with looking to infantile component-instincts, however, whereas Lacan discusses the gaze in conjunction with the *objet a* and a desire ultimately derived from the subject's association with the symbolic order. Lacan does discuss Freud's concept of *Schaulust* in the seminar, but only to reject any connection with organic need or "instinct" in favor of a more subtle phenomenological orientation of the scopic drive as directed "outward and back" in an intersubjective relation that links the subject to the Other (see B22, page 177; tr. B22b, page 194).

[20]Lacan's comments on the scopic field of the imaginary in this seminar provided the basis for Christian Metz's enormously influential elaboration of Lacan's work within the field of film theory; see K1270. For the importance of the Lacanian notion of "suture" to film theory in France, see G789. Lacan also influenced film theory in England and the United States through the British journal *Screen,* which published translations of Metz's work and many other essays dealing with Lacan's work. See especially the work of Stephen Heath (G636, G638, and F1211) and Annette Kuhn (K1231).

[21]The idealized function of women in cultural representation had been discussed by Lacan earlier in Seminar VII (1959-1960), where he analyzes the role of the lady in courtly love as a specialized form of the object of desire. See B18, esp. pages 167-84.

[22]For a general discussion of feminist issues in Lacanian psychoanalysis, see F370.

[23]Lacan's use of the figure of the knot and his later appropriation of the topological figure of the Borromean knot have been described by Mitchell and Rose in a footnote to their translation of Lacan's seminar session from 21 January 1975. It is a succinct and clear explanation of this issue and deserves quoting at length: the difficulty of Lacan's work, they say,

> in many ways became greater in direct proportion to his increasingly elaborated use of the theory of knots which he took from Alexander (1928) [J.W. Alexander, "Topological Invariants of Knots and Links," *Transactions of the American Mathematical Society* 30 (1928): 275-306], and developed in relation to a possible topography of the unconscious in his later work . . . . Lacan's preoccupation with knots is part of what has been his continuous attempt to find a formula for the difficulty of unconscious processes which is not immediately cancelled by its own immediacy or presence—hence his rejection of geometrical optics in favour of topology ("a set of continous deformations" [Seminar XXI] . . .), and the recourse to mathematics ("I do not want to write up anything which could be taken for a signified, nor lend to the signified any authority whatsoever" [Seminar VIII] . . .). More recently the theory of knots has been used to stress the relations which bind or link Imaginary, Symbolic and Real, and the subject to each, in a way which avoids any notion of hierarchy, or any priority of any one of the three terms: "These three terms: what we imagine as a form, what we hold as circular in language, and that which ex-ists in relation both to the imaginary and to language, have led me to bring out the way in which they are linked together" (*Scilicet* 6/7, 1976, page 56). Above all, the emphasis is, as always, on the intricate and inextricable nature of the ties which make the subject both subject *of* and *to* the unconscious: "the unconscious, this knot of our being—the word 'knot,' rather than the word 'being,' is the one that matters—the being of this knot which is driven by the unconscious alone" [Seminar XXI]. (F370, page 171, no. 6.)

[24]Despite the obvious meta-theoretical dimension of Lacan's later work, he continued to reject the possibility of attaining a "metalanguage." One can only speak of *a* language ("*une langue* ") in another "*langue,* " Lacan said, and the possibility of a metalanguage would depend on "language"—"*le langage* "— which does not exist (B36a). See no. 15.

[25]The spoken quality of this passage renders a literal translation of the words virtually useless: "They [women] are real, and terribly so. They are only that. They consist only insofar as the symbolic ex-sists, that is to say, the unconscious. That is exactly how they ex-sist, as [a] symptom from which the unconscious elicits consistency, apparently in the field extracted [i.e., mapped or projected] from the real."

Lacan's French provides a more pointed illustration of his argument, since "con" is a vulgar pun meaning "cunt." Its presence in words such as "*consistent*" and "*consistance*" literally inserts the feminine into terms for the phallocentric qualities of stability or essence, undermining the ontological pretensions of the terms just as Lacan's neologism "ex-sist" disrupts the certainty of "*existence*." The syllable "con" may also be intended to echo in "unconscious," associating that realm with feminine resistance to symbolization.

JACQUES LACAN

Section A

Books and Collections of Essays

A1. <u>De la psychose paranoïaque dans ses rapports avec la personnalité</u>. Thèse de Doctorat en Médecine, Faculté de Médecine de Paris. Paris: Le François, 1932. 381 pages.

Claims that paranoiac psychosis is integrally related to the development of an individual's whole personality as it evolves through the stages described in psychoanalysis, and stresses the role of social relations in the formation and structure of paranoid delusions. Part I traces the historical background and latest developments of psychiatric attitudes towards paranoia and the psychology of personality, and carefully distinguishes the developmental origin of psychoses as defined by Lacan from the two most influential explanations of the time: (1) that of a "constitution" innate in the individual that can be determined as "paranoiac"; and (2) that of a" kernel" or "nucleus" (<u>noyau</u>) of delusional conviction that functions as a "mental automatism."
Part II presents a detailed case history of "Aimée," a woman who had been hospitalized after trying to stab a prominent actress who she felt had been plotting against her young son. Lacan diagnoses the case as the prototype of a new clinical category, "auto-punitive paranoia," which he explains in the context of his careful exposition of Freud's theories regarding the formation of the ego and libidinal cathexis. Part III recapitulates the theoretical conclusions derived from this application of psycho-analytic doctrine in psychiatry and defends its utility as a tool of diagnosis and therapy.
The survey of issues and debates in Part I establishes the background against which Lacan proposes a comprehensive definition of personality that draws upon common beliefs as well as psychiatric categories. He distinguishes among three dimensions of personality:

(1) the biographical development of the individual, which assumes "comprehensible relations" among the events, situations and behavior in a person's life;

(2) the individual's concept of his or her self as defined by a "dialectical progress" between the individual's experience of the world and an ideal image of the self (Freud's ego-ideal). Lacan says that this ideal image manifests itself internally as guilt and externally in the form of idealized role models with which the individual identifies;

(3) a "certain tension" in social relations stemming from the pragmatic autonomy of individual conduct that confronts the ethical requirements of one's social responsibilities.

Lacan insists on the absolute interaction of all three dimensions at every stage of the development of the personality, and he argues that paranoiac psychosis must be understood as a fundamental disturbance of all three levels taken together as a whole. In Part III he elaborates on this holistic model and defines personality as the "totality constituted by the individual and his immediate (propre) milieu."

Lacan later observed that the extensive and painstaking analysis of the biographical details that make up the case history of Part II is the most original part of the thesis (E131) because it demonstrates the concrete basis of paranoiac psychosis, which he considers as a highly structured reaction of a personality to a specific situation that the individual encounters in his or her environment (p. 98 [Note: these page references refer to the edition listed below as A1c]). Aimée was extremely close to her mother, and Lacan claims that their intense, relatively isolated relationship resulted in Aimée's fixation at what Freud called the state of "secondary narcissism," which is constituted by the "turning around upon the ego of libido withdrawn from the objects which it has cathected hitherto" (see Freud's "On Narcissism" (1914) and K1239, p. 337).

This psychic orientation appeared in Aimée's tendency to identify with a series of women who entered her life and towards whom she felt the deep ambivalence that is characteristic of narcissistic attachment. This ambivalence eventually extended to prominent people whom she had never met and finally gave way to delusions of persecution in which she felt that these public figures planned to attack her son as a means of punishing her. Once she is hospitalized after attacking the actress, Aimée's symptoms suddenly disappear, and Lacan takes this mysterious recovery as evidence of the symbolic character of her crime. He says that Aimée tried to stab the actress because she was an image of the self

that Aimée desired to punish. Once that urge was
satisfied, Lacan argues, the unconscious guilt from
which it stemmed was assuaged, and that satisfaction
also alleviated the tension within Aimée's divided
sense of her self which had resulted in her projection of hostility onto these ego-images in the first
place.
   The theoretical importance of this analysis lies in
Lacan's association of delusion with a disturbance in
the subject's perception of the real and also with
what Lacan calls the "syntax" of social relations
represented in paranoiac crime. General psychiatric
knowledge of the time considered the delusory
interpretations characteristic of paranoia to be the
result of a hypertrophy of the patient's rational
capacities, but Lacan argues that the delusions
result from an elementary misperception of the difference between the self and the world of objects
that constitutes the subject's sense of the "real."
This failure to distinguish between the self and
others in the world is the crux of narcissistic
fixation. It also has specific implications for
social relations as well, as Freud explains in an
essay that Lacan had translated a year earlier (D99),
and in this double association Lacan links one's
perception of the real to one's accession to the
social order through their common determination by
the "general energetic of the libido" or, more
simply, through "desire" (pp. 256-57, 273).
   This close causal connection between the status of
the real and one's place in society presages Lacan's
later interest in the relation between the real and
symbolic registers of experience as it is determined
by the properties of the signifier. In the thesis,
social relations and the real are viewed "phenomeno-
logically," as effects of the structure of an
individual's personality, and Lacan claims that this
phenomenological perspective grounds the intentionality of "true consciousness" ("connaissance vraie")
in the real and grants it an objectivity in the
social order.
   Even at this point in his career, however, Lacan
assumes that there is a symbolic or signifying
function inherent in this "concrete" ground of
consciousness. He defines delusion as "the expression, in the form of language forged by the comprehensible relations of a group, of concrete tendencies
that manifest an insufficient conformity to the
necessities of the group but that are misunderstood
by the subject" (p. 337). The emphasis in this
passage is, of course, on the relational structure of
the individual's sense of place in her social
context, and Lacan is most interested in what he will
later characterize as the imaginary register of
psychotic delusion. But as his description of the

delusion as a linguistic expression suggests, Lacan's
thesis imports into his application of Freud's work
an emphasis upon signifying mechanisms that looks
forward to his later claims that the unconscious is
"structured like an language" and that delusionary
disturbances derive from the subject's failure to
assume his or her place in the symbolic order of
language, rather than from some "psychic" disorder in
the conventional psychiatric sense.

In part, this emphasis on the linguistic expression
of paranoid delusion responds to the importance of
writing in Aimée's particular case. She had dreamed
of becoming a famous novelist and actually had
written two novels, the first of which Lacan analyzes
in some detail and praises for its literary quality.
Drawing upon the methodological defense proposed in
C40, Lacan unveils in Aimée's writing stylistic
features that reflect the structure of her psychosis,
such as the "iteration of the object" that leads her
repeatedly to identify with other women as the "same"
reflection of herself. In a subsequent discussion of
his thesis (E131), Lacan claimed that the method for
analyzing the writing of paranoiacs which he developed there and in C40 could be applied equally
well to the stylistic analysis of poetry (C41). This
interest in the poetic dimension of "schizographic"
writing reflects Lacan's close association with the
surrealist movement in Paris during the 1920s and
1930s, and he takes up the application of psychoanalytic perspectives to stylistic analysis in two
essays published in the surrealist art journal Le
Minotaure: C41 and C42.

Aimée's case also resembles other cases of "délires
à deux" that Lacan studied; see E122 and especially
C42, where he uses newspaper reports to analyze
murders committed by the Papin sisters, which created
a sensation in France in 1933. Catherine Clément
discusses all of these essays in terms of Lacan's
treatment of women in F316, pp. 55-8, 67-78.

Forty years later, when his thesis was reprinted,
Lacan commented ironically on the naiveté of this
work in a presentation at Yale University; see E270a.
His psychotics led him to Freud, he remarks, and in
his thesis he was applying "freudisme" without
knowing it (p. 15). He also said he had resisted the
republication of his early work because he now
believes that "la personnalité" and paranoid psychosis are not just related, but essentially the
same; see B34, 16 December 1975.

This thesis was awarded "mention très honorable"
and a bronze medal by the Faculté de Médecine.

A1a.   De la psychose paranoïaque . . .suivi de Premiers
        écrits sur la paranoia. Le Champ freudien. Series
        directed by Jacques Lacan. Paris: Editions du

Seuil, 1975.   412 pages.

Includes C40, C41, C42, and a list of works published by Lacan through 1933.

A1b.   A brief excerpt from A1 was reprinted in F305, pp. 4-14.

A1c.   Another edition of A1, without the supplementary material in A1a.   Collection Points.   Paris: Editions du Seuil, n.d. [1980?].   369 pages.

A1d.   Partial translation into Japanese as "Shorei eme." A7.

A**.   De l'usage de la parole et des structures de langage dans la conduite et dans la champ de la psych-analyse.   Paris: Presses universitaires de France, 1956.   291 pages.

This item is listed by the National Union Catalog for 1953-1957 but could not be verified and does not appear in Dor or in the holdings of the Bibliothèque de l'Ecole de la Cause freudienne.

A2.   Ecrits.   Le Champ freudien.   Series directed by Jacques Lacan.   Paris: Editions du Seuil, 1966. 920 pages.

Collects most of Lacan's major "writings" from 1936 to 1965, as well as pieces of seminars and several contributions to conferences, etc., all edited by Lacan for publication in this volume.   With a few significant exceptions, Lacan arranges the collection in approximate chronological order and presents the texts with various prefaces, explanatory notes, and reflections on the way the texts have been received since their first publication.   In the "Repères bibliographiques" Lacan furnishes full biblio-graphical information on the original publication all of the texts.   Jacques-Alain Miller provides an index of major concepts discussed in the book and a list of the various graphs used by Lacan, with brief explana-tions of each graph and references to its various appearances in the texts.
Despite the title this collection and its con-venient presentation of Lacan's texts, Ecrits is not an ordinary anthology and the texts it includes are not all "essays" or even "writings" in the usual sense.   The first piece listed in the chronological order of the "Repères bibliographiques," for example, is C44, "Le stade du miroir."   Lacan describes the item as having been "produced" for the first time at the fourteenth Congrés psychanalytique international, 3 August 1936.   There follows a reference to The

International Journal of Psycho-Analysis 18, part 1
(1937): 78, where "cette communication est inscrite
sous la rubrique 'The Looking-glass Phase.'" It
turns out, however, this issue of the IJP simply
contains a reference to the paper and nothing more.
Lacan explains in a note on p. 67 of Ecrits that he
never got around to submitting the text of the paper;
what the reader finds in Ecrits under the title of
"Le stade du miroir comme formateur de la fonction du
Je" is in fact a paper presented at the sixteenth
Congrès international de psychanalyse, 17 July 1949,
thirteen years after the first item titled "Le stade
du miroir."

A somewhat different problem is exemplified by the
second appendix to the volume, "La métaphore du
sujet," which is the "text" of an oral discussion
that took place 23 June 1960 and that was not written
by Lacan until June 1961 (E170). Similarly, his
introduction to Jean Hyppolite's paper on Freud's
Verneinung, based on a seminar session of 10 February
1954, clearly bears the mark of his subsequent work
and is not the same text as is published for that
date in B12. Usually the revisions and interpolations are carefully noted as such, but not always,
and at times it is impossible to determine the exact
date of composition for a particular paragraph or
reference. Even the relatively few texts that were
originally written for publication possess their own
difficulties, since Lacan occasionally inserted
passages after their original appearance or revised
them for publication in Ecrits, as he did for other
items "based on" typescripts of seminar sessions.
Finally, this collection omits a number of items that
Lacan wrote expressly for publication in various
journals or encyclopedias, and so cannot be considered a comprehensive representation of Lacan's
work during these years.

Such difficulties limit the utility of Ecrits as a
retrospective look at Lacan's career up to 1966, but
they also emphasize its most important dimension.
For this collection is best studied as a book in its
own right, a group of items composed at different
times but integrated by Lacan here in a comprehensive
vision that uses his past work to articulate his
current (1966) understanding of the issues and topics
discussed in the book. To be sure, as Lacan notes in
the last item included in the collection, one of the
main differences between science and psychoanalysis
is that science forgets the turning points, "les
péripéties," of the subjective dramas in which it is
born, whereas psychoanalysis elevates its own
"dramas" as an important dimension of truth. Readers
can trace much of the drama of Lacan's own career in
Ecrits as he comments on the conditions in which an
earlier comment emerged or the controversies it

engendered. His willingness to violate chronology in
the arrangement of the items, however, as well as the
separate sections, the various prefaces, and the
running commentary conducted in notes and afterwords,
all suggest a more immediate intervention on Lacan's
part in the role of an author rather than an editor.
And the chronological evolution of concepts that can
be traced at times across various pieces tends to
function more as a dialectical presentation of a
continuous argument than as intellectual biography or
an explanatory archaeology of ideas prior to some
"final" form.

Contents

   The following table describes most of the apparatus
Lacan wrote to accompany the items included in
Ecrits, but it does not list footnotes and other
brief comments appended to remarks in the texts
themselves.

I

"Ouverture de ce recueil"......................9-10

   The first words in Ecrits are quoted by Lacan from
Buffon: "Le style est l'homme même." He has invoked
them, Lacan says, so he can extend the phrase with
"l'homme à qui l'on s'adresse." Lacan claims that
this extension satisfies his familiar principle that,
in language, our message comes to us from the Other
in an inverted form. But if man is reduced to being
nothing other than the place of the return of our
discourse, Lacan adds, what good is it to address him
in the first place? He takes this question as the
main challenge that will be posed to him by readers
of the Ecrits who are unfamiliar with his work, and
he responds by offering C69 as a starting point ("un
palier dans notre style") despite the generally
chronological order of the other pieces.

"Le séminaire sur 'La lettre volée'" (C69)......11-61

   In addition to C69, this item includes the seminar
lesson of 26 April 1955 (though not in the same form
as the lesson for that day published in B13). The
lesson is preceded by its own introduction, "Présentation de la suite," and accompanied by several
explanatory notes, the longest of which is the
"Parenthèse des parenthèses".

"Présentation de la suite"....................41-44

   Notes that the preceding item was part of a seminar
in which it was introduced by the text that follows

it here. All of his writings, Lacan says, take their
place within "an adventure which is that of psychoanalysis," and he claims to have taken the detours of
that adventure as a principle of instruction. This
item also includes remarks on the analytic experience
and the goals of the analyst.

"Parenthèse des parenthèses"....................54-57

   Notes the utility of using parentheses to mark
relations within the signifying chain he is discussing in the text.

II

"De nos antécédents"...........................65-72

   Describes the topics and issues that interested him
at the beginning of his career, his debt to Clérambault ("notre seul maître en psychiatrie") and his
concept of "automatisme mental," and Lacan's eventual
migration toward the work of Freud. Lacan cites his
first intervention in psychoanalytic theory, the
account of the mirror stage in C44, as a point of
resistance to current notions of the ego that was
both technical and theoretical, even though it was
not recognized as such until later (p. 67); and he
offers the first few articles in Ecrits as samples of
his interests at that time.
   Lacan says that in his early work he was particularly concerned with the mistaken notions about the
subject's relation to the real that were associated
with Freud's Beyond the Pleasure Principle (1920),
and he connects these misconceptions to equally
mistaken notions of the ego and of Freud's attempt to
associate it with the perception-consciousness
system. His mirror stage clarified the role of the
ego and its relation to reality by distinguishing
between the imaginary and the symbolic, Lacan claims,
and it also shifted emphasis away from biology and
stages of development toward a recognition of what
came to be called the "field of the Other."
   Despite this retrospective account of his early
work, Lacan claims that his students have erred in
trying to find his current ideas in these old pieces,
and he suggests that people should be satisfied that
what is actually there did not bar the way to his
later work. In conclusion, Lacan says that this
collection has simply replaced these texts in a
"futur antérieur" in which they will have preceded
his insertion of the unconscious into language, and
he offers these biographical remarks only in a desire
to clarify the reader's way.

"Au-delà du 'Principe de réalité'" (C43)........73-92

III

IV

Comments on the position of the subject in the
training analysis, and emphasizes that the "reforme
du sujet" begun in the following article (C58) must
be conducted from the "scientific position" that is
implied in the psychoanalytic discovery. The
relation of psychoanalysis to science, Lacan says,
inevitably raises questions of truth, and in psychoanalysis the symptom is articulated as it represents
the "return of truth as such in default of knowledge"
("le retour de la vérité comme tel dans la faille
d'un savoir" [p. 234]). The symptom can be interpreted only within the order of the signifier, he
adds, and since one signifier has meaning only in
relation to another, the truth of the symptom lies in
this articulation of the signifying chain (pp. 234-
5).
     This introductory section includes other comments
on the subject as a sexed being, castration in
relation to the subject and his symptom, and the
necessary identification between teaching psychoanalysis and the training analysis.

Points out the link between psychoanalysis and
language that unified the various contributors to the
first issue of La psychanalyse (F386), and claims
that it is the importance of language, at the level
of the signifier, that motivates his return to the
texts of Freud rather than some regressive search for
the origin. One reads Freud as one writes in
psychoanalysis, Lacan says, and that says it all.

"Introduction au commentaire de Jean Hyppolite sur

V

Recounts the importance of Silberer's concepts of
material phenomena and functional phenomena as Freud
adopted them in The Interpretation of Dreams (1900),
especially as they mark the passage of the symbol
from its existence in a material domain to a condition in which it becomes an influence on the
subject's psychic state. This section also describes
Jones's role in debates on the topic of symbolism
during the later controversy, focussing on his
disagreements with Kleinians and followers of Anna
Freud, whom Lacan describes as the movement of
"l'anafreudisme."

VI

VII

"La science et la vérité" (C85)...............855-77

Appendice I

Jean Hyppolite, "Commentaire parlé sur la _Verneinung_
de Freud" (L1897)..........................879-87

Appendice II

"La métaphore du sujet" (E170)...............889-92

"Index raisonné des concepts majeurs."
Compiled by Jacques-Alain Miller...........893-902
Jacques-Alain Miller, "Table commentée des
représentations graphiques".................903-08
Termes de Freud en allemand.................909-10
Index des noms cités........................911-16
Repères bibilographiques dans l'ordre
chronologique...............................917-20

Editions and translations

A2a.   _Ecrits_ I. Collections Points: Sciences Humaines.
Paris: Editions de Seuil, 1970. 289 pages.

Contains a new introduction by Lacan (D104) and the
following items from A2, selected by Lacan: "Ouverture de ce recueil," C69, "De nos antécedents," C53,
"Du sujet enfin en question," C58, C65, and C71. A
second volume appeared as A2g.

A2b.   _Escritos I: Lectura estructuralista de Freud_.
Translated by Tomas Segovia, in collaboration with
Juan David Nasio. Mexico: Siglo Vientiuna
Editores, 1971. A second volume appeared as A2h.

A2c.   _Ekuri_ I. Japanese translation directed by M. Sasaki.
Kobundo, 1972. See A2k.

A2d.   _Schriften_ I: Selected and edited by Norbert Haas.
Translated by Haas, Rodolphe Fasché, et al. Suhr-
kamp-Taschenbucher Wissenschaft 137. Olten,
Switzerland: Walter-Verlag, 1973. 240 pages.

Contains C53, C58, C69, C74. Volumes II and III
appeared as A2i and A2n.

A2e.   _Escritos_ I. Buenos Aires: Siglo xxi, 1974.

A2f.   _Scritti_ I and II. Edited by Giacomo Contri. Einaudi
Paperbacks 52. Turin: G. Einaudi, 1974. 927
pages.

A2g.   Ecrits II. Collection Points: Sciences humaines.
       Paris: Editions du Seuil, 1975. 244 pages.

       Selected by Lacan, contains the following items
       from A2: C68, C72, C73, C83, C80, C81, and C85.
       Volume I appeared as A2a.

A2h.   Escritos II. Translated by Tomas Segovia, in
       collaboration with Juan David Nasio. Mexico:
       Siglo Vientiuna Editores, 1975; rpt. 1978. See
       A2e.

A2i.   Schriften II. Edited by Norbert Haas. Translated by
       Chantal Creusot, Wolfgang Fietkau, Norbert Haas,
       Hans-Jörg Rheinberger and Samuel M. Weber. Olten,
       Switzerland: Walter-Verlag, 1975. 277 pages.

       Contains the following items from A2: C71, C72,
       C73, C80, C81, C83, and C85. Volume I appeared as
       A2d, Volume III as A2n.

A2j.   Ecrits: A Selection. Translated by Alan Sheridan.
       New York: Norton, 1977; and London: Tavistock,
       1977. 338 pages.

       Contains a brief glossary and the following items
       from A2: C51, C53, C58, C65, C71, C72, C73, C74,
       C80, and Miller's commentary on the graphs.

A2k.   Ekuri, II. Japanese translation directed by M.
       Saski. Kobundo, 1977. See A2c and A2o.

A2l.   Escritos. Translated by Inês Oseki-Depré. Sao
       Paulo, Brazil: Ed. Perspectiva, 1978. 346 pages.

A2m.   Escritos. Reprint of A2b and A2e. 1978.

A2n.   Schriften III. Edited by Norbert Haas. Translated
       by Haas, Franz Kaltenbeck, Friedrich A. Kittler,
       Hans-Joachim Metzger, Monika Metzger, and Ursula
       Rutt-Förster. Olten, Switzerland: Walter-Verlag,
       1980. 252 pages.

       Contains C45, C46, and C82, and the following items
       from A2: C43, C47, C61, C62, and C77. Volume I
       appeared as A2d, Volume II as A2i.

A2o.   Ekuri, III. Japanese translation directed by M.
       Sasaki. Kobundo, 1987. See A2c and A2k.

A**.   Other translations in the following languages have
       been reported but could not be verified:

       Serbo-Croation: Yugoslavia, Naprijed editions.
       Norwegian: Norway, Gyldendal Norsk editions.

A**.   The Language of the Self.   Translated with notes and
       commentary by Anthony Wilden.   Baltimore: The
       Johns Hopkins University Press, 1968.   338 pages.

       This book contains a translation of C58 and was
       originally issued under Wilden's name, but it was
       later re-issued under Lacan's name.   See F420 for a
       full description of Wilden's apparatus and essay.

A**.   Las formaciones del inconsciente, seguido de El deseo
       y su interpretacion.   Introductions by Charles
       Melman, Jan Miel, and Jean Reboul.   Buenos Aires:
       Ediciones Nueva Vision, 1970.   See B16a and B17d.

A**.   La cosa freudiana e altri scritti.   Translated by
       Giacomo Contri.   Nuovo politecnico 48.   Turin: G.
       Einaudi, 1972.   248 pages.

A3.   Télévision.   Interview with Jacques-Alain Miller for
       the Service de recherche of the O.R.T.F [Office de
       la Radiodiffusion-Télévision Française].   Directed
       by Benoît Jacquot, 1973 [120 minutes].   Miller's
       note to the edition dated Christmas, 1973.   Le
       Champ freudien.   Paris: Editions du Seuil, 1974.
       72 pages.

       Consists of seven separate segments, listed below.
       Each segment focuses on a general topic but usually
       includes remarks on several issues.

       I.   [Je dis toujours la vérité]....................9

       Comments on the role of the audience of his
       seminars and claims that there is not much difference
       between them and television: "un regard dans les
       deux cas: à qui je ne m'adresse dans aucun, mais au
       nom de quoi je parle."   I expect nothing from these
       "analystes supposés" who come to listen to me, Lacan
       says, except that they be "this object thanks to
       which my teaching is not an autoanalysis" (p. 10).
       This segment begins with a statement that was later
       used in a memorial notice by Le Seuil in La quinzaine
       littéraire (see J1122):   Lacan says that he always
       speaks the truth, though not all the truth, because
       one can never say that.   To say all, he explains, is
       materially impossible because the words are lacking.
       But he adds that it is by this very impossibility
       that the truth holds fast to ("tenir au") the real.
       ("Je dis toujours la vérité: pas toute, parce que
       toute la dire, on n'y arrive pas.   La dire toute,
       c'est impossible matériellement: les mots y man-
       quent.   C'est même par cet impossible que la vérité
       tient au réel" [p. 9].)

II.   [L'inconscient, <u>chose fort précise</u>]...........15

Explains his concept of the unconscious and its
relation to langauge and speech, comments on the
relation between analysis and therapy, and discusses
the signifying function of <u>lalangue</u> and the "<u>chiffre
du sens</u>" derived from it.

III.   [<u>Etre un saint</u>].............................25

Compares the psychoanalyst to a saint, and returns
to the topic of the unconscious to caution that the
idea of discourse is not founded on the "ex-sistence"
of the unconscious. Lacan says instead that the
unconscious ex-sists only in relation to discourse
(p. 26). Noting the hostility between the International Psychoanalytic Association and himself,
Lacan describes the international society as the
SAMCDA, a society of mutual assistance against
analytic discourse (p. 27).

IV.   [<u>Ces gestes vagues dont de mon discours on
      se garantit</u>].................................33

Responds to objections that the unconscious
consists of more than words, and describes his
understanding of topics usually associated with the
unconscious: psychic energy, affect, and drive.

V.   [<u>L'égarement de notre jouissance</u>].............47

Insists on the priority of <u>le refoulement</u> over <u>le
répression</u> ("<u>le refoulement qui produise la répres-
sion</u>"); comments on his characterization of transference as the "<u>sujet supposé savoir</u>," and describes
the Oedipus complex as a necessary myth that gives
form to the operations of structure. Lacan says that
the sexual impass secretes fictions that rationalize
the impossible from which it comes (p. 51). In this
segment Lacan also observes that he has made his
fortune from analytic discourse and so is a genuine
"self-made man" (English in the text). For a
critical response to this claim, see G611.

VI.   [Savoir, faire, espérer].....................57

Comments on three questions from Miller based on
Kant's first critique: What can I know? What must I
do? What may I hope for? In response, Lacan
dismisses the first as irrelevant to psychoanalysis,
since it starts with the assumption that the subject
is unconscious. He then discusses the second in
relation to the ethic of "<u>Bien-dire</u>," and says of the
third question that he has seen hope lead to suicide
in the cases of men whom he has respected. "<u>Le</u>

suicide est le seul acte qui puisse réussir sans
ratage," he adds (pp. 66-67).

VII. [Ce qui s'énonce bien, l'on le conçoit
      clairement]................................71

   Briefly comments on the topic of his style and the
problem of interpretation.

   According to Miller's note at the beginning of the
text, the interviews were conducted under the aegis
of the Service de la recherche de l'O.R.T.F and were
to be broadcast at the end of January, 1974, as
Psychanalyse.
   Translated by Denis Hollier, Rosalind Krauss, and
Anette Michelson in October 40 (1987): 5-50 (see
A11). The videotape was shown in the United States
for the first time on 9 April 1987. Also translated
into Italian under the supervision of Giacoma Contri
and published by Einaudi.

A**. Ecrits inspirés. Besançon: Editions AREP, 1977.
      Listed in F371, p. 1055.

A**. With Henri Claude, P. Mignault, and Henri Ey.
      Travaux et interventions. Paris: l'Association
      régionale de l'éducation permanente (AREP), 1977.
      Listed in Répertoire bibliographique de la phil-
      osophie.

 A4. Lacan in italia 1953-1978/En Italie Lacan. Edited by
      Giacomo B. Contri. Milan: La Salamandra, 1978.
      261 pages.

   Reprints various papers and addresses Lacan
presented in Italy during his visits there from 1953
to 1974, and translates them into Italian. Introductory and explanatory apparatus also appears in
French and in Italian. Includes several essays
printed earlier (most importantly, C58, C65) and a
number of texts that appear here for the first time:
E229, E238, E239, E240, E248, E249, and G515.

 A5. Seminari di Jacques Lacan (1956-59). Translated by
      Lamberto Boni. Parma: Pratiche Ed., 1979. 192
      pages.

   Translation of the summaries of the seminars for
1956-59 by J.-B. Pontalis.

A**. Speech and Language in Psychoanalysis. Translated
      with notes and commentary by Anthony Wilden.
      Baltimore: The Johns Hopkins University Press,
      1968; re-issued 1981.

This is a reprint of the translation of C58, which
first appeared under Wilden's name in 1968 as F420
and was reissued under Lacan's name with this title
in 1981. See F420 for a complete description of this
item.

A6.   <u>Les complexes familiaux dans la formation de l'in-
      dividu: essai d'analyse d'une fonction en psy-
      chologie</u>. Paris: Editions du Seuil, 1984. 112
      pages. Reprint of C45 and C46.

      <u>Répertoire bibliographique de la philosophie</u> lists
      a translation by Victor Fishman as <u>La Familia</u>,
      Argonauta, Métodos Viventens, second edition 1979,
      144 pages. Also translated into Japanese by T. Saski
      as <u>Kazoku fukugono byori</u> (Kobundo, 1986). A trans-
      lation into English is forthcoming from Norton.

A7.   <u>Futaridearu kotono yamai</u> [<u>Le délire à deux</u>.] Japan:
      Asahi shuppau, 1984.

      Includes Japanese translations of C40, C41, C42,
      and a partial translation of A1.

A8.   <u>Reseñas de enseñanza (1964-68)</u>. Buenos Aires: Hacia
      el tercer encuentro del Campo Freudiano, 1984.   58
      pages.

      Based on a translation of "Comptes rendus d'en-
      seignement," a collection of Lacan's abstracts for
      Seminars XI-XV from the <u>Annuaire de l'Ecole pratique
      des hautes études</u> that were published together in
      <u>Ornicar?</u> 29 (1984): 7-25.

A9.   <u>Acte de fondation, et autres textes</u>. Paris: Ecole
      de la Cause freudienne, 1985. 45 pages.

      A collection of texts related to the foundation of
      the Ecole freudienne de Paris and of the Ecole de la
      Cause freudienne.

      Contents

A10. Disukuru [Discourses]. Japan: Kobundo, 1985.

Includes Japanese translations of E211 and E215.

A**. Jacques Lacan parle. Conférence de Louvain, 13
October 1972. Vidéo-Durée 55. Paris: MK2 Vidéo,
1986.

A11. October 40 (1987): 5-133. Television and Dossier on
the Institutional Debate.

Includes the English translation of A3 and translations of the following items, all related to the
crises in institutional affiliations that mark
Lacan's career: B38a, B38b, E157, E159, E170/171,
E172, E178, E179, E203/204, E204, E288, and J1063.

Section B

Seminars

B12. Seminar I (1953-54): Les écrits techniques de
      Freud. Edited by Jacques-Alain Miller. Paris:
      Editions du Seuil, 1975. 316 pages.

Contents

Focuses on Freud's work from 1910-20, emphasizing his conceptualization of narcissism, transference, and resistance. Lacan treats those phenomena as products of the subject's imaginary identification with an other, which is structured by--and finally transcended through--la parole, the speech of analytic discourse. He also discusses the relations among the imaginary, symbolic, and real registers of experience; the substitution of the signifier for the thing; and the aggressivity endemic to imaginary relations and the paranoiac structure of human knowledge, all within the context of analytic practice.

Le moment de la résistance

Lacan begins by stressing the fundamental role of language in Freud's discoveries and insisting that language has its own order of reality quite apart from things. This point leads to an attack on ego psychology and the idea that analysis should adjust the patient's ego to some autonomous standard, whether that standard be conceived as "reality" or as an ego-ideal associated with the analyst. Lacan invokes the work of Michael Balint as a useful critique of this more traditional concept of analytic work, but he criticizes what he sees as the exclusively "objective" relations postulated by Balint's "two-body psychology." Rather than these dualistic objective relations, Lacan describes subjective interrelations that join patient and analyst in a triadic structure consisting of the patient, the analyst, and speech (la parole).

Lacan claims that the central discovery in Freud's accounts of analytic treatment was his perception that most of his patients' difficulties stemmed from "the problematic relations of the subject with himself" (p. 39). The goal of analysis thus became the patient's assumption of his past through its reconstruction in the present of analytic discourse (p. 55), and Lacan follows Freud in defining "resistance" as anything which interrupts the construction of this spoken history.

He goes on to note Freud's association of resistance with transference in "The Dynamics of
Transference" (1912), but Lacan explains transference in terms of the patient's imaginary
identification with the analyst, who at this level
is viewed as "the other." The other is thus
essential to what Lacan calls the "system of the
ego," and he says that in fact the ego exists for
the subject only at the level at which the other is
situated. As a result, resistance "is incarnated
in the system of the ego and the other" (p. 61).

Lacan argues that this relation of the ego to the
other is "an essential structure of the human condition" (p. 64), but he also says that the fundamental function of this ego is a méconnaissance
that obscures the alienation inherent in imaginary
relations. (Lacan's discussion of this point is
informed by Jean Hyppolite's commentary on Freud's
essay "Verneinung," which Lacan translates as
dénégation and associates with méconnaissance. See
L1897 and C61 and C62.) This first group of
seminar sessions then concludes with an extended
critique of Anna Freud's concept of the ego and
with a more sympathetic account of Melanie Klein's
analysis of the role played by the mother's body in
her essay "The Importance of Symbol-Formation in
the Development of the Ego." Here Lacan observes
during a discussion of hallucination that the
real, "or that which is perceived as such, is that
which resists symbolization absolutely," and he
claims that the true stake of analysis is not the
ego but "the recognition of what function the
subject assumes in the order of symbolic relations
which pervade the field of human relations" (p.
80).

La topique de l'imaginaire

The second group of sessions in this seminar
deals with the "junction of the symbolic and the
imaginary in the constitution of the real" (p. 88).
Lacan uses Freud's theories about narcissism
(especially "On Narcissism: An Introduction"
[1914]) to explain how the individual comes to
assume his place in the symbolic order of culture
through a modulation of his earlier relations to
objects and other people. Having already explained
the origins of the ego in the imaginary register,
Lacan now analyzes the way objects are constituted
as such in the field of human perception. Lacan
stresses the subjective character of the object
relations described by Freud as part of the narcissistic structure of the ego, and he argues that
our sense of the "real" is determined by our
relation to the other that is situated within the

imaginary identification described above. The
formation of the object, Lacan says, is "con-
temporaneous with the formation of the ego" (p.
188).

Lacan also observes that the imaginary identification of the ego is the driving force of the
sexual instinct that Freud called the libido (p.
141). That identification appears in Freud's work
as "primary narcissism," the source of the subject's sense of self and the basis of our ability
to organize reality into "a certain number of
preformed categories" (p. 144). At this point,
however, Lacan is more interested in a stage of
"secondary narcissism" which he admits is less
closely tied to Freud's theory. Rather than the
schema or _Gestalt_ of one's place in the world that
is provided by the _moi-idéal_ (Freud's _Idealich_)
within the identifications of primary narcissism,
secondary narcissism offers the individual an
"alter-ego," a different kind of "other" that Lacan
distinguishes as the _idéal du moi_ (Freud's _Ich-
ideal_). He calls this _Ichideal_ the _autre qui parle_
(written in next year's seminar as the _Autre_, or
"Other" with a large O/A), and he claims that it
enables the individual to transcend the imaginary
and enter into the symbolic liaisons that constitute human society.

Lacan says that the subject's position in the
imaginary structure, and the desire that is
concomitant with that position, can only be
conceived with the aid of a "guide" beyond the
imaginary and located at the level of the symbolic
order (p. 162). Thus he concludes a few pages
later that "the subject becomes conscious of his
desire in the other, by the intermediary of the
image of the other which gives to him the phantom
of his proper mastery" (p. 178). When this
relation to the other is named by the subject, it
takes on a symbolic dimension characterized by the
introduction of a third element into the imaginary
dyad, the _élément de médiation_, which situates the
couple in its presence and so transforms them onto
another plane (_"les fait passer sur un autre plan,
et les modifie"_). At this moment, Lacan says, they
enter language, are subjected to the law, and so
become fully human (p. 178).

Lacan discusses this move from the imaginary to
the symbolic by describing the subject's relation
to the imaginary other in terms of what Melanie
Klein identified as the "appeal" (_"l'appel"_ in
Lacan's text, which also connotes naming and
"calling" in the several senses of that term).
Also drawing upon Heidegger's concept of "calling
into being" as a property of language, Lacan
describes the appeal that constitutes the imaginary

relation to the other as indicative of the subjective dimension of all human relations and their
proto-linguistic nature.

Lacan also notes the role of the appeal in the
sado-masochistic dimension of subjective inter-
actions, since the appeal necessarily carries with
it the possibility of being refused. This possibility assumes the subjectivity of the other,
Lacan says, and it introduces the element of
dependence that subjects one to the other in what
Hegel described as the master/slave relation. In
addition to proving the "fundamental Hegelian
thesis--the desire of man is the desire of the
other" ("le désir de l'homme est le désir de
l'autre" [p. 169]), Lacan claims that his account
of the interaction between imaginary relations and
the symbolic order of language reveals why subjection and exploitation are inevitable in human
relations. They are structural properties of
civilization itself, he says; they underlie the
very notion of "work" and orient our lives toward
the limit of absolute mastery, death.

Au-delà de la psychologie

The third section of the seminar stresses the
constitutive role of the symbolic order in what are
usually considered to be the "psychological"
aspects of human behavior and identity. Focussing
on the transition in which the individual moves out
of the mirror stage, with its imaginary identification with the other, and into the symbolic order
of language and the law, Lacan describes what he
calls la bascule du désir, the "swing" or "swerve"
of desire. This occurs at a moment in the mirror
stage when the other's image produces in the infant
a "jubilatory assumption [l'assomption jubilatoire]
of a mastery that he has not yet obtained" (p.
192). Through this assumption, the subject proves
fully capable of possessing that mastery à l'in-
terieur, i.e., of "introjecting" it.

In this exchange, man recognizes his own desire
inverted in the other, and this recognition is the
first step toward the naming of desire and toward
the subject's accession to the symbolic. At this
point, Lacan says, the subject's desire is "susceptible to the mediation of recognition" that
replaces the indefinite longing for the destruction
of the other as such (p. 193). Desire will
therefore return to the subject mediated through
the other, "verbalized" within the symbolic order
(p. 194). This is how man's desire enters into the
mediation of language. Desire is named "in the
other, by the other," and so enters into the "order
of a law already set to include the history of each

individual" (pp. 200-01). Our relations with
objects are constituted the same way, Lacan adds,
and illustrates his point by commenting on Freud's
discussion of the Fort/Da game from Beyond the
Pleasure Principle (1920). Lacan claims that the
child plays not with the object but with its
presence and absence, thus transforming it into a
symbolic function in which "the symbol emerges, and
becomes more important than the object itself" (p.
201).

Lacan then moves on to discuss the role of speech
in analysis. "Speech is this mill-wheel by which
human desire is ceaselessly mediated by re-entering
the system of language," he says (p. 203), but he
also claims that the law of free association
loosens a certain number of the moorings that
usually bind the subject to speech (see p. 205).
This allows the subject to see, in succession, the
diverse parts of his self-image as it has been
formed in the imaginary, and as a result he can
obtain to the state of maximal narcissistic
projection that Freud described as essential for
analytic progress (p. 205).

In short, analytic discourse allows the subject
to constitute the history of his ego, to assume his
"past" quite literally as a "form" in and of the
future. By introducing the third element--the
speech of the subject--into the relation of self
and other, the analysis can progress beyond the
cul-de-sac of imaginary relations in which the
subject has been trapped. As the patient flounders
in the impasse of the reconstituted imaginary bond,
and as desire emerges in the confrontation with the
image, the analyst must intervene through an
interpretation, breaking the cycle of repetition
and restoring the subject to the symbolic with his
history intact (see p. 212).

Les impasses de Michaël Balint

The next section of the seminar begins with an
extended critique of Michael Balint's concept of
"primary love," a pre-genital stage in which the
infant relates to the mother (or anything else)
strictly as an object that satisfies its desire.
Lacan objects that such a model cannot explain how,
or why, the infant ever moves beyond that stage,
and he insists that even the earliest relations are
in fact intersubjective, a relation between two
subjects. Citing Sartre's Being and Nothingness as
essential reading for any analyst, Lacan describes
the imaginary identification with an other in terms
of Sartre's dualistic concept of le regard," the
"look" or "gaze." Lacan supplements Sartre's
theory, however, by noting that within the recipro-

cal structure of the "double-gaze" which joins two
subjects looking at each other there is always a
third element.   This <u>tiers</u> is established in the
fact that "I see that the other sees me, and that
this third intervening term sees me being seen."
There are never just two terms, Lacan says, because
I always see the other seeing me; that is, the
other is experienced as possessing a subjectivity
modelled on our own (and on which our own is
modelled in turn).   This subjectivity stands
outside the imaginary relation between the two
objects of the reciprocal gaze.   This triadic
structure institutes a certain lack or "<u>béance</u>"
within the imaginary identification, and this lack
makes way for the symbolic.
   Lacan continues to emphasize the priority of the
symbolic over the imaginary in human experience.
Contrary to what we generally think, he says, even
for the infant the imaginary comes into being only
within the poles of the symbolic and the real (p.
244).   Even Hegel's account of the master-slave
relation, which is paradigmatic of the imaginary
order of experience, is circumscribed by the
symbolic because it depends on the notion of work
and the economic order in which the roles of master
and slave are defined (p. 249).   Furthermore, the
death towards which the relation tends is structured as "risk" (<u>risque</u>), the stakes of the game
(<u>enjeu</u>), rather than fear of biological catastrophe.   Thus there is at the very origin of the
struggle between the master and the slave <u>une règle
du jeu</u> that testifies to the presence of the
symbolic.
   Hegel's discussion of the master/slave relation
bears obvious ontological implications in the
context of his argument, and Lacan pursues those
implications to establish a link between the symbolic order of speech and being.   "It is speech
that institutes the lie in reality," he says,
because it introduces "that which is not."   On the
other hand, the possibility of negation is what
allows for the corollary, i.e., "what is."   Before
speech, "nothing is, nor is it not . . . it is only
with speech that there are things which are--
which are true or false. . . --and some things that
are not." Speech introduces the "cavity of being
into the texture of the real . . . . It is with the
dimension of speech that truth is hollowed out in
the real" ("<u>le creux de l'être dans la texture du
réel</u> . . . . <u>C'est avec la dimension de la parole
que se creuse dans le réel la vérité</u>" [p. 254]).
Similarly, the "truth" of the subject is dependent
on speech as well, but Lacan is careful to explain
that it is not the "psychological" properties of
the subject he is concerned with; rather, psycho-

analysis works with "that which is hollowed out in the experience of speech," which is the analytic experience per se (p. 256).

La parole dans le transfert

The last section of the seminar deals with the concept of analysis itself. Lacan claims that analysis consists of the subject's search for his truth and so must start from the position of ignorance that marks the junction of the symbolic and the real (p. 306). (Lacan identifies two other "fundamental passions" in addition to ignorance: love, which exists at the borderline [ligne d'arrête] of the imaginary and the symbolic; and hatred, which exists at the juncture of the imaginary and the real [p. 298]). The very fact that the patient is willing to put himself in that position indicates the ouverture au transfert necessary for a successful analysis, Lacan says, and he warns the analyst that he must not try to guide the subject towards knowledge (savoir). Rather, he can only start the subject on the path to knowledge by engaging him in a dialectical operation in which the subject will be able to "totalize" the diverse accidents and traumatic events that are closed to him in the imaginary form of his memory (p. 312; cf. pp. 215, 222): "It is by the spoken assumption of his history that the subject is engaged in the path of the realization of his truncated imaginary. This complement to the imaginary is accomplished in the other, to the extent that the subject assumes the other in his discourse, as he makes it understood to the other" (p. 312).

This summary of theoretical points raised by Lacan in the course of the seminar tends to distort the general focus of Lacan's teaching, which is consistently directed toward analytic practice. It also ignores Lacan's frequent recourse to what he calls the "diagram of the inverted bouquet," with which he illustrates his theory of the relationship between the image of the self situated within the imaginary order and the position of the subject in the symbolic order.

Throughout the seminar Lacan also discusses a number of subsidiary points as well: the role of traumatic events in the "truncation" of the imaginary order (pp. 215, 222); the distinction between psychosis and neurosis (Lacan says that the psychotic subject completely lacks the capacity for imaginary experience and so conflates the symbolic with the real, whereas the neurotic tends to collapse the real into the imaginary); and the running joke about elephants. Early in the seminar, Lacan illustrates the substitutive function that gives rise to the possibility of signification by pointing out that the signifier "elephant" allows him to let elephants into the room even though the door is not big enough, and that example comes to stand for the "murder of the thing" by the signifier (see pp. 196, 244). (The cover of the published text carries a picture of a huge elephant looking directly at the reader, and at the end of the seminar Lacan distributed little elephant figurines to the participants.)

During this seminar Jean Hyppolite presented a paper on Freud's Verneinung that was published in A2, pp. 879-87, and later in Hyppolite's Figures de la pensée philosophique. An expanded version of Lacan's introduction and response to the paper appeared separately as C61 and C62. For a general critique of the text of this seminar as established by Miller vs. the stenographer's transcript, see G430.

B12a. Das Seminar, Buch I: Freuds technische Schriften. Edited by Norbert Haas. Translated by Werner Hamacher. Olten: Walter, 1978. 364 pages.

B12b. Il seminario, vol. I: Gli scritti tenici di Freud (1953-54). Edited by Giacomo Contri. Translated by Antonello Siacchitano and Irene Molina. Turin: G. Einaudi, 1978. 354 pages.

B12c. El seminaro, I: Los escritos ténicos de Freud. Translated by Rithée Cevasco and Vincente Mira Pascual. Barcelona: Paidos Ibéric, 1981.

B12d. Seminario: Los excritos técnicos de Freud. Col. Analitica. Caracas: Anteneo, 1982.

B12*. According to J1053, a translation into Portuguese has been published by Dom Quixote Press, and another edition is forthcoming in Brazil from Zahar. A translation into Greek is forthcoming from Kedros Press.

B13. Seminar II (1954-55): Le moi dans la théorie de Freud et dans la technique de la psychanalyse. Edited by Jacques Alain-Miller. Paris: Editions du Seuil, 1978. 375 pages.

Contents

Introduction

Focuses on the period in Freud's career following what Lacan calls the "crisis in analytic technique" that occurred in 1920, and emphasizes Freud's conceptualization of the ego, consciousness and the unconscious, the death drive, and the repetition-compulsion as necessary supplements to the "de-centering of the subject" that Freud had begun in The Interpretation of Dreams (1900). In addition to extended close readings of sections from Beyond the Pleasure Principle (1920) and of Freud's dream about Irma's injection and other dreams from Chapter VII of The Interpretation of Dreams, this seminar introduces Lacan's own concepts of "le grand Autre" (as opposed to the "autre" of imaginary relations); the "L-schema" described below;

and further remarks on the problems of resistance
and regression in analysis, the function of the
symbolic order, and relations among the symbolic,
the imaginary and the real. The seminar also
includes an abbreviated version of C69; Lacan's
reflections on the intersubjective strategy behind
the game of pair ou impair (even-or-odd); and
several discussions of cybernetics as a model for
the symbolic order that characterizes human speech
in terms of the possibility of its "meaning" or
"significance" rather than the mere communication
of "information."

Introduction

   The introductory section describes Freud's work
as a "Copernican revolution" because it "decenters"
the subject in relation to the individual, and
Lacan insists that the unconscious always eludes
the certitudes that usually characterize man's
sense of himself as ego (comme moi [p. 16]). The
ego exists only on an imaginary plane, Lacan says,
where réminiscence informs what we generally think
of as the "eternal form" of the world and of our
being. He argues that the imaginary plane is
absolutely heterogeneous with that of the symbolic,
and he claims that the symbolic constitutes a
rupture (forçage) when it is introduced into
reality. However, the symbolic also constitutes
the subject as such through speech (la parole), and
Lacan draws upon the work of Lévi-Strauss to argue
that the "founding speeches" ("les paroles fon-
datrices") which envelop the subject also determine
his relations with everyone around him. The
symbolic even structures the way human beings
couple among themselves, Lacan adds. Though these
relations lead to the creation of real beings,
infants come into the world bearing an étiquette (a
little tag or label but also "etiquette" in the
sense of "ceremony") which is their name, "the
essential symbol for that which is their lot" (p.
30).

Au-delà du principe du plaisir, la répétition

   The first two chapters of this section continue
to emphasize the constitutive role of the symbolic
in human experience and insist on the absolute
distinction between the "je" of the subject and the
individual ego. Lacan defines subjectivity as an
"organized system of symbols" that animates
experience and gives it meaning (p. 56), and he
says that Lévi-Strauss has taught us to understand
human experience as coterminous with that system
(p. 43).

   Lacan associates the symbolic plane with the
unconscious in this section largely on the basis of
Freud's distinction between the ego and the unconscious.   Lacan claims that everything Freud wrote
emphasized the <u>excentricité</u> of the subject in
relation to the ego (<u>moi</u>) (p. 60), and it is in the
unconscious, excluded from the system of the ego,
that the subject speaks (p. 77).   There is a <u>dis-
symétrie absolue</u> between the subject of the unconscious and the organization of the ego, Lacan
says; "<u>le</u> je <u>du sujet inconscient n'est pas</u> moi"
(p. 59).
   Unlike the symbolic function of the subject, the
ego must be considered as an "object" that consists
in an imaginary function, characterized by an
identification with an "other" based upon the
"dialectic of jealousy-sympathy" Lacan described in
C53.   Lacan argues that this rivalry constitutes
"connaissance" in a pure state, since it establishes a relation between the ego and an object on
the basis of the desire of this other (p. 67).   The
imaginary dimension of this object-relation traps
the ego in an endless conflict with the other,
however, since the desire of the other is not
recognized as such.
   That recognition requires a "third" ("<u>un troi-
sième</u>"), which Lacan says we find in the unconscious.   The "third" grounds the position of the
"je" in speech, and it interrupts the destructive
cycle of the imaginary and transforms the relation
between the moi and the other into the symbolic
order.   Although the moi is an imaginary function,
Lacan insists that it intervenes in the psychic
life only as a symbol from the moment the symbolic
world is founded--which is to say, from the first
(p. 68).   This inevitable priority of the symbolic
is what distinguishes the imaginary function of the
ego in human experience from the image of the
"other" that allows animals to identify themselves
as part of a species by imprinting.   This difference between the way animals and humans relate
to others in the earliest stages of development is
the great discovery of analysis, Lacan says (p.
50).   Human experience always begins with a crack
(<u>fêlure</u>), a profound disturbance in the vital
order, and it was this notion of a break or rupture
at the foundation of human life that led Freud to
the death-instinct (<u>l'instinct de mort</u>) (p. 50).
   Lacan claims that Freud's essentially biological
perspective on the death-instinct and the repetition compulsion resulted in a confusion of the
biological and human orders of experience.   As a
result, Freud failed to formulate the concept of
the symbolic that is actually implied in his work
(pp. 51, 35).   Lacan would substitute cybernetics

for biology as the constitutive ground of subjectivity, and in fact he claims at one point that
freudian biology has nothing to do with biology but
is instead an "energetic myth" which implies "the
metaphor of the human body as machine"--though
Lacan reminds us that the most complicated machines
are made out of words (p. 63).

The point of Lacan's comparison between the
symbolic and a machine is that both a symbolic and
a mechanistic order operate independent of the
individual subject through a closed circuit of
systematic relations. Lacan says that this closure
is the basis of our "need for repetition" ("le
besoin de répétition"), and, in that need, we
rediscover that "the unconscious is the discourse
of the other" (p. 112). Hence Lacan claims that
the repetition compulsion is introduced only by the
register of language and the function of the symbol
and cannot be traced to some biological mechanism
(p. 112).

Les schémas freudiens de l'appareil psychique

In this section Lacan briefly comments on the
diagrams Freud presented in the Entwurf of 1895 and
in Chapter VII of The Interpretation of Dreams
(1900), and he focuses on the interpretation of
dreams as a means of determining the relation
between the imaginary, the symbolic, and the real.
Lacan begins by recalling his claim that repetition
derives from the closure of a symbolic circuit
exterior to the subject (p. 123), but he adds that
the imaginary and the symbolic cross (pp. 131-2).
It is therefore crucial to analysis, Lacan says,
that the analyst know whether his relation to the
speaking subject is structured as an imaginary
opposition or as a symbolic mediation (p. 131).

Lacan pursues the theoretical relation between
the imaginary and the symbolic with a revisionist
reading of Freud's comments on dream interpretation, using Freud's analysis of his own dream of
Irma's injection as an example. Lacan's reading of
Freud's dream exemplifies his central assertion
that the "psychic place" in which the dream occurs
is really the symbolic dimension. "The structural
laws of the dream, as those of language, are
inscribed elsewhere, in another place," Lacan
argues (p. 160), and that other place is the
symbolic. At one level, Lacan simply means to
emphasize that we always deal with a reconstruction
of the dream in an analysis, one that obviously
takes place in the symbolic order through the
subject's speech (see p. 195). But we never know
for sure "who" is speaking, or to whom the speech
is addressed. For Freud, Lacan says, it is not

important that one dreams of being a butterfly but
that the dream means, that it means for someone.
The essential question is who, or what, is that
someone (p. 154). Lacan briefly discusses Freud's
observations on the censor, the superego, and
resistance in the light of this question, but then
suspends his discussion of dreams in favor of an
extended commentary on the schema presented in
Chapter VII of The Interpretation of Dreams.
  When Lacan returns to this topic in the chapter
on Freud's dream of Irma, it is to counter those
who would read the dream as a stage in the development of Freud's ego. To be sure, Lacan said, Freud
insisted that the dream was based on an unconscious
desire, but for whom does this desire exist?
Rather than a single coherent ego holding the dream
together, there seems to be at least three different places to situate Freud's ego, i.e., in each
of the three colleagues he mentions. Lacan says
that this point reinforces Freud's own argument
that "the ego is the sum of the identifications of
the subject" (p. 187), but what Freud's dream
illustrates is not a coherent summation of the ego
so much as a "spectral decomposition of the
function of the ego" into a series of imaginary
identities (p. 197).
  The importance of this "imaginary plurality of
the subject," this "Freudian crowd," can be seen in
Freud's comments on mass-psychology in Group
Psychology and the Analysis of the Ego (1921). It
appears at first as the destruction of the subject
as such, but Lacan explains that it is the subject
who speaks in this dream, and it is to him that
this unconscious discourse is addressed (p. 200).
The imaginary decomposition of the subject represented in this dream thus marks the junction of the
symbolic and the imaginary, a point that is
dramatized at the end of the dream when the cryptic
symbols of a chemical formula suddenly appear to
Freud as a conclusion to his imaginary quandary.
  The appearance of the formula marks what Lacan
calls the second summit of the dream. The first
comes when Freud gazes down Irma's throat and
experiences a curious horror at what he sees, an
anatomical formation that properly is situated in
the nose. Drawing upon other details offered by
Freud himself, Lacan reads this passage as Freud's
encounter with the image of death, which lies
behind the imaginary trio Freud calls up to obscure
it. Like the symbolic, death here lies beyond the
imaginary, but at this point Lacan associates death
with the real. What Freud sees, Lacan says, is an
image that evokes what Lacan calls the revelation
of the real "without any possible mediation," a
discovery of an "essential object" that is not an

object at all but "this something before which all
the words halt and all the categories run aground,
the object of anguish par excellence" (p. 196).   At
this point, Lacan says, the dream is experienced as
an approach to the <u>dernier réel</u>, and the "imaginary
decomposition" evinced by Freud's account uncovers
the composite quality of ordinary perception that
is usually masked by the illusory coherence of the
ego.   That is why I teach analysts to analyze
dreams, Lacan observes (p. 199).

Lacan then turns to the "fundamental uncertainty"
inherent in object relations as they are constituted within the imaginary register of experience.   Fortunately, Lacan says, the symbolic
intervenes in the dual relation between the self
and other, the <u>toi</u> and <u>moi</u>, which would otherwise
paralyze the individual within a "vast concentric
hallucination" (p. 201).   The symbolic interjects
<u>un tiers régulateur</u> into that binary couple and
restructures perception within a "zone of nomina-
tion," and in that zone things are imbued with a
certain identity that carries with it a temporal
dimension.   When two subjects agree to recognize
the same object at the same time, Lacan says, a
symbolic pact is thus constituted by naming, and
this event marks the emergence of the symbolic in
relation to the imaginary.

To exemplify this conjunction between the
imaginary and the symbolic in terms of Freud's
dream, Lacan notes that the chemical formula
appears to Freud at the moment when the dream
approaches the greatest point of chaos within the
imaginary identifications.   At this point, he says,
the formula represents discourse as such and so
marks the pressure of the symbolic on imaginary
stability.   But it is a <u>un discours insensé</u> and
seems to come from nowhere; it exists as "<u>une voix</u>
<u>qui n'est plus que</u> la voix de personne," and Lacan
quotes Freud's own explanation for the source of
the formula and of the whole dream as illustrative
of the subject's relation to the symbolic: "the
creator is someone greater than me.   It is my
unconscious, it is that speech which speaks in me,
beyond me" ("<u>qui parle en moi, au-delà de moi</u>" [p.
203]).   A distinction between the ego and the
speaking subject thus emerges in Freud's own
account, and a few pages later Lacan rephrases
Freud's remarks to conclude that "the unconscious
subject is the subject who speaks, and this subject
who speaks is beyond the ego" (p. 207).

<u>Au-delà de l'imaginaire, le symbolique, ou du petit</u>
<u>au grand Autre</u>

The next section of the seminar elaborates on

Lacan's postulation of a subject "beyond the ego,"
which he now begins calling "le grand Autre." He
writes it with capital A (i.e., the Other) to
distinguish it from the imaginary other which he
identifies as the ego, and Lacan associates the
Other with the function of speech (p. 276). In
analysis, Lacan says, the subject usually sees
himself as an ego (moi). But because the ego is
always recognized in the form of a specular other,
or the "semblable," the ego never exists alone. It
is always in relation to a symmetrical, homogeneous
image, and so is structured along the lines of an
imaginary plane.

Sketching this relation in what came to be called
the "L schema," Lacan distinguishes another plane
from the imaginary, which he calls the "wall of
language" ("le mur du langage"), and he claims that
it crosses the imaginary, disrupting the imaginary
union of the ego and its image. The ego and its
objects or "others" that make up the "false
reality" of the imaginary all in fact derive from
the wall of language, Lacan says; they become
objects because they are named as such in the
organized system of the symbolic.

When the subject speaks with his "semblables," he
speaks in what Lacan calls the "common language,"
where these imaginary egos are taken to be real and
where the subject identifies himself with everyone
to whom he speaks. As analysts, however, Lacan
says that we must believe that there are other
subjects besides us. We must address ourselves to
these "true subjects," the "véritables Autres,"
despite the fact that they are ultimately inaccessible: "Le sujet est séparé des Autres, les vrais,
par the mur du langage" (p. 286). Nevertheless,
Lacan adds, language is made as much to found us in
the Other as to prevent us from understanding it,
and that is what makes the analytic experience
possible (p. 286). So, Lacan concludes, analysis
must aim for "the passage of a true speech, which
joins the subject to an other subject (rather than
an objectified other), on the other side of the
wall of language. It is the ultimate relation [la
relation dernière] of the subject to a true Other,
to the Other who gives a response that one does not
expect, which defines the terminal point of
analysis" (p. 287-88). Lacan sums up this goal by
rewriting Freud's famous dictum, "Wo Es war, soll
Ich werden" as "Là où le S[subject] était, là le
Ich doit être ("There where the subject was, the I
must be." (p. 288).

To sum up Lacan's central point in this section,
we might say that there are a number of things
"beyond" the imaginary order of the coherent ego
which it is the job of the pleasure principle to

maintain: the symbolic, the other, death, and the
real.   The crucial point of analysis is the passage
from the imaginary to the symbolic, which is
achieved by getting the subject to assume his true
position through a speech founded in and addressed
to the Other rather than to the imaginary others
with whom he usually identifies and whom he
mistakes for real.   This is not a simple developmental model of ego-development, however, since the
symbolic always precedes the subject's imaginary
experience.

In fact, Lacan insists that the "imaginary
economy" has a meaning "only insofar as it is
inscribed in a symbolic order which imposes a
ternary relation" (p. 296).   Despite the way it may
appear, the subject never has a dual relation with
an object because it is only in relation to another
subject that his relations with objects take on
their meaning (p. 297).   Thus in addition to
establishing the identity of the object, as
described above, naming also inserts it into the
symbolic order of language.   Naming also raises the
question of what remains unnamed in our experience,
however, and Lacan declares that this unnameable is
death (p. 247).

Death is thus intimately involved with the very
possibility of speech that is associated with the
act of naming, and Lacan repeatedly remarks on the
persistent association in human culture between
"the speech [la parole] which dominates the
destiny of man, and death" (p. 241).   Lacan claims
that we can find this connection indirectly in
Beyond the Pleasure Principle when we consider that
the Widerholungswang (which Lacan translates as
"insistance répétitive, insistance significative")
is the principle characteristic of the symbolic
order.   Lacan also connects death to the formation
of the ego by noting that death is presented to us
only in a wound (le béance) that is produced in the
imaginary by the symbolic (p. 245).

The béance that marks the presence of death in
human experience is also the site of desire, as
Lacan explains in Chapter XVIII.   Earlier in this
section Lacan notes that all human knowledge and
especially conscious relations are based on the ego
and its imaginary identification with the other
because it is from the perspective of this ego that
all objects are regarded.   But Lacan also claims
that it is from the position of the subject, "a
subject primitively at odds with itself [désac-
cordé] and fundamentally dismembered [morcelé] by
this ego, that all the objects are desired" (pp.
209-10).   Moreover, the subject cannot desire
without dissolving itself and displacing the object
as well.   Hence for Freud, Lacan says, desire is

not sexual; rather, it is a relation of being to
lack, a "lack of being by which being exists" (p.
261).

Based as it is on a lack within the being of the
subject, Lacan argues that desire therefore cannot
be attributed to the ego, nor can it even be
considered strictly "human." Instead, Lacan says
that desire emerges at the moment when the individual is incarnated in a word (une parole).
Desire emerges from the roll of a die, Lacan
remarks. I do not say human desire, he adds,
"since, in the end, the man who plays with the die
is a captive of the desire thus put in play. He
does not know the origin of his desire, rolling
with the written symbol on the six faces" (p. 273).

(This section of the seminar also contains an
abbreviated version of C69, in which Lacan emphasizes how different individuals can come to
occupy different places as determined by the
circulation of the letter. Also included are a
provocative reading of Oedipus Rex and Oedipus at
Colonus that illustrates the close connection
between death and being in Oedipus's realization of
his fate; and Lacan's meditation on the game of
odd-or-even (pair ou impair), in which he points
out the strategic identification with the "subjectivity" of his opponents that allows a young boy to
win far beyond what would be predicted on the basis
of the calculation of probability. This latter
point raises the problem of language in human
relations, which is discussed in the last section
of the seminar.)

Final

Most of this last section deals with the interaction between the symbolic and the imaginary in
actual human discourse and its implications for
analytic practice. Lacan begins by distinguishing
between the symbolic order of language (langage)
and what he calls "universal discourse" (p. 328),
the concrete langues that we manipulate with all
their ambiguity, emotional content, and human
significance (leur sense humain [p. 351]). He
describes le langage as a cybernetic calculating
system which operates as a closed circuit completely independent of the human subject--and,
consequently, completely lacking signification (p.
328). What gives that world of signs its signification, Lacan says, "is the moment when we stop the
machine. It is the temporal cuts which we fashion
there . . . the intervention of a scansion which
permits the insertion of that which can have a
meaning (sense) for a subject" (p. 328).

Lacan argues that the existence of signification
in language demonstrates the importance of the
imaginary (p. 352), and explains why there is
always some resistance to the restitution of the
integral text of the symbolic exchange. Because we
are incarnated beings, Lacan says, we always think
with "some imaginary go-between, which arrests,
stops, entangles symbolic mediation" (p. 367).
Thus, unlike cybernetic systems which are governed
by the science of syntax, human discourse possesses
a semantic dimension "furnished with the desire of
men" (p. 351).

Lacan explains that, in analysis, these interruptions of the imaginary appear as resistance,
which arises from the fact that "the ego is not
identical to the subject" but is in fact caught up
in an imaginary relation with the other. That is
why Freud associated resistance with transference,
Lacan says. Resistance occurs when the "imaginary
circuit" of the ego's relation to the other--the
identification of transference--blocks the "fundamental discourse" that would otherwise pass from
the Other to the Subject (see p. 374).

Ideally, in the process of analysis the analyst
will refuse to occupy the position of the imaginary
other, "resisting," in other words, the ego's
attempt to identify with him. This is why Lacan
insists that the "only true resistance in analysis
is the resistance of the analyst" (p. 373). This
tends to put the analyst in the position of the
Other rather than that of the other, "insofar as he
is that which is the most difficult to gain access
to." The imaginary projections of the ego are
frustrated by this Other, who is veiled to the ego,
and the analysis overcomes what Lacan calls the
"inertia of the imaginary" (p. 353). As the ego
comes into accord with the fundamental discourse
that joins the subject with the Other, it approaches the position of the subject itself, and
this is the end of analysis.

Lacan concludes with an exposition on analytic
technique which focuses on the analyst's refusal to
assume the position of the "<u>sujet supposé à savoir</u>"
that comes to figure prominently in Lacan's
technical essays of the late 1960s, and this leads
to further reflections on the ego and its relation
to death and resistance. Lacan says that Freud's
emphasis in <u>Beyond the Pleasure Principle</u> on
<u>Wiederholung</u>, repetition, changes his focus from
the opposition of consciousness and unconsciousness
to a new opposition between "something that is
repressed" and tends only to be repeated, and
something which forms an obstacle to it, i.e., the
ego. If you reread Freud's text in this new light,
Lacan says, you will see that "the ego is strictly

situated as part of the order of the imaginary and
Freud emphasizes that all resistance comes from
this order" (pp. 369-70). More important, however,
is Lacan's association of the symbolic with the
death instinct introduced by Freud in this text.
Earlier, Lacan had claimed that we must conceive
of repetition, which Freud associates with the
death-instinct, as "tied to a circular process of
the exchange of speech" which he describes as a
"symbolic circuit exterior to the subject" in which
the subject is caught up and his fate determined
(p. 123). Here, Lacan directly links death and the
symbolic and claims that "the death-instinct is
only the mask of the symbolic order insofar as--
Freud wrote it--it is mute, that is to say insofar
as it is not realized" (p. 375). The symbolic
order is what lies beyond the pleasure principle,
which tries to preserve the imaginary harmony of
the ego. Like death, the symbolic is precisely
that which cannot be recognized (p. 370); it is the
repressed, which "insists, and demands to be" (p.
354).

For a detailed critique of Miller's version of
the seminar for 16 March 1955, see G430. F357 is
devoted to the general question of establishing
authoritative texts for Lacan's seminars.

B13a.   Das Seminar, II (1954-55): Das Ich in der Theorie
        Freuds und in der Technik der Psychoanalyse.
        Translated by Hans-Joachim Metzger. Olten:
        Walter, 1980. 419 pages.

B13b.   Seminario. Yo en la teoria de Freud y en la
        technica psicoanalitica. Translated by Irene
        Agoff. Buenos Aires: Paidos, 1983. 481 pages.

B14.   Seminar III (1955-56): Les psychoses. Edited by
        Jacques-Alain Miller. Paris: Editions du Seuil,
        1981. 363 pages.

        Contents

            Introduction à la question des psychoses

Describes psychosis as a disturbance in the
subject's relation to the signifier that results
from the "foreclosure" (Verwerfung) of a primordial
signifier, the "nom-du-père." Lacan illustrates
his theory of psychosis with a close reading of
Schreber's Memoirs, which shows that "what is
refused [refusé] in the symbolic order, re-emerges
[resurgit] in the real" (p. 22). Many of Lacan's
remarks focus on passages from the Memoirs that are
not discussed in Freud's own analysis of the text,
"Psycho-Analytic Notes on an Autobiographical
Account of a Case of Paranoia (Dementia Paranoides)" (1911), and Lacan argues against Freud's
conclusion that the delusions are a defense against
latent homosexual desires. It is Schreber's
inability to assume a place in the symbolic order
of language, Lacan claims, with its concomitant

status of symbolic castration, that results in his
fantasies about becoming the wife of God.   The
auditory hallucinations he hears murmuring ceaselessly around him are nothing other than imaginary
manifestations of the symbolic functions that he
lacks.

Throughout the seminar, Lacan uses the pathological state of psychosis and its differences from
neurosis to identify crucial points in the ordinary
subject's relation to the symbolic order.   In
psychosis, Lacan says, what is ordinarily repressed
is completely foreclosed or rejected from the symbolic order, and it reappears in "another place
(un autre lieu), the imaginary-real, without a
mask."   Neurosis, on the other hand, always remains
strictly within the symbolic, and the repressed
always reappears amidst the symbols where it was
originally repressed (Verdrangung) even though it
is usually masked there in the form of the symptom
(p. 120).

The fact that "foreclosure" is possible at all
leads Lacan to claim that there is a stage prior to
all symbolization at which the subject can either
accept (Bejahung) or reject (Verwerfung) the
signifier in place of the object or the "other."
Lacan associates this stage with what Freud identified as the Oedipal phase, and he claims that it
is the site of symbolic castration, in which the
subject must give up the fantasy of being the
phallus for another and assume the phallus as
signifier if he is to gain access to the symbolic.
An individual's sexual identity is formed at this
stage, Lacan says, because that identity is
determined by the network of signifiers that
subordinate the subject to the constraints of the
symbolic order.   Access to that order hinges on
one's response to the name-of-the-father, which is
the signifier that marks the intervention of the
"law" within the bond of mother and child.   This
signifier, which Lacan implicates with the signifier of the phallus, replaces the imaginary
identification between self and other with a
symbolic recognition of the place of the Other as
the locus of speech and as the ground of one's
being as subject in and to language.   Lacking that
recognition, the psychotic remains trapped within
the imaginary, where he encounters the Other in
the various forms of imaginary, totalized others
who engage him in endless rounds of mutually
destructive emulation.   (Lacan comments on psychosis and Schreber's Memoirs again in C72.)

Introduction à la question des psychoses

Lacan claims that the psychotic subject ignores

the language that he speaks, but the real question
is how that language appears in the real to the
psychotic.   To explain this phenomenon, Lacan
distinguishes among Bejahung, Verneinung, and
Verwerfung, and he argues that behind the process
of verbalization and before the "denegation" of
Verneinung, there is a "Bejahung primordiale," an
"admission into the meaning [sens] of the symbolic,
which itself can fail" (p. 21).   This failure
results in foreclosure or Verwerfung, a total
exclusion in which the subject refuses to admit
into the symbolic something that he nevertheless
experiences.   In the cases of Schreber and the
Wolf-man, what is foreclosed is the possibility of
symbolic castration.   What is thus foreclosed then
reappears in the real where it cannot be assumed by
the "je" or, in other words, where it cannot be
recognized and articulated because the individual
cannot assume the role of the subject who speaks
about it (pp. 21-22).

Lacan claims that this is why Freud posed the
problem of psychosis at the level of speech (la
parole) and why verbal hallucinations usually play
such a prominent role in psychotic experience.
Psychosis has its source in "the history of the
subject in the symbolic," Lacan says (p. 22), and
he argues that neurosis can be distinguished from
psychosis according to where the moment of repression occurs in the subject's accession to the
symbolic order (p. 22).

Alluding to the L-schema introduced in the
seminar for last year (see B13), Lacan reminds his
audience that the full speech between the subject
and the Other is usually interrupted by the
imaginary relation between the ego and the other.
This interruption yields a "triplicity" (vs. the
duplicity of the imaginary relation) in which the
ego of the subject speaks to an other about the
subject, which appears in that speech as the third
person.   In psychosis, however, the subject
identifies completely with his ego, and Lacan
asserts that this results in the verbal hallucination of some third party out there, who speaks and
comments on the subject's activity but who is
unrelated to the subject (p. 23).

Returning to this point in a slightly different
form, Lacan observes that "the fundamental structure of speech" is that "the subject receives his
message from the other under an inverted form" (p.
47).   To speak as such is to speak to an other,
Lacan says, or, in fact, to "make the other speak
as other" (p. 48).   So, to say "you are my wife"
implies the inverted version of the same claim made
by the other, "you are my husband."   What ordinarily distinguishes this particular "other" from

the objects that are the "others" in our field of
knowledge--i.e., what makes this relation of speech
an intersubjective relation rather than objective
knowledge--is the possibility of being wrong.
There is always a chance that the other will not
answer, that it is not what it seems, or that it
can trick us: that it can lie.
     The result of this uncertainty is that the other
can be recognized, but not known. It is experienced as an absolute Other, and it is this
"unknown" (cette inconnue) that characterizes
normal speech at the level where it is spoken to
the other (p. 48). Thus Lacan describes the Other
as "beyond the known" (au-delà du connu). "It is
in recognition that you institute the Other," Lacan
says. It is not an element of "reality," but "an
irreducible absolute, on whose existence as
subject depends the very value of the speech in
which you make the recognition" (p. 63).
     Applying these remarks to psychosis, Lacan claims
that hallucinatory speech (la parole délirante) is
characterized by the complete exclusion of the
Other. There is no "behind" or "beyond" such
speech, Lacan says. The psychotic subject is
concerned exclusively with the other of the
imaginary. Instead of significations being linked
with other significations through a dialectical
function of the signifier, for the psychotic
certain elements of the signifier break off, become
isolated, and take on a peculiar weight all their
own. The result is a curious inertia of signification (p. 66), in which the same elements are
repeated over and over again (see pp. 31, 43).
     Lacan distinguishes two poles of such concrete
manifestations of psychosis: intuition, and
formula. Psychotics frequently report interrupted
phrases or isolated syntactic formulas, Lacan says,
and these phrases repeat themselves continuously,
with no apparent connection to anything beyond
themselves. At the other extreme is the "intuition" of significance surrounding something in the
psychotic's experience. Instead of connecting one
signification to another, the psychotic tends to
become fixated on the intuition of signification
itself, even though it is "ineffable" and so
remains isolated, irreducible, and perpetually
mysterious. In such a state there is no possibility of the psychotic being able to recognize
this imaginary discourse as his own because he
cannot relate to it as a subject.

Thématique et structure du phénomène psychotique

     The second section of the seminar focuses on the
psychotic's relation to elements foreclosed from

symbolization. In neurosis, elements are repressed
or subjected to "denegation" (Verneinung) but only
after being admitted to the level of discourse.
Thus the neurotic, confronted with the repressed,
can simply substitute another signifier in its
place. This substitution is what makes up the
symptom. Psychosis, however, derives from a stage
in the subject's history when something fundamental
to his being was subjected to "foreclosure" (Verwerfung) before it even made it to the level of
discourse. When this "non-symbolized" element
"re-appears," it is perceived as part of the real
rather than the symbolic, and the only relation to
it that is available for the psychotic is imaginary
(pp. 94-95). This is why Lacan claims that psychotic experience is trapped in the desperate
effort to cover the real with the imaginary order.
    Ordinary human relations also possess an imagi-
nary dimension, of course, and Lacan spends a
considerable part of this section of the seminar
tracing the connections between psychotic and
ordinary varieties of human experience. Noting
Freud's claim that the narcissistic structure of
early object relations leaves us perpetually
"refinding" the same objects (see Three Essays on
the Theory of Sexuality [1905]), Lacan argues that
reality possesses a hallucinatory quality in all
human perception. But Freud's emphasis on the
reality principle insures that the subject will
never find the object he desires, Lacan says; he
will always be finding another object because
"reality is marked from the first by symbolic
annihilation [néantisation]" (pp. 98, 168).
    Given this inevitable dislocation in the object
of our desire, Lacan claims that even the most
"natural" relation between human beings, that of
the male to the female, must be referred to a third
perspective that lies beyond the dualism of the
imaginary and that can provide a model of harmony
and stability. This perspective is that of the
symbolic order, the name-of-the-father (see p.
111). That is exactly the signifier that Schreber
is lacking, and Lacan returns to the Memoirs to
show how the fragmentation and dispersion described
there indicate the imaginary character of
Schreber's relation to the world of his delusion.
    Lacan's analysis of Schreber's text is detailed
and specific, but several general issues emerge.
Lacan identifies the "God" that presides over the
speaking birds and articulate rays of Schreber's
delusion as an imaginary manifestation of what is
ordinarily experienced as the Other who makes
speech possible. In normal circumstances, we
relate to that Other as a third person, the lui or
"him" to whom we address our speech "indirectly."

That "lui" provides the occasion for us to assume
the position of the "je," the place of the subject
in speech. Schreber's world contains no such
"lui," however, but only a "tu" (second person
familiar pronoun) to which Schreber is bound in an
imaginary union. (Cf. Lacan's contradictory claim
in A2, where Lacan alludes to the "astonishing
absence" of the "tu" in Schreber's text [A2j, p.
215].) Lacan thus describes Schreber's relation to
this God as an "imaginary degradation of alterity"
and insists on distinguishing it from any kind of
"stage" preceding the subject's confrontation with
the other. (This distinction also allows Lacan to
differentiate his theory of psychosis from more
traditional Freudian accounts that locate the
source of psychotic delusion in pre-Oedipal stages
of ego development.)
     Lacan repeatedly returns to what Schreber de-
scribes as a "fundamental language" supported by
this God, and while recognizing the obvious
delusional qualities of Schreber's hallucination,
he argues that it suggests a property of the
unconscious central to Freud's work. Freud's use
of the phrase "unconscious thought" makes sense
only if we understand that "thought" to be "the
thing that is articulated in language," Lacan says.
The unconscious as Freud described it is "structured, woven, enchained by language" (p. 135). To
admit the existence of the unconscious is to
realize that "la phrase" continues to circulate
even when consciousness turns away from it. In
Chapter XI, Lacan describes this discourse as a
"strange twin" ("un étrange jumeau") that always
accompanies the ego, a "fantasy that speaks" and
that is "pregnant with delusion" (p. 165). It is a
function of the ego that we do not have to listen
to this perpetual "articulation that organizes our
actions as spoken actions," says Lacan (p. 128),
but that function is most evident when it breaks
down, as in Schreber's case. Analysts know, Lacan
adds a little later, that the "normal" subject is
simply someone who is in the position "of not
taking seriously the biggest part of his interior
discourse. . . . That is the main difference
between you and the insane" (p. 140).

Du signifiant et du signifié

     This section describes the function of the
signifier, its role in the formation of sexual
identity in the Oedipal complex, and the metaphoric
and metonymic properties of language. It is
followed by a paper Lacan presented at a conference
on the centenary of Freud's birth, "Freud dans le
siècle" (Chapter XIX).

Lacan begins by noting that a distinction between the signifier and the signified is essential to the structure of the unconscious, which is "like a language" (p. 187).   The signifier operates according to its own laws, independently of any signified; it is "a "sign which returns to another sign, which is as such structured to signify the absence of another sign" (188).   This network of signifiers grounds the human reality found in analysis, Lacan says, and he goes on to discuss the role of the signifier in psychosis and hysteria and, more generally, in the cultural determination of feminine identity.

Recalling his earlier explanation that psychosis derives from the foreclosure of a "primordial signifier" which creates a "hole" or "lack" (un trou, un manque) at the level of the signifier, Lacan says that the psychotic tries to compensate for this lack through an imaginary identification with an other rather than seeking to establish a "fundamental speech" with the symbolic Other. (This is why analysis can actually trigger psychosis if the analyst is not careful to resist the patient's effort to treat him as an imaginary other.)

Lacan also argues that sexual identity is formed, or deformed, according to the subject's relation to the symbolic order, a point discovered in Freud's account of the Oedipal struggle.   According to Freud, Lacan says, the Oedipus complex shows us that "the subject finds his place in a preformed symbolic apparatus which installs the law in sexuality" (p. 191).   Within this apparatus, the symbolic role of the father (the nom-du-père, not the actual father) serves a crucial function because it is the point towards which imaginary conflict is oriented (p. 240).

Lacan claims that this conflict stems from an imaginary identification between the subject and the father, which both males and females experience but which is resolved differently for the two sexes.   That resolution hinges on castration because it is the possibility of something "missing" or "lacking" that introduces the role of the phallus as a signifier and so "literally rips out [the function of man and woman] from the imaginary to situate it in the domain of the symbolic" (p. 200).   But the positions that men and women occupy in the symbolic are not symmetrical, Lacan adds, and he describes the feminine sex as possessing the character of absence, of emptiness, of a "hole" ("Le sexe féminin a un caractère d'absence, de vide, de trou" [p. 199]).

For a more extended discussion of sexual identification in relation to the symbolic order, see

B31.   Lacan's analysis of the symbolic functions of
metaphor and metonymy in this seminar emphasizes
(1) the priority of metonymy in language and (2)
the essential function of the signifier as the
basis for the "transfer of the signified" that
constitutes the usual explanations of metaphor.
See C71 for a full account of Lacan's argument.

    "Freud dans le siècle," which concludes this
section, emphasizes what Lacan calls Freud's "true
originality," his recours à la lettre (p. 272).
Alluding to his own distinction between the other
and the Other, Lacan claims that there is a double
alienation traced in Freud's work.   One form of
alienation is associated with the imaginary other,
which is the source of what we generally call our
sense of self or "self-consciousness."   The second
is linked to what Lacan has identified as the
Other, "the other who speaks from my place" and is
completely different from the semblable of the
imaginary other.   (According to Miller's text of
Lacan's seminar, Lacan was not at this point
consistently capitalizing the symbolic "other,"
though he had introduced that device in last year's
seminar.)   That is what Freud taught us about
analytic technique, Lacan says, and it reminds us
that the unconscious is essentially speech, a
parole de l'autre that can be recognized only when
the other returns it to you (p. 274).
    Lacan also argues that Freud's repetition
compulsion, his "automatisme de répétition," has
nothing to do with the repetition of needs but is
"fundamentally the insistence of a speech" (insistance d'une parole [p. 275]).   The last word of
Freudian anthropology, Lacan adds, is not that man
is supported by un irrationnel, but that he is
possessed by the "discourse of the law," "une
raison" of which he is more victim than master (p.
275).

Les entours du trou

    Much of the last section of the seminar is given
over to a detailed analysis of Schreber's Memoirs
that shows how the loss of a signifier can result
in the specific delusions Schreber describes.
Lacan distinguishes between two planes in the
hallucinations: the reconstruction of a world, and
the imaginary figuration of the other in that
world.   Psychotic delusions are always constructed
as imaginary versions of the psychotic's self,
Lacan argues, but they are not derived from
"object relations."   Rather, the delusions stem
from the psychotic's inability to distinguish
between the "other" and the "Other" and from his

consequent expulsion from the order of signifiers
that organizes the ordinary experience of reality.
Nevertheless, the symbolic does appear to the
psychotic in imaginary form. In Schreber's case,
it underlies two different manifestations of speech
he describes: the "mot révélateur" of pure signification, and "le refrain," which retains the
purely formal qualities of the signifier. Lacan
says that a third manifestation of speech described
by Schreber, the "divine rays" and other detached
voices he hears, suggests the continuous discourse
of the unconscious, what Saussure called "la masse
amorphe" of the signifier as it endlessly circu-
lates apart from any significatory function (p.
330).

After spending most of the seminar emphasizing
the separation of the signifier and the signified,
near the end of the seminar Lacan turns to the
relation between them. He explains that the two
domains are linked only through a "point de
capiton," an "anchoring point" (literally an
upholstery button) or "point of convergence which
allows us to situate retroactively and prospec-
tively everything that happens in this discourse"
(pp. 303-04; for further comments on the point de
capiton see C80). In Freud's terms this point is
occupied by the function of the father, Lacan says,
and that is why Schreber's inability to incorporate
the signifier "être père" into his chain of discourse led to the radical split between signifier
and signified that characterizes his delusion.

In the last session, Lacan directly contrasts his
theory of psychosis to more traditional concepts,
returning to his earlier discussion of castration
and the phallus in the symbolic determination of
sexual identity. Lacan disagrees with Freud's
contention that Schreber's psychosis can be attributed to a disturbance in the pre-Oedipal stage
of narcissistic fantasy and that it served as a
defense against homosexual desire. Instead, Lacan
argues that the prevalence of verbal hallucinations
and the importance of the father-function in
Schreber's account suggests that the psychosis
results from Schreber's failure to accept the
castration which is absolutely central to the
emergence of the signifier and hence to the
subject's accession to the symbolic (see p. 351).
The function of the father is crucial, Lacan says,
because it introduces "the third" (un tiers) into
the narcissistic structure of the mother-infant
dyad. It possesses a signifying element that is
"irreducible to all forms of the imaginary condition"--this element is, of course, the phallus
(see p. 355)--and it has no other function in the
Oedipal triad than to represent "le porteur, le

détenteur du phallus" (p. 359).   (The phrase
literally means "the bearer, the keeper of the
phallus.")   So, since sexual identity is constituted within the realm of the signifier, the
foreclosure of the name of the father that
Schreber's text illustrates resulted both in
confusion regarding his own gender and in the
delusional fragmentation of symbolic functions.

B14a. Il seminaro, Libro III: Le psicosi, 1955-56.
       Italian translation directed by Giacomo Contri.
       Einaudi paperbacks, 160. Turin: Giulo Einaudi,
       1985. 382 pages.

B14b. A brief portion of this seminar was translated in
       Lacan Study Notes 1, no. 1 (1982): 1, 3.

B14*. A translation into Spanish is forthcoming from
       Paidos in Buenos Aires and in Barcelona, under
       the direction of Jacques-Alain Miller and Diana
       Rabinovich.

 B15. Seminar IV (1956-57):   La relation d'objet et les
       structures freudiennes. Abstract by J.-B.
       Pontalis approved by Lacan. Bulletin de psychol-
       ogie 10 (1957): 426-30, 602-05, 742-43, 851-54;
       11 (1957): 31-34.

B15a. Sessions for 21 November-19 December 1956.
       Bulletin de psychologie 10 (1957): 426-30.

       Notes Lacan's emphasis on the central importance
of the "object" in contemporary psychoanalysis and
argues that Freud's own remarks concerning the
status of the object are more complex than those
currently in fashion. Citing "Finding the Object"
from Freud's Three Essays on the Theory of Sexuality (1905), Lacan argues that Freud never
considered the object as a source of complete
satisfaction. Rather, Lacan claims that Freud
described the subject's relation to the object as a
"nostalgia" that makes every search for the object
a "re-search," the repetition of a doomed effort to
retrieve an object that is always lost "before" the
present experience (p. 426). (See B14 for further
remarks on the "refinding" of the object). The
subject's relation to his world is thus marked with
a profound conflict, Lacan says, an opposition
between reality and that which is "obscurely sought
by the 'tendency'" (p. 426).
       Pontalis then describes Lacan's observation that
there is one domain where the subject-object
relation is direct and unmediated: the imaginary.
But Lacan also says that Freud introduced a third
term between the mother-child dyad of the imagi-

nary: the phallus (p. 427).   Functioning as a
signifier, the phallus disrupts the imaginary union
of the subject with the object and institutes the
symbolic order in human experience.   The result is
a sense of "privation," of the "lack of the object," and this constitutes the essential point of
analytic experience and forms its point of departure.   This moment is experienced as "castration"
in the imaginary; "privation" in the symbolic; and
"frustration" in the real (p. 428).

As a result of this lack, Lacan claims that the
real can never be comprised within the analyst's
experience but always exists at its limit.   He says
that we radically misunderstand analysis if we seek
some ultimate reality beyond that which is structured by the signifier.   Even the id (le Es) cannot
be considered the ground of signification but instead merely designates "that which, in the subject, is susceptible of becoming I, and not a
brute reality" (p. 427).   In other words, he adds,
there is nothing present in the signified that is
not marked by the signifier.

Pontalis says that these sessions concluded with
Lacan's critique of D. W. Winnicott's theory of
transitional objects (see L2510) and with a discussion of the imaginary function of the phallus in
the development of feminine identity.   For further
remarks on the difference between the imaginary
dimension of masculine and feminine identity see
B14, B31, and F370.

B15b.   Sessions for 9-23 January 1957.   Bulletin de
         psychologie 10 (1957):   602-05.

Describes Lacan's discussion of the "feminine
object" as it emerges in the cases of feminine
homosexuality reported by Freud in "Fragment of an
Analysis of a Case of Hysteria" (the Dora case,
1905) and "The Psychogenesis of a Case of Female
Homosexuality" (1920).   Lacan notes Freud's
emphasis on the "phallic assumption" (l'assomption
phallique) that defines both self and object for
men and women, and he argues that Freud's comments
can only be understood in reference to the symbolic
order.   The role of frustration in the etiology of
phobias and perversions must also be treated from
the perspective of the symbolic order, Lacan says,
because frustration always implies an "other" and
so involves a "gift" rather than a simple object
(p. 602).   Frustration has nothing to do with the
failure to satisfy a need, Lacan argues.   Rather,
frustration derives from the possibility of the
other's refusing to make a gift of the object to
the subject (p. 743).   When the infant realizes,
for example, that the mother can refuse its demand,

it recognizes the possibility of a lack of the
object, a crucial stage in the individual's access
to the symbolic.

Pontalis describes Lacan's explanation of this
notion of the object as "gift" in the first group
of sessions. Freud's notion of penis envy, for
example, is recast by Lacan into an account of the
young girl's relation to the signifier. According
to Lacan, it is because she realizes that she does
not have the phallus that the young girl can
recognize the function of the father as one who can
give her that object. The symbolic order of the
gift, with its reference to the place of the Other
as the locus of the missing object, thus also
introduces the girl to the Oedipal complex as Freud
described it. (See p. 603.)

Lacan also distinguishes between the frustration
of love and the frustration of "jouissance de
l'objet." The frustration of jouissance can renew
desire, Lacan says, but it can never constitute any
form of an object. In the frustration of love,
however, there is an object of sorts: the gift.
At its extreme limit "there is no greater sign of
love than the gift of that which one does not have"
(p. 604).

B15c. Sessions for 30 January-27 February 1957. Bulletin
       de psychologie 10 (1957): 742-43.

       Explains how Lacan uses the paradoxical combina-
tion of presence and absence characteristic of the
fetish to describe the symbolic function of the
phallus. According to Freud in Three Essays on the
Theory of Sexuality (1905) and "Fetishism" (1927),
Lacan says, the fetish is the woman's phallus
insofar as she doesn't have one; or, in other
words, it is the phallus the woman does not have
(p. 742). Lacan claims that the fetishist loves in
the object precisely what it lacks, and he compares
the fetishistic object to a curtain that takes on
value by being "that on which absence is projected"
(p. 742). The phallus thus serves as the perfect
model for signifiers, Lacan adds, because it is
"never wholly present there where it is, nor wholly
absent there where it is not" (p. 742-43).

B15d. Sessions for 6 March-10 April 1957. Bulletin de
       psychologie 10 (1957): 851-54.

       Describes how Lacan uses Freud's case history of
Little Hans ("Analysis of a Phobia in a Five-Year-
Old Boy" [1909]) as an illustration of the way
castration is integral to the subject's assumption
of a role in the symbolic order as the child passes
through the Oedipal conflict. The path through

the Oedipal complex is relatively simple for the
girl, Lacan claims. It begins with the mother's
lack of a phallus and ends with the woman receiving
the "gift" of an infant, which substitutes for the
phallus. The boy passes through the Oedipal
complex less directly because he has a phallus.
That is, he possesses a penis, which enables an
imaginary identification with the father. To
resolve the Oedipal conflict, however, the boy must
come to accept the phallus as the property of
someone else, an "other" or the nom-du-père. This
is the origin of what Lacan calls the "symbolic
debt" that makes castration the formative crisis of
the Oedipal complex (p. 851).

B15e.   Sessions for 8 May-3 July 1957. Bulletin de
        psychologie 11 (1957): 31-34.

Recounts Lacan's further comments on the myths
described by Little Hans and Lacan's explanation
that those myths enable Hans to manipulate the
order of signifiers and so modify his relation to
the world around him. To understand his phobia
about horses, for example, we need to understand
how the horse operates as a signifier for Hans, not
to seek for some hidden, absolute meaning or origin
of the horse in Hans' past. More generally, Lacan
argues that Hans's story shows us the importance of
the symbolic dimension in one's constitution of a
world of objects and of the name-of-the-father as
essential to the structure of the symbolic (p. 33).

The seminar concludes with a brief reading of
Freud's Leonardo da Vinci and a Memory of his
Childhood (1910) in which Lacan comments on Freud's
theory of narcissism and the concept of sublimation.
        Pontalis' whole summary is translated in A5.

B16.   Seminar V (1957-58): Les formations de l'incons-
        cient. Unpublished. Abstract by J.-B. Pontalis
        in Bulletin de psychologie 11, no. 4/5 (1958):
        293-96; 12, no. 2/3 (1958): 182-92; 12, no. 4
        (1958): 250-56.

Comments at length on the word play discussed by
Freud in Jokes and Their Relation to the Unconscious (1905), and shows how the laws of the
unconscious that we see at work in dreams, symptoms, and puns are the same as those that govern
language and that produce meaning through the
agency ("l'agence") of the signifier: metaphor and
metonymy (Bulletin 11, pp. 295-96). (Lacan also
insists on the primacy of metonymy, which makes
possible metaphorical substitution. See B14, where

Lacan claims that metonymy is there from the
beginning and is what makes metaphor possible [p.
259].) Reflecting on the importance of the
interlocutor in word play as the one who unveils
the sense of a pun behind what is actually said,
Lacan also distinguishes among demand, desire, and
need as they determine different relations between
the subject and the other to whom speech is
addressed (Bulletin 12, p. 183).

Comparing this Other to the ideal spectator
addressed in comedy, Lacan says that this Other
which is addressed by "le trait d'esprit" is never
the real and living subject but rather a quasi-
anonymous, symbolic place ("lieu symbolique") that
is the storehouse of received ideas ("trésor
d'idées reçues")(Bulletin 12, p. 184). Thus,
although demand addresses the Other as an ideal
reference and presumes the possibility of total
satisfaction, desire is always refracted as it
passes through that demand and encounters the Other
not as subject but as the locus of the code in
which the demand is cast. That is why Lacan claims
that the satisfaction of all human desire depends
on the harmony ("l'accord") of the signifying
system as it is articulated in the speech of the
subject and manifested in the code itself, and he
diagrams the relation between the two manifestations of the signifying system in the "graph of
desire" discussed in C80.

The central part of the seminar is devoted to
Lacan's notion of the "name-of-the-father" and the
"paternal metaphor," Lacan's terms for the symbolic
function of the Father and the role of the phallus
as distinct from a child's actual father and the
penis. He describes the three moments of the
Oedipal crisis and their attendant disturbances
according to traditional psychoanalytic accounts,
and he contrasts those accounts with his own, which
stresses the desire of desire itself, the "desire
of the other," and the function of the phallus as
the signifier of desire. Freud's discovery, Lacan
says, was that desire is alienated in the signifier. The primary mistake of those such as
Ernest Jones, who would derive sexual identity on
the basis of biological difference, is that they do
not understand the privileged character of the
phallic signifier (Bulletin 12, p. 190). Similarly, those such as Melanie Klein, who account for
the subject's relation to objects as an outgrowth
of an identification with the mother, neglect the
fact that the "exterior" is always given for the
subject as the place where the desire of the other
is situated and where the subject will encounter
the third member of the oedipal group ("le tiers"),
the father. So, as Pontalis describes Lacan's

conclusion, beyond the captivating dualism is
introduced a third term by which the subject
demands to be signified. Thus the phallus is the
point, Lacan says, which marks that my desire must
be signified. It is the symbol of the lack of my
desire which insists that the signified is always
signified obliquely ("à coté"), and that it is, in
fact, the phallus (Bulletin 12, p. 190).

The closing sessions of the seminar focus on the
irreducible quality that distinguishes desire from
demand and need, or, in other words, on the alienation of desire in the signifier. Lacan also
distinguishes between the obsessive character and
the hysteric on the basis of their relation to the
phallus. He claims that the frontier of analysis
is situated on the difference between wanting to be
the phallus (which can only lead to the distortions
of hysteria and obsession and the disturbances of
neurosis and psychosis) and wanting to have the
phallus (which is the first step towards the subject's accession to the symbolic).

Lacan's distinction between desire, demand, and
need appears in most of his works during this
period. For a more detailed account, see C73.
This seminar also contains several remarks about
Gide's childhood that explain how disturbances can
result from an irregular identification with the
mother and the "desire of the other," which in
Gide's case stemmed from reaction to his aunt's
attempted seduction of him as a small boy (see
C76). In addition, Lacan's account of the Oedipal
conflict distinguishes between the experience of
boys and girls at specific moments, particularly
during the intervention of the name-of-the-father,
and Lacan emphasizes the purely symbolic basis of
sexual identity that becomes a prominent part of
his discussion of femininity in Seminar XX. For
his earlier but compatible analysis of Oedipal
relations see C45 and C46, where the role of the
phallus is suggested but not so prominent.

B16a.   Las formaciones del inconsciente, seguido de El
          deseo y su interpretacion. Introductions by
          Charles Melman, Jan Miel, and Jean Reboul.
          Buenos Aires: Ediciones Nueva Vision, 1970.

B16b.   Le formazioni dell'inconscio. A5, pp. 49-103.

B17.   Seminar VI (1958-59): Le désir et son interpréta-
          tion. Sessions 12 November 1958-11 February
          1959 have not been published but are described by
          J.-B. Pontalis in Bulletin de psychologie 13, no.
          5 (1960): 263-72; and 13, no. 6 (1960):   329-35.
          Sessions 4 March-29 April 1959 are edited by
          Jacques-Alain Miller and published as follows:

"Hamlet: Le canevas (I)."   Ornicar? 24 (1981):
     7-17.
"Hamlet: Le canevas (II)."   Ornicar? 24 (1981):
     18-31.
"Hamlet: le desir de la mère."   Ornicar? 25
     (1982):   13-25.
"Hamlet: il n'y a pas d'Autre de l'Autre."
     Ornicar? 25 (1982): 26-36.
"Hamlet: l'objet Ophélie."   Ornicar? 26/27
     (1983):   7-19.
"Hamlet: le désir et le deuil."   Ornicar? 26/27
     (1983):   20-30.
"Hamlet: phallophanie."   Ornicar? 26/27 (1983):
     31-44.

B17a.   Sessions for 12 November 1958- 7 January 1959.
        Bulletin de psychologie 13, no. 5 (1960):   263-
        72.

        Discusses the graph of desire presented at length
in C80, and comments on the dream of the dead
father described by Freud in "Formulations Regarding the Two Principles in Mental Functioning"
(1911).   The comments on both topics focus on
distinctions among need, demand, and desire as
those terms designate the subject's different
relations to objects and language, which are
determined by the signifier.   The analytic experience does not define the object in its generality as a correlative of the subject, Lacan says,
but in its particularities as that which supports
the subject at the moment when he has to confront
his existence (in the radical sense of "ex-sisting"
in language).   This is the moment when the individual, as subject, must be effaced behind a signifier.   It is at this panic-point, Lacan notes,
that the subject clings to the object of desire (p.
269).
        These sessions contain more brief comments on the
role of fantasy in Freud's "A Child is Being
Beaten" (1919) and on the importance of Ernest
Jones' concept of aphanisis.   Lacan claims that
Jones was mistaken in his belief that men and
women have the same relation to their desire--
rather, Lacan insists, they are irreducibly
different because of their asymmetry in relation to
the signifying phallus--but he admits that the
concept of aphanisis obliges us to conceive of a
subject that "ex-sists" outside of his desire.
(For further comments on Freud's essay, see B16.)

B17b.   Sessions for 14 January-11 February 1959. Bulletin
        de psychologie 13, no. 6 (1960):   329-35.

Comments on a dream analysis by Ella Sharpe in
Dream Analysis. The dream is described, and Lacan
emphasizes the essentially imaginary character of
Sharpe's interpretation and her attention to the
fantasy of impotence attributed to the patient as
the meaning of his dream. Lacan rejects Sharpe's
interpretation and establishes the role of the
signifier and the patient's relation to the Other
as central to the patient's account of the dream.
   The abstract concludes with a precise commentary
on Klein's notion of the breast and its role in the
child's identification with the unified image of
the mother. There are four, not two, elements in
this primitive relation to the object, Lacan
insists. The subject conceives of the object, the
maternal breast, not only as being there or not,
but as inscribed in a relation with some other
thing which can be substituted for it. Lacan
claims that this possibility of substitution is
crucial to the subject's access to the symbolic
because it is only insofar as the breast can be
substituted for the totalized image of the mother's
body that the image of the other can be substituted
for the subject. In addition, Lacan says, it is
this substitutive function that determines the
inexhaustible desire which characterizes the
individual's existence as a speaking being (p.
334). He then concludes with several observations
on the role of the phallus and the asymmetrical
relation to the phallus experienced by males and
females. For the male, Lacan says, "il n'est pas
sans l'avoir," whereas the female "est sans
l'avoir."

B17c.   Sessions on Hamlet. Ornicar 24-27 (1981-1983),
        passim. See the main entry above for page
        numbers in specific issues.

        Notes the similarity between the dilemma facing
        Sharpe's patient--whether to be or not to be the
        phallus--and the one articulated by Hamlet in the
        formula "to be or not to be." Lacan claims that
        Shakespeare's play reinforces his own theory of the
        castration complex, and he demonstrates how that
        complex is manifested in concrete experience.
           Lacan begins with Freud's observation that the
        difference between Oedipus and Hamlet lies in the
        degree of repression that is explicit in the plot.
        In Oedipus, the desire of the child to murder his
        father and sleep with his mother appears and is
        realized by the characters on stage, as it might be
        in a dream. In Hamlet, that desire is never
        spoken--in other words, it is repressed--and it is
        manifest instead through Hamlet's procrastination,
        his unexplained inability to carry out the revenge

demanded by the ghost of his father. (Later Lacan
aligns this demand with the social law that condemns Hamlet's desire for his mother, thus aligning
the Law of the Father with social constraint; see
Ornicar 25, p. 20). Hamlet's "scruples of conscience" may therefore be read as a translation of
what remains unconscious in his soul.

To this distinction Lacan adds one of his own.
Oedipus's crime is "unconscious" because he does
not know that he has committed it, whereas Hamlet
begins with Hamlet's discovery of the crime through
the ghost of his father. This immediately establishes Claudius as a "form" of Hamlet because he
has accomplished Hamlet's desire. Claudius is thus
a "rival," but one who has done precisely what
Hamlet has not done because of his "scruples of
conscience." It is in Hamlet's relation to
Claudius, then, expressed through the various
detours by which Hamlet delays his act, that his
unconscious desire takes shape before our eyes, and
Lacan describes the action of the play as a
"canevas diffus" upon which castration is finally
realized as the necessary end of Hamlet's story
(Ornicar? 24, p. 17).

After a brief survey of other psychoanalytic
readings of Hamlet, Lacan goes on to observe that
Shakespeare has modified the eternal conflict of
the son with the father to reveal the fact that
desire is always found at the limit where action
leads to death. Lacan illustrates this point with
a lengthy plot summary in which he emphasizes the
various death-scenes in the play and their connection to Hamlet's unconscious desire (Ornicar?
24, pp. 18-31.). In the session of 19 March 1959
(Ornicar? 25, pp. 13-25), however, Lacan identifies
the desire with which Hamlet is concerned as "le
désir de sa mère," the desire "of" his mother in
the sense of being his mother's desire. Lacan
focuses on Hamlet's meeting with his mother after
the play he stages for the king to show how Hamlet
tries to redirect his mother's desire away from
Claudius and to a more righteous mode of behavior.
That redirection inevitably implies Hamlet's own
incestuous desire for the mother's desire, however,
and Lacan points to the fact that their exchange is
governed by the ghost of Hamlet's father as proof
that this scene stages the "Oedipal" subordination
of imaginary identification to the law of the
symbolic, a vivid illustration of the formula "the
desire of man is the desire of the Other" ("le
désir de l'homme est le désir de l'Autre") (p. 23).

The session of 19 March 1959 also contains an
intriguing discussion of the psychoanalytic interpretation of dramatic literature. Lacan agrees
with Ernest Jones' observation that we are not

dealing with a real person when we analyse Hamlet's
motivations, and he goes on to claim that the hero
of the play "is strictly identical to the words of
the text" (p. 15). We are thus dealing with the
order of illusion, he adds, and when such a work
moves us, it is always on the unconscious plane
governed by its "composition." Lacan cautions that
this does not mean that we are dealing with the
poet's unconscious, although events in the author's
life (such as the death of Shakespeare's father)
can help us understand drastic changes in the
course of an author's career. Rather than relying
on such biographical facts, though, the play itself
moves us by reason of its being a structure where
desire can find its place, a composition so rigor-
ously articulated that all the desires, or more
exactly all the problems of the subject's relation
to desire, can be projected there ("<u>Une structure
telle que le désir puisse y trouver sa place, une
composition assez rigoureusement articulée pour que
tous les désirs ou plus exactement tous le problèmes du rapport du sujet au désir, purissent s'y
projeter</u>" [p. 17]). Similarly, later in the
session Lacan warns us against treating Hamlet as a
clinical case. This character is not a real
being, Lacan observes. It is a drama which is
present to us as a pivot (a "<u>plaque tournante</u>")
where a desire is situated (p. 25).

This effect is even more pronounced when we see
the play staged, Lacan adds. How better to
illustrate the function of the unconscious as the
"discours of the Other" than in the audience's
relation to Hamlet? Clearly, the unconscious is
presented there as the discourse of the Other, and
the hero is present only by this discourse. Lacan
argues that this representative dimension--i.e.,
the staging of the discourse--is strictly analogous
to the way that each of us is aware of his or her
own unconscious, and he adds that, because our
relation to the unconscious is woven from our
imaginary, this representative dimension of the
play also figures our relation of our own body.

Lacan explains this reference to the body to
stress the corporeal nature of his psychoanalysis.
Despite objections that his theory is purely
abstract, Lacan insists that he has always claimed
that it is we who furnish the material for the
signifier. It is with our own members that we
fashion the alphabet of this discourse which is the
unconscious, Lacan says. That is what the imaginary is. In the same way, the actor lends his body
to his role not simply as a marionette but "with
his unconscious," a gesture which links his members
with a certain story which is his own ("<u>l'acteur
prête ses membres . . . avec son inconscient bel et</u>

bien réel, à savoir le rapport de ses membres avec une certaine histoire qui est la sienne" [p. 18]).

The last group of sessions published in Ornicar? focuses again on the role of the object in relation to the subject's desire, approaching that topic through Freud's accounts of the experiences of mourning and jealousy. The intolerable dimension of human experience, Lacan says, is not the experience of one's own death, which no one ever has, but that of the death of an other. Such a loss opens up a hole in the real, and it is this hole that "mobilizes" the signifier. The hole provides a place where the signifier of the lack-- most generally, the phallus--is projected, and that lacking signifier is essential to the structure of the Other because it renders the Other impotent (impuissant) to give you a response. Projected into that hole in the real, it is the signifier that you can pay for only with your flesh and blood, the signifier that is essentially the phallus under the veil (p. 30). Lacan claims that Ophelia stands for that signifier and that the whole play turns around it. That is why Hamlet begins and ends with mourning and why Hamlet first struggles with his imaginary double, Laertes, in Ophelia's grave.

These sessions also contain a detailed account of the objet a and the phallus as fantasms. (Lacan says that the object of the fantasm, which he describes as "image et pathos," is this other which takes the place of the object that the subject lacks; see p. 11.) Lacan also discusses the dimension of time in the subject's relation to the object (pp. 17-18); distinctions between perversion and neurosis; and the importance of Hamlet's punning as a way of deferring "the fatal signifier" (pp. 26-27).

B17d.   Las formaciones del inconsciente, seguido de El deseo y su interpretacion. Introductions by Charles Melman, Jan Miel, and Jean Reboul. Buenos Aires: Editiones Nueva Vision, 1970.

B17e.   The sessions of 15-29 April 1959 were translated by James Hulbert as "Desire and the Interpretations of Desire in Hamlet," Yale French Studies 55/56 (1977): 11-52.

B17f.   Pontalis's abstract was translated into Italian in A5.

B17g.   The session of 15-29 April 1959 was also translated by Laszlo Kalman as "Hamlet: Az anya vagya: A Masiknak nincs Masikja," Helikon: Vilagirodalmi Figyelo (Hungary): 29 (1983): 374-84.

B17h.   "Desiderio e interpretazione del desiderio in
        Amleto," Calibano (Rome) 4 (1979):   108-41.

 B18.   Seminar VII (1959-60):   L'éthique de la psych-
        analyse.   Paris: Editions du Seuil, September
        1986.   375 pages.

Contents

Rejects traditional ethical and therapeutic goals
of psychoanalysis and argues that the central moral
issue of psychoanalysis lies in the relation between action and desire. Lacan claims that the
moral dimension of psychoanalysis derives from
Freud's discovery that human action always has a
hidden meaning, a point towards which the subject
tends but which always remains just beyond the
reach of desire. Thus the central ethical judgment
of psychoanalysis is not based on Aristotle's
"Sovereign Good," the more modest humanistic aim of
"doing good," or even the customary demand of the
analysand for "happiness." Rather, Lacan says, the
revisionary ethical thrust of psychoanalysis centers upon a single question: "Avez-vous agi con-
formément au désir qui vous habite? ("Have you
lived in conformity with the desire that inhabits
you?"). Throughout the seminar, Lacan pursues this
question in conjunction with ethical implications
raised by several key psychoanalytic concepts:
jouissance, sublimation, and "Das Ding," the
"thing" that eludes signification and that is
distinct from the imaginary objects of desire. In
addition, he devotes a substantial portion of the
seminar to a close reading of Antigone, which he
claims dramatizes the ethical consequences of man's
relation to the unconscious, his determination by
the signifier, and the function of the "second
death" though which man confronts the limit of his
being.

Section One: Introduction de la chose

After an introductory chapter that describes the
ethic of psychoanalysis as based on the energy of
desire and the effects of guilt and repression,
Lacan establishes the influence of moral law in
psychoanalysis through associations among analytic
practice, action, and the real (pp. 28-30). Most
of Chapter II is devoted to a discussion of the
distinction between the primary and secondary
processes distinguished in Freud's early work and
their relation to the pleasure principle and the
reality principle. The relevance of these topics
becomes apparent in Lacan's discussion of Freud's
place in the tradition of ethical thought that
begins with Aristotle, where Lacan argues that a
determining principle of that tradition is a
connection between pleasure and the good.
Aristotle's search for a universal ethical "voie"
toward the Sovereign Good resembles Freud's
elevation of the wish (Wunsch) to be the determining principle of psychoanalytic experience,
Lacan says, and this Wunsch can be considered as
the moral ground of psychoanalysis, though not in a

direct sense (p. 33).

Lacan argues that the moral function of the wish
is not direct because Freud does not see it as
leading to action. While the pleasure principle
leads us towards the "realization" of the wish, the
reality principle postpones or detours the culmi-
nation of the pleasure principle and so "corrects"
it. Left unchecked, the pleasure principle would
eventuate in pure hallucination, whereas Lacan
argues that the reality principle guides the
subject towards truly "possible action" (p. 40).
Thus Lacan argues that the "moral law" is grafted
onto the real and in effect constitutes our access
to that domain: "ma thèse est que la loi morale,
le commandement moral, la présence de l'instance
morale, est ce par quoi, dans notre activité en
tant que structurée par le symbolique, se pré-
sentifie le réel--le réel comme tel, le poids du
réel" (p. 28). Because analysis stops short of
access to the real, however, it can only be a
prelude to moral action as such, and Lacan claims
that "the ethical limits of analysis coincide with
the limits of its praxis" (p. 30).

Lacan continues this argument in the third
chapter, focussing on a reading of Freud's "Entwurf
einer Psychologie" (1895) that suggests Freud's
true interest in distinguishing between primary and
secondary processes was more ethical that psychological (see p. 45). The principal topic of
Chapters IV-VI, however, is Lacan's commentary on
Freud's distinction between Das Ding and Sach,
German words for "thing." The point of Freud's
distinction, Lacan says, is that "things" (Sach)
associated with words and identified within the
selective parameters of conscious perception do not
constitute the real as such. There remains an
aspect of things (Ding) that is left out and that
escapes incorporation into the symbolic; it remains
"hors-signifié," "dehors," and functions as the
"absolute Other" of the Subject (p. 65). Thus the
split that constitutes our relation to reality does
not occur between the things "imaged" in the pre-
conscious and the words of the conscious; rather,
the split occurs between Sach and Ding occasioned
by our relation to language and results from the
influence of the signifier at work well below the
level of consciousness and prior to the designation
of specific "things" as the content of a "pre-
conscious" realm. Lacan can therefore argue that
Das Ding "fait la loi" at the level of the unconscious (p. 89), and he proposes as a thesis that
"moral law is articulated in relation to the real
as such, the real insofar as it can be the
guarantee of the Thing" (p. 92).

For Lacan, Das Ding comes to represent the very

possibility of an "Other" realm barred from the
subject. He associates it with the Mother understood as an object of desire and so portrays Das
Ding as the ground of the incest prohibition (pp.
83-83) and of "negative moral law" in general,
which he illustrates with the Ten Commandments (see
pp. 82-84). This forbidden Thing, Lacan says,
functions exactly as the divine Sovereign Good did
in the Aristotelian ethical tradition, i.e., as "le
bien interdit," and it was Freud's recognition of
the importance of the negation inherent in desire
that enabled him to overturn the very foundation of
moral law (p. 85). This distance between the
subject and the object of its desire that is
installed as the very possibility of law--and its
representation in speech--thus comes to occupy the
center of ethical obligation in psychoanalysis, and
it renders impossible one of the most pervasive
moral instructions of Christian ethics: love thy
neighbor as thyself. (Lacan returns to this
obligation throughout the seminar; see below.)
    The concluding chapter of this section deals with
sublimation, which is portrayed as the positive
counterpart to the negative interdiction of moral
sentiment (p. 105). Lacan claims that sublimation
is encountered on the field of the drive and hence
establishes a relation between the subject and the
objects that constitute its sense of reality.
Whereas the function of the Law poses obstacles to
the realization of desire in Das Ding, sublimation
promises the satisfaction of desire through objects
that are "inseparable from the imaginary elaborations and especially cultural [i.e. collective]
elaborations" that link the subject to the object
in the fantasm (p. 119). Sublimation is the topic
of the following section and is not explored in
detail here, though Lacan does pause long enough to
condemn psychoanalysts who would propose as an
ethical goal the "adequation" of the subject to the
world of objects constituted in this way. Such a
goal, Lacan says, is nothing more than a "pastoral
fantasy" (pp. 106-07).

Section Two: Le problème de la sublimation

    Lacan defines sublimation most simply as "that
which raises an object to the dignity of the Thing"
(p. 133) or, in other words, that represents the
object in an idealized form which would overcome
the barrier separating the subject from the Thing
and so be totally adequate to the desire that seeks
it. The representational dimension of this idealization is crucial to Lacan, for it is what enables
one object to be substituted for another in the
process of sublimation. This substitution is

possible only as the objects come to be represented
by signifiers, Lacan says, and he therefore claims
that sublimation seeks its idealized object through
the paths of the signifier.   (Lacan repeatedly
refers to these paths as "les voies," the same term
he uses to describe the way to the Sovereign Good
in classical ethics.)   The very substitution of
signifier for thing that makes sublimation
possible, however, necessarily separates Das Ding
from the signifier and so constitutes a "beyond" to
both the signifying chain and the pleasure principle.   This separation installs the barrier
between subject and Thing that insures the insufficiency of any single signifier or object of desire
even as it elevates the signifier to the status of
a fantasm that can satisfy the desire it evokes.

Lacan treats the representational basis for
sublimation as a generalized case of the purportedly mimetic function at the heart of the beaux
arts, and he claims that the primitive end of all
art is to "cerner la Chose" by organizing forms
around the hole introduced in the real by the
signifier.   Art is thus never simply mimetic, Lacan
argues, but always establishes a relation between
the object (of sublimation) and the Thing that
remains beyond the realm of the signifier (p. 169).
He claims this function is evident in the fashion
for perspective and architectural illusion in
painting, where the forms are literally composed
about a vide or empty space that gives them shape.
But the paradigmatic form of sublimation in western
culture is courtly love, Lacan says, and he
discusses the conventions of courtly love at length
throughout this section, stressing the role of the
unattainable Lady as the perfect object of the
lover's desire (see esp. Chapter XI).

Lacan's emphasis on the inadequacy of the
signifier to satisfy desire leads him to speculate
on one of the most troublesome questions of theological ethics: What is the origin of evil?   Or,
more modestly, if God made the world, how come
things go so badly?   Lacan's answer is that
creation of any sort, human or divine, necessarily
brings about its negation, "ex nihilo."   This point
is illustrated by the being of the signifier, which
introduces a hole or wound ("béance") in the real
and functions only in relation to that hole.   In
the terms introduced earlier in the seminar, the
signifier comes into being only through the foreclosure of the Thing; in ethical terms, Lacan
suggests that the principle means that the good
must bring with it the possibility of the bad, and
he goes on to claim that evil ("le mal") comes to
exist in the very being of the "human" and the
making of signifiers (p. 150).

Section Three: Le paradoxe de la jouissance

   After a brief chapter on Bernfeld's theory of
sublimation, Lacan continues his speculation on
theological ethics and notes Freud's own interest
in religious discourse, as exemplified in <u>Moses and
Monotheism</u> (1937-39).   The central point of Freud's
interest in religion, according to Lacan, is that a
God comes into being only through his murder.
(Furthermore, as Lacan notes in Chapter XIV, it is
the very absence of God in death that makes a
message about belief in his life possible; see p.
212.)   This is the moral paradox behind <u>Totem and
Taboo</u> (1912-13), and Lacan generalizes it into the
principle that links desire to the Law: whenever
the obstacle to <u>jouissance</u> is overcome, it is
thereby reinforced; conversely, the prohibition
arises only in its transgression (pp. 207-08).
Lacan says that this is why Law has its origins in
the murder of the Father, and although he claims
that this myth was simply invented by Freud, Lacan
also claims that it serves as the perfect ethical
rationale for an age in which God is dead.
   Useful as Freud's myth of transgression is,
however, Lacan notes that it led Freud repeatedly
to an insurmountable obstacle: the moral commandment to love one's neighbor as oneself (p. 209; cf.
p. 100).   Lacan claims that Freud was horrified by
the "<u>amour du prochain</u>" because he realized that
the aggressivity in the subject's own heart--which
was to be controlled by this command--was inherent
in all humans, and this meant that one's neighbor
would necessarily be "<u>un être méchant</u>," a being as
evil as "<u>ce plus prochain des prochains qui est en
moi</u>" ("this most neighborly of neighbors which is
in me," a phrase made heavily ironic in English by
the positive connotations of the term "neighbor,"
which might be more accurately rendered here as
"proximate other"; see pp. 218-219.)
   Lacan is referring here to the emergence of the
very category of "other" through the identification
that takes place at the mirror stage, where the
self emerges only in and through the "desire of the
other."   Thus he claims that the commandment to
love one's neighbor "<u>est de la loi du rapport du
sujet humain à lui-même qu'il se fasse lui-même,
dans son rapport à son désir, son propre prochain</u>"
(p. 92).   The aggressivity endemic to this imaginary relation with the other in the mirror stage
thus insures that an "evil" inheres in the very
being of humanity, and Lacan says this is why Freud
found this command "inhuman" (p. 229).   The subject
recoils before the commandment, Lacan says, just as
he recoils before the specter of his own <u>jouis-</u>

sance.

Lacan's account of the paradox of jouissance and
the impossibility of "loving one's neighbor"
emphasizes the barrier to the satisfaction of
desire that is installed by man's relation to the
signifier. Throughout the seminar, but especially
in this section, Lacan argues that Kant and Sade
both identified the function of that barrier in
their work and posited a "beyond" to human experience that is deferred from our grasp but that
nevertheless orients our lives and gives them
meaning. For Kant, this "beyond" was an ideal form
of behavior or "the Good," an "ethical imperative"
that informed our action in this world but only
because we project that perfect form onto the world
of nature, idealizing it through our fictions.
(For this reason Lacan returns several times to
Kant's theory of art in the Critique of Judgment,
though he defers a complete discussion of the
work.)

For Sade, the "beyond" was death, not the death
of a specific victim but a "second death" that
included the position of the spectator and always
lay just beyond his or her experience. That is why
torture is always endless in Sade, Lacan says. The
object of desire is always a fantasm, a "part
object" that dramatizes the barrier to jouissance
and allows the Other to be glimpsed in the suffering of one's victim, and this Other is as
indestructible as it is unobtainable. Thus Lacan
argues that the confrontation of Kant with Sade
leads "to the point of apocalypse, or revelation,
of something called transgression" and so returns
us to the importance of desire in his "ethical
interrogation" (see p. 245). (Lacan draws a
parallel between the function of this "beyond" in
Kant and especially in Sade, and the Last Judgment
described in the revelation of St. John; see p.
340. For a comparison among Kantian disinterested-
ness, Sadean suffering, and the crucifixion of
Christ, see p. 304.)

The remainder of this section is explicitly
devoted to two specific barriers to desire as
identified by traditional philosophical discourse:
beauty and the good ("le bien et le beau"). The
association of these two functions suggests a close
link between ethics and aesthetics that Lacan notes
is already apparent in Kant's third critique, but
Lacan also points out Freud's curious reserve when
confronted with the question of beauty and argues
that beauty may take us much closer to desire than
the good (p. 256). In Chapters XVI-XVIII, however,
Lacan comments at length on two more general topics
related to the transgression of these barriers:
the "creationist" insistence on an absolute discon-

tinuity between the world of nature and the world
constituted by the subject's relation to the
signifier, and a link between the "good" and
"goods" that aligns Marx with Freud and exposes the
function of power inherent in the moral ambition to
do/produce good/goods.

   The first of these topics leads Lacan immediately
to argue for the causal association between the
function of the signifier and what Freud described
as "beyond" the pleasure principle, the death
drive. There is a "will to destruction" that leads
us beyond pleasure, Lacan says, a "<u>Volonté d'Autre-
chose</u>" that is generated by the signifying chain
and that constitutes the origin of the world as
posited within a "creationist sublimation" (p.
251). His point here is that evolutionary theory
proposes a continuity between the worlds of nature
and culture that contradicts the absolute discontinuity introduced by the function of the signifier. The signifier thus "creates" through a
<u>Spaltung</u> that splits off the subject from his
desire and locks <u>jouissance</u> within this field
behind inaccessible barriers (p. 247), and Lacan
goes on to identify this field as the unconscious
(p. 252), the field of the Thing (p. 253; cf. pp.
264-64).

   Lacan's remarks on the similarity between Marx
and Freud turn upon his claim that both men
realized that need and reason could not account for
human behavior. Hence they both recognized the
importance of desire in the production of "<u>les
biens</u>" ("goods" in Marx's sense and something
closer to what Freud might have called satisfaction
or well being), and Lacan claims that this desire
has the same basis in Marx as it does in Freud:
"Production is an original domain," Lacan argues,
"a domain of creation <u>ex nihilo</u>, insofar as it
introduces into the natural world the organization
of the signifier" (p. 253). It was this realization, Lacan says, that led both Marx and Freud to
an awareness of the inevitable links among production, signification, and power:

> <u>Nous avons la dernière fois défini le bien dans
> la création symbolique, comme l'initium d'où part
> la destinée du sujet humain dans son explication
> avec le signifiant. La véritable nature du bien,
> sa duplicité profonde, tient à ce qu'il n'est pas
> purement et simplement bien naturel, réponse à un
> besoin, mais pouvoir possible, puissance de
> satisfaire. De ce fait, tout le rapport de
> l'homme avec le réel des biens s'organise par
> rapport au pouvoir qui est celui de l'autre,
> l'autre imaginaire, de l'en priver</u>. (p. 274)

(Last time we defined the good in symbolic
creation as the _initium_ that gives rise to the
destiny of the human subject in his articulation
[literally "explanation"] with the signifier.
The true nature of the good, its profound
duplicity, derives from that which is not purely
and simply a natural good, a response to a need,
but which is a possible power, the power to
satisfy. Hence, every relation of man with real
goods is organized by relation to a power which
is that of the other, the imaginary other, who
deprives him of it.)

Thus in the subject's eyes this "other" is always
someone happier than himself and who inspires a
profound and bottomless jealousy (p. 278), an
attitude similar to what Marx identified as a
class-based _ressentiment_ and one that renders the
"_amour de prochain_" a social as well as psychic
impossibility.

Section Four: L'essence de la tragédie

   This section is devoted to a reading of
Sophocles' _Antigone_ as a dramatization of the way
suffering can suspend being above the nothing from
which it emerged, and Lacan claims that Sophocles'
play illustrates the similarity between the tragic
vision of life and the psychoanalytic ethic. Both
are based on the will to do good, Lacan says (p.
300), but both tragedy and psychoanalysis inevitably return man to confront the _coupure_ ("cut" or
"break") that installs the presence of language
into the life of man and so links him to his death
(see pp. 328, 325). This death is not the end of
the organic individual but is the "second death"
Lacan discussed earlier in relation to Sade's work.
It is the position from which we can see death
infringing on life, a field of the Other that is
occupied by Antigone and identified by Lacan as the
zone described in Freud's account of the death
drive.
   In Lacan's reading, _Antigone_ is thus staged on
the inevitable barrier that both separates and
joins human life to a realization of its death, and
recalling his earlier comments on this barrier
Lacan points out that it is no accident that
Antigone is recognized for her beauty as well as
for her implacable determination to do a "good"
that undermines the whole structure of Law represented by Creon. Both beauty and the good thus
mark the transgression that brings the power of
that Law to life even as they challenge the extent
of its authority over death, an awareness that
Antigone suffers as a "second death" in the tomb.

Section Five: La dimension tragique de
   l'expérience psychanalytique

   The concluding section of the seminar begins with
Lacan reminding his audience of the central issue
at stake: the ethical consequences of the relation
to the unconscious that was opened up by Freud's
work (p. 238).   He notes that the most basic demand
people make of psychoanalysis is for individual
happiness, but he also observes that this demand
has a political dimension as well because it
demands a satisfaction of the basic needs of all
people (p. 338).   The problem with this demand is
that it is not need that must be satisfied but "la
tendance,"   the orientation or "tendency" of the
drive that testifies to the mark of the signifier.
That mark, in turn, establishes sublimation as the
process through which satisfaction is pursued, and
that process institutes the endless change of
objects that makes the discourse of demand essentially metonymic (p. 340).   The ethical end of
psychoanalysis cannot, therefore, promise happiness, nor "normality," nor "adaptation" to
reality, nor the release of instinctual energy.
Metonymic discourse can only lead to the "second
death" that will somehow lend significance to death
itself, a point of view that language requires of
each human being if he or she is to "rendre compte
. . . ce qu'il nest pas" (p. 345).   The end of
analysis--and Lacan is speaking here especially of
the training analysis--can only be to put the
analysand face to face with the human condition and
so reveal the desperate chaos that joins death to
desire and measures what man is against what he is
not (p. 351).

B18a.   "Compte rendu avec interpolations du Séminaire de
        l'Ethique." Ornicar? 28 (1984):   7-18.

        Comments briefly on issues related to an "ethic"
of psychoanalysis that would be derived from
Freud's account of the pleasure principle, its
relation to the reality principle, and the position
of the subject vis-à-vis the real and jouissance.
Desire would be the sole principle of such an
ethic, Lacan says (p. 8), but he adds that the
moral law is that by which the symbolic act finds
support "du pur réel" (p. 12).   This essay also
includes several references to Aristotle, especially the Ethics, and to Jeremy Bentham's Theory
of Fiction, which Lacan praises for its recognition
that man takes pleasure only from his fictions (p.
15).
        For further comments on the ethic of psycho-

analysis, see C79. A brief but exceptionally clear account of Lacan's discussion of ethics during this period can be found in F344. For a summary of Lacan's seminar that situates it within the context of ethical debates in contemporary psychoanalysis see Jean Clavreul's essay for the recent _Encyclopédie française_, "Les enjeux de la psychanalyse: une éthique du sujet," translation forthcoming by William Richardson.

In an explanatory note, Jacques-Alain Miller says that this abstract is based on nineteen typed pages of uncertain date that include two "interpolations" apparently written after 1968. The pages were discovered in a box containing a typescript of the seminar, and a note in the manuscript refers to an introductory address that was to accompany the abstract but that has not been found.

B18b. Brief section translated by Dennis Porter. _Newsletter of the Freudian Field_ 1, no. 1 (1987): 11-13.

B19. Seminar VIII (1960-61): _Le transfert_. Unpublished.

B20. Seminar IX (1961-62): _L'identification_. Unpublished except as noted below.

B20a. "Le clivage du sujet et son identification." _Scilicet_ 2/3 (1970): 103-36.

Focuses on the splitting of the subject in relation to the _objet a_ and its association with the Other, the locus of speech. An introductory section (pp. 103-07) briefly establishes the radical nature of the subject that has been derived from the psychoanalytic discovery of the unconscious: that subject is constituted by what it cannot know, and a principle correlative of that discovery is the profound dependence of the subject on the order of language. The result of that dependence is the "splitting" of the subject (alternately called "_le refente_" or "_le clivage_"), which is the basis of the psychoanalytic concept of identification. The _objet a_ is an effect of that split, a remainder ("_un reste_") that functions as the cause of desire. "_Dissimulé dans l'Autre_," this _objet a_ thus comes to orient the movement of identification at the same time that it serves as its terminus ("_point d'arrêt_").

The first section of this article focuses on "_le trait unaire_," the "pure difference" fundamental to the order of the signifier as described by Saussure. This difference can only be articulated through repetition of an apparent identity, how-

ever, and this paradox yields the endless repetition of identity in the form of an "eternal
return" through the repetition of difference.
Since this is how the subject appears in the real,
it further establishes his identity upon the basis
of a loss, infinitely repeated through the chain of
signifiers.

The second section of the article distinguishes
the identification fundamental to the ego-ideal
from the function of desire associated with the
objet a, and it links Freud's three kinds of
identification to the three moments Lacan describes
as the series "privation-frustration-castration."
In the first moment, privation, the subject
experiences the absence of an object: something is
simply not in its place. Frustration is derived
from the subject's conception of that absence as a
loss of unity, and hence is based on an imaginary
identification with an other. The object is thus
perceived as a lack in the image of the other,
where the subject alienates his own image and, at
the same time, bases his desire (p. 120). The
Other is thus introduced here as a metaphor of "le
trait unaire," the locus of the succession of "les
uns" ("tous les uns que se succèdent") for which
the subject himself is the metonymy (p. 122) and to
which he addresses his demand. The third moment,
castration, derives from a "radical discordance"
between demand and its object. That discordance
results from the impossibility of the Other
responding to the demand, which is in the first
place based on an object the Other lacks, a
"défaillance" in the Other.

The third section of the article describes the
function of the phallus as a "medium" between
demand and desire (p. 125). What starts out as an
object of need (the real breast, for example)
becomes the object of desire by being taken up
within the repetitions of the demand--i.e., the
order of the signifier. The function of the
phallus supports this transmutation (p. 129), and
this support is what yields the logical structure
of the analytic experience. The same "coupure" or
cut--castration--that situates the object of desire
as radically lost also, through that same detachment, creates a remainder, a "scrap" ("lambeau
restant") that can yield a mirror image and so
serves as the subject's access to the world of
"reality" as he comes to know it. All of this
"logic of desire" hinges on the relation between
the objet a and the Other, as noted earlier, and
the concluding paragraphs of the article focus on
the subject's relation to the Other as implied in
Freud's three types of identification.

(Much of this article proceeds through an

analysis of a topographical model of the torus.
The model is used to indicate the complex relations
generated by the subject's relation to the object
of desire through time, and to demonstrate the
paradoxical results of simplistic models of unity
and surface when they encounter the functions of
absence and repetition inherent in the logic of the
signifier.)

B20b.   "Presentation brève du séminaire de J. Lacan sur
        l'identification." Abstract by Gérôme
        Taillandier (June 1986). Les identifications
        (F343), pp. 9-22.

        Briefly describes Lacan's comments on Freud's
        distinctions among three kinds of identification
        and discusses in more detail the role of the
        signifier and desire in Lacan's account of identi-
        fication. Taillandier's précis is much shorter and
        more accessible than the dense and detailed account
        in B20a, but it clearly makes no attempt to render
        the process of Lacan's own exposition as Scilicet
        does.

B21.   Seminar X (1962-63): L'angoisse. Unpublished.

B22.   Seminar XI (1964): Les quatre concepts fonda-
        mentaux de la psychanalyse. Paris: Editions du
        Seuil, 1973. 254 pages.

        Note: This seminar began on 15 January 1964,
        following Lacan's "excommunication" from the
        Société française de psychanalyse. He had sus-
        pended the seminar begun at Saint Anne's Hospital
        in the fall of 1963 as the "Noms du Père" (see
        E172), and he began a new series of seminars on
        this day at the Ecole Normale Supérieure in
        response to an invitation from Louis Althusser and
        a section of the Ecole pratique des Hautes Etudes
        chaired by Fernand Braudel. In his opening
        remarks, Lacan thanks Braudel for welcoming him and
        says that without Braudel's help and that of Claude
        Lévi-Strauss, who brought his case to Braudel's
        attention, he would have remained a refugee reduced
        to silence.
        At Saint Anne's Hospital before the move, Lacan
        had addressed an audience composed mostly of
        psychoanalysts, and he had focussed on more
        narrowly defined topics such as "transference,"
        "identification," and "anxiety." After moving to
        the Ecole Normale Supérieure, his audience
        broadened to include a wider range of the French
        intelligentsia, and the seminars also began to
        range more widely in philosophical topics, as his
        commentary on Merleau-Ponty and on Sartre's dis-

cussion of "the gaze" in this seminar suggests.
Lacan's work had always been infused with references to philosophical and literary sources, of
course, and this new series of seminars remained
closely focussed on Freud's work and the practice
of psychoanalysis. Lacan himself periodically
remarks on the more general nature of his audience
for this seminar, however, and he takes some pains
to distinguish between remarks directed to those
who have followed his seminars since the beginning,
and those attending for the first time this year.
   This was the first of Lacan's seminars to be
published. The volume includes a brief note by
Lacan's editor, Jacques-Alain Miller, that explains
the difficulty in establishing a printed text from
Lacan's oral presentations (see p. 249, tr. p. xi).
Miller says that this text is based on a shorthand
record filled with inaccuracies, and he claims to
have corrected and expunged sections of that
"original" text--though the expunged passages
amount to less than three pages. He also notes the
difficulty of devising a system of punctuation that
would produce a readable text but that would also
inevitably determine the meaning of the text in a
somewhat new form. (For the controversy surrounding Miller's editing practices and the status
of the texts produced by it, see F357.

<u>Contents</u>

The first session of the seminar, titled "Excommunication," addresses the issues surrounding
Lacan's departure from Saint Anne's Hospital and
his split with the Société française de psychanalyse over his method of training analysts.
Implicit in this controversy is the desire of some
members of the SFP to gain recognition from the
International Psychoanalytic Association, which had
required Lacan's removal from the list of those
qualified to train new analysts, and Lacan comments
on the experience of being part of a deal between
these two organizations (see F379). He also
explores various relations among psychoanalysis,
religion, and science, focussing his remarks on the
role of the analysts's desire in psychoanalysis and
especially on the role of Freud's desire in
relation to the development of psychoanalytic
concepts. Lacan concludes by promising to investigate the conceptual status of Freud's four
fundamental concepts: the unconscious, repetition,
transference, and the drive.

L'inconscient et la répétition

The next four sessions discuss the concepts of
the unconscious and repetition as they involve the
function of the signifier. Nature provides the
signifiers that organize human experience, Lacan
says. The unconscious appears to us in the form of
a discontinuity or gap within the chain of signifiers. Freud identified this gap as the "navel" of
dreams, an unknown, unrealizable center that is
entirely different from other concepts of the
unconscious that preceded (and followed) Freud, and
Lacan points out that it is this discontinuity
itself that is the basis for notions of totality or
wholeness. The unconscious is neither being nor
non-being, Lacan argues, but is instead "pre-

ontological," the "non-réalisé" (pp. 31-32; tr., p.
29-30). Its status is ethical, as suggested in
Freud's insistence that "I must be" there where the
id is. Lacan also claims that this unconscious
possesses a "pulsative" function in which anything
that appears within its gap is destined to disappear, and he introduces what he calls the
"conjectural science of the subject" in relation to
this function (p. 44; tr. p. 43).

After commenting briefly on the subject as
conceived first by Descartes and then by Freud,
Lacan goes on to discuss the function of repetition
and its relation to remembering proposed in Freud's
"Remembering, Repeating, and Working-Through"
(1914). He stresses the difference between
repetition and transference despite their close
connection in analytic experience. He also
distinguishes between repetition and reproduction,
denying the possibility of true reproduction and
arguing that repetition tends toward an "act" that
forever remains on the horizon. It is in this
"act" of repetition, Lacan says, that we discover
the resistance of the subject (p. 51; tr. p. 51).

To explain this relation between the subject and
repetition, Lacan turns to the game of Fort/Da
described in Beyond the Pleasure Principle (1920).
Lacan claims that the game symbolizes repetition,
but not the repetition of some instinctual need
that demands the return of the mother. Instead,
what is repeated in the game is the mother's
leaving as it constitutes the originary cause of a
splitting in the subject. The spool thrown over
the back of the chair is not a representation of
the mother; it is a small piece of the subject, one
that is detachable and yet still connected precisely through the repetition of its detachment (p.
60; tr. p. 62-3). "The man thinks with his
object," Lacan says, and he identifies this object
as the objet a discussed in the next group of
sessions.

The repeated return of the spool is related to
the split within the subject that marks the child's
access to the order of signifiers, and it indicates
what Lacan calls an "encounter" ("la rencontre")
with the real. The function of the real, Lacan
says, is a failed encounter with that which is
always "unassimilable" in the traumatic experience:
"The real is that which always comes back to the
same place--to the place where the subject in so
far as he thinks . . . does not meet it" (p. 49;
tr. p. 49). Lacan comments on this point with an
extended discussion of the dream of the burning
child reported by Freud in his Interpretation of
Dreams (1900), and he briefly links the general
relation of the real and the order of signifiers to

Aristotle's connection between the _tuché_ and _auto-
maton_ in his _Physics_.

Du regard comme objet petit a

   The sessions of 19 February-11 March 1964 deal
with "le regard," the "look" or "gaze," and its
relation to the object, the _objet a_. Inspired by
his reading of Merleau-Ponty's posthumously
published work _Le visible et l'invisible_, Lacan
claims that the function of the gaze is inherent in
the _méconnaissance_ of narcissistic identification
that he characterizes as the "scopic field" of the
Imaginary. In short, Lacan claims that "we are
beings who are looked at . . . that which makes us
conscious institutes us by the same token as
speculum mundi" (p. 71; tr. p. 75). In this sense,
the spectacle of the world appears to us as omniscient, all-seeing, as well as seen. In dreams, on
the other hand, we perceive the world as being
shown to us; there, "what characterizes the images
is that _it_ [i.e, the id, "_ça_"] _shows_ (p. 72; tr. p.
75). (Lacan calls this "given-to-be-seen" quality
"_la tache_," "the stain" [p. 71; tr. p. 74].) The
subject, on the other hand, is relegated by the
dream to the position simply of someone who does
not see, and Lacan promises to discuss this fading
of the subject in relation to the identity between
the gaze and the _objet a_.
   The gaze can be considered as the _objet a_, Lacan
says, the "underside [_cet envers_] of consciousness"
(p. 79; tr. p. 83), and it is imagined by the
subject in the field of the Other. (Lacan also
claims that at the scopic level we are at the level
of desire, "of the desire of the Other" [p. 96; tr.
p. 104].) Referring to Sartre's discussion of the
"look" or gaze in _Being and Nothingness_, Lacan says
that the gaze does not mark the presence of an
"annihilating subject" who objectifies us within
his look; it is instead "the subject sustaining
himself in a function of desire," as Sartre himself
suggests. It is no accident, Lacan adds, that the
science of perspective grew up about the same time
as Descartes, and he parallels the emergence of
Renaissance theories of perspective with the
formulation of the Cartesian subject as a geometrical point, a point of perspective that cannot be
identified with "consciousness" in the usual sense.
He illustrates his remarks with a brief discussion
of Hans Holbein's _The Ambassadors_ and relates the
optical effect of anamorphosis to his analysis of
the geometrical properties of the gaze. "This
picture," Lacan says of Holbein's painting, "is
simply what any picture is, a trap for the gaze"
(p. 83; tr. p. 89).

Lacan then goes on to distinguish between the eye
and the gaze, a distinction analogous to the more
general distinction between the organ and its
function in relation to the subject. In painting
or in any visual scene, Lacan says, the point of
the gaze is always outside the picture, and the
picture and the gaze are related through (or on)
what Lacan calls "l'écran"("the screen"), which he
parallels with the "stain" introduced above (p. 89;
tr. p. 96). Lacan argues that when a painter
offers up his painting, he does give something for
the eye to feed on, but he also "invites the person
to whom this picture is presented to lay down [à
déposer] his gaze there as one lays down one's
weapons. This is the pacifying, Apollonian effect
of painting" (p. 93; tr. p. 101), which Lacan calls
the "dompte-regard," the "taming of the gaze," in
contrast to the trompe-l'oeil in which the eye is
misled (see p. 100; tr. p. 109, and cf. p. 95; tr.
p. 103.) In the dialectic of the eye and the gaze,
he concludes, we find not coincidence, but a "lure"
(leurre): "You never look at me from the place
from which I see you. Conversely, what I look at
is never what I wish to see." (p. 95; tr. p. 103).

In the context of his discussion of the lure,
Lacan comments in some detail on the phenomenon of
mimicry in nature (see pp. 91-92; tr. pp.97-99),
and he returns to this topic on 11 March to distinguish between the lure produced by one animal to
attract another and the way the lure functions in a
human context. The human, Lacan says, is not
entirely caught up in this imaginary capture the
way an animal is. The human "maps himself in it .
. . In so far as he isolates the function of the
screen and plays with it. Man, in effect, knows
how to play with the mask as that beyond which
there is the gaze. The screen is here the locus of
mediation" (p. 99; tr. p. 107). "If one wants to
deceive a man," Lacan observes some time later,
"what one presents to him is the painting of a
veil, that is to say, something that incites him to
ask what is behind it." What makes a painting
commercially successful is that, somehow, it
satisfies a desire to contemplate on the part of
the viewer, an "appetite of the eye" that must be
fed (pp. 102, 105; tr. p. 111-12, 115. In this
same session, Lacan also comments on the gesture
and on the myth of the evil eye.)

Le transfert et la pulsion

The sessions of 15 April-29 May 1964 focus on the
other two fundamental concepts identified by Lacan,
transference and the drive. Lacan begins by

arguing that transference may be the product of the
analytic experience itself, but that it also bears
a close relation to possibilities inherent in
experience outside of analysis and only depends on
the presence of the analyst in its most narrow,
psychoanalytic sense.   Lacan rejects transference
both as the basis for rectifying the patient's
relation to reality and as an arena in which the
patient's ego can or should be strengthened.
Instead, he describes transference in relation to
the more general repetitive function of the "missed
encounter" ("du même ratage"), a "temporal pulsation" in which the unconscious closes up like a
shutter (pp. 131, 119; tr. pp. 143, 131).   This
closure is effected by the ego (p. 119; tr. p. 131)
or by the objet a (p. 132; tr. p. 145), and it
constitutes both an obstacle to remembering (p.
133; tr. p. 145) and the initial moment at which
interpretation achieves its full force (p. 119; tr.
p. 131).   Born of the subject's relation to the
signifier, transference situates the subject in the
position of error vis-à-vis his discourse.   This
position usually results in the lying and misleading speech through which the analyst must
identify the true subject that is constituted as
secondary in relation to the signifier (pp. 127-30;
tr. pp. 138-42).
   Lacan redefines transference as that which
"manifests in experience the enacting of the
reality of the unconscious, in so far as that
reality is sexuality," and he claims that sexuality
is consubstantial with the dimension of the
unconscious (pp. 159, 133; tr. pp. 174, 146).
Lacan briefly discusses the link between sex and
death in the individual and then introduces the
function of desire as a "last residuum of the
effect of the signifier in the subject."   "Desidero
is the Freudian cogito," Lacan says, and desire may
be figured as the locus of a junction between the
field of demand and sexual reality (pp. 141, 143;
tr. pp. 154, 156).   He then claims that the desire
he is concerned with here is that of the analyst,
not the analysand (p. 143; tr. p. 156), and this
observation leads him to the topic of the drive.
   Lacan notes that the notion of a drive has been
seen as contradictory to the "intellectualization"
of his own theory, (p. 148; tr. pp. 161-2), but
that is only because the drive is so often conceived as organic, contrary to Freud's own argument.   He briefly discusses Freud's presentation of
the concept of the drive, stressing the difference
between the object of need and that of the drive,
in which the object itself is of no importance (p.
153; tr. p. 168).   Lacan then compares the drive to
a montage (p. 154; tr. p. 169), which is the way

"sexuality participates in the psychical life, in a way that must conform to the gap-like structure that is the structure of the unconscious" (p. 160; tr. p. 176). This is why, in relation to the biological finality of sexuality, drives are always partial drives, and Lacan claims that sexuality is realized through the drives only in so far as they are partial because subjects deal only with that part of sexuality that passes into the networks of the signifier (p. 161; tr. p. 177).

In contrast to the object-oriented notion of the drive as a manifestation of organic need, Lacan describes the drive as structured by a movement "outward and back" ("l'aller et retour" [p. 162; tr. p. 177]). This movement is realized most dramatically in sadomasochistic relations and in the relations with an other constituted in the Schaulust, or pleasure of seeing, associated with the scopic drive. Lacan comments on those relations in some detail, and rejects the notion of relating various drives through some process of maturation or natural metamorphosis (pp. 164-65; tr. pp. 180-81). In the last session of this group, Lacan describes the partial drive as a circular movement that emerges, circles about the objet a, and returns to its source, and he claims that it is in this pulsation that the subject attains to the dimension of the Other (p. 177; tr. p. 194).

In the session of 29 May 1964, Lacan sums up much of what he has said about the drive and sexuality, and introduces the issue of sexual differentiation. The partial drives with which sexuality is associated are distinct from "love," Lacan explains. Love is structured at its biological level by the opposition active/passive, in which Freud claims that we recognize the parallel opposition masculine/feminine. The libido is distinct from such oppositions, however, and may be characterized by what Lacan calls a "lamella," which is represented by the objet a "as related to what the sexed being loses in sexuality" (p. 180; tr. p. 197). (He claims that this lamella is the serious side of what he describes as the "hommelette" in B17.) In response to a question, Lacan elaborates on this mysterious lamella and says that it is the "organ of the libido," adding that "the lamella has a rim, it inserts itself into the erogenous zone, that is to say, in one of the orifices of the body, in so far as these orifices . . . are linked to the opening/closing of the gap of the unconscious" (pp. 181-82; tr. p. 200).

Le champ d l'Autre, et retour sur le transfert

The sessions for 27 May-17 June 1964 return to the topic of transference, this time in the context of the subject's relation to the field of the Other. Lacan begins by reminding his audience that the partial drive cannot represent the totality of the sexual tendency, i.e., reproduction, and in fact there is nothing in the psyche at all by which the subject may situate himself as male or female. There is only Freud's division between activity and passivity (p. 186; tr. p. 204). As a result, Lacan says, gender identity is entirely dependent on the scenario situated in the field of the Other, the Oedipus complex. In short, sexuality is represented in the psyche by something other than sexuality itself and is established through the overlap of two different "lacks": one inherent in the subject's dependence on a signifier that can be found only in the field of the Other; and the second, the "real lack," derived from what the living being loses in reproduction, "namely, that the living being, by being subject to sex, has fallen under the blow of individual death" (p. 186; tr. p. 205). The myth intended to embody this "missing part," Lacan adds, is precisely that of the lamella.

The rest of the first session in this group is given over to a discussion of aphanisis as what Lacan calls, in English, the "fading" of the subject, and to the circular relation of the subject to the Other that Lacan describes here as a combination of "joining" and "separation," functions that Lacan adopts from symbolic logic (see pp. 191-93; tr. p. 210-211. (These two functions are associated with what Lacan calls the alienation of the "vel," a logical alternative which involves mutually exclusive terms which overlap to form a third region different from both.) In the next session, Lacan claims that there simply cannot be a subject without this aphanisis occurring somewhere and that it is in the alienation of this fundamental division that the "dialectic of the subject" is established (p. 201; tr. p. 221).

Later in the seminar, Lacan returns to this topic and claims that alienation derives from the originary signifying dyad. This pair of signifiers, which Lacan represents as "S_1 . . . S_2," constitutes a couple in which the subject is represented by one signifier for another signifier, and Lacan distinguishes that kind of alienation from a second, "what appears first as lack in what is signified by the dyad of signifiers, in the interval that links them, namely, the desire of the Other" (p. 213; tr. p. 236).

Several other remarks focus on Freud's Vorstellungsreprasentanz (which Lacan translates "le

représentant de la représentation" or "representative of the representation" [p. 198, tr., p.
217]) and on the role of desire, doubt, and
certainty in Descartes' notion of the function of
God. Lacan then turns to that figure produced
within the transference of the analytic situation,
the sujet supposé savoir, or "subject supposed to
know." The subject supposed to know is the
precondition of transference, Lacan says, and
whenever that status is conferred on an individual,
whether or not an analyst, transference occurs (p.
211; tr. p. 233). What he is supposed to know,
Lacan explains later, is simply "signification" (p.
228; tr. p. 253), which is not knowledge but is
absolute despite that because it constitutes a
"point of attachment" that joins the analyst's
desire "to the resolution of that which is to be
revealed" (p. 228; tr. p. 253). Thus the subject
is supposed to know by the fact that it is a
subject of desire, and this position yields the
"transference effect" or, more simply, love. Lacan
claims that love is essentially the wish to be
loved, and he claims that behind this love known as
transference "is the affirmation of the link
between the desire of the analyst and the desire of
the patient" (p. 229; tr. p. 254).
    Lacan devotes much of the last session in this
group to the issue of interpretation, and he is
careful to reject the criticism that his approach
undercuts the possibility of interpretation. Lacan
says that although meaning may be simply an effect
of an operation in the field of the signifier, and
interpretation therefore not open to "meaning" per
se, this does not mean that all interpretations may
be equal. "The fact that I have said that the
effect of interpretation is to isolate in the
subject a kernel . . . of non-sense, does not mean
that interpretation is in itself nonsense" (p. 226;
tr. p. 250). Instead, interpretation "has the
effect of bringing out an irreducible signifier"
and is an "interpretation significative." What is
essential is that the subject should see, beyond
the signification of interpretation, "to what
signifier--to what irreducible, traumatic, non-
meaning--he is, as a subject subjected" (p. 226;
tr. pp. 250-51). (In this session Lacan also
comments on the effect of metaphor in lines from
"Booz endormi" that he discussed in C71, and on the
field of pleasure and the ego [Ich] that he had
introduced in the preceding session.)

Reste à conclure

    Lacan begins the last session of the seminar by
posing the question to psychoanalysts in his

audience, "how can we be sure that we are not
imposters?" (p. 237; tr. p. 263). The issue of
imposture always looms over the analyst's head,
Lacan says, and the analyst usually wards it off
with ceremonies, forms and rituals. Lacan then
returns to the relations among science, religion,
and psychoanalysis, comparing psychoanalysis and
religion according to the oblivion and mystery
common to each, yet denying that psychoanalysis is
a religion and insisting instead that psychoanalysis, like La science, science in general, "is
engaged in the central lack in which the subject
experiences himself as desire" (p. 239; tr. p.
265).

In analysis, this lack reveals the presence of
the objet a, repeatedly rediscovered in the
movement of transference (p. 242; tr. p. 269). It
is present as soon as the subject addresses his
demand to the analyst as the subject supposed to
know, a demand that always takes the form of "I
love you, but, because inexplicably I love in you
something more than you--the objet petit a--I
mutilate you" (p. 241; tr. p. 268). This objet a
covers the gap instituted by the inaugural division
of the subject but never crosses the gap. "This a
is presented precisely, in the field of the mirage
of the narcissistic function of desire, as the
object that cannot be swallowed, as it were, which
remains stuck in the gullet of the signifier. It
is at this point of lack that the subject has to
recognize himself" (p. 243; tr. p. 270). Lacan
goes on to add that this "remainder" marked by the
objet a means that considering an analysis to be
terminated by identification with the analyst
elides its true motive force. "There is a beyond
to this identification, and this beyond is defined
by the relation and the distance of the objet petit
a to the idealizing capital I of identification"
(p. 244; tr. pp. 271-72). (The "I" to which Lacan
refers here is the capital I of identification, not
the pronoun "I" or "je" which would mark the
subject's place in discourse. This distinction is
obvious in French but invisible in the English
translation.)

For the publication of this seminar in 1973,
Lacan wrote a short afterword (which was not
translated); see D107.

B22a. Abstract by Lacan in Annuaire de l'Ecole pratique
        des hautes études. Section des sciences econo-
        miques et sociales, 1964-65. Pp. 249-51.

Claims that the purpose of this seminar is to
restore "l'abrupt du réel" to the field established
by Freud, and more particularly to determine its

subversive status through an examination of the
four functions fundamental to that subversion.
Lacan briefly characterizes psychoanalytic concepts
of the unconscious, repetition, transference, and
the drive, and he proposes to redefine them and
then link them through the topology of "le bord,"
the "rim." Lacan mentions several other topics
covered in the seminar including his remarks on the
scopic drive, the place of the Other, and his
account of alienation in the subject's relation to
the Other.
Reprinted on the back cover of B22.

B22b.   The Four Fundamental Concepts of Psycho-Analysis.
        Translated by Alan Sheridan. Preface by Lacan
        (see D111). London: Hogarth Press, 1977. 290
        pages.

B22c.   Cuatro conceptos fundamentales del psicoanalisis.
        Translated by Francisco Monge. Breve biblioteca
        de reforma. Barcelona: Barral ed., 1977. 292
        pages.

B22d.   American edition of B22b. New York: Norton, 1978.
        290 pages.

B22e.   Die vier Grundbegriffe der Psychoanalyse. Trans-
        lated by Norbet Haas. Olten: Walter, 1978. 301
        pages.

B22f.   Il seminaro II: Libro XI--I quattro concetti
        fondamentali della psicoanalisi. Edited by
        Giacomo Contri. Translated by Sciana Loaldi and
        Irène Molina. Turin: Einaudi paperbacks, 1979.
        286 pages.

B22g.   Paperback edition of B22b. London: Penguin, 1980.
        239 pages.

B22h.   American paperback edition of B22b. New York:
        Norton, 1981.

B22i.   Chapter XI on anamorphosis was translated into
        Japanese as "Anamorufozu" in Gendai shiso.

B22*.   Other translations have appeared or are forthcoming
        in the following languages:
        Spanish (Paidos editions in Buenos Aires and
            Barcelona, under the direction of Jacques
            Alain Miller and Diana Rabinovich; another
            edition is published in Spain by Barral.)
        Portuguese (published by Zahar in Brazil)
        Serbo-croation (published by Naprijed)
        Slovene (published by Cankarjeva)
        Greek (published by Kedros in 1983)

B23.   Seminar XII (1964-65):   <u>Problèmes cruciaux pour la</u>
        <u>psychanalyse</u>. Unpublished except as noted below.

B23a.   Abstract by Lacan in <u>Annuaire de l'Ecole pratique</u>
        <u>des hautes études</u>.   Section des sciences écono-
        miques et sociales, 1965-66.   Pp. 270-73.

        Focuses on the being of the subject ("<u>l'être du</u>
        <u>sujet</u>") as the central problem for psychoanalysis,
        and insists that Freud's discovery that the
        unconscious could only be translated in knots of
        language led him repeatedly to speak of that
        subject as split ("<u>refendu</u>").   Lacan claims that
        the being of the subject is the "suture of a lack"
        ("<u>la suture d'un manque</u>"; see G739), and he says
        this is the same lack that sustains the subject in
        its recurrence and serves as "<u>le trait unaire</u>," a
        mark of primary identification that comes to
        function as an ideal (see C86).   This mark, Lacan
        says, is "<u>ce qui manque au signifiant pour être</u>
        <u>l'Un du sujet</u>," and he argues that the subject is
        split by being at the same time the effect of the
        mark and the support of its lack (<u>Ornicar?</u>, p. 10).
        Lacan also insists that the being of the psycho-
        analyst represents the being of the subject in the
        analytic experience, and he reminds us that the
        experience of analysis is always an engagement of
        being, not thought.   The two sides of the subject
        are split here between truth and knowledge
        (<u>savoir</u>), and Lacan adds that the problematic
        character of the analyst's being comes from what he
        encounters as the being of the subject in the
        symptom.
        Reprinted in <u>Ornicar?</u> 29 (1984):   9-12.

B24.   Seminar XIII (1965-66):   <u>L'objet de la psych-</u>
        <u>analyse</u>.   Unpublished except as noted below.

B24a.   Opening session published as C85.

B24b.   Abstract of whole seminar by Lacan in <u>Annuaire de</u>
        <u>l'Ecole pratique des hautes études</u>.   Section des
        sciences économiques et sociales, 1966-67.   Pp.
        211-12.

        Describes the function of object-relations in
        psychoanalytic experience.   Lacan notes that
        object-relations dominate the subject's relation to
        the real and that oral and anal objects are asso-
        ciated with demand.   Lacan adds, however, that
        other objects such as the gaze and the voice ("<u>le</u>
        <u>regard et la voix</u>") require a more complex theory,
        since they stem from a division of the subject
        which supports desire.   He also remarks on the
        importance of the scopic drive and on the topology

he has developed to represent the structure of
perception and its relation to the subject, and he
stresses the importance of autocriticism to the
position of the analyst as he responds to demand
and desire in the analytic experience.
    Reprinted in Ornicar? 29 (1984): 12-13. See
also "El objeto del psicoanalisis," preceded by
Louis Althusser, "Freud Y Lacan," tr. Muria
Garreta, revised with notes by Ramon Garcia. Coll.
Cuadernos Anagrama 5 (Barcelona: Ed. Anagrama,
1970), 58 pages.

B25.   Seminar XIV (1966-67): La logique du fantasme.

    The three descriptions listed below differ enough
to make a precise account of the seminar difficult.
B25a appeared first and was published in the
official journal of the Ecole freudienne de Paris.
There is no evidence that Lacan approved this text,
however, as he did the summaries for Seminars IV
and V. B25b is more precise and detailed and
resembles ordinary exposition much more closely
than B25a, which approaches the more extemporaneous
style of the published seminars. At the level of
generality on which these annotations are written,
however, both versions describe the same topics in
roughly the same order, so the annotation for this
essay is based on B25a with occasional references
to B25b for clarifying details.
    The third description of this seminar listed
below possess the obvious authority of being
written by Lacan himself, but its brevity and particular emphases suggest an independent text rather
than a full account of the seminar itself, and it
is annotated as such.

B25a.   Summary by Jacques Nassif. Lettres de l'Ecole
        freudienne de Paris 1 (1967):   11-17; 2 (1967):
        7-23; 3 (1967):   3-33; 4 (1967):   2-23; 5 (1968):
        62-108.

    To facilitate reference to the appropriate issue
of the Lettres, the annotations are divided according to the way Nassif grouped the seminar
sessions. These divisions seem arbitrary at times
and should not be taken as signifying radical
shifts in the topics under discussion.

16-23 November 1966. Lettres 1 (1967): 11-17.

    Establishes the logical status of the subject
that is barred from discourse by the operation of
the signifier ($) and that therefore functions as a
lack in the chain of signifiers which constitutes

the "universe of discourse." Actually, Lacan adds,
there is no coherent "universe" of discourse, nor
any signifier which can contain significance itself
(p. 13). Invoking Russell and using set theory as
an analogy, Lacan argues that the subject functions
as the paradoxical element of the set that contains
all sets and yet is not contained in a set, and he
says that the subject arises at the limit of the
universe of discourse, rooted there in the function
of repetition described by Freud. In effect, Lacan
says, what repetition seeks to repeat is precisely
what always eludes it (p. 17), and he asserts that
we must try to determine the logical function of
the lack that results.

7 December 1966-18 January 1967. Lettres 2 (1967):
   7-23.

Continues to develop the link between psychoanalysis and contemporary symbolic logic, emphasizing the similarity between the signifier's
relation to the truth and the paradoxical impossibility of a set containing its own limits. Only an
"effect" of truth is possible, Lacan says, and the
only signifier of that effect is the signifier of
what is missing from the universe of discourse (p.
12). Lacan attacks the identification of thinking
and existence manifest in the Cartesian cogito, and
he distinguishes between the id--as the position
"je ne pense pas"--and the unconscious--the
position "je ne suis pas." That distinction is
necessary, Lacan says, if we are to understand
Freud's discovery of a "pensée qui n'est pas 'je,'"
i.e., the Other, the site of speech ("le lieu de la
Parole"), which Lacan identifies as Freud's "other
scene." He concludes by defining alienation as the
unavoidable choice between "je ne pense pas" and
"je ne suis pas."

25 January 1967-8 March 1967. Lettres 3 (1967):
   3-33.

Opens by claiming that the "truth" of alienation
is supported by the objet a and that there is no
place where the truth constituted by speech can be
assured or where that which is only words can be
put into question. Lacan formulates this point as
S(Â), and he claims that it is the sole point of
departure for the logic of the fantasm.
Alienation, Lacan continues, is the operation
which marks the field of the Other with the same
finitude that marks the subject himself, the finitude that defines, in the subject, the fact of
dependence on the effects of the signifier (p. 11).
Thus the Other is fractured in the same way that

the subject is marked by the double bind of repetition (p. 11), and that repetition is the path
from the act to the "acting out" which establishes
the significance of the act for the subject (p.
13).   Lacan elaborates on the relations among the
passage to the act, repetition, sublimation, and
acting out, and he concludes with a long analysis
of the "sexual act" and its relation to _jouissance_
and the effect of the subject, focussing on the
role of repetition in sexual desire as an effort to
overcome the lack inherent in the subject (p. 33).

12 April 1967-26 April 1967.   _Lettres_ 4 (1967): 3-
   23.

   Notes that the subject is a fact or creation of
language ("_un fait de langage, un fait_ du _lan-
gage_"), but adds that one can attribute the
function of speech to the subject only by seeing
that he acquires this mode of being through the act
in which he is situated ("_dans l'acte où il se
tait_").   The discovery of the unconscious showed
us, Lacan says, that the subject can only speak
from the depths of silence that characterize the
sexual act (p. 5), and he claims that the great
secret of psychoanalysis is that there is no such
thing as the sexual act (p. 5).   Lacan explains
this claim by noting that his definition of "act"
implies the doubling of the signifier that will
permit the subject to be inserted in a signifying
chain where he is inscribed.   Consequently, the
sexual act is impossible because there is always a
third object between man and woman whose substitutive function creates a slippage that prohibits
them from being related in an essentially fixed
opposition.   This third object is the phallus--the
sign of a lack (B25b, p. 248).

10 May 1967-21 June 1967.   _Lettres_ 5 (1968): 62-
   108.

   Begins with a brief discourse on masochism that
leads Lacan to his present topic, the structuration
of the act whereby the subject comes to light
through the relation of one signifier to another.
To commit an act, Lacan says, is in effect to
introduce a relation among signifiers.   This is
true even when those signifiers are "man" and
"woman," and that is why their relation always
depends on a third, which lends significance to
their relation.   The pleasure of that relation is
also dependent on this "third," which lifts the
pleasure from mere satisfaction to _jouissance_ (p.
66).
   Here Lacan declares that this third is the place

of the Other, which he defines as the "reservoir of
material for the act." The Other is equivalent to
the body, which Lacan claims is in effect the first
signifier, and he says that the Bible tells us the
body is made to receive something that one can call
the "mark" and that hence supplants the body with
the signifier.
Lacan then reworks the problem of alienation
introduced earlier, this time from the Hegelian
perspective of the master/slave relation (see B25b,
pp. 262-64). He also notes that his insistence on
the necessity of the subjective articulation of the
signifier is only a preface to the more fundamental
relation between the subject and the body. Lacan
observes that this is the traditional site of
corporeal symbolism, but he adds that the association of the body and the subject can only pass
through the paths of structure, across the inci-
dents of the signifier in the real as it introduces
the subject there (p. 84).
The seminar concludes with a long discussion of
jouissance in relations between men and women. In
the sex act, Lacan says, there is always a jouissance that remains in suspense: that of the other.
As a result, the body of each individual is turned
into a metaphor for the jouissance of the other.
Jouissance thus comes to be suspended between the
two, dependent on the body of the other, so that
the jouissance of this other remains adrift ("reste
à la dérive" [p. 94]). Jouissance thus functions
as the limit of pleasure, and the objet a always
remains beyond that limit, instituting the principle of repetition and always eluding the pleasure
principle. (Lacan does insist on distinguishing
between male and female alienation in this
relation, arguing that the male is doubly alienated
because "his" body incarnates a second alienation,
that of the objet a.) The objet a, Lacan says, is
that part of the body where jouissance can take
refuge ("se réfugier"), and the (barred) subject's
conjunction with the objet a is engendered there,
at the disjunction in the field of the Other
between the body and jouissance" (p. 107).

B25b.   "Pour une logique du fantasme." Dated "Christmas-
        Easter 1968." Scilicet 2/3 (1970): 223-73.

        See note to B25.

B25c.   Abstract by Lacan, Annuaire de l'Ecole pratique des
        hautes études. Section des sciences économiques
        et sociales, 1967-68. Pp. 189-94.

        Invokes the schema of alienation presented in B22
        to open the juncture between the id and the

unconscious, and comments on his formula "<u>ou je ne
pense pas ou je ne suis pas</u>" as it relates thinking
and being through negation. Lacan says that
psychoanalysis usually postulates that the unconscious is where "I am not" has a substance, and
that it can be invoked in the "I am not thinking"
insofar as the unconscious is conceived as "<u>maître
de son être</u>," i.e., as not being language.
However, Lacan adds that the "<u>manque à être</u>" that
constitutes alienation takes place through the
incarnation of the subject that is called castration, and it is not simply "not thinking."
Within the "content" created by castration are the
droppings ("<u>les chutes</u>") that testify to the fact
that the subject is only an effect of language, the
<u>objet a</u>.   Centered upon this emptiness, these
objects take on the function of the "cause" of
desire as they are perceived to be "<u>solidaires</u>" of
the split within the subject--i.e., as they become
fantasms.

Lacan then comments on repetition and its role in
"the act" (specifically the sexual act) through
which the "inmixing" of difference is produced in
the signifier. (For further comments on "inmixing," see C86). He describes the importance of
this act within the difference between two formulas: (1) There is no sexual act, in the sense
of certifying the subject as a single sex.   (2)
There is only the sexual act, which implies a split
within the subject and the structure of the
fantasm.

Lacan mentions several graphs that diagram these
formulas and their relevance for the subject's
relation to the objects of his desire, and he
stresses the importance of the fantasm in the
analysis of neuroses. He also notes that this
seminar is the first time he has associated the
place of the Other with the body rather than
treating it as pure intersubjectivity:

> <u>nous avons pour la première fois appuyé que ce
> lieu de l'Autre n'est pas à prendre ailleurs que
> dans le corps, qu'il n'est pas intersubjectivité,
> mais cicatrices sur le corps tégumentaires,
> pédoncules à se brancher sur ses orifices pour y
> faire office de prises, artifices ancestraux et
> techniques qui le rongent</u>. (Ornicar?, p. 17)

Reprinted in <u>Ornicar?</u> 29 (1984):   13-18.

B26.   Seminar XV (1967-68):   <u>L'acte psychanalytique</u>.
        Unpublished except as noted below.

B26a.   Abstract by Lacan in <u>Annuaire de l'Ecole pratique
        des hautes études</u>. Section des sciences écono-

miques et sociales, 1968-69. Pp. 213-220.

Defines the psychoanalytic act as the moment when the analysand becomes an analyst ("moment électif où le psychanalysant passe au psychanalyste"), and explains the theory behind the process of "la passe" proposed in C88. Within this moment lies the subject's relation to knowledge, Lacan says, and at the heart of this act is the perception of the fault ("la faille," failing, bankruptcy) of the sujet supposé savoir (the subject-supposed-to-know), which in turn is derived from the fact that the very notion of an unconscious means that there can be knowledge without a subject. Within psychoanalysis, Lacan adds, the psychoanalyst is not a subject, and the notion of a "self" (English in the text), so important to the psychoanalytic community, is really the loss ("la perte") of the analyst. The only way an analyst can exist, Lacan claims, is through the logic with which the act is articulated before and after, and he says that the psychoanalyst is formed in relation to the objet a: "Le psychanalyst se fait de l'objet a. Se fait, à entendre: se fait produire: de l'objet a; avec de l'objet a" (Ornicar?, p. 21).
Lacan goes on to discuss the ethical dimension of the psychoanalytic act, its relation to "acting out," and the role of jouissance and castration in analysis.
Reprinted in Ornicar? 29, (1984): 18-25.

B27. Seminar XVI (1968-69): D'un Autre à l'autre.
Unpublished except for a brief excerpt which appeared as "Extraits de la séance du Séminaire" [26 February 1969]. Littoral 9 (1983): 33-37.

Notes the relevance of Freud's work to the question Foucault raised about the author's function in discourse. Lacan also claims to have noticed an allusion to his own work in Foucault's promise to discuss the "retour à . . . " as a decisive moment in the transformation of a field of discourse.
This item consists of two versions of Lacan's remarks, one based on a transcript edited by Lacan and the other a "source-text" apparently based on a shorthand record of the discussion. The texts differ mainly in syntax and punctuation. This item is preceded by E203.

B28. Seminar XVII (1969-70): L'envers de la psychanalyse. Unpublished.

B29. Seminar XVIII (1970-71): D'un discours qui ne serait pas du semblant. Unpublished.

B30.   Seminar XIX (1971-72):   <u>. . . ou pire</u>. Unpublished
        except as noted below.

B30a.   Abstract by Lacan in <u>Annuaire de l'Ecole pratique
        des hautes etudes</u>. Section des sciences
        économiques et sociales, 1972-73. Pp. 287-91.

        Stresses the importance of the concept of the One
        as it differs from (and in relation to) zero, and
        refers to the mathematical models developed by
        Frege and Cantor. Lacan says that this first "One"
        creates an originary split (the "<u>coupe du deux</u>")--
        One and zero makes two, he notes--and this split is
        what engenders the numerical series as this
        original difference is repeated. Lacan parallels
        this mathematical model to the structure of the
        symbolic, where this One is repeated but not
        totalized in the repetition. The signifier One is
        not just a signifier among others, either, nor is
        it an autonomous monad. Rather, "<u>cet Un-là</u>", the
        "<u>entre-d'eux</u>" of the signifiers, is "<u>le savoir
        supérieur au sujet, soit inconscient en tant qu'il
        se manifeste comme ex-sistant</u>" ("knowledge above
        the subject, unconscious in so far as it is
        manifest as ex-sistant"). Thus the "<u>Un-dire</u>" is
        that which makes ex-sist those which insist in
        repetition.
        The rest of this abstract focuses on Lacan's
        claim that there are no sexual relations and on the
        role played by <u>jouissance</u> in relation to the body,
        speech, and thought. Knowledge (<u>le savoir</u>) affects
        the body of the being who is made out of words by
        cutting up its <u>jouissance</u>, Lacan says. This "cut"
        produces "<u>les chutes</u>," the droppings that he calls
        the <u>objet a</u>. That which thinks, calculates and
        judges, Lacan adds a few lines later, is <u>jouis-
        sance</u>, <u>jouissance</u> of the Other, and this requires
        the One, which in turn makes the subject function
        as castrated. This situation is symbolized by the
        imaginary function that incarnates impotence--that
        is, by the phallus.
        Reprinted as ". . . Ou pire," <u>Scilicet</u> 5 (1975):
        5-10. At the beginning of the abstract, Lacan
        claims that this seminar is accompanied by another
        entitled "Savoir du psychanalyste," which Dor lists
        as having been presented at Hôpital Sainte-Anne,
        1971-72, but which has not been published.

B30b.   The session for 3 March 1972 has been translated by
        Denise Green in <u>Semiotext(e)</u> 4, no. 1 (1980):
        208-18.

B31.   Seminar XX (1972-73):   <u>Encore</u>. Edited by Jacques-
        Alain Miller. Paris: Editions du Seuil, 1975.
        133 pages.

Contents

Argues that sexual relations are impossible--"<u>il n'y a pas de rapport sexuel</u>" (pp. 35, 53, etc.)--because the very notion of joining together to make "One" ignores the fundamental gap ("<u>la béance</u>") that is the cause of the subject's desire and the origin of his demand for love (see p. 16). Man's desire is the desire of the Other, Lacan says in the first chapter of this seminar; that is why the unconscious was invented. But love ignores that; it is "<u>une passion qui peut être l'ignorance du désir</u>" (p. 11). As a result, love always demands more love, "again" ("<u>encore</u>"); and in fact, Lacan observes, "<u>encore</u>" "is the proper name of the fault line [<u>la faille</u>] in the Other from which the demand for love originates" (11).

Lacan next turns to the issue of sexual differentiation and focuses on two closely related topics: the site of sexual difference, and the origin of femininity. Lacan begins by recognizing that the "<u>l'être du corps</u>," the "being of the body," is sexed, but he claims that this is "secondary" since experience teaches us that these biological traces are not the origin of the <u>jouissance du corps</u> "insofar as it symbolizes the Other" (12). Rather, one of these sexed beings, man, is marked as such because he is "provided with" the organ "<u>dit phallique--j'ai dit</u> dit," Lacan reminds us, just as the other being is marked by the possession of "<u>le sexe corporel, le sexe de la femme--J'ai dit</u> de la femme." He emphasizes these figures of speech because they testify to the fact that there is no transcendent essence behind the difference between the sex (genitals, but also the category) and the being that possesses it--a difference implied by the phrase "<u>le sexe</u> de <u>la femme</u>."

The point of Lacan's attention to these phrases is that sexual identity has its origin in language, not the body. This is true for both sexes, but in this seminar Lacan emphasizes the discursive con-

stitution of femininity, which he characterizes as
"<u>pas-toute</u>," not-all: "<u>l'être sexué de ces femmes</u>
<u>pas-toutes ne passe pas par le corps, mais par ce</u>
<u>qui résulte d'une exigence logique dans la parole</u>"
(15).   Thus the very notion of making One of these
"two" sexes is misleading, since they are not "two"
at all but are situated within the logic of speech.
The transcendence of their division in the logic of
speech is thus rendered impossible by the way they
are constituted: being, Lacan concludes, a being
that would be posed as absolute, "is ever only the
fracture, the break, the interruption of the
formula "sexed being" insofar as the sexed being is
interested in <u>jouissance</u>."

The second chapter of the seminar is devoted to a
formula Lacan proposed in the opening session:
"the <u>jouissance</u> of the Other is not the sign of
love."   After a brief critique of traditional
theories of signification in which Lacan describes
substantive semantic categories as modes of
"collectivizing" the signifier rather than desig-
nating a signified, he concludes by observing that
the "substance of the body" can be defined only as
that which "<u>se jouit</u>."   This "substance" is what
experiences <u>jouissance</u> ("<u>se jouit</u>") and so
"corporealizes" the body in the mode of the signifier ("<u>de façon signifiante</u>").   The signifier
therefore may be considered the cause of <u>jouissance</u>
because without the signifier this aspect of the
body could not be delimited.
Thus, Lacan argues, in the experience of <u>jouis-</u>
<u>sance</u> one's body must "<u>jouit</u>" with a part of the
body of the Other ("<u>le corps de l'un qui jouit</u>
<u>d'une part du corps de l'Autre</u>").   That part must
"<u>jouit</u>" also, Lacan adds, and he notes that Sade in
fact taught us that it is always the Other who
experiences <u>jouissance</u>.   Nevertheless, because it
is only a part of the Other that is involved, this
<u>jouissance</u> precludes the unifying fantasy of love.
This is why Lacan insists the "<u>jouissance</u> of the
Other" is not a sign of love.   Remembering that
will lead to a consideration of phallic <u>jouissance</u>,
Lacan remarks, and he promises further discussion
of the association between the <u>jouissance</u> of the
Other and the "<u>pas-tout</u>" he has identified as the
role of women in speech.

The third chapter of the seminar is devoted to
the function of writing (<u>l'écrit</u>) in analytic
discourse.   Writing is not the same thing as the
signifier, Lacan claims. The signifier is a
dimension of language that was proposed by linguistics and is supported by a scientific discourse
that has introduced into speech the distinction

between a signifier and a signified. Saussure said
the relation between these elements of the sign is
arbitrary, but Lacan argues instead that the
signified is merely an effect of the signifier and
that there is no relation at all. According to
Lacan, "reference" is simply that which constitutes
discourse as a bond ("lien"), and he says that the
signifier as such refers to nothing if not to the
use of language as just such a bond (p. 32).

To treat discourse as a bond is not, however, to
assume that there is a prediscursive collection of
entities waiting to be ordered by language. Lacan
is careful to avoid the "mythic" dream of returning
to any "prediscursive reality." Each reality is
founded and defined by a discourse, he says; every
dimension of being is produced in the course of the
discourse of the master ("dans le courant du
discours du maître," p. 33). This includes the
sexual and familial divisions of men, women, and
children, which Lacan claims are only signifiers
(p. 34). A man is nothing other than a signifier,
and a woman seeks a man under the title of
signifier ("au titre de signifiant"). A man seeks
a woman, however, under the title of something
which can only be situated by discourse since the
woman ("la femme") is "pas-toute," not-whole;
therefore, there is always something about her that
eludes discourse. (p. 34). That is why analysis
teaches us that there is no such thing as sexual
relations ("il n'y a pas de rapport sexuel") in
discursive relations. In fact, Lacan adds, it is
the very impossibility of rendering sexual
relations in writing that makes writing (here
termed "l'écriture") possible as a specific effect
of discourse (p. 36).

The general import of Lacan's remarks seems to be
that the function of writing or, more simply, "la
lettre" in analytic discourse derives from its
discursive function as a bond or connection among
signifiers--which implies, of course, a bond among
subjects as well. He also notes its importance as
a way of figuring the structure of analytic
discourse in his own writing through the use of
letters such as A, a, S, etc., but toward the end
of this chapter he turns to the importance of
reading as the basis of analytic discourse.

The importance of reading to analytic discourse
is illustrated by Joyce's Finnegans Wake. Lacan
describes this novel as an "illegible" text that
produces what analytic discourse has taught us to
read as "le lapsus" rather than a specific
signified, and he says that this lapsus is what
signifies that there is something to be read at
all. It is this "to be read" (se lire) that
constitutes the register of analytic discourse,

Lacan claims, because that discourse is always
concerned with reading what is enunciated by the
signifier as something other than what it
signifies.

In your analytic discourse, Lacan says to the
analysts in his audience, you suppose that you know
how to read the subject of the unconscious. Your
story or history ("histoire") of the unconscious is
nothing other than that. Not only do you suppose
that you know how to read it, but you also suppose
that you can teach it how to read (p. 38).

The fourth chapter of the seminar contains
observations on the functional similarity between
God and the Other, and on the radical insufficiency
of language to being. It is an effect of writing,
Lacan says, that being is always presented beside
itself ("être . . . par-être," p. 44), and it is in
relation to this par-être that we must articulate
that which supplements sexual relations (insofar as
they do not exist): love ("l'amour").

Lacan situates the subject's relation to love
through the difference between the sign and the
signifier. The signifier represents a subject for
another signifier, Lacan reminds his listeners, and
that representation is what constitutes the sign.
The sign is thus not the sign of some thing but of
an effect, i.e., the subject. The subject is
nothing other than that which slides ("glisse")
within a chain of signifiers, and this subject-
effect is what distinguishes one signifier from
another. In other words, the subject is the
differentiating effect that characterizes each
signifier as a separate element (p. 48). Described
as such, Lacan concludes, the subject does not have
much to do with jouissance; to the contrary, the
sign of the subject provokes desire, and that is
the domain of love (p. 48).

This chapter also contains Lacan's notorious
attack on History, which is related to remarks he
made earlier about Marxism. On p. 32 Lacan
observes that to him Marxism has never seemed to be
a conceptualization of the world. Rather, it seems
more like a "gospel" in which "history" instituted
another dimension of discourse, one that would completely overturn philosophical discourse and the
sense of the world based on it (p. 33). In this
later chapter, Lacan claims that he detests the
philosophical formation of "History" precisely
because it gives us the idea that it possesses a
meaning of some sort. The first thing we have to do
in the face of such proclamations, Lacan says, is
to realize that we are dealing with nothing other
than the effects of a saying ("un dire"). Such
sayings, he adds, as well as their effects--such as

History--we can see in the way that "ça" agitates,
shakes up, and bothers speaking beings ("en quoi ça
agite . . . "les êtres parlants" [p. 45]).
    Lacan's remark is difficult to translate because
the pronoun "ça" refers to the "id" as well
functioning in its usual grammatical capacity, and
Lacan exploits that ambiguity as well as the
deliberately general referent of this phrase. To
be sure, he says, this ça gives a little life to
the sentiment called love, but that sentiment only
leads to the necessity of perpetuating this ça
through the dead end of reproducing bodies. Cannot
language have some other effects, Lacan asks, than
to lead men by the nose to reproduce themselves
again from body to body? There is indeed another
effect, Lacan says: writing (45).
    (Lacan's remarks about History as a collection of
sayings whose effects can be see in the way "ça
agite, ça remue . . . les êtres parlants" suggest
some connection between History and the unconscious. Lacan does not explicitly make that
association here, but cf. Fredric Jameson's
characterization of history as the real, that which
resists desire [see G660]. Luce Irigaray has
denounced Lacan's rejection of History in this
passage and claims that it illustrates the way
psychoanalysis tends to universalize phallocentricism by ignoring the historical determinants
of discourse [see G658].)

    In the fifth chapter of the seminar, Lacan turns
to what he describes as another satisfaction that
is associated with jouissance and that is supported
by language at the level of the unconscious, quite
apart from the issue of need. Language is the
mechanism of jouissance, Lacan says (p. 52), and he
goes on to relate this function of language to
Freud's account of the pleasure principle, claiming
that it is precisely this jouissance that is
repressed by speech as impossible or "unnecessary."
    Lacan defines the necessary as that which never
ceases to be written (p.55), and he says that
jouissance is referred centrally to that which is
not necessary, that which does not follow in
speech. He connects this elliptical definition
(which he says he borrowed from Aristotle) to the
topic of feminine sexuality, and says that the
failure of women analysts ("les dames analystes")
to speak about feminine sexuality stems directly
from the mechanism of jouissance itself--i.e.,
language. There is no other to phallic jouissance,
Lacan claims, except that about which woman is
utterly silent (p. 56).

    The sixth chapter of the seminar is devoted to

the jouissance of woman, which Lacan describes as
something more ("en plus"), beyond the phallus
("au-delà du phallus"). It is a supplementary
jouissance, Lacan says, one that is derived from
the woman's role as the not-all, the "pas toute" of
language. Anytime a speaking being of any sort,
male or female, assumes a role under the banner of
women, that being is situated within the phallic
function as not-all (p. 68). This role is what
defines the woman, except that we can only speak of
"The woman" with the "The" crossed out if that
article is supposed to designate any universal
category. Lacan claims that "Woman" exists only as
excluded by the nature of things, which is in fact
the nature of words.

In this chapter Lacan also remarks on F348 and on
the persistent criticism by materialists that his
Other is just like the "good old God" theology gave
us. Lacan says that he proposed the Other at the
time of C71 as a means of exorcising that God, but
he does go on to comment on the tradition of
Christian mysticism (in which he places his Ecrits)
and its relation to feminine jouissance. We call a
"mystic" one who experiences a jouissance that
"goes beyond" ("qui soit au-delà") Lacan says, and
like Bernini's Saint Theresa (which appears on the
cover of this seminar), mystics experience this
jouissance without knowing anything about it (p.
71). Could not this jouissance be the very thing
that puts us on the path to ex-istence, Lacan asks?
Why not interpret the face of the Other, he says,
the face of God, as supported by feminine
jouissance? (p. 71).

(This chapter and the following one were
translated with brief commentaries as B31c.)

The question of knowledge and the relation
between woman and the Other is taken up in the
seventh chapter, where Lacan designates the
jouissance of the woman with the formula S(∅).
(The ∅ refers to the Other, which is barred to
represent the fact that it is inaccessible to the
subject.) The similarity between the ∅ and the
crossed-out article of the phrase "Là femme" marks
what Lacan calls the opaque place of the jouissance
of the Other--the Other that woman might be if she
existed (p. 77). As the place where everything
that articulated by the signifier comes to be
inscribed, the Other is, at its basis, radically
Other (p. 75). Similarly, Woman's relation to God
stems just from the fact that her jouissance is
radically Other, and Lacan draws together these two
observations by noting that the symbolic has
undoubtedly always been the support of what
Christian theology has called God.

The question that really polarizes his topic,
Lacan concludes, is just what does the woman know
of the place of the Other, of the God "dont elle
jouit" (p. 82).   But he has already answered this
question: "There is a jouissance proper to her, to
this 'her' which does not exist and which signifies
nothing.   There is a jouissance proper to her and
of which she herself may know nothing, except that
she experiences it--that much she does know" (p.
69, tr. B31c, p. 145).   This is the ignorant bliss
that she shares with the mystics and that is
figured on Saint Theresa's face in Bernini's
statue, as described in the preceding section.
Lacan says that the ultimate question always
involves what there is to know about the knowledge
of feminine jouissance ("de savoir, dans ce qui
constitue la jouissance féminine . . . ce qu'il en
est de son savoir" [p. 81]).   And if the unconscious has taught us anything, Lacan adds, it is
that somewhere there is something that knows more
than the speaking being knows.   This somewhere is
in the Other, and there, "it [ça] knows" (p. 81).
It knows, Lacan says, because it (the ça) is supported by the signifiers that constitute the
speaking being as subject.   Because she experiences
this knowledge without knowing it, however, woman
finds herself situated between two poles: the S(∅)
that marks the place of the Other, supported by
feminine jouissance; and the phallus, the signifier
that marks the place of man in the symbolic and
that is supported by phallic jouissance (p. 75),
which Lacan calls the jouissance of the idiot.

Lacan's remarks about knowledge and truth in the
eighth chapter shift the focus of the seminar
somewhat.   He distinguishes between the "truth"
("la vérité") of "being" and what he calls a
knowledge supported entirely by the signifier as
such, which has jouissance as its limit (p. 85).
Thus he claims that the question of knowledge is
that of love, not being (p. 84).   Oriented towards
that jouissance, this knowledge obtains a power far
beyond the illusory fantasm of a "whole truth," and
Lacan emphasizes the difference by labelling the
domain of knowledge a "mi-dire," a "half-speech"
which recognizes its limit as the cause of desire
rather than the fantasy of being.   That limit is
marked with the objet a, the cause of desire, which
Lacan here defines as the "semblant" of being.   A
trace of the imaginary form in which the ego
"envelops" the object and situates it as the object
of desire, this objet a constitutes reality for the
subject, and Lacan is careful to distinguish
between this reality and the real, which he says is
inscribed only as an "impasse de la formalisation"

(p. 85). This impasse opens up between the <u>sem-blant</u>, constituted by the symbolic, and the reality that is supported by the concrete experience of human life (p. 87).

This chapter also contains Lacan's distinction between contingency and necessity, a topic he returns to throughout his later work. Contingency, he says, is "ceasing to not be written" ("<u>ce cesse de ne pas s'écrire</u>"). Necessity is "not ceasing to be written" ("<u>ne cesse pas de s'écrire</u>"). The impossible, however, is "not ceasing to not be written" ("<u>ne cesse pas de ne pas s'écrire</u>"), which is the plight of sexual relations. As a result of these formulas, Lacan notes that the apparent necessity of the phallic function actually emerges as pure contingency, the "corporeal contingency" in which the phallus "ceases to be not-written" (pp. 86-87).

In the ninth section Lacan returns to the question of knowledge. The unconscious derives not only from the fact that being thinks ("<u>que l'être pense</u>") but also from the fact that being, by thinking, experiences <u>jouissance</u>. That does not mean that being knows any more that we thought, he adds; in fact, it knows nothing at all (p. 95). Lacan claims that there is no desire to know, despite Freud's remarks about the <u>Wissentrieb</u>. The significance of the unconscious is that in addition to already knowing all there is to know, man's knowledge is perfectly limited to this insufficient <u>jouissance</u> constituted by the fact that he speaks (p. 96). Reworking Freud's famous "<u>Wo es war</u> . . . ", Lacan says that "there where the id speaks, it/the id experiences <u>jouissance</u>" ("<u>Là où ça parle, ça jouit</u>" [p. 104]). There is a hole that is called the Other, he adds, which is the Other insofar as it is the place where speech ("<u>la parole</u>") underlies truth and with truth the pact that supplements the non-existence of the sexual relation (p. 103).

Lacan goes on to refer to the wound ("<u>la béance</u>") proper to the sexuality of the speaking being, and he claims that this wound is inscribed as the very law of <u>jouissance</u> insofar as <u>jouissance</u> is the "<u>dit-mension</u>" of the body (pp. 105, 104). ("<u>Dit-mension</u>" puns on "dimension" and the said ["dit"] or spoken experience.). This chapter of the seminar frequently discusses the role of the body as a central element in baroque art, and Lacan notes the recurrent association of the suffering and pleasure of the body--its <u>jouissance</u>--with traditional representations of wisdom, knowledge, and the soul. (The soul is nothing other than the supposed identity of the body with whatever explains it, Lacan says; the soul is that which one thinks à propos the body [p. 100].) This is why Lacan agrees with those who have characterized his discourse as "baroque," (p. 102), and he traces the importance of the body to symbolic discourse all the way back to Aristotle. It was Aristotle, Lacan observes, who was intelligent enough to see that the symbolic was exactly what intelligence was concerned with, although he was not intelligent enough to realize that speech, the support of langauge, was concerned with jouissance (p. 102).

The tenth chapter of the seminar focuses on the relation between being and saying, and it proceeds through a series of reflections illustrated by the figure of the Borromean knot, which Lacan had introduced to the seminar the year before. For me, Lacan begins, being is just a fact of speech ("un fait de dit" [p. 107]). The symbolic must not be confused with being; rather, it supports only the "ex-sistance" of speech ("dire") because, Lacan says, analysis has shown that I speak without knowing it. I speak with my body without knowing it, too, and thus I always say more than I know (p. 108). That is how I arrive at the meaning of the subject in analytic discourse, he adds. That which speaks without knowing it makes me "I," subject of the verb, and that has nothing to do with being. This "I" is not a being; it is a supposition of that which speaks ("un supposé à ce qui parle").
  Such an "I" cannot "know" in the usual sense, and Lacan describes knowledge as forbidden, "inter-dit," in the sense of slipping between the cracks of speech, "inter-dit," between the lines (p. 108). This is the only truth accessible to us, he says, and he admits to not knowing how to take this truth anymore than he knows what to do with la femme, which Lacan claims is the same thing, at least for man. They are the same because the partner of the other sex always remains Other, he adds (109). Man always believes that he creates the woman, but in fact he simply puts her to work, the work of the One; that is why this Other must remain barred, as illustrated by the formula $S(\emptyset)$ (p. 118).
  The barring of the Other that Lacan describes here not only stems from the inaccessibility of the truth with which woman is associated. Lacan also explains the barring as an inevitable result of the subject's function in speech and its imaginary relation to the body. Discussing his formula "I ask you to refuse that which I offer because it is not it" ("parce que se n'est pas ça"), Lacan says that the ça here is the objet a, the missing object of desire related to demand through metonymy (p. 114). The phrase "ce n'est pas ça" means that the

desire inherent in all demands is only the request
for the _objet a_, for the object that will come to
satisfy _jouissance_. The partner of the "I" that is
the subject of speech is never recognized as the
Other, however, but is in fact experienced as that
which substitutes for the Other as the cause of
desire--i.e., as the _objet a_, which appears in
Freudian theory as the nursing-object ("_objet de la
succion_"), the object of excretion, of the gaze,
and of the voice ("_la voix_"). These "objects,"
Lacan says, are all the other "Ones" that
substituted for the Other of desire.

These remarks bear directly on Lacan's
distinction in Chapter V between the way men and
women view each other. There Lacan argued women
pursue men under the title of the signifier, but
from the point of view of the male, the missing
partner is replaced by the object _a_, which appears
in the real as the fantasm. Nevertheless, although
Lacan admits that these objects are what constitute
the world for the subject, he insists that this is
not a world of sexual relations. This world is the
work of speaking bodies ("_les corps parlants_"), and
such a world, the world full of knowledge, is only
a dream of the body insofar as it speaks. There is
no knowledgeable subject ("_sujet connaissant_"),
only subjects that are the correlates of the _objet
a_, correlates of the speech of _jouissance_ insofar
as it is the _jouissance_ of speech ("_corrélats de
parole jouissante en tant que jouissance de
parole_"). The reciprocity between the subject and
the _objet a_ is thus total (p. 114). For the
speaking being, the cause of its desire is strictly
equivalent to the division of the subject that
constitutes the world in this way, that is, as a
perfectly symmetrical mirror of the subject and its
thought. The speaking body reproduces itself there
only by accident, as it were, only through a
misunderstanding of its _jouissance_.

The tenth chapter of the seminar contains remarks
on many of the themes introduced earlier, especially regarding the association between love and
knowledge. Lacan also returns to the impossibility
of sexual relations as such, and he argues again
that such relations are impossible because the
jouissance of the Other, taken as body, is always
inadequate. That _jouissance_ is perverse on the one
side insofar as the Other is reduced to the _objet a_
and enigmatic on the other side (p. 131). Most of
Lacan's remarks, however, are directed towards the
topic of "_lalangue_," a term he introduced earlier
without explanation as what distinguishes his work
from that of the structuralists, who would reduce
language to semiology (p. 93).

It is generally stated that language serves to communicate, Lacan says, but language ("le langage") is made from lalangue, and lalangue has nothing to do with communication. Lacan claims that language is that which one tries to learn from lalangue, and he adds that if he said that language is structured the same way as the unconscious is structured, it is because language does not exist in the first place. Language is an "élucubration de savoir sur lalangue," a mere hypothesis based on the lalangue which supports it, while the unconscious is a "savoir-faire avec lalangue" (p. 127). If we can say that the unconscious is structured like a language, it is only because the effects of lalangue, some of which are already there as knowledge and some of which remain enigmatic, go far beyond all that the being who speaks is capable of enunciating.

Returning to the issue of the unconscious, Lacan describes it here as the evidence of a knowledge that escapes the speaking being (p. 126). Yet we can say nothing of the unconscious without an hypothesis, Lacan adds a few pages later, and his hypothesis is that the individual which is affected by the unconscious is the same thing as the subject of the signifier. Hence the formula "a signifier represents a subject for another signifier." But the signifier can be defined as nothing other than a difference from another signifier, and it is the introduction of that difference as such that allows us to extract from lalangue that which we call the signifier itself (p. 129).

In this sense, Lacan says, we can call the signifier the sign of the subject, a subject which exists but only for the speaking being, a being for whom being is always elsewhere ("le sujet se trouve être, et seulement pour l'être parlant, un étant dont l'être est toujours ailleurs" [130]). Knowledge of the "one" therefore cannot come from the body, he adds, but only from the signifier One, the "master-signifier," which is incarnated in lalangue as something which remains undecided among the phoneme, the word, and the phrase, not to mention thought (p. 131). Lacan concludes the seminar with this cryptic allusion to the Y a d'l'Un of last year's seminar and with a few brief remarks about love as the approach to being, "l'abord de l'être" (p. 133).

Sections VI and VII were translated and printed with a brief introduction in F370. For an extended commentary on Lacan's remarks about feminine sexuality in this seminar, see F333 and G658.

B31a. Lacan's remarks on Jakobson were translated by Louise Vasvair Fainberg as "On Jakobson," Gradiva

1, no. 2/3 (1977): 152-60.

B31b. Seminario XX--Aun. Buenos Aires: Paidos, 1981.
       177 pages.

B31c. Chapters 6 and 7 were translated by Jacqueline Rose
       as "God and the Jouissance of The Woman" and "A
       Love Letter" in F370, pp. 137-61.

B31d. [Seminar XX (Serbo-Croatian).] Ljnbl jana: Zbirka
       Analecta, 1985. 121 pages.

B31e. Chapter Six was translated into Japanese as "Kamito
       joseino kairaka," Gendai shiso 13, no. 1 (1985).

B32.   Seminar XXI (1973-74): Les non-dupes-errent.
       Unpublished.

B33.   Seminar XXII (1974-75): R.S.I. Ornicar? 2 (1975):
       87-105; 3 (1975): 95-110; 4 (1975): 91-106; 5
       (1975): 15-66. Edited by Jacques-Alain Miller.

B33a. Sessions for 10 and 17 December 1974. Ornicar?
       (1975): 87-105.

       Claims that his general topic for the year will
be connections among the real, the symbolic, and
the imaginary (R, S, and I), and observes that the
only way to designate their common measure is the
Borromean knot (p. 93). Much of these sessions--
and of the whole seminar--is devoted to topographical permutations on the simple Borromean knot
of three loops, which Lacan uses to show that the
link between the symbolic and the real hinges on
the "third dimension" where the imaginary is rooted
(p. 94).
       Lacan also describes Freud's distinctions among
inhibition, anxiety, and the symptom, and associates these three terms with the triad of the RSI,
which he diagrams on p. 99. Within that diagram,
he also situates three other terms which he
discusses throughout the seminar: meaning
("sens"), jouissance of the Other, and phallic
jouissance. Following up other implications of
this diagram, Lacan claims that his goal for the
year is to show how phallic jouissance is tied to
the production of existence (p. 102). The jouissance of the Other, Lacan says, is the key to what
he has designated as the "hole" in the real around
which the effect of existence emerges, and he adds
that it is a jouissance insofar as it concerns not
the Other of the signifier but the Other of the
body, the Other of the other sex (p. 104).

B33b. Sessions for 14 and 21 January 1975. Ornicar? 3

(1975):   95-110.

Continues his discussion of the knots, and claims
that all three "somethings" he designates as RSI
share a "consistance," a consistency that he
identifies as "la corde" from which the knots are
made (p. 98). Unlike the line, Lacan says, the
cord exists in three dimensions, a fact that
renders tangible the dilemma of the speaking being,
which is uneasily situated between two and three
dimensions. (Lacan explains that this is why he
writes the word dimension "dit-mension, mension du
dit" (p. 99).
Lacan also reminds his audience of the intimate
relation between numbers and the real--"science
counts," he says--though he insists it takes
language to convey the numbers and their meaning.
So, since the unconscious is structured like a
language, there may also be something countable,
"comptable," about the unconscious. Lacan adds a
few remarks about the suitability of the knot as a
means of addressing this aspect of the unconscious,
returns briefly to the terms diagrammed above, and
then admits that his RSI cannot be found in Freud's
work. Contrary to a prodigious number of people
from Plato to Tolstoy, Lacan observes, "Freud
n'était pas lacanien" (p. 102).
The session for 21 January focuses on several
topics derived from the diagram described above,
and from Lacan's continuing interest in the
question of femininity, which he developed at
length in B31. Lacan begins by proposing the objet
a as one of two entrées to the Other, a point based
on the fact that the subject is always only
"supposed" ("supposé"). If the subject knows
something, Lacan says, it is only that he is
himself a subject caused by an object which is not
what he knows, the objet a. This object is not the
other of connaissance; it is the Other. The fact
that the subject is caused by this "object," Lacan
adds, is notable only by "une écriture" (p. 106).
Lacan also discusses here what he calls the
"père-version" of "mi-dieu" (a demigod or literally
a "half-god"), the function of the father that is
also the function of the symptom (p. 108). The
woman's relation to the objet a, closely related to
the paternal père-version of "le juste mi-dieu,"
also involves her submitting to castration just as
much as any man, but it remains to be said just
what corresponds, for her, to "cette ex-sistence de
réel qu'est le phallus" (p. 109). After briefly
discussing several kinds of belief and love, Lacan
concludes by stating flatly "a woman is a symptom"
(p. 111).

B33c. Sessions for 11 and 18 February 1975. <u>Ornicar?</u> 4
       (1975): 91-106.

       Briefly comments on Lytton Strachey's <u>Queen
       Victoria</u> and the function of woman illustrated
       there, and says that women do not necessarily have
       to try to integrate themselves into the categories
       of man. The have a special relation to the uncon-
       scious, he claims; "<u>elles traitent ça avec une
       sauvagerie, une liberté d'aillure tout à fait
       saisissante</u>." If I had to embody the idea of
       freedom, Lacan adds, I would obviously choose a
       woman (p. 95).
       Lacan then turns to the question of a "mental
       knot" and its relation to the real, and to the link
       between meaning and the real. The effect of
       meaning required by analytic discourse is neither
       imaginary nor symbolic, he says. What will occupy
       him this year will be the task of conceiving how
       the real can be an effect of meaning (p. 96). I
       say that the effect of meaning ex-sists, Lacan
       notes, and in that, it is real (p. 98). The
       session then concludes with brief remarks on the
       function of the <u>Nom-du-Père</u>, the topic of last
       year's seminar, and Lacan says that it was under
       the function of the <u>Nom-du-Père</u> that Freud elided
       the imaginary, the symbolic, and the real (p. 99).
       Most of the second session in this issue is
       devoted to geometrical implications of the
       Borromean knots. It concludes with several remarks
       on the symptom, where Lacan insists again that his
       notion of the symptom has its origin in Marx's
       analysis of capitalism, specifically in the link
       Marx draws between capitalism and feudalism (p.
       106).

B33d. Sessions for 11 and 18 March, 8 and 15 April, and
       13 May 1975. <u>Ornicar?</u> 5 (1975-76): 15-66.

       Continues his reflections on the <u>nom-du-père</u> and
       its relation to the symbolic, imaginary, and real
       as they are joined in the Borromean knot. Lacan
       also traces the religious dimension of the <u>nom-du-
       père</u> as the Bible connects it to its most radical
       function, "naming" (English in the text, p. 21),
       and he raises the question of "order" among the
       three loops of the simple Borromean knot. Lacan
       concludes with several remarks about women, their
       relation to the real ("<u>Elles sont réelles, et même
       terriblement</u>"), and their ex-sistence as symptom
       (p. 25).
       In the next session, Lacan says that he supposes
       the knot to be the real by virtue of the fact it
       determines "ex-sistence," a certain mode of
       "<u>tourne-autour</u>" (p. 33). This association with the

real is what distinguishes the knots from models
because models always draw upon the "l'imaginaire
pur" (p. 34).   (Lacan also dwells upon his use of
color in diagramming some of the knots, a point
that comes up repeatedly throughout this seminar
but that remains somewhat obscure because the
drawings are reproduced in black and white.)
    In the last three sessions, Lacan continues to
discuss relations among the real, the symbolic, and
the imaginary through various form of the Borromean
knot, which he continues to insist is not a model
but a "support."   The knot is not reality, he says;
it is the real, and in fact the knot is what demonstrates the distinction between the two terms (p.
50).   He claims that the real emerges only through
the idea of a knot (p. 49) and is characterized by
being knotted ("se nouer").   Lacan says that the
unconscious, too, is supported by the knot, and he
goes on to identify the real with the unconscious,
arguing that the unconscious is the real in so far
as the real is "troué" (literally "holed" [p. 50]).
This connection between the real and the unconscious is peculiar to speaking beings, "le
parlêtre," because they are "incarnated" within the
symbolic and so subject to the only thing that can
make a hole in the real, i.e., the signifier.   As
the support of the hole, le trou, Lacan claims that
the knot thus cannot be imaginary, cannot be a
"representation," but in fact is what supports the
real and what links the unconscious to the symbolic
(p. 50).
    The concluding portions of the seminar raise a
number of issues, including remarks on the difference between the Jewish and the Christian
concepts of God; the structural rather than
historical sources of the incest taboo as an effect
of the naming function of the name-of-the-father
(p. 54); and the role of the number series 1-2-3 in
the formation of the group.   Elaborating on the
role of the hole in the group of three, Lacan
reflects on the various proportions inherent in the
group of three and then briefly discusses the
implications of introducing a fourth element into
the group (p. 64).   He concludes with a promise to
discuss what it might mean to situate the name-of-
the-father as a substance among the three pairs of
terms introduced at the beginning of this year's
seminar: the imagination as inhibition, the real
as anxiety, and the symbolic as symptom (p. 66).

B33e.   The session for 21 January 1975 was translated by
        Jacqueline Rose in F370, pp. 162-71.

B34.   Seminar XXIII (1975-76):   Le sinthome.   Ornicar? 6
        (1976):   3-20; 7 (1976):   3-18; 8 (1976):   6-20;

9 (1977):   32-40; 10 (1977):   5-12; 11 (1977):
2-9.   Edited by Jacques-Alain Miller.

B34a.   Sessions for 18 November and 9 December 1975.
        Ornicar? 6 (1976):   3-20.

Explains that "sinthome" is an old way of writing
"symptom," and that the change in spelling marks
the infusion of Greek into French, much as Joyce
desired for English in Ulysses. (For further
remarks on Joyce, see C95.) Lacan comments on the
myth of the fall and the role of language and the
serpent (which he designates "comme faille ou mieux
phallus"); on Portrait of the Artist as a Young
Man; and on the division between the symbol and the
symptom, the conjunction of which constitutes a
"false hole." The symptom supports one of the two
signifiers of symbolism, Lacan says, alluding to
the S_2 that replaces the prior signifier in the
signifying chain S_1 . . . S_2 (p. 19). He also
briefly remarks on his visit to the United States
and his meeting with Chomsky, and notes his surprise that Chomsky considers language an "organ."
One can understand the operation of language only
if one treats it as making a hole in the real,
Lacan says. Language is not, in itself, a message
of any kind, genetic or otherwise, but functions
simply as a hole. (For Lacan's addresses to
various groups during his visit to the United
States, see E270.)

B34b.   Sessions for 16 December 1975, 13 and 20 January
        1976: Ornicar? 7 (1976):   3-18.

Addresses objections raised by Michel Thomé and
Pierre Soury during last year's seminar regarding
his failure to recognize the importance of orientation in certain kinds of Borromean knots and the
difficulty going from three to four loops in the
models of knots he proposes. Lacan recalls the
diagram described in B33 and notes that phallic
jouissance is situated at the conjunction of the
symbolic with the real and is experienced as para-
sitical ("parasitaire") by the subject supported by
the "parlêtre."
In the sessions for January, Lacan admits to
being "embarrassé" by Joyce's work, and he returns
to it on several occasions before introducing a
paper by Joycean Jacques Aubert. Lacan's interest
in Joyce stems from what he calls the "lalangue" in
which Joyce wrote, but he also refers to Joyce as
"the symptom" and traces the link between God and
the artificer suggested in Ulysses and Portrait.
Lacan cites Robert M. Adams' Surface and Symbol as
a useful work because it calls attention to the

problem of the surface and its relation to the
symbolic that has occupied him for some time during
this seminar, and he remarks on the curious relation between the concrete, the surface, and the
body in the "parlêtre's" relation to his own body
and to the body of the other in sexual attraction.

B34c.   Sessions for 10 and 17 February 1976. Ornicar? 8
         (1976): 6-20.

   Raises the question of the role of the redeemer
in Joyce's fiction and of a faith in the true, and
briefly discusses Joyce's relation with his wife.
Lacan also claims that he was led to the idea of
the knots by the fact that the real is found within
the convolutions of the true (p. 11), and that the
Borromean knot is really a chain, "une chaînoeud"
(p. 12).
   Recalling one of his recent cases in which the
symptom was that of "paroles imposées" or "imposed
speech," Lacan points out that Joyce's daughter
suffered from the same symptom and that Joyce
defended her by claiming that she was genuinely
telepathic. Lacan claims that Joyce's defense of
his daughter ironically reflects what appears to
have been his own situation as a writer, since his
work reflects the pressure of a parole imposed upon
him and decomposing itself in his writing (p. 17).
At any rate, Lacan concludes, in the context of his
other case, Joyce's defense of his daughter appears
to be a "carence du pére."
   (At the end of the session for 17 February, Lacan
once again describes woman, une femme, as a
symptom, but here he notes that for a woman, man
must be something else, something worse than a
symptom, perhaps "un ravage.")

B34d.   Session for 16 March 1976. Ornicar? 9 (1977): 32-
         40.

   Returns to the issue of orientation in the
Borromean knots, and claims that there is something
that can be oriented in our experience but only
because the real serves as a limit, an absolute
zero. This orientation is not meaning, however,
because it excludes the sole fact of the "copulation" between the symbolic and the imaginary in
which meaning consists (pp. 33-34). (Lacan
observes that "le sense comme tel que j'ai défini
tout à l'heure de la copulation du langage, puisque
c'est de ça que je supporte l'inconscient, avec
notre propre corps" [p. 34].) In fact, Lacan adds,
the orientation of the real forecloses meaning, and
he describes the real as "toujours un bout." This
"bout," or end, is also related to death, and Lacan

claims that the death drive described by Freud <u>is</u>
the real in so far as it can only be thought as
impossible: "<u>chaque fois qu'il montre le bout de
son nez, il est impensable</u>" (pp. 37-38).

B34e.   Session for 13 April 1976. <u>Ornicar?</u> 10 (1977):   5-
        12.

Claims to have invented what is represented in
writing as "the real," and says that the real is
what holds together the imaginary and the symbolic.
Commenting on the English phrase "I have to tell,"
Lacan observes that one creates a language ("<u>une
langue</u>") as one speaks and gives it meaning, and it
must be recreated at every moment. This means that
there is no collective unconscious, Lacan adds,
only particular unconsciousnesses. He repeats his
assertion that the real has no meaning and claims
that meaning is the Other of the real (p. 9). In
response to questions, Lacan remarks that psychoanalysis is a practice but the psychoanalyst is a
symptom (p. 9); that each act of speech is a "<u>coup
de force</u>" of a particular unconsciousness; and that
the true real ("<u>le vrai réel</u>") implies the absence
of law. The real is not an order, he says; that is
what he means when he refers to "<u>un bout de réel</u>"
(p. 11).

B34f.   Session for 11 May 1976. <u>Ornicar?</u> 11 (1977):   2-9.

Claims that his "<u>noeud-bo</u>," the Borromean knot,
is a support for thought, a kind of writing that
grants a certain autonomy to "<u>la dite écriture</u>."
There is another kind of writing, Lacan admits, one
that results from what might be called a "precipi-
tation" of the signifier, and he claims that he
showed Derrida the way to study that (p. 3). The
kind of writing he is discussing, though, comes
from somewhere besides the signifier. It comes
from the "<u>trait unaire</u>," or the infinite line ("<u>la
droite infinie</u>") which appears in the Borromean
knot and which is the most simple support for the
hole ("<u>le trou</u>") that surrounds it.
There is another logic, however, beyond that of
<u>la droite infinie</u>, and Lacan designates it as "<u>une
logique de sac et de corde</u>." He claims that this
logic will help us understand how Joyce functions
as a writer. Writing is essential to Joyce's ego,
Lacan claims, and he argues that Joyce's text is
made like a Borromean knot, although that figure
never appears in Joyce's work. Joyce is
"<u>l'écrivain par excellence de l'énigme</u>," Lacan
adds, and he says that this enigma is situated in
the relation between the enunciation and the statement or <u>énoncé</u> and thus lends to the power of

writing "<u>la peine qu'on s'y arrête</u>" (p. 9).
(This session also contains several remarks on
the drives (<u>les pulsions</u>) and their relation to
language and the body. Lacan claims that man's
relation to the body is not simple because the body
has its own holes, which figure prominently in
psychoanalysis. Psychology, he remarks, is nothing
other than the confused image that we have of our
own body.)

B35.   Seminar XXIV (1976-77): <u>L'insu que sait de l'une-</u>
       <u>bévue s'aile à mourre</u>. <u>Ornicar?</u> 12/13 (1977):
       4-16; 14 (1978): 4-9; 15 (1978): 5-9; 16
       (1978): 7-13; 17/18 (1979): 7-23. Edited by
       Jacques-Alain Miller.

B35a. Sessions for 16 November and 14 December 1976.
       <u>Ornicar?</u> 12/13 (1977): 4-16.

       Begins by introducing something that goes beyond
the unconscious: the "<u>Insu-que-sait de l'une</u>
<u>bévue</u>," which may be translated roughly as
"ignorance that knows the blunder." (Lacan claims
that "<u>l'une-bévue</u>" is as good a translation of
Freud's <u>Unbewusst</u> as any other and better than
"<u>l'inconscient</u>," which is too close to "<u>l'incon-</u>
<u>science</u>." "<u>S'aile à mourre</u>" is a near homonym for
"<u>c'est l'amour</u>," as Lacan explains at the end of
the seminar.) A dream constitutes a "<u>bévue</u>" as an
<u>acte manqué</u>, Lacan says, or as a <u>trait d'esprit</u> by
virtue of the fact that it is tied to "<u>lalangue</u>."
       Lacan also promises to explore the relation
between what is often considered our "interior" and
"identification," and he describes Freud's
distinctions among three kinds of identification:
the identification with the father, which is
associated with love; a participatory identification that is designated "hysterical"; and
identification based on a single trait, which Lacan
calls the "<u>trait unaire</u>."
       In passing, Lacan further comments on the end of
analysis, which he describes here as equipping the
patient to "<u>savoir y faire avec son symptôme</u>,"
i.e., to live with his symptom. I have proposed
that the symptom can be the sexual partner, Lacan
says. In this sense, the symptom is that which one
knows, even that which one knows best--which is not
to say, he adds, that going to bed with a woman
means you know her. He concludes with a brief
commentary on several kinds of Borromean knots and
with a defense of his topological reflections on
the torus and the mathematical model of the Klein
bottle.
       The second lesson in this issue elaborates
further on several varieties of knots, most of

which employ the torus. There is no progress even
in psychoanalysis, Lacan says, because everything
keeps turning around on itself. The structure of
man and of the world is "torique," based on the
torus, and Lacan claims that even Freud realized
that the conscious and the unconscious are
supported and communicated by a "toric" world.
Lacan also observes that there are only two types
of signifiers, which are embodied in the énoncés
"same" and other," and he says that the only thing
differentiating the same from the other is the fact
that the same is the same "materially." He emphasizes the fundamental role of materiality ("le
matériel") to the signifier and claims that the
material is present to us as "corps-sistant," the
subsistence of the body, which is "consistent" (p.
10). Man always knows more than the thinks he
does, Lacan says, but the substance of this knowledge, the substance that supports it, is nothing
other than the signifier. "L'homme parle-être"
simply means that "il parle signifiant," Lacan
concludes, and in "speaking (with) the signifier"
in this way man confounds the notion of being with
his speech.

B35b.   Session for 11 January 1977. Ornicar? 14 (1978):
        4-9.

        Briefly remarks on the experience of reading some
        of his earlier work and on the material published
        in F379. Lacan also comments on several other
        topics, among them the hope that psychoanalysis
        will become a science. That is impossible, he
        claims; such a wish is only a "délire scien-
        tifique."

B35c.   Session for 18 January 1977. Ornicar? 15 (1978):
        5-9.

        Introduces the braid ("la tresse") as the
        fundamental principle of the Borromean knot and
        discusses several variations of a knot in the form
        of a ball. Lacan comments on the difficulty of
        situating the holes constituted by the knots, and
        in response to a question Lacan claims that art is
        beyond the symbolic because "l'art est un savoir-
        faire, le symbolique est au principe du faire."

B35d.   Session for 8 March 1977, "Nomina non sunt
        consequentia rerum." Ornicar? 16 (1978): 7-13,

        Comments on several topics, including the "face"
        by which the real is distinguished from that which
        is knotted to it, and the connection between the
        real and "structure." The real is defined as being

incoherent insofar as it is structured, Lacan says,
and he observes that the real does not constitute a
universe except as it is knotted to two other
functions, one of which is the living body ("le
corps vivant"). Hence the "consequence" of the
phrase used for a title of this session cannot be a
"real" consequence, and Lacan reminds his audience
that the real excludes all species of meaning. He
concludes with several controversial remarks
regarding analytic discourse, which he diagrams
differently from his customary way of
distinguishing it from the three other discourses
(see E210-211).

B35e.   Sessions for 15 March, 19 April, 10 and 17 May
        1977, "Vers un signifiant nouveau." Ornicar?
        17/18 (1979):   7-23.

Begins by defending his remarks about analytic
discourse from the preceding session and his
observation to an audience in Belgium that psychoanalysis might be an "escroquerie," a fraud.
Psychoanalysis is no more a fraud than poetry,
Lacan says, since poetry is founded on a "double
meaning" based on the relation of the signifier to
the signified. One could say that poetry is
"imaginairement symbolique" because it relies on a
violence done to the customary usage of language
("la langue"). Poetry is a pure knot, Lacan adds,
a knot that joins one word with another word (p.
11).
    Later in the seminar, Lacan goes on to distin-
guish among the "réellement symbolique," the
symbolic that is included in the real and that is
called a lie; the "symboliquement réel," which is
anxiety; and the "symboliquement imaginaire," which
is geometry. The symptom is real, Lacan observes,
and he claims that it is the only thing that is
truly real, which is to say that it conserves a
meaning in the real. "C'est bien pour cette raison
que le psychanalyste peut, s'il a de la chance,
intervenir symboliquement pour le dissoudre dans le
réel" (p. 9).
    During the first session, Lacan also remarks that
sexual relations, "le rapport sexuel," do not exist
except in the form of incest or as murder. That is
what the myth of Oedipus means: the only person
you want to sleep with is your mother, and one
kills the father. But Lacan claims that what gives
the myth its meaning is the fact that Oedipus kills
someone he does not know and sleeps with someone
whom he does not recognize as his mother (p. 9).
    The second session in this issue focuses on
psychoanalytic discourse and the place of the true.
The analysand thinks he speaks the truth, Lacan

says, but the analyst knows that he speaks only
beside the truth; what he imagines as true is what
Freud designated as the traumatic kernel. Lacan
asks if psychoanalysis is not thus an "<u>autisme à
deux</u>." Lacan also notes that analysands always
speak of their parents, a point related to the fact
that it is their parents that teach them to speak.
The session continues with several remarks on the
"contamination" of discourse by sleep and puns made
by the analysand. Lacan then returns to the topic
of poetry and concludes that writing cannot be the
support of poetry since poetry is the resonance of
the body, "<u>la résonance du corps</u>," and he suggests
that we turn to Chinese writing to find out what
poetry is.
   In the third session, Lacan briefly comments on
the theory of undecidability proposed by Godel and
observes that it holds true on the most mental of
all planes, that of the "countable." Freud identified the unconscious as mental, Lacan says,
though nobody knows why, and he says that the
mental is "<u>tissé</u>" with words, among which "<u>bévues</u>,"
mistakes, are always possible. Everything that is
mental, he adds, I write under the name of symptom,
that is to say, a sign. Lacan goes on to argue
that negation itself is a sign and is the principle
of telling the truth as well (p. 17).
   The rest of the session describes the problematic
status of knowing (<u>savoir</u>) in analysis and the
notion of the Other as the <u>sujet supposé savoir</u>.
Lacan also claims that there is only the One,
nothing of the Other, and that the One "<u>dialogue
tout seul</u>," dialogues alone, because it always
receives its own message under an inverted form.
That is what "knows," Lacan says, not some subject
possessed with the supposed knowledge. He links
this notion of the One with what he calls the
sentiment of hatred, but he also says that this
hatred is parent to love, the love inscribed
obliquely in the title of this seminar, "<u>l'Insu-
que-sait de l'une bévue, c'est l'amour</u>" (p. 18).
Nothing is more difficult to grasp than this trait
of a <u>bévue</u>, Lacan adds, but it is crucial because
consciousness has no other support than what is
permitted by these blunders.
   The last session in this issue, titled "<u>Un
signifiant nouveau</u>," begins with several observations on Julia Kristeva's book <u>Polylogue</u> and then
moves on to the question of why we cannot invent a
new signifier. Our signifiers are always received
by us, Lacan says, and we never invent new ones
despite our efforts in puns such as "<u>une bévue</u>" for
<u>Unbewusst</u>. Lacking a metalanguage that would make
this invention possible, Lacan claims that such a
signifier, which would come into being lacking all

meaning, could only come from the real--and the
real is "that which never ceases being not
written."

B36.   Seminar XXV (1977-78): Le moment de conclure.
        Unpublished except as noted below.

B36a.   "Une pratique de bavardage" (15 November 1977).
        Ornicar? 19 (1979): 5-9. Edited by Jacques-
        Alain Miller.

        Comments generally on psychoanalysis, sex, and a
        number of other topics raised in preceding
        seminars. Lacan begins by announcing that
        psychoanalysis is not a science but a practice, a
        "pratique bavardage" ("babbling practice") that
        puts speech on the rank of slobbering or sput-
        tering, though he admits that this splashing around
        has its consequences. Analysis does say something,
        Lacan adds, and "to say" or "to tell" implies time.
        He goes on to observe that the absence of time is
        only something that one dreams, a dream that
        consists in imagining that one is awakening. One
        passes his time dreaming, and the unconscious is
        derived precisely from the hypothesis that one does
        not dream only when one is asleep. (Lacan also
        notes, however, that what we call reasonable, "la
        raisonable" is a fantasm, and a fantasm is not a
        dream but an aspiration [p. 5]).
        Lacan remarks further on the role of saying
        ("dire") and words. An idea has a body, he says;
        it is the word that represents it, and this word
        has the curious property of making the thing ("il
        fait la chose"). Noting that "I love to équivo-
        quer" and to write, Lacan claims that using writing
        to "équivoquer" can be useful because the
        definition of analysis is just this:
        "l'équivoque." ("Equivoquer" might be translated
        here "equivocate" or "to make ambiguous.") Sex,
        too, is "un dire," but not a relation. Because of
        the existence of the signifier, the ensemble (set,
        but also more generally "group") that could
        constitute the sexual relation is empty, an
        "ensemble vide," and it is this notion of an empty
        set that is most appropriate to sexual relations.
        Emphasizing the importance of speech in analysis,
        Lacan goes on to claim that the psychoanalyst is
        "un rhéteur," a rhetorician who "rhetoricizes" to
        equivocate. One tries to tell the truth, Lacan
        remarks, but that is not easy since the truth is
        associated with ("a affaire avec") the real, and
        the real is doubled by the symbolic. (A few lines
        later Lacan comments that it is just the "inadé-
        quation" of words to things that analysts are
        concerned with.) Furthermore, Lacan says, one can

only speak of one language ("_une langue_") in
another language; there is no metalanguage because
"_le langage_" does not exist.
   The rest of the seminar deals with several other
topics including enigmatic remarks about "_un
signifiant nouveau_" that was introduced in the
seminar of last year. Here Lacan says that the
ego, consciousness, could identify with this new
signifier, but he then says that the only property
of the signifier he has identified as S_1 is that it
relates to S_2, and the subject is divided between
them. Consequently, one cannot say that the
subject is represented by just one of the two
signifiers. Lacan also claims that life is comic,
not tragic, and says he cannot imagine why Freud
used a tragedy, _Oedipus_, to designate the link
among the symbolic, the imaginary, and the real.

B37.   Seminar XXVI (1978-79):   _Le topologie et le temps_.
       Unpublished.

B38.   Seminar XXVII (1980):   _Dissolution_. _Ornicar?_ 20/21
       (1980):   9-20; 22/23 (1981):   7-14.

       Consists of letters and brief, informal remarks,
       some of which were originally published in _Le monde_
       and others in the internal newsletter of La Cause
       freudienne, as noted below.

B38a. "Lettre de dissolution."   5 January 1980. _Le
       monde_, 9 January 1980. Reprinted _Ornicar?_ 20/21
       (1980):   9-10.

       Says that there is a problem with the Ecole
       freudienne de Paris and that the solution is the
       dis-solution of the whole Ecole. Lacan claims that
       his decision is motivated by a desire to control
       deviations from the original praxis opened by Freud
       and instituted under the name of psychoanalysis.
       Also reprinted in A9, pp. 29-30. Translated by
       Jeffrey Mehlman in _October_ 40 (1987):   128-30 (see
       A11).

B38b. "L'autre manque."   15 January 1980. _Le monde_, 26
       January 1980. This is the second session of
       Seminar XXVII but was originally published
       separately in _Le monde_ accompanied by E288.
       Reprinted in _Ornicar?_ 20/21 (1980):   11-12.

       Comments on the difference between the real
       (which can be counted) and a totalized whole, "un
       univers," which does not exist; and observes that
       "'_la' femme_," "the" woman, is not deprived of
       phallic _jouissance_ nor is there any trace of an
       "antiphallic" nature in the unconscious. Most of

this session, however, is devoted to remarks about
the dissolution of the Ecole freudienne de Paris
and about the desire of people to follow him in a
new group. There seem to be people who need me,
Lacan says, but he asks who believes that enough to
put it in writing. If I should ever leave you, he
remarks, "say that it is in order to be the Other
at last."
     Also reprinted in A9, pp. 31-32. Translated by
Jeffrey Mehlman in October 40 (1987): 131-33 (see
A11).

B38c. "D'écolage." 11 March 1980. Ornicar? 20/21
       (1980): 14-16.

       Demands a work of mourning from those who would
       follow him "pour la Cause freudienne," and claims
       that this phrase denotes not a School but a field,
       a "champ" where each will have the chance to
       demonstrate the knowledge his experience has made
       available to him. Lacan sketches the principles
       behind the formation of cartels and elaborates on
       his remark during the preceding seminar about the
       possibility of women experiencing phallic
       jouissance. This does not mean that I think they
       are men, as some have imputed to me, Lacan says,
       and he goes on to explain briefly what "la satis-
       faction véritable--phallique" might mean for women.
       It is a "Satisfaction qui se situe de leur ventre.
       Mais comme répondant à la parole de l'homme," Lacan
       says, which means roughly a satisfaction situated
       in their womb but answering to the speech/word of
       man (p. 16). This item also contains the text of
       E290.
       Reprinted in A9, pp. 34-36.

B38d. "Monsieur A." 18 March 1980. Ornicar? 20/21
       (1980): 17-20.

       Rejects the imputation of a surrealism that is
       far from his tastes, and also proclaims himself to
       be against philosophy as well. Lacan responds to
       several written questions submitted to him since
       the last session, and he describes the various
       paraphernalia that constitute the Cause freudienne:
       a box of his letters, a newsletter, a forum, and
       the publication of the records.
       Reprinted in A9, pp. 37-38.

B38e. "Lumière!" 15 April 1980. Delenda [?] (Described
       in Ornicar? as having already appeared in Delenda
       and listed by Dor as published in no. 4, pp. 1-4,
       though it does not appear there.) Reprinted in
       Ornicar? 22/23 (1981): 7-10.

In response to a letter from Françoise Dolto,
denies that he ever identified himself with the
Ecole freudienne, and in response to another letter
denies that he believes himself to be infallible.
I do not take myself for the <u>sujet du savoir</u>, Lacan
says, and the proof of that is the fact that I
invented the <u>sujet supposé savoir</u>.

B38f.   "Le malentendu."   10 June 1980.   <u>Courrier de la</u>
        <u>Cause freudienne</u> (July 1980).   Reprinted in
        <u>Ornicar?</u> 22/23 (1980):   11-14.

Announces his plans to go to Venezuela to see how
his writings have gotten along without him (see
C98), and claims he will return because he has his
practice in Paris, along with the seminar, which
complements it.   Lacan claims never to have said
that the word (<u>la verbe</u>, associated with the <u>verbum</u>
of "Let there be light!" discussed in the last
session) is creative, precisely because he said
that the word is unconscious and hence
"<u>malentendu</u>," misunderstood.   Lacan claims that the
mission of psychoanalysis is to exploit this
misunderstanding with a revelation which is the
fantasm.   Man is born misunderstood, he adds, and
the body appears in the real ("<u>fait apparition dans</u>
<u>le réel</u>") only as misunderstanding.
     Translated in the <u>Papers of the Freudian School</u>
<u>of Melbourne</u> (1980):   97-101.

B**.   Seminar at Caracas (1980).   See C98.

B**.   "Comptes rendus d'enseignement 1964-1968."
        <u>Ornicar?</u> 29 (1984):   7-25.

Reprints Lacan's abstracts for Seminars XI
(1964)-XV (1967-68) from the <u>Annuaire de l'Ecole</u>
<u>pratique des hautes études</u>.   See B22-B26.

Section C

Primary Works: Essays

C39.   "Structure des psychoses paranoïaques."   Le semaine
       des hôpitaux de Paris 14 (7 July 1931):   437-45.

       Claims that paranoia is often confused with a
       notion of deviant character, and proposes instead to
       define paranoia phenomenologically in terms of the
       structure of delusional states (états délirants).
       Lacan describes those states and more briefly traces
       the genesis and treatment of paranoiac psychosis as
       described in A1.

C40.   With Lévy-Valensi, J., and Pierre Migault.   "Ecrits
       'Inspirés':   Schizographie."   Texte intégral de la
       communication à Société médico-psychologique, 12
       November 1931.   Annales médico-psychologiques 2,
       no. 5 (1931):   508-22.

       Argues that sometimes psycho-pathological mech-
       anisms are evident only in written language, not
       oral speech, and offers examples from the case of
       "Marcelle C."   The authors observe that the pa-
       tient's regular handwriting and the rapid, uninter-
       rupted composition of her letters support her claim
       that she is simply expressing words and phrases that
       are already formulated and "inspired" in her by some
       external force.   Although the letters are always
       addressed to a specific person and make special
       pleas for her cause, the patient claims to know no
       more about the meaning of their apparently inco-
       herent language than any other reader.
       The authors speculate that the patient's sense of
       being inspired and the agitated mental state which
       accompanies the composition of the letters may stem
       from the rhetorical situation of pleading her case
       before an auditor, and they point out that the
       distortions of language in the letters resemble the
       systematic and/or deliberate deformation of normal
       syntax, semantics and grammar characteristic of

poetic discourse and especially surrealism. A
detailed linguistic analysis of some of the letters
shows that the long word chains, neologisms, and odd
associations can be attributed to rhythmic patterns
and image clusters that are generated by the
language itself but that would be suppressed as
irrelevant or unreal in ordinary discourse.

On the origin of the term "schizographie" used to
denominate the disjunction between an individual's
oral and written discourse, see E124. For a subsequent elaboration of the philosophical implications
behind the patient's perception of her writing and
thoughts as coming from somewhere else, see C49,
where Lacan connects it to his concept of "méconnaissance." For a more extended discussion of
verbal distortions as a form of communication
between the patient and the doctor, see C49, pp.
167-8.

Reprinted in A1a, pp. 365-82. Translated into
Japanese as "'fukikomareta' shuki" in A7.

C41. "Le problème du style et la conception psychiatrique
      des formes paranoïaques de l'expérience." Le
      minotaure 1 (1933): 68-9.

Argues that paranoiac forms of experience depend
on a perception of the world that imbues objects
with a "personal significance" that is quite different from the "affective neutrality" of objects in
rational consciousness, and claims that this alternative mode of perception causes the persecutory
delusions typical of paranoia. Lacan considers this
perception and the symbolic forms in which it is
expressed (delusions, etc.) as an "original syntax"
that represents actual conflicts and tensions
present in the human community, and this connection
with ordinary social relations explains the curious
attraction that these expressions (such as
Rousseau's work) have always held for the societies
in which they appear.

These points echo claims made earlier in A1 and
recall Lacan's emphasis there on the social dimension of paranoiac delusion and on the need to
analyze the symbolic character of delusory expressions. In this essay, Lacan emphasizes two other
implications of his argument that are especially
appropriate for the audience of the surrealist art
journal Le minotaure:

(1) He notes the inevitable complicity between
traditional psychiatric categories and "the laws
proper to the development of the whole ideological
superstructure," and he proposes a more phenomenological psychology that will focus instead on the
local relations that constitute the patient's place
in the immediate social context of his or her life.

(2) He claims that one of the central representative strategies used by paranoiacs in their
writing is the "iterative identification of the
object" (i.e., the tendency to substitute several
objects for the same original or "true" object), and
he says that this tendency is fundamental to all
poetic creation and constitutes one of the "conditions of typification" that create style.
Consequently, an understanding of the original
syntax of paranoia offers an indispensible introduction to the symbolic value of art and especially
to the problems of artistic style, which will remain
impenetrable to any analysis not freed from a naive
realism of the object.

For Lacan's earlier work on the linguistic
analysis of writing by paranoiacs, see C40 and Part
II, Chapter I of A1. C41 is reprinted with C40 and
C42 in A1a, pp. 383-88. Translated in Japanese as
"Yoshikino mondai" in A7.

C42. "Motifs du crime paranoïaque: le crime des soeurs
      Papin." Le minotaure 3/4 (1933): 25-28.

Recounts the brutal murders committed by Christine
and Léa Papin, two sisters who lived as domestic
servants in the house of a provincial soliciter.
One night, they attacked the solicitor's wife and
daughter, mutilated their faces, and gouged out
their eyes. The Papins then slashed the thighs and
buttocks of one of the women and smeared the blood
all over the genitals of the other. After their
frenzy abated, the sisters washed off the hammer,
carving knife, and other weapons used in the attack
and went to bed together, as usual.

The murders created a sensation in the newspapers,
and on the basis of those reports Lacan diagnoses
the case as another example of the délires-à-deux
such as those he presents in E122. Noting Christine's belief that in another life she could be her
sister's husband, Lacan claims that that fantasy
suggests an unconscious homosexual attraction
between the two women. He attributes the murderous
impulse to a narcissistic fixation similar to the
one he discussed in his thesis (A1), in which the
ambivalence of the narcissistic bond manifests
itself in persecutory delusions. Ordinarily, Lacan
says, that ambivalence is directed towards the
actual other with which the ego identifies, but in
this case the sisters were so close, and so isolated, that neither of them could serve as an
"other." Consequently, Lacan argues that the
affective ambivalence of the bond was transferred to
the mother and daughter in the same way that Aimée
transferred her own "amorous hatred" for her sister
onto a succession of people (see A1).

Lacan derives several general observations from this case:

(1) He emphasizes the "primordial" influence of social relations in the formation of the personality and claims that the aggressive drive (pulsion) is "imprinted" with a social relativity manifest in the moral logic that structures delusions of vengeance and self-punishment. He accounts for the social and ethical character of the delusions by citing Freud's analysis of the origin of the social impulse in the fraternal conflict that gives way to a certain type of homosexuality in the development of the child.

(2) He observes the symbolic character of the murders, which realized certain metaphorical expressions of vengeance such as "I'll tear your eyes out," and he argues that the act itself cannot exactly be considered "real." Instead, the sisters had attacked images of themselves, literally representations of an ideal self whose attractive power was experienced in the inverse form of hatred.

(3) He describes the Papins' act as an effort to resolve the "human enigma of sex," which is his interpretation of Christine's remarks during their trial that they had searched their victims' wounds for "the mystery of life." Comparing the mutilation of the victim's eyes to a bacchant castration, Lacan claims that the strange declarations of such tortured women reveal the madness that their enchained consciousnesses can build up around "the enigma of the phallus and of feminine castration."

Reprinted in A1a, pp. 389-98, and in Obliques 2 (1972): 100-63. For a dossier of photographs and other materials related to the trial of the Papin sisters, see K1179. Translated into Japanese as "Paranoia scihanzaino doki" in A7.

C43.   "Au delà du 'Principe de réalité.'" Evolution psychiatrique 3 (1936): 67-86.

Condemns associationist psychology because it dismisses too much psychic experience as "illusion," and claims that Freudian psychoanalysis has revolutionized our understanding of such phenomena through its law of free association.

Lacan's critique of associationist psychology focuses on the transcendental character of the category of "truth" by which it distinguishes among various psychic phenomena. Unlike the category of the "real," which functions in most contemporary sciences, Lacan says that "truth" is a value-laden term inherited from the metaphysical assumptions of scholastic psychology and has nothing to do with scientific knowledge of any kind. The free association introduced by Freud as the foundation of the analytic experience, however, operates according to

the rules of non-omission and non-systematization
and so valorizes all of the subject's experiences by
recognizing the "proper reality of the psychic
reactions."

This recognition takes place within the analytic
experience, and Lacan devotes most of the essay to a
phenomenological description of that experience and
the "specific reality of inter-human relations" that
emerges within it. Psychology must define its
proper object and its method of analysis in that
reality, Lacan claims, and he concludes by describing the function of two "relativistic" (as
opposed to "subjective") concepts associated with
this object and method: the image, and the complex.

Lacan's account of the analytic experience
explains how the image emerges as an object of
psychoanalytic knowledge within the discourse of the
subject. "The given of this experience is first of
all language," Lacan says, and the primary characteristic of that language is that it "signifies
for someone" (A2, p. 82). This is not to say that
there is a single meaning to be discovered in the
subject's words; instead the analyst must refuse to
"hear" what the subject thinks he is saying in order
to discover "the subject's intention as a certain
tension of the social relation." That intention may
be punitive, propitiatory, demanding, or purely
aggressive. It will, however, inevitably be
expressed, though unconsciously; and it will be
conceived (conçué) though denied by the subject.
Thus language, "being approached by its function of
social expression, reveals at the same time its
significative unity in the intention, and its
constitutive ambiguity as subjective expression,
confessing against thought, lying with it" (p. 83).

In an ordinary dialogue, the subject would suspend
his discourse when he failed to get a response from
his partner, but Lacan claims that in analysis the
analyst's persistent refusal to respond in any way
leads the subject to pursue his monologue by
addressing himself to some other imaginary listener.
The analyst's refusal to respond can therefore force
the subject to recognize the image that he has
substituted for the analyst, and Lacan defines
therapeutic action essentially as this "double
movement" by which the image first emerges as the
"real" listener in the analyst's silence only to be
progressively "disassimilated from the real" (see
pp. 83-85).

The emergence of the image in this manner demonstrates its importance as a pattern for the subject's development and for his "intuition" of the
world around him. Lacan claims that the image first
serves that function in the identifications by which

the subject emerges from an undifferentiated state
of sensation into the world of social relations.
The earliest and most important identifications are
those involving the subject's parents, which
determine the particular form of his relations with
other humans, "otherwise called his personality" (p.
89). The specific nature of those parental identifications is determined by the actual situations in
existence at the time the identifications are
formed, Lacan says. The "constellation" of
behavioral traits informed by these identifications
is called a "complex," and Lacan claims that it is
through the complex that "the images which inform
the broadest unities of behavior are established in
the psyche [le psychisme]" (p. 90).
   In addition to describing these phenomenological
attributes of what he calls "freudisme," Lacan also
notes the importance of Freud's metaphyschological
critique and especially his notion of the libido.
Although Lacan largely dismisses the "substantialist
hypothesis" of the libido as irrelevant to psychology, he praises Freud's "energetic concept" of
the libido as "the symbolic notation of the equiv-
alence among the dynamisms that the images invest in
behavior" (p. 91). Lacan also dismisses the possibility of truly "objective" knowledge in psychology (or in any science) and defines the structure of analytic knowledge in the strictly rela-
tivist terms of social interaction: the analytic
experience, he says, must be described as a "constant interaction between the observer and the
object."
   Lacan expanded these remarks on the complex, on
the image or the "imago," and on the importance of
familial identifications in C45 and C46. His
interest in the importance of these identifications
to the development of the personality alludes to his
theory of the mirror stage, which was first articulated in C44 and later expanded in C45 and especially in C53. For his discussion of the reality
principle much later in his career, see C92.
   Reprinted in A2, pp. 73-92.

C44.   "Le stade de miroir: théorie d'un moment struc-
       turant et génétique de la constitution de la
       réalité, conçu en relation avec l'expérience et la
       doctrine psychanalytique." Fourteenth Congrès
       psychanalytique international, Marienbad, 3 August
       1936. Unpublished. Cited as "The Looking-glass
       Phase" in a summary of the conference printed in
       The International Journal of Psycho-Analysis 18,
       part I (1937):   78.

C45.   "Le complexe, facteur concret de la psychologie
       familiale." Encyclopédie française VIII: La vie

mentale. Edited by Henri Wallon. Paris:
Larousse, Société de gestion de l'Encyclopédie
française, 1938. Pp. 8.40.5-8.40.16.

Argues that the human family must be understood at
"the original order of reality where social relations are constituted," and that that reality is
based on culturally conditioned "complexes" rather
than on biological instincts. Lacan distinguishes
among three different types of complexes:
  (1) "le complexe de sevrage," which is associated
with weaning but generalized by Lacan to cover the
anxiety of any separation, including most importantly that of birth itself.
  (2) "le complexe de l'intrusion," which is formed
in the "mirror stage" (le stade du miroir) anywhere
from six to eighteen months of age and accounts for
the jealousy inherent in the original perception of
the "imago of the other." This "other" is usually a
brother or sister with whom the child identifies as
a rival and a twin.
  (3) the Oedipal complex, which occurs around four
years of age and involves a fantasy of castration,
the sublimation of reality, and the repression of
sexuality, all of which help situate the individual
within the social order.
  Lacan defines the complex as a specific form of
reality that was objectified at a given stage of
psychic development, and the function of the complex
is to repeat this organization of reality in the
subject's subsequent experience. The complex thus
organizes one's relations to objects through a
dialectical process that constantly tests affective
forms of psychic organization against the "obstacle
of the real" ("au choc du réel"), and Lacan claims
that the "subversion of all instinctive fixities"
that results from this dialectical process is the
source of culture and the distinctive mark of the
human order (p. 8.40.5).
  Lacan notes his debt to Freud's definition of the
complex as an essentially unconscious structure of
interpersonal relations based upon the representation of the "imago," i.e., an imaginary set of
attributes (affective as well as visual) that
constitutes the subject's view of another person.
(For the earliest use of this concept in psychoanalysis see Jung's Psychology of the Unconscious
[1911].) Lacan departs from Freud, however, by
insisting that the subject also is conscious of what
the complex represents as reality, and by insisting
that the instincts must be understood in the light
of the complex instead of treating the complex as a
product of the instincts. (The distinction between
this "reality," organized and represented in the
form of the complex, and "the real," invoked here

only as an obstacle to the subject's desire, becomes
an increasingly important theme in Lacan's work,
though the distinction is only implicit here despite
Lacan's consistent separation of the two words.)

The first section of this essay is devoted to le
complexe du sevrage. Lacan claims that the separation (or weaning) complex is the most primitive
complex in the development of the psyche, and he
notes that even here the cultural determination of
psychic organization is apparent, since the time and
methods of weaning vary widely from culture to
culture. Lacan agrees with Freud that weaning
leaves in the human psyche a permanent trace of the
biological relation to the mother that it interrupts, but he observes that this physical crisis
(crise vitale) is doubled by a psychic crisis in
which the physical tension of the situation resolves
itself in mental intention. This produces the
earliest form of the dialectical structure that
determines our sense of otherness, i.e., of the
autonomy of objects and/or other people.

Lacan also claims that the trauma of weaning is
only the psychic expression of the even earlier
trauma of birth, which possesses a special intensity
in human infants because their "prematuration"
leaves them insufficiently adapted to extra-uterine
life relative to other new-born animals. Thus,
Lacan says, "anxiety is born with life," and the
maternal breast takes on a dominant but highly
ambivalent role as the first imago of this separation, marking the loss of unity as well as the
possibility of retrieving it.

Most of Lacan's remarks about the separation
complex and its origin in birth follow Freud's own
argument proposed first in a footnote to the second
edition of The Interpretation of Dreams (1909), then
near the end of The Ego and the Id (1923), and at
greatest length in Inhibitions, Symptoms, and
Anxiety (1926), where Freud also raises the issue of
prematuration. See also Otto Rank's The Trauma of
Birth (1924). While generally following the
arguments proposed by Freud, Lacan directly criticizes Freud's effort to establish the "appetite for
death" as a biological function and claims that it,
too, can be understood instead as a response to "the
congenital insufficiency of those [biological]
functions"--that is, as a complex rather than an
instinct. Thus death, like motherhood ("la mere et
la mort") functions as an imago of separation which
reveals an underlying "nostalgia for the Whole" (du
Tout) that is expressed in forms as various as
family affection, the "metaphysical mirage of
universal harmony," utopian social visions, and
obsessions with lost paradises.

The second section of the essay is devoted to le

complexe de l'intrusion, which Lacan associates with
the mirror stage. (Lacan first used the term
"mirror stage" or sometimes "mirror phase" in a
paper read in 1936 [see C44], and a more extended
treatment of the concept appeared ten years later as
C53.) In this complex the subject recognizes
himself as such for the first time, and it usually
begins when the infant sees his "semblables"--
usually his siblings--participating with him in
domestic relations. Infantile jealousy is the most
obvious expression of this complex, which Lacan
claims comes to serve as the "genesis of sociability
and, hence, of consciousness [connaissance, which
might also be translated "knowledge" here] itself
insofar as it can be considered human" (p. 8.40.8).

Lacan's main point is that this jealousy represents not so much a physical rivalry as a mental
identification between the infant and a "semblable"
who is perceived here for the first time as an
"other" self. The "imago" of the other that results
from this identification is linked to the child's
emergent sense of the structure of his or her own
body, and the child's relation to this imago/other
can be characterized as "homosexual" in the psychoanalytic sense; it combines both a pure identification that fuses the self with the other and a
"love" that determines the other as an "object"
apart from the self. The aggressive, sado-masochistic component of the homosexual bond that Freud
identified thus can be considered secondary to the
identification of the self with the other, which is
the object of the ambivalence of the affective bond.
The infant's recognition of a coherent body-image
in his reflection is a crucial means of overcoming
the sense of physical and psychical fragmentation
that emerges in the separation complex. Lacan notes
that the unity resulting from this identification
with an other is purely imaginary, however, and
introduces a "temporary intrusion of a tendency
towards alienation [tendance étrangère]" into the
"specular satisfaction" of the imaginary identification. The ego is thus formed out of a paradoxical
combination of identification and alienation, and
Lacan claims that "the ego constitutes itself at the
same time as the other in the drama of jealousy" (p.
8.40.10). (Lacan uses the term "l'autrui" here,
which literally means "the others," but it takes on
the specialized sense of "l'autre," "the other,"
that he later develops at length. This special
usage is signaled by Lacan's use of the article with
the noun, which is used familiarly by itself as
"autrui" [see G800]. Similarly, his emphasis on
the"imaginary" quality of the specular identification in the mirror stage presages the more complex

use of that term in his later work.)

The third section of the essay is devoted to the Oedipal complex. As the subject works through the mirror stage and moves toward the Oedipal stage that usually occurs about three years later, Lacan claims that a "third object" is introduced that substitutes "the concurrence of a triangular situation" for the specular ambiguity and affective confusion endemic to the imaginary identification between the self and the other. In this triangular situation, the maternal object is replaced by a "communicable" object which is recognized within a social context, and an entirely new order of reality emerges.

Lacan's account of the choice between the maternal and the social objects is based on Freud's description of the "triangular character" of the Oedipal complex in Chapter III of The Ego and the Id. Before reaching the Oedipal stage, Freud says, the young boy develops an "object-cathexis" for his mother and simply identifies with his father. As the boy's sexual wishes for his mother become more intense, the father is perceived as an obstacle to them, and the boy's relation to the father becomes more ambivalent. This tension progresses until the boy has to give up the early object-cathexis of the mother and make a choice that Lacan describes as "either an identification with his mother or an intensification of his identification with his father."

Lacan emphasizes the consequences of this choice for the subject's perception of reality, but this emphasis is entirely consonant with Freud's own concerns, as is evident from the description of "reality testing" as one of the major institutions of the ego (see especially Chapter II of The Ego and the Id, "A Metaphyschological Supplement to the Theory of Dreams" [1917], and "An Outline of Psycho-Analysis" [1940].) Lacan goes on to claim, however, that the permanence and substantiality of the object is based on its "socialization," which differs significantly from the more positivistic attitude usually found in Freud. That claim also accentuates the distinction Lacan makes between the real and what might be called the "subjective" sense of reality that is constituted in and through the affective bonds described above, and it attributes those bonds more to the social and cultural contexts in which they occur than to the sexuality that Freud described as their basis (see below).

Lacan's analysis of the Oedipal situation closely follows Freud, except on two central points:

(1) Lacan puts an extraordinary emphasis on the ambivalence of the child's relation to the parent of the same sex, which consists in the paradoxical union of identification and aggression charac-

teristic of the mirror stage. Lacan sees this
ambivalence resolving itself in two separate
formations: the aggression takes the form of sexual
repression associated with the super-ego; and the
identification sublimates the parental image as a
representative ideal, the ego-ideal. (Freud usually
blurs distinctions between these two terms, especially in The Ego and the Id, which seems to be
Lacan's principal reference for this essay. But see
Freud's effort to keep the terms separate in Group
Psychology and the Analysis of the Ego [1921] and
New Introductory Lectures on Psycho-Analysis
[1933].)
    (2) Lacan's analysis of the repressive function
focuses on the castration complex and departs
radically from Freud by insisting on the imaginary
basis of the complex rather than on any real source
of danger understood either biologically or historically. Lacan observes that the repression of
sexuality associated with the mastery of the Oedipal
complex derives from the difference between the pre-
Oedipal, imaginary identification of the son with
the mother and the "double affective movement" that
links the son to the father. According to Freud's
account of the Oedipal complex, that bond of son
with father is characterized by the son's resentment
of the father as a sexual rival for the mother, and
by the son's equally intense fear that the father
feels the same aggressive resentment toward him as a
rival.
    What Lacan objects to in this account is Freud's
insistence on the real basis for the son's fear,
which is derived from Freud's assumptions about the
biological superiority of adult males in primitive
society and from the hypothetical premise of a
primal murder described in Totem and Taboo. Citing
several sources of objections to Freud's hypothesis,
including the difficulty Freud has in accounting for
the presence of "castration" anxiety in young girls,
Lacan proposes that the fantasy of castration,
rather than deriving from any real threat, is "in
effect preceded by a whole series of fantasies about
the fragmentation of the body [morcellement du
corps]" that are interesting for "the evident
irreality of their structure" (pp. 8.40.13-14).
These fantasies are not related to any threat to a
real body, Lacan says, but to "a heteroclitic
mannequin, a baroque puppet" that must be recognized
as the narcissistic object described above, and to
the defensive values the subject gives these forms
against "the anxiety of vital dismemberment stemming
from its prematuration" (p. 8.40.14).
    As a corollary to his revision of Freud's account
of the Oedipal threat, Lacan claims that the fantasy
of castration does not depend on a threat to any

real organ nor does it depend on the sex of the
child.   Rather, Lacan claims that the castration
anxiety endemic to the Oedipal complex derives from
the earlier separation complex and represents the
narcissistic ego's defense against threats to its
imaginary coherence.   Lacan denies that Oedipal
tensions are brought on by a sudden irruption of
genital desire and argues instead that they stem
from the object that "reactualizes" the separation
complex: the mother.   Thus Lacan concludes that the
genesis of repression must be situated even earlier
than the Oedipal complex and that we must recognize
what he calls "the maternal origin of the archaic
super-ego."   (For Freud's account of castration
anxiety as a fear of separation from the mother, see
Chapter VIII of Inhibitions, Symptoms and Anxiety
[1926]).
     After his analysis of the repressive plane of the
Oedipal complex, Lacan turns to the second plane,
the sublimation of reality.   Assuming as his
starting point the identification of the subject
with the parent of the opposite sex, Lacan recalls
the paradoxical roles of the parental imago: it
inhibits the sexual function, but only unconsciously
as the super-ego; and it preserves that function,
but only under the guise of a "misperception"
("méconnaissance") embodied in the ego-ideal.   His
main point here is that the object of identification
in the Oedipal situation is not the object of
desire, but that which opposes desire in the Oedipal
triangle.   This observation leads Lacan to claim
that sublimation occurs when the mimetic identification with the parent has become "propitiatory"
("propitiatoire").   "The object of sado-masochistic
participation is disengaged from the subject [and]
takes its distance from him in the new ambiguity of
fear and love.   But, in this step towards reality,
the primitive object of desire appears lost.   This
fact defines for us the originality of Oedipal
identification: it appears to indicate to us that,
in the Oedipal complex, it is not the moment of
desire that erects the object in its new reality,
but that of the narcissistic defense of the subject"
(p. 8.40.14).
     Lacan's account of the Oedipal stage has specific
implications for the differences between the experiences of boys and girls at this moment.   For both
sexes, the mother (or the maternal breast) is the
first object towards which the subject is directed.
For boys, the mother is also the object of Oedipal
desire, which simplifies the mental organization of
the subject.   However, the Oedipal desire for the
mother also provides a singular occasion for the
reactivization of tendencies associated with the
separation complex.   These fundamentally narcis-

sistic tendencies oppose the attitude of exterior-
ization toward which the Oedipal complex leads and
can be the occasion for a regression in sexual
development of the child.

The situation is much different for what Lacan
calls "the other sex." The fact that the Oedipal
desire of girls is directed toward the father, i.e,
an object different from that of the pre-Oedipal
tendencies, makes the transition to and through the
Oedipal complex easier for them. The genital
sexuality emerging at this stage separates more
easily from the primitive tendencies associated with
the maternal object, and consequently girls are not
mixed up with the regressive interiorization characteristic of the boy's Oedipal struggle (p.
8.40.13). Lacan also claims that the anxiety
associated with separation can be assuaged to a
greater extent by the adult woman in the act of
nursing and contemplating her own infant, acts in
which she "receives and satisfies the most primitive
of all desires" (p. 8.40.7). (Cf. Freud's claim in
The Ego and the Id that the consequences of the
Oedipal conflict in girls was "precisely analogous"
to those of boys [p. 22], and his later distinction
between the experiences of the sexes in "Some
Psychical Consequences of the Anatomical Distinction
between the Sexes" [1925].)

Despite these distinctions between the experiences
of boys and girls, Lacan concludes his essay by
insisting that the structure of the Oedipal complex
and the psychic equilibrium it normally yields are
strictly relative to social structure, and he
briefly cites Malinowski's work on matriarchal
societies to confirm the possibility of alternative
social models. What is unique about patriarchal
societies, Lacan says, is that they unite the two
functions of sublimation and repression in the same
figure, the father. Hence "this antinomy is played
out within the individual drama . . . but its
effects extend far beyond that drama, integrated as
they are in an immense cultural patrimony: normative ideals, juridical statutes, creative inspi-
rations" (p. 8.40.15).

Lacan concludes by observing that modern man can
best be understood as the product of the "conjugal
family" taken in its existence as a concrete and
historically specific form of social organization.
Noting the recent decline of the paternal imago that
can be traced in the "political catastrophes" of the
time, Lacan cites this decline and its impact on the
family as the source of "major contemporary neuroses." He observes that it is probably no accident
that the Oedipal complex itself was discovered by
the son of a patriarchal Jew in the heart of a city
that had become a melting pot for the most diverse

familial forms (p. 8.40.16).
Reprinted with C46 as <u>Lex complexes familiaux</u> in
A6.   The last third of this article, on the Oedipus
complex, was translated by Andrea Kahn as "The
Oedipus Complex." in <u>Semiotext(e)</u> 4, no. 1 (1980);
190-200.

C46.   "Les complexes familiaux en pathologie." <u>Encyclo-
       pédie française</u> VIII: <u>La vie mentale</u>. Edited by
       Henri Wallon. Paris: Larousse, Société de
       gestation de l'Encyclopédie française, 1938. Pp.
       8.42.1-8.42.8.

Claims that the familial complexes formed through
the evolution of the ego in the Oedipal stage can be
directly linked to specific forms of psychoses and
neuroses. Although Lacan insists on an organic
factor in etiology of psychoses, he argues that
familial complexes structure such disturbances and
so determine the specific form of the obstacle
(<u>l'arrêt</u>) that psychosis will pose to the development of the ego and to the object-relations that
make up "reality" for the subject. In neuroses, on
the other hand, the complexes serve a <u>causal</u>
function that determines the symptoms and structures
of later disturbances in the personality.
Lacan says that the mental forms constituting
psychoses are actually <u>re</u>constitutions of stages in
the ego's development, and that the objects of
psychotic delusion correspond to the different
object-relations correlative to those stages within
the "normal genesis of the object in the specular
relation of the subject to others" (<u>l'autrui</u>). (See
remarks on the "mirror stage" in C45 and C53.)
Delusional objects thus "manifest the primordial
constitutive character of human consciousness," but
they may also reflect distortions in the "secondary
integrations" that determine the subject's relations
to objects and his "reality." Lacan observes that
familial complexes can play either of two roles in
psychosis: they can motivate the subject's reactions to his environment, or they can become the
themes of his delusions. And while Lacan stops
short of claiming that the complexes actually
determine the eruption of psychosis, he does note
the clinical evidence of the correlation between
psychosis and anomalous family situations, and he
attributes that correlation not to heredity but to
the purely "social" dimension of interpersonal
relations among family members.
After discussing the role of familial complexes in
psychosis, Lacan turns to "familial neuroses"--i.e.,
neuroses related to specific "deformations" of the
nuclear family assumed in Freud's account of the
Oedipal complex--and he emphasizes the role of the

symptom and the ego ideal. He briefly describes
Freud's argument that symptoms are not only an
expression of a repressed memory but also a defense
against anxiety, and Lacan explains how Freud linked
the symptom to the primordial separation associated
with birth and represented later in the danger of
castration (see Freud, Inhibitions, Symptoms and
Anxiety [1926] and Lacan's remarks on le complexe du
sevrage in C45.) Lacan also argues that the trauma
associated with separation from the mother is
extended to the infant's more general state of
functional disintegration (morcelage fonctionnel),
and in the mirror stage this results in two corollary manifestations: "the assumption of the
original fragmentation under the game of rejecting
the object, and the affirmation of the unity of the
body proper under the identification with the
specular image." Lacan associates this specular
image with the ego ideal that Freud relates to the
superego (see The Ego and the Id [1923] and "On
Narcissism" [1914]), and he claims that it is
engaged with the subject's rejection of the object
in a "phenomenological knot" that retains a
"structural deformation" characteristic of the
concrete reality in which the "drama of the individual" is lived (see pp. 8.42.4-5).
     This "dialectical play" between the ego and the
object makes up the subject's relation to reality,
and it is structured by the family complexes Freud
grouped together as the Oedipal complex. The
Oedipal complex serves a double purpose in Freud's
work, Lacan claims. The occurrence of the Oedipal
conflict in the narcissistic progress of the
subject's psychic development influences the
structural evolution of the ego; and the images
introduced into that structure by the Oedipal
conflict determine a "certain affective animation"
of reality. These effects can be disrupted by the
exigencies of specific cultural forms, however, and
Lacan claims that the "caprices" of this Oedipal
regulation of the ego have increased as "social
progress" has moved the family towards a more
narrowly defined conjugal unit with a wider variety
of individual variations. Lacan says that this
evolution of the family towards the "conjugal" or
nuclear form characteristic of modern society has
yielded two specific forms of "degradation" within
the Oedipal stage, which in turn lead to two
specific forms of neuroses: (1) an incomplete
repression of the desire for the mother coupled with
a reactivization of the anxiety inherent in the
relation of birth, which leads to transference
neuroses; and (2) a narcissistic degeneration of the
idealization of the father, which results in the
aggressive ambivalence immanent in the primordial

relation to the "semblable" and leads to character
neuroses.

Although it is clear that the form and content of
a neurotic symptom are determined by some trauma
within the narcissistic process of ego-formation,
Lacan admits that it usually impossible to establish
a single event as the origin of a transference
neurosis. The typical forms of character neuroses,
on the other hand, can be connected fairly consistently to the structure of the subject's family (p.
8.42.5). Lacan discusses three abnormal family
situations that can interrupt the successful resolution of the Oedipal conflict: (1) Excessively
rigorous patriarchal domination or a tyrannical
system of prohibitions, which can lead to an
exaggerated super-ego. (2) A mother who is either
too aloof or too solicitous, or more generally any
sexual disharmony between the parents which interrupts the sublimation of sexuality and the consequent "imaginative animation of reality." (Lacan
says that this can also lead to the "eternal being
[entité] of desire," i.e., an excessive libidinal
attachment to "reality" or to any object [including
one's body]). (3) An unchecked identification with
the parent of the opposite sex, most often determined by a domineering mother who usurps the
position of authority in the family. This results
in a conflict between the imaginary personality of
the subject and his or her biological sex, which in
turn serves as the "psychological determination" of
homosexuality.

Lacan's emphasis on the social basis of familial
relations substitutes culture for Freud's sexuality
in the etiology of neuroses. After briefly discussing the way our fundamentally patriarchal traditions elevate the male principle and represent the
female principle under a masculine ideal (as in the
image of the Virgin), Lacan observes that the
psychic inversion of such principles can threaten
the whole weight of the superstructure that supports
them and so can be connected with the "utopian turn
in the ideals of a culture." The psychoanalyst may
base his recognition of psychic discordances on
patent forms of homosexuality, Lacan says, but "it
is as a function of a social antinomy that we must
understand this imaginary impasse of sexual polari-
zation, since it is there that are engaged, invi-
sibly, the forms of a culture, the morals and the
arts, struggle and thought."

Reprinted with C45 as A6.

C47.   "Le temps logique et l'assertion de certitude
       anticipée: un nouveau sophisme." Cahiers d'art
       (1945).

Critiques the classical solution to a famous logic problem and insists on the importance of the temporal dimension of the logical process as the ground for the subject's identification of himself in terms of others.   The problem consists of a dilemma faced by three prisoners.   Their warden brings into their cell five disks, three white and two black.   He places a disk on the back of each prisoner in such a way that only the other two can see it, and he tells them they cannot talk to each other.   He then says he will free the first one who comes to him and is able to explain how he figured out the color of the disk on his back.   A short time after the warden leaves the cell, all three pris- oners come to the door together, claim that the disks on their backs are all white, and explain their solution.   The warden has to set them all free.

The usual solution is as follows: If any one of the three prisoners, Prisoner A, were to see black disks on Prisoners B and C, then he would immedi- ately know that the disk on his own back was white and run to the warden.   If A saw a black disk on B and a white disk on C, and if C did not immediately leave, then A would know that the disk on his own back was white, since if it were black C would have seen two black disks and immediately known that his own disk was white.   Since no one heads to the door as soon as they see the disks on the backs of the other prisoners, A can conclude that they all face the same uncertainty that he does, which means that they all see two white disks.   Thus, all of their disks must be white.

Lacan argues that this solution is really a sophism and is not strictly "logical" in the sense of a timeless relation among abstract terms. Rather, the solution described above involves intersubjective identifications among the three individuals as those relations evolve through time. Lacan thus distinguishes among the "instant du regard," the "moment de conclure," and the "temps pour comprendre," or logical time.   These terms designate three moments in the process by which each of the prisoners establishes the certainty of his own color (i.e., his "identity") by identifying with the subjective process of perception and doubt going on in the other two.

In terms of the solution, Lacan argues that absolute certainty can come about only if the group hesitates twice before going to the warden's office so that each man can express the doubt they all share.   In terms of the problem's relevance for psychoanalysis, Lacan claims that the means by which a prisoner's identity, his "I," emerges in this game is similar to its "psychological birth" in the formation of the subject (A2, p. 208).

In C58, Lacan returns to this point when criti-
cizing Freud for slighting the time interval between
an event recalled by the subject and the restruc-
turing of the event later (nachträglich). He refers
to this essay again the following year in B13 and
returns to it throughout his career to emphasize
both the logical structure of identity and the
importance of time in the formation of the ego.
Wilden comments on this point and briefly summarizes
"Les temps logique" in F420, pp. 105-6, n. 47. For
Lacan's subsequent analysis of another logical
problem, see C48. For a more complex discussion of
a similar instance of reciprocal identification, see
C69. Reprinted in A2, pp. 197-213.

C48.   "Le nombre treize et la form logique de la suspi-
       cion." Cahiers d'art (1945/46):   389-93.

Continues the investigation of "collective logic"
begun in C47 by way of "the problem of twelve
pieces." Given a collection of twelve items which
are identical except for one which differs in weight
from the others, the problem is to discover the odd
piece using only a balance scale and only three
weighings. Lacan solves the problem by developing a
method of weighing that he then abstracts into a
mathematical formula that can be applied to similar
problems regarding groups that contain any number of
items.

Lacan's interest in the solution to this problem
lies in the fact that it involves the isolation of a
single member of a group through a process of
reasoning that discovers the pure difference of the
item--whether it is heavier or lighter than the
other items--and he claims that the numerical com-
binations leading to this discovery manifest the
"logical form of suspicion" and that they lead to
"the absolute idea of difference, the root of the
form of suspicion." The essay concludes with an
ironic note that this solution proves the weighing
of sins in the Last Judgment need not last very
long, and with a more serious defense of the ancient
faith in mathematical analysis as a means of inves-
tigating the "generative function of phenomena."

This essay and C47 demonstrate Lacan's early
interest in mathematical logic as a model for the
structure of psychological processes and other
"subjective" states such as doubt and suspicion. In
his subsequent discussions of algebraic formulas and
"mathemes," however, Lacan tended to treat mathematical symbols more metaphorically, as in his claim
that the vertical stroke of the + signifies the
"crossing of the bar" between the signifier and the
signified (see C71).

C49.   "Propos sur la causalité psychique." Journées
       psychiatrique à Bonneval, 28 September 1946.
       Evolution psychiatrique 1 (1947):   123-65.

       Posits the imago as the central object of a
       "scientific psychology" (A2, p. 162), and compares
       the psychological insights granted by his theory of
       the mirror-stage to philosophical arguments concern-
       ing being and truth. The essay is divided into
       three parts.

       Part One:
       Criticizes Henri Ey's notion of "organo-dynamism"
       as simply another form of organicism, and attack's
       Ey's dualistic assumption that we can discover the
       reality of the ego at a level of "psychical cau-
       sality" apart from somatic phenomena. Ey describes
       this "structural duality" as a relation between "le
       monde et le Moi," and he claims that this "antinomy"
       between the world and the ego animates the dialec-
       tical movement of the spirit. Lacan objects that
       "there is no antinomy between the objects that I
       perceive and my body, the perception of which is
       justly constituted by an accord with [those ob-
       jects]" (p. 159).

       Part Two:
       Criticizes Ey's emphasis on the importance of
       belief and the role of error in delusion, and
       insists that delusional belief is really "méconnais-
       sance," a misperception based on an essential
       antinomy of its own: "to misperceive supposes a
       perception," Lacan says. This is especially
       apparent in the case of systematic misperceptions or
       delusions, where that which is denied is, in some
       fashion, also recognized. Lacan claims that the
       phenomena of automatism involves a similar mécon-
       naissance (see E115 and C40), since there the
       patient fails to perceive his speech or writing as
       his own. The reality that the patient confers on
       these phenomena does not depend on the sensible
       impressions that he experiences in them or on the
       belief that he attaches to them, Lacan says;
       instead, it depends on the fact that these phenomena
       seem to address him personally. "They double him,
       respond to him" as he identifies and questions them,
       and Lacan claims that the remarkable thing about
       this state is that the patient can understand the
       phenomena without recognizing himself in them. This
       example of the way automatism raises the issues of
       self-perception and signification leads Lacan to
       focus and extend his earlier interest in the
       importance of language to psychological analysis
       (see C41). He argues that the metaphysical import

of such phenomena lies in the way they show that
"the phenomena of madness is not separable from the
problem of signification for being in general, that
is to say, of language for man" (p. 166). Lacan
claims that the language of man, "this instrument of
his lying," is pervaded by the problem of his truth,
since the word "is not a sign, but a knot of signification" where meaning lies hidden and must be
unveiled to be discovered (p. 166). Thus Lacan
argues that one must define psychology concretely as
the "domain of madness, in other words of all that
makes a knot in discourse," and he invites his
audience to join him in a study of the significations of madness, the verbal distortions by which
the patient would communicate with us (p. 168). He
cites his thesis (A1) as an example of one such
study, and he claims that we can find the general
structure of méconnaissance in the "dialectic of
being" that informs other cases of paranoid delusion
as well.

Lacan says that this méconnaissance is revealed in
the rebellion of the madman who would impose "the
law of his heart" onto the world that seems so
disordered to him. He adds, however, that this
enterprise is not mad (insensée) because it is a
"defect" in the man's adaptation to life. Rather,
it is mad insofar as the subject does not recognize
his own being in the chaos of that world, nor does
he recognize that the order he would impose is
merely the "inverted, virtual" image of that same
being" (p. 172). (Lacan cites Hegel as the source
for his general formulation of madness as a "dialectical development" of the human being. Much of
Lacan's argument here and even some of his phrasing
derives directly from Part 5.B of Hegel's Phenomenology of Spirit; see especially section "b," "Das
Gesetz des Herzens, und der Wahnsinn des Eigen-
dunkels" ["The Law of the Heart, and the Frenzy of
Self-conceit"].)

Lacan cites Molière's Alceste as an example of a
madman who recognizes the dependence of his being on
this kind of perception, but Lacan also insists that
a similar recognition underlies Napoleon's self-
conscious "production of Napoleon" (p. 171). Thus
he observes that the risk of madness is also closely
aligned with the freedom of greatness, and he claims
that the stakes of that risk can be measured in the
attractions of identifications "where man engages
both his truth and his being." Far from being the
"contingent issue of the fragility of his organism"
(i.e., of somatic disturbances), madness is "the
permanent virtuality of an open fissure in his
essence." "The being of man," Lacan concludes, "not
only cannot be understood without madness, but it
would not be the being of man if it did not carry

madness within itself as the limit of its freedom"
(p. 176).

Part Three:
   Continues his attack on Ey's account of the ego as
an integrative function that adapts the individual
to reality, and emphasizes instead the purely
imaginary function of the imago as part of the
"ideal identifications" that constitute the history
of the subject's development.   Lacan cites Merleau-
Ponty's Phénoménologie de la perception (Paris:
Gallimard, 1945) in support of his claim that these
"illusory" or imaginary forms constitute the category of the "real," and he insists that the "formal
negation" or méconnaissance inherent in these imaginary forms also establishes the relation between
the ego and "the other."   Lacan goes on to compare
this relation to the general phenomenon of "transitivism" as described by other psychologists such as
Charlotte Buhler, who has recognized this transitivism "under the striking form of a veritable
capture [captation, which also connotes a seductive
lure] by the image of the other" (p. 180).   Lacan
says that this theory of transitivism closely
resembles his own work on the mirror stage, where he
described how the child's specular identification
with the other moves from jealousy to sympathy.   As
the subject finds a sense of himself in the image of
the other, Lacan adds, that image comes to captivate
this sense in itself (p. 181; see C45).
   The essential point of Lacan's emphasis on the
mirror stage in opposition to Ey's model of an
integrative ego is that Lacan links the effect of
early images of the self to a sense of "alienation"
rather than integration.   Because the subject first
experiences a sense of himself in the other, Lacan
follows Hegel and claims that "the very desire of
man is constituted . . . under the sign of mediation, it is desire to have his desire recognized.
It has for its object a desire, that of the other"
(p. 181).
   In psychoanalytic terms, this means that the
Oedipal complex, which plays a crucial role in the
progress through the mirror stage (see C45 and C53),
not only provokes the somatic effects of hysteria in
atypical instances but also constitutes the sense of
reality in the normal evolution of the subject.
And, Lacan argues, since the Oedipal relations
described by Freud are specific to the modern
patriarchies of Western Europe, the institution of
the Oedipal complex in the history of the subject
can also be said to mark "the recuperation of the
biological and the social in the cultural."   Thus
even the earliest objects that emerge in the field
of the subject's tendencies carry with them "the

double possibility of a symbolic use and an instrumental use" that reflects the subject's position in
culture, and those objects simply do not exist for
him apart from that possibility.

Lacan concludes with a brief discussion of the
importance of visual identification in the process
of imprinting in birds and insects and with a short
coda in which he defends his use of Descartes, Hegel
and philosophical sources in general.

Reprinted in Le problème de la psychogénèse des
névroses et des psychoses, edited by Henri Ey
(Paris: Desclée de Brouwer, 1950), pp. 123-65.
Lacan's "Allocution de clôture" for the conference
appears in this book, pp. 215-16. Reprinted without
the "allocution de clôture" in A2, pp. 151-93. For
a much more positive discussion of Ey's work, especially as it regards the relation between language
and madness, see D100. For an extended comment on
Le problème, see G472.

C50.   "La psychiatrie anglaise et la guerre." Evolution
       psychiatrique 1 (1947):   293-312; discussion 313-
       18.

Recounts the experience of psychiatrists associated with the British army during World War II, and
describes their theoretical and practical innovations in the group treatment of mental illness.
Lacan argues that their emphasis on group solidarity
among the patients in the military hospitals and
their calculated refusal to intervene directly in
the organization and operation of those groups
reflects Freud's account of group psychology (see
Group Psychology and the Analysis of the Ego [1921])
and of the detached role of the analyst in psychoanalysis. Lacan also discusses the role of psychological concepts in the testing processes by which
recruits and officers were selected when England
mobilized, and he argues that the British situation
during and just after the war demonstrates the
increasingly public and even political position
psychology can occupy in society. In the discussion
that follows Lacan's paper, Henri Ey objects to
broadening the domain of psychiatry beyond strictly
pathological phenomena, and others warn that psychiatrists must be restricted to advisory roles and
should not accept governmental appointments.

Much of this essay is based on Lacan's tour of
several British military hospitals, though he also
cites the work of British psychiatrists Bio and
Rickmann as useful examples of military psychiatry
during the war. For a more theoretical discussion
of the effect of war on modern society, see C51.

C51.   "L'agressivité en psychanalyse." Eleventh Congrès

des Psychanalystes de langue française, Brussels,
May 1948. Revue française de psychanalyse 12
(1948):   367-88.

Attributes aggressivity to the specular identifications by which a coherent ego is formed in the
image of an other (see C53). Lacan argues this
point in five theses that approach aggressivity
through its manifestation in the analytic experience:
(1) Aggressivity is present within the "dialectical grasp of meaning" that constitutes "psychoanalytic action." Since "only a subject can
understand a meaning," the psychoanalytic experience
must presuppose a "subject who manifests himself as
such to the intention of another," though one of
these subjects, the analyst, must play the role of
the "ideal impersonality."
(2) This aggressivity is manifest to the analyst
as the "pressure of an intention" on the patient's
part. That intention reflects the "images" by which
the subject has conceived himself in relation to the
world around him. Certain of those images or
"imagoes" "represent the elective vectors of aggressive intentions," such as castration, dismemberment, and other imagoes of the corps morcelé, the
"fragmented body." Lacan claims that together these
images constitute a "Gestalt proper to aggression in
man" and that this Gestalt serves the specific
"imaginary function" elucidated in the remaining
theses.
(3) Analysts must "efface themselves" in the
dialogue of analysis in order to discern this
Gestalt and its function in the subject. Refusing
the patient's appeal will bring into play his
aggression toward the analyst, Lacan says, and that
will, in turn, yield the "negative transference"
that is the initial knot of the analytic drama.
Lacan explains that the phenomenon of transference
derives from the patient's imposing onto the analyst
one of the "archaic imagoes" which have been infused
with the "symbolic overdetermination that we call
the subject's unconsciousness" (p. 107-8). He goes
on to argue that this imago will be revealed in
analysis "only insofar as our attitude offers the
subject the pure mirror of an unruffled surface."
(4) Aggressive reactions of all sorts retain "the
original organization of the forms of the ego and of
the object" as those forms are determined by stages
in the subject's "mental genesis" (see p. 111).
Among the most important of those stages is the
child's passage from an essentially undifferentiated
experience in the first six months to an increasing
awareness of "others" with whom the child identifies
in a "dialectic of identifications." This passage

includes an "ambivalent aggressivity" expressed as
jealousy and envy when the child encounters siblings
of about the same age. These reactions are codified
at six months in what Lacan calls the "mirror stage"
(see C44 and C53), in which the image of the other
can emerge either in the mirror or in the actual
presence of another child with whom the infant
identifies. In either case, Lacan says, the image
captivates the subject and represents an "ideal
unity" that is "invested with all the original dis-
tress resulting from the . . . physiological natal
prematuration" peculiar to human infants (p. 113,
tr. p. 19). Lacan describes this moment as a
"structural crossroad" in which we discover the
nature of aggressivity and its connection to the
formulation of the ego and its objects. He claims
that the individual's relation to the other is
erotically charged, and that the image he fixes upon
himself in this manner is inherently alienating.
The ego emerges as an organization of these conflic-
ting passions, Lacan says, and he claims that the
form of this ego "will crystallize in the subject's
internal conflictual tension, which determines the
awakening of his desire for the object of the
other's desire" (p. 113, tr. p. 19).
     Lacan goes on to argue that this "aggressive
relativity" which marks the very origin of the ego
manifests itself at each stage of its development,
and it also bears witness to the composition of the
ego out of "a conjunction of the subject's history
and the unthinkable innateness of his desire" (p.
114, tr. pp. 19-20). He says that aggressivity
constitutes the "primary identification that
structures the subject as rival with himself," and
that it must be transcended by the secondary Oedipal
identification. At that point, the child introjects
the imago of the parent of the same sex in the guise
of an ego-ideal or superego, thereby sublimating
aggression into socially acceptable associations.
     (5) Aggressivity is one of the preeminent
attitudes in modern society and was first formulated
in Hegel's theory of the master/slave relation. From
the conflict of the master and the slave, Lacan
argues, Hegel realized that "the satisfaction of
human desire is possible only when mediated by the
desire and the labour of the other," and Lacan
condemns the current "promotion of the ego" in the
name of utilitarian individualism.
     Lacan observes that narcissistic structure of the
ego entails a specifically social orientation of the
individual to the space around him, which Lacan
claims rejoins the "objective space of reality."
(In other words, the narcissistic structure of the
ego informs the subject's perception of objects that
make up his sense of the world.) This spatial

dimension of human experience is thus crossed by a
"subjective tension," anxiety, which lends it a
temporal dimension as well. Lacan claims that it is
at the intersection of these two "tensions," i.e.,
spatial and temporal, that we should envisage "that
assumption by man of his original splitting [déchir-
ement]," and he associates this splitting with what
Freud formulated as the "death instinct." (On
Lacan's theory of the alienation inherent in the
primordial ego and the "suicidal" dimension of the
discordance between the ego and being, see C49. For
a more elaborate account of the splitting that
occurs at the intersection of these tensions, see
C80.)
     Most of what Lacan says in this essay about desire
and its place in the recognition of the other
derives directly from Alexandre Kojève's Introduction à la lecture de Hegel (Paris: Gallimard,
1947). Kojève's remarks about the place of death in
the desire for recognition are especially relevant:
"all human, anthropogenetic Desire--the Desire that
generates Self-consciousness, the human reality--is,
finally, a function of the desire for 'recognition,'
And the risk of life by which the human reality
'comes to light' is a risk for the sake of such a
Desire" (p. 7; see F374, p. 65).

C52. "Essais sur les réaction psychiques de l'hyper-
      tendu." Congrés français de chirurgie, 4-9
      October 1948. Actes des Congrès (n.d.): 171-76.

C53. "Le stade du miroir comme formateur de la fonction
      du Je telle qu'elle nous est révélée dans l'expér-
      ience psychanalytique." Paper read at the Six-
      teenth International Congress of Psychoanalysis,
      Zurich, 17 July 1949. Revue française de psych-
      analyse 13 (1949): 449-55.

      Describes the child's "jubilant assumption"
      (l'assomption jubilatoire) of his specular image in
      a mirror as an essential step in the development of
      the ego, and stresses the "alienating destination"
      inherent in the "fictional direction" of this iden-
      tification of the self with an "other." Other psy-
      chiatrists had studied this phenomenon before Lacan
      (see K1239, p. 250-52), but Lacan treats it as a
      "convenient symbol" (C45, p. 10) of the "symbolic
      matrix in which the I is precipitated in a primor-
      dial form, before it is objectified in the dialectic
      of identification with the other, and before lan-
      guage restores to it, in the universal, its function
      as subject" (A2, p. 92; A2j, p. 2). Following
      Freud, Lacan says that we may call this I the "I-
      ideal," but the crucial point of this iden-tifi-
      cation is the fact that it makes the ego irre-

ducible to the individual alone, who from now on
will approach "the coming-into-being (le devenir) of
the subject asymptotically" (A2, p. 94; A2j, p. 2).
  Lacan's discussion of the mirror stage here
focuses on two different aspects of the experience:
why it begins, and how it ends. Motivated by the
child's sense of organic discord stemming from the
"prematuration" of the infant, the "certain dehis-
cence at the heart of the organism, a primordial
Discord," the mirror stage allows the child to
overcome that uneasiness in the totalizing "mirage"
of the image, which catches up the subject in "the
lure of spatial identification." This imaginary
identification establishes a relation between the
"organism and its reality," but that relation is
obviously based on a fundamental "méconnaissance"
(i.e., in this case, a mistaken identity) that
results in a "succession of phantasies that extends
from a fragmented body-image [the corps morcelé] to
a form of its totality that I shall call ortho-
paedic--and lastly, to the assumption of the armor
of an alienating identity, which will mark with its
rigid structure the subject's entire mental development" (A2, p. 97; A2j, p. 4).
  The mirror stage ends with the assumption of that
identity, a process which Lacan calls the "deflection of the specular I into the social I" (A2, p.
98; A2j, p. 5). In C51 Lacan describes this as the
secondary identification that resolves the Oedipal
conflict when the child introjects the imago of the
parent of the same sex; here, he describes it as
"the dialectic that will henceforth link the I to
socially elaborated situations" and claims that "it
is this moment that decisively tips the whole of
human knowledge into mediatization through the
desire of the other" (A2, p. 98; A2j, p. 5).
  This essay should be read in conjunction with C51,
where Lacan discusses the aggressivity inherent in
imaginary relations with the other and where he
argues that Hegel's theory of desire shows how one's
relations to objects and to one's self are constituted through the mediation of the other. The
earliest discussion of the mirror stage in Lacan's
career occurs in C44, but his first published
account was C45. This whole concept of identification derives from Freud's account of the narcissistic structure of the ego; see especially "Psycho-
Analytic Notes on an Autobiographical Account of a
Case of Paranoia" (1911), "On Narcissism" (1914),
and D99.
  See F374 and K1239 for more detailed descriptions
of this essay and for further references to relevant
work by others including Otto Rank and Charlotte
Buhler. The concept of the mirror stage itself
derives from Henri Wallon's "Comment se développe

chez l'enfant la notion des corps propre," _Journal de psychologie_ (1931): 705-48. The mirror stage remained a prominent theme in Lacan's work and is discussed by most commentators, though few go as far as Catherine Clément, who claimed that it was a revolutionary idea but the only one that Lacan ever had (F316). An important analysis of the para- doxical interaction between the anticipation of coherence and the retrospective anxiety of fragmen- tation can be found in F334.

Abstract in _International Journal of Psycho- Analysis_ 30 (1949): 203. Reprinted in A2, pp. 93- 100, A2j, pp. 1-7. Also translated into Greek by Andromaque Skarpalezou in _O politis_ 25 (1979).

C54. With M. Cénac. "Introduction théorique aux fonc- tions de la psychanalyse en criminologie." Thir- teenth conference of the Psychanalystes de langue française, 29 May 1950. _Revue française de psych- analyse_ 15, no. 1 (1951): 7-29. Discussion, 30- 84. Lacan's response to comments and questions, 84-88.

Claims that crime and the law are joined in a fundamentally dialectical relationship, and notes that Freud recognized the importance of that relation to the origin of Man in _Totem and Taboo_ (1912-13). The authors trace Freud's concept of the superego to this origin, and they argue that the superego links the individual with the social and so takes on a "generic" signification as that which constitutes the dependence of man "in relation to the human milieu" (p. 136). The authors also claim that criminal acts reveal a juncture of nature and culture, and an Oedipal interpretation of the acts shows that their psychopathic structure derives from their "symbolic" character or their "_irréel_" mode of expression rather than the criminal situation they create (p. 131). "The structures of society are symbolic," they add, and "insofar as the individual is normal, he makes use of them for his real acts; insofar as he is psychopathic, he expresses them by symbolic acts" (p. 132).

This emphasis on the symbolic character of criminal action leads the authors to define a "criminogenetic object" (pp. 141-42) that is constituted within the "dialectical negativity" by which the ego is formed through an identification with an other. The emotional ambivalence of that identification, which is an essential stage in the narcissistic structure of the ego described by Freud, generates an intensely aggressive attitude in the ego toward the other; if the tension of that identification is inadequately resolved, the dialectical evolution of the ego is suspended.

Consequently, the sense of reality determined by the
ego's relation to the other is profoundly alienating
and can result in criminal behavior such as Lacan
studies in A1 and C42. There he explains that the
real identity of the victims is irrelevant to the
symbolic function that the victims serve in the
criminals' perception of the world around them.

For Lacan's response to the discussion following
his paper, see E152. On aggression in the dialectical evolution of the ego, see C51; for the
importance of identification as a stage in the
development of the ego, see C53; and on the alienated reality of the subject, see C49. Freud
discussed these issues throughout his career, but
the following works are especially important to
Lacan's theory of identification and aggression in
the formation of the ego and in the subject's sense
of reality: "Psycho-Analytic Notes on an Autobiographical Account of a Case of Paranoia (Dementia
Paranoides)" (1911), "On Narcissism: An Introduction" (1914), and "Some Neurotic Mechanisms in
Jealousy, Paranoia and Homosexuality" (1922; see
D99).

Reprinted in A2, pp. 125-49, and in Ornicar? 31
(1984):   23-27.

C55.   "Some Reflections on the Ego." Translated by Nancy
       Elisabeth Beaufils. The British Psycho-Analytical
       Society, 2 May 1951. International Journal of
       Psycho-Analysis 34 (1953):   11-17.

Describes Lacan's theory of the mirror stage and
emphasizes the importance of these early identifications to the subject's sense of reality. Lacan
alludes to his earlier study of "paranoiac knowledge" and the role of desire in our relation to
objects (C53), and he observes that all human
knowledge depends on "the mechanism of paranoiac
alienation of the ego" in the image of an other that
emerges in the mirror stage. In fact, Lacan adds,
the jealousy inherent in the triangular nature of
the earliest relationship between the ego, the
object and "someone else" insures that "the object
of man's desire . . . is essentially an object
desired by someone else" (p. 12).

This essay touches upon most of the issues raised
by Lacan in his work after the war, including that
of the corps morcelé and of the function of aggressivity in narcissistic identification (see C51).
Lacan also raises two other issues in this essay
that will become increasingly important in his work:
the dangers associated with a strong ego and with
the celebration of the ego as a primary mechanism of
psychic integration; and the centrality of language
in the psychoanalytic experience.

In his discussion of this second topic Lacan
insists that the "structure of language" gives us a
clue to the function of the ego, which he associates
with Verneinung (denial) and claims that "the
essential function of the ego is very nearly that
systematic refusal to acknowledge reality [mécon-
naissance systématique de la réalité] which French
analysts refer to in talking about the psychoses"
(p. 12). Language has a "retrospective effect" on
what is finally considered "real," Lacan concludes,
and the ego can either be the subject of the verb or
qualify it. (Lacan illustrates this grammatically
in the difference between active and passive voice.)
In either case, however, Lacan says that the person
who speaks appears in a relationship of some sort,
"whether one of feeling or doing" (p. 111).
     Reprinted in Le coq héron 78 (1980): 3-13. For a
discussion of this essay in conjunction with C53,
see F374, pp. 32-34.

C56.   "Le symbolique, l'imaginaire et le réel." Confé-
       rence à la Société française de psychanalyse, 8
       July 1953. Bulletin de l'Association freudienne 1
       (1982): 4-13.

C57.   "Discours de Jacques Lacan." First Congrès de la
       Société française de psychanalyse, Rome, 26
       September 1953. La psychanalyse 1 (1956): 202-
       11. Discussion, 211-232. For Lacan's response to
       comments on 27 September 1953, see E160.

       Briefly recounts the central themes of C58,
emphasizing the intersubjective character of human
relations as it emerges in analytic discourse.
Lacan also stresses the constitutive role of speech
or language--here called "the symbolic order" (p.
206)--as the field and fundamental "material" of
psychoanalysis. He opposes his theory of the ego as
an imaginary function to the objectifying tendencies
of ego psychology, and he claims that "the real
which analysis confronts is a man who must be
allowed to speak" (p. 204). Analysis consists
precisely in distinguishing the person lying on the
analytic couch from the one speaking, Lacan adds,
and he insists that there are at least three members
in any analytic session: the analyst, the patient,
and the "je" who speaks.
     To this triad Lacan adds a fourth, "le mort" (the
dummy hand in bridge, but also, of course, death),
and he recalls Freud's connection between the symbolic order and the death instinct in Beyond the
Pleasure Principle (1920) (pp. 207-8; see F420, p.
100). Lacan also distinguishes between psychology
and the totalizing scope of psychoanalysis, which
deals with the whole experience of the human indi-

vidual, and he concludes that "psychoanalysis, if it is the source of truth, is also a source of wisdom. . . . It is all language." He tells analysts to nourish themselves in all forms of language from Rabelais to Hegel, popular songs, and the language of the streets, for it is there, he concludes, that analysts will encounter "the style by which the human is revealed in man" (p. 211).

For other papers associated with this conference see F386. Key passages from this essay are translated in the notes to F420. (Note: References to the "Discourse of Rome" usually mean C58, not this item.)

C58.   "Fonction et champ de la parole et du langage en psychanalyse." Paper distributed at the Congrès de la Société française de psychanalyse, Rome, 26-27 September, 1953. La psychanalyse 1 (1956): 81-166. For Lacan's oral address and the subsequent discussion of this essay, see E160.

Explains and defends his claims that the psychoanalytic experience is constituted by a dialectical relationship between two subjects within the field of language (see C51), and prescribes a role for the analyst based on the "subject" that emerges in the symbolic order rather than on the objectified notion of an autonomous "ego" that was becoming especially influential at the time among psychoanalysts in the United States.

Preface
Briefly describes the controversy that split the Société psychanalytique de Paris and led to the formation of the Société française de psychanalyse (see F379 and F412). Lacan accuses the SPP of authoritarian training methods that blunt the authenticity of the students' research and keep them in the state of "une minorisation perpétuée" (A2, p. 238). Rather than trying to rigidify some institutional hierarchy, Lacan says, the teacher's most urgent task is a re-examination of the history behind concepts that have been deadened by routine, and an exploration of their subjective foundations (A2, p. 240; A2j, p. 33).

Introduction
Claims that contemporary psychoanalysts have abandoned the foundation of speech (la parole), and describes his effort to show how the concepts of psychoanalysis function only in a "field of language [langage]" and in relation to "the function of speech [la parole]" (A2, p. 246; A2j, p. 39). (Note: The earlier translation of this item by Wilden [see below] renders la parole as "the Word,"

which can be misleading in the context of Lacan's
argument because he is focussing here on the act of
speaking rather than on the words spoken.)

Section I: Parole vide et parole pleine dans la
  réalisation psychanalytique du sujet.
Describes the goal of analysis as the patient's
realization of his truth as subject in and to the
symbolic order of language, and characterizes the
discourse of the analytic session as either "empty
speech" (la parole vide) or "full speech" (la parole
pleine). In empty speech, the subject always seems
to be talking about someone else and addresses the
immediate "here and now" of the session. Full
speech possesses a historical component in which the
subject verbalizes past events, restages them in the
presence of an other, and so comes to recognize his
unconscious in--and more importantly as--his
history. Lacan claims that psychoanalysis is in
fact based on this "assumption of his history by the
subject, insofar as it is constituted by the speech
addressed to the other" (A2, p. 257; A2j, p. 48).
  Lacan claims that "psychoanalysis has only a
single medium: the patient's speech," and he says
that all speech calls for a reply (A2, p. 247; A2j,
p. 40). In other words, the patient's speech takes
on significance only as it is addressed to another
subject, the analyst (see C51). This relationship
is constituted in the field of speech, but the
patient initially experiences it on an imaginary
plane through the mechanism of transference, in
which the analyst becomes the imago of the "other"
where the patient sees himself reflected as an ego-
ideal, a coherent "moi." Lacan says that the art of
the analyst is to "suspend the subject's certainties
until their last mirages have been consumed" (A2, p.
251; A2j, p. 43), and as the mirages dissipate, the
subject can recognize the imaginary character of
that coherent being. Thus Lacan defines the role of
the ego in analysis as "frustration in its essence.
Not frustration of a desire by the subject, but
frustration by an object in which his desire is
alienated" (A2, p. 250; A2j, p. 42).
  The subject's passage from empty speech to full
speech occurs at the moment when he brings "the
origins of his own person" into the present of analytic discourse. This happens through what Freud
described as a nachträglich recollection of past
events in reference to present circumstances, or in
Lacan's words through a reordering of past contingencies by conferring on them "the sense of necessities to come" (A2, p. 256; A2j, p. 48).
  This "historicization" has both a primary and
secondary function for Lacan. The primary function
is simply the emergence of an event within a

chronological sequence at a particular moment.
Secondary historicization reconstitutes those events
within a present context that depends on the subject's relation to an other, as in the anamnesis of
the analytic session. But this distinction is
blurred by Lacan's insistence that all events or
past moments are immediately historicized in this
second sense even as they occur because they always
are experienced within intersubjective contexts
(i.e., as part of human culture). Thus Lacan claims
that the anal stage "is no less purely historical
when it is actually experienced than when it is
reconstituted in thought [repensé]" (A2, p. 262;
A2j, p. 53), and he describes the "so-called"
instinctual stages as "stigmate historique" (A2, p.
261). Since those stages constitute the subject's
"history"--and hence his unconscious--only in relation to another subject, Lacan arrives at his famous
formula, "the unconscious of the subject is the
discourse of the other" (A2, p. 265; A2j, p. 55).

Section II: Symbole et langage comme structure et
   limite du champ psychanalytique.
   Redefines the field of psychoanalysis as "the
symbolic order," which Lacan identifies with
language but extends to include the most general
organizational principles of human culture. He
insists on the fundamental place of language in
Freud's understanding of human behavior, and he
claims that the symbolic order functions as the
primary law governing all forms of human interaction. This order pervades all social relations,
Lacan says. It is autonomous of and antecedent to
the arrival of any individual into the world of
culture, and it persists after the individual is
gone. In fact, Lacan adds, it would totally
overwhelm the living being "if desire did not
preserve its part in the interferences and pulsations that the cycles of language cause to
converge on him (A2, p. 279; A2j, p. 68).
   Thus what is at stake in an analysis is "the
advent in the subject of that little reality that
this desire sustains in him with respect to the
symbolic conflicts and imaginary fixations as the
means of their agreement, and our path is the
intersubjective experience where this desire makes
itself recognized. From this point on," Lacan
concludes, "the problem is that of the relations
between speech and language in the subject" (A2, p.
279; A2j, p. 68). Those "relations between speech
and language" are what position the individual in
culture as a subject, and the last half of Section
II argues that psychoanalysts are best equipped to
define that position because "we are practitioners
of the symbolic function" (p. 72).

Section III: Les résonances de l'interprétation et
le temps du sujet dans la technique psychanalytique.
Focuses on "the junction between the symbolic and
the real" in psychoanalysis, and situates that
junction in two ways: (a) through the "analyst's
abstention," i.e., his refusal to reply to the
patient's "demand for love" or, more generally, his
dialectical position vis-à-vis the patient's speech;
and (b) through the function of time in analytique
technique, specifically the time of the analytic
session but also the subject's own "time" as a
historical subject situated in a chronological
sequence of past-present-future that is limited by
death.
The first of these points depends on the dialectical character of analytic speech, in which the
analyst's aim is not some prise de conscience beyond
language but instead must be an effort to "decenter"
the subject from his consciousness-of-self (i.e.,
his "ego) and so to "free the subject's speech" by
introducing him into "the language of his desire"
(A2, p. 293;, A2j, p. 81).
The rest of this section is largely devoted to a
discussion of the second point at which Lacan marks
the junction of the symbolic and the real: the
"time" of the subject and his relation to death as
constituted within the symbolic order of language.
Lacan denies that language functions as a refe-
rential sign connected to the "real world," and he
argues instead that language is principally evoca-
tive, not informative: it "evokes" both the subjects and the objects of our experience rather than
simply communicating information about them.   Hence
Lacan says that "what I seek in speech is the
response of the other" (A2, p. 299; A2j, p. 86), and
it is that "question" addressed to the other than
constitutes the individual as subject.
In analysis, the analyst is the other, or, more
accurately, he represents that other for the
subject.   As such, the analyst has the power to
"recognize" or "abolish" the patient as subject, and
that is the responsibility of the analyst when he
does intervene in the patient's speech.   He can do
that, however, only as an echo of the subject's own
message (hence the "resonance of interpretation"
mentioned in the title of this section).   He must
play the role of an echo because the analyst himself
is caught up in the dialectical subjectivity of
language and does not occupy a privileged position
that is more "real" or "true" than the patient's.
Thus the goal of analysis can never be the revelation of a "real" or "true" meaning behind the
patient's speech, but only "the advent of a true

speech and the realization by the subject of his
history in his relation to a future" (A2, p. 302;
A2j, p. 88). Lacan argues that this effect can be
brought about best in sessions of variable length,
his controversial "short sessions." Terminating the
session at different times, Lacan says, is a means
of "punctuating" the patient's speech, fixing its
meaning at a point beyond the control of the patient
himself and so forcing him to distinguish between
his sense of himself and the position of the subject
of speech.

Although most of Lacan's remarks are directed
towards the practice of psychoanalysis, throughout
the essay he extends his observations to the subject's more general relation to the symbolic.
Drawing upon Freud's account of the game of Fort/Da!
in Beyond the Pleasure Principle (1920), Lacan
describes the child's fascination with these sounds
and the spool they designate as a paradigm for our
experience of words in general, which inevitably
emerge as a "presence made of absence." It is out
of such words, he claims, that our world comes to be
arranged. "It is the world of words that creates
the world of things. . . . Man speaks, then, but it
is because the symbol has made him a man" (A2, p.
276; A2j, p. 65). Echoing Alexander Kojève's
immensely influential lectures on Hegel (which Lacan
attended), Lacan describes the child's "birth into
language" as a "murder of the thing," and he says
that "this death constitutes in the subject the
eternalization of his desire" (A2, p. 319; A2j, p.
104). (For Kojéve's discussion of the word as the
death of the thing, see Introduction à la lecture de
Hegel [Paris: Editions Gallimard, 1947], pp. 372-
76.)

As the child's first experience of limit, this
moment is repeated continuously and comes to
constitute his place as subject in human culture,
or, in the terms Lacan has just introduced, the
symbolic order. And as a limit, the word also
reflects and anticipates the subject's relation to
the ultimate limit, death. "The first symbol in
which we recognize humanity in its vestigial traces
is the sepulture, and the intermediary of death can
be recognized in every relation in which man comes
to the life of his history. . . . Therefore, when
we wish to attain in the subject what was before the
serial articulations of speech, and what is primordial to the birth of symbols, we find it in death,
from which his existence takes on all the meaning it
has" (A2, pp. 319-20; A2j, pp. 104-05).

Lacan goes on to add that this "mortal meaning"
reveals a center in speech that is exterior to
language itself, and he cautions that such a claim
is more than a metaphor; "it manifests a structure"

(A2, p. 320; A2j, p. 105). This structure is the
focus of psychoanalysis, and Lacan concludes that
psychoanalysis may therefore be the loftiest of all
work undertaken in this century. The analyst
functions in society as "interpreter in the discord
of languages," and as a result

> [t]he psychoanalytical experience has redis-
> covered in man the imperative of the Word as the
> law that has formed him in its image. It manipu-
> lates the poetic function of language to give to
> his desire its symbolic mediation. May that
> experience bring you to understand at last that it
> is in the gift of speech that all the reality of
> its effects resides; for it is by way of this gift
> that all reality has come to man and it is by his
> continued act that he maintains it. (A2, p. 322;
> A2j, p. 106)

"Fonction et champ de la parole" is certainly the
most influential single essay of Lacan's career. It
established his independence from most contemporary
movements in the psychoanalytic community, and as
the "Discours de Rome" it became a manifesto to his
followers. Theoretically, the essay draws upon his
earlier accounts of the imaginary and the alienation
of the subject in the imago of the other (see C45
and C53). It also draws upon the role of the
analyst as he outlined it in C51 and upon the
importance of language in intersubjective relations,
a topic that pervades Lacan's work throughout his
career. But "Fonction et champ" differs significantly from most of Lacan's earlier work by treating
the imaginary as part of a "triad" of "elementary
registers" of experience--the symbolic, the imaginary, and the real--and by emphasizing the subject's
passage from the imaginary to the symbolic as his
entry into the world of culture.
Here Lacan begins to use the symbolic order as a
synonym not only for language but also for "law,"
"culture," or the "social order," and he also begins
to discuss it in distinct contrast to the imaginary
couple of self and other that constitutes the
"mirage" of a coherent ego. Though similar gestures
may be found in earlier essays, his more systematic
and consistent opposition of the symbolic and the
imaginary in this essay marks a crucial turning
point in Lacan's thought. Reading the essay retro-
spectively, the form of that opposition as it
appears here also suggests his later elaboration of
terms such as the real and the Other, though these
two terms remain rather loosely determined at this
point.
The best commentary on this essay is Lacan's own
address, E161, which supplemented the written

version of the paper that was distributed at the
conference.   The paper itself was reprinted and
slightly revised in A2, pp. 237-322, accompanied by
a brief introduction written for that collection.
It was first translated into English in F420 with
extensive notes by the translator and a long
monograph on Lacan's work.   It was subsequently
translated in later editions of A2 and as "Funzione
e campo della parola e del unamaggio in psycanalisi"
in La cosa freudiana, Turin: Einaudi, 1972, pp. 81-
178.

C59. With R. Lévy and H. Danon-Boileau.   "Considerations
     psychosomatiques sur l'hypertension artérielle."
     Evolution psychiatrique 3 (1953):   397-409.

     Claims that hypertension must be treated with a
combination of somatic and psychiatric medicine, and
observes the importance of Lacan's work on aggressivity within narcissistic identification to an
understanding of the psychological factors behind
arterial hypertension.

C60. "Le mythe individuel du névrosé."   Presented at the
     Collège philosophique de Jean Wahl and distributed
     without permission in 1953.   Paris: Centre de
     documentation universitaire, 1953.   30 pages.

     Describes psychoanalysis as more of a liberal art
in the medieval sense than a modern science because
it is based on the measure of man in relation to
himself, an intersubjective yet internal relation
comprised by the practice of speech ("l'usage de la
parole").   As a result, Lacan says, the analytic
experience is never objectifiable and instead is
based on what can be called "myth."   Lacan defines
myth as that which gives a discursive formula to
something that cannot be transmitted as truth, and
he says that the primary myth of psychoanalysis is
the Oedipal complex.   Lacan goes on to test the
Oedipal myth as an explanatory formula for neurotic
obsession through a close reading of Freud's case of
the Rat Man and of an episode from Goethe's youth
recounted in Poesy and Truth, and he concludes that
a radical critique of the Oedipal schema is necessary.   Instead of the triangular formula articulated
by traditional freudians, Lacan says, we must
introduce a fourth term into the Oedipal relation:
death.   Death is essential to the "second great
discovery of psychoanalysis," the narcissistic
relation, and is first experienced as the sense of
chaos and disarray that emerges against the image of
an ideal self in the mirror stage (see C53).
     Much of this article investigates the imaginary
doubling behind the obsessive relations described in

the case of the Rat Man, and Lacan carefully traces
the parallels between the family relations of the
Rat Man and the social situation in which his
obsessive behavior erupts years later. Lacan
concludes that the fantastic scenario of the Rat
Man's obsession functions as a little drama, a
script based on the initial constellation of relations that constituted his subjectivity, and Lacan
calls this pattern "the individual myth of the
neurotic."
    Reprinted with an introductory note by Jacques-
Alain Miller in Ornicar? 17/18 (1979): 289-307.
Translated by Martha Evans in Psychoanalytic
Quarterly 48 (1979): 405-25. Translated into
Italian as "Il mito individuale del nevrotico," with
commentary by Miller, Michel Silvestre, and Colette
Soler, edited by Antonio Di Ciaccia (Rome: Astrolabio, 1986).

C61. "Introduction au commentaire de Jean Hyppolite sur
      la Verneinung de Freud." Presented as part of
      B12, 10 February 1954. La psychanalyse 1 (1956):
      17-28.

    Notes the centrality of resistance to the tech-
nique of psychoanalysis, and argues that one
completely misunderstands the phenomenon unless it
is taken within the context of analytic discourse.
Lacan cites Freud's argument that resistance in-
creases as the patient's discourse approaches its
unconscious "nodal points" and is manifested
"radially" through breaks in the chain of discourse.
These breaks mark the point when the speech of the
subject swings toward (bascule vers) the presence of
the auditor, the analyst. Lacan says this moment is
usually indicated by a suspension of discourse that
is often accompanied by anxiety, and it betrays the
essentially imaginary identification with an other
that constitutes the ego.
    Through the transference that occurs at such
moments, the analyst can learn "qui parle et à qui,"
who speaks and to whom in the analysis. As a result, he can identify the imaginary dialectic in
which the subject is trapped. This is the progress
of analysis as defined by Lacan. The subject begins
analysis, Lacan says, "en parlant de lui sans vous
parler à vous, ou en parlant à vous sans parler de
lui. Quand il pourra vous parler de lui, l'analyse
sera terminée" (p. 21, n. 1).
    Turning to Hyppolite's paper, Lacan associates the
dialectic of analytic discourse with the Hegelian
notion of a mediated self-consciousness, and he
raises a question about the relation between the
"non-being" manifested in the symbolic order and
"the reality of death" as it bears upon the emer-

gence of self-consciousness in Hegel. For Hyppolite's commentary see L1897; for Lacan's response
to Hyppolite see C62.
    Reprinted in A2, pp. 369-80, with the significant
alteration of a capital "A" for the original lower
case "a" in the formula "l'inconscient c'est le
discourse de l'Autre" (p. 379). Also reprinted in
an abbreviated form in B12, pp. 63-68, which includes a more extended discussion of the "bascule"
of the subject's speech towards the other (pp. 185-
98).

C62.   "Réponse au commentaire de Jean Hyppolite sur la
        Verneinung de Freud." Presented as part of B12,
        10 February 1954. La psychanalyse 1 (1956): 41-
        58.

    Departs from Hyppolite's emphasis on the relation
between negation and affirmation in the creation of
the symbol (see L1897) to focus on Freud's account
of the affective organization of the real. For
Freud, Lacan argues, "l'affectif" is conceived as
that part of the "primordial symbolization" that is
preserved even within the "discursive structuration." That structuration, Lacan adds, is designed
"to translate under the form of méconnaissance that
which this first symbolization owes to death" (p.
43). We are thus led to an intersection of the
symbolic and the real where we encounter, "in a form
that denies itself" (i.e., through denegation or
Verneinung), what was excluded at the origin of
symbolization.
    Lacan offers two examples of this phenomenon:
hallucination, and acting out. Discussing Freud's
account of hallucination in his analysis of the
Wolf-man, Lacan distinguishes between repression
(refoulement, Verdrangung) and foreclosure (retranchement, Verwerfung). He argues that the effect of retranchement is a total abolition of the
symbolic, as if the castration inherent in the
substitution of the signifier for the signified
never existed. In such cases there is a complete
lack of the "inaugural affirmation" (Bejahung) that
is the "primordial condition by which something
comes from the real to offer itself to the revelation of being" (p. 47), and the subject is incapable of distinguishing between the "sentiment
d'irréalité" and the "sentiment de réalité." As a
result, Lacan says, what is normally constituted by
remembrance (rémemoration) within the symbolic text
is experienced by the subject as part of the real, a
condition Lacan recognizes by the formula "ce qui
n'est pas venu au jour de symbolique, apparaît dans
le réel" (p. 48).
    For further comments on Hyppolite's paper (L1897),

see C61.   Lacan's response was reprinted in A2, pp.
381-400, and in an abbreviated form in B12, pp. 68-
73.   Translated as "Riposta al commento di Jean
Hyppolite sulla 'Verneinung' di Freud," Nuova
corrente (Milan) 61/62 (1973):   128-38.

C63.   "Variantes de la cure-type."   Easter 1955.   Encyclo-
       pédie médico-chirurgicale, psychiatrie, tome III,
       2-1955, fasicule 37812-C10.   Edited by Henry Ey.

Notes the lack of agreement among different
schools of psychoanalysts regarding the therapeutic
criteria for analysis, and proposes a model for
analytic practice based on the centrality of speech
(la parole) in the experience of analysis itself.
Lacan is especially critical of theorists who would
have the analyst become the ally of the "healthy
part" of the patient's ego, or who would have the
patient model his ego on that of the analyst.   Such
approaches, he says, are based on a "naive objectification" of the imaginary formation of the ego into
a synthetic function (A2, p. 345).   In fact, Lacan
says, the ego is derived from a narcissistic
relation that gives rise to an aggressivity inherent
in the "splitting (déchirement) of the subject
against himself, a splitting that he knew from the
primordial moment in which he saw the image of the
other" (p. 345).
Lacan claims as a result that modelling the
subject's sense of himself on the ego of the analyst
will just be an alibi for narcissism, and he insists
that this situation can be corrected only by
mediating between the two subjects constituted
within analytic speech.   That mediation is possible,
however, only by the introduction of a third term
that interposes itself between the two subjects:
"the reality, the death-instinct."   In order for the
relation of transference to escape the imaginary
trap of ego-to-ego mirage, the analyst must strip
from the narcissistic image of his ego the various
forms of desire through which it is constituted and
"reduce it to the sole figure which, under the masks
of those desires, sustains that image: that of the
absolute master, death" (p. 348).
In concrete terms, the analyst's occupying the
place of death simply means that he doesn't speak,
but Lacan is careful to point out that this silence
must be situated in the place of a response (p.
351).   It is a silence that calls forth (comporte, a
pun on an earlier remark that the analyst must
"porte la parole") the speech of the subject, and
Lacan claims that that speech is always manifested
in the analytic situation as a "communication" in
which the subject offers his message in an inverted
form, hoping that the other will render it true (p.

351).

Lacan illustrates these inversions by statements such as "you are my wife," which carries with it the inverted claim "I am your husband."   True speech is thus paradoxically opposed to true discourse by the fact that true speech "constitutes the subjects' recognition of their being in so far as they are intér-essés in it" (an un-translatable pun that conflates "interested" and "mixed-essences"). Discourse, on the other hand, is "true" insofar as the subject aims it at objects in what can be called an "adequation to things" (p. 351).   In true speech, Lacan concludes, "signification always returns to signification" rather than to things.   Hence man, in the subordination of his being to the law of recognition by an other, is traversed by speech, and Lacan claims that it is in that crossing that man is open to suggestion.

Lacan concludes the essay with an attack on the function of knowledge (le savoir) in analytic practice.   The analyst acquires a knowledge about the imaginary in his experience, Lacan says (p. 357), and that knowledge can exert its own allure as it is explored by the patient.   This is why Freud emphasized that the science of analysis must be put in question in every case.   In the place of "savoir," Lacan recommends "le non-savoir," the "positive fruit of the revelation of ignorance" (A2, p. 358).   Otherwise, the "robot analyst," proceeding according to some imaginary knowledge, can never "porte la parole."   The unconscious remains closed off from him, silent, since he thinks he already knows what it has to say.   Lacan says that this is what Freud discovered in the "turning point" of his work on analytic technique, and it is the source of his "magical" success: to succeed, analysis must be based on a speech that is true for both the patient and the analyst.   That is why the analyst must aspire "to such mastery of his speech that it becomes identical to his being. . . . the analyst, better than any other, must know that he can be himself only in his words (ses paroles)" (p. 359).

For other remarks on the formation of the analyst, see C88; also see F395, F396, and F397.   Lacan's essay was reprinted in A2, pp. 323-362.   According to Lacan's note in A2, p. 918, this essay was deleted from the Encyclopédie in 1960.

C64.   "Psychanalyse et cybernétique ou de la nature du langage."   Société française de psychanalyse, 22 June 1955.   First published as part of B13, pp. 339-54, edited by Jacques-Alain Miller.

Claims that the possibility of a scientific order derives from the moment when man imagined natural

processes carrying on without him, and notes that
symbols have always kept to their own path despite
man's effort to join them to the real. Lacan compares symbolic systems to cybernetic calculation,
which is based on syntax rather than semantics, and
he contrasts those systems to semantics, which
governs "concrete language" and is "furnished with
the desire of men" (B13, p. 351). Lacan insists
that for a message to have a meaning instead of
being just pure information, it cannot simply be a
sequence of signs (see C65 in A2, pp. 413). It must
be an oriented sequence, and that orientation is
established through the imaginary dimension of the
subject's discourse (pp. 352-54).
    On the role of desire as an "anchoring point" of
discourse, see C73.

C65.   "La chose freudienne ou sense de retour à Freud en
       psychanalyse." Expanded version of a paper
       presented at a conference at the Neuro-psychiatric
       Clinic at Vienna, 7 November 1955. Evolution
       psychiatrique 1 (1956): 225-252.

       Explains what his "return to Freud" entails for
our understanding of the place of the ego and speech
in analytic practice, and for the role of "truth" in
the field of psychoanalysis. Although Lacan's recourse here to a mythological narrative makes any
attempt to describe his argument even more reductive
than usual, it is clear that the opening sections of
the essay intend to problematize the very issue of
"truth" as it bears on traditional analytic theory
that would relegate it to some ahistorical, pre-
Oedipal reality underlying the subject's speech.
    Despite these criticisms of traditional notions of
Truth, however, Lacan claims that truth is "inscribed at the very heart of analytic practice."
He says that Freud's discovery began with a "particular truth" that changed our understanding of
reality forever (A2, p. 408; A2j, p. 120). Rather
than naming this truth, however, Lacan has it
"speak" a highly cryptic message that promises to
teach the listener the signs by which truth can be
recognized. I appear in the dream, truth says, in
jokes and in "the profile of Cleopatra's nose" (an
allusion to Pascal's aphorism). In Freud's work we
find that "things are my signs, but I repeat, signs
of my speech. If Cleopatra's nose changed the
course of the world, it was because it entered the
world's discourse, for to change it in the long or
short term, it was enough, indeed, it was necessary
for it to be a speaking nose" (A2, p. 411; A2j, p.
123).
    Lacan's effort to identify truth with the phrase
"I speak" leads him directly to a consideration of

the intersection between speech and language. He
tells his audience that "There is no speech that is
not language" ("Il n'est parole que de langage"),
but that is just to remind us that "language is a
order constituted by laws" (A2, p. 413; A2j, p.
125). He describes those laws using Saussure's
distinction between the synchronic order of language
and what Lacan calls the diachronic order of the
signified, that of "concretely pronounced discourses, which reacts historically on the first
order of the signifier" (A2, p. 414; A2j, p. 126).
The dominant factor here, Lacan claims, is "the
unity of signification," which can never simply
indicate the real but always refers back to another
signification. Thus signification can only be
realized by grasping things "in their totality."
Its origin cannot be a mere redundancy with things,
i.e., some level where signification simply stands
in for them, "for it always proves to be in excess
over the things that it leaves floating within it"
(A2, p. 414; A2j, p. 126).

After insisting on the "omnipresence" of this
symbolic function for the human being and on the
"immixture of subjects" that makes the psychoanalytic ethic something other than individualistic
(A2, p. 414; A2, p. 127), Lacan offers a re-reading
of Freud's slogan Wo Es war, soll Ich werden that
emphasizes the importance of translating Ich as "I"
rather than le moi or "ego" (A2, p. 416-19; A2j, p.
129): "là où était ça, le je doit être." He then
carries the distinction between the subject and the
ego into a critique of ego psychology, which tends
to objectify the ego. If the ego is an object,
Lacan argues, it has no special privileges over any
other object, and he impersonates a desk to dramatize this point. Acknowledging that the ego, and
not a desk, is the seat of perceptions, Lacan
insists nevertheless that, as the locus of perception, the ego "reflects the essence of the objects
it perceives and not its own" (A2, p. 424; A2j, p.
134). His point, of course, is that our perception
of objects, our object-relations, are essentially
narcissistic in nature, and in the next section of
the essay he makes this point explicit.

Lacan says there that our relations to the objects
that make up our world is based on the "imaginary
passion" generated by our own image of our body, and
that image depends on a relation to the other that
"links all the objects of my desires more closely to
the desire of the other than to the desire that they
arouse in me" (A2, p. 427; A2j, p. 137). The libidinal alienation arising from this condition, he
concludes, leads to the "paranoiac principle of
human knowledge, according to which its objects are
subjected to a law of imaginary reduplication."

Most of the concluding pages of the essay deal
briefly with analytic practice as it raises the
issue of relations among the four poles of the L-
schema: S, the subject; A, the Other; a(moi), the
ego; and a'utre, the imaginary other. Lacan argues
that the analyst must refuse to deal with the
patient as an imaginary other. Rather, he must be
imbued with the difference between the Other he
addresses in his speech and the other whom he sees
before him. Instead of giving in to the patient's
effort to trap him in an imaginary identification,
Lacan says that the analyst must intervene "concretely in the dialectic of analysis by pretending
he is dead . . . either by his silence when he is
the Other with a capital O, or by annulling his own
resistance when he is the other with a small o." In
either case, Lacan adds, he makes death present (A2,
p. 430; A2, p. 140).

Lacan then briefly introduces the notion of a
"symbolic debt" incurred by any subject during his
accession to the symbolic order. He concludes than
any analysis of the means by which speech recovers
the debt that engenders it must return to "the
structures of language so manifestly recognizable in
the earliest discovered mechanisms of the unconscious." That is why Freud insisted on a famil-
iarity with languages and institutions, Lacan says,
and also why he was so interested in art. He then
ends by recommending a greater role for the lin-
guist, the historian, and the mathematician in the
training of analysts.

Reprinted in A2, pp. 401-436. Translated into
Italian in A2f; and into English in A2j, pp. 114-
145. Lacan also presented this paper in his
seminar, 14 December 1955. See his brief introduction to that presentation, B14, pp. 81-82.

C**. "Freud dans le siècle." Seminar session for 16 May
      1956. See B14, pp. 263-77.

This session of Lacan's seminar for 1955-56 has
achieved some prominence of its own and stands apart
from the rest of the sessions to some extent. For a
description of Lacan's remarks, see the comments on
B14 referring to these pages.

C66. "La grand'route et le Nom du Père." Based on the
      seminar of 20 June 1956. L'âne 3 (1981): 4-5

Compares the signifier to a highway that cuts
across a country, determining the location of cities
and villages and governing the relations among
social groups along predetermined paths. Like la
grand'route, the signifier "être-père" or "le nom-
du-père" determines the sexual relations between men

and women as constituted within the symbolic order.
Also printed as part of Chapter XXIII in B14, pp.
323-331.

C67.   With Wladimir Granoff. "Fetishism: The Symbolic,
the Imaginary, and the Real." Perversions:
Psychodynamics and Therapy. Edited by Sandor
Lorand, M. D. Associate Editor, Michael Balint,
M. D. New York: Gramercy Books, 1956. Pp. 265-
76.

Uses the case of little Harry to show how Freud's
concept of the fetish can be clarified by Lacan's
distinction among the symbolic, imaginary, and real
registers of experience. Noting Freud's insistence
that the fetish had to be deciphered like a symptom-
-that is, as a phrase or message--the authors account for Harry's mutism as an "imaginary capta-
tion" in which Harry "gives reality to the image"
and refuses to place himself within the register of
the symbolic (p. 169; see Lacan's similar definition
of psychosis in B14). Fetishism is born between
imaginary and symbolic relationships, they argue,
and between the affects of anxiety and guilt that
characterize those orders respectively. "As soon as
a third person is introduced into the narcissistic
relationship, there arises the possibility of real
mediation," the authors say, and they claim that
Harry's entire clinical history turns on this
moment, which is, of course, that of the Oedipal
conflict: "Will the fear of castration thrust
[Harry] into anxiety? Or will it be based and
symbolized as such in the Oedipal dialectic? Or
will the movement rather be frozen in the preeminent
memorial (i.e., the fetish) which, as Freud puts it,
fear will build for itself?" (p. 273).
This essay is particularly interesting for the
connections it draws between Lacanian theories of
the Oedipal conflict and of the role of language in
analysis, and those of other authors such as Karl
Abraham. See too the authors' ethological distinction between the imaginary and symbolic registers of
experience: "behavior can be called imaginary when
its direction to an image, and its own value as an
image for another person, renders it displaceable
out of the cycle within which a natural need is
satisfied. . . . Behavior is symbolic when one of
these displaced segments [i.e., a sudden interruption of a behavioral pattern, such as the abrupt
substitution of parade behavior for a portion of a
combat cycle enacted between two birds] takes on a
socialized value. It serves the group as a reference point for collective behavior. This is what we
mean when we say that language is symbolic behavior
par excellence" (p. 272).

Second edition, London: Ortolan Press, 1965.

C68. "Situation de la psychanalyse et formation du
      psychanalyste en 1956." Etudes de philosophiques
      11 (1956): 567-84.

      Attacks several of the concepts introduced into
      psychoanalysis since Freud's death, primarily the
      emphasis on the ego associated with American
      psychoanalysis and, less significantly, the notions
      of frustration and intuition. Lacan also ridicules
      the bureaucratic organization of the International
      Psychoanalytic Association, along with its hier-
      archical structure through which candidates must
      find their way to be recognized as analysts. In
      place of this rigid bureaucracy, Lacan proposes that
      psychoanalysts return to Freud's own emphasis on the
      role of speech in analysis and on the "procédure
      langagière" endemic to the unconscious (p. 466). "A
      psychoanalyst must be assured that man is, before
      his birth and beyond his death, taken into the
      symbolic chain," Lacan claims; "this exteriority of
      the symbolic in relation to man is the very notion
      of the unconscious" (pp. 468-69).
      Reprinted in A2, pp. 459-91.

C69. "Le séminaire sur 'La letter volée.' La psychanalyse
      2 (1957): 1-44. Based on the seminar of 26 April
      1955 (see B13) and written May-August 1956.

      Uses Poe's story "The Purloined Letter" to
      illustrate a central thesis: the position of the
      subject is determined by the signifier or, more
      generally, by the chain of signifiers that makes up
      the symbolic order. Comparing the letter in Poe's
      story to the signifier, Lacan shows how the posses-
      sion of the letter leads to one's being possessed by
      the letter, i.e., to one's inadvertent assumption of
      a position vis-à-vis others that is determined
      wholly by one's relation to the signifier.
      What Freud teaches us in Beyond the Pleasure
      Principle (1920), Lacan says, "is that the subject
      must pass through the channels of the symbolic."
      However, in Poe's story we see that "not only the
      subject, but the subjects, grasped in their inter-
      subjectivity . . . model their very being on the
      moment of the signifying chain which traverses
      them. If what Freud discovered and rediscovers with
      a perpetually increasing sense of shock has a
      meaning, it is that the displacement of the sig-
      nifier determines the subjects in their act" (tr.
      p. 60). Lacan calls this the "immixture of sub-
      jects" that he introduced in the analysis of the
      dream of Irma's injection in B13, and the fact that
      the various subjects come to occupy the same

position in relation to the letter confirms the
power of the "repetition automatism" which "finds
its basis in what we have called the <u>insistence</u> of
the signifying chain" (tr. p. 39). As he says in
conclusion, a "letter always arrives at its destination" (tr. p. 72).
   This is one of Lacan's best-known essays and has
been discussed at length by a number of commentators
beginning with Derrida's critical reading (G544).
For a reading of Derrida's reading, see G661. See
also F424 and K1356 for related essays. Most of
these essays are reprinted in F374/375, where the
place of Lacan's essay in the more general context
of his work is discussed and where the editors
provide a detailed reading of the essay, along with
commentary on the various disputes it engendered.
   C69 was reprinted, with a lengthy commentary and
other apparatus by Lacan, in A2, pp. 9-61. It also
appeared in Daniel Hameline, ed., <u>Anthologie des
psychologues français contemporains</u> (Paris: Presses
Universitaires de France, 1969), pp. 324-29. An
abbreviated version presumably based on Lacan's
seminar presentation appears in B13, pp. 225-40.
Translated by Jeffrey Mehlman as "Seminar on 'The
Purloined Letter,'" <u>Yale French Studies</u> 48 (1972):
39-72. Also translated in Italian in A2f, pp. 13-
80.

C70.   "La psychanalyse et son enseignement." Société
       française de philosophie, 23 February 1957.
       <u>Bulletin de la Société française de philosophie</u>
       51, no. 2 (1957): 65-85. Discussion pp. 86-101.

   Claims that psychoanalysis has posed a unique
problem to philosophy ever since <u>The Interpretation
of Dreams</u> (1900): within an unconscious that is
"not so much profound as inaccessible" to consciousness, "<u>ça</u> parle," i.e., the id (or more simply "it")
speaks as a "subject within the subject, transcending the subject" (p. 65). Even before Saussure,
Lacan says, Freud distinguished the signifier from
the signified and taught us to understand the
function of the signifier quite apart from any
"natural meaning" it might have. "In effect," Lacan
adds, Freud's discovery led us directly to the
symbolic order (p. 73). That is why Freud taught
that we must "read" a symptom as it is supported by
a structure identical to the structure of language.
Lacan claims that the symptom itself is already
"inscribed in a process of writing" because it is a
particular formation of the unconscious: it does not
possess a specific signification, but functions only
in relation to the signifying structure that determines it. "If you will allow the play on words,"
Lacan says, we might say that the symptom is always

concerned with the "agreement" between the subject
and the verb (p. 73).

Lacan also briefly sketches his distinction
between the other and the Other and explains that
the analyst must be situated in the place of the
Other if he is to avoid turning the transference
into simply another imaginary trap for the subject's
ego. Any psychoanalysis that proposes the ego as
its point of stability distorts's Freud's teaching,
Lacan insists, since Freud's whole theory of narcissism denounces such imaginary identifications in
favor of establishing the subject's position in the
register of the signifier.

This item also includes a brief discussion of the
differences between hysteria and obsession and an
attack on the usual curriculum of psychoanalytic
institutes, which Lacan considers too narrowly
focussed on therapeutic ends more appropriate to a
school for dentists: "Any return to Freud that
gives substance to a teaching worthy of the name
will be produced only by the path by which the most
hidden truth is manifested in the revolutions of
culture. This path is the only formation that we
can pretend to transmit to those who follow us. It
is called: a style" (p. 85).

In the discussion following his presentation (see
J1092), Lacan defends his emphasis on the determin-
ative role of language in Freud's thought and claims
that "The truth of the unconscious is thus not
imposed as an ineffable profundity of reality. It
is truth because it is produced according to the law
of truth in a structure of language" (p. 90).

Reprinted in A2, pp. 437-58.

C71.   "L'instance de la lettre dans l'inconscient ou la
       raison depuis Freud." Presented at the Sorbonne
       to the Groupe de philosophie de la Fédération des
       étudiants ès lettres, 9 May 1957. La psychanalyse
       3 (1957): 47-81.

       Explains the connection between Freud's account of
       the unconscious and Saussure's distinction between
       the signifier and signified, and argues that the
       psychoanalytic experience discovers in the uncon-
       scious "the whole structure of language" (A2, p.
       495;A2j, p. 147). Reminding his audience that
       language exists long before the entry of any
       individual subject (A2, p. 495; A2j, p. 148), Lacan
       attacks the notion of an integrated self as repre-
       sented in Descartes's Cogito ergo sum and claims
       instead that Freud discovered "the self's radical
       ex-centricity to itself" in relation to language
       (A2, p. 524; A2j, p. 171). Freud identified a
       "radical heteronomy . . . gaping within man," Lacan
       says, a split that results from the subject's

relation to the signifier or the "letter," which
Lacan defines here as "the essentially localized
structure of the signifier" (A2, p. 501; A2j, p.
153).

Lacan represents the function of the signifier
with the "algorithm" S/s, which he uses to represent
Saussure's theory of what Lacan describes as "the
primordial position of the signifier [S] and the
signified [s] as being distinct orders separated
initially by a barrier resisting signification" (A2,
p. 497; A2j, p. 149).   What is important about
Saussure's discovery, Lacan says, is not the celebrated arbitrariness of the connection between
signifier and signified.   Rather, it is the notion
of a barrier between them.   The signifier does not
immediately refer us to some signified as its fixed
meaning; instead, the chain of signifiers operates
according to "the laws of a closed order" in which
the signifier never crosses over to the realm of the
signified but "always anticipates meaning by unfolding its dimension before it" (A2, pp. 501-02;
A2j, pp. 152-53).   As a result, meaning "insists"
[insiste] in the chain of signifiers but never
"consists" in any one of them   (A2, p. 502; A2j, p.
153).   Consequently, Lacan concludes, we must accept
the idea of an "incessant sliding [glissement
incessant] of the signified under the signifier"
(A2, p. 502; A2j, p. 154).

Lacan's emphasis on the barrier that separates the
signifier from the signified leads him to distinguish metaphor from metonymy as the two sides or
"slopes" (les versants) of the field of the signifier.   Saussure stressed the horizontal linearity
of the chain of discourse, Lacan argues, but there
is in fact a "polyphony" of discourse that also
aligns it vertically along the several staves of a
musical score (A2, p. 503; A2j, p. 154).   These two
vectors are derived from Roman Jakobson's distinction between the metonymic (the "linear") and the
metaphoric (the "vertical") poles of language (see
Jakobson's "The Metaphoric and Metonymic Poles,"
Chapter Five of Fundamentals of Language, by
Jakobson and Morris Halle [1956]).   Lacan also
briefly alludes to the linearity of discourse being
marked by "anchoring points" (points de capiton), a
concept he introduced in B14 and will elaborate on
in C73.

In a detailed analysis of what he calls the
"creative spark" of metaphorical substitution, Lacan
denies that metaphor allows the simultaneous
presentation of two signifiers, much less any
presentation of two signifieds within the realm of
discourse.   Instead, metaphor "flashes between two
signifiers one of which has taken the place of the
other in the signifying chain, the occulted sig-

nifier remaining present through its (metonymic) connection with the rest of the chain" (A2, p. 507; A2j, p. 157). In other words, one signifier has replaced another, driving the first "beneath the bar" where it occupies the place originally occupied by the signified--in short, where it functions as the "meaning" of the current signifier. Lacan says this is how the effect of meaning or signification is achieved without ever actually crossing over from the realm of the signifier into that of the signified.

Lacan represents these two functions of metonymy and metaphor by two formulas. Metonymy is represented by the formula $f(S \ldots S') \doteq S(-)s$. Lacan explains that this means that the relation between two signifiers is what "installs" the "manque de l'être" or "lack-of-being" in the subject's relation to the object. The relation does this through the "valeur de renvoi" of signification, the "reference back" from the second signifier to the first that gives rise to the effect of meaning and invests signification with a "desire aimed at the very lack it supports" (A2, p. 515; A2, p. 164). That "lack-of-being" is represented here by the "(-)," which Lacan says stands for a minus-sign (the lack) and also for the bar between the S and s.

Metaphor is represented by the formula $f(S'/S)S \doteq S(+)s$, which means that the substitution of one signifier for another produces an effect of signification that we call "creative" or "poetic." The sign "+" represents here the apparent crossing of the bar that gives rise to that effect (A2, p. 515; A2j, p. 164). (In light of Lacan's later interest in "mathemes" it is interesting to note that his own use of mathematical formulas here is at least partially figurative, as exemplified in his reading of the plus-sign as a crossing of the bar represented by the minus-sign. When this essay was translated into English for the first time, the line separating the signifier from the signified was not reproduced in Lacan's diagrams. For a comment on the implications of that slip, see G820.)

Lacan next turns to the place of the subject as defined in relation to the order of the signifier. Instead of Descartes's "I think therefore I am," Lacan substitutes "I think where I am not, therefore I am where I do not think" (A2, p. 518; A2j, p. 166). The radical ex-centricity of the subject suggested by this paradox derives from what Lacan calls "this signifying game" between metonymy and metaphor, insofar as it includes "the active edge that splits my desire between a refusal of the signifier and a lack of being" (A2, p. 517; A2j, p. 166). Language thus poses the question of being to the subject or, more accurately, "in place of the

subject," and Lacan claims that man is caught "in
the rails--eternally stretching forth towards the
desire for something else [le désir d'autre chose]-
-of metonymy" (A2, p. 518; A2j, p. 167).
    Lacan notes that this relation of the subject to
the chain of signifiers has specific implications
for our understanding of neurosis and the symptom.
It also raises the issue of the Other, and in the
concluding pages of the essay Lacan describes man's
relation to the Other as one in which the Other is
always mediating between the subject and his double,
a constant source of agitation that lies at the
heart of the subject's sense of identity and that
turns it into a sense of something missing. "If I
have said that the unconscious is the discourse of
the Other," Lacan remarks, "it is in order to indicate the beyond in which the recognition of
desire is bound up with the desire for recognition"
(A2, p. 524; A2j, p. 172).
    In addition to these claims, Lacan discusses the
linguistic dimension of Freud's treatment of dream-
analysis in The Interpretation of Dreams. He
identifies Verdichtung (condensation) with metaphor,
the "superimposition of the signifiers," and
Verschiebung (displacement) with "that veering off
of signification that we see in metonymy" (A2, p.
511; A2j, p. 160). He also analyzes some lines by
Valéry and Hugo to illustrate the effects of signification achieved by poetic metaphor, including a
line from Hugo's "Booz endormi" that reappears
frequently in Lacan's work: "Sa gerbe n'était pas
avare ni haineuse" ("His sheaf was neither miserly
nor spiteful") (A2, p. 506; A2j, p. 156). Lacan
also exemplifies the constitutive power of the
signifier in our perception of reality with a story
about two children who look out of the window of a
train, each seeing a different sign (the Hommes/
Dames on some public rest rooms), and so arrive at
very different conclusions about where they are.
    This is one of Lacan's most famous essays, second
only perhaps to C58. His introductory remarks are
often cited as a justification of his complex prose
style, which he describes here as existing somewhere
between the written and spoken word in a form that
leaves the reader "no other way out than the way in,
which I prefer to be difficult" (A2, p. 493; A2j, p.
146).
    Reprinted in A2, pp. 493-528. For a more detailed
description see F374. First translated by Jan Miel
as "The Insistence of the Letter in the Unconscious," Yale French Studies 36/37 (1966), pp. 112-
47; reprinted in Structuralism, edited by Jacques
Ehrmann (New York: Anchor Books, 1970), pp. 101-37
(see G734). Miel's translation was also reprinted
in The Structuralists from Marx to Lévi-Strauss,

edited by Richard and Fernande DeGeorge (Garden
City, NY: Anchor Books, 1972), pp. 287-323. A
later translation by Alan Sheridan drew heavily on
Miel to the extent of reproducing some of Miel's
editorial notations and much of his phrasing.
However, Sheridan translated "l'insistance" as
"agency" instead of Miel's "insistence" and made
several other substantial changes. See "The Agency
of the Letter in the Unconscious or Reason Since
Freud," A2j, pp. 146-78. For an extended commentary
see F348. Also translated by Norbert Haas as "Das
Drangen des Buchstabens im Unbewussten oder die
Vernunft seit Freud," in Anselm Haverkamp, ed.,
Theorie der Metapher (Darmstadt: Wissenschaftliche
Buchges, 1983), pp. 175-215; and into Italian in
A2f, pp. 488-523, reprinted in Psicanalisi come
filosofia del linguaggio, edited by A. Pagnini
(Milan: Longanesi, 1976), pp. 115-28.

C72. "D'une question préliminaire à tout traitement
      possible de la psychose." Based on B14, edited
      for publication December 1957-January 1958. La
      psychanalyse 4 (1959): 1-50.

      Claims that the preliminary question of the title
is how to designate the defect or "fault" (le
défaut) that gives psychosis its essential structure
and distinguishes it from neurosis. As an answer
Lacan proposes "the foreclosure of the name-of-the-
father in the place of the Other, and in the failure
of the paternal metaphor" (A2, p. 575; A2j, p. 215).
      Lacan begins by criticizing traditional psycho-
analytic explanations of psychosis, which have been
based on antiquated models of perception that
assumed an absolute distinction between the per-
ceiver and the perceived, the subject and the
object. He also rejects the equally simplistic
models of projective perception in which objects are
constituted within and by an autonomous subjectivity, a position that blurs the distinction
between perception and hallucination. Lacan says
that in phenomena such as verbal hallucination
(which he had studied thirty years earlier) it is
clear that the "perception" of speech depends on
something other than the conscious, unified subject.
      The crucial point in such cases, Lacan argues, is
"that the sensorium being indifferent in the
production of a signifying chain . . . this signifying chain imposes itself, by itself, on the
subject in its vocal dimension" (A2, p. 533; A2j, p.
181). In other words, the hallucinations characteristic of psychosis are dependent on and organized
by effects of the signifier or, more simply, by
language. "In the place where the unspeakable
object is rejected in the real," Lacan says, "a word

makes itself heard" (A2, p. 535; A2j, p. 183). He
supports this thesis with an analysis of Schreber's
Memoirs. (See his earlier and more extended
comments on Schreber's book and Freud's analysis of
it in B14.)

Lacan then turns to an attack on psychologists who
have proposed the ego as a synthesizing faculty
whose job is to adapt the subject to the external
world and whose failure can explain the "loss of
reality" that is termed psychosis. Lacan objects
that such theories ignore Freud's insistence that
the ego "is constituted according to the other," and
that they also "ignore the symbolic articulation
that Freud discovered at the same time as the
unconscious, and which, for him, is, in effect,
consubstantial with it: it is the need for this
articulation that he signifies for us in his
methodical reference to the Oedipus complex" (A2, p.
546; A2j, p. 191). The result of this ignorance is
an excessive emphasis on the organ represented by
the phallus in the Oedipal complex rather than on
the symbolic function of the phallus, and a consequent emphasis on homosexuality as a determinant of
paranoiac psychosis rather than as "a symptom
articulated in its process" (A2, p. 544; A2j, p.
190).

The third section of this essay introduces a
complex network among elements of Lacan's argument
that defies summary. (For an attempt at a systematic summary and explanation, see F374, pp. 209-
212.) Starting with a simplified form of the L-
schema, Lacan situates relations among the imaginary, the symbolic, and the real registers according
to corollary relations among the Subject, the Other,
the ego, and its objects, and he formulates the
result in what has come to be called the "R-
schema."

At its simplest level, Lacan's point about this
formidable array of terms is that the subject's
imaginary sense of "self" is separated from the
symbolic register by the real. The real is experienced by the subject as a gap within the
imaginary identification with the other, a wound or
"béance" opened up by the prematuration of the human
individual in the face of the idealized coherence of
the imaginary other (see C53). This experience
leads to the subject's identification with the
phallus, which is the point of insertion into the
Symbolic. "It is by means of the gap opened up by
this prematuration in the imaginary . . . that the
human animal is capable of imagining himself as
mortal, which does not mean that he would be able to
do so without his symbiosis with the symbolic, but
rather that without this gap that alienates him from
his own image, this symbiosis with the symbolic, in

which he constitutes himself as subject to death,
could not have occurred" (A2, p. 552; A2j, p. 196).

   Ignoring Lacan's extended commentary on a number
of points raised by the configurations of his
diagrams, his conclusions may be summarized as
follows:
   (1) The R-schema reveals the importance of
Freud's emphasis on the _imaginary_ function of the
phallus as the pivot of the subject's relation to
the symbolic process, rather than as a real organ
that one either has or wants. The "phallocentricism" of this model is "entirely conditioned by
the intrusion of the signifier in man's psyche,"
Lacan says, and it is "strictly impossible to deduce
from any pre-established harmony of this psyche with
the nature that it expresses" (A2, pp. 554-5; A2j,
pp. 198).
   (2) "The attribution of procreation to the father
can only be the effect of a pure signifier, or a
recognition, not of a real father, but of what
religion has taught us to refer to as the name-of-
the-father" (A2, p. 556; A2j, p. 199; see also
K1350). "Of course," Lacan adds, "there is no need
of a signifier to be a father, any more than to be
dead, but without a signifier, no one would ever
know anything about either state of being."
   (3) That Freud himself recognized the affinity
between the place of the father and the presence of
death is apparent "when the necessity of his re-
flexion led him to link the appearance of the
signifier of the Father, as author of the Law, with
death, even to the murder of the Father--thus
showing that if this murder is the fruitful moment
of debt through which the subject binds himself for
life to the Law, the symbolic Father is, insofar as
he signifies this Law, the dead Father" (A2, p. 556;
A2j, p. 199).
   The third part of this essay is given over to a
detailed analysis of the delusional phenomena
described in Schreber's _Memoirs_, with special
emphasis on the foreclosure of the name-of-the-
father and the way this foreclosure determines the
psychotic subject's distorted relations to the
symbolic and imaginary orders. Lacan says that
ordinarily "the signification of the phallus . . .
must be evoked in the subject's imaginary by the
paternal metaphor" (A2, p. 556; A2j, p. 199). If
that does not occur, there will be a "hole" in the
symbolic order exactly at that point where the name-
of-the-father would ordinarily function, and Lacan
turns to the details of Schreber's delusional world
to show how many of its details--including
Schreber's "homosexual" fantasies of becoming a
woman--can be explained as the subject's effort to

reconstruct itself around "the hole dug in the field
of the signifier" by the foreclosure that lies at
the origin of the psychosis. Foreclosed, "never
having attained the place of the Other," the name-
of-the-father therefore "must be called into
symbolic opposition to the subject. It is the lack
of the name-of-the-father in that place which, by
the hole that it opens up in the signified, sets off
the cascade of reshapings of the signifier . . . to
the point at which the level is reached at which
signifier and signified are stabilized in the
delusional metaphor" (A2, p. 577; A2j, p. 217).
   Reprinted in A2, pp. 531-83, A2j, pp. 179-225.
For a more detailed account of Lacan's argument in
this essay, see F374, esp. pp. 238-62. The R-schema
is discussed further by Lacan in C73, and he adds a
long explanatory footnote when this essay is reprinted in A2 (see pp. 553-54; A2j, pp. 223-24).
Jacques-Alain Miller discusses the R-schema in A2,
pp. 905-07 (A2j, pp. 333-34), and another extended
discussion of the schema may be found in F420, pp.
293-98. B14 is the best commentary on this difficult essay, but on the general topic of psychosis
in Lacan's work see F392. Schreber's memoirs, first
published in 1903, have been translated as Memoirs
of My Nervous Illness, tr. Ida Macalpine and Richard
Hunter (London: W. M. Dawson and Sons). Lacan
complements Macalpine's commentary on that text, but
most of his remarks are addressed to Freud's
analysis of the memoirs in "Psycho-Analytic Notes
upon an Autobiographical Account of a Case of
Paranoia (Dementia Paranoides)" (1911).

C73.   "La signification du phallus" ("Die Bedeutung des
       Phallus"). Presented in German, 9 May 1958, at
       the Max Planck Institute in Munich. A2, pp. 685-
       695.

   Insists that Freud's theory of the castration
complex marks a "disturbance of human sexuality, not
of a contingent, but of an essential kind," one that
is "insoluble by any reduction to biological
givens." Lacan also claims that clinical facts
"reveal a relation of the subject to the phallus
that is established without regard to the anatomical
difference of the sexes" (A2, p. 686; A2j, p. 282).
In addition, he briefly recounts the issues debated
by Freud, Jones, Horney, and Klein regarding the
phallic stage and the definition of feminine
sexuality, and then he demonstrates the importance
of Saussure's distinction between the signifier and
the signified as a theoretical formulation of
Freud's own discoveries.
   Lacan begins by claiming that it is "Freud's
discovery that gives to the signifier/signified

opposition the full extent of its implications:
namely, that the signifier has an active function in
determining certain effects in which the signifiable
appears as submitting to its mark, by becoming
through that passion the signified" (A2, p. 688;
A2j, p. 284). This "passion of the signifier" marks
a new dimension of the human condition, Lacan says,
because we find that man's nature "is woven by
effects in which is to be found the structure of
language, of which he becomes the material" (A2, pp.
688-89; A2j, p. 284). He distinguishes between this
position and the "culturalist" argument associated
with Karen Horney, and argues that his own approach
stems from "a question of rediscovering in the laws
that govern that other scene (ein andere Schauplatz,
i.e., the unconscious) . . . the effects that are
discovered at the level of the chain of materially
unstable elements that constitutes langauge." Lacan
identifies these effects as metonymy and metaphor,
the "determining effects for the institution of the
subject" (A2, p. 689; A2j, p. 285).
     The subject is instituted in speech in this way
only in relation to a "signifying place" that is the
locus of the Other, and it is in this splitting of
the subject that the phallus reveals its function.
Insisting that Freud distinguished between the
phallus and "the organ that it symbolizes," Lacan
says that "the phallus is a signifier" and it
designates the effects of the signified "in that the
signifier conditions them by its presence as a
signifier" (A2, p. 690; A2j, p. 285). (On Lacan's
curious and perhaps inadvertent allusion to an
organic basis for the phallus as the symbol of the
penis, see G750.) The effects of the phallus's
presence as a signifier proceed from what Lacan
calls a "deviation" of man's needs that occurs as a
result of the fact that he speaks. As needs are
"subjected" to demand, Lacan argues, they return
alienated from the speaker, a consequence not of any
"real" dependence but of the fact that "it is from
the locus of the Other that its message is emitted"
(A2, p. 690; A2j, p. 286). What is thus alienated
in need reappears as "desire," which is irreducible
to need despite attempts by some psychoanalysts to
equate the two, especially in relation to the notion
of "frustration."
     Lacan elaborates on these distinctions among need,
desire, and demand, associating demand with an
"Other as already possessing the 'privilege' of
satisfying needs." Such an assumption, he claims,
serves as a definition of love. Desire, on the
other hand, is a closed field occupied by the sexual
relation, which is thus also to be distinguished
from biological need as well as from love and which
cannot be ordered by reference to any "genital"

organization. "In any case," Lacan concludes, "man
cannot aim at being whole . . . while ever the play
of displacement and condensation to which he is
doomed in the exercise of his functions marks his
relation as a subject to the signifier. The phallus
is the privileged signifier of that mark in which
the role of the logos is joined with the advent of
desire" (A2, p. 692; A2j, p. 287).

This essay extends the emphasis on a semiotic or
"structural" articulation of psychoanalytic theory
that occupied much of Lacan's attention during the
1950s and early 1960s, but it also establishes the
importance of sexual identity and its relation to
the splitting of the subject in the face of demand
(and the symbolic order) that Lacan began emphasizing more consistently in his later work. The
concluding sections of this essay comment on the
"masquerade" of feminine sexuality and the observation that "man finds satisfaction for his demand for
love in the relation with the woman, in as much as
the signifier of the phallus constitutes her as
giving in love what she does not have." These
remarks look forward to Lacan's critique of the
idealization of "The woman" as the Other and his
discussion of the impossibility of sexual relations
in B31.

Translated in A2j, pp. 281-91, and in F370, pp.
74-85. For additional commentary on many of the
issues raised in this essay, see the other items in
F370, especially Rose's introduction.

C74. "La direction de la cure et les principes de son
      pouvoir." Presented at the Colloque international
      de Royaumont, 10-13 July 1958. Revised 1960. La
      psychanalyse 6 (1961): 149-206.

Describes several misconceptions regarding
analytic practice as proposed by various Freudian
schools, and discusses in detail relations among
desire, demand, and need as they bear on the role of
the analyst. Lacan begins with a particularly
vicious attack on American ego psychology and the
corollary notion that the analyst must provide a
"good" or "strong" ego as a model for the patient's
"cure" ("treatment" in the English translation").
The analyst directs the treatment, not the patient,
Lacan says, and that means that the direction cannot
be formulated as a univocal line of communication
(A2, p. 586; A2j, p. 227). Instead, the analyst,
too, must "pay" with his words but also with his
person as he "lends it as a support for the singular
phenomena that analysis has discovered in the
transference" (A2, p. 587; A2j, p. 227). And
whereas the analyst is "always free in the timing,
frequency and choice of my interventions," this

second kind of payment requires that "my freedom is
alienated by the duplication to which my person is
subjected" in the handling of transference--and it
is there, Lacan adds, that the "secret of analysis"
must be sought (A2, p. 588; A2j, p. 228).

Lacan then briefly describes the role of the
"dummy" ("_le mort_") as an aid to the analyst and as
a means of introducing the fourth member of the
analytic game (the patient's unconscious) (A2, p.
590; A2j, p. 229).   Moving on to the place of
interpretation in analysis, Lacan argues that
"interpretation is based on no assumption of divine
archetypes" but on the fact that "the unconscious is
structured in the most radical way like a language"
(A2, p. 594; A2j, p. 234).   Interpretation must
therefore accept "a concept of the function of the
signifier" in all of its most radical implications
if it is to "grasp where the subject is subordi-
nated, even suborned, by the signifier" (A2, p. 593;
A2j, p. 233).   Hence, Lacan argues,

> in order to decipher the diachrony of unconscious
> repetitions, interpretation must introduce into
> the synchrony of the signifiers that compose it
> something that suddenly makes translation pos-
> sible--precisely what is made possible by the
> function of the Other in the concealment of the
> code, it being in relation to that Other that the
> missing element appears.   (A2, p. 593; A2j, p.
> 233)

This appearance is paradoxical, of course, since the
sign always "establishes presence against a background of absence, just as it constitutes absence in
presence."   This is what Freud discovered in the
Fort! Da! game described in Beyond the Pleasure
Principle (1920), and it is "the point of insertion
of a symbolic order that pre-exists the infantile
subject and in accordance with which he will have to
structure himself" (A2, p. 594; A2j, p. 234).

Using this account of the function of the signifier and the Other in interpretation, Lacan then
comments on various concepts of transference,
focussing on transference love and the function of
desire and demand.   It would seem that the analyst
supports the subject's demand by his very presence,
Lacan begins, but this is not done simply to
frustrate the subject.   Instead, it is to "allow the
signifiers in which his frustration is bound up to
reappear."   Lacan explains this remark by recalling
that primary identification is produced "in the
oldest demand," that of the infant for the mother--
or, more specifically, in the mother's omnipotence.
It is this identification, however, "that not only
suspends the satisfaction of needs from the signi-

fying apparatus, but also that which fragments
them, filters them, models them upon the defiles of
the structure of the signifier" (A2, p. 618; A2j, p.
255).   Thus, Lacan concludes, "there is now no need
to seek further for the source of the identification
with the analyst. That identification may assume
very different forms, but it will always be an
identification with signifiers" (A2, p. 619; A2j, p.
256).

Lacan devotes the last section of the essay to
Freud's contention that dreams are wish-
fulfillments, and he comments at length on Freud's
reading of the dream of the butcher's wife from The
Interpretation of Dreams. In the course of his
discussion, which turns on Freud's discovery of the
"desire for desire" that lurks beneath the wife's
demand, Lacan remarks again on the complex interaction among desire, demand, and the Other that
underlies analytic discourse:

> Desire is that which is manifested in the interval
> that demand hollows within itself, in as much as
> the subject, in articulating the signifying chain,
> brings to light the want-to-be ["le manque à
> être"], together with the appeal to receive the
> complement from the Other, if the Other, the locus
> of speech, is also the locus of this want, or
> lack." (A2, p. 627; A2j, p. 263)

"That which is thus given to the Other to fill,"
Lacan adds, "and which is strictly that which it
does not have, since it, too, lacks being, is what
is called love, but it is also hate and ignorance.
It is also what is evoked by any demand beyond the
need that is articulated in it . . . . Furthermore,
the satisfaction of need appears only as the lure in
which the demand for love is crushed" (A2, p. 627;
A2j, p. 263).

This is why Lacan claims two pages later, "Desire
is produced in the beyond of the demand . . . But
desire is also hollowed within demand." Or more
dramatically, "desire is the furrow inscribed in the
course . . . the mark of the iron of the signifier
on the shoulder of the speaking subject" (A2, p.
629; A2j, p. 265). On the basis of such claims,
Lacan distinguishes between the desire that oriented
the subject toward the Other as the locus of speech
and the demand for love that reflects primary
identification, and he derives the following
principle from that distinction.

> --if desire is an effect in the subject of the
> condition that is imposed on him by the existence
> of the discourse, to make his need pass through
> the defiles of the signifier;

--if, on the other hand . . . by opening up the
dialectic of transference, we must establish the
notion of the Other with a capital O as being the
locus of the deployment of speech (the other
scene, ein andere Schauplatz, of which Freud
speaks in 'The Interpretation of Dreams');
--it must be posited that, produced as it is by an
animal at the mercy of language, man's desire is
the desire of the Other.
This principle involves a quite different
function from that of the primary identification
referred to above, for it does not involve the
subject's assuming the insignia of the other, but
rather the condition that the subject has to find
the constituting structure of desire in the same
gap opened up by the effect of the signifiers in
those who come to represent the Other for him, in
so far as his demand is subject to them." (A2, p.
628; A2j, p. 264)

Reprinted in A2, pp. 585-645, and translated in
A2j, pp. 226-80. Abstract by Jean-Bertrand Pontalis
in Bulletin de psychologie 12, no. 2/3, pp. 160-62.
For a detailed reading of this essay, see F374.

C75.   "Remarque sur le rapport de Daniel Lagache:
        'Psychanalyse et structure de la personnalité.'"
        Presented at the Colloque international de Royau-
        mont, 10-13 July 1958. Revised 1960. La psych-
        analyse 6 (1961): 111-47.

Uses the occasion of Lagache's paper to clarify
his own differences from more traditional psychoanalytic accounts of the ego; of the ego-ideal and
the ideal ego (especially as described by Nunberg in
Principles of Psycho-Analysis [1932]); of the id (le
ça); and of the relation between negation, the unconscious, and the subject. Lacan praises Lagache's
recognition of the importance of "others" in the
development of the child, but he insists that he and
Lagache differ considerably regarding the function
they attribute to intersubjectivity. Whereas
Lagache understands it as a symmetrical relation "à
l'autre du semblable" in which the subject learns to
be treated as an object for the other, Lacan
emphasizes the subject's emergence from the given
("la donée") of the signifiers, which recover him in
an Other which is their transcendental place (A2, p.
656).
The second section of the essay, entitled simply
"Ou ça," focuses on the nature of the id, especially
as it marks the subject's relation to the chain of
signifiers. Rather treating it as a reservoir of
drives, Lacan situates the id at the juncture of the
subject's entry into the symbolic and ties it

closely to the paradoxical function of affirmation
(<u>Bejahung</u>) and negation or, as Lacan translates it,
<u>de</u>negation (<u>Verneinung</u>). He illustrates this
function with the phrase "<u>Je crains qu'il ne</u>
<u>vienne</u>," and he distinguishes between the subject of
the statement, the "<u>Je</u>," and the subject of desire,
indicated by the "<u>ne</u>" that registers the desire by
defending against it, an example of denegation.
Lacan warns us, however, that the "place" of the
subject marked by this negation cannot be described
simply as the absence of a coherent subject, despite
Lagache's suggestions. Instead, Lacan claims it is
the place that makes absence itself possible and
that poses the first contradiction, which is summed
up in the phrase "to be or not to be" (A2, p. 666).
The third section of the essay consists of a
detailed analysis of how the ego-ideal and the ideal
ego come about through the subject's misperception
of his relation to objects and his place in the
world of objects. Using the optical models he will
return to in Seminar XI (see B22), Lacan explains
relations between the imaginary and the symbolic
registers of experience by tracing the difference
between actual and projected "points of view"
relative to an object that is situated within the
field of vision according to idealized optical
positions. (For a detailed summary of Lacan's use
of optical models in this context, see B22.)
The fourth and final section of the essay is quite
brief and merely suggests the ethical dimension of
Lacan's critique of traditional psychoanalytic
concepts, a topic that he takes up as the theme for
Seminar VII.
Reprinted in A2, pp. 647-84.

C76.   "Jeunesse de Gide ou la lettre et le désir."
        <u>Critique</u> 131 (1958):   291- 315.

Comments on Jean Delay's <u>La jeunesse d'André Gide</u>
(Paris: Gallimard, 1956), pointing out the often
reciprocal relation between the "message" of Gide's
writing and the experiences of his life that are
described in Delay's study of Gide's "private"
papers. The importance of those papers, Lacan
contends, is not in their content but in their mode
of address. Like other famous people who seem to
keep records for future biographers, Gide wrote them
"<u>à un autre à venir</u>," addressing his purportedly
private thoughts and experiences to an "other" in
and for whom they take on their significance. Delay
realizes that, Lacan notes, and that is what
differentiates his study from works of "applied
psychoanalysis": in Delay's work, psychoanalysis is
"applied" in the proper sense, that is, as "treatment," and hence is applied to a subject who speaks

and who listens. Lacan goes on to discuss the links
between Gide's accounts of his youth and certain
themes in his work, such as that of the double,
death, and the ideal woman.
(In B16, Lacan uses Delay's account of Gide's
childhood [especially the attempted seduction of
young Gide by his aunt and Gide's relation to his
cousin] to show why the infant's desire of the
mother's desire is an important formative moment in
the child's emerging sense of itself.)
Reprinted in A2, pp. 739-64.

C77.   "Propos directifs pour un Congrès sur la sexualité
        féminine." Written in 1958. Presented at the
        Colloque international de psychanalyse, 5-9 Sep-
        tember 1960, at the Municipal University of
        Amsterdam. La psychanalyse 7 (1962).

        Objects to the usual psychoanalytic formulations
        of issues related to feminine sexuality such as
        passivity, masochism, and frigidity, and argues that
        they are merely biologistic distortions of Freud's
        concepts. Furthermore, Lacan argues that such
        formulations contradict the evidence presented by
        analysis itself, which leads to the following
        principle: "castration cannot be deduced from
        development alone, since it presupposes the subjec-
        tivity of the Other as the place of its law. The
        otherness of sex is denatured by this alienation.
        Man here acts as the relay whereby the woman becomes
        this Other for herself as she is this Other for
        Him."
        Reprinted in A2, pp. 725-36. Translated by
        Jacqueline Rose in F370, pp. 87-98. For further
        remarks on the imaginary notion of woman as the
        Other see B31 and Rose's introduction to F370, as
        well as the other items by Lacan in F370. On the
        more general issue of feminine sexuality, see items
        listed in the index under that topic.

C78.   "A la memoire d'Ernest Jones: sur sa théorie du
        symbolisme." January-March, 1959. La psych-
        analyse 5 (1960): 1-20.

        Praises Jones's work for a logical power which
        transcends the uses to which he put it, and de-
        scribes Jones's efforts to establish a new way of
        using symbolism in analytic interpretation that
        would go beyond the fixed meanings assumed by Jung,
        Rank, and Sachs. Focussing on Jones's essay "The
        Theory of Symbolism" (British Journal of Psychology
        9, no. 2 [1916]), Lacan explains how Jones resisted
        the tendency to return symbolism to a primitive
        mysticism and proposed instead to treat the symbol
        as a substitute for a "concrete idea"--in other

words, as what Lacan came to call a signifier.
Jones recognized from the first, Lacan says, that
analytic symbolism is conceivable only in relation
to the linguistic fact of metaphor (A2, p. 703).
Lacan claims however that Jones went astray following the metaphor through a false law of a
"displacement" in which its function was understood
in reference to a "semanteme" that systematically
passed from the particular to the general and the
concrete to the abstract.

What Jones failed to understand, according to
Lacan, is that the network of the signifier is the
most concrete of all ideas. It is there that the
subject is already implicated even before he comes
to be constituted in the form of a self within a
genealogical order or as the representative of a sex
(A2, p. 704). Both the subject and the world must
submit to the substitutions by which the signifier
serves its metaphorical function, and Lacan says
that the "primary ideas" Jones discovered at the
foundation of symbolism designate the points where
the subject disappears under the being of the signifier and so comes to be sustained by discourse
itself (A2, p. 709). What analysis has revealed
about the phallus, Lacan adds, is that it functions
as the signifier of the lack-of-being ("manque-à-
être") that determines the subject's relation to the
signifier, and in this sense we can understand that
all of the symbols Jones studied were in fact
"phallic symbols," though not in the sense that
Jones himself struggled with. Jones's search for a
"true symbolism" through distinctions between
positive and negative conditioning returned him
repeatedly to that fact, but Lacan says that Jones
could never see it because he mistakenly accorded a
primacy to the real over thought and to the signified over the signifier. Instead, he should have
realized that the effects of the signified are
created by the permutations of the signifier (A2, p.
705).

Reprinted in A2, pp. 697-717, with a long note by
Lacan, pp. 717-24. There he elaborates on connections among the works of Silberer, Jung, and
Jones regarding the topic of symbolism, and on the
relevance to this debate of his distinctions among
the real, imaginary, and symbolic registers of
experience. Lacan also explained his motives for
writing this essay and its primary points in a
letter to D. W. Winnicott (see E170). For further
comments on aphanisis as proof that the subject "ex-
sists" outside of desire, see B17, Bulletin de
psychologie, pp. 270-71.

C**.   "Hamlet." Lacan's reading of Hamlet occurred in the
       course of Seminar VI and is annotated at B17.

C79.   "Ethique de la psychanalytique: leçons publiques du
        Docteur Jacques Lacan à le Faculté Universitaire
        St. Louis, à Bruxelles, les 9 et 10 mars 1960."
        <u>Quarto: supplement à la Lettre mensuelle de
        l'Ecole de la cause freudienne</u> 6 (1982):   5-24.

        Describes in Part I Freud's emphasis on the
        paradoxical relation between the death of the Father
        and the severity of the Law as proposed in <u>Totem and
        Taboo</u> (1912-13), and traces the function of iden-
        tification that underlies the formation of the
        super-ego which subjects individuals to that law.
        Lacan rejects the characterization of Freud's
        thought as humanist and insists instead that there
        is a "Logos" that serves as the "substructure" of
        man in Freud's work.
        Part II is devoted to the question of whether or
        not psychoanalysis can provide an ethic for our
        time, and Lacan argues that the mirror stage is
        implicit in the identification demanded by the
        command to "Love your neighbor as yourself." Man
        has long since given up seeing the world as a
        reflection of himself, Lacan observes, but now sees
        his image in the form of signifiers.
        For a more extended treatment of this topic see
        B23.

C80.   "Subversion du sujet et dialectique du désir dans
        l'inconscient freudien." Congrès de Royaumont,
        Les Colloques philosophiques internationaux, 19-23
        September 1960. A2, pp. 793-827.

        Begins with a brief critique of the unified
        subject assumed by modern science, and denies that
        subject was challenged either by Copernicus or
        Darwin. It was Freud who first subverted that
        notion of a unified subject, Lacan says, and he did
        it by conceiving of the unconscious as a chain of
        signifiers (A2, p. 799; A2j, p. 297). Lacan claims
        that a similar effect is visible today in modern
        linguistics, but the contemporary formulations of
        that discipline have simply articulated Freud's
        earlier discovery with their distinction between the
        signifier and the signified and with their emphasis
        on metaphor and metonymy. Although Freud lacked
        such formulas, Lacan argues that his discovery of
        the structure of language in the unconscious was
        even more radically subversive because it required a
        new kind of subject (A2, p. 800; A2j, p. 298), and
        Lacan locates this subject in relation to the series
        of cuts ("<u>coupures</u>") in which the unconscious
        "interferes" with the signifying chain. The
        strongest of these cuts "acts as a bar between the
        signifier and the signified," Lacan says, and it is

there that the subject is bound in signification.
The analytic session itself is instituted as a "cut
in a false discourse," and it is this cut in the
signifying chain alone that "verifies the structure
of the subject as discontinuity in the real" (A2, p.
799; A2j, p. 299).

Having explained the subversive thrust of the
Freudian unconscious, Lacan moves on to describe its
dialectical character. He begins with a brief
commentary on Hegel's notion of absolute knowledge.
Knowledge was traditionally conceived as a knowledge
of objects, Lacan says, but with Descartes knowledge
began to involve an element of doubt within the
knower himself, which then had to be resolved into
certainty. Knowledge thus came to rest on the
subject's own assurance, apart from the object. The
dialectical character of knowledge described by
Hegel codified this shift toward a knowledge that
knows itself, which Lacan characterizes as a passage
from connaissance to that of savoir. This is the
passage of truth, Lacan points out, and in Hegel it
is motivated by desire and directed by the "cunning
of reason," which means simply that "the subject
knows what he wants" (A2, p. 802; A2j, p. 301; see
F374, p. 361-62).

Lacan claims that Freud reopened this juncture
between truth and knowledge by showing how desire
"becomes bound up with the desire of the Other" and
by showing that the desire to know (savoir) lies in
this loop ("cette boucle") that joins the subject to
the Other (A2, p. 802; A2j, p. 301). For Freud,
Lacan says, knowledge (savoir) does not involve
connaissance but is inscribed in discourse, and
hence desire is not based on any biological instinct
but instead is connected to "drive." This connection, in turn, implies not a coincidence of the
subject with its object but instead the inevitable
"fading" of the subject in the face of the object of
desire. Lacan emphasizes the non-biological
character of desire further by distinguishing it
from need, but he also insists that it cannot be
reduced to demand either because it constantly
eludes articulation.

Lacan then turns to the graph of desire first
introduced in B17 to show "where desire, in relation
to a subject defined in his articulation by the
signifier, is situated" (A2, p. 805; A2j, p. 303).
The diagram and Lacan's comments are exceptionally
detailed and complex, but his essential aim is to
define the subject's position vis-à-vis the diachronic and the synchronic dimensions of the
signifying chain. In so doing, Lacan also situates
the subject's relation to "meaning" or the signified
as the product of desire, but this desire is
structured through the precise functions of the

signifier.

Lacan's discussion of the graph thus complements
his insistence that the signified is related to the
signifier only through a constant sliding ("glissement"), and he extends that observation by
introducing what he calls "points de capiton" or
"anchoring points." These points mark the moments
at which the subject's desire crosses the signifying
chain and stops that endless sliding by orienting
the chain towards meaning. Further elaborations of
the graph situate the Other within this orientation
as well as locating the imaginary relations of the
ego and its other, and Lacan uses the graph to show
how the symbolic position of the subject reflects
the dynamic tension of the imaginary and so remains
vulnerable to the distortions characteristic of
pathological states.

The imaginary struggle of the ego and the other
can be understood in terms of Hegel's master-slave
dialectic, and Lacan discusses that dialectic
briefly to show how it presumes the exclusion of
death from the relation (A2, p. 810; A2j, p. 308).
He cites that exclusion as proof that this imaginary
conflict is based on a symbolic pact that precedes
the imaginary and makes it possible, and he generalizes from this example to claim that in all cases
the symbolic dominates the imaginary (A2, p. 810;
A2j, p. 308). The dynamics of the imaginary
struggle necessarily imply desire, of course, and
Lacan goes on to determine the function of desire in
relation to both the imaginary and the symbolic as
desire is "structured" by the Oedipus complex.

Referring to his familiar distinction between the
real father and the name-of-the-father that represents the Law, Lacan explains how man's desire is
always the desire of this Other in the sense of
desire "belonging to" or "coming from" the position
of the Other. So instead of seeking what the ego
wants, the subject asks "what do you, the Other,
want of me?" and the stage is set for a conflict
between the ego and the subject that is at the heart
of fantasy and psychosis. Lacan's discussion of
fantasy leads to further elaborations of the graph
of desire that situate the subject's "fading" in
relation to objects that are determined by the
signifying chain, and Lacan redefines "part-objects"
and their role in fantasy by attributing their
partial quality to the "cut" that marks the subject's separation from the real (and hence the
origin of his desire), rather than considering them
in relation to some "whole" that would supplement
their partiality (A2, p. 817; A2j, p. 315).

Lacan has already pointed out that the cut with
which part-objects are associated is the bar between
the signified and signifier, and as such the cut

reflects the subject's more general "lack" as he is
constituted within the symbolic order. Lacan marks
that lack as S(Ø), which he reads as the "signifier
of a lack in the Other, inherent in its very
function as the treasure of the signifier" (A2, p.
818; A2j, p. 316). This signifier is the signifier
"for which all the other signifiers represent the
subject," which is also the symbolic function of the
phallus. Lacan goes on to explain how the symbolic
and imaginary functions of the phallus relate his
formulation of the imaginary and symbolic registers
of experience to the more traditional Freudian
account of castration and its role in the socialization of the individual through the Oedipal
complex.

Castration, Lacan says, simply marks the possibility of being detached; it is what establishes
the phallus as "negativized" ("négativé") in its
place in the specular image. Thus castration is
what "predestines the phallus to embody jouissance
in the dialectic of desire" (A2, p. 822; A2j, p.
319). "Jouissance is forbidden to him who speaks as
such," Lacan says, "although it can only be said
between the lines for whoever is subject of the Law,
since the Law is grounded in this very prohibition"
(A2, p. 821; A2j, p. 319). Finally, citing castration or "primary repression" as the limit to
jouissance and hence as the mark of human finitude,
Lacan claims it is what makes desire "human." He
concludes with the observation that "Castration
means that jouissance must be refused, so that it
can be reached on the inverted ladder ["l'échelle
renversée] of the Law of desire" (A2, p. 827; A2j,
p. 324).

This item is one of the densest and most subtle of
Lacan's essays. In many ways its summarizes most of
the themes introduced in his earlier work, and the
various positions diagrammed here recall the
formulas of the R-schema Lacan introduced five years
earlier. The most significant difference between
the R-schema and the graph of desire is that the
later graph introduces a temporal vector into the
relations that is invisible in the earlier diagram.
The temporal dimension in the subject's relation to
the signifying chain was always an important aspect
of Lacan's thought, and this later diagram enables
him to define its function more precisely than
before and to determine its connection to the
synchronic dimension of the subject's desire.

The most useful commentary on the topics of this
essay is a paper Lacan presented shortly after the
colloquium at Royaumont, C81. The abstract of
Seminar VI published in the Bulletin de psychologie
contains a useful discussion of the graph of desire;
see B17, pp. 264-67. For a detailed and excep-

tionally clear discussion of Lacan's argument, see
F374. F334 contains an extended discussion of
Lacan's treatment of the Dead Father in relation to
dreams discussed by Freud in "Formulations Regarding
the Two Principles in Mental Functioning" (1911) and
in The Interpretation of Dreams (1900). A more
extended discussion of Freud's analysis of the dream
of the dead father appears in B17, pp. 269-70.
Translated in A2j, pp. 299-325.

C81. "Position de l'inconscient." Text based on Lacan's
response to S. Leclaire and J. Laplanche, "L'inconscient, une étude psychanalytique" and Conrad
Stein, "Langage et inconscient." Sixth Colloque
de Bonneval, "The Freudian Unconscious," 30
October-2 November 1960. Edited by Lacan for
publication in L'inconscient, ed. Henri Ey.
Paris: Desclée de Brouwer, 1966. Pp. 143-77,
159-79.

Briefly criticizes the notion that the unconscious
is a form of psychic reality and the corollary
notion that the subject is a unified, coherent
consciousness, which Lacan calls the "central error"
of psychology. Lacan traces the philosophical basis
for the unitary subject in the Cartesian cogito and
in the dialectical sequence that underlies absolute
knowledge in Hegelian phenomenology, but he claims
that the only homogenous element of consciousness is
the imaginary capture of the ego by its specular
reflection and the méconnaissance that is associated
with that reflection. (For a more detailed discussion of these points, see the opening section of
C80.)
After a few comments on his alternative doctrine
of the unconscious and its role in the analytic
experience, Lacan briefly describes the synchronic
and diachronic aspects of the subject's relation to
language. That relation consists of two "movements." The first is an effect of language born out
of the original splitting of the subject ("cette
refente originelle"). In this movement, the
subject translates the synchronic signifying system
of Saussure's langue into "this primordial temporal
pulsation" ("pulsation temporelle") that is "the
fading that constitutes his identification." In the
second movement, desire "makes its bed" from "the
signifying cut" where metonymy is born, and it is
here that diachrony--"dite 'histoire'"--is inscribed
in the fading and returns to the fixity that Freud
established as the unconscious wish--i.e., to the
inanimate state constituting the goal of the death
drive ("fiat retour à la sorte de fixité que Freud
décerne au voeu inconscient" [p. 835]).
Lacan then discusses at greater length the two

"fundamental operations" in the causation of the
subject: alienation and separation. Alienation, he
argues, is "le fait du sujet" and is the consequence
of the subject's relation to the signifier. This
priority of the signifier over the subject also
explains the originary division of the subject and
gives rise to the place of the Other (p. 840).
Separation, Lacan says, is more closely related to
what Freud called Ichspaltung and arises from the
subject's realization of a loss or a lack that implies his "disparition" and death but that is first
perceived as a "fault" in the Other. As that lack
in the Other comes to be seen as the subject's own
loss, however, separation rejoins alienation and
returns the subject to the loss inherent in his own
origin.
     In the remaining sections of this article, Lacan
introduces the terms "l'Hommelette," a pun invoking
the myth of a unitary "egg" as the genesis of
creation, and the corollary "lamelle," a cellular
membrane separating and yet joining cells or,
apropos Lacan's pun, eggs as they divide and become
two. (Cf. the pun on "l'Hamlette" in Seminar VI.)
Lacan's point is subtle and complex, but essentially
he is attempting to undermine the simplistic
division of human experience along biological lines
that would yield an absolute and fixed distinction
between male and female. The topic of sexual difference emerges explicitly in the closing remarks of
the article, where Lacan insists on the non-
biological basis of sexual difference and claims
that male and female are best distinguished along
lines of activity and passivity. (For a more
extended discussion of this topic, see B31.)
     Reprinted with brief introductory remarks and
notes in A2, pp. 829-50.

C82.   "Maurice Merleau-Ponty." Les temps modernes 184/185
       (1961): 245-54.

     Comments on the phenomenology of perception
developed in Merleau-Ponty's work from The Phenomenology of Perception (1945) to the essay "L'oeil et
l'esprit" (Art de France, 1961, pp. 187-208, and
reprinted in this issue of Les temps modernes).
Lacan distinguishes that phenomenology from more
traditional theories of knowledge and claims that
Merleau-Ponty has shamed psychoanalysts by his
incisive analysis of the painter's relation to the
unconscious in his art. Nevertheless, Lacan argues
that Merleau-Ponty has failed to account for the
importance of the signifier in determining the
subject's relation to the body in speech, and that
he has also failed to recognize the function of the
"third" in what he understands as a more direct

relation of body to body (see p. 249-50). Lacan
notes, however, that Sartre's critique of Merleau-
Ponty is lacking as well, since it ignores the
function of the fantasm. Lacan expands on these
topics at length in B22.
    Translated by Wilfred Ver Eecke and Dirk de
Schutter as "Merleau-Ponty: In Memoriam," Review of
Existential Psychology and Psychiatry 28, no. 1/2/3
(1982-83):   73-81.

C83. "Kant avec Sade." Critique 191 (1963):   291-313.

    Situates the work of Sade between that of Kant and
Freud, and argues that Sade showed how moral law,
the ethical imperative Kant attributed to an
internal voice, necessarily is derived from the
voice of the Other and is suspended upon the
"combinatoire" constituted by the endless multi-
plicity of victims in Sade's stories. Lacan claims
that the Sadean maxim of a "droit à la jouissance"
is thus more honest that Kant's universal moral
sense because this appeal to the Other unmasks the
split ("la refente") within the subject that is
occluded by Kant's notion of an inner conscience
(A2, p. 770).
    Similarly, Lacan claims that Kant's invocation of
a transcendental ground of being behind the phenomena of objects is echoed by the final inaccessibility of the object of desire in Sade's work, but
Sade represents that inaccessibility as a "étrange-
ment séparé du sujet" (A2, p. 772). Consequently,
Sade links desire and death and so discovers the
"fading" of the subject before the object of his
desire that is described by Lacan as the structure
of the fantasm. Lacan thus claims that the fantasm
is at the heart of the Sadean narrative because the
fantasm depends on a point (the point of aphanisis)
at which the object must be indefinitely deferred.
Lacan argues that this deferral is the motivation
behind the endless tortures Sade inflicts on the
victims of his narratives. Whether those victims
are unique (Justine) or multiple, the victim's
suffering is characterized by the monotony of the
subject's relation to the signifier and hence must
be repeated indefinitely as desire--and death--are
endlessly deferred.
    "Kant avec Sade" also contains a running commen-
tary on Antigone and the way that play challenges
the notion of morality as an ethic of the social
good, as well as more detailed comments on the
doctrine of Will in Kant's work. For more extended
remarks on these topics see B18. A good though
brief commentary on this extremely difficult essay
can be found in F344, Part Three, where Julien
situates the themes of the essay in the context of

Lacan's seminars during this period and emphasizes
the contrast between Lacan's reading of <u>Antigone</u> and
his use of Plato's <u>Symposium</u> shortly after this
essay was written.   F345 is also useful for a more
general discussion of Lacan's readings of Kant; see
p. 96ff.
    Reprinted as the afterword to <u>Oeuvres complètes du
Marquis de Sade</u>, Vol. 2, Tome III (Paris: Cercle du
Livre précieux, 1966), pp. 551-77; and in A2, pp.
765-90.   Translated into Italian in de Sade, <u>La
filosofia nel boudoir</u> (Rome: Newton Compton, 1974):
313-34.

C84.   "Hommage fait à Marguérite Duras du <u>Ravissement de
        Lol. V. Stein</u>." <u>Cahiers Renauld-Barrault</u> 52
        (1965):   7-15.

    Describes the "<u>ravissement</u>" of the title not so
much as an event as a "knot" ("<u>noeud</u>") which
organizes the subjectivity of the characters within
a "triangulation," an "<u>être à trois</u>."   The members
of this triangle are Lol, Tatiana, and Jacques Hold,
who are joined in an interdependent relation that is
circumscribed about a "<u>centre des regards</u>," a center
of gazes or looks.   The geometry of this triangle is
peculiar, however, and actually is structured
according to the topography of a knot or an "en-
velope" with neither an inside nor an outside and
in which Lol's gaze is reflected through the gaze of
others.
    Reprinted in <u>Marguerite Duras</u> (Paris: Albatios,
1979), pp. 131-38.

C85.   "La science et la vérité."   1 December 1965.
        Typescript of the leçon d'ouverture of Seminar
        XIII (see B24).   <u>Cahiers pour l'analyse</u> 1 (1966):
        7-30.

    Observes that the split ("<u>la refente</u>") of the
subject is the basis for psychoanalysis, but argues
that to know that split as it appears in its praxis
we cannot take it for an empirical fact.   Instead,
Lacan says that a certain "reduction" must be
carried out, and it is through that reduction that
the proper object of psychoanalysis is constituted:
the <u>objet a</u> (A2, pp. 855, 863).
    Much of this lesson is given over to a comparative
analysis of how the subject is constituted within
several fields of knowledge: science, game theory,
linguistics, anthropology, magic, religion, and
psychoanalysis.   Unlike most of the others, Lacan
says, psychoanalysis takes its point of departure
from a distinction between knowledge and truth that
is born in the constituent division of the subject
(p. 856).   Nevertheless, despite the traditional

view that Freud departed radically from the scientism of his time, Lacan claims that it was the
scientific subject that guided Freud to his discoveries, and that the subject of science is the
same one that psychoanalysis practices on (A2, pp.
858, 863).   Rejecting the humanistic implications of
the phrase "sciences of man," Lacan claims that the
"man" of science doesn't exist, only "his subject."
By this rejection, Lacan seems to have in mind the
contemporary paradoxical models of scientific
knowledge such as described by Godel and certain
kinds of linguistics and game theory (A2, pp. 860-
61), though he invokes structuralism in general for
the "very special mode" in which it conceives the
role of the subject.

Lacan then discusses the nature of truth,
especially as it is understood in psychoanalysis.
Starting with the phrase, "Moi, la vérité, je
parle"--which he derives from Freud's suggestions
that the unconscious is language (A2, p. 866)--Lacan
says that the phrase simply means that there is no
"metalanguage," no way of saying the "truth of
truth" because, in fact, truth is founded simply on
what it says ("le vérité se fonde de ce qu'elle
parle") (A2, p. 868).   He then compares this
psychoanalytic truth to that of magic and religion.
In magic, Lacan observes, truth is the "efficient
cause."   In religion, truth is the "final cause,"
and those different roles for truth yield different
relations between the subject and knowledge.   The
scientific role of truth in causality is less
simple, he adds, but truth can be recognized in
science under the aspect of a formal cause (A2, p.
875).   Psychoanalysis, on the other hand, accentuates "truth" under the aspect of its material
cause, which is what distinguishes it from conventional forms of science.   This material cause is, of
course, "la forme d'incidence du signifiant que j'y
définis" (A2, p. 875).

In the course of his discussion, Lacan makes an
observation about the history of science that takes
on increased importance in the light of more philosophical concerns with epistemological patterns in
the work of Thomas Kuhn and Michel Foucault.
Commenting on the economic science inspired by
Marx's Capital, Lacan remarks that if we examine it
closely, science "has no memory."   It forgets the
turning points ("les péripéties") from which it is
born and in which it is constituted.   In other
words, it lacks the very dimension that psychoanalysis takes as its central concern.   Each of
these turning points is a drama, he adds, a subjective drama, and each is "le drame du savant.   Il a
ses victimes dont rien ne dit que leur destin
s'inscrit dans le mythe de l'Oedipe" (A2, p. 870).

Reprinted in A2, pp. 855-77.

C86.   "Of Structure as an Inmixing of an Otherness
        Prerequisite to Any Subject Whatever." Presented
        at a colloquium on "The Languages of Criticism and
        the Sciences of Man," Johns Hopkins University,
        18-21 October 1966. <u>The Languages of Criticism
        and the Sciences of Man</u>. Edited by Richard
        Macksey and Eugenio Donato. Baltimore: Johns
        Hopkins University Press, 1970. [Reprinted as <u>The
        Structuralist Controversy: The Languages of
        Criticism and the Sciences of Man</u>. Baltimore,
        1972; rpt. 1975, 1977.] Pp. 186-95, discussion
        pp. 195-200.

        Begins by insisting on Freud's discovery that
        words "are the object through which one seeks for a
        way to handle the unconscious," and by emphasizing
        that it is words "in their flesh, in their material
        aspect," that are "the only material of the uncon-
        scious" (p. 187). This is what he means when he
        claims that the unconscious is structured like a
        language, Lacan says; there is only one kind of
        language, not a meta-language but a "concrete
        language," French or English, the kind people talk
        (p. 188). In addition to being structured like a
        language, Lacan adds, the unconscious is <u>langagier</u>
        because it raises the question of the subject, a
        subject that cannot simply be identified with the
        speaker or the personal pronoun in a sentence or
        énoncé. As Freud showed, the unconscious consists
        precisely in the fact that something thinks, but
        that "something" is barred from consciousness and is
        an "other subject" (p. 189).
        The problem, then, according to Lacan, is to find
        this subject, and he says that it is always neces-
        sary to find it as a lost object. He therefore
        attacks psychological models of subjectivity that
        stress unity and argues instead that human life
        proceeds <u>à la dérive</u>, irregularly and without
        understanding, and not according to the scandalous
        lie of some unifying entity. Instead of such
        metaphysical concepts of unity, Lacan proposes
        instead that we consider unity in terms of the unit,
        as a countable unit such as makes up the chain of
        integers. As Frege showed, Lacan says, integers are
        not based on discrete empirical data. Rather, the
        sequence of integers is based on the formula (n +
        1), which constitutes each integer as a "plus-one"
        that is repeated throughout the chain in conjunction
        with different units in the place of n. Lacan's
        point is that the "unit" of the chain of integers is
        made up of repetition with a difference, of a mark
        that appears repeatedly but only in the guise of
        difference. "The trait, I insist, is identical, but

it assures the difference only of identity--not by
effect of sameness or difference but by the difference of identity" (p. 192).

Claiming that language is constituted by the same
kind of unitary trait as the chain of integers--with
the difference that the unitary trait of the
integers is replaced by the differential trait of
the signifier--Lacan says that the collection of
signifiers as a whole constitutes the Other (p.
193). Within this universe of signifiers, however,
"nothing contains everything," and in this gap is
constituted the subject. The subject thus introduces a "loss" in reality, a loss introduced by the
word, and Lacan claims that this lack may therefore
serve as the definition of the subject (p. 193). He
says that the inherent "otherness" in the sphere of
language makes of the subject a "fading thing"
running under the chain of signifiers, and Lacan
describes the function of the signifier as "something that represents a subject for another signifier" (p. 194).

Lacan concludes with brief remarks on desire and
jouissance, focussing on the fading of the subject
before the object of desire as it appears in the
fantasm. The fantasm thus supports desire, Lacan
says, and sustains the subject in the endless
pursuit of jouissance. But as we approach our goal,
the law of the pleasure principle poses a barrier to
all jouissance, and in this barrier speech is born.
We would probably all be as quiet as oysters, Lacan
adds, if not for this curious organization that
disrupts the barrier of pleasure (or makes us dream
of disrupting it), and he ends by observing that
"all that is elaborated by the subjective construction on the scale of the signifier in its relation
to the Other and which has its root in language is
only there to permit the full spectrum of desire to
allow us to approach, to test, this sort of forbidden jouissance which is the only valuable meaning
that is offered to our life" (p. 195).

The discussion of Lacan's paper focuses on several
topics raised in the presentation, particularly on
Lacan's use of Frege and the system of integers and
on the relation of Lacan's work to the "nothingness"
described by Sartre. Lacan elaborates a bit on his
debt to Frege but denies having spoken of "nothingness" at all. (For further remarks about Sartre,
see E187.

This text was delivered in a combination of French
and English and published for the first time in
English.

C**. "Comptes rendus de seminaire 16-23 Novembre 1966."
      Text established by Jacques Nassif, not reviewed
      by Lacan. Lettres de l'Ecole freudienne de Paris

1 (1967):   11-17. See B25.

C87. "Proposition du 9 Octobre 1967, première version."
      Analytica 8 (1978): 3-26.

      Substantially the same as C88, with minor dif-
      ferences at the sentence-level.

C88. "Proposition du 9 octobre 1967 sur le psychanalyse
      de l'Ecole." Scilicet 1 (1968), pp. 14-29.

      A central document in the evolution of the Ecole
      freudienne because here Lacan formally proposes his
      new method for certifying analysts, "la passe." The
      proposition immediately generated controversy inside
      and outside the school. The International Psycho-
      Analytic Association considered the procedure
      irresponsible and unprofessional because Lacan
      claimed that analysands could authorize themselves
      to practice psychanalysis whenever they felt they
      were ready. At that point, Lacan said, the Ecole
      will recognize the new analyst as an "A.M.E."
      (Analyste membre d'Ecole). If and when the analyst
      aspired to be recognized as an "A.E." (Analyste de
      l'Ecole), he had to complete the "pass" by choosing
      two or three other members of the school and re-
      lating the story of his analysis to them. These
      "passers" then represented the analyst before a jury
      of A.E.s (which in fact always included Lacan), who
      judged the applicant's ability to use his experience
      for theoretical research on the basis of what the
      passers reported. Some members of the Ecole
      resented this procedure because they considered it
      arbitrary, and, more importantly, because they felt
      that it imposed a hierarchy of authority that
      violated the Ecole's anti-institutional principles
      and put Lacan in the role of le Maître. When the
      Ecole finally voted to adopt the procedure in
      January 1969, some of Lacan's closest followers
      split off and formed Le Quatrième Groupe, which
      became known as the "Lacanians without Lacan."
      Sherry Turkle's Psychoanalytic Politics: Freud's
      French Revolution (F412) describes the political
      impact of this proposition on the psychoanalytic
      community in France, but her sociological orienta-
      tion tends to slight the major theoretical dimension
      of Lacan's argument: his claim that the self-
      authorization of the analyst is a necessary conse-
      quence of the fundamental structure of psycho-
      analysis. Starting with the claim that transference
      is the origin of psychoanalysis ("au commencement de
      la psychanalyse est le transfert" [p. 19]), Lacan
      argues that the "intersubjectivity" at the heart of
      traditional accounts of transference necessarily
      implies the use of speech. Consequently, the actual

relation between the two partners in the "training"
analysis, the analysand and the analyst, must be
constituted in terms of the symbolic order of
language rather than through any unmediated intuition of one subject by another.

The position of the analyst in this relation,
ordinarily conceived as the "subject supposed to
know" ("le sujet supposé savoir"), does not depend
on anything the analyst really knows. In fact, the
analyst knows nothing, and Lacan says that is why
Freud advised analysts to come to each case as if
they had learned nothing from previous cases. The
"subject supposed to know" is rather produced by the
analysand's speech, a formation not of deliberate
artifice but "de veine," by chance, as a "détachée"
of the analysand. The end of the training analysis,
which is literally the passage of the analysand to
the position of the analyst, thus involves the
analysand's recognition of his "self" in and as the
analyst, and Lacan notes that no one is in a better
position to recognize that self than the analysand.

This dialectical process of self-recognition
undermines the authority of traditional psychoanalysis in two ways:

(1) It renders the institutional structure by
which most psychoanalytic organizations govern the
admission of candidates irrelevant and even impossible. This vitiates the power and prestige of
those organizations, and Lacan also claims that it
exposes their regulations for what they are--
repressive strategies that reflect the collusion
between those organizations and other repressive
structures such as the Church and the Army which
depend on their own "subject supposed to know."

(2) It displaces the analyst from the position of
power, since he is only represented in transference
as the omniscient subject by the speech of the
analysand, who, as Lacan reminds us, always speaks
first. In Lacanian terms, this means that the
subject supposed to know is present in transference
only as a signifier, and the relation between that
signifier and the "signified" (the knowledge that
the analysand supposes the analyst knows) is
constituted only within the chain of signifiers that
is the analysand's speech. The role of the analyst
is thus reduced to that of a "rapport tiers," a sort
of catalyst that facilitates the analysand's
association of one signifier (the analyst) with
another that represents the analyst's "knowledge."
Lacan compares this role to that of Socrates in the
Symposium when he leads Alcibiades to the truth of
his desire simply by letting him speak, and elsewhere Lacan characterizes the role of the analyst as
that of the dummy [le mort] in a game of bridge.

This explanation of transference in the training

analysis (<u>analyse didactique</u>) precludes any didactic
purpose because the analyst does not possess anything he can teach. Lacan does claim, however,
that we can see illustrated in this process the
"pure bias" or "slant" of the subject's relation to
the signifier, especially as that relation identifies the desire to know with the desire of the
Other ("<u>le désir du savoir comme désir de l'Autre</u>").
This phrase is a stock formula for Lacan and is
associated with a wide range of topics, but it
derives from his generally Hegelian understanding of
desire as a desire for recognition by an Other. One
wants to be the object of the Other's desire, to
assume the desire of the Other as one's own desire,
in short to be the Other. The flexibility of the
French "de," which can be translated either as "of"
or "for" in the phrases "<u>le désire de l'Autre</u>" or
"<u>le désir du psychanalyste</u>," evokes all of these
alternatives at once.

  Lacan's emphasis on the role of the "desire of the
analyst" in transference aligns the analysand's
desire to be an analyst with the more immediate and
passionate desire for the analyst, for what the
analyst "knows," and for what the analyst wants to
know--in other words, for what the analysand
"supposes" the analyst wants/has. In his effort to
satisfy that desire, which Lacan describes as "the
desire for the desire of the Other," the analysand
proceeds through several steps. He first perceives
the analyst as the subject supposed to know. He
identifies with that subject as his Imaginary other.
He then realizes that that subject does not know
what the analysand originally supposed him to know,
and in fact that the analyst wants to know what the
analysand wants to know. At that moment, Lacan
concludes, "<u>ce savoir supposé, il l'est devenu</u>"; the
analysand has become the knowledge he supposed to
belong to the analyst.

  This stage marks the "<u>virage</u>," the turning point
or conversion in the analysand's accession to the
position of the subject. Lacan claims that it joins
"<u>l'être du désir</u>" with "<u>l'être du savoir</u>" as the two
ends of a Möbius strip along whose single side is
inscribed the "<u>manque</u>" or "lack" realized in the
analysand's experience of his own "being" as an
analyst. The passage from analysand to analyst thus
rests upon the more generalized division or "splitting" of the subject that characterizes the entry of
any individual into the symbolic order, and Lacan
insists that any effort to terminate the analysis in
some absolute judgment of an external authority can
only mystify psychoanalytic practice by obscuring
the "desire of the analyst" on which it is based.

  Reprinted in A9, pp. 15-27. See E190.

C89. "Introduction de Scilicet au titre de la revue de
      l'Ecole freudienne de Paris." Scilicet 1 (1968):
      3-13.

      Describes the intended audience for the journal;
      establishes its oppositional relation to official
      organs of the International Psychoanalytic Associ-
      ation; and declares its policy of publishing only
      unsigned articles--with the exception of essays by
      Lacan himself. Much of the introduction simply
      rehearses the ongoing antagonism between Lacan and
      the psychoanalytic establishment, but his explana-
      tion of why his articles will be signed offers an
      astute account of the way "knowledge" is con-
      stituted, disseminated, and governed by the symbolic
      order of language. Separating his person from the
      name "Lacan," Lacan ironically notes the economic
      importance of that name for the success of the
      journal. However, he also recognizes the power of
      that name to open up psychoanalytic practice at
      precisely those points that are usually considered
      untouchable and to consolidate a new practice by
      identifying certain terms and attitudes as
      "Lacanian" and so controlling their use.
      Despite this open desire to centralize Lacanian
      psychoanalysis under a single authority, Lacan also
      claims that his name will have the same effect as
      the lack of name on the other articles: both
      "Lacan" and the lack of a name prohibit the easy
      reduction of revolutionary gestures to the predeter-
      mined place of the subject in the signifying chain.
      Hence this practice will inaugurate "l'épopée de la
      débandade" or the "jeu de massacre" (the "epoch of
      confusion" or the "play of massacre") within
      psychoanalysis. Recalling the rumor that
      Shakespeare once played the ghost of Hamlet's
      father, Lacan observes wryly that he is also signing
      his work to let people know that he is not ready to
      play the ghost yet.

C90. "La méprise du sujet supposé savoir." Scilicet 1
      (1968): 31-41.

      Claims that the possibility of interpretation
      depends on the assumption that there is a subject
      who can know what is being interpreted, and de-
      nounces psychoanalysis for harboring the "universal
      obscenity" of hermeneutics under the deluded concept
      of the analyst as just such a "subject supposed to
      know." Lacan claims that it is only in that mis-
      taken supposition that the analyst finds support
      for the practice of psychanalysis, and he charac-
      terizes that support as "on-tique," i.e., as
      structured upon the being of some absolute subject
      represented by the indefinite pronoun "on": "Mais

qu'il puisse y avoir un dire qui se dise sans qu'on
sache qui le dit, voilà à quoi la pensée [of
psychoanalysis] se dérobe: d'est une résistance on-
tique" (pp. 36-7: "But that it might be possible to
have a statement that states itself without one
knowing who says it, that is what psychoanalytic
thought cannot face: it is an on-tique resistance."
"On" is usually translated as "one," though it is
used more like "they" in phrases such as "they say .
. ." or "they know . . . ." Lacan goes on to
explain that he is punning on the Greek on, present
participle of einai, to be.)
     Lacan compares the on-tique status of the subject
supposed to know to that of God or, in his terms,
the Other. He says that the unconscious effaces
this subject as well as all others in the endless
dialectic of appearance and disappearance that
characterizes the effect of the unconscious on our
awareness. Thinking that it has "discovered" the
unconscious, psychoanalysis perpetuates the illusion
of the subject by protecting it from this
(dis)appearance, Lacan says, and that insures the
continuation of the "psychoanalytic act" of interpretation because it reserves a place for the
analyst as the subject supposed to know. Thus Lacan
concludes "l'interprétation, il la reparot sur le
transfert qui nous ramène à notre on" ("interprétation is carried on [at its source] by the transference that leads us back to our on," i.e., to the
ground of our being as subjects).

C91. "De Rome 53 à Rome 67: La psychanalyse. Raison
       d'un échec." Scilicet 1 (1968): 42-49.

     Recalls the themes of his earlier address in Rome
(C58)--specifically his effort to describe the
isomorphic relation between language and the
unconscious and to determine the ex-centric basis of
man's desire as it arises in the place of the Other-
-and briefly describes the controversy surrounding
his critique of the "absolute subject supposed to
know" in the structure of analytic transference.
Lacan discusses his own position as a precursor of
many contemporary intellectual fashions and claims
that his work remains a beacon atop the mounting
flood of jargon such as the "ça parole," the
signifier and signified, the trace, and différance
with an a, which Lacan calls that "Aphrodite from
the foam." This essay is primarily interesting as
an example of Lacan's sense of his own place in the
intellectual milieu of France in the 1960s, which
includes his ironic deflation of Lévi-Strauss,
Derrida, and Foucault as fashionable late-comers to
truths he has been propounding for thirty years.
But the demagogic tone of the essay also exemplifies

Lacan's condescending attitude toward his own
followers, which was creating dissention within the
Ecole freudienne and would contribute to a major
rift among its members in 1969.

C92. "De la psychanalyse dans ses rapports avec la
      réalité." Scilicet 1 (1968): 51-9.

Defines "reality" and describes its function
within the analytic process as it determines the
role of the analyst, the structure of transference,
and the alienating effect of the analysand's
recognition of his desire in the discourse of the
analytic session. Lacan begins by noting that the
spontaneity of the process of free association
precludes the analyst's bringing any sort of
knowledge to bear on it or preparing any strategy
for intervening in the process beforehand. In fact,
"non-preparation" is the ideal preparation, Lacan
says, and he specifically criticizes the ego-
psychology of American psychoanalysis for its
assumption that the analyst helps the patient or
analysand "adapt" to reality in the sense of an
absolute norm.
    That norm is constructed by the discourse of
analysis, Lacan argues, and he says that we can
think of reality as "material" or "solid" only in
the sense of its being an uninterpretable or totally
opaque limit to language. Just as nothing from
dreams can be admitted to analysis without being
represented by the patient's narrative, and just as
desire is present only as it is articulated in the
form of a demand, "reality" is present for interpretation only at the very spot where it is "cut off
and inscribed in the nature of the signifier," or,
more simply, where the "real" is replaced by the
signifier which represents it as reality in
language. Reality thus forms an impenetrable
barrier to knowledge in the same way that the
unconscious does, and Lacan claims that reality in
this sense is where the unconscious "inscribes
itself."
    This relatively simple point becomes more compli-
cated when Lacan traces its implications for the
psychic processes of the subject and the formation
of that subject in the analytic discourse. Observing that an individual perceives the existence
of his body as a coherent image in the world, the
Dasein or "being there" of the Imaginary other,
Lacan says that the signifier cuts off the world
from language and the individual experiences that as
a cutting off from the body, or castration. Instead
of recognizing himself as a coherent moi or ego in
an imaginary other, with the advent of the signifier
the individual perceives his "self" in scattered

pieces discarded and lost in some "other" place
beyond the boundaries of the ego, where it appears
as mere left-overs, excrement, "our being without
essence."

This "corporeal residue" Lacan identifies as the
"objet (a)," which we can only perceive as lost or
as a general lack (manqué) that generates desire.
The "other" place is, of course, the place of the
Other, the unconscious, and the individual's
perception of a part of himself being lost "over
there" is a result of his relation to the signifiers
of his speech. The perception marks the splitting
(Spaltung) of the subject as the individual assumes
his place in the Symbolic order of language, the
"discourse of the Other." Thus Lacan describes the
"reality of the subject" (an ambiguous phrase that
refers to both the "reality" perceived by the
subject and to the subject's existence within the
order of language) as the "figure d'aliénation"
formed in the relation between the "false subject"
of the "I think" (an allusion to Descartes' "I
think, therefore I am") and the "objet (a)" cut off
by the signifier in the representation of reality.
Lacan concludes that this "thought reality" is in
fact "the truth of the alienation of the subject,
its rejection in the désêtre, the renunciation of
the 'I am'" ("La réalité pensée est la vérité de
l'aliénation du sujet, elle est son rejet dans le
désêtre, dans le 'je suis' renoncé" [p. 58].
"Désêtre" puns on "désert" [the ontological no-man's
land in which the objet a is perceived as lost],
"dés-être" [from-being, since-being, or non-being],
and perhaps "déserter" [to desert].)

The divided subject appears as a frequent motif in
Lacan's work, but here it specifically characterizes
the analysand's position in the discourse of the
"training analysis" (analyse didactique). Through
transference, the analysand's desire to be an
analyst becomes a desire for the analyst; as the
analysand comes to identify with the analyst as his
imaginary other, he begins to see his desire as the
desire of the analyst, that is, as a desire that has
been "lost" and must be recovered in the place now
occupied by the analyst as a "subject supposed to
know." Lacan describes this place as the place of
the objet a, and he defines the analysand as one
"who comes to realize his 'I think' as alienation,
that is to say, to discover the fantasm as the motor
of psychic reality, that of the divided subject" (p.
59). This can only happen, however, if the analyst
refuses to give in to the analysand's fantasy of a
"subject supposed to know," if he plays the role of
the "I think not"; if, in short, the analyst refuses
to be the measure of reality. In fact, Lacan
concludes, the analyst can open up the road to truth

for the analysand only by offering himself as "the
support of the désêtre, by virtue of which the
subject subsists in an alienated reality." "Psychoanalysts are the wisemen of a wisdom they cannot
engage," Lacan says; if they try to be anything more
than the equal of those they guide on the road to
truth, neither analysand nor analyst will get
anywhere.

This essay is one of Lacan's most difficult texts
because it raises most of the central issues in his
work within the narrow context of his critique of
analytic practice. Lacan also repeatedly but
cryptically directs his remarks to Freud's explanations of the reality principle, its relation to the
pleasure principle, and its place in the distinction
between primary and secondary processes; see C43.
The most useful commentary on Lacan's concept of the
analyst's role can be found in F396. For a fas-
cinating sample of Lacanian analysis in action, see
F397, which includes a collection of clinical
reports by Lacanian analysts and a transcript of a
patient interview by Lacan.

C**. "Pour une logique du fantasme." Scilicet 2/3
       (1970): 223-73. See B25.

Published anonymously two years after Nassif's
summary of Seminar XIV (see B25a), this essay has
achieved a semi-official status as the text of
Seminar XIV. The general topics of the essay and
its organization follow those described by Nassif in
B25a, but the argument of this text is more systematic and the style approaches ordinary exposition
much more closely than Nassif's text or than the
published seminars.

C93. "Lituraterre." Littérature 3 (1971): 3-10.

Reflects on the relation between psychoanalysis
and literature through Joycean permutations on the
metaphor of the letter as a "littoral" or shoreline
that joins territories that are simplistically
distinguished in psychology as Innenwelt and Umwelt.
Lacan claims that the letter is the metaphorical
support of the signifier and of discourse, too, as
discourse is associated with "le semblant." "Ce qui
de jouissance s'évoque à ce que se rompe un semblant," Lacan says, "voilà ce qui dans le réel se
présente comme ravinement. C'est du même effect que
l'écriture est dans le réel le ravinement du
signifié, ce qui a plus du semblant en tant qu'il
fait le signifiant" (p. 7). Lacan refers to the
relation between the letter and the unconscious that
he explained in C71, but he also contrasts the role
of the letter in alphabetical writing to the

function of the ideogram in Japanese.

C94.   "L'étourdit." 14 July 1972. Scilicet 4 (1973): 5-
        52.

    Repeats his claim that sexual relations do not
exist ("il n'a pas de rapport sexuel") and explains
that "relations" of any kind exist only in statements ("énoncés"), where the real is inaccessible
except as the limit of their logic. The immediate
manifestation of this limit is negation (represented
by the French "n'y a"), and that "nothing" makes
relations between men and women impossible because
they inhabit the language of those statements (p.
11). Human life is, of course, reproduced, but
Lacan claims that the question of how it is reproduced can be answered only by reproducing the same
question--or, Lacan adds, "pour te faire parler" (p.
12).
    Lacan argues that sexual relations are also
blocked by the fact that the body of speaking beings
("des parlants") is subjected to a division of the
organs, and one of these organs, the phallus, is
made into a signifier. Thus turned into a signifier, this organ hollows out the place where the
effect of being occurs for le parlant, a being that
Lacan calls the "l'inexistence" of sexual relation
(p. 13).
    Lacan pursues the issue of symbolic differenti-
ation between the sexes and the consequent impossibility of a sexual relation that would somehow reach
across that difference, and he describes the
connection between this symbolic difference and what
Freud designated as castration. Briefly alluding to
the debate among Karen Horney, Helen Deutsch and
other Freudians in the 1930's regarding the biological vs. symbolic ground of sexual difference (p.
20), Lacan goes on to describe the symbolic function
of women as the "pastout" (see B31).
    In the later portions of this essay, Lacan
comments on his use of topology, describing it as a
"n'espace" derived from mathematics (p. 28). He
comments briefly on the topological function of the
"cross-cap" as he uses it, and distinguishes at
greater length between topology and structure (p.
40ff.). Structure is the real that is brought to
light in language, Lacan says ("La structure, c'est
le réel qui se fait jour dans le langage," [p. 33]),
and according to Lacan topology is the fiction of a
surface in which structure is dressed (p. 41).
Lacan concludes this section on topology with a
discussion of the way the torus serves as the
structure of neurosis, in which desire loops back on
itself in two turns through an endless repetition
("la ré-pétition indéfiniment énumérable") of demand

(p. 42).

Also of note in this essay is Lacan's distinction between le <u>langage</u> and languages. "Le <u>langage</u>," Lacan says, "<u>ne peut désigner que la structure dont il y a effet de langages</u>" (p. 45). Le <u>langage</u>, he adds later, has no effect at all other than that of the structure from which the incidence of the real is derived, and he insists on the historical basis for the persistence of any one language among others in relation to the real. Being structured <u>like</u> a language, the unconscious is also subject to the vagaries [<u>l'équivoque</u>] that distinguish each particular language, Lacan says. What makes one language different from others is nothing more than the sum of the vagaries that make up its history, and it is there, Lacan concludes, that we find "<u>la veine dont le réel, le seul pour le discours analytique à motiver son issue, le réel qu'il n'y a pas de rapport sexuel, y a fait dépôt au cours des âges</u>" (p. 47).

C**.   "La mort est du domaine de la foi." Grande Rotonde de l'Université de Louvain, 13 October 1972. <u>Quarto: supplement belge à La lettre mensuelle de l'Ecole de la Cause Freudienne</u> 3 (1981): 5-20.

This item is listed separately by Dor but appears in <u>Quarto</u> under the title of E236 and is annotated there.

C**.   "Texte sur l'inconscient." April 1974. Listed by Dor, p. 83, as forthcoming in Spanish in "Freud et la psychanalyse."

C95.   "Joyce, le symptôme." Fifth International Symposium on James Joyce. Paris, 16-20 June 1975. <u>Actes du 5ème symposium James Joyce</u>. Paris: Editions du C.N.R.S., 1979.

Briefly recounts his meeting Joyce and observes of that chance encounter that it was just one of the accidents ("<u>les hasards</u>") that we fashion into our destiny by virtue of the fact that we speak and, more precisely, that we are spoken. Most of the talk is devoted to Lacan's notion of Joyce as symptom or, as Lacan says it was originally spelled, "<u>sinthome</u>." Joyce may be considered a "symptom," Lacan says, in the sense that a symptom is an effect of language. The symptom is purely that which conditions "<u>lalangue</u>," he adds, though to a certain extent Joyce transports it to the power of language and in doing so refuses analysis. Lacan also comments on the use of puns in <u>Finnegans Wake</u> and more briefly on the figure of the circle and cross, which Lacan has been using to sketch the relations among

the real, the imaginary, and the symbolic.
     Reprinted in L'ane 6 (1982): 3-5, where it
appears with a short comment by Jacques Aubert, the
Joycean who invited Lacan to speak at the symposium.
See J1010. Lacan discusses Joyce at greater length
throughout B34.

C**.   "Desire and the Interpretation of Desire in Hamlet."
       K1356, pp. 11-52. French text Edited by Jacques-
       Alain Miller. Translation by James Hulbert.
       Based on B17.

C96.   "C'est à la lecture de Freud." Cahier cistre:
       cahiers trimestrels du lettres differentes 3
       (1977): 7-17.

       Stresses the importance of Freud's discovery of
the link between the unconscious and language, and
claims that is the heart of his teaching. Lacan
attacks the institutionalization of psychoanalysis
in the "anafreudisme" of the International Psychoanalytic Association, and he claims that the issue
of institutionalization is important because it
bears on the transmission of psychoanalysis itself
through the training analyses governed by various
societies. He briefly recounts his own troubles
with the IPA and comments on several other topics.
       First, Lacan distinguishes between language and
speech and argues that the unconscious may be said
to be structured like a language because it is
deployed ("se déploie") in the effects of language.
It is useless to ask it why, Lacan says, because it
will just respond, "pour te faire parler." One
forgets that speech is not language, he adds, and
that language "fait drôlement parler l'être qui dès
lors se spécifie de ce parlage" (p. 13).
       Next, he praises Descartes' discovery of the
subject and its relation to the phrase "therefore I
am," but Lacan claims that Descartes failed to
realize the implication of his dictum, "I think,
therefore I am." It happens, Lacan says, that the
id thinks there where it is impossible for the
subject to articulate the "I am" ("ça pense là où il
est impossible que le sujet en articule ce 'donc je
suis.'"). In other words, the id thinks where the
subject cannot know it, which implies that there
must be some "other" that can have knowledge besides
the subject. Lacan therefore rewrites Descartes's
saying as "je pense où, là où je ne puis dire que je
suis." That is what it means to be a speaking
being, Lacan says, and that is why in every statement the subject of the enunciation (i.e., that
which makes the statement) is always separated from
being by the bar. (For an explanation of the
subject's being situated on the bar between the

signifier and the signifier, see C71.)

Lacan concludes with a few remarks on the real and on literary criticism. The real is the impossible, Lacan says, and it is impossible to say. That is why psychoanalysis is called the "science of the impossible." Addressing literary criticism, Lacan claims that it is interested in the promotion of the structure of language, just as science is. But although the unconscious necessitates the primacy of "une écriture" and criticism tends to treat written texts as the unconscious, the very fact that such texts are written means that they cannot imitate the effect of the unconscious (pp. 15-16). He briefly compares interpreting a text to interpreting a symptom and then concludes that the literary work is no more a metaphor of structure than structure is the metaphor of the reality of the unconscious. "Elle en est le réel," Lacan says, and in that sense the literary work imitates nothing: "Elle est, en tant que fiction, structure véridique," and he refers his audience to C69 for an explanation.

This item is based on an unedited text, but one that was authorized by Lacan; the title is by the editors of Cahier cistre. Reprinted in F336, pp. 7-17.

C**. "Une pratique de bavardage."   15 November 1977. Ornicar? 19 (1979): 5-9. See B36.

C**. "Nomina non sunt consequentia rerum." Ornicar? 16 (1978): 7-13. See B35.

C**. "Vers un signifiant nouveau." Ornicar? 17/18 (1979): 7-23. See B35.

C97. Remarks for the catalog of the exhibition François Rouan, Musée Cantini, Marseille, 1978. Rouan. Paris: Centre Georges Pompidou, Musée national d'art moderne, 1983. Pp. 88-94.

Observes that Rouan paints on bands but says that if he dared he would advise him to paint on braids ("les tresses") instead. Lacan reflects on the topographical properties of the braid and relates it to several varieties of Borromean knots, a topic discussed at greater length in B35, especially in the lesson of 18 January 1977 (Ornicar? 15 [1978]: 5-9). This item is a facsimile of a holographic text.

C98. "Le séminaire de Caracas." 12-15 July 1980. L'ane 1 (1981): 30-31.

Opening address for a conference on Lacan's teaching, held in Caracas. Lacan notes that his

presence has annoyed many people, especially those
who profess to represent him without ever asking his
opinion, and he says that his audience can be
Lacanians if they want to, but he is a Freudian
("<u>C'est à vous d'être lacaniens, si vous voulez.
Moi, je suis freudien</u>", p. 30). Lacan comments on
the misleading implications of Freud's diagram of
"the sack" in <u>The Ego and the Id</u>, which treats the
drives as if they were little balls to be expelled
once digested, and he says that he prefers Freud's
association of the drives with the orifices of the
body. Instead of a sack, Lacan proposes a Klein
bottle, with no inside or outside, or perhaps a
torus. He contrasts the sexual peace ("<u>la paix
sexuelle</u>") of animals with the less certain sexuality of the speaking being--"<u>qui sait que faire
d'un corps de parlêtre</u>," he asks--and concludes with
brief remarks on the death drive.

   Translated in <u>The Papers of the Freudian School of
Melbourne</u> (1980):   103-06.

C**.   "Comptes rendus d'enseignement 1964-1968." <u>Ornicar?</u>
       29 (1984):   7-25.

       Reprints Lacan's abstracts for Seminar XI (1964)-
Seminar XV (1967-68) from the <u>Annuaire de l'Ecole
pratique des hautes études</u>. See B22-26.

Section D

Primary Works: Reviews, Translations and Prefaces

D99.   "De quelques mécanismes névrotiques dans la
        jalousie, la paranoïa et l'homosexualité."
        Translation of Freud's "Uber einige neurotische
        Mechanismen bei Eifersucht, Paranoia und Homosex-
        ualität" (1922) ("Some Neurotic Mechanisms in
        Jealousy, Paranoia and Homosexuality"). Revue
        française de psychanalyse 3 (1932):   391-401.

D***.   Translation of the chapter on schizophrenics in
        Otto Fenichel's Perversionen, Psychosen, Charak-
        terstorungen. Cited in A1, p. 260, n. 3, as
        forthcoming in Revue française de psychanalyse.
        Listed by Dor, p. 39.

D100.   Review of Henri Ey, Hallucinations et délire.
        Paris, 1935. Evolution psychiatrique 1 (1935):
        87-91.

        Praises Ey's book as a major contribution toward
        our understanding of psycho-motor hallucinations,
        and defends Ey's emphasis on a historical grasp of
        the issue vs. the pseudo-scientific "observations"
        of clinical psychiatrists (see D101).   Lacan agrees
        with Ey that the essential character of a halluci-
        nation is the patient's belief in its reality, and
        he claims that the sense of a "split" or "doubling"
        (dédoublement) in the self which is reported so
        often by patients suffering from these halluci-
        nations can be attributed to disturbances in the
        subject's integration of his personality.
        Lacan says that one of the consequences of such
        disturbances is that the patient experiences a real
        "movement," such as speech, as alien or even as
        being forced upon him from somewhere else.   Lacan
        agrees with Ey's claims that this "powerful factor
        of the doubling of the personality" is situated in
        "the very structure of the function of language, in
        its phenomenology, which is always imprinted with a

duality," and he notes the relevance of this idea
to his own work on "graphic automatisms." For more
commentary on the role of language in madness, see
C40 and C49; C49 also contains a more extended and
much more critical analysis of Ey's work.

D101. Review of E. Minkowski's Le temps vécu: études
       phénoménologiques et psychopathologiques.
       (Collection de l'Evolution psychiatrique. Paris,
       1933. 401 pages.) Recherches philosophique 5
       (1935/66): 424-31.

       Claims that the methodological novelty of
Minkowski's work lies in his structural point of
view, which is manifest in his observations about
the formal parallels among different types of
morbid consciousness. Lacan praises Minkowski for
distinguishing among those types according to the
way each conceives of the ego, the character
(personne), objects, (the "intentionalization of
the obstacles of reality"), and logical, causal,
spatial, and temporal assertions. Lacan objects,
however, to Minkowski's hostility to psychoanalysis
and to his consequent refusal to consider the
"affective history" of the subject as a factor in
"mental troubles."
       Lacan also claims that Minkowski has introduced a
new dualism into psychiatric theory by insisting on
an exclusive opposition between organicism and
psychogenesis. As a preferable alternative, Lacan
offers his own work on the "object-conflict" in
paranoiac consciousness, which proposes a "triangular" situation of the object between the other
and the ego ("entre le toi et the moi"). Lacan
insists that the "substantial structure" of man's
intelligence is not so much determined by his grasp
of "solid" things as by an affective dialectic
which leads him away from an egocentric assimi-
lation of his milieu and towards the sacrifice of
the ego to others ("la personne l'autri"). He also
suggests that Minkowski would have profited from a
close reading of Heidegger, Freud, and other
contemporary German thinkers.
       This essay is marked by an overt and intense
hostility to the scientistic rhetoric of psychiatric discourse and by the ambitious parallels
Lacan draws between psychoanalytic and philosophical claims about the relation between the self
and the world. Both characteristics will become
more prominent in Lacan's post-war discourse but
are surprising in the context of his earlier work.

D102. Translation of Martin Heidegger's "Logos." La
       psychanalyse 1 (1956): 59-79. See F386.

D103.   "Presentation" to D. P. Schreber, Memoires d'un
        névropathe. Cahiers pour l'analyse 5 (1966):
        69-72.

        Welcomes the French translation of this text,
        which he had discussed at length in B14. Lacan
        calls Schreber's book "un grand texte freudien" not
        so much for what Freud was able to clarify in it
        but for the way it illuminated the pertinence of
        the categories Freud had forged for other reasons.
        Lacan notes Freud's own defense of his using a
        written text as the basis for his analysis of
        Schreber's case, and he briefly discusses the
        relevance of Schreber's text to his own work on
        paranoia, especially as presented in A1.

D**.   "Ouverture de ce recueil," etc. for Ecrits (A2),
        1966.

        The introductory sections, notes, and other
        material written for this collection constitute a
        running commentary (and at times critical per-
        spective) on the essays and have been annotated in
        A2.

D104.   Introduction to Ecrits I (A2a).   14 December 1969.
        Pp. 7-12.

        The introduction addresses the issue of femi-
        ninity and its relation to the signifier and to the
        Other in terms of Poe's "The Purloined Letter," and
        comments on the distortions that Lacan's own terms
        have suffered at the hands of other psychoanalysts.
        Lacan also comments on his difficulties with the
        psychoanalytic establishments he has confronted
        during his career and on the charges of incompre-
        hensibility that have been levied against him.

D105.   Preface to F392. Dated Christmas, 1969. Pp. 9-20.

        Claims that the Ecrits is unsuitable for a thesis
        such as F392 because of the essays' antithetical
        nature and because they were originally conceived
        within the structure of a discourse aimed at a
        specific audience: psychoanalysts. Lacan de-
        scribes the institutional and political dimensions
        behind the complicated relation between psychiatry
        and psychoanalysis, and he alludes obliquely to
        several of the controversies that have surrounded
        his own work and to the work of some of his
        students, especially that of Laplanche and Leclaire
        (see G681). Lacan also recounts his argument with
        Perelman over the function of metaphor (see E169),
        and he recalls with irony the reaction of those who
        first blamed him for not quoting Jakobson as a

source for his own concept of metaphor and then
blamed him--after they read Jakobson--for differing
from a theory he never claimed as his source.

Much of this essay is virtually opaque for anyone
not familiar with Lacan's career because many of
his remarks consist of cryptic references to names
and places associated with various papers and
conferences. Nevertheless, his tone of amused
ambivalence towards those who have followed his
work is clear, and he concludes by observing that
Freud was fortunate not to have the university pack
at his heels (tr. p. xiv).

Translated in the English edition of F392, pp.
vii-xv. See E205.

D106. "Avis au lecteur japaonais." Introduction to A2c,
       1972. La lettre mensuelle de l'Ecole de la Cause
       freudienne 3 (1981): 2-3.

       Brief preface to the Japanese translation of the
       Ecrits. Lacan claims to be perplexed by being
       translated into Japanese because "c'est une langue
       dont je me suis approché à la mesure de mes
       moyens." He comments on the centrality of punning
       to Japanese, which dramatizes the tendency of the
       meaning of any discourse to "ne se procure jamais
       que d'un autre." "Telle qu'y est faite la langue,"
       he concludes, "on n'aurait à ma place besoin que
       d'un style. Moi, pour la tenir, cette place, il me
       faut un style."

D107. "Postface." B22 (1973), pp. 251-54.

       Notes his ambivalence about rendering his speech
       into writing. "Or ce qui se lit," Lacan says,
       "c'est de ça que je parle, puisque ce que je dis
       est voué à l'inconscient, soit à ce qui se lit
       avant tout" (p. 251).

D108. "Introduction à l'édition allemande d'un premier
       volume des Ecrits (Walter Verlag)." 7 October
       1973. Scilicet 5 (1975): 11-17.

       Begins by posing the question of the meaning of
       meaning, which he says in his practice is grasped
       in "ce qu'il fuie" in the sense of a "leak" rather
       than flight. Meaning is always an enigma, Lacan
       says, and he substitutes for the more usual
       question one of his own: what is the sign of the
       sign? Lacan answers that the sign of a sign is
       that another sign can be substituted for it, and
       that the whole scope of a sign is its ability to be
       decoded. Even so, he adds, a decoded message can
       still remain an enigma, as in the case of the
       formations of the unconscious.

Lacan goes on to discuss the "decodable" character of the structure of the unconscious and
argues that Freud discovered the sexual "meaning"
of that structure. Sex is linked to meaning, he
says, and is not inscribed in relations. He then
distinguishes between coding and counting and
argues that numbers have a special relation to the
real. (A few pages later, he says that "le langage
véhicule dans le nombre le réel dont la science
s'élaborer.") Numbers also possess a "meaning"
that offers an insight ("ouvre un aperçu") into
what makes sense ("rendre compte") of the entry of
the real in the world of the speaking being, the
"l' 'être' parlant" (p. 12).
Lacan goes on to discuss the relation between
psychoanalysis and science; the relation between
love and knowledge in the analytic experience (as
opposed to the common misperception of a link
between desire and knowledge suggested by Freud's
Wisstrieb); and the être parlant's passion for
ignorance. He concludes with brief remarks on
contingency and lalangue (see B31).

D109. "L'éveil du printemps." Préface à la pièce de
       Wedekind. L'éveil du printemps (Paris: Gal-
       limard, 1974). Reprinted in Bulletin de l'As-
       sociation freudienne 2 (1983): 11-12.

D110. "Faire mouche." Le nouvel observateur, 29 March
       1976, p. 64.

       Praises Benôit Jacquot's film L'assassin musicien
       for its ability to "convince" the viewer about the
       reality of its experience and to make "the true"
       (le vrai) emerge from fantasy. Lacan observes that
       the fantasm always underlies "le vraisemblable" and
       that it engenders "the truth" that makes Jacquot's
       film so convincing. For a fully developed theory
       of film and cinematic effect based on Lacanian
       principles, see K1270.

D111. Preface to the English language edition of B22. 17
       May 1976. Pp. vii-ix.

       Observes that "the unconscious, I would say, is
       the real," and notes that despite Freud's belief
       that he was carrying the plague to America,
       psychoanalysis turned out to be adopted (or
       adapted) quite painlessly as an anodyne. Lacan
       rejects the possibility of anyone deciding for
       someone else when that person is an analyst, and he
       claims that "the analyst hystorizes [sic] only from
       himself" (p. viii). Lacan also rejects the need
       for any certification, even that of his own birth,
       and proclaims "I am not a poet, but a poem. A poem

that is being written, even though it looks like a
subject" (p. viii). Commenting on several other
aspects of analysis and the program of the pass
(see C88), Lacan concludes by claiming to be
occupied with urgent cases at this time and says
that he writes "in so far as I feel I must, in
order to be on a level [au pair] with these cases,
to make a pair with them" (p. ix).
    Reprinted (in French) in Ornicar? 12/13 (1977):
124-26.

Section E

Primary Works: Interviews and Miscellaneous Works

E112. With Alajouanine, Th., and P. Delafontaine.
"Fixité du regard avec hypertonie, prédominant
dans le sens vertical avec conservation des
mouvements automatico-réflexes; aspect spécial du
syndrome de Parinaud par hypertonie associé à un
syndrome extrapyramidal avec troubles pseudo-
bulbaires." Société neurologique, 4 November
1926. Revue neurologique 2 (1926):   410-428.

Proposes several schemas for this disturbance
that are discussed again by Alajouanine and M.
Thurel in "Révision des paralysies des mouvements
associés des globes oculaires (contribution à
l'étude de la dissociation des activités volontaire
et réflexe)," Revue neurologique 1 (1931):   125-66.

E113. With J. Lévy-Valensi and M. Meignant.   "Roman
policier: du délire type hallucinatoire chro-
nique au délire d'imagination." Société de
psychiatrie, 26 April 1928. Abstract by André
Reiller. Revue neurologique 35, T. I, no. 5
(1928):   738-9.

Describes a man who suffered from the delusion
that he was a detective. He was committed when he
informed that Parisian police of his investigations
into several crimes. This is an interesting case
in the light of Lacan's later work on psychosis
because the authors note that fantasies are perceived by the patient as grounded in the external
world. Lacan will later attribute such perceptions
to the collapse of the imaginary into the real in
A2, p. 18; also see F392, pp. 230-46.
Also printed in Annales médico-psychologiques 1
(1928):   474-6; and in L'encéphale 5 (1928):   550-
1.

E114. With Trenel, M.   "Abasie chez une traumatisée de

guerre."   Société neurologique, 2 November 1928.
Revue neurologique 1 (1928):   233-37. Listed by
Dor, p. 35.

E115.   With L. Marchand and A. Courtois. "Syndrome
comitio-parkinsonien encéphalique." Société
clinique de médecine mentale, 17 June 1929. Revue
neurologique 2 (1929): 128. Annales médico-
psychologique 2 (1929):   185.

Describes the treatment of a young woman suffering from ambulatory automatism and numerous
other symptoms. Abstract in L'encéphale 9 (1929):
672. On the philosophical implication of automatism, see C49.

E116.   With George Heuyer. "Paralysie générale avec
syndrome d'automatisme mental." Société de
psychiatrie de Paris, 20 June 1929. L'encéphale
9 (1929):   802-3.

Briefly describes the symptoms of a 40 year-old
woman suffering from a general paralysis that was
preceded by hallucinatory syndromes and delusions
of grandeur and persecution.

E117.   "hiatus irrationalis." Dated H.-P, August 1929.
Le phare de Neuilly 3/4 (1933):   37.

A thirteen-line sonnet addressed to "things" in
which the poet finds a current whose "torrent is no
sweeter than my dreams." If I "saddle you with an
unceasing desire," he says to things, "I cross your
waters, I fall towards the shore" where "my
thinking demon . . . crashes on the hard soil where
being arises./But as soon as every word perishes in
my throat . . . I lose myself in the flux of an
element." "That which flows in me, the same
sustains you," he concludes; "it is the fire that
makes me your immortal lover." Influenced by the
surrealist movement, this poem also depicts
affective bonds between a subject and objects as
structured by the narcissistic ego.
Reprinted in Le magazine littéraire 121 (1977):
11.

E118.   With René Targowla. "Paralysie générale pro-
longée." Société de psychiatrie, 19 December
1929.

Describes a 52 year-old man whose early trouble
with speech and memory led to a general paralysis
of extraordinary duration, and recounts the medical
treatment of the patient in full detail.
Reprinted in L'encéphale 1 (1930):   83-5.

E119. With A. Courtois. "Psychose hallucinatoire
    encéphalitique." Société clinique de médecine
    mentale, 17 November 1930. Annales médico-
    psychologiques 1 (1930): 284-85.

    Describes a patient suffering from hallucinatory
    psychosis with important oneiric elements, visual
    phenomena, and complete insomnia. Abstract in
    L'encéphale 4 (1930): 331.

E120. "Crises tonique combinées de protrusion de la
    langue et de trismus se produisant pendant le
    sommeil chez une parkinsonnienne post-encépha-
    litique. Amputation de la langue consécutive."
    Société de psychiatrie, 20 November 1930.
    Annales médico-psychologiques 2, no. 5 (1930):
    420.

    Describes a 53 year old woman suffering from
    Parkinson's disease who has nocturnal seizures in
    which her jaws clamp down on her protruding tongue.
    Lacan notes that this case is unique because such
    seizures have never been reported occurring during
    sleep. See E123.
    Reprinted in L'encéphale 2 (1931): 145-6.

E121. With P. Schiff and Mme. Schiff-Wertheimer.
    "Troubles mentaux homochromes chez deux frères
    hérédosyphilitiques." Société de psychiatrie de
    Paris, 20 November 1930. L'encéphale 1 (1931):
    151-54.

    Describes the similar mental disturbances of two
    brothers suffering from hereditary syphilis and
    explains their treatment. The facts that the
    brothers were born within two years of each other
    and that the behavior of one reflects that of the
    other so closely foresees Lacan's later interest in
    the psychogenetic "délires à deux." See C42 and
    E122.

E122. With Henri Claude and P. Migault. "Folies simul-
    tanées." Société médico-psychologique, 21 May
    1931. Annales médico-psychologiques 1 (1931);
    483-90.

    Describes two cases, each of which involved a
    mother and her illegitimate daughter who both
    suffered from delirium. Lacan claims that these
    cases differ from the classical pattern of mental
    contagion because the symptoms of each mother and
    daughter persist even when the women are apart.
    Lacan briefly elaborates on the theoretical
    points of this essay in A1. There he emphasizes

the formative importance of the social isolation of
the two couples and the "law of reinforcement" that
intensifies the psychic abnormalities of the
daughters during their cohabitation with their
mothers.
Abstract in L'encéphale 7 (1931):   557.

E123.   With Henri Ey. "Parkinsonisme et syndrome dé-
        mentiel. (Protrusion de la langue dans un des
        cas.)" Société médico-psychologique, 12 November
        1931. Annales médico-psychologiques 2, no. 4
        (1931):   418-28.

        Claims that these cases are distinctive because
        encephalitis ordinarily manifests itself as motor
        disturbances or character disorders, but in these
        cases psychic syndromes affect the intellectual
        sphere with a minimum of affective or instinctual
        disorders. The authors note the rarity of tongue
        protrusion and cite E120 as one of the few other
        cases reported.
        Abstract in L'encéphale 10 (1931):   822.

E124.   With Pierre Migault and J. Lévy-Valensi. "Trouble
        du langage ecrit chez une paranoïaque presentant
        des éléments délirants du type paranoïde (schizo-
        graphie)." Société médico-psychologique, 12
        November 1931. Annales médico-psychologique 2,
        no. 4 (1931):   407-8.

        Introduces the term "schizographie" to describe
        the disjunction between the patient's oral dis-
        course, which is coherent, and his written dis-
        course, which is incoherent. A complete discussion
        of the case and this term appeared later as C40.
        Abstract in L'encéphale 10 (1931):   821, under
        the title "Délire et écrits à type paranoïde chez
        une malade à présentation paranoïaque."

E125.   With Henri Claude and Pierre Migault. "Spasme de
        torsion et troubles mentaux post-encéphali-
        tiques." Société médico-pyschologique, 19 May
        1932. Annales médico-psychologiques 1, no. 5
        (1932):   546-551.

        Describes the congeries of symptoms following an
        encephalitic illness. The symptoms included long
        periods of mutism in which the patient would
        communicate only through writing.

E126.   With Georges Heuyer. "Un cas de perversion
        infantile par encéphalite épidémique précoce
        diagnostiqué sur un syndrome moteur fruste."
        Société médico-psychologique, 13 July 1933.
        Annales médico-psychologiques 2 (1933):   221-23.

Describes a 14 year-old boy who has repeatedly
attacked other children and who suffers from a
slight but notable trembling in the eyes, tongue
and hands. The authors argue that this case
involves a complex set of causes for the boy's
behavior that are usually just grouped together as
the "perversions instinctives essentielles" of
children.
Abstract in L'encéphale 8 (1933):   617.

E127.   With H. Claude and G. Heuyer.   ""Un cas de démence
        précocissisme." Société médico-psychologique, 5
        September 1933. Annales médico-psychologique 1
        (1933):   620-24.

        Describes the symptoms of a ten-year-old boy
        suffering from dementia praecox, which includes
        delusions of persecution, mutism, and periodic
        outbreaks of violence. The authors speculate that
        the patient's exposure to his cousin's infectious
        encephalitis might be the origin of the illness,
        and they observe that the patient himself suggested
        this etiology after examining himself in a mirror.
        This case illustrates Lacan's early interest in
        the phenomenon of the mirror stage, and it also
        exemplifies the curiously "contagious" character of
        psychic disturbance that he will later explore in
        the case of the Papin sisters.
        Abstract in L'encéphale 6 (1933):   469.

E128.   "Compte-rendu de la 84ème assemblée de la Société
        suisse de psychiatrie tenue à Nyons-Prangins."
        7-8 October 1933. L'encéphale 11 (1933):   686-
        95.

E129.   With G. Heuyer.   "Alcoolisme subaigu à pouls normal
        ou ralenti. Co-existence du syndrome d'automa-
        tisme mental." Société médico-psychologique, 27
        November 1933. Annales médico-psychologique 2,
        no. 4 (1933):   531-46.

        Notes several unusual cases in which alcoholic
        delusions are combined with a normal or slow pulse,
        and claims that this unusual association of
        symptoms possesses an important diagnostic value
        when they appear with certain elements of mental
        automatism.
        Abstract in L'encéphale 1 (1934):   53.

E130.   Discussion of J. Piaget, "La psychanalyse et le
        développement intellectuel." Eighth Congrés des
        psychanalystes de langue française, 19 December
        1933. Revue française de psychanalyse 1 (1934):
        1-34.

Notes that paranoiac disturbances have a representative social value. Reprinted in Ornicar? 31
(1984): 8.

E131.   "Exposé général de nos travaux scientifiques."
         Dated 1933. Appendix to Ala, pp. 399-403.

Describes his thesis and the work published
through 1932, stressing his use of a "phenomenological analysis" that allowed him to determine the
"mental structure" beneath different clinical
syndromes. Lacan claims that this phenomenological
perspective led him to apply linguistic methods of
analysis to written manifestations of delusional
language, and that it also suggested a profound
connection between the content of psychic phenomena
and the patient's whole personality. He defines
personality as an "ensemble of specialized functional relations" that adapt the man-animal to the
human milieu called "society," and he concludes
that the psychology of personality can be described
in terms of a highly organized reaction to specific
situations which reflects a "conflict of moral
conscience" regarding one's relationship with other
people.
Lacan claims that he is the first to interpret
the phenomena of delusion in the context of a
detailed analysis of the patient's concrete
history. He does cite Piaget and psychoanalysis,
however, as sources for his claim that the psychology of personality is related to one's sense of
morality and social relations, especially as that
sense is determined by discrete stages in the early
development of the individual. The predisposition
to psychosis can be located in any interruption in
that development that is occasioned by the concrete circumstances of the subject's history, and
Lacan says that psychosis itself emerges under the
influence of a situation that parallels the one
that caused the earlier interruption. Among the
benefits claimed by Lacan for this socially-
oriented psychology of personality is the light it
throws on the contagious quality of paranoia, which
can be related to the expressive value of paranoia
as an eminently human conflict.

E***.   With G. Heuyer. "Compte-rendu du Congrès inter-
         national pour la protection de l'enfance: impor-
         tance des troubles du caractère dans l'orien-
         tation professionnelle." Listed as forthcoming
         in the bibliography of Ala, p. 405.

E132.   Discussion of C. Odier, "Conflits instinctuels et
        bisexualité." Société psychanalytique de Paris,
        20 November 1934. Revue française de psych-
        analyse 4 (1935): 683.

        Brief remark. Reprinted in Ornicar? 31 (1984):
        9.

E133.   Discussion of M. Friedman, "Quelques réflexions sur
        le suicide." Société psychanalytique de Paris,
        18 December 1934. Revue française de psych-
        analyse 4 (1935): 686.

        Notes the importance of a structured conception
        of narcissism in suicide. Reprinted in Ornicar? 31
        (1984): 9.

E134.   Discussion of O. Codet, "A propos de trois cas
        d'anorexie mentale." Société psychanalytique de
        Paris, 18 June 1935. Revue française de psych-
        analyse 1 (1936): 127.

        Brief remarks on anorexia mentale. Reprinted in
        Ornicar? 31 (1984): 10.

E135.   Discussion of P. Schiff, "Psychanalyse d'un crime
        incompréhensible." Société psychanalytique de
        Paris, 18 November 1935. Revue française de
        psychanalyse 4 (1935): 690-91.

        Briefly notes the similarities between the case
        Schiff presents and that of Aimée, which he
        described in his thesis (A1). Lacan also notes the
        similarity of these cases to that of the Papin
        sisters (see C42) and points out the importance of
        determining the value of the incident that precipi-
        tates the crime, however absurd it may seem.
        Reprinted in Ornicar? 31 (1984): 9-10.

E136.   Discussion of M. Cénac, "La neuvième conférence des
        psychanalystes de langue française." Evolution
        psychiatrique 1 (1935): 79-86; see especially p.
        85.

        Briefly comments on "la tension sociale" and its
        importance in social contact for the paranoiac, and
        emphasizes the role of personality and "structural
        formations" in various psychoses.

E137.   Discussion of M. Bonaparte, "Vues paléobiologiques
        et biopsychiques." Société psychanalytique de
        Paris, 19 January 1937. Revue française de
        psychanalyse 3 (1938): 551.

        Relates the threat of "ce morcellement" (fantasms

of dismemberment, castration, etc.) to the imaginary unity of the human body conceived in the mirror stage (see C53), and argues that anxiety is fixed in the first six months of biological prematuration.
Reprinted in <u>Ornicar?</u> 31 (1984): 10-11.

E138.   Discussion of D. Lagache, "Deuil et mélancolie." Société psychanalytique de Paris, 25 May 1937. <u>Revue française de psychanalyse</u> 3 (1938): 564-65.

Brief remark on the way Lagache's case illustrates how certain people who have not resolved the Oedipal crisis remain in two dimensions: maternal fixation, and narcissism. Reprinted in <u>Ornicar?</u> 31 (1984): 11.

E139.   Discussion of R. Loewenstein, "L'origine du masochisme et la théorie des pulsions." Tenth Conférence des psychanalystes de langue française, 21-22 February 1938. <u>Revue française de psychanalyse</u> 4 (1938): 750-52.

Briefly remarks on Freud's concept of the death drive, which Lacan notes was unusually speculative but cannot easily be divorced from analytic doctrine. The biological dimension of Freud's speculation is especially problematic, Lacan says, because man is unique: he is the only animal that kills himself, and that has a superego.
Reprinted in <u>Ornicar?</u> 31 (1984): 12-13.

E140.   "De l'impulsion au complexe." Société psychanalytique de Paris, 25 October 1938. <u>Revue française de psychanalyse</u> 11, no. 1 (1939): 137-41.

Describes two cases Lacan presented to the SPP, and includes a brief summary of the discussion that followed (by J. Leuba). Lacan stresses the importance of fantasies of dismemberment and claims that the cases illustrate and confirm his theoretical formula for the primordial stage of the "<u>corps morcelé</u>" in the genesis of the ego. In the discussion with Hartmann, Loewenstein, and others, Lacan admits a close relation between this stage and the "mirror stage" described in C44 and C45.
Reprinted in <u>Ornicar?</u> 31 (1984): 14-19.

E141.   Discussion of F. Pasche, "La délinquance névrotique." Société psychanalytique de Paris, 17 February 1948. <u>Revue française de psychanalyse</u> 2 (1949): 315.

Notes Lacan's interest in distinguishing between
"normal" and "neurotic" delinquents, especially in
relation to the connection between a psychic disturbance and the actual commission of the criminal
act. For a discussion of this "passage à l'acte"
in response to a later paper by Lacan, see comments
by S. A. Shentoub in J1016.
Reprinted in Ornicar? 31 (1984): 19.

E142. Discussion of J. Leuba, "Mère phallique et mère
       castratrice." Société psychanalytique de Paris,
       20 April 1948. Revue française de psychanalyse 3
       (1949):   317.

Briefly notes that the maternal imago is more
castrating than the paternal. Lacan claims that
some form of the myth of Osiris has appeared at the
end of each of his analyses, and he says that some
deficiency of the father is usually behind the most
serious neuroses. For Lacan's own account of the
castrating mother and the pathological effect of
the absent father, see C46.
Reprinted in Ornicar? 31 (1984): 19.

E143. Discussion of Ziwar, "Psychanalyse des principaux
       syndromes psychosomatiques." Société psych-
       analytique de Paris, 19 October 1948. Revue
       française de psychanalyse 2 (1949):   318.

Reports Lacan's endorsement of Ziwar's attempt to
describe the structure of typical syndromes, and
describes Lacan's distinction between two different
kinds of hypertension, "red" and "white." Lacan
claims that this difference cannot be fully understood without a more complete awareness of their
psychic structures.
Reprinted in Ornicar? 31 (1984).

E144. Discussion of S. A. Shentoub, "Remarques méthodo-
       logiques sur la socioanalyse." Société psych-
       analytique de Paris, 14 December 1948. Revue
       française de psychanalyse 2 (1949): 319.

Notes that psychoanalysis must bring to sociology
an apparatus suitable for attacking the subject on
the plane of subjective experience.
Reprinted in Ornicar? 31 (1984): 20.

E145. Discussion of R. Held, "Le problème de la théra-
       peutique en médecine psychosomatique." Société
       psychanalytique de Paris, 20 June 1949. Revue
       française de psychanalyse 3 (1949):   446.

Reports Lacan's agreement with Held's claim that
mothers possess a "mortifying" character, espe-

cially in the relationships between mothers and
daughters, but notes Lacan's objection to the
suggestion that this character can be explained by
the emancipation of women. Lacan argues instead
that this phenomenon is too recent to be at the
origin of such an old problem. For Lacan's own
analysis of the relationship among contemporary
social forms, the role of the mother, and certain
forms of neuroses, see C46.
Reprinted in Ornicar? 31 (1984).

E146. Discussion of F. Dolto, "A propos de la poupée-
fleur." Société psychanalytique de Paris, 18
October 1949. Revue française de psychanalyse 4
(1949): 566-67.

Notes Dolto's use of a flower-puppet [i.e., a
small doll with a daisy where the face should be]
as a therapeutic aid in her treatment of narcissistic children, and claims that her technique
supports his own research on the mirror stage, the
imago of the body-proper, and the dismembered body.
Lacan also remarks that the flower-puppet is a
sexual symbol and that it masks the human face.
Reprinted in Ornicar? 39 (1984).

E147. Discussion of M. Bonaparte, "Psyché dans la nature
ou les limites de la psychogénèse." Société
psychanalytique de Paris, 16 November 1949.
Revue française de psychanalyse 4 (1949): 570.

Reports Lacan's observations that a living being
(le vivant) cannot be conceived without an "umwelt"
or environment that surrounds him on all sides and
that influences him through what is usually called
the "psychism."
Reprinted in Ornicar? 31 (1984).

E148. Discussion of M. Bouvet, "Incidences thérapeutiques
de la prise de conscience de l'envie de pénis
dans des cas de névrose obsessionnelle féminine."
Société psychanalytique de Paris, 20 December
1949. Revue française de psychanalyse 4 (1949):
571-72.

Reports Lacan's question about Bouvet's failure
to speak of the phallic-mother stage in his report
of the case under discussion.
Reprinted in Ornicar? 31 (1984).

E149. "Réglement et doctrine de la commission de l'enseignement de la Société psychanalytique de
Paris." Revue française de psychanalyse 3
(1949): 426-35.

Describes the procedures by which the Committee
on Teaching must oversee the selection and training
of candidates seeking admission to the SPP as
practicing analysts. After being interviewed by
each member of the committee and passing this preliminary examination, the candidate chooses a
member of the Society as his analyst, gets the
choice approved by the committee, and begins his
"analyse didactique," the "training analysis."
This analysis lasts at least two years and includes
theoretical training as well as three to five
weekly sessions. During this time, at a point
determined by the analyst, the candidate begins
seeing his own patient(s) for "une analyse sous
contrôle," i.e., an analysis supervised by two
other members of the society who evaluate the
candidate's performance. When they decide the
candidate is ready, the Committee authorizes him to
present an original work before the Society, which
then votes on his admission.

These regulations resemble those of most other
psychoanalytic societies of the time but take on a
special significance in the light of the radically
different plan Lacan proposed to the Ecole freudienne de Paris in 1967, "la passe" (see C88).
Lacan had joined the SPP in 1934 and became a
member of the Committee on teaching in 1948.

Reprinted in F380, pp. 29-36. For the controversy that surrounded these training statutes, see
E154.

E150.   With the Commission de l'Enseignement de la Société
        psychanalytique de Paris. Revue française de
        psychanalyse 3 (1949): 436-41.

        Suggests a series of provisions designed to train
        people to meet the immediate demand for child
        analysts. The provisions reduce the time and
        expense usually involved in the training analysis
        but require a significant amount of theoretical as
        well as practical study.

E151.   Discussion of papers by Franz Alexander, Anna
        Freud, Melanie Klein, and Raymond de Saussure
        during a meeting on "Psychothérapie, psych-
        analyse." Premier Congrès mondial de psychi-
        atrie. Paris, 1950. Actes du Congrès 5 (A.S.I.,
        no. 1172). Paris: Hermann, 1952.

        Argues that the essential point of departure for
        the study of the "psychisme de l'enfant" is the
        fact that the child must use the syntactic forms of
        the adult from the moment it speaks and so is
        already part of the experience structured by those
        forms. Thus, Lacan says, language determines

psychology more than psychology explains language.
Lacan also claims that the ego is an illusion, a
"superstructure engaged in social alienation," and
insists that the biological basis of need is
predestined to be organized by symbolic combi-
nations and the law.
　　Reprinted in <u>Ornicar?</u> 30 (1984): 7-10.

E152.　Extended response to comments on C54. <u>Revue</u>
　　<u>française de psychanalyse</u> 15, no. 1 (1951): 84-
　　88.

　　Focuses on the narcissistic character of the
crimes discussed in the preceding article (C54),
especially as it bears on the individual's sense of
reality and his relation to culture. Such crimes
have meaning only within the "closed structure of
subjectivity," Lacan says, specifically the
structure that "excludes the neurotic from the
authentic realization of the other by occluding in
him the experiences of social conflict and communication, the structure which leaves him prey to the
truncated root of the moral conscience that we call
the superego" (p. 85). Lacan says that this is why
these crimes are never exclusively "social" in the
usual sense.
　　Lacan refers to such criminals as "<u>les criminels</u>
<u>du</u> moi," criminals of the ego, and he claims that
they are the mute victims of an evolution in
cultural forms toward constraints that are increasingly exterior to the self. Hence "the society
where these criminals are produced cannot without
bad conscience take them as scapegoats, and the
role of vanguard (<u>vedette</u>) that it confers on them
so easily clearly manifests the real function they
serve" (p. 86). In these scapegoats society
recognizes the "intentions of all," Lacan adds, and
he argues that the major determining factor of
these crimes or any others is the very conception
of responsibility that the subject receives from
the culture in which he lives.
　　These remarks clarify the central theoretical
points of Lacan's earlier essays on "criminals of
the ego," A1 and C42.

E153.　Discussion of a paper by March Schlumberger,
　　"Introduction à l'étude du transfert en clinique
　　psychanalytique." Fourteenth Conférence des
　　psychanalystes de langue française, 1951. <u>Revue</u>
　　<u>française de psychanalyse</u> 16, nos. 1/2 (1952):
　　154-63.

　　Uses Freud's history of the Dora case to show how
the "dialectical experience" of psychoanalysis
hinges on the subject-to-subject relation exposed

by the phenomenon of transference in analysis.
This subject-to-subject relationship that emerges
in transference is constitutive of human experience
as such, Lacan observes, because it is the demand
to be recognized by another that constitutes man as
man.

Lacan argues that in psychoanalysis the subject
is constituted by a discourse through which the
simple presence of the analyst establishes the
dimension of dialogue before any intervention even
takes place. He insists on the analyst maintaining
this position of a "non agir," i.e., of non-
intervention, in view of what he calls the "orthodramatization of the patient's subjectivity."
("Orthodramatization" is a neologism that may
allude to the term "orthopsychiatry." If so, the
term would suggest the corrective import of the
patient's working through the interrupted narcissistic evolution of the ego in the process of
transference.)

Lacan discusses Freud's account of the Dora
analysis as an illustration of how Freud recognized
the phenomena of transference without entirely
understanding his own role in it, and he describes
the account as a "scansion of the structures where
truth is transmuted for the subject." Lacan says
that those structures not only determine Dora's
comprehension of things but also determine her
position as the subject for which those things
function as "objects." Thus he concludes that
Freud's account is "identical to the progress of
the subject, that is to say to the reality of the
cure."

Lacan's revisionist reading of the Dora case is
intriguing because it marks the strategic function
of various interventions that Freud makes in Dora's
descriptions of her experiences. On the role of
the analyst as a "non agir," see C88, C92, F395,
F396 and F397.

Reprinted as "Intervention sur le transfert" in
A2, pp. 215-26; translated as "Intervention on
Transference" by Jacqueline Rose in Feminine
Sexuality (see F370, pp. 61-75).

E***.   Discussion of M. Benassy, "Sur la théorie des
        instincts," and M. Bouvet, "Le Moi dans la
        névrose obsessionnelle, relations d'objets et
        mécanismes de défense." Fifteenth Conférence des
        psychanalystes de langue française, Paris, 1952.
        Unpublished.

        Dor lists this as unpublished but with a ref-
        erence to Revue française de psychanalyse 1/2
        (1953):   212.

E154.   "Statuts proposés pour l'Institute de psych-
        analyse." Société psychanalytique de Paris,
        January 1953. F379, pp. 52-63.

        Includes "Projet d'amendement aux status proposés
        par le docteur Sacha Nacht pour l'Institute de
        Psychanalyse," "Exposé des motifs--Psychanalyse et
        enseignement," and the statutes themselves. The
        importance of this document can only be understood
        within the context in which it was delivered, which
        Turkle describes in F412, p. 104-06. Sacha Nacht
        was the original director of the training institute
        associated with the SPP, and he had proposed to
        restrict the analytic diploma to physicians, who
        would have to complete a rigorously structured
        curriculum.
        This proposal contradicted the society's own
        training statutes, which Lacan had written in 1949
        (see E149), and it enraged Marie Bonaparte, who
        advocated lay analysis and was providing much of
        the money for the training institute. Bonaparte
        and Lacan joined against Nacht, who resigned as
        head of the institute, and Lacan was appointed to
        head the institute temporarily. The new statues he
        proposed in this item reflect the ones of 1949,
        though their appearance at this time must be read
        as a direct rejection of Nacht and as an effort by
        Lacan to return the society to the broader, less
        regimented goals of its earlier periods.
        The "project" is a witty effort to affirm Lacan's
        interest in maintaining a unified society, and he
        describes his proposal as presenting to "our corps
        morcelé the instrument of a mirror where, god
        willing, it will look forward to its unity."
        The "exposé" is a more polemical introduction in
        which Lacan insists on the value of a flexible
        program for the preparation of analysts and claims
        that psychoanalysis can never be reduced to any
        single "science," as Nacht desired. Psychoanalysis
        is situated "at the center of all the sciences of
        man," Lacan says, and that is why the training
        institute must be considered as the "designated
        host of all confrontations with affiliated disci-
        plines." To this end, Lacan describes the mode of
        teaching proposed here as a means of restoring "the
        primacy of speech" to the analytic experience and
        of recognizing the "institution of a dialogue"
        between two subjects in analytic discourse.
        The statutes themselves recall most of the points
        Lacan raised in E149, with detailed accounts of the
        administrative relations between the Société and
        the proposed Institute.
        On 20 January 1953 Lacan was elected president of
        the SPP, but his plans for the institute had failed
        to give Marie Bonaparte a significant role and she

shifted her allegiance to Nacht. Nacht was then
reinstated as the leader of the new institute and
proceeded to enact his original proposal for the
strict curriculum. This tension finally led Lacan
to resign the presidency in June, 1953, and to form
a new group, the Société française de psychanalyse.
(For a more detailed account of this controversy,
see the introduction to this volume and F379.)

E***.   "Le stade du mirror en action." Société psych-
          analytique de Paris, 19 May 1953. Unpublished.
          Indexed in <u>Revue française de psychanalyse</u> 3
          (1953): 369.

          The bibliography in <u>Magazine littéraire</u> 121
          (1977): 29ff. reports that this presentation was
          accompanied by a film by Gesell, "The Discovery of
          Self in Front of the Mirror."

E155.   "Lettre de Jacques Lacan à Madame Roudinesco (24
          May 1953)." F379, pp. 76-20.

          Describes the debates between the groups as-
          sociated with Nacht and Lacan concerning the
          statutes Lacan proposed for the Teaching Institute
          of the Société psychanalytique de Paris. Roudi-
          nesco was a student at the society during the
          controversy and had written an open letter to Nacht
          and Lacan in which she accused Lacan of being
          responsible for the conflict dividing students of
          the society even if he hadn't directly instigated
          it. Roudinesco's letter is printed in F379; see
          Turkle's description of the controversy in F412, p.
          106.

E156.   Letter of Michael Balint, 14 July 1953. F379, pp.
          119.

          Thanks Balint for his support and insists that
          his group did everything they could to avoid a
          split with the Société psychanalytique de Paris.

E157.   Letter to Rudolph Loewenstein, 14 July 1953. F379,
          pp. 120-35.

          Describes the events surrounding Lacan's split
          from the Société psychanalytique de Paris and
          condemns Sacha Nacht as a hypocrite for scheming to
          take over the Society's training institute. As a
          result of Nacht's dissembling and partly as a
          result of Marie Bonaparte's sudden reversal of
          allegiance from Lacan to Nacht, in early June the
          Society issued a vote of no confidence in Lacan,
          who was then president. He immediately resigned
          and joined the newly formed Société française de

psychanalyse, and this letter recounts the bitter-
ness and disappointment behind his decision. He
insists that he and his supporters never intended
to split from the Society and were in fact expelled
by Nacht, but he also notes that a majority of the
students associated with the old society came with
him and claims that Nacht's incompetence will
disaffect many others. (Loewenstein had been
Lacan's analyst twenty years earlier, and he
supported the new society--to no avail--before the
executive committee of the International Psychoanalytic Association in London when it met to
decide whether or not to recognize the SFP). See
Turkle's account of the controversy, F412, p. 110,
and the related documents in F379.
    Translated by Jeffrey Mehlman in October 40
(1987):   55-69 (see A11).

E158. Letter to Professor N. Perrotti, 14 July 1953.
       F379, pp. 117-18.

    Defends the decision to split off from the
Société psychanalytique de Paris and form a new
group as a consequence of obligations that the
analysts felt toward their students, and agrees to
follow Perrotti's solution to the conflict that had
resulted in Lacan's being forbidden to appear at
the business meeting of the Eighteenth International Psychoanalytic Congress in London. (Lacan
had been notified of that decision only a week
before this letter was written.)   It was at that
meeting that the IPA refused to recognize the newly
formed Société française de psychanalyse, largely
at the urging of Anna Freud and the group surrounding Nacht, which was allowed to attend. Anna
Freud strongly objected to the "irregular training"
of students under Lacan's supervision and to the
fact that Lacan's supporters had made the controversy public. For an account of the IPA's decisions, see J1063 and F412, p. 110. For related
letters and documents, see F379.

E159. Letter to Heinz Hartmann, 21 July 1953. F379, pp.
       136-37.

    Appeals to Hartmann for support and defends
himself and the new Société française de psychanalyse by insisting that they had never wanted to
split up the Société psychanalytique de Paris and
by maintaining that they had been driven out by
Nacht and his followers. Later that month,
Hartmann voted against the SFP during the administrative session of the London congress of the
International Psychoanalytic Association, and two
years later, as president of the IPA, he again

refused to recognize the SFP for membership.
Translated by Jeffrey Mehlman in October 40
(1987):   70-71 (see A11).

E160.   Response to comments on C57 and C58.   27 September
         1953.   La psychanalyse 1 (1956):   242-55.   (For
         the comments by Pr. Perrotti and Serge Leclaire,
         see pp. 232-42).

         Defends his emphasis on language in psycho-
         analysis by distinguishing between treating
         language as merely a methodological tool and his
         considering it as the locus of the analytic ex-
         perience itself.   Language is neither "signal, nor
         sign, nor even sign of the thing insofar as the
         thing is an exterior reality," Lacan says; "the
         relation between the signifier and signified is
         entirely enclosed in the order of Language itself,
         which completely conditions its two terms" (p. 243,
         tr. p. 123).   He goes on to stress the materiality
         of the signifier and attacks the notion that the
         human brain is the locus of language.   If not
         there, then where? Lacan asks, and, "replying for
         the signifier," he responds "'everywhere else.'"
         Where is the signified from this perspective?
         "'Nowhere,'" Lacan says.
         Lacan argues that despite all grammatical
         appearances, no part of speech has the power to
         "denominate" a thing.   "No doubt discourse is con-
         cerned with things," he adds, and it is even in
         this encounter that things emerge as such.   But he
         goes on to say that this is so true that the word
         no longer can be considered merely the sign of the
         thing; instead, "the word tends to become the thing
         itself" (p. 144, tr. p. 123).   Lacan concludes with
         a brief discussion of the Fort/Da game from Beyond
         the Pleasure Principle (1920) to demonstrate the
         primacy of the signifier over what it signifies and
         to illustrate the equation between the symbol and
         death that he proposed in C58.
         See F386.   Many of the central passages in this
         item are translated in the notes to F420.

E161.   Discussion of Jean Hyppolite, "Phénoménologie de
         Hegel et psychanalyse." Société française de
         psychanalyse, 11 January 1955.   Reference to
         Lacan's comment in La psychanalyse 3 (1957):   32.

         Brief remark.

E162.   Discussion of Juliette Favez-Boutonier, "Psych-
         analyse et Philosophie" (see L1683).   Société
         française de philosophie, 25 January 1955.
         Bulletin de la Société française de philosophie
         49 (1955):   37-41.

Briefly summarizes several of his major claims
including the notion of Freud's work as a
"Copernican revolution" whose central truth, "the
subject who speaks is not the conscious subject,"
fundamentally decenters the human subject. Lacan
says this truth is why psychoanalysis emphasizes
the constitutive role of speech in the subject's
sense of "self," and that emphasis in turn is what
disturbs traditional humanism and its faith in
individual autonomy.

E163.   Discussion at the Colloque sur l'anorexie mentale,
        28 November 1955. Indexed without description in
        La psychanalyse 1 (1956): 290.

E164.   Discussion of Claude Lévi-Strauss, "Sur les
        rapports entre la mythologie et le rituel"
        (L2019). Société française de philosophie, 21
        May 1956. Bulletin de la Société française de
        philosophie 3 (1956): 113-19.

        Agrees with Lévi-Strauss's emphasis on the role
        of the signifier in L2018, and says that this study
        of the combinatory laws common to myths from
        several societies shows how the order of the
        signifier can determine the way reality is repre-
        sented quite apart from the effect of the signi-
        fied. Nevertheless, Lacan suggests that the
        current paper tends to admit the "massive in-
        trusion" of an element from the real into the for-
        mation of the myth, and for that reason it seems to
        retreat from the principles of the earlier essay.
        For Lévi-Strauss's response, see L2019.

E165.   Discussion of A. Hesnard, "Réflexions sur le 'Wo Es
        war, soll Ich verden' de Sigmund Freud." Société
        française de psychanalyse, 6 November 1956. La
        psychanalyse 3 (1957): 323-24.

        Notes that the ego, le Moi, is essentially a
        structural notion that goes beyond its definition
        as consciousness, and says that the ego plays the
        role of a screen (l'écran) in relation to reality.
        Lacan claims that the "war" is very important in
        Freud's phrase because the pastness it designates
        is an essential dimension of the Es, which is tied
        to the construction of the symptom and its nach-
        träglich nature.

E166.   Discussion of Daniel Lagache, "Fascination de la
        conscience par le Moi." Séance scientifique du 8
        January 1957, Société française de psychanalyse.
        La psychanalyse 3 (1957): 325-29, passim.

Comments on the difficulty of situating the subject in relation to an object, and insists that its proper dimension is to exist in intersubjectivity. In some ways, Lacan says, the ego is a "perversion," although the confusion of the "je" with the "moi" is not so much a perversion as a madness (une folie).

E167.   Discussion of G. Favez, "Le rendez-vous avec le psychanalyste." Société française de psychanalyse, 5 February 1957. La psychanalyse 4 (1958): 308-13.

Praises the use of the term "rendez-vous" to describe the relation between the analyst and the analysand, but balks at the idea that the "real" character of the analyst is finally revealed at the end of analysis. Analysis brings about the confrontation of one subject with an other, Lacan says, but it is not the analyst that meets with the patient there.

E168.   Discussion of J. Favez-Boutonier, "Abandon et névrose" and P. Matussek, "La psychothérapie des schizophrènes." Société française de psychanalyse, 7 May 1957 and 4 June 1957. La psychanalyse 4 (1958): 318-20, 332.

Objects that the neurosis of abandonment described by Favez-Boutonier cannot be supported from a psychoanalytic perspective because man does not relate to objects as such but to the lack assumed as the path of desire. Lacan also says that if the analyst withdraws during analysis, it is not to provoke stress or frustration but to give way to the fundamental ambiguity of the coexistence of the real and the symbolic.

E169.   Discussion of C. Perelman, "L'idée de rationalité et la règle de justice." Société française de philosophie, 23 April 1960. Bulletin de la Société française de philosophie 1 (1961): 29-33.

Compares Perelman's analysis of metaphor to his own explanation in C71, and notes that the "heterogeneity" among the four elements of a metaphorical comparison consists of a division between three signifiers and the effect of a signified that their substitution engenders, not of a division between a set of two signifiers and a set of two signifieds.
Reprinted as "La métaphore du sujet" in A2, pp. 889-92.

E170. Letter to D. W. Winnicott, 5 August 1960.
       Translated by Jeffrey Mehlman in <u>October</u> 40
       (1987): 76-78 (see A11).

       Thanks Winnicott for his invitation to address
       the London Society and expresses regret that
       Winnicott claims to have been unable to understand
       C78. Lacan attempts to explain the motives and
       essential thrust of the essay, and in an aside he
       briefly describes his concern and pride that his
       step-daughter and nephew have been arrested for
       acts of political resistance.

E***. Discussion of Conrad Stein, "Langage et incon-
       scient" and of S. Leclaire and J. Laplanche,
       "L'inconscient, une étude psychanalytique."
       Sixth Colloque de Bonneval, 30 October-2 November
       1960. See C81.

E171. Letter to Serge Leclaire, 10 November 1963. F380,
       p. 91.

       Notes that today is the first time he has ever
       missed a plenary session of "<u>notre Société</u>," the
       Société française de psychanalyse. Lacan explains
       that his presence would have required the Society
       to disavow the motion of order of October 14.
       (Presumably Lacan is referring to the motion
       removing Lacan from the Society's list of training
       analysts, passed on 13 October 1963. The motion
       was instigated by Wladimir Granoff and signed by
       Juliette Favez-Boutonier, Daniel Lagache, and
       Georges Favez. See F380.)

E172. "Le séminaire des noms-du-père." 20 November 1963.
       F380, pp. 110-11.

       Announces the end of the seminar, which has been
       meeting for ten years, and attributes his decision
       to the vote to remove his name from the list of
       training analysts for the Société française
       psychanalyse. Lacan reconvened his seminar in
       January 1964 at the Ecole Normale Supérieure (see
       B22). Translated by Jeffrey Mehlman in <u>October</u> 40
       (1987): 81-95 (see A11).

E173. Discussion of Paul Ricoeur, "Technique et non-
       technique dans l'interprétation." Colloquium on
       "Technique et Casistica," University of Rome, 7-
       12 January 1964. <u>Tecnica e casistica: actes du
       congrès du Rome</u>. Padova: Cedam, 1964. P. 44.
       See K1314.

E174. "Du 'Trieb' de Freud et du désir du psychanalyste."
       Based on discussions during a Colloquium on

"Technique et Casistica," 7-12 January 1964.
Tecnica e casistica: actes du congrès du Rome.
Padova: Cedam, 1964.   Pp. 51-53, 55-60.   See
K1341.

Comments on several mistaken readings of concepts
described by Freud, especially that of "Trieb" or
"la pulsion," which some analysts have mistakenly
tried to reduce to a form of instinct.   Such concepts are our "myths," Lacan says; they mythify the
real in such a way that desire reproduces there the
relation of the subject to the lost object.   This
is the case even for the concept of libido.   Lacan
claims that libido is not the sexual instinct but
is conceived by Freud as an energy.   Its sexual
coloring is a "coleur-de-vide," suspended in the
light of a wound ("une béance").   He also notes
that desire is intimately related to castration,
and in fact it is the assumption of castration that
creates the lack in which desire is instituted.
"Le désir est désir de désir," Lacan says, "désir
de l'Autre, avons-nous dit, soit soumis à la Loi."
Reprinted with explanatory note in A2, pp. 851-
54.

E175.   Discussion of A. de Waelhens, "Note pour une
        épistémologie de la santé mentale."   Colloquium
        on "Technique et Casistica," 7-12 January 1964.
        Tecnica e casistica: actes du congrès du Rome.
        Padova: Cedam, 1964.   Pp. 87-88.   See K1341.

E176.   Discussion of Filiasi Carcano, "Morale tradizionale
        et Societa Contemporanea."   Colloquium on "Tech-
        nique et Casuistique," 7-12 January 1964.
        Tecnica e casistica: actes du congrès du Rome.
        Padova: Cedam, 1964.   P. 106.   See K1341.

E177.   Discussion of R. Marlé, "Casuistique et morales
        modernes de situation."   Colloquium on "Technique
        et Casistica," 7-12 January 1964.   Tecnica e
        casistica: actes du congrès du Rome.   Padova:
        Cedam, 1964.   P. 117.   See 1341.

E***.   "L'excommunication."   15 January 1964.   See B22.

        The opening address of Lacan's eleventh seminar,
        which began after his departure from the Société
        française de psychanalyse.   For a description of
        the whole address, see B22.   Excerpt reprinted on
        the fourth coverpage of F380.   Translated in B22b,
        pp. 7-17.

E178.   "Fondation de l'EFP."   21 June 1964.   F380, pp.
        149-52.

Known as the "Acte de fondation," this document
founded the Ecole freudienne de Paris seven months
after Lacan left the Société française de psychanalyse (see F380). Lacan explains the name of the
new society as an indication of his intention to
return to the "original praxis" that Freud instituted under the name of psychoanalysis, and to
guard against deviations from that praxis. Lacan
promises that members will find the freedom and
support for any work that is valuable, and he
describes a "circular organization" of small groups
that will replace the usual vertical hierarchy of
such associations.

Lacan says there will be three sections of the
EFP: a section of "pure psychoanalysis," primarily
concerned with the training of new analysts; a
section of applied psychoanalysis devoted to therapeutic and clinical medicine; and a section of the
"recensement du champ freudien," which will explore
connections between psychoanalysis and work being
done in other disciplines.

Reprinted in A9, pp. 7-10, where it appears with
"Note adjointe" and "Préamble" (pp. 10-14). The
"Note adjointe" consists of a "guide de l'usager"
in seven parts which specifies various definitions
and rules regarding the training analysis, candidates for the school, etc. The "Preamble" briefly
describes the discord among groups practicing
purportedly "Freudian" psychoanalysis and the
resistance faced by the "sujets formés par Lacan"
from "une certaine 'Internationale'" (p. 13). The
new group will be a "school" in the antique sense,
Lacan promises: a place of refuge or a base of
operations against what even in ancient times could
be called the malaise in civilization.

Translated by Jeffrey Mehlman in October 40
(1987): 96-105 (see A11).

E179. "Reponse à des étudiants en philosophie sur l'objet
       de la psychanalyse." 19 February 1966. Cahiers
       pour l'analyse 3 (1966): 5-13.

Distinguishes between the "subject" defined by
psychoanalysis and various "consciousnesses"
proposed by philosophers, claiming that all of the
philosophical theories of consciousness have no
other function than that of suturing up the wound
("la béance") left by the split ("la refente") that
inaugurates the subject as defined by psychoanalysis.

Lacan also distinguishes the subject from the
autonomous ego proposed by Hartmann and other
American analysts, and he claims that ego psychology, with its dream of the autonomous ego as a
free sphere of conflict, is nothing more than the

ideology of a class of immigrants who long for the
prestigious place they formerly occupied in central
European society. Lacan says that these immigrants
still regret losing the comfortable world which
they gave up during the war only to install themselves in a society where values are based on the
scale of the income tax (p. 8). Hartmann could
have understood that from his paper on the mirror
stage at the conference at Marienbad, Lacan adds.
However, he says, nothing can resist the appeal of
diversifying the forms of the concentration camp,
and "l'idéologie psychologisante" is one of those
forms (p. 8).

In response to questions regarding the revolutionary and Marxist implications of psychoanalysis,
Lacan insists that his theory of language is, in
itself, materialist and so consonant with Marxism
in that respect, but he refuses any transcendental
or utopian possibility of obviating the alienating
dimension of work. That is no more possible, Lacan
says, than transcending the alienation of discourse
in which the subject is constituted in the first
place.

A large portion of this exchange is translated in
G690. A complete translation by Jeffrey Mehlman
appears in October 40 (1987): 106-13 (see A11).

E180.   "Psychanalyse et médecine." Roundtable discussion
at the Collège de Médecine, 16 February 1966.
Lettres de l'Ecole freudienne de Paris 1 (1967):
34-61.

Responds to an attack on his effort to "democ-
ratize" the teaching of psychoanalysis by declaring
that it is "extraterritorial" to medicine, and
invokes Foucault's work to illustrate that the
field of medicine has been constituted by doctrinal
assumptions rather than by absolute scientific
truth. Medicine is simply in its "scientific
phase" at the moment, Lacan says (p. 37), and he
observes that its empiricist epistemology has
limits because the body is not characterized simply
by the dimension of extension ("l'étendue"). Lacan
claims instead that a body is something made to
experience jouissance by itself ("fait pour jouir,
jouir de soi-même"), and he completely excludes the
dimension of jouissance from what he calls the
"epistemo-somatic." That exclusion is the point of
departure for psychoanalysis, Lacan concludes, and
that is why doctors must take Freud's discoveries
into account.

Throughout his comments, Lacan clarifies several
of his arguments regarding desire, the subject, and
the Other. He says that the unconscious does not
exist because there is an unconscious desire, but

234 Section E: Miscellaneous Works

desire exists because there is an unconscious.
That is to say, he adds, that there is language
which eludes the subject's mastery in its structure
and its effects, something that is beyond consciousness, and it is there that we can situate the
function of desire. That is why it is necessary to
introduce what he calls the "place of the Other"
(pp. 45-6).

E181.   Discussion of Charles Morazé, "Literary Invention."
        International Symposium on "The Languages of
        Criticism and the Sciences of Man," Johns Hopkins
        Humanities Center, 18-21 October 1966. <u>The
        Languages of Criticism and the Sciences of Man</u>.
        Edited by Richard Macksey and Eugenio Donato.
        Baltimore: The Johns Hopkins University Press,
        1970. Reprinted as <u>The Structuralist Contro-
        versy: The Languages of Criticism and the
        Sciences of Man</u>, Baltimore, 1972. Pp. 41-44.

        Praises Morazé for raising the central question,
        "Who invents?," and claims that Morazé has proposed
        the definition "one invents to the degree that he
        puts a number of signs in relation to each other"
        (p. 42). Lacan praises the suggested distinction
        between the subject and the flesh-and-blood
        individual who "invents," and he relates that
        distinction to the "passion of signs" discussed in
        Morazé's paper. Lacan also makes passing reference
        to the concept of "inmixing" (glossed here in
        French as "<u>inmiction</u>") and defines it as the
        structural form of the subject. See E182 and C86.

E182.   Discussion of Lucien Goldmann, "Structure: Human
        Reality and Methodological Concept." Inter-
        national Symposium on "The Languages of Criticism
        and the Sciences of Man," Johns Hopkins Human-
        ities Center, 18-21 October 1966. <u>The Languages
        of Criticism and the Sciences of Man</u>. Edited by
        Richard Macksey and Eugenio Donato. Baltimore:
        The Johns Hopkins University Press, 1970.
        Reprinted as <u>The Structuralist Controversy: The
        Languages of Criticism and the Sciences of Man</u>,
        Baltimore, 1972. Pp. 120-22.

        Contrasts the unified subject described by
        Goldmann with his psychoanalytic understanding of
        the subject, and recalls Derrida's question to him
        "Why do you call <u>this</u> the subject, this uncon-
        scious? What does the subject have to do with it?"

E183.   "Entretien avec Jacques Lacan." 26 November 1966.
        <u>Les lettres française</u> 7 December 1966, pp. 1, 16-
        17.

Acknowledges his debt to Freud and discusses his relation to Sartre and structuralism. Lacan says he wants to be known mainly as "the one who read Freud," and he praises Freud for the logical coherence and consistency of his work. "The unconscious is a new _fact_ and it gives the lie to the old structure of subject-object," Lacan says, and he claims that contemporary psychoanalysts have an aversion for the unconscious because they do not know where to put it: "It doesn't belong to Euclidian space," he remarks. "It is necessary to construct a space proper to it, and that is what I am trying to do today."

In response to a question about the influence of Sartre on his work, Lacan claims to owe nothing to Sartre although he praises the analysis of sado-masochistic relations in _Being and Nothingness_. Lacan also acknowledges similarities between his own work and that of figures often grouped with him as "structuralists," but he claims they are pursuing entirely different paths. His only serious objection to Sartre's attack on struc-turalism (see L2343), Lacan says, regards Sartre's claim that all structuralists ignore history and neglect the role of the subject. I have spoken of a "decentered subject," Lacan says, but only through its disappearance in the "detour" of desire, and in the Discourse of Rome (C58) he insisted that "the event, in its earliest eruption, is already experienced by the speaking being _as inscribed_ in history, in a primary historicity." See E184.

E184.   Interview with Gilles Lapouge. _Le figaro lit-téraire_, 1 December 1966, p. 11.

Offers an account of Lacan's career and the central concepts of his work, with explanations of various points by Lacan. The interview begins with Lapouge's observations about the relative rarity of Lacan's work appearing in print and about the in-timidating bulk and austerity of A2. Lacan notes that Freud's work had marked an inconceivable opening in reality when it appeared, but that Freud's earliest students set about reducing its radical character by stressing his connections with earlier thinkers. This is why he has stressed a return to Freud "_au pied de la lettre_," Lacan says, and he goes on to stress Freud's attention to language, calling him "_un linguiste_." Lapouge also comments on the ex-centric nature of subjectivity, the distinction between desire and need, and Lacan's claims that the unconscious is the dis-course of the Other.

E185.   "Petit discours à l'O.R.T.F." Interview with
         Georges Charbonnier, 2 December 1966. Revue
         recherches 3/4 (1967):   5-9.

         Insists on the importance of speech (la parole)
         to psychoanalysis as described in C58, and asserts
         that language is a milieu as real as the world
         called "exterior." We cannot elude the fact that
         man develops as much in a bath of language ("un
         bain de langage") as in a milieu called "natural,"
         Lacan says (p. 7), and he claims that desire arises
         within the milieu of language as "the passion of
         the signifier." Lacan argues that the subject is
         derived through the "practice" of language ("la
         pratique du langage") and is just the effect of the
         signifier on the animal that it marks, but he also
         adds that a subject not simply decentered. Rather,
         the subject is dedicated to sustaining itself
         through a signifier that is repeated ("se répéte"),
         i.e., divided. Lacan says that this division and
         repetition is the basis for his formula "the desire
         of man is the desire of the Other," and he explains
         that the Other is the cause of desire from which
         man is precipitated as a remainder ("d'ou l'homme
         choît comme reste") (p. 7).

E186.   "Interview à la RTB," 14 December 1966. Quarto:
         supplement belge à la Lettre mensuelle de l'Ecole
         de la cause freudienne 7 (1982):   7-11.

         Briefly describes the unrest among members of the
         Société française de psychanalyse that has resulted
         from his split with the group, and comments on the
         way he conceives, after Freud, the unconscious as
         structured like a language. Lacan expresses an
         interest in the structuralist enterprise of pro-
         moting the importance of language structures and
         professes his aspirations toward scientific rigor.

E187.   "Sartre contre Lacan." Interview with Jacques
         Lacan by Gilles Lapouge. Le figaro littéraire,
         29 December 1966, p. 4.

         Combines brief observations by Lacan and ex-
         tensive quotations from his work with remarks on
         the philosophical import of Lacan's teaching, which
         Lapogue notes derives from science, not philosophy.
         Lacan claims that Bataille and Merleau-Ponty had
         urged him to publish his seminars for years, but
         that he finally decided to publish A2 now to pre-
         vent further exploitation and distortion of his
         ideas and terms. This book, Lacan says, forms a
         critical apparatus "assez rude pour empêcher des
         utilisations malhonnêtes."
         Lapouge comments on the difficulty of A2 though

he denies that its precise language is needlessly
obscure, as some have charged. Let's say, Lacan
responds, that everything about these texts is
organized to prohibit them from being read "en
diagonale"; they are the texts of my seminars, but
submitted to the laws of writing, which are essentially different from those of speech. After
all, he adds, people don't grind their teeth when a
mathematician uses a formal apparatus. Toward the
end of the interview, Lacan returns to this topic
and insists that psychoanalysis must be conceived
as a science and psychoanalysts trained within that
context.

The main importance of this interview lies in
Lacan's remarks about Sartre and Sartre's brief
criticism of Lacan in L2343. In an interview that
was advertised as "Existentialism vs. Structuralism," Sartre had objected to "Structuralists"
such as Lacan, Lévi-Strauss, and Foucault because
they emphasized structure over history. Lacan
accepts the title of structuralist for this hetero-
genous group, but he observes that each has his own
definition of structure. My definition, Lacan
says, designates "structure" as the incidence of
language as such in the phenomenal field that is
analyzable in the analytic sense. In the field of
my research, Lacan adds, "structured like a
language" is a pleonasm.

Lacan strenuously objects, however, to Sartre's
charge that he ignores history. In the "Discours
de Rome" (C58), Lacan says, you can see that I
grant considerable importance to history because
history appears to me as coextensive with the
register of the unconscious: "L'inconscient est
histoire," he exclaims. Lacan then briefly
criticizes Sartre for identifying the subject with
consciousness and for proposing a phenomenology of
sadistic passion that contradicts the clinical
experience of any doctor. Nevertheless, Lacan
calls Sartre's work brilliant and observes that,
even though he is older than Sartre, one might
consider him a sort of successor to the younger
man. See E186.

E188. Interview with François Wahl. Broadcast on radio 8
       February 1967. Bulletin de l'Association freud-
       ienne 3 (1983): 6-7.

E189. "Discours de clôture des journées sur les psychoses
       chez l'enfant." Journées d'études, 21-22 October
       1967, with an additional note from 26 September
       1968. Revue recherches 2 (1968): Enfance
       alienée, l'enfant, la psychose, et l'institution,
       pp. 143-50. Additional note from 26 September
       1968, pp. 151-2.

Posits a connection between Freud's concept of
the pleasure principle and jouissance, and notes
the importance of "l'objet a" to the infant's
experience, which necessarily takes place in a
field organized according to the structures of
langauge. Lacan briefly notes the relevance of
Winnicott's concept of the transitional object as a
clinical trait in small children (see L2510), but
claims that he was the first to determine its
theoretical importance. Reprinted in Enfance
aliénée, edited by Maud Mannoni (Paris: U.G.E.
[10/18], 1972), pp. 295-306.

E190.   [Response to comments about C88.]   6 December 1967.
         Scilicet 2/3 (1970):   9-24.

Remarks on the controversy surrounding "la passe"
and the distinction between the A.E. and the A.M.E.
outlined in his proposition of 9 October 1967, and
tries to clarify his intentions regarding the place
of non-analysts in the Ecole freudienne de Paris.
Lacan rejects charges that his proposition is autocratic and insists that his solitude was exactly
what he renounced in forming the Ecole. If I were
alone, he asks, for whom would I speak? "Il n'y a
pas d'homosémie entre le seul et seul" (p. 11).
This item includes other remarks on the desire of
the psychoanalyst and its relation to the psychoanalytic act, and on the disruptions that followed
the earlier controversy surrounding his split from
the Société française de psychanalyse (see F380).
     This item is followed here by E213.

E191.   "Jacques Lacan commente la naissance de Scilicet."
         Interview with R. Higgins. Le monde, 16 March
         1968, p. 6.

Briefly comments on the origin and purpose of the
journal Scilicet, noting the resistance of other
psychoanalytic societies to the discourse of the
Ecole freudienne de Paris. What they are really
resisting, Lacan says, is the discourse of Freud
himself. (Higgins notes the practice of publishing
articles in Scilicet anonymously--except Lacan's
essays which are published under his name--and he
compares this practice to the anonymous publications of the mathematician Bourbaki.)

E192.   Discussion of P. Benoit, "Thérapeutique--
         Psychanalyse--Objet." Congrès de "Psychanalyse
         et psychothérapie" de l'Ecole freudienne de
         Paris, Strasbourg, 12 October 1968. Lettres de
         l'Ecole freudienne de Paris 6 (1969):   39ff.

Brief remark.

E193.   General discussion.   Congrès de Strasbourg, 12
        October 1968.   _Lettres de l'Ecole freudienne de_
        Paris 6 (1969):   42-48.

        Briefly describes some of the difficulties in
        establishing a clear set of therapeutic criteria
        for psychoanalysis and alludes to his more extended
        discussion of this problem in C63.   Lacan also
        notes the paradoxically inverse relation between
        psychoanalytic theory and the presence of "truth."
        Truth is by its very function unknowable, Lacan
        says, but that doesn't keep it from being "there,"
        in front of the analyst, in the person of the
        patient.

E194.   Discussion of M. Ritter, "Du désir d'être psych-
        analyste, ses effets au niveau de la pratique
        psychothérapique de 'l'élève analyste.'"   Congrès
        de Strasbourg, 12 October 1968.   _Lettres de_
        l'Ecole freudienne de Paris 6 (1969):   92-94.

        Objects to a phrase introduced in the discussion,
        "_la nature mensongère du symptôme_," the lying
        nature of the symptom.   If psychoanalysis exists,
        Lacan says, the symptom, far from having a "lying
        nature," is veracious, and in fact the first
        presence of truth is in the symptom.

E195.   Discussion of J. Nassif, "Sur le discours psych-
        analytique."   Congrès de Strasbourg, 12 October
        1968.   _Lettres de l'Ecole freudienne de Paris_ 7
        (1970):   40-42.

        Briefly remarks on the importance of the cate-
        gories of "heterogeneity" and "event" to modern
        logic and to the relevance of logic for psycho-
        analysis.

E196.   Discussion of M. de Certeau, "Ce que Freud fait de
        l'histoire."   Congrès de Strasbourg, 12 October
        1968.   _Lettres de l'Ecole freudienne de Paris_ 7
        (1970):   84.

        Observes that the relation to the father de-
        scribed by Freud is less simple and unified than
        appears, and suggests that the "scar of the
        father's evaporation" today would be called
        segregation.   We believe that modern universalism
        has homogenized relations among men, Lacan says,
        but he asserts that segregation is stronger than
        ever at all levels and that barriers have even been
        reinforced.

E197.   Discussion of J. Rudrauf, "Essai de dégagement du
        concept psychanalytique de psychothérapie" and J.
        Oury, "Stratégie de sauvetage de Freud." Congrès
        de Strasbourg, 12 October 1968. Lettres de
        l'Ecole freudienne de Paris 7 (1970): 136-37,
        146, 151.

        Briefly insists on maintaining the polyvalence of
        the objet a in multiple situations.

E198.   "En guise de conclusion." Closing address at the
        Congrès de Strasbourg, 12 October 1968. Lettres
        de l'Ecole freudienne de Paris 7 (1970):   157-
        66.

        Recounts the various issues raised at the
        conference regarding the relation between psycho-
        analysis and psychotherapy.

E199.   "Notes prises aux presentations de malades du Dr.
        Lacan à l'hôpital Sainte-Anne." Scilicet 1
        (1968): 173-77.

        Notes (apparently not written by Lacan) on two
        cases of persecutory hallucination that Lacan
        presented in 1968 at Sainte Anne's Hospital.

E200.   "Note de lecture sur le numéro de L'arc consacré à
        Freud." Scilicet 1 (1968): 192. Listed by Dor,
        p. 68.

E201.   "Adresse au jury d'accueil à l'assemblée avant son
        vote (le 25 janvier 1969)." Scilicet 2/3 (1970):
        49-51.

        Explains and defends the proposals set forth in
        C88 regarding la passe and the distinction between
        the A.E. and the A.M.E., just before the Ecole
        freudienne de Paris was to vote on it. See J1018.

E202.   Discussion of Michel Foucault, "Qu'est-ce qu'un
        auteur?" Société française de philosophie, 22
        February 1969. Bulletin de la Société française
        de philosophie 3 (1969): 104.

        Observes that whether or not one calls the
        current topic "structuralism," the point is not the
        negation of the subject but rather its dependence
        on the signifier. Lacan also denies the legitimacy
        of the slogan "les structures ne descendent pas
        dans la rue," which was popular during May 1968 and
        expressed the radical left's disaffection with
        intellectual discourse. If the events of May de-

monstrated anything, Lacan says, it was precisely a descent of structures into the street. The fact that this slogan is written in the streets proves nothing except that, as is often the case, within every act is a fundamental misunderstanding of itself. Lacan does not mention Foucault's essay in his comments, but he does discuss it briefly in B27.

Reprinted in Littoral 9 (1983): 31-32.

E203. Letter to Le monde, 5 July 1969.

Objects to Le monde's account of his seminar session for 26 June 1969, at which Lacan announced that he had been prohibited from teaching at the Ecole Normale Supérieure by Robert Flacelière, who was director of the ENS at that time. Several people from the seminar then occupied Flacelière's apartment and stayed there until he called the police. Le monde published this letter with a brief note defending its report.

Translated by Jeffrey Mehlman in October 40 (1987): 116-17 (see A11).

E204. "L'impromptu de Vincennes."   3 December 1969. Magazine littéraire 121 (1977):   21-24.

Amidst frequent hostile interruptions, begins to sketch out his theory of the four discourses, focussing on the discourse of the university. In response to constant challenges from the audience, Lacan makes several remarks on the relation of psychoanalysis to revolutionary themes current at the time, including the status of the university. The university is a certain kind of discourse, Lacan says, and psychoanalysis has taught us that you cannot escape discourse without becoming aphasic. Hence there is no "outside" to the university in a radical sense. Experience shows us, Lacan remarks just before leaving, that revolutionary aspirations lead only to the discourse of the master, and he claims that what his audience aspires to, as revolutionaries, is a Master. You will have one, he concludes. (See E246).

This article is particularly interesting as an example of the tension and revolutionary rhetoric that pervaded the French universities in the late 1960s, and it also demonstrates Lacan's fondness for contentious performances in his response to hecklers.

This item is based on one of several different versions of Lacan's talk and is published with G622. This article is the first of four planned conferences, but only two took place. The second, unpublished, was held on 14 March 1970 and is

listed by Dor as "Des Unités de valeur."
Reprinted in F354. Translated by Jeffrey Mehlman
in <u>October</u> 40 (1987): 116-27 (see A11).

E205. ["Appendix: general purport of a conversation with
Lacan in December 1969."] Description of Lacan's
remarks during an interview with Anika Rifflet-
Lemaire. F392, pp. 401-07.

Rejects Laplanche's claim in G681 that the
unconscious is the condition of language. Rather,
Lacan says, language is the condition of the
unconscious. Lacan also resists Laplanche's idea
that conscious language can somehow approach the
system of the unconscious. Instead, Lacan emphasizes a "double inscription" in which the signifier
is reduplicated in completely different "bat-
teries", and he claims that the import of the
signifier is completely different in both of them.
On the other hand, Lacan argues that his notion of
a "mythical" anchoring point (see C80) concerns
conscious language only, and he says that only
through conscious language is it possible to arrive
at "a particularly successful signifying montage
which is more effective than another and which
proves itself in praxis" (tr. 250).
This last point is also reflected in Lacan's
hostility toward those who would convert his
teaching into a finite set of propositions. He
claims that his <u>Ecrits</u> are "merely stones scattered
along the way" and are deliberately incomplete and
unfinished. Instead of the didactic position of
those who would peddle his thought, especially in
the university, he prefers what Lemaire calls "the
intuitive, 'impressionist' and essentially practical elaboration of scientific theses concerning
psychoanalysis."
Translated in the English edition of F392, pp.
249-53. See D105.

E206. "La psychologie au jugement de la psychanalyse:
'l'illusion d'une psychologie des profondeurs.'"
K1206, pp. 322-23.

Briefly mentions A1, A2, and the seminars to
introduce an excerpt from C69. This item is accompanied by a short comment from the editor of the
anthology.

E207. Discussion of Ph. Rappard, "De la conception
grecque de l'éducation et de l'enseignement de la
psychanalyse." Congrès de l'Ecole freudienne de
Paris sur "L'enseignement de la psychanalyse,"
17-19 April 1970. <u>Lettres de l'Ecole freudienne
de Paris</u> 8 (1971): 8-10.

Briefly remarks on the relation proposed by
Rappard between Eros and Agapé and on the connection between instruction and initiation in
analysis.

E208.   Discussion of M. Montrelay and F. Baudry, "Sur
        l'enseignement de la psychanalyse à Vincennes."
        Congrès de l'EFP, 17-19 April 1970. Lettres de
        l'Ecole freudienne de Paris 8 (1971):   187.

        Brief remark.

E209.   Discussion of Ch. Melman, "Propos à prétention
        roborative avant le Congrès." Congrès de l'EFP,
        17-19 April 1970. Lettres de l'Ecole freudienne
        de Paris 8 (1971):   199, 203-4.

        Brief remarks.

E210.   Closing address at the Congrès de l'EFP, 17-19
        April 1970. Scilicet 2/3 (1970): 391-99.

        Describes the problematic relation between knowl-
        edge and teaching, and distinguishes among the
        discourses of the university, the master, the
        hysteric, and the analyst. These four discourses
        differ, Lacan says, according to various relations
        they establish among the barred subject, the objet
        a, and the signifiers S^1 and S^2.
        In response to a remark by Rabant, Lacan rejects
        the suggestion that the signifier is the sign of
        the impossibility of jouissance. The signifier is
        not what prohibits jouissance, he says; rather, it
        is that which splits jouissance ("ce qui fait le
        clivage de la jouissance," p. 217).
        Reprinted in Lettres de l'Ecole freudienne de
        Paris 8 (1971): 205-217.

E211.   "Radiophonie." Interview with M. Georgin. Parts
        1-4 broadcast by the R.T.B., 5, 10, 19, and 26
        June 1970. Parts 5-7 broadcast by O.R.T.F., 7
        June 1970. Scilicet 2/3 (1970): 55-99.

        Expresses surprise that Georgin's questions
        indicate that he has actually read A2, and responds
        to inquiries on a number of different topics.
        Lacan explains his claim that Freud anticipated
        Saussure's discoveries in linguistics; qualifies
        the notion of "structure" as a common ground among
        psychoanalysis, anthropology, and linguistics;
        distinguishes his use of metaphor and metonymy from
        that of Jakobson; and explains why Freud's dis-
        covery of the unconscious subverts theories of
        knowledge (connaissance):   "L'inconscient, on le

voit, n'est que terme métaphorique à désigner le
savoir qui ne se soutient qu'à se présenter comme
impossible, pour que de ça il se confirme d'être
réel (entendez discours réel)" (p. 77). Lacan also
describes the incompatibility between knowledge
(savoir) and truth (vérité), and briefly describes
the four discourses introduced in B28 and E210.
    A brief excerpt was translated into English by
Stuart Schneiderman in On Signs, ed. M. Blonsky
(Baltimore: Johns Hopkins University Press, 1985),
pp. 203-06. Translated into Japanese as "Radio-
foni" in A10.

E212. "Liminaire." September 1970. Scilicet 2/3 (1970):
       5-6.

       Briefly notes the controversy surrounding the
vote on C88, and comments on the items included in
this issue of Scilicet (see E211).

E213. [Comment on E190]. 1 October 1970. Scilicet 2/3
       (1970): 24-29.

       Briefly comments on the theoretical basis of la
passe and on the controversy surrounding its
acceptance within the Ecole freudienne de Paris.
See C88.

E214. "Pour l'annuaire." 28 February 1971. Annuaire de
       l'Ecole freudienne de Paris (1975): 19.

       Comments briefly on the resistance to the Ecole
freudienne de Paris by other groups, and compares
it to the more general resistance to Freud's work
that has persisted for a half-century. That
controversy just proves Freud's accomplishment,
Lacan says, and he claims that this resistance
would have proceeded unchecked without "l'assiette
d'une formation où l'analyse s'articule d'un
décalage du discours dont Lacan dresse l'acte."
       Reprinted in Annuaire de l'Ecole freudienne de
Paris (1977): 87; in the Annuaire et textes
statutaires de l'Ecole de la Cause freudienne
(1982): 79; and again in A9, p. 28.

E215. "Tokyoni okeru disukuru" [Discourse of Tokyo]. 21
       April 1971. A10, 1985.

E216. Discussion of Ch. Bardet-Giraudon, "Du roman conçu
       comme le discours même de l'homme qui écrit."
       Congrès de l'Ecole freudienne de Paris sur "La
       technique psychanalytique," Aix-en-Provence, 20-
       23 May 1971. Lettres de l'Ecole freudienne de
       Paris 9 (1972): 20-30.

A long series of exchanges on the role of women
in Balzac's novels, concludes with a brief observation on Balzac's contribution to the direction of
the novel and its early engagement with the
capitalist economy of the modern era.

E217.   Discussion of P. Lemoine, "A propos du désir du
        médecin." Congrès de l'EFP, 20-23 May 1971.
        Lettres de l'Ecole freudienne de Paris 9 (1972):
        69, 74-78.

        Brief remarks on the role of desire in medicine,
        especially the "desire of the doctor." Lacan
        insists on the distinction between the analyst and
        the medical doctor, which he says has been lost by
        non-Lacanian analysts since the war.

E218.   Discussion of J. Guey, "Contribution à l'étude du
        sens du symptôme épileptique." Congrès de l'EFP,
        20-23 May 1971. Lettres de l'Ecole freudienne de
        Paris 9 (1972): 151, 154, 155.

        Brief remarks on the distinction between the
        theoretical articulation of death and of castra-
        tion.

E219.   Discussion of S. Ginestet-Elsair, "Le psychanalyste
        est du côté de la vérité." Congrès de l'EFP, 20-
        23 May 1971. Lettres de l'Ecole freudienne de
        Paris 9 (1972): 166.

        Brief remark.

E220.   Discussion of A. Didier-Weill and M. Silvestre, "A
        l'écoute de l'écoute." Congrès de l'EFP, 20-23
        May 1971. Lettres de l'Ecole freudienne de
        Paris 9 (1972): 176-182 passim.

        Brief remarks on the special character of
        analytic discourse and the difference between
        speech that occurs between "l'intercontrôle" and
        "le contrôle" itself.

E221.   Discussion of P. Mathis, "Remarques sur la fonction
        de l'argent dans la technique analytique."
        Congrès de l'EFP, 20-23 May 1971. Lettres de
        l'Ecole freudienne de Paris 9 (1972): 195, 196,
        202-05.

        Brief remarks on the historically specific
        character of the way money and desire are related
        in the upbringing of children in bourgeois culture
        (pp. 195, 196). This item also contains a more
        extended observation on the relation between money
        and analytic discourse especially as that discourse

relates to the university discourse of the liberal
professions, which Lacan claims are defined by a
systematic misunderstanding of money (203).

E222. Discussion of S. Zlatine, "Technique de l'inter-
       vention: incidence de l'automatisme de répéti-
       tion de l'analyste." Congrès de l'EFP, 20-23 May
       1971. Lettres de l'Ecole freudienne de Paris 9
       (1972):   254, 255, 256.

       Brief remarks.

E223. Discussion of C. Conté and L. Beirnaert, "De
       l'analyse des résistances au temps de l'analyse."
       Congrés de l'EFP, 20-23 May 1971. Lettres de
       l'Ecole freudienne de Paris 9 (1972):   334, 336.

       Briefly notes that psychoanalysis participates
       intimately in the "temps pour comprendre" and "le
       moment de conclure" that characterizes "logical
       time" as described in C47.

E224. Discussion of J. Rudrauf, "De la règle fonda-
       mentale." Congrès de l'EFP, 20-23 May 1971.
       Lettres de l'Ecole freudienne de Paris 9 (1972):
       374.

       Brief remark.

E225. Discussion of S. Leclaire, "L'objet a dans la
       cure." Congrès de l'EFP, 20-23 May 1971.
       Lettres de l'Ecole freudienne de Paris 9 (1972):
       445-50.

       An extended observation on the origin of his idea
       of the objet a in Freud's Three Essays on the
       Theory of Sexuality (1905), and on the implications
       of the objet a for the relation between desire and
       demand, for the function of castration, and for
       distinctions among the four discourses Lacan de-
       scribed in the seminar of last year (see B28, E210,
       E211).

E226. Discussion of P. Delaunay, "Le moment spéculaire
       dans la cure, moment de rupture." Congrès de
       l'EFP, 20-23 May 1971. Lettres de l'Ecole freud-
       ienne de Paris 9 (1972):   471-73.

       Brief remarks.

E227. Closing address to the Congrès de l'EFP, 20-23 May
       1971. Lettres de l'Ecole freudienne de Paris 9
       (1972):   507, 513.

       Summary remarks on themes of the conference,

especially that of the position of analysts in
"medical reality" and that of the cut ("<u>coupure</u>")
between truth and knowledge ("<u>vérité et "savoir</u>").

E228.   "L'opinion de Jacques Lacan." <u>Le monde</u>, 19
        November 1971, p. 17.

        Briefly comments on Dominique Desanti's <u>Un métier
        de chien</u>, saying he enjoyed it as a novel but not
        as a book about psychoanalysis because her heroine
        addresses a topic that psychoanalysts find impos-
        sible to talk about: love.

E229.   "Du discours psychanalytique."   12 March 1972. A4,
        pp. 32-55.

        Opens with brief remarks about A2 and then re-
        hearses his insistence on man's being constituted
        in and by language, a fact Lacan claims is proven
        by psychoanalysis (p. 36). The whole world thinks
        that Freud offered "sexuality" as the answer to all
        questions, Lacan says, but Freud himself insisted
        that he did not even know what the word meant. The
        reason he did not know, Lacan adds, is that it led
        him to discover the unconscious, i.e., to discover
        that the effects of language play ("<u>jouent</u>") in
        this place where the word "sexuality" might have a
        meaning.
        Lacan then describes how his work on his thesis
        led to his encounter with psychoanalysis before the
        war (p. 42) and how his work with the analysis of
        dreams taught him about the "priority of the sig-
        nifier." Now everybody is talking about the sig-
        nifier, Lacan says, even Sartre; and everybody
        knows that the signifier signifies "lacanisation"
        (43).
        This item concludes with a number of remarks
        about the four discourses (see B28, E210, E211) and
        describes a fifth discourse, that of capitalism.
        Lacan points out that the position of the master
        depends on the existence of language, and that
        obedience hinges on one's engagement in the order
        of language (p. 47). In response to questions,
        Lacan says that capitalist discourse is a substi-
        tute for the discourse of the master, and he aligns
        "<u>le plus de jouir</u>" with Marx's theory of surplus
        value, "<u>la plus value</u>" (p. 49).

E230.   Opening address to the Journées de L'Ecole freud-
        ienne de Paris, 29 September-1 October 1972.
        <u>Lettres de l'Ecole freudienne de Paris</u> 11 (1973):
        2-3.

        Briefly calls on members of the EFP to make their
        work accessible to those in attendance who are not

part of the school but who want to know what is
going on.
(Note: The title page of this issue of Lettres
de l'Ecole freudienne de Paris incorrectly lists
the dates of the Journées as 1973. They occurred
in 1972 and were not published until the next
year.)

E231.   Discussion of C. Conté, "Sur le mode de présence
        des pulsions partielles dans la cure." Journées
        de l'EFP, 29 September-1 October 1972. Lettres
        de l'Ecole freudienne de Paris 11 (1973): 22-24.

        Notes that Conté has based some of his remarks on
        B22, and observes that the stenographer left out
        certain questions and comments from the seminar, as
        well as some of the dialogue. Lacan asks anyone in
        the audience who was there in 1964 and still has
        notes on the questions to let him see them.

E232.   Discussion of M. Safouan, "La fonction du père
        réel." Journées de l'EFP, 29 September-1 October
        1972. Lettres de l'Ecole freudienne de Paris 11
        (1973): 139-41 passim.

        Brief remarks.

E233.   Closing remarks to the Journées de l'EFP, 29
        September-1 October 1972. Lettres de l'Ecole
        freudienne de Paris 11 (1973): 141-44.

        Briefly notes his satisfaction that the school
        finally has a place to exist, and describes the
        importance of Lettres de l'Ecole freudienne de
        Paris to the formation of the school as such.

E234.   Discussion during a roundtable meeting. Journées
        de l'EFP, 29 September-1 October 1972. Lettres
        de l'Ecole freudienne de Paris 11 (1973): 215.

        Brief remarks.

E235.   Discussion of J. Allouch, "Articulation entre la
        position médicale et celle de l'analyste."
        Journées de l'EFP, 29 September-1 October 1972.
        Lettres de l'Ecole freudienne de Paris 11 (1973):
        230.

        Brief remark.

E236.   "Jacques Lacan à Louvain." 13 October 1972. Text
        based on transcript of a tape, authorized by
        Jacques-Alain Miller. Quarto: supplement belge
        à la Lettre mensuelle de l'Ecole de la cause
        freudienne 3 (1981): 5-20.

Argues that the primacy of language in the constitution of the human subject structures social
relations because they are established through
discourse.   Lacan claims that at the bottom of all
these relations is "le discours du maître" and the
relations of power that it entails, including a
second sort of discourse: that of the slave (p. 7).
The discourse of the slave, Lacan says, is in a
dialectical relation to the discourse of the master
and to the position of knowledge.   Lacan also observes that Freud's description of the object of
mourning in Mourning and Melancholy (1917) guided
him towards his invention of "l'objet petit a" as a
term for the lost object, and he says that the
whole process of an analysis turns on this objet a
(p. 19a).

This item is a long and complex address, self-
consciously presented as an oral discussion, that
touches upon a number of issues including the connection between jouissance and the relation of both
sexes to a third, as "ce tiers vous le fixiez dans
l'Autre" (p. 19a-b).

E237.   "Jacques Lacan à l'Ecole belge de psychanalyse."
         Text based on a tape of a discussion recorded at
         Louvain, 14 October 1972.   Quarto: supplement
         belge à la Lettre mensuelle de l'Ecole de la
         cause freudienne 5 (1981):   4-23.

         A series of exchanges with the audience in which
         Lacan explains and defends the system of la passe
         (see C88).   Lacan briefly comments on the discourse
         of the master and the relations of power inherent
         in discourse, and he expands on his remarks about
         aggressivity from C51 and on his use of the phrase
         "le corps sans organes" (p. 22).   He also discusses
         the four discourses--that of the master, the hys-
         teric, the university, and analytic discourse--as
         they depend on different relations among what Lacan
         calls his "quadripodes," S_1, S_2, $\cancel{S}$, and a.

E238.   "La psychanalyse dans sa reference au rapport
         sexuel."   Milan, 3-4 February 1973.   A4, pp. 58-
         77.

         Briefly describes the relation between the ego
         and the function of the imaginary capture, but
         notes that our participation in "la langue" keeps
         the domination of the image from being all powerful
         (p. 67).   That allows us to envisage another mode
         of access to the real, Lacan notes.

         This item also includes a number of remarks on
         the relation between sexuality, jouissance, and
         language, including Lacan's famous dictum, "Un être

parlant n'a pas de rapport sexuel" (p. 75).

E239. "Excursus." Milan, 3-4 February 1973. A4, pp. 78-
       97.

Notes the curious power of "l'affect" and the
power of psychotherapy to make an impact through
speech alone, and accounts for that power by
pointing out Freud's own argument that the repressed is always of the order of the signifier (p.
79). Freud defined the affect, Lacan says, as
something which is not repressed, something which
remains at large ("errant") (p. 80). Lacan claims
that it is not the affect that is repressed, but
always something on the order of the signifier.
Returning to his remarks about jouissance earlier
that morning (see E238), Lacan again insists on its
difference from sexual relations, and he centers
that distinction on the effect of language. That
which language introduces and situates in the
world, he says, can be qualified as writing
("ecriture"), and we can characterize this language
as the accumulation--the "cumulus"--of jouissance.
After several more remarks on sadistic jouissance
and its difference from love, Lacan characterizes
the objet a as the "autre du désir," the cause of
desire that permitted Freud to distinguish object-
love from narcissistic love. Lacan says that
although most people think of their partner of the
opposite sex as their love-object and the object of
their fantasies, you do not have to analyze very
many people to realize that their desire is always
aimed a little to the side of what they imagine.
We all enter the world as the objet a's of our
parents, Lacan adds, and that is how we take our
place in reality. It is no wonder, then, that our
reality is always anthropomorphic, and that it
enters into our experience as the fantasm. There
is no reason for any of our actions other than the
fantasm (93).
This item concludes with several remarks about
the difficulty of the position of the analyst, and
then observes that "the exploitation of desire is
the grand invention of capitalist discourse" (p.
97). Once desire has been industrialized, "on ne
pouvait rien faire de mieux pour que les gens se
tiennent un peu tranquilles" (p. 97).

E240. "Una riunione." Milan, 4 February 1973. A4, pp.
       98-100.

Briefly comments on the heterogeneity of his
audience and on the necessity of centering his
remarks on analytic discourse.

E241. Remarks to France-Culture regarding the Twenty-
       eighth International Congress of Psychoanalysis.
       July, 1973. Le coq héron 46/47 (1974):   3-8.
       Listed by Dor, p. 80.

E242. Discussion of introductory remarks by J. Clavreul
       and J. Oury. Congrès de l'Ecole freudienne de
       Paris, La grande motte, 1-4 November 1973.
       Lettres de l'Ecole freudienne de Paris 15 (1975):
       16, 18-19.

       Brief remarks on the term "indécidable."

E243. Discussion of introductory remarks by S. Leclaire.
       Congrès de l'EFP, 1-4 November 1973. Lettres de
       l'Ecole freudienne de Paris 15 (1975):   26- 27,
       27-28.

       Brief remarks on the procedure of la passe and
       the designation of an analyst as a passeur.

E244. General address.   Presented 2 November 1973.
       Congrès de l'EFP, 1-4 November 1973. Lettres de
       l'Ecole freudienne de Paris 15 (1975):   69- 80.

       Comments on his television appearance in A3 and
       on the publication of A2 in German.   Lacan claims
       that anytime he writes something, he usually
       rewrites it at least twelve times, but that the
       preface to the German edition is a first draft.
       When he mentioned that earlier to another group,
       Lacan says, someone replied that it is a good thing
       it is a first draft, since if he had rewritten it
       probably nobody could have understood it.
           Lacan also attacks Ogden and Richards' book The
       Meaning of Meaning as "neo-positivist" and says
       that instead of seeking the "meaning of meaning" we
       should look for the "sign of the sign."   The sign
       does not lead to meaning, he warns; it is de-
       cipherable because it is connected to other signs.
       What the analyst must know is that there is some-
       thing that encodes, the unconscious, not that there
       is something that calculates, thinks, or judges.

E245. Discussion during a debate on the formation of
       analysts. Congrès de l'EFP, 1-4 November 1973.
       Lettres de l'Ecole freudienne de Paris 15
       (1975):   132, 139.

       Brief remarks.

E246. Discussion during a panel on "la passe." Congrès
       de l'EFP, 1-4 November 1973. Lettres de l'Ecole
       freudienne de Paris 15 (1975):   185-93.

Explains the conditions in which he first
proposed <u>la passe</u> and the "prudence" with which he
addressed its intended audience, those designated
"l'Analyste de l'Ecole" (see C88). Lacan denies
that he was acting as the Master when he made the
proposal, and claims that he was in fact trying to
escape the mastery inherent in societies structured
along more traditional lines. He explains the
self-authorization of the analyst inherent in the
system of <u>la passe</u>, the role of the <u>juré d'agré-
ment</u>, and the way <u>la passe</u> is modelled on analytic
discourse.
    Lacan discusses the four discourses at length
(See B28, E210, E211), focussing on a subdivision
of the discourse of the master, capitalist discourse, and the "<u>plus-de-jouir</u>" inherent in it.
Comparing this term to Marx's "<u>plus-value</u>" (surplus
value), Lacan claims that the <u>plus-de-jouir</u> has a
more radical function in capitalist discourse than
surplus value and insists on the importance of that
function in man's relation to language. In the
discourse of the master, he adds, the <u>plus-de-jouir</u>
is replaced by the <u>objet a</u>.
    Lacan concludes with further comments on the
pass, insisting on its difference from the "mag-
isterial character" of other methods of recruiting
analysts. (Lacan also recalls his warning that the
students of Vincennes were using revolutionary
rhetoric to mask their desire for--and of--a
Master; see E204.)
    Reprinted as "Sur l'expérience de la passe,"
<u>Ornicar?</u> 12/13 (1977):   117-23.

E247. Discussion of C. Melman, "Le dictionnaire."
       Congrès de l'EFP, 1-4 November 1973. <u>Lettres de
       l'Ecole freudienne de Paris</u> 15 (1975):   206, 208,
       210.

       Brief remarks.

E***. <u>Télévision</u>. Interview with Jacques-Alain Miller.
       Miller's preface dated Christmas, 1973. Paris:
       Editions de Seuil, 1974. See A3.

E248. "Alla 'Scuola freudiana.'" Milan, 30-31 March
       1974. A4, pp. 104-47.

       A collection of extended comments by Lacan and
shorter exchanges with his audience in response to
a list of questions printed on pp. 259-61. Lacan
opens with a brief series of remarks on the nature
of our contact with the real, and says that analysis is the only thing that can permit us to survive
in the real (p. 106). Lacan attacks the notion
that the analyst is an ally of the patient's ego

and criticizes the more general concept of an
autonomous ego (pp. 109-11), and he emphasizes the
importance of the analyst receiving the dream
through the spoken "lalangue" (see B31).
   Lacan then turns to the Borromean knot and to
relations among the real, the symbolic, and the
imaginary that the knot establishes topologically.
The symbolic passes its time knotting and unknot-
ting the real and the imaginary in "lalangue,"
Lacan says (p. 115), and he warns against slighting
the imaginary or any one of the three registers
that are interlocked there. After several more
remarks on the fact that "êtres parlants" know
nothing of death or sexual reproduction because
they think they are immortal, Lacan comments on the
constraining character of the analyst's role and
returns to the topic of language and its relation
to the imaginary and the real.
   There can be no language of the body, Lacan says,
and he also rejects the importance of "code" in
language. Nevertheless, he insists that there is a
"palpitation langagière" in the body, but this
"palpitation" is inscribed in reality only under
the form of the fantasm. Lacan claims that the
fantasm takes on substance ("son épanouissement")
in love, which here functions as the language of
the body, and he says that this is the way that the
body is truly implicated in the fantasm--and the
way that the image and the imaginary take on a role
in love (p. 142).
   Lacan concludes with several remarks on the relation of the real to language and on the difference between God and the Other.

E249. "Directives." 1 April 1974. A4, pp. 155-64.

   Addresses the problem of conducting an Italian
school of psychoanalysis along Lacanian lines, and
describes the principles according to which the
formation of the analyst must take place. Among
those principles Lacan mentions the absolute self-
authorization of the analyst, which he describes as
the cornerstone of Lacanian psychoanalysis; the
distinction between the A.M.E. (l'Analyste Membre
de l'Ecole) and the A.E. (l'Analyste de l'Ecole);
and the importance of les passeurs in the procedure
of la passe. (For a more detailed account of these
principles, see C88).
   Reprinted with E250 as "Note italienne," Ornicar?
25 (1982): 7-10.

E250. "Lettre adressée à trois psychanalystes italiens."
       Dated 1974 (but see the version in Ornicar? noted
       below). Spirales 9 (1981): 60.

Affirms the importance of <u>la passe</u> to any school based on the analytic technique developed by Lacan, and briefly describes other tenets crucial to the formation of an analyst. See C88. For other comments by Lacan to Italian analysts, see A4.
Reprinted in <u>La lettre mensuelle de l'Ecole de la cause freudienne</u> 9 (1982): 2. Also reprinted with E249 as "Note italienne" in <u>Ornicar?</u> 25 (1982): 7-10, but this version is dated April 1973.

E251.   "Conference de presse." Interview on 29 October 1974. Seventh Congrès de l'Ecole freudienne de Paris, Rome, 31 October-3 November 1974. <u>Lettres de l'Ecole freudienne de Paris</u> 16 (1975): 6-26.

Notes Freud's emphasis on the difficulty of psychoanalysis and the "untenable" position of the analyst. Lacan claims that the sciences always struggle for more prestige because they really do not know what they are doing, and he argues that the analyst is much more closely concerned with the "truth" than the scientist is. Lacan also notes the opposition between psychoanalysis and religion and comments on the differences between confessing to a priest and talking to an analyst. In response to a question about the difficulty of understanding the <u>Ecrits</u>, Lacan says that he did not write them to be understood, he wrote them to be read (p. 17).

E252.   Opening address. Congrès de l'EFP, 31 October-3 November 1974. <u>Lettres de l'Ecole freudienne de Paris</u> 16 (1975): 27-28.

Brief introductory remarks.

E253.   "La troisième." Transcript of a discussion during the Congrès de l'EFP, 31 October-3 November 1974, not reviewed by Lacan. <u>Lettres de l'Ecole freudienne de Paris</u> 16 (1975): 177-203.

Situates the <u>objet a</u> at the intersection of the imaginary, symbolic, and the real, and diagrams the space of their coincidence as the shared space of a Borromean knot. This "<u>a</u>" is what separates phallic <u>jouissance</u> from the <u>jouissance</u> of the body, Lacan says, since it marks the introduction of the body into the economy of <u>jouissance</u> through the <u>image</u> of the body. Lacan claims that this detour is necessitated by prematuration, as he explained in C53, and he adds that phallic <u>jouissance</u> is always outside the body, "<u>hors corps</u>." Lacan also distinguishes a third form of <u>jouissance,</u> the "<u>jouissance de l'Autre</u>," and he argues that this <u>jouissance</u> of the Other is outside language, outside the symbolic, just as phallic <u>jouissance</u> is always outside the body.

E254. Closing address. Congrès de l'EFP, 31 October-3
       November 1974. Lettres de l'Ecole freudienne de
       Paris 16 (1975): 360-61.

       Briefly comments on the success of the conference
       and regrets that so few Italians came.

E255. Interview. Panorama, 21 November 1974. Cited in
       F354. Cf. G716.

E256. "Improvisation: désir de mort, rêve et réveil."
       Answer to a question posed by Catherine Millot,
       1974. F303, p. 3.

       (Millot asked Lacan whether the desire for death
       was associated with the desire to sleep or the
       desire to wake. This item is based on her notes of
       his response.)
       Claims that death is situated on the side of
       waking and that death is a dream among other dreams
       that perpetuate life. Total awakening is the death
       of the body, Lacan says, and when Freud said that
       life aspires to death, he meant that in so far as
       life aspires to a total and full consciousness.
       Lacan claims that Freud erred, however, when he
       thought that life could aspire to return to in-
       animate material in the death-drive.
       According to Lacan, life in the body subsists
       only through the pleasure principle. Among
       speaking beings, though, the pleasure principle is
       submitted to the unconscious, i.e., to language,
       and that language remains ambiguous. It sup-
       plements the absence of sexual relations and in
       doing so masks death. Lacan says that language is
       tied to death through the repression of the "non-
       rapport sexuel" and that without language we could
       not even dream of death as a possibility. He also
       suggests, however, that the existence of language
       is what allows us not to think about death.

E257. "Peut-être à Vincennes . . . " January 1975.
       Ornicar? 1 (1975): 3-5.

       Briefly describes his hope that "perhaps at
       Vincennes" the following sciences will find an
       occasion for their renewal in the contact with
       psychoanalysis: topology, logic, and, most im-
       portantly, linguistics.

E258. Response to a question. Strasbourg, 26 January
       1975. Lettres de l'Ecole freudienne de Paris 17
       (1976): 221-23.

Briefly comments on the difference between
méchant and méprise, and claims that "L'homme n'est
pas méchant. Il est méprisant, bien sur."

E259. Opening address. Journées de l'Ecole freudienne de
       Paris, Paris, 12-13 April 1975. Lettres de
       l'Ecole freudienne de Paris 18 (1976): 1-3.

       Briefly notes the general topics of the con-
       ference and describes his own contribution to one
       of them, the ethic of psychoanalysis (see B18).

E260. Response to comments by M. Ritter. Journées de
       l'EFP, 12-13 April 1975. Lettres de l'Ecole
       freudienne de Paris 18 (1976): 8-12.

       Based on comments made in Strasbourg 26 January
       1975 (see E258). Lacan explains Freud's reference
       to the Unerkannte in The Interpretation of Dreams
       (1900). It is not a form of the real, Lacan says,
       but is instead the Urverdrangt, the primordial re-
       pressed. He claims that it is the destiny of the
       Urverdrangt to be at the roots of language and that
       it functions as a hole ("un trou"), the limit of
       analysis. Only in that sense, Lacan adds, does the
       Unerkannte have anything to do with the real. Like
       the "réel pulsionnel," the Unerkannte--as the
       Urverdrangt--functions under a double negative that
       may best be described as "ne cesse pas de ne pas
       s'écrire," not ceasing not to be written.
       Lacan also comments on Freud's notion of the
       drive as it relates to sexual drives between men
       and women, and he notes the existence of a third
       element between them, the phallus. The presence of
       the phallus means that sexual relations are never
       biological, Lacan concludes, but are always struc-
       tured by language, the impossibility of the real,
       and death (p. 11).

E261. Discussion of "Les concepts fondamentaux et la
       cure." Journées de l'EFP, 12-13 April 1975.
       Lettres de l'Ecole freudienne de Paris 18 (1976):
       35, 36, 36 bis, 37.

       Brief remarks.

E262. Discussion of "La forclusion." Journées de l'EFP,
       12-13 April 1975. Lettres de l'Ecole freudienne
       de Paris 18 (1976): 89.

       Brief remarks.

E263. Discussion of "L'éthique de psychanalyse."
       Journées de l'EFP, 12-13 April 1975. Lettres de
       l'Ecole freudienne de Paris 18 (1976): 154.

Brief remarks.

E264. Discussion of "Du plus une." Journées de l'EFP,
       12-13 April 1975. Lettres de l'Ecole freudienne
       de Paris 18 (1976): 220-47, passim.

       Brief remarks on several topics, with more
       extended comments on the study-groups within the
       EFP.

E265. Discussion of "Du plus une et de la mathématique."
       Journées de l'EFP, 12-13 April 1975. Lettres de
       l'Ecole freudienne de Paris 18 (1976): 248-59.

       Brief remarks.

E266. Closing remarks. Journées de l'EFP, 12-13 April
       1975. Lettres de l'Ecole freudienne de Paris 18
       (1976): 262-70.

       Comments on the real, the hole ("le trou") in the
       typology of Borromean knots, and death; and notes
       that in the symbolic, there is no opposition, only
       "le trou." To be and its negation, Lacan says, are
       exactly the same thing.

E267. Opening address. Journées d'Etudes de l'Ecole
       freudienne de Paris, Paris, 14-15 June 1975.
       Lettres de l'Ecole freudienne de Paris 24 (1978):
       7.

       Brief remarks.

E268. Discussion of A. Albert, "Le plaisir et la règle
       fondamentale." Journées d'Etudes de l'EFP, 14-15
       June 1975. Lettres de l'Ecole freudienne de
       Paris 24 (1978): 22-24.

       Claims that one can be no more precise about
       defining the pleasure principle than Freud was, who
       said it is the "principle of moderation, the block-
       age of stimulation." The trap, Lacan says, is not
       pleasure, but jouissance (p. 22). He notes a dis-
       tinction between Albert's use of "singularity" and
       Aristotle's notion of the "particular," and he
       claims that the symptom is that "particularity"
       insofar as it is a sign of the relation to the real
       that distinguishes each of us as speaking beings
       ("parlêtres"). There would be no symptom, Lacan
       adds, without the symbolic; that is, without this
       injection of signifiers in the real with which we
       are forced to work ("composer"). He concludes that
       the symptom is thus at the heart of the fundamental
       law of psychoanalysis because that law aims at the

very thing of which the subject is the least dis-
posed to speak: his symptom, his particularity
(pp. 23-24).

E269. Closing discourse. Journées d'Etudes de l'EFP, 8-9
November 1975. Lettres de l'Ecole freudienne de
Paris 24 (1978): 247-50.

Brief remarks on the function of the cartels and
on the symptom as it relates to the real, the symbolic, and the imaginary.

E270. "Conférences et entretiens dans des universités
nord-américaines." Edited by Jacques-Alain
Miller. Scilicet 6/7 (1976): 5-63.

Based on a series of conferences and discussions
in the United States. The texts are transcribed
from typescripts and recordings and retain the extemporaneous style of Lacan's oral responses.

E270a. "Yale University, Kanzer Seminar." 24 November
1975. Scilicet 6/7 (1976): 7-31. Address by
Lacan, pp. 7-16. Discussion, pp. 17-31.

Begins by apologizing for his English and claims
that he has been practicing by reading Joyce, a
paradoxical method at best (for further remarks on
Joyce see B34). Lacan introduces the question of
how one comes to want to be an analyst and discusses his own career as it began with his thesis
A1. Like Freud, Lacan says, he studied the
writings of psychotics, and his psychotics eventually led him to Freud. In fact, he adds, he was
applying "le freudisme" in his thesis without even
knowing it.
Lacan goes on to discuss briefly the verbal basis
of Freud's interpretation of dreams and the
linguistic character of the unconscious as it
emerges in Freud's first three major works. That
discovery, Lacan says, is what led him to the conclusion that the unconscious is structured like a
language (p. 13). Lacan also insists that the most
fundamental aspect of so-called sexual relations is
associated with language as well. He concludes
with a few remarks on the end of analysis, in which
Lacan warns against pushing analysis too far; when
the analysand thinks that he is happy to live,
Lacan says, that is enough.
The discussion following Lacan's address touches
on several issues, among them the place of psychoanalysis in medicine; the impossibility of sexual
relations in human experience (which is implied by
the lack inherent in any human "act"); the necessity of writing for history and for the relations

between history and psychoanalysis; and the difference between science and psychoanalysis. On the
issue of science, Lacan observes that up to now,
everything produced as science has been non-
verbal, a product of little letters and mathematics
rather than language. Thus science has a special
relation to the real, he says, which has no
"meaning" and so cannot be described with words.
That is why he has tried to introduce mathemes into
psychoanalysis in imitation of science: not to
mathematize everything, but to begin to isolate a
"mathematizable minimum."
    In response to questions about the connections
among discoveries in history, science and psychoanalysis, Lacan observes that psychoanalytic
discoveries are limited to the experience of
analysis itself, and we have no way of knowing
whether or not the unconscious exists outside of
psychoanalysis.
    For further discussion with students from Yale,
see E270b.

E270b. Discussion with students at Yale University. 24
        November 1975. Scilicet 6/7 (1976): 32-37.

        Brief answers to a series of questions. In
        response to a question about the importance of
        literature in his writing, Lacan says that his
        writings must be literature rather than science
        since they are written and then sold as such.
        Commenting on the "theoreticians" who have in-
        fluenced him, he names only Marx as the first one
        who had an idea of the symptom. Lacan also
        observes that "truth" has the structure of a
        fiction because it passes through language, and
        language itself has a fictional structure.
        Commenting on Freud's auto-analysis, Lacan also
        notes that it was a "writing-cure" (in English in
        the text) and says that he doesn't believe in it.
        Writing is different from speaking, he adds, and
        reading is different from listening.
        For Lacan's address to a group of faculty and the
        discussion that followed see E270c.

E270c. "Yale University, Law School Auditorium." 25
        November 1975. Scilicet 6/7 (1976): 38-41.

        Comments briefly on the symptom as the fourth
        loop that joins the real, the imaginary and the
        symbolic into a Borromean knot, but says that he is
        searching for another geometry to approach this
        issue. Lacan also describes the status of the
        hysteric as an effect, like that of any subject,
        but he claims that the hysteric is a subject who
        produces knowledge. Socrates began the discourse

of the hysteric, Lacan says, though this does not
mean that he was necessarily a hysteric himself
despite some evidence to support that supposition.
Lacan claims that, in fact, Socrates was something
even worse, a subtle master and, in a certain
fashion, not too bad of an analyst. In addition,
Lacan pronounces cryptically that the id is the
real ("<u>le ça de Freud, c'est le réel</u>") and that
phallic <u>jouissance</u> is at the junction of ("<u>au joint</u>
<u>de</u>") the symbolic and the real.

E270d.   "Columbia University, Auditorium School of Inter-
          national Affairs." 1 December 1975. <u>Scilicet</u>
          6/7 (1976):   42-52.

          Describes a "new dimension" of speech in analysis
          that he calls the "<u>dit-mension</u>," and associates
          this <u>dit-mension</u> with the truth that constitutes
          what the analyst has to say in analysis. Lacan
          says that truth begins from the moment that the
          analyst has something to say to the analysand, and
          their relation is based on an agreement, a social
          bond, in which this "truth" will circulate. But
          the "<u>dire de la vérité</u>" is always only a "<u>mi-dire</u>,"
          i.e., a partial statement, and Lacan says that the
          most difficult thing about analysis is convincing
          the analysand that his particular truth is not the
          "whole truth."
          Lacan comments on a number of other issues: the
          function of the father and its relation to the
          real, which is the only case where the real is more
          important that the true; the close link between
          scientific discourse and the discourse of the hys-
          teric (see the four discourses described in B28,
          E210, E211); and a number of permutations on the
          topography of the Borromean knots. However, this
          presentation is especially interesting for its
          emphasis on the political dimension of speech and
          its distinction between language as structure and
          the rhetorical nature of "<u>lalangue</u>."
          Beginning with the assumption that the analysand
          attends analysis to be freed from his symptom,
          Lacan asks what it means to be "freed" from a
          symptom. He warns against treating the resistance
          of the symptom as a duel between some inner and
          outer world. From the beginning, Lacan says, all
          experiences consist of the subject's relation to
          "<u>lalangue</u>," which deserves to be called "maternal"
          (as in "our mother tongue") because the infant
          receives it from the mother. This relation is what
          constitutes the human as a "<u>parlêtre</u>," a speaking
          being. What the infant learns is not grammar,
          however, but a rhetoric of speech; that is why
          Lacan says that the unconscious is structured like
          <u>a</u> language, not <u>the</u> language. <u>The</u> language would

imply some abstract universal structure such as
logic, rather than the closer and more particular
relation between lalangue and the social situation
in which it functions.

E270e.   "Massachusetts Institute of Technology."   2
         December 1975. Scilicet 6/7 (1976):   53-62.

         Briefly comments on a number of issues. Lacan
         claims that psychoanalysis is not a science but a
         practice; notes his debt to Lévi-Strauss but in-
         sists that their notions of structure are quite
         different from one another; denies any connection
         to philosophy because it seeks a wisdom he believes
         is impossible; and insists on the importance of
         what Freud discovered as narcissism. I have em-
         phasized that concept, Lacan says, because the
         human notion of the world depends on a prior iden-
         tification with the surface of the body and on the
         extrapolation of that surface into the perfect form
         of the sphere. He also comments on the topography
         of the sphere and substitutes for it a series of
         Borromean knots that describe relations among the
         real, the imaginary and the symbolic. Lacan treats
         those relations as an overlapping of three separate
         loops that are joined by a fourth, which he iden-
         tifies as the symptom.

E271.   "Impromptu sur le discours analytique."   2 December
         1975. Scilicet 6/7 (1976):   62-63.

         Brief remarks on analytic discourse as one of the
         four discourses (see B28, E210, E211).

E272.   "Sur le noeud borroméen: 'Un ratage dans l'étab-
         lissement d'une figure de noeud ou un méfait de
         perspective,' 'Le noeud borroméen orienté,' 'Une
         propriété non demontrée.'" Ornicar? 5 (1975):
         3-15.

         Beginning with a reproduction of Borromean
         figures from B31, presents a number of diagrams
         listing permutations on the chain of loops dis-
         cussed in the seminar. The next two subsections,
         "Le noeud borroméen orienté," and "Une propriété
         non demontrée," use related figures to pose prob-
         lems derived from "invertability" of relations
         traced with the Borromean knots.

E273.   Discussion of Jacques Aubert, "Galeries pour un
         portrait." Conférences du Champ freudien,   9
         March 1976. Analytica 4 (1977):   16-18.

         Comments on the impossibility of analyzing anyone
         raised as a strict Catholic, and discusses the

relation between Catholicism and the function of
Stephen Dedalus as an imaginary form of Joyce's
ego.   Lacan claims that Stephen can serve as a
"strong ego," as the Americans would say, precisely
because he is a fabricated ego.   This item also
includes brief remarks on the English translation
of Freud's Ich as "I."   (Note: Analytica 4 is a
supplement to Ornicar? 9.)

E274.   Closing address.   Ninth Congrès de l'Ecole freud-
        ienne de Paris, Strasbourg, 21-24 March 1976.
        Lettres de l'Ecole freudienne de Paris 19 (1976):
        555-59.

        Brief remarks on the topics of inhibition,
        acting-out, and other issues raised by the papers
        delivered at the conference.

E275.   Discussion of M. Ritter, "A propos de l'angoisse
        dans la cure."   Journées de l'Ecole freudienne de
        Paris, Paris, 31 October-2 November 1976.
        Lettres de l'Ecole freudienne de Paris 21 (1977):
        89.

        Brief remark.

E276.   Discussion of J. Petitot, "Quantification et
        opérateur de Hilbert."   Journées de l'EFP, 31
        October-2 November 1976.   Lettres de l'Ecole
        freudienne de Paris 21 (1977):   129.

        Brief remark on the difficulty of defining the
        topological function of a hole ("un trou").

E277.   Response to questions about knots and the uncon-
        scious.   Journées de l'EFP, 31 October-2 November
        1976.   Lettres de l'Ecole freudienne de Paris 21
        (1977):   472-75.

        Observes that a hole ("un trou") is not consti-
        tuted by repression but by what surrounds it, which
        Lacan calls the symbolic (p. 473).   He also claims
        that it is the function of number that gives us
        access to the real, though that access is always
        indirect, and that it is this real that he has
        tried to "articulate" in the Borromean chain (p.
        473).   This chain is not a knot, Lacan insists, but
        simply a chain that falls apart if one of its links
        is broken.   Man is effectively enchained by this
        chain, he adds, and he says that it allows the pos-
        sibility for the appearance of "false-holes" when
        two true holes overlap.

E278.   Closing address.   Journées de l'EFP, 31 October-2
        November 1976.   Lettres de l'Ecole freudienne de

Paris 21 (1977):   506-09.

Brief remarks on the use of the matheme and on the S_1, which is not a "prime signifier" ("la signifiant qui prime") but rather the signifier in whose name the subject is manifest.

E279.   "Note liminaire" to La scission de 1953 (F379), p. 3.

Claims that he won the battle documented in the articles collected here, since he has succeeded in conveying what he thinks of the unconscious. Lacan does, however, express an aversion towards the memory of that controversy, which led to his departure from the Société psychanalytique de Paris.

E280.   "Ouverture de la section clinique."   5 January 1977. Ornicar? 9 (1977):   7-14.

Comments on various topics associated with psychoanalytic practice, including the fact that "free" association is presumed to be determined by the unconscious; the relatively limited power of a written signifier compared to its spoken function; and the confusing nature of Freud's Traumdeutung. In response to questions, Lacan notes the loose relation of truth to the real; comments on the function of the signifier in psychosis; and admits that he has, indeed, claimed to be psychotic, but he to tries to be as little psychotic as possible even though it might make him a better analyst.

E281.   "Propos sur l'hysterie."   Presented at Brussels, 26 February 1977, with discussion.   Text based on notes transcribed by J. Cornet and I. Gilson, authorized by Jacques-Alain Miller.   Quarto: supplement belge à la Lettre mensuelle de l'Ecole de la Cause freudienne 2 (1981):   5-10. [An unauthorized version was published as "Extraits d'une conférence . . .," Le nouvel observateur, 19 September 1981, p. 50.   See G784.]

Emphasizes the importance of hysterics to Freud's work and to the birth of psychoanalysis.   The unconscious originated from the fact that the hysteric does not know what she says, Lacan argues, even when she says something perfectly well by the words she lacks.   He adds that the unconscious is a sediment of language (p. 5), but the real is at the opposite extreme of our practice.   It is an idea, a limit-idea of what has no meaning.   Following these remarks are Lacan's answers to several questions on his relation to Freud, on castration (we must al-

ways speak of castrations, Lacan says), and on his
use of Borromean knots.

E282.   Closing address.   Journées d'Etudes de l'Ecole
        freudienne de Paris, Lille, 23-25 September 1977.
        Lettres de l'Ecole freudienne de Paris 22 (1978):
        499-501.

        Brief remarks on the themes of the conference and
        on the distance between language ("la langue") and
        logic.

E283.   Discussion of M. Safouan, "La proposition d'Octobre
        1967 dix ans après." Assies de l'Ecole freud-
        ienne de Paris sur "L'expérience de la passe,"
        Deauville, 7-8 January 1978. Lettres de l'Ecole
        freudienne de Paris 23 (1978): 19-20.

        Brief remarks.

E284.   Discussion of J. Guey, "Passe à l'analyse infinie."
        Assies de l'EFP, 7-8 January 1978. Lettres de
        l'Ecole freudienne de Paris 23 (1978): 94.

        Brief remarks.

E285.   Closing address. Assies de l'EFP, 7-8 January
        1978. Lettres de l'Ecole freudienne de Paris 23
        (1978): 180-81.

        Brief remarks on the procedures for the formation
        of the analyst.

E286.   Closing address. Ninth Congrès de l'Ecole freud-
        ienne de Paris, Paris, 6-9 July 1978. Lettres de
        l'Ecole freudienne de Paris 25, no. 2 (1979):
        219-20.

        Brief remarks on his belief that psychoanalysis
        is "intransmissible," on the "sinthome," and on the
        obscure connection between the position of the
        analyst, the operation of the signifier, and the
        cure.

E287.   "Lacan pour Vincennes!" 22 October 1978. Ornicar?
        17/18 (1978): 278.

        A brief remark on the proposed transfer of the
        Université de Paris VIII from Vincennes to Saint-
        Denis. Lacan hopes that the university campus can
        remain at Vincennes, and he recounts the accom-
        plishments of the Department of Psychoanalysis in
        the four years since he began generally directing
        its activities. Overall, Lacan says, the exper-
        ience has been positive, but he admits that

analytic discourse has nothing to teach.   "How can one teach something that even Freud believed cannot be taught?" Lacan asks.   Rather than imparting knowledge, the goal is to "corriger l'objet," which is why he has introduced set theory into psycho-analysis.

This item is accompanied by other documents regarding the proposed change of sites.

E***.   "Lettre de dissolution."   5 January 1980.   Le monde, 9 January 1980.   See B38.

This is the first session of Seminar XXVII but was originally published separately in Le monde. Reprinted in B38b, Ornicar? 20/21 (1980):   9-10. Translated in Papers of the Freudian School of Melbourne (1979):   2-5.

E***.   "L'autre manque."   15 January 1980.   Le monde, 26 January 1980.   See B38b.

This is the second session of Seminar XXVII but was originally published separately in Le monde accompanied by E288.   Reprinted in B38, Ornicar? 20/21 (1980):   11-12.

E288.   Letter to Le monde.   24 January 1980.   See B38.

Offers B38b for publication, and claims that the psychoanalyst feels a horreur of his act to the point of badmouthing the one who recalls him to it: Lacan.   Lacan also claims that this horror is re-sponsible for the clamor against Jacques-Alain Miller, who is considered odious for being at least one who has read Lacan.

Translated by Jeffrey Mehlman in October 40 (1987):   133 (see A11).

E289.   "Statuts de la Cause freudienne," with cover letter to the Préfecture de Police, 21 February 1980. F324, pp. 35-36.

Announces the formation of the Cause freudienne under his direction, and briefly describes the aims and organizational principles of the new group. The statutes were elaborated in E291.

E290.   "Delenda est."   10 March 1980.   Le monde, 17 March 1980.

An announcement addressed to those who would follow him in the formation of the Cause freud-ienne.   Lacan proclaims that the dissolution of the Ecole freudienne de Paris is irreversible, and he describes steps to thwart any attempt to preserve

the EFP. Reprinted in "D'écolage," B38c, 11 March
1980, and in <u>Delenda</u> (Bulletin temporaire de la
Cause freudienne) 1 (1980): 1. Translated in
<u>Papers of the Freudian School of Melbourne</u> (1979):
2-5.

E291. "Jacques Lacan explique ses décisions." <u>Le matin
de Paris</u>, 18 March 1980, p. 23.

Welcomes the group meeting on 15 March 1980 at
P.L.M. St. Jacques, where he had called together
those who wanted to follow him after the dissolution of the Ecole freudienne de Paris. The EFP
was dead and did not know it, Lacan says, and he
adds that his letter of 5 January 1980 (B38a) was a
"love-letter" even though no one recognized that at
the time. Lacan goes on to comment that the
failure of the school was inevitable because "the
effect of a group is contrary to the effect of the
subject . . . . a group is defined as a syn-
chronous unity of which the elements are individuals. But a subject is not an individual." He
announces his decision to pursue the <u>cause freud-
ienne</u>, but he adds that this new thing he is doing
is "<u>always the same thing</u>," well understood, but
"<u>autrement</u>."

E292. Presentation during the Seminar of 10 June 1980 to
inaugurate the first issue of the <u>Courrier de la
Cause freudienne</u> (29 June 1980). <u>Courrier de la
Cause freudienne</u>, July 1980, p. 1. Listed by
Dor, 98.

E293. Invitation to the Rencontre Internationale de
Février 1982 in Paris. Issued at the Rencontre
de Caracas 12-15 July 1980. <u>Courrier de la Cause
freudienne</u>, September 1980, p. 2. Listed by Dor,
p. 99.

E294. "Statuts de la Cause freudienne" (long version),
with cover letter to the Préfecture de Police, 22
October 1980. F324, pp. 37-42.

Articulates more fully the aims and procedures
listed in E289 and announces the appointment of
various people to official posts in the new group.

E295. "Il y a du refoulé. Toujours. . . . " Letter for
la Cause freudienne. 23 October 1980. <u>Courrier
de la Cause freudienne</u> October, 1980, p. 3.

Notes the irreducibility of the repressed and
claims that the elaboration of the unconscious in
analysis is nothing other than the production of
this hole ("<u>trou</u>"). Lacan associates this hole

with death as something that cannot be looked at
directly, like the sun. He also briefly comments
on the progress of the Ecole de la Cause freudienne
in organizing a group for the training of analysts
and the granting of the A.M.E. and the A.E. (see
C88).
Reprinted in A9, p. 41.

E296. Letter to members of the S.C.I. _Courrier de la_
Cause freudienne, December 1980. Listed by Dor,
p. 99.

E297. "A Lacanian Psychosis: Interview by Jacques
Lacan." Undated. Translated by Stuart Schneiderman from an unedited transcript of Lacan's
interview with a hospitalized psychiatric
patient. F397, pp. 19-41.

Presents Lacan's dialogue with a man suffering
from what Lacan calls a "Lacanian" psychosis, with
"imposed speeches" and notable manifestations of
the subject's troubled relations to the real, the
symbolic, and the imaginary. For that reason,
Lacan concludes, we cannot be optimistic about the
outcome of the case. This item offers a rare
glimpse into Lacan's actual analytic practice. For
accounts of Lacanian analyses by other psychoanalysts, see the other items collected in F397.

E298. Letter regarding the Forum of the Ecole de la Cause
freudienne. ("Voilà un mois que l'ai coupé avec
tout. . .") 26 January 1981. _Le matin de Paris_,
29 January 1981, p. 23. _Courrier de l'Ecole de_
la Cause freudienne, January, 1981.

Notes the continuing controversy surrounding his
work, and endorses the Ecole de la Cause freudienne
as "l'Ecole de mes élèves, ceux qui m'aiment
encore." He proclaims the doors of the Ecole open
to "les Milles" and establishes a forum where open
discussion can flourish, though without him.
Reprinted in _Le monde_, 31 January 1981, p. 35; in
Actes du Forum de l'Ecole de la Cause freudienne,
28-29 March 1981, p. 1; and in A9, p. 42.

E299. Letter regarding the Forum of the Ecole de la Cause
freudienne. ("Mon fort est de savoir ce qu'at-
tendre signifie.") 11 March 1981. _Actes du_
Forum de l'Ecole de la Cause freudienne, 28-29
March 1981, p. 1. _Courrier de l'Ecole de la_
Cause freudienne, March, 1981.

Reaffirms his recognition of the Ecole de la
Cause freudienne as the sole group responsible for
carrying on his teaching, and sets the date for the

first forum.
Reprinted in A9, p. 43.

E***.   "Interventions de Lacan à la Société psychana-
         lytique de Paris." <u>Ornicar?</u> 31 (1984): 7-27.

         Collects Lacan's discussions of papers presented
         to the society that were published in <u>La revue</u>
         <u>française de psychanalyse</u>, with a brief intro-
         duction by Jacques-Alain Miller (p. 7). Includes
         E130, E132, E133, E134, E136, E137, E138, E140,
         E141, E143, E144, E145, E147, E148.

E***.   "Extraits de la séance du Séminaire" [26 February
         1969]. <u>Littoral</u> 9 (1983):   33-37. See B28.

E***.   "Le séminaire 'D'un Autre à l'autre': extraits de
         la séance du 26 February 1969. <u>Littoral</u> 9
         (1983):   33-37. See B31.

Secondary Works

Section F

Books, Journals, and Collections of Essays

F300.   Actuel. Spring, 1980. Special issue on Lacan.

F301.   Analytica. Supplement to Ornicar?.

        Published irregularly as a supplement to Orni-
        car?.

F302.   Analytiques.

        Devoted to the mathematical exposition of psycho-
        analytic concepts begun by Lacan, and centered upon
        the work of the mathematician Daniel Sibony.

F303.   L'âne 3 (1981). Special section on Lacan's death.
        See pp. 1-9.

        Includes G509, G628, G686, G824 as well as an
        excerpt from B14, E256, and a brief note on the
        importance of Lacan's work that focuses on the
        lasting impact of his clinical methods.

F304.   Annual of Lacanian Studies. Forthcoming.

        Edited by Patrick Colm Hogan and Jacques-Alain
        Miller, and intended to serve as a primary journal
        for Lacan studies in the United States.

F305.   L'arc 58 (1974): 1-88. Jacques Lacan.

        Exemplifies the effect of Lacan's influence on a
        number of women working in fields ranging from
        psychoanalysis to linguistics and literary criti-
        cism.

        Contents

        Catherine Clément, "Un numéro"....................1
        Jacques Lacan, "'Aimée'" (excerpts from A1).......4

F306.   Archard, David. <u>Consciousness and the Unconscious</u>.
        Problems of Modern European Thought.   London:
        Hutchinson and Co., Ltd., 1984. 136 pp.

        Surveys various accounts of the unconscious
        beginning with Freud and including Sartre, Lacan,
        Laplanche, Leclaire, and the Italian Marxist
        Sebastiano Timpanaro. Archard complains that
        "Freudian energetics" is largely ignored by Lacan,
        and that this aspect of Freud is incompatible with
        Lacan's notion of Freud as "a hermeneutist of the
        unconscious" (p. 83). More generally, Archard
        claims that the very premise of the "primacy of the
        signifier" is finally incoherent as a theory of
        meaning and if taken seriously renders Lacan's work
        "an untranslatable, rhetorical text" (p. 84). See
        especially Chapters 4 and 5.

F307.   <u>Aut-Aut</u> 177/178 (1980).   <u>A partire de Lacan</u>.

        <u>Contents</u>

F***.   Backès-Clément, Catherine. Le pouvoir des mots:
         symbolique et idéologique. Repères sciences
         humaines idéologies. Paris: Maison Mame, 1973.
         173 pages.   See F315.

F308.   Beirnaert, Louis. Aux frontières de l'acte
         analytique: la Bible, Saint Ignace, Freud et
         Lacan. Paris: Editions du Seuil, 1987.   246
         pages.

         Collects a number of articles mostly published
         during the 1970s that discuss various topics common
         to religion and psychoanalysis. Beirnaert (1906-
         1985) was a contemporary of Lacan who became a
         Jesuit in 1923 and then undertook the study of
         psychoanalysis, joining Lacan and Lagache when they
         founded the Société française de psychanalyse in
         1953. He remained with Lacan's groups until the
         dissolution of the Ecole freudienne de Paris in
         1980, when he joined another group of analysts,
         Errata. This biography is relevant to the col-
         lection of essays listed here because it suggests
         an inverted parallel to Lacan's own career, with
         his early education by Jesuits at the Collège
         Stanislas and his continuing interest in religion.
         Beirnaert addresses a number of issues directly
         raised in Lacan's work, such as the importance of
         desire to a psychoanalytic theory of ethics (see
         B18), but many of the most interesting essays
         entail Beirnaert's reflections on religious texts
         by figures such as Saint Ignatius and his careful
         comparison between theological tenets and psycho-
         analytic concepts.
         For Beirnaert's discussion of topics raised in
         Lacan's work, see especially the essays in Section
         II, "De l'éthique: désir indestructible et loi non
         écrite"; Section III, "Aux frontières de l'acte
         analytique"; and Section V, "Relire Ignace après
         Freud, Lacan, et quelques autres."

F309.   Benvenuto, Bice, and Roger Kennedy.   <u>The Works of</u>
        <u>Jacques Lacan: An Introduction</u>.   London: Free
        Association Books, 1986.

        Reviewed in <u>TLS</u> 4350 (1986):   880.

F310.   Bowie, Malcolm.   <u>Freud, Proust and Lacan: Theory</u>
        <u>as Fiction</u>.   Cambridge: Cambridge University
        Press, 1987.   224 pages.

        Focuses on theoretical models of desire and their
        connections to imaginative literature.

F311.   <u>Cahiers pour l'analyse</u> 1 (1966):   <u>La vérité</u>.   Pp.
        1-70.

        Contains C85, G739, L1649, and L1995.   Published
        by the Cercle d'epistémologie de l'Ecole Normale
        Supérieure, this journal devoted most of its first
        five issues to psychoanalytic topics that are
        discussed from a Lacanian perspective.

F312.   Caruso, Paulo.   <u>Conversaciones con Claude Lévi-</u>
        <u>Strauss, Michel Foucault, y Jacques Lacan</u>.   Il
        Cammino: Pensiero e civilta 4.   Milano: U.
        Mursia, 1969.   Barcelona: Editorial Anagrama,
        1969.   190 pages.

F313.   <u>Che Vuoi?:   Journal of Psychoanalysis in the</u>
        <u>Freudian Field</u>.   First issue Fall 1984.

        Includes a variety of works, generally oriented
        towards a Lacanian approach to psychoanalysis.

F314.   Cipoletta, Patrizia, et al.   <u>La struttura della</u>
        <u>soggettivita: linguaggio e desiderio.   Saggio su</u>
        <u>Freud, Lacan, Deleuze</u>.   Rome: La Parola, 1981.
        212 pages.

F315.   Clément, Catherine Backès.   <u>Le pouvoir des mots:</u>
        <u>symbolique et idéologique</u>.   Repères sciences
        humaines idéologies.   Paris: Maison Mame, 1973.
        173 pages.

        Discusses the power of words as manifest in the
        relation between ideology and the symbolic order
        that is described by Lacan.   Although Clément also
        comments on the importance of Marxism, literature,
        and the ethnology of Claude Lévi-Strauss to this
        topic, most of the book focuses at least indirectly
        on Lacan's theories of the subject and its relation
        to language.

F316.   Clément, Catherine.   <u>Vies et légendes de Jacques</u>
        <u>Lacan</u>.   Paris: Editions Bernard Grasset, 1981.

Traces Lacan's initial accounts of the mirror
stage and his frequent recourse to that concept in
the early stages of his career, and claims that it
was the only original idea Lacan had. Clément
explores Lacan's work on the imaginary in general,
focussing on the aggressivity that Lacan claimed
was inherent in imaginary identification, and she
devotes a long chapter to Lacan's interest in vio-
lent crimes committed by women. Clément moves
between personal reflections on Lacan's influence
in her own life to more critical and theoretical
analyses of Lacan's work, and she directs her most
vehement criticism towards the "mathemes" and what
she considers to be the scientistic fantasies that
obsessed Lacan and his followers in the last decade
of his career.
     Translated by Arthur Goldhammer as The Lives and
Legends of Jacques Lacan (New York: Columbia
University Press, 1983), 225 pages. For a comment
on Clément's work and a comparison with F396, see
G505. Reviewed by Jane Gallop in Sub-stance 32
(1981), 77-78. Also translated by Joaquin Jorda as
Vidas y Legendas de Jacques Lacan (Barcelona:
Anagrama, 1981), and by Sergio Benenuto as Vita e
leggenda di Jacques Lacan (Rome: Laterza, 1982).

F317. David-Menard, Monique. L'hystérique entre Freud et
       Lacan: corps et langage en psychanalyse. Paris:
       Editions universitaires, 1983. 215 pages.

       Reviewed by R. Gentis in Quinzaine littéraire 435
       (1985): 23-25.

F318. Davis, Robert Con, ed. The Fictional Father:
       Lacanian Readings of the Text. Amherst, Mass.:
       The University of Massachusetts Press, 1981. 206
       pages.

       Includes an introduction and epilogue by Davis,
       two reprints of earlier essays (G531 and L1909),
       and four original essays: G465, G555, G631, G808.
            Davis's introduction--"Critical Introduction:
       The Discourse of the Father" (pp. 1-26)--argues
       that the triadic relationship constituted by
       Freud's model of the family is the paradigm for
       literary textuality, and that the function of the
       father as defined in Lacan's concept of the
       "symbolic father" is the "single principle of
       meaning that precedes the plurality of narrative
       meanings and stands behind all narrative develop-
       ments" (p. 25). This claim leads to what Davis
       describes as the major theoretical premise behind
       all of the essays in this volume: a "psycho-
       analytic anthropomorphism of the text" that under-

stands "textuality is an inscription of the subject." Hence Davis asserts that "the operations of
the psychoanalytic subject and the text are
synonymous . . . [and] a literary narrative shows
aspects of such unconscious processes as seduction,
primal scene, and castration" (p. 3). Davis supports and illustrates these claims with a brief
reading of The Odyssey.
   Davis's epilogue, "The Discourse of Jacques
Lacan" (pp. 183-89), briefly mentions several
extensions and critiques of Lacanian criticism. He
discusses the reader's relation to the narrative
text as a desire that "seeks complete satisfaction
in its object" but that is endlessly suspended
through "the process of negotiating the gap between
need and demand and of binding desire to the law,
to the father" (pp. 187-88).

F***.   Davis, Robert Con, ed. Lacan and Narration: The
        Psychoanalytic Difference in Narrative Theory.
        MLN 98, no. 5 (1983):   843-1063. See F371.

F319.   De Waelhens, Alphonse. La psychose: essai
        d'interprétation analytique et existentiale.
        Louvain, Belgium: Editions Nauwelaerts, 1972.
        227 pages.

   Claims that his project is "to reflect, from a
philosophical and phenomenological perspective, but
with the help of psychoanalysis, on several
dimensions of behavior which . . . we will call
here 'irrational,' but which, in fact, will be
mainly psychotic behavior. . . . It is our wish
that this interpretation should clarify the
potentiality for madness lying at the very heart of
the structures that are constitutive of the human
condition" (tr., p. x).
   Most of the book consists of detailed commentaries on theories of psychosis from a Lacanian
perspective which emphasizes the subject's relation
to the signifier and the foreclosure of the name-
of-the-father, see the Table of Contents below.
Part of Chapter Four is devoted to Lacan's reading
of the Schreber case (C72 and B14), emphasizing the
link between the Oedipus complex and the mirror
image that precedes it as they both attempt to fill
a "gap" in the subject's being. Part of Chapter
Six focuses on two definitions of the unconscious
in Lacan's work: that the unconscious is structured
like a language, and that the unconscious is the
discourse of the Other. Lacan's work is the focal
point for all of the book, however, and informs not
only the chapters devoted to psychoanalysis but
also De Waelhens's comments on existential and
phenomenological approaches to the issues of

language and the real in human experience.
Translated by W. Ver Eecke as Schizophrenia: A
Philosophical Reflection On Lacan's Structuralist
Interpretation, Duquesne Studies, Philosophical
Series, Volume 35 (Pittsburgh: Duquesne University
Press, 1978), 261 pages. The translation includes
a preface, introduction, and bibliography by the
translator, who traces De Waelhens's debt to Lacan
in detail. Consequently, this text offers the
English reader the most extended and concrete
introduction to Lacan's theory of psychosis and its
philosophical and psychoanalytic sources.

Contents (based on the Ver Eecke translation)

F320. Deho, Giorgio. Lo strutturalismo dalla matematica
       alla critica letteraria: un saggio introduttiuo
       con i confronti antologici da I. Adler . . .
       [and] Jacques Lacan. Tangenti 61. Messina,
       Italy: G. D'Anna, 1975. 192 pages.

F321. Le discours psychanalytique. Paris: founded
       September, 1981.
       Directeur de la publication: Charles Melman.

       A journal devoted to psychoanalysis and orig-
       inally edited by a committee made up of analysts
       and non-analysts associated with Le Centre d'études
       et de recherches freudiennes (CERF). The founding
       group was Charles Melman, Claude Landman, and
       Contardo Calligaris. The journal caused a split
       within that organization, and in 1982 it became
       totally independent of CERF, which soon dissolved.
       Begun in reaction against the tendency to popu-
       larize psychoanalysis as an accessible approach to
       popular culture, most of the issues contained
       articles on clinical themes, the ethical and

pedagogical implications of Lacan's teaching, and
more general notes on internal debates among
analysts themselves.   In 1982, many of those
associated with the journal joined together to form
l'Association freudienne.

F322.   Dor, Joël.   Bibliographie des travaux de Jacques
        Lacan.   Paris: InterEditions, 1983.   207 pages.

        Lists but does not describe most of Lacan's pub-
        lications, and includes an alphabetical list of
        essay titles by Lacan and a calendar of seminar
        sessions with titles.

F323.   Dor, Joël.   Introduction à la lecture de Lacan,
        Volume 1:   L'inconscient structuré comme un
        langage.   L'Espace Analytique.   Paris: Denoël,
        1985.   265 pages.

        Offers a general introduction to Lacan's work.
        Reviewed by A. Reix in Revue philosophique de la
        France et de l'étranger 110 (1985):   352-53.

F324.   Dorgeuille, Claude.   La second mort de Jacques
        Lacan: histoire d'une crise octobre 1980-juin
        1981.   Paris: Actualité freudienne, 1981.   167
        pages.

        Recounts in detail the events surrounding the
        dissolution of the Ecole freudienne de Paris 1980-
        81; lists most of the documents and letters pro-
        duced during that controversy; and prints the most
        important of those items, with a running commentary
        about the conditions in which they were written.
        Among the items by Lacan published for public dis-
        tribution for the first time in this collection are
        E292, E293, E294, E295.   (Although all of these
        items appeared under Lacan's name, there was some
        debate about who actually wrote them; see pp. 42-
        43.)   This collection also contains Melman's bitter
        letter to Lacan denouncing the manipulative power
        struggles with which his name has become associated
        (J1090).

F325.   Entre-temps.   25 issues, March 1980-September 1982.

        Founded by Claude Rabant and Marianne Monnet as a
        forum for members of the Ecole freudienne de Paris
        who rejected Lacan's decision to dissolve the
        group.

F326.   L'éthique de la psychanalyse et la question du coût
        freudien.   Paris: EVEL, 1984.

        Discusses issues in analytic practice related to

Lacan's propositions about the position of the
analyst, logical time, and other topics that challenge more traditional methods of psychoanalysis.
This collection includes papers and transcripts of
discussions from colloquia held in 1982 and 1983.
The major essays are listed below.

Contents (selected)

F327. Etudes freudiennes 25 (1985): 7-140. Incidences
de l'oeuvre de Lacan sur la pratique de la psychanalyse.

Testaments from a number of practicing analysts
about the way Lacan's theoretical innovations have
changed their analytic work.

Contents

F***. L'excommunication. Edited by Jacques-Alain Miller.
Supplement to Ornicar? 8 (1977). See F380.

F328. Fages, Jean-Baptiste. Che cosa ha veramente detto
Lacan. Translated by Orio Buonomini. Che cosa
hanno veramente detto 47. Rome: Ubaldini, 1972.

147 pages.

F329.   Fages, Jean-Baptiste. <u>Comprendre Jacques Lacan</u>.
        Talouse: Edouard Privat, 1971.   123 pages.

        Discusses Lacan in the contexts of psychoanalysis
        and structuralism, and more generally as a prom-
        inent literary figure of the twentieth century.
        The first part of the book describes the develop-
        ment of central tenets in Lacan's work throughout
        his career, starting with the mirror stage. The
        second part discusses Lacan's relation to more
        traditional forms of psychoanalysis and to the
        institutional structure of psychoanalysis as a
        discipline. Fages comments at length on Lacan's
        use of linguistics, the concepts of neurosis and
        psychosis as derived from Lacan's theory of the
        symbolic, and on Lacan's distinction between
        metaphor and metonymy. Reprinted 1979.

F330.   Felman, Shoshana. <u>Jacques Lacan and the Adventure
        of Insight: Psychoanalysis in Contemporary
        Culture</u>. Harvard University Press, 1987.

        Discusses the importance of Lacan's work for
        psychoanalysis and for the study of literature,
        especially as it can provide the grounds for larger
        cultural observations. (This book reprints several
        of Felman's earlier articles from <u>Yale French
        Studies</u>, <u>MLN</u>, <u>Poetics Today</u>, and elsewhere.)

F331.   Fougeyrollas, Pierre. <u>Contre Lévi-Strauss, Lacan
        et Althusser: trois essais sur l'obscurantisme
        contemporain</u>. Rome/Paris: Librarie de la Jon-
        quière, 1976.   216 pages.

F332.   Francioni, Mario. <u>Psicanalisi linguistica ed
        epistemologia in Jacques Lacan</u>. Filosofia della
        Scienze 34. Turin: Edizioni di Filosofia, 1973.
        51 pages. Reprinted Turin: Boringhieri, 1978.
        81 pages.

F***.   <u>French Freud: Structural Studies in Psycho-
        analysis</u>. Edited by Jeffrey Mehlman. <u>Yale
        French Studies</u> 48 (1972).   202 pages. See F424.

F***.   <u>Freud/Lacan: quelle articulation?</u> <u>Littoral</u> 14
        (1984):   5-56.
        See F357.

F333.   Gallop, Jane. <u>The Daughter's Seduction: Feminism
        and Psychoanalysis</u>. Ithaca, New York: Cornell
        University Press, 1982.   164 pages.

        Discusses the relationship between various

notions of feminine sexuality and principle theoretical generalizations of psychoanalysis, primarily through critiques of other feminist works
inspired by or responding to Lacanian theory.
There are chapters on works by Juliet Mitchell (see
K1274), Luce Irigaray, Michèle Montrelay, Catherine
Clément, Stephen Heath, Hélène Cixous, and Eugénie
Lemoine-Luccioni, and a concluding essay on the
case of Dora as reported by Freud and discussed by
Clément in La jeune née.
    Although Gallop claims to mistrust unifying
themes as a phallocentric ruse of stability and
coherence, the book repeatedly returns to an opposition between two forms of discourse: the
phallocentric law of the symbolic, with its unitary
principles of order and closure and the universa-
lizing generality of its epistemological claims;
and the counter-discourse of the feminine, which is
open-ended, inherently unstable and incoherent, and
eschews closure in favor of an endless prolifera-
tion of specific, disconnected utterances. This
opposition reflects similar polarities proposed by
Cixous and Kristeva, but Gallop resists valorizing
the feminine as an independent realm free of symbolic determination. Instead, she insists on the
necessarily dialectical interaction between the
phallocentric and feminine positions. No one can
escape from power, she argues; instead, it must be
exercised and criticized through what Kristeva
calls the role of the intellectual as "dissident"
(see p. 119). This strategy will "dephallicize"
power, Gallop says, and she claims that she intends
to "assume the phallus and unveil that assumption
as presumption, as fraud" (122).
    Gallop's analyses of other feminist arguments are
often instructive in their refusal to grant the
authors' convenient reductions of Lacan's indirect
assertions. Her account of B31 and A3 also offers
a lucid account of the significant playfulness in
Lacan's claim that "woman does not exist." More
important than these expository readings, however,
is Gallop's insistence on restoring (or establishing) the political dimension of psychoanalysis
that was lost in Lacan's distinction between the
penis and the phallus and, more generally, in his
privileging symbolic exchange over the unruly
pleasures and specificity of the body. The division between "political" and "psychoanalytic"
reading is not totally inescapable, Gallop concedes
(p. 101), but we can avoid treating the phallus as
"some fundamental, transcendental truth" beyond the
political materiality of the penis and the specific
contingencies it embodies in its "ups and downs"
(p. 98).
    Gallop self-consciously offers her own discourse

as one example of what such an alternative might
look like. She notes her refusal to resolve contradictions in the texts she reads or to exclude
one avenue of discussion for another, and she deliberately pursues often fanciful etymological
reflections at the expense of any more general
focus or purpose. Most of the book, however,
offers a sophisticated yet accessible overview of
the complex debates generated by the confrontation
between feminism and Lacanian psychoanalysis. On
this point see G751. For an extended review by
John Muller see <u>Psychoanalytic Quarterly</u> 53 (1984):
588-94.

F334.   Gallop, Jane. <u>Reading Lacan</u>. Ithaca, New York:
        Cornell University Press, 1985. 198 pages.

    Discusses various themes in Lacan's work through
readings of passages from C53, C65, C69, C71, C73,
and C80. Gallop claims that her "ultimate project
is to foster some sort of dialogue between Lacan
and America," and to that end she addresses a
number of the problems confronted by efforts to
translate Lacan's writings. She lends those problems a substantial theoretical significance, however, by focussing most of her attention on the
more general task of reading Lacan in a Lacanian
manner.
    Gallop argues that such a reading must subord-
inate interpretation to an understanding of the
structure of transference by which readers seek the
presence of an author that would lend coherence to
the text before them--to identify with Lacan, in
other words, much as an analysand would identify
with the analyst. That goal reproduces the imaginary identifications of the mirror stage, Gallop
says, and must be replaced or pursued in conjunction with a more properly symbolic understanding of
the lure of identification itself.
    To illustrate such a reading, Gallop frequently
refers to her personal experiences while reading
Lacan's work and while writing the manuscript. She
does, however, direct this general strategy towards
a critique of contemporary theories of the "death
of the author," which she describes as disguised
attempts to replace the author with the reader
through transference and so reclaim the author's
mastery for the reader. In opposition to this
fundamentally conservative strategy, which would
maintain the structure of mastery as an invisible
truth of reading, Gallop proposes the notion of a
"fading" author who cannot be identified with the
text and remains an obstacle to the reader's own
security.
    Gallop associates this attack on the traditional

notion of authority with feminist critiques of
Lacan's phallocentrism, and in the introductory
chapter she argues that work done under the ambiguous title of "women's studies" has raised the
possibility of a new kind of subject--one that is
not only female but also plural--against the mono-
lithic individual of a phallocratic cogito. She
objects to those who would simply dismiss Lacan's
work as a blind reproduction of sexist ideology,
however, and defends Lacan's notion of the phallus
as deliberately ambivalent, a "signifier" that
cannot be identified with the penis despite the
customary association between the phallus and the
male individuals that dominate our culture (p.
140).

Gallop addresses two kinds of readers: one who
is approaching Lacan's work for the first time and
so needs an elementary introduction to the most
general aspects of Lacan's writing; and another who
is equipped to worry about vagaries of Lacan's
style and the various translations that have presented Lacan to readers of English. Her book is
useful on both levels, and particularly enlight-
ening on two persistently misconstrued issues: the
"sequence" of the imaginary and symbolic experiences in the life of the infant, and the relation
among desire, demand, and repression. In Chapter
Three Gallop observes that the familiar understanding of the mirror stage as the moment in which
the child overcomes the chaos of a fragmented body
(the "corps morcelé") by recognizing a coherent
image of the self is oversimplified, and she claims
that, in fact, this "moment" consists of two contradictory attitudes of anticipation and retro-
action. The body is not experienced as fragmented,
Gallop says, until there is a coherent image
against which to measure the fragmentation. Thus
the individual looks both forward to the ideal coherence and backward to the anguish of dismemberment, each perspective depending on the other.

Gallop's remarks about desire and repression are
more subtle and focus upon familiar passages from
C73. At issue is the status of "Urverdrangung,"
usually translated as primary repression. Lacan
argues that the Urverdrangung is, as Gallop says,
"that part of needs which is left out in the articulation of a demand, and which man experiences
as desire" (p. 151). For this reason, commentators
have understood desire as a "reappearance" of the
Urverdrangung, and they have even translated
Lacan's "apparaître," "appears," as "reappears."
Gallop shows how that translation distorts Lacan's
point, which is that the primary repressed can only
appear as desire. The appearance of the repressed
cannot therefore be a "return" in any sense, but

only marks the secondary, alienated quality that is the Urverdrangung (see pp. 150-52).

In addition, Gallop also discusses more general aspects of the mirror stage, the curiously "inter-subjective" quality of anxiety in transference, Lacan's objections to American ego psychology, the priority of metonymy over metaphor, and Lacan's remarks about two dreams discussed by Freud: the dream of the dead father from "Formulations Re-garding the Two Principles in Mental Functioning" (1911), and the dream of the burning child from The Interpretation of Dreams (1900).

F335.   George, François. L'effet 'yau de poêle: de Lacan
        et des lacaniens. Paris: Hachette, 1979.   204
        pages.

        Expanded version of G612.

F336.   Georgin, Robert. Lacan: théorie et pratiques.
        Lausanne: Editions l'Age d'homme, 1977.

        Surveys fundamental concepts in Lacan's work, especially those of the subject, the signifier, the function of the phallus, and desire ("Théorie: le champ lacanien," pp. 19-66), and then uses Lacan's work as the basis for four less analytic essays. Georgin combines Lacanian psychoanalysis and the mythic thought identified by Lévi-Strauss to write "a new myth" out of the elemental structures common to Christianity, Greek mythology, and other sources. He also composes an autobiographical sketch by Shakespeare and offers other imaginative pieces intended to illustrate or dramatize Lacanian principles of analysis. Includes C96. Reprinted as Lacan, CISTRE-Essais (Petit-Poeulx, Belgium, 1984), 118 pages.

F337.   Georgin, Robert. Le temps freudien du verbe. Le
        Sphinx. Lausanne: Editions l'Age d'homme, 1973.
        164 pages.

        Focuses on the "Copernican revolution" in the human sciences that took place in the years 1950-1980 and traces the effect of Saussure's Cours de linguistique générale on linguistics (through the work of Jakobson), anthropology (through the work of Lévi-Strauss), and psychoanalysis (through the work of Lacan). Georgin claims that Lacan's re-formulation of Freud in terms of Saussurean lin-guistics constitutes the major event in contemp-orary human sciences, not only because Freud's work finds its full meaning in that reformulation but also because Lacan's return to Freud has undermined our most fundamental concepts of what constitutes

knowledge itself.
Chapters III and IV (pp. 88-148) are devoted to
Lacan's work, though the whole book is dedicated to
Lacan. Reprinted, with several corrections and a
brief note in memory of Lacan, as De Lévi-Strauss à
Lacan, Ecrits/CISTRE (Paris: CISTRE, 1983).

F338. Godino Cabas, Antonio. Curso y discurso de la obra
       de Jacques Lacan. Buenos Aires: Helguero, 1977.
       298 pages.

F339. Granon-Lafont, Jeanne. La topologie ordinaire de
       Jacques Lacan. Paris: Point Hors Ligne, 1985.

       Discusses Lacan's use of mathematical formulas
and topology.

F340. Hesnard, Angelo. De Freud à Lacan. Horizons de la
       Psychologie. Paris: Editions ESF, 1970; 3rd
       edition, 1977. 148 pages.

       Describes the history of psychoanalysis in France
from just after World War I to the late 1960s, with
the second half of the book devoted to Lacan's
teachings and the formation of his own school.
Written by a founding member of the Société psychanalytique de Paris and a former President of the
Société française de psychanalyse (1959-60), this
book focuses on the debates among various psychoanalytic societies during the first half of the
twentieth century, but Hesnard notes that the
debates surrounding Lacan's work were of a different sort. Lacan made fidelity to Freud's work
itself the stakes of the controversy, Hesnard
notes, and the Ecole freudienne de Paris was in
that sense a new kind of psychoanalytic institution, one that opened up a deep and potentially
destructive split within the psychoanalytic
community.
       Despite its polemical effect, however, Lacan's
work is in Hesnard's eyes a "faithful continuation
of the ideas and discoveries of the Master" (p.
85), and he hopes that his brief description of
Lacan's central concepts will open up a debate that
the international psychoanalytic community has so
far refused.
       Translated into Spanish by Carmen Cienfuegos in
the collection "Novicurso" (Barcelona: Editions
Martinez Roca, 1976), 160 pages.

F341. Huber, Gérard. Conclure dit-il: sur Lacan.
       Paris: Galilée, 1981.

F342. Hystérie et obsession: les structures cliniques de
       la névrose et la direction de la cure. Collected

Papers from the Fourth International Congress of
the Champ freudien, Paris, 14-17 February 1986.
Fondation du Champ freudien. Paris: Bibliothèque des <u>Analytica</u>/Navarin Editeur, 1985[?].
468 pages.

Presents forty-eight papers from the fourth
international congress of the Champ freudien,
grouped according to the topics listed below. All
of the papers address their respective topics from
perspectives informed by Lacan's work, and most
invoke Lacan's texts in detail as the basis for
their argument. In addition, a number of the
papers address specific issues and claims from
Lacan's work and offer extended commentaries on a
wide range of passages.

F343.   <u>Les identifications: confrontation de la clinique
        et de la théorie de Freud à Lacan</u>.   L'espace
        analytique. Paris: Denoël, 1987. 232 pages.

        Contains clinical and theoretical contributions
        on the topic of identification, especially as dis-
        cussed by Lacan in B20. The book opens with a de-
        scription of Lacan's seminar on identification by
        Gérôme Taillandier (see B20b) and then presents a
        series of papers and transcripts of discussions
        from a conference sponsored by the CFRP. The major
        essays are listed below and are not annotated sep-
        arately in this bibliography.

        Julia Kristeva, "Le réel de l'identification"....47
        Monique David-Ménard, "Identification et
          hystérie".......................................79
        Jean Florence, "Les identifications"............149

        The collection also includes discussions and
        comments by Ginette Michaud, Jean Oury, Conrad
        Stein, and Jacques Schotte.

F***.   <u>Incidences de l'oeuvre de Lacan sur la pratique de
        la psychanalyse</u>. <u>Etudes freudiennes</u> 25 (1985):
        7-140. See F327.

F***.   <u>Jacques Lacan</u>. <u>L'arc</u> 58 (1974): 1-88. See F305.

F344. Julien, Philippe. <u>Le retour à Freud de Jacques</u>
       <u>Lacan: l'application au miroir</u>. Collection
       <u>Littoral</u>: Essais en psychanalyse. Toulouse:
       Editions Erès, 1985. 239 pages.

       Claims that Lacan's teaching is, from beginning
       to end, "a debate with the imaginary. Posed at
       first as such, associated with the narcissism of
       the ego, the imaginary is then submitted to the
       primacy of the symbolic, to return with a dif-
       ference when Lacan links it finally to the relation
       between the symbolic and the real" (p. 225).
       Julien surveys this evolution in Lacan's attitude
       toward the imaginary and divides his career into
       three stages.
       The first ranges from 1938, when Lacan published
       his remarks about the mirror stage in C45 and C46,
       to 1952, when Lacan is most interested in de-
       scribing the imaginary mode as a "psychic object"
       with its own causality. From 1953 to 1960, Julien
       says that Lacan described the effect of the sym-
       bolic <u>on</u> the imaginary, portrayed the mirror stage
       as submitted to the symbolic order, and formalized
       the imaginary with an optical schema. From 1961-
       80, Lacan inscribed the mirror stage within a topo-
       logical schema, Julien says, and he began to treat
       the gaze as the <u>object petit a</u> while treating the
       imaginary as inseparable from the symbolic and the
       real (see pp. 58-59).
       Julien's book is one of the few studies of
       Lacan's work to discuss key concepts as they
       evolved throughout his career. For this reason,
       his remarks about Lacan's earliest published works
       are particularly interesting. See especially Part
       One, "<u>L'ombre de Freud</u>," pp. 27-59.

F345. Juranville, Alain. <u>Lacan et la philosophie</u>.
       Philosophie d'aujourd'hui. Paris: Presses
       Universitaires de France, 1984. 496 pages.

       Claims that philosophy and psychoanalysis are
       symptoms of each other, and that Lacan's theory of
       the Borromean knot joins the two discourses through
       the function of the real. Juranville argues that
       Lacan's concept of the real as a "<u>non-sens irréduc-</u>
       <u>tible</u>" underlies his theory of the signifier and of
       the unconscious as well, and that it codifies con-
       temporary philosophies of the world such as pro-
       posed by Heidegger and Levinas. Yet Juranville
       also claims that psychoanalysis has no way of
       theorizing the real as anything other than a
       "beyond"--beyond the pleasure principle, beyond the
       Oedipal complex--and this is where philosophy pro-
       vides a necessary supplement to psychoanalytic

discourse. Psychoanalysis thus lends to philosophy
its awareness of the function of "partial truth"
and the possibility of a "pure signifier" that is
not supported by some realm of being beyond itself,
and philosophy offers a conceptual rigor unknown in
psychoanalytic theory.
  Juranville pursues this thesis through detailed
analyses of issues central to Lacan's work, de-
voting most of the book to a sustained close
reading of most of Lacan's published texts.
Chapter One examines Lacan's use of linguistics,
but Chapters Two through Four are devoted to a
comparison between specific Lacanian concepts and
the work of various philosophers, as suggested by
their titles: "Le champ philosophique comme lieu
où prend son sens la théorie de l'inconscient"; "Le
désir et son sujet"; and "Le désir et l'objet."
Chapter Five discusses Lacan's theories of neurosis, transference, and other psychoanalytic issues
as "structures existentiales," and Chapter Six
attempts to establish a "discourse on the unconscious" beyond the simple negation with which
psychoanalysis marks the effect of the unconscious
on speech. The last two chapters continue this
line of inquiry, tracing connections among the
psychoanalytic theory of Borromean knots and the
philosophical discourse of total truth, and among
psychoanalytic discourse, philosophical discourse,
and history.
  Translated as Lacan und der Philosophie (Munich:
Boer, 1985). An excerpt from the French text was
published, with a brief comment, in L'âne (1985).

F346.   Kremer-Marietti, Angèle. Lacan et la rhétorique de
        l'inconscient. Paris: Aubier Montaigne, 1978.
        250 pages.

        Argues that Saussurean linguistics, especially as
developed by Lévi-Strauss and Lacan, can provide
the basis for a more general theory of signs that
cuts across different disciplines. Kremer-Marietti
claims that Lacan's theory of discourse and the
"rhetoric of the unconscious" that is its foundation offers a fully articulated semiological model
for the subject of science, one that underlies all
of the human sciences. She also comments on
Lacan's work under the following rubrics: his
thesis on paranoia, his commentary on the case of
Schreber and Freud's own analysis of Schreber's
memoirs, the unconscious as language, the rhetoric
of the unconscious, and the links between psychoanalysis and philosophy.

F***.   Lacan lesen. Der Wunderblock. Collected papers
        from a symposium in Berlin, April 1978. Edited

by Norbert Haas.   Berlin: Verlag Der Wunderblock, 1978.   139 pages.   See F423.

F347.   Lacan Study Notes.   Founded 1982.

Associated with the New York Lacan Study Group,
the first numbers of this journal were edited by
Helena Schulz-Keil and Stuart Schneiderman, who was
later replaced by Ellie Ragland-Sullivan.   LSN
contains essays about Lacan, book reviews, and
notices about conferences held by Lacanian groups
around the world.   All major essays from this
journal have been listed in this bibliography.

F348.   Lacoue-Labarthe, Philippe, and Jean-Luc Nancy.   La
titre de la lettre: une lecture de Lacan.
Paris: Editions Galilée, 1973.   148 pages.

Describes Lacan's appropriation of Saussure's
work for his psychoanalytic theory of the signifier, and criticizes Lacan for retaining rather
traditional humanistic assumptions about the subject.   The authors claim that such assumptions are
undermined by the function of the signifier as proposed by Saussure and even as theorized by Lacan
himself.

F349.   Lang, Hermann.   Die Sprache und das Unbewusste
[Language and the Unconscious: the Fundamentals
of Psychoanalysis According to Jacques Lacan].
Frankfurt/Main: Suhrkamp, 1973, rpt. 1986.   326
pages.

F350.   Leclaire, Serge.   Démasquer le réel: un essai sur
l'objet en psychanalyse.   With an essay by Juan-
David Nasio.   Le Champ Freudien.   Paris:
Editions du Seuil, 1971.   188 pages.

Discusses the relation between the psychoanalyst
and the real, especially as established through
what Lacan designated as the objet a.

F351.   Leclaire, Serge.   Psychanalyser: un essai sur
l'ordre de l'inconscient et la pratique de la
lettre.   Collection Points.   Paris: Seuil, 1958.
189 pages.

Cites several works by Lacan throughout, especially on the centrality of language and the
function of the signifier in psychoanalytic speech
as it constitutes the subject's relation to objects
and to the body.   See "Le corps de la lettre," pp.
77-96, and "Le refoulement et la fixation, ou l'articulation de la jouissance et de la lettre," pp.
147-70.

F352.   Lefort, Rosine, and Robert Lefort.   <u>Naissance de</u>
         <u>l'Autre: deux psychanalyses</u>. Le Champ freudien.
         Paris: Editions du Seuil, 1980.

         Relates several case histories exploring the role
         of the analyst as Other and the place of the mirror
         stage at the moment of the individual's entry into
         the symbolic.

F***.   Lemaire, Anika. <u>Jacques Lacan</u>. Preface by Lacan
         (D105).   Foreword by Antoine Vergote. Brussels:
         Charles Denart, 1970. See F392.

F353.   <u>Lettres édifiantes et curieuses adressées au</u>
         <u>Docteur Lacan pour s'inscire à son école</u>. Edited
         by Bernard de Fréminville. Editions Solin, 1980.

         A collection of fictional satiric letters os-
         tensibly attributed to thinly veiled public figures
         associated with Lacan and to famous his-torical
         figures who have "applied" for membership in the
         new group being formed according to Lacan's request
         in B38.   For a mock-serious review of this pam-
         phlet, see J1068; also see J1026.

F354.   <u>Libération</u>. 11 September 1981. Pp. 1-9.

         A special issue on Lacan's death, with several
         commentaries, interviews, and brief reflections on
         Lacan's importance to psychoanalysis and on his
         place in the contemporary intellectual scene in
         Paris.   Contains G447, G470, G474, G554, G643, G716
         and other brief comments by prominent French
         psychoanalysts.

F355.   Lipowatz, Athomosios. <u>Diskurs und Macht: Jacques</u>
         <u>Lacans Begriff der Diskurses</u>. Marburg/Lahn:
         Guttandin and Hoppe, 1982.   370 pages.

F356.   <u>Littoral</u>. Founded May 1981.

         Originally associated with AREL, the Association
         de recherche et d'étude du langage, this journal
         (and AREL) was conceived as a forum for a wide
         range of contributors and readers, not simply
         psychoanalysts. The first editorial board included
         Philippe Julien, Guy Le Gaufey, Erik Porge, Mayette
         Viltard, and the editor, Jean Allouch.   <u>Littoral</u>
         has continued to contest the proclaimed hegemony of
         the Ecole de la Cause freudienne over Lacan's work,
         and in particular it has criticized Jacques-Alain
         Miller's editing of the seminars. Special issues
         have been devoted to the "Translation of
         Freud/Transcription of Lacan" (no. 13 [1984]) and

"Freud/Lacan: What Articulation?" (no. 14 [1984]).
See F357.   Other issues have been devoted to
Lacanian topics such as the importance of typology
to psychoanalysis (no. 5 [1982]) and a conference
on "L'instance de la lettre," based on C71.
Littoral also sponsors the publication of two
smaller journals as less formal newsletters,
stécriture and La transa.

F357.   Littoral 13 (1984):   63-126.   Traduction de Freud,
transcription de Lacan.

Discusses the problems involved in efforts to
establish a reliable text of the seminars and is
generally critical of the versions edited by
Jacques-Alain Miller.   For specific criticism see
the items listed below.

Contents (Selected)

Marcelo Pasternac, "L'édition des Ecrits
en espagnol" (G792)............................63
Danièle Arnoux, "Sur la transcription" (G440)....79
Danièle Cerf-Bruneval, "La place du
lecteur" (G493)................................87
Danielle Hébrard, "Transcription et
ponctuation" (G639)............................99
Jean Allouch, "Lacan censuré" (G430)............109
Gérôme Taillandier, "Quelques problèmes de
l'établissement du séminaire de
J. Lacan" (G912)...............................121

F358.   Littoral 14 (1984):   5-56.   Freud/Lacan: quelle
articulation?

Compares specific concepts discussed by Freud and
Lacan, especially their attitudes towards representation and signs.

Contents

Jean Allouch, "Freud déplacé" (G429)..............5
Philippe Julien, "Lacan, Freud: une rencontre
manquée" (G665)................................17
Danièle Lévy, "L'étrange altérité de
l'expérience" (G703)...........................25
Guy Le Gaufey, "Représentation freudienne et
signifiant lacanien" (G691)....................41

F359.   MaccCabe, Colin, ed.   The Talking Cure: Essays in
Psychoanalysis and Language.   New York: St.
Martin's Press, 1981.   230.

A collection of essays based on papers presented
in a seminar on psychoanalysis and language at

King's College, Cambridge, 1976-77. Includes G527,
G583, G644, G684, G710, G845, G913, G914 and L2331.

F360.   MacCannell, Juliet Flower. Figuring Lacan:
Criticism and the Cultural Unconscious. London:
Croom Helm 1986. 182 pages.

Emphasizes the importance of Lacan's work for an
understanding of social relations, focussing on his
concepts of love and desire.

F361.   Magazine littéraire 121 (1977):   8-36.   Lacan.

Contents

Philippe Sollers, "Hommage à Lacan" (G898)........9
Gilles Romet, "Un démon pensant" (G843)..........10
Jacques Lacan, "Hiatus irrationalis" (E117)......11
Marc Rouanet, "Lacan et Freud: expérience d'un
    savoir et division du sujet" (G850)............12
Paméla Tytell, "Lacan et l'anglais tel qu'on
    le parle" (G920)................................14
Catherine Clément, "Lettre à Lacan ou l'oiseau
    pris" (G507)....................................18
Jacques Lacan, "L'impromptu de
    Vincennes" (E204)...............................21
Dominique Grisoni, "Politique de Lacan" (G622)...25
Michel de Wolf, "Essai de bibliographie
    complète".......................................28

F362.   Mannoni, Maud. La théorie comme fiction: Freud,
Groddeck, Winnicott, et Lacan. Le Champ freudien. Paris: Editions du Seuil, 1979. 183
pages.

Argues that theory can function as a defense
against listening carefully to what the analysand
says, but that Freud's use of theory as a "fiction"
has led psychoanalysts such as Lacan and Winnicott
to an alternative practice that makes room for the
imaginary within a large ludic arena, an "espace de
jeu" that escapes the "langage 'psy'" which isolates psychiatrists and psychoanalysts from their
patients.

F363.   Marini, Marcelle. Jacques Lacan. Paris: Pierre
Belfond, 1986.

F364.   Massota, Oscar. Introduccion a la lectura de
Jacques Lacan. Buenos Aires: Proteo, 1974, rpt.
1977. 177 pages.

Reviewed by B. Alazet in Revue des sciences
humaines 202 (1986): 188-90.

F365.   Miller, Jacques-Alain. Cinco conferencias Cara-
        queñas sobre Lacan. Buenos Aires: Letra Viva,
        1980. Caracas: Ateneo, 1981.

F366.   Miller, Jacques-Alain. Entretien sur le Séminaire
        avec François Ansermet. Paris: Navarin, 1984.

F367.   Miller, Jacques-Alain, ed. Nouveaux documents sur
        la scission de 1953. Paris: Navarin Editeur,
        1978. 64 pages.

        Collects several documents not included in F379
        and F380, some of which provide additional informa-
        tion about the circumstances in which C58 was first
        presented.

F368.   Milner, Jean-Claude. L'amour de la langue.
        Connexions du Champ Freudien. Paris: Editions
        du Seuil, 1978. 133 pages.

        Distinguishes between la langue, the objective,
        formal descriptive concept used by linguists and
        grammarians to define the structure of language,
        and Lacan's concept of "lalangue," the link between
        desire and speech by which a "being" becomes a
        "speaking being."

F369.   Milner, Jean-Claude. Les noms indistincts. Paris:
        Editions du Seuil, 1983.

        Discusses several concepts central to Lacan's
        work that derive from three "suppositions": (1)
        that something is "there" beyond the symbolic,
        which leads to Lacan's notion of the real; (2) that
        there is a language, which leads to the symbolic;
        and (3) that there is anything "du semblable,"
        which leads to the imaginary. Much of this book is
        devoted to reflections on the political dimension
        of Lacan's work, especially regarding the concepts
        of the Master, freedom, and "multiplicity" as em-
        bodied by "les vraisemblements."

F370.   Mitchell, Juliet, and Jacqueline Rose, eds.
        Feminine Sexuality: Jacques Lacan and the Ecole
        Freudienne. New York: W. W. Norton and Co.,
        1982. 187 pages.

        Contains essays by Lacan and others on feminine
        sexuality, especially as that topic was debated by
        Freud and Jones in the 1920s and 1930s, and as it
        bears on the issues of castration and the symbolic
        constitution of sexual difference.
        In a long introductory survey of this topic,
        Mitchell briefly describes Freud's accounts of the
        origin of sexual difference, and she claims that

Freud's rejection of biology as a determing factor
and his theory of the castration complex were crucial influences on Lacan's own theory of a "fragmented subject of shifting and uncertain sexual
identity." MItchell's essay includes a brief
analysis of the "great debate" over female sexuality that arose among psychoanalysts following
Freud's preliminary conclusions, and she argues
that ego-psychologists as well as theorists interested in object-relations have assumed a biologically intrinsic sexual difference between males
and females that is antithetical to the theory of
sexual identity and subjectivity Freud developed
after 1915.

     A second introduction by Rose argues that most
psychoanalysts have failed to understand the
"essential interdependency" between subjectivity
and femininity in Freud's work, and that that
failure has led to a misperception of Freud's
"corresponding stress on the division and precar-
iousness of human subjectivity itself." Rose describes fundamental tenets in Lacan's work as they
bear on the relation between sexuality and the
unconscious, and she claims that Lacan pursued that
relation to the point of conceiving sexuality
purely in terms of the divisions in and between
subjects as they are situated in the symbolic order
of language.

     Rose also argues that this conception of sexu-
ality led Lacan in his later work to consider any
possibility of unity, "One," "Love," or Woman (La
femme) as merely a myth promoted by the symbolic to
disguise the fundamental split or lack that is its
original link to the subject. (Earlier, Rose says,
Lacan tended to assign such effects to an imaginary
register that was disrupted by the symbolic.)
Despite the arguments of some feminists, she concludes, in Lacan's later work there is no prediscursive reality, no possibility of a realm of
freedom such as the mother's body or a feminine
realm "outside language" because Lacan argues that
"the unconscious severs the subject from any unmediated relation to the body as such . . . [and]
because the 'feminine' is constituted as a division
in language, a division which produces the feminine
as its negative term" (p. 55).

     Also contains E153, C73, C77, and selections from
B31, B32, and G864. A selective bibliography lists
the major essays from the earlier debates on feminine sexuality among Freud and other analysts as
well as many related recent works from the debates
over Lacan's declarations on the topic of femininity. For other contributions to the contemporary version of this controversy, see F333,
K1219, and the other items listed in the index

under "feminine sexuality." See also a review by
Christopher Culler, Lacan Study Notes 4 (1985): 13-
15.

F371. MLN [Modern Language Notes] 98, no. 5 (1983): 843-
       1063. Lacan and Narration: The Psychoanalytic
       Difference in Narrative Theory. Edited by Robert
       Con Davis.

       A special issue of MLN devoted in part to Lacan's
       work and its influence on narrative. Contains a
       brief preface by Richard Macksey, an editor of the
       journal; an introduction by Davis; and the fol-
       lowing articles: G530, G566, G580, G712, G715,
       G872, and L2105. There is also a selective
       bibliography by Davis and Macksey (pp. 1054-63).
       Macksey's introduction, "'Sur un terrain en
       friche': Liminal Note" (pp. 843-47), briefly de-
       scribes the controversy surrounding Lacan's first
       presentation of a paper to an American conference
       (see C86) and suggests a few of the implications of
       his work for narrative analysis, the topic of the
       collection.
       Davis's introduction, "Introduction: Lacan and
       Narration" (pp. 848-59), describes Lacanian ap-
       proaches to narrative based on Lacan's claim that
       the unconscious is structured like a language, and
       claims that they are derived from three basic pro-
       positions: (1) "Narration is structured like a
       (subject in) language" (p. 853); (2) the manifest
       content of any narrative is produced by its un-
       conscious discourse; and (3) that unconscious is
       manifest in gaps or lapses that disrupt any nar-
       rative text. A Lacanian narratology must thus
       produce a "triple reading," Davis says: a reading
       of the manifest text, of the unconscious discourse
       that is its precondition, and finally of a recon-
       stituted text that is produced through this inter-
       pretive reading.

F372. Mooij, Antoine. Taal en Verlangen: Lacans theorie
       van de psychoanalyse. Meppel: Boom, 1975. 263
       pages.

F373. Mounin, Georges. Quelques traits du style de
       Jacques Lacan. 1969; rpt. Editions de Minuit,
       1970.

F374. Muller, John P., and William J. Richardson. Lacan
       and Language: A Reader's Guide to Ecrits. New
       York: International Universities Press, Inc.,
       1982. 443 pages.

       Describes in detail the essays translated in A2j
       and identifies most of Lacan's explicit (and often

implicit) references and intellectual sources.
Each essay in A2j is the subject of a separate
chapter, and each chapter contains several sections: a general overview of the essay and its
place in Lacan's career; a "Map of the Text" that
describes the argument in the form of an outline;
and "Notes to the Text," which identifies and
explains philosophical, literary, and psychoanalytic sources used in the essay. In addition,
there are an introduction, an afterword, and three
indexes: Name, Works of Freud, and Subject.
Translations into French and Japanese forthcoming.

F***.   Muller, John P., and William Richardson, eds. The
        Purloined Poe: Lacan, Derrida and Post-Structur-
        alist Reading. Baltimore: The Johns Hopkins
        University Press, forthcoming.

        Includes essays on C69 by Felman (G568), Derrida
        (G544), Johnson (G661), Muller and Richardson's own
        "Overview" to C69, notes, and a "map" of Lacan's
        text similar to the commentaries in F374. An ap-
        pendix to this apparatus provides an introduction
        to the very difficult mathematical argument Lacan
        presents in the essays that accompany C69 in A2,
        and in "Negation in 'The Purloined Letter': Hegel,
        Poe, and Lacan," Muller discusses Hegel's concept
        of negation to explain why the subjects in Poe's
        story shift places within the fundamental triadic
        structure identified by Lacan.

F375.   Nasio, Juan-David. Les yeux de Laure: le concept
        d'objet a dans la théorie de J. Lacan. Paris:
        Aubier, 1987. 243 pages.

        Explores the function of what Lacan identified as
        the objet a in a case history and at greater length
        through various topographical figures. The first
        section of the book discusses the role of trans-
        ference in analysis, especially as it involves the
        imaginary and the sujet-supposé-savoir. The second
        section focuses on the objet a and its relation to
        foreclosure, and the third section proposes a
        "psychoanalytic topology" that defines the function
        of the objet a in terms of what Lacan called the
        "cross-cap" and its role in the topological
        manipulation of surfaces.
        This item offers a detailed and carefully il-
        lustrated introduction to one of the more arcane
        aspects of Lacan's topological reflections. Much
        of Nasio's argument draws upon discussions of the
        cross-cap in unpublished seminars (Seminar IX, X,
        and XII), but see A2, pp. 366-67 and 553-54; B22,
        p. 143; and C94.

F376.   Newsletter of the Freudian Field. Edited by Ellie
         Ragland Sullivan, Henry W. Sullivan and Jacques-
         Alain Miller. Sponsored by the Foundation of the
         Freudian Field. First issue spring, 1987.

         Intended for English-speaking readers interested
         in clinical and theoretical issues from a Lacanian
         perspective. The journal covers literary, cul-
         tural, and cinematic work as well as psycho-
         analysis, and it has special sections devoted to
         abstracts of relevant books and a "Calendar of
         Events" for Lacanian groups around the world.

         Contents of issue 1, no. 1 (1987)

         Editorial...1
         Interview with Jacques-Alain Miller..............5
         Jacques Lacan, Excerpts from The Ethics of
            Psychoanalysis (B18)..........................11
         Russell Grigg, "Freud's Problem of
            Identification"...............................14
         Bruce Fink, News from Over
                           Seas...........................19
         Abstracts of Books and Articles.................21
         Calendar of Events..............................26

F377.   Nodal: revue de l'Association freudienne 1 (1984).
         Certaines conséquences de l'enseignement de
         Lacan. Edited by Joseph Clims. Paris: Editions
         Joseph Clims, 1984. 283 pages.

F***.   October 40 (1987): 5-133. Television. See
         A11/B12

         Contains a translation of A3 by Denis Hollier,
         Rosalind Krauss, and Annette Michelson. In a
         section titled "Dossier on the Institutional De-
         bate," this issue also includes translations by
         Jeffrey Mehlman of the following items related to
         various controversies concerning Lacan's affilia-
         tions with psychoanalytic groups and other institu-
         tions: B38a, B38b, E157, E159, E170, E171, E172,
         E178, E203, E204, E288, and J1063.

F378.   Ornicar? bulletin périodique de Champ freudien.
         Founded 1975.

         Named after a mnemonic slogan used to teach
         conjunctions to schoolchildren ("Mais ou et donc or
         ni car"), Ornicar? is directed by Jacques-Alain
         Miller and associated with the Department of
         Psychoanalysis of the University of Paris VIII at
         Vincennes (now at Saint Denis). All of the ma-
         terial published in this journal is devoted to

Lacan's work, but only selected items (in addition
to all items by Lacan) have been listed in this
bibliography.

F379.   Ornicar? 7 (1976), supplement. La scission de
        1953. Edited by Jacques-Alain Miller.

        Collects documents related to Lacan's split with
        the Société psychanalytique de Paris in 1953.
        Lacan had joined the SPP in 1934 and was elected
        President in January 1953, but at that time he was
        embroiled in a controversy over his advocacy of a
        variable length for the analytic session, a policy
        that became known as the "short session." Lacan
        was also involved in a dispute with another member
        of the SPP, Sacha Nacht, who wanted to move the
        organization and especially the training of new
        analysts more towards the format of traditional
        medical training, while Lacan insisted on a less
        rigid and more individualized program. Lacan's
        policies enraged the International Psychoanalytic
        Association, which refused to recognize the SPP as
        long as Lacan was responsible for training ana-
        lysts. The struggle for recognition divided the
        members of the SPP, and in June 1953 the Society
        returned a vote of no confidence in Lacan. He then
        resigned and helped form a new group, the Société
        française de psychanalyse. (For a more detailed
        account of this conflict, see the biographical
        sketch at the beginning of this bibliography; also
        see F412 and F393.)
        Most of the official documents produced during
        this controversy are reprinted here, including
        items by Lacan (E154-E159 and E279) as well as a
        number of letters to Lacan (see J1059). Lacan
        comments on the material in this volume in B35, and
        related items were collected and published as F367.
        E157 and E159 are translated in October 40 (1987):
        55-71, and various documents from the International
        Psychoanalytic Association related to this matter
        are reprinted there as well; see F377/378 and
        J1063.

F380.   Ornicar? 8 (1977), supplement. L'excommunication.
        Edited by Jacques-Alain Miller.

        Collects documents related to Lacan's split with
        the Société française psychanalyse at the end of
        1963 and to the founding of the Ecole freudienne de
        Paris in 1964. Includes a chronological summary of
        Lacan's "excommunication" from the IPA as well the
        "Edinburgh demands" issued by the International
        Psychoanalytic Association following its twenty-
        second Congress in that city in 1959, when the SFP
        requested formal recognition by the international

body. After considering the request, the Central
Committee of the IPA refused to recognize the SFP
because of "unhealthy" elements in the group--i.e.,
Lacan. In 1961, however, the IPA offered to recon-
sider the SFP's request for recognition if the
society followed a number of demands which included, among other controversial requirements, the
requirement that Lacan and Françoise Dolto be
phased out as training analysts. After the
Stockholm Congress of 1963, the IPA intensified its
campaign against Lacan by issuing an ultimatum to
the SFP: either permanently ban Lacan from
training analysts by 31 October 1963 or lose all
chances of recognition by the IPA.

   These demands brought to a climax the hostility
between Lacan and the IPA that had been festering
since 1953 (see C58), and it created a tension
within the SFP between those willing to sacrifice
Lacan for the recognition and those remaining
faithful to him and to the independence of the SFP
from what many considered the authoritarian demands
of the IPA. Those favoring recognition won, and
Lacan left the SFP to form the Ecole freudienne de
Paris, taking with him a number of followers. The
ones who remained in the SFP reorganized as the
Association psychanalytique de France, which was
officially recognized by the IPA in Amsterdam in
1965. On 21 June of 1964, Lacan founded the Ecole
freudienne de Paris (see E178), and this period of
controversy came to a close.

   This collection contains more than forty documents from this controversy including E172, E178,
and "La directive de Stockholm," which is reprinted
in October 40 (1987): 79-80 (see F377/378). For
an account of this period, see F412.

F381.   Palmier, Jean-Michel. Lacan: le symbolique et
        l'imaginaire. Collection Psychothéque. Paris:
        Editions Universitaires, 1969. 156 pages.

        Describes fundamental tenets of Lacan's work,
including the mirror-stage, the supremacy of speech
and the signifier, and the role of language and the
Other in relation to the unconscious. Palmier
focuses on Lacan's role as a theoretician of psychoanalysis in dialogue (at least implicitly) with
others such as Karl Abraham, Ernest Jones, and
Melanie Klein. An appendix discusses Lacan's link
with the work of Lévi-Strauss and with the structuralist movement in general.
        5th edition, Paris: J.-P. Delarge, 1979.
Translated by Maria Grazia Meriggi as Guida a
Lacan: il simbolico e l'immaginario (Milano:
Biblioteca universale Riqqoli, 1975), 164 pages.

F382. <u>Patio</u>. Paris: founded September, 1983.   Directeur
       de la publication: Claude Rabant.

       A journal devoted to psychoanalysis and con-
       taining articles, brief papers and notes, and
       translations of articles using terms and themes
       from Lacan's work.   Although the first issue in-
       cludes an article critical of the "amour du Maître"
       that it claims is characteristic of l'Ecole freud-
       ienne (see G466), in the introduction Rabant claims
       "<u>Il y a du divers dans la psychanalyse</u>" and says
       that the journal will explore many different kinds
       of writing about psychoanalysis.   His aim is not to
       unify them or measure them against each other,
       Rabant says, but "<u>pour y tracer des parcours et y
       trouver des libertés, pour y rejouer peut-être des
       circulations autour du trou même qu'ils déplacent</u>"
       (p. 5).

F383. Perrier, François.   <u>Voyages extraordinaires en
       Translacanie</u>.   Paris: Lieu commun, 1985[?].   192
       pages.

       Recounts his adventures in the world of Lacanian
       analysis, exclaiming that "I am a refugee from
       Lacanism!" and proposing to expose the posing and
       hypocrisy surrounding the cultic presence of Lacan
       among French psychoanalysts.   Perrier was a member
       of the Quatrième Group and was purportedly among
       those who founded the Ecole freudienne de Paris.
       Reviewed by Didier Eribon, "Les naufragés du
       'Jacques Lacan,'" <u>Le nouvel observateur</u>, 7 June
       1985, pp. 58-59; by C. J. Stivale in <u>French Review</u>
       60 (1986):   154-55; and in <u>Critique</u> 41 (1985):
       1084-89.

F384. <u>Poinçon: bulletin de liaison</u>.   Founded October
       1981.

       Devoted to the question "what are the articula-
       tions between the theoretical work of a psycho-
       analyst with the written word and the act of
       writing itself?"   <u>Poinçon</u> began as a product of a
       cartel working on B18, which included D. Ruff, J.M.
       Jadin, and others.

F385. Pontalis, Jean-Bertrand.   <u>Après Freud</u>.   Paris:
       Gallimard, 1968.

F386. <u>La psychanalyse</u> 1 (1956).   <u>De l'usage de la parole
       et des structures de langage dans la conduite et
       dans le champ de la psychanalyse</u>.   291 pages.

       Contains the papers and transcripts of discus-
       sions from the first meeting of the Sociéte

française de psychanalyse, Rome, 26-27 September
1953, and a number of other items produced by
members of the new society during its first three
years. The documents from the conference are
especially important in the light of the controversy surrounding the formation of the SFP following Lacan's split with the Société psychanalytique de Paris and the International Psychoanalytic Association. See F379.

Contents

[The volume concludes with two essays apparently
not delivered at the conference:]

Elane Amado Lévy-Valensi, "Vérité et langage du
    dialogue platonicien au dialogue

psychanalytique"............................257
Silvan S. Tomkins, "La conscience et
l'inconscient représentés dans un modèle
de l'être humain." Translated from English
by Muriel Cahen............................275

F387. Psyche. (October, 1980). Special issue on Lacan.

F388. Rabinovich, Diana, ed. Actas de la reunion sobre
       la enseñanza de Lacan y el psicoanalisis en
       América Latina. Collection Analitica. Caracas:
       Anteneo, 1982.

F389. Ragland-Sullivan, Ellie. Jacques Lacan and the
       Philosophy of Psychoanalysis. Urbana: Uni-
       versity of Chicago Press, 1986. 358 pages.

       Describes and illustrates five important topics
       in Lacan's work, as indicated by the following
       table of contents. Ragland-Sullivan quotes from
       Lacan's seminars at length and supports her ex-
       planations and commentary with corollary concepts
       and examples from a variety of disciplines. In
       addition to the primarily descriptive emphasis of
       the book, the concluding chapter also addresses
       feminist charges of phallcentricism in Lacan's
       work, arguing that "Lacanian theory provides a
       particular key for understanding the socialization
       and symbolization processes that have shaped male
       and female specificity through the ages" (p. 269).
       Ragland-Sullivan's text provides one of the most
       substantial close reading of Lacan's work available
       in English and aims to "synthesize the major con-
       cepts by which Lacan built a bridge between psycho-
       analysis and philosophy" (p. xxi; for an extended
       analysis of Lacan's relation to philosophical tra-
       ditions in France, see F345). She goes beyond the
       citations and sources provided by Wilden in F420
       and demonstrates Lacan's importance to a broad
       range of intellectual disciplines, though Ragland-
       Sullivan stops short of Lacan's later interest in
       topology and does not explore his interest in
       formal mathematics. She does stress Lacan's in-
       terest in the effect of meaning and signification
       throughout the book, but unlike Lemaire's "semi-
       otic" Lacan (F392), Ragland-Sullivan portrays
       Lacan's interest in language as the consequence of
       his insights into the function of desire and the
       Other as derived from philosophy and psycho-
       analysis--not from the mechanistic application of
       Saussurean linguistics onto the Freudian uncon-
       scious as suggested in F392 and F348.
       Ragland-Sullivan does not, however, attempt to
       explore the clinical basis of Lacan's work or to
       account for its applications in analytic practice

(except as an illustration for specific concepts),
nor does she dwell on the stylistic dimension of
Lacan's argument that occupies readers such as
Gallop (F334).

Contents

1. What Is "I"? Lacan's Theory of the Human
    Subject.....................................1
2. Lacan's Four Fundamental Concepts of
    Psychoanalysis.............................68
3. A Lacanian Theory of Cognition.............130
4. The Relationship of Sense and Sign.........196
5. "Beyond the Phallus?" The Question of
    Gender Identity............................267

F***.   Ragland-Sullivan, Ellie, ed. Newsletter of the
        Freudian Field. See F366.

F***.   Regards sur la psychanalyse en France. Nouvelle
        revue de psychanalyse 20 (1979). 288 pages. See
        F377.

F390.   Regnault, François. Dieu est inconscient: études
        lacaniennes autour de saint Thomas d'Aquin. La
        collection du Studiolo. Paris: Navarin, 1985.
        160 pages.

        Discusses the work of Galileo, Newton, and others
        as it joins the realms of science and religion,
        focussing on the issues of subjectivity and know-
        ledge as raised by Lacan's remarks about God and
        the subject of science. Throughout the book,
        Regnault also uses his observations about theology
        and epistemology to comment on specific Lacanian
        formulas such as the distinctions among the real,
        the symbolic, and the imaginary, and the function
        of the Borromean knots.

F391.   Rella, Franco. Il mito dell'altro: Lacan,
        Deleuze, Foucault. Opuscoli marxist 26. Milan:
        Feltrinelli, 1978. 66 pages.

F392.   Rifflet-Lemaire, Anika. Jacques Lacan. Preface by
        Lacan (D105). Foreword by Antoine Vergote.
        Brussels: Charles Dessart, 1970. 419 pages.

        Introduces the reader to basic aspects of Lacan's
        work, emphasizing his use of Saussurean linguistics
        and the similarity between his treatment of the
        symbolic function of the Oedipal complex and the
        model of cultural relations proposed by Claude
        Lévi-Strauss. Major sections of the book are de-
        voted to the following topics: "Some elements and
        some problems of general linguistics"; "Lacan's use

of the general data of linguistics"; "The constitution of the subject by accession to the symbolic--
the Spaltung--the role of the Oedipus in this
transition"; "The engendering of the unconscious by
primal repression (or accession to language) in
accordance with the process of metaphor"; "The
elementary signifiers constituting the unconscious"; "The transition from lack to desire and
to demand"; "The mechanisms of the formations of
the unconscious: structure and organization of the
unconscious signifying network"; "The general conception of the cure in Lacan"; and "The Lacanian
conception of neurosis and psychosis."
      Second edition, revised and augmented by the
author with a preface by Lacan (D105), re-issued
under the name "Lemaire" (Brussels: Mardaga,
1978), 379 pages.   Translated by David Macey
(London: Routledge and Kegan Paul Ltd., 1977),
266 pages.   Translated into Italian by Roberto
Eynard (Rome: Astrolabio, 1970), and into Spanish
by J. Millet (Barcelona: E. D. HASA, 1971; and
Buenos Aires: Sudamericana, 1979).

F393.   Roudinesco, Elisabeth.   La bataille de cent ans:
      histoire de la psychanalyse en France.   Volume
      One, 1885-1939.   Paris: Editions Ramsay, 1982.
      Volume Two, 1984.

      Describes the history of psychoanalysis in France
from roughly 1885, when Freud came to study with
Charcot, to 1981, the year of Lacan's death.
Volume One briefly mentions Lacan several times,
generally to identify his subsequent development of
themes and issues suggested by the early events
that are discussed in more detail.   Through such
references, Roudinesco establishes Lacan's connection to a wide variety of psychoanalytic positions, but her interest in this volume is more
generally restricted to major influences that
emerged in France before World War II.
      Volume Two is devoted to the "second generation"
of psychoanalysts in France, those that emerged as
powerful forces after World War II; it deals ex-
tensively with Lacan, his work, and his relations
to other forms of psychoanalysis.   This is by far
the most detailed and ecumenical account of Lacan's
place in the development of psychoanalysis, and it
provides both a detailed account of the institutional relations that govern the transmission of
psychoanalysis in France and a sophisticated
analysis of the theoretical continuities and conflicts among the different groups. (In this attention to the sociological dimension of psychoanalytic controversies, this book resembles F412,
which remains the best study of French psycho-

analytic movements associated with Lacan in
English.)

F394.   Roustang, François.   <u>Lacan: de l'équivoque à
        l'impasse</u>.   Paris: Les éditions de Minuit, 1986.
        118 pages.

        Argues that Lacan's effort to found psycho-
        analysis on a science of the real eludes attempts
        to reduce his work to simplistic formulas, and
        claims that Lacan's thought proceeds through a
        rigor paradoxically marked by "<u>une systématisation
        des équivoques</u>."   Roustang devotes most of the book
        to analyzing Lacan's science of the real, and he
        emphasizes the "impossibility of the real" and its
        link to the stylistic strategies--the equivoca-
        tions--by which Lacan withheld the very possibility
        of "concluding" psychoanalytic discourse from his
        readers and listeners.

F395.   Safouan, Moustapha.   <u>Jacques Lacan et la question
        de la formation des analystes</u>.   Paris: Editions
        du Seuil, 1983.

        Discusses the training of the analyst and its
        relation to the institutional structures that moti-
        vate and inform that training.   Safouan traces the
        issues and variations in psychoanalytic institu-
        tions and training "before Lacan" and then de-
        scribes in detail the innovations introduced by
        Lacan and embodied in the Ecole freudienne de
        Paris.
        Translated by Claude Schneider in <u>Papers of the
        Freudian School of Melbourne</u> (1983/84):   155-221.

F396.   Schneiderman, Stuart.   <u>Jacques Lacan: The Death of
        an Intellectual Hero</u>.   Cambridge, Mass.:   Harvard
        University Press, 1983.   182 pages.

        Speculates on the role of death in psychoanalytic
        theory and practice, focussing on the death of
        Lacan and its impact on French psychoanalysis as
        well as on his own position as an analyst trained
        by Lacan.   Schneiderman recounts a number of anec-
        dotes about Lacan by way of explaining his peculiar
        prominence and the effect of his teaching, and he
        suggests a number of links between Lacan's theoret-
        ical positions and the institutional and personal
        controversies over his work.   See G505.

F397.   Schneiderman, Stuart, editor and translator.
        <u>Returning to Freud: Clinical Psychoanalysis in
        the School of Lacan</u>.   New Haven: Yale University
        Press, 1980.   263 pages.

Collects a number of case histories and essays by
Lacanian analysts exemplifying the issues and, to a
lesser extent, the concrete techniques associated
with Lacanian psychoanalysis. Includes a preface
and brief essay on Lacan's early work by Schneiderman and a rare transcript of an interview by
Lacan with a psychotic patient (E297). Also included are an essay on Lacan's case presentation
(G737), as well as other clinical essays on neurosis (L1997, L1998, L2007, L2108, L2143, L2328,
L2330, L2332); on psychosis (L1598, L2329, L2349);
and on perversion (L1563, L2109, L2457).

F398.   Scilicet. Founded 1968.

Devoted to publishing work by members of the
Ecole freudienne de Paris, the slogan of this
journal is "tu peux savoir ce qu'en pense l'Ecole
freudienne du Paris." The articles are published
unsigned, with the exception of Lacan's own texts.
All of the work published in Scilicet is directly
related to Lacan's work, but only selected items
(in addition to all items by Lacan) have been
listed in this bibliography. Published by Editions
du Seuil.

F399.   Sédat, Jacques, ed.   Retour à Lacan?. L'analyse au
        singulier. Paris: Librairie Arthème Fayard,
        1981. 282 pages.

Publishes for the first time a number of essays
on Lacan by different authors, most of which focus
on the tempestuous history of the Ecole freudienne
de Paris and the controversy surrounding its dissolution. The essays range from personal memoirs
and polemical attacks to theoretical analyses of
specific Lacanian concepts, though they all take
the institutional, the theoretical, or the clinical
dimension of psychoanalysis as their point of departure. (Note: these essays are not numbered as
separate items.)

Contents

Translated into Spanish by Irene Agoff, Col.
Psicoteca Serie Freudiana (Barcelona: Gedisa,
1982), 288 pages.

F400.   Seitter, Walter.   Jacques Lacan und.   Berlin:
Merve-Verlag, 1984.

F401.   Sichère, Bernard.   Le moment lacanien.   Figures.
Paris: Grasset, 1983.   210 pages.

Explores the meaning of Lacan's "intervention on
a general scene which is not only that of psychoanalysis, but which is at the same time that of
history as well, of our history, to the extent that
history itself has an unconscious" (p. 24).
Sichère claims that Lacan's theory of the subject
retrieves the radical character of Freud's work,
but he insists that this idea of the subject "in
general" is also the idea of a "certain historical
moment of subjectivity" and is closely linked with
the way discourse was rearranged in the late 1960s.
Sichère also argues, however, that Lacan's
tripartite apparatus--theory of the subject, theory
of speech (la parole), theory of the Law--main-
tained a radical heterogeneity with the moment of
its emergence, and in doing so became the sole
source for an "ethic of truth" that can oppose the
illusory "ethics of jouissance" that have dominated
utopian revolutionary schemes since that time.
Much of Sichère's book is devoted to tracing this
ethical and political dimension of Lacan's work
through a discussion of the relations among speech,
Law, and subjectivity, but his rhetorical focus is
a polemic against certain forms of French leftist
thinking that grew out of May '68 and adopted, if
briefly, the Maoist politics of the Cultural Revolution in China.   Excerpt reprinted in Infini 3
(1983):   78-86.   See G889.

F402.   Significante y sutura en el psicoanalisis.   Buenos
Aires: Siglo XXI Editores Argentina, 1973.   84
pages.

A collection of essays on psychoanalytic issues
related to Lacan's work.

F403.   Smith, Joseph H., and William Kerrigan. Inter-
        preting Lacan. Psychiatry and the Humanities,
        Volume 6. New Haven: Yale University Press,
        1983. 289 pages.

Contents

Analysis

Philosophy and Psychoanalytic Theory

Lacan in Use

    Kerrigan's "Introduction" provides a brief sketch
of Lacan's belated recognition by the English-
speaking world and describes the collected essays.
Smith's "Epilogue" describes three potential stum-
bling blocks in Lacan's work for new readers--his
concept of the ego, his use of a linguistic rather
than an economic point of view, and his concept of
reference--and proposes several points of consensus
between ego psychology and Lacan's thought.

F404.   Stanton, Martin. Outside the Dream: Lacan and
        French Styles of Psychoanalysis. London:
        Routledge and Kegan Paul, 1983. 131 pages.

Offers an impressionistic commentary on topics
and styles of discourse popular in French psychoanalysis associated with the work of Lacan.
Stanton discusses several changes in the institutional structure of psychoanalysis in France from
the early years of the IPA through the dissolution
of the Ecole freudienne de Paris (pp. 52-73), and
he focuses in particular on the place of psychoanalytic discourse and issues in the contemporary
social order.

F405.   stécriture.   Published by Littoral (F356).

Devoted to the problem of establishing texts for
Lacan's seminars, especially from the perspective
of theoretical issues regarding the written representations of oral speech.   This bulletin is intended as a corrective to the texts established by
Jacques-Alain Miller for Editions de Seuil.   For a
general description of its aims, see G902 and the
issue of Littoral on this problem, F357.

F406.   Teichmann, Gottfried.   Psychoanalyse und Sprache
        [Psychoanalysis and Language: From Saussure to
        Lacan].   Wurzburg: Koenigshausen and Neumann,
        1983.

Reviewed by H. Weiss and S. Stretz in Zeitschrift
für Klinische Psychologie Psychopathologie und
Psychotherapie 32 (1984):   366-68.

F407.   This, Bernard.   Le père: acte de naissance.
        Paris: Editions de Seuil, 1981.

Describes the birth of the Ecole de la Cause
freudienne.

F408.   Topique: revue freudienne.   Founded in 1969.

Official journal of Le Quatrième Groupe, which
was composed of Lacan's followers who became disillusioned with the Ecole Freudienne de Paris and
in 1969 split off to form their own group, which
became known as "Lacanians without Lacan."   They
opposed the "pass" and its distinction between
practicing analysts and "pure analysts," and they
vehemently criticized the institution of the
"Psychoanalytic Clinic" at Vincennes.

F409.   La transa.   Published by Littoral (F356).

Published as a bulletin under the aegis of
Littoral, La transa is devoted to publishing and
critiquing translations of Freud's work.

F410.   <u>Transitions</u> (Paris) 8 (1981).   <u>Hommage à Jacques</u>
        <u>Lacan</u>.

F411.   <u>Tribune</u> 1 (1985).   <u>L'institution en question</u>.
        Cartels Constituants de l'Analyse Freudienne.

        Traces the evolution of psychoanalytic institu-
        tions in France since the dissolution of the Ecole
        freudienne de Paris in 1980.   This issue includes
        discussions of the dissolution and subsequent
        events by A. Rondepierre, J. Nassif, D. Saadoun,
        and C. Dumézil; a synoptic table of groups formed
        during and after the dissolution; descriptions of
        journals devoted to psychoanalysis in France; and a
        collection of reprinted by-laws, constitutions,
        statements of purpose, etc. drawn up by various
        psychoanalytic associations, groups, and schools
        during the early 1980s.   Subsequent issues continue
        this descriptive survey and bring it up to date.

F412.   Turkle, Sherry.   <u>Psychoanalytic Politics: Freud's</u>
        <u>French Revolution</u>.   New York: Basic Books, 1978.

        Describes the impact of psychoanalytic theory and
        practice on university education and everyday life
        in France, especially as that theory has been in-
        fluenced by the work of Lacan.   Turkle focuses on
        the controversies surrounding Lacan since his elec-
        tion as president of the Société psychanalytique de
        Paris in 1953, and she explains those controversies
        in terms of the theoretical issues at stake and
        "the more overtly political concerns that separated
        the various psychoanalytic societies that struggled
        for dominance of the French intellectual scene"
        after Lacan split with the SPP.   (See the biograph-
        ical sketch for this bibliography and F379.)
        Turkle identifies the short session and, later,
        "<u>la passe</u>" as the central issues at stake in
        Lacan's conflicts with the psychoanalytic estab-
        lishment.   Both policies undermined the possibility
        of institutional supervision in the practice of
        analysis and the training of new analysts, Turkle
        argues.   As a result, Lacan's policies opened up
        what Turkle calls a "psychoanalytic protestantism"
        that raises a central and perennial conflict within
        psychoanalysis itself.   On the one hand, psycho-
        analysis carried a subversive thrust within it from
        the beginning, with its emphasis on the unconscious
        and on forces beyond the realm of rational order
        and control.   Yet, on the other hand, psycho-
        analysts always emphasized the necessity of insti-
        tutional governance, allegiance to doctrine, and
        the role of centralized authority in the training
        of analysts and the dissemination of theoretical
        concepts.   Lacan himself lived this paradox, Turkle

concludes, since he insisted on the utter individuality of his discourse and at the same time insisted on playing the role of an absolute Master
who dominated the societies under his control as
well as the students and colleagues who worked with
him.
   Although Turkle focuses on Lacan's career, her
book also discusses the broader topic of psychoanalysis as a social phenomenon in France today.
She explores the connections among psychoanalysis
as a theoretical project, as an influence on radical politics (especially after May 1968), and as
the crucial factor that determines how people
conceive of themselves and the world around them.
Her point that "existentialists' cafes have given
way to the psychoanalysts' couches" marks an important shift in the intellectual discourse of
France, one that has changed not only the vocabulary used by a wide range of intellectuals but also
the topics that they discuss. More generally,
Turkle's survey of the internal politics of psychoanalytic movements in France constitutes a precise
if narrow history of the institutional structure of
medical training and university education in
France. For a broader and more de-tailed history
of psychoanalysis in France since the nineteenth
century, see F393.
   Reprint Cambridge, Mass.: MIT Press paperback
edition 1981. Based on I1003.

F413.   Vallejo, Américo. Topologia de Jacques Lacan.
        Buenos Aires: Helguero Editores, 1979.

F414.   Vallejo, Américo. Vocabulario Lacaniano. Buenos
        Aires: Helguero Editores, 1980. 180 pages.

F415.   Vapperlau, Jean Michel. Essais: le groupe
        fondamentale du noeud. Topologie en extension.
        Paris: Point Hors Ligne, 1985.

        Discusses Lacan's use of mathematical formulas
        and topology.

F416.   Verdiglione, Armando. Psychanalyse et sémiotique.
        Col. 10/18. Colloquium at Milan, May 1974.
        Paris: Union generale d'éditions, 1975. 309
        pages.

        Contains a number of articles by various authors
        that focus on implications of Lacan's theory of the
        signifier in psychoanalytic discourse. Not all of
        the articles focus on Lacan's work itself, but all
        assume the importance of issues and topics derived
        from Lacan, and most recognize his influence
        explicitly.

F417.   Vivien, C.   Question au docteur Lacan.   Vandoevre,
        1968.

        Listed in Biblio: Catalogue des ouvrages parus
        en langue française . . .   (Paris: Hachette,
        1967).

F418.   Weber, Samuel.   Rückkher zu Freud: Jacques Lacans
        Ent-stellung der Psychoanalyse.   Frankfurt/
        Berlin/Wien, 1978.   144 pages.

        A general though sophisticated introduction to
        Lacan that appeared at a time when Lacan's work was
        not well known among German readers.   See G781.

F419.   Weyergans, François.   Le pitre.   Paris: Gallimard,
        1973.

        Portrays the exploits of a central character who
        is clearly Lacan.

F420.   Wilden, Anthony.   The Language of the Self.   With
        Jacques Lacan, The Function of Language in
        Psychoanalysis.   Translated with Notes and
        Commentary by Anthony Wilden.   Baltimore: The
        Johns Hopkins University Press, 1968.

        Translates C58 into English for the first time,
        with an extensive set of notes and a long essay by
        Wilden, "Lacan and the Discourse of the Other" (pp.
        159-311).   The "Translator's Notes" (pp. 89-156)
        trace the philosophical, linguistic, and literary
        sources of Lacan's essay; establish specific con-
        nections with Freud's terms; and refer readers to
        similar points in other works by Lacan, often
        translating long passages from essays that were
        little known outside of France.
        This book began Lacan's influence among intel-
        lectuals in the United States and remains an
        excellent introduction to the philosophical di-
        mensions of his work.   It generated considerable
        controversy when it appeared, however, because it
        was published under Wilden's name instead of
        Lacan's.   It was later re-issued as a book by
        Lacan, with apparatus by Wilden, under the title of
        Speech and Language in Psychoanalysis (Baltimore:
        Johns Hopkins University Press, 1981), 338 pages.
        An earlier edition was issued by Dell (New York,
        1975).

F421.   Wilden, Anthony.   System and Structure: Essays in
        Communication and Exchange.   London: Tavistock
        Publications, 1972.   540 pages.

Describes many fundamental tenets of Lacan's work
through the 1960s, and comments more specifically
on several issues raised by Lacan that are particularly important for the theories of communication
and social interaction proposed by Gregory Bateson
and Réné Girard.   Several chapters are devoted to
Lacan's work:

Chapter One, ""The Symbolic, the Imaginary, and
the Real: Lacan, Lévi-Strauss, and Freud," provides a general overview of Lacan's work that
follows F420 but dwells at more length on Lacan's
debt to Lévy-Strauss and the "communicational
content" of Lacan's work (pp. 1-10).

Chapter Two, "Metaphor and Metonymy: Freud's
Semiotic Model of Condensation and Displacement,"
obviously owes a great deal to Lacan's own reading
of Freud's terms in the light of rhetorical functions, as Wilden points out (p. 47ff.), though
Wilden claims that much of Lacan's argument is
untenable from "a critical semiotic perspective"
(pp. 31-62).

Chapter Nine, "Nature and Culture: The Emergence
of Symbolic and Imaginary Exchange," invokes
Lacan's distinction between the symbolic and the
imaginary to propose an alternative model of
structural exchange and of relations among structures (pp. 230-277).   (This chapter is followed by
an appendix written by Gerald Hall, "The Logical
Typing of the Symbolic, the Imaginary, and the
Real" [see G629]).

Chapter Ten, "Critique of Phallocentrism,"
focuses on Wilden's repeated charge that Lacan's
theory is culture-bound by its phallocentric insistence on the Law of the Father and the determinant power of the Oedipal complex.   Wilden
comments at length on Lacan's theory of the phallus
and his perpetuation of the myth that a "lack" is
the essential aspect of the symbolic position of
"woman," and he illustrates the phallocentric limi-
tations of psychoanalysis with an extended discussion of Schreber's case as analyzed by both Freud
and Lacan.   "Schreber's philosophy is an ethical
commentary on the organization of aggressivity in
nineteenth-century society," Wilden says, and he
claims that Schreber "deserves a place among the
great mystics and the great utopian socialist
philosophers" (pp. 278-301).

Chapter Sixteen, "Linguistics and Semiotics: The
Unconscious Structured Like a Language," systematically explores the sources of Lacan's famous
proclamation in Freud's work (pp. 445-461).

Chapter Seventeen, "The Ideology of Opposition
and Identity: Critique of Lacan's Theory of the
Mirror-Stage in Childhood," uses Lacan's theory of
the mirror stage to explore the process of self-

identity as it is determined by ideological constraints.   The mirror stage is "an <u>alienation</u> of
the subject," Wilden argues (p. 465), and he
sprinkles his arguments with allusions to several
works by and about oppressed minorities, including
Frantz Fanon's <u>Wretched of the Earth</u> (pp. 462-488).

F422.   <u>Der Wunderblock</u> [<u>The Mystic Writing Pad</u>].

A German journal of psychoanalysis oriented
toward Lacan's work.   For a brief discussion of its
importance, see G781.

F423.   <u>Der Wunderblock</u>. <u>Lacan lesen</u>. Collected papers
from a symposium in Berlin, April 1978.   Edited
by Norbert Haas.   Berlin: Verlag Der Wunderblock, 1978.   139 pages.

Contents

Norbert Haas, "Vorwort"...........................5
Manfred Frank, "Das 'wahre Subjekt' und sein
Doppel: Jacques Lacans Hermeneutik".............12
Franz Kaltenbeck, "Wahrheit als Ursache".........38
Norbert Haas, "Was heisst Lacan ubersetzen?".....49
Lutz Michael Mai, "Psychoanalyse und Institution
    am Beispiel der 'Kassenanalyse'"...............59
Peter Muller, "Die genehmigte Analyse und der
    erlaubte Genuss"...............................69
Jutta Prasse, "Bericht: Zur Lacan-Rezeption
    in Italien"....................................83

Also includes transcripts of discussions and
comments by these authors and others attending the
conference.

F424.   <u>Yale French Studies</u> 48 (1972). <u>French Freud:</u>
<u>Structural Studies in Psychoanalysis</u>. Edited by
Jeffrey Mehlman.   202 pages.

Contents

Jeffrey Mehlman, "French Freud"...................5
Jeffrey Mehlman, "The 'Floating Signifier':
    From Lévi-Strauss to Lacan" (G728).............10
Jacques Lacan, "Seminar on 'The Purloined
    Letter'" (C69)................................39
Jacques Derrida, "Freud and the Scene of
    Writing".......................................74
Jean Laplanche and Serge Leclaire, "The Uncon-
    scious: A Psychoanalytic Study" (G681).......118
Appendices (definitions of key terms
    from K1239)...................................179

Mehlman's introductory essay briefly describes

the implications of Lacan's emphasis on the function of repression in Freud's work, and of the substitution of language for biology in the theoretical models of contemporary French psychoanalysis.

Section G

Secondary Essays

G425. Akoun, André. "Le veritable approt de Lacan."
       Psychologie 120 (1980): 30.

G426. Alexandre, Laurent. "Psychanalyse et pratique
       scientifique (questions à propos d'un Ecrit de
       Jacques Lacan)." Lénine et la pratique scien-
       tifique. Actes du Colloque d'Orsay. Edited by
       the Centre d'études et de recherches marxistes
       (C.E.R.M.). Paris: Editions sociales, 1974.
       650 pages.

G427. Allouch, Jean. "De la translittération en psych-
       analyse." META: Journal des traducteurs 27, no.
       1 (1982): 77-86.

G428. Allouch, Jean. "Enfants du parladit." F327, pp.
       97-113.

       Discusses Lacan's influence on analytic practice
       in general as the source of a paradigm shift in
       psychoanalysis. See G430.

G429. Allouch, Jean. "Freud déplacé." F358, pp. 5-15.

       Claims that Lacan's distinctions among the real,
       symbolic, and imaginary registers introduced a new
       paradigm into psychoanalysis, and discusses the im-
       plications of that paradigmatic shift in the light
       of Thomas Kuhn's Structure of Scientific Revolu-
       tions.

G430. Allouch, Jean. "Lacan censuré, ou quand une
       imprécision s'ajoute à une autre imprécision,
       puis à une autre encore . . . ." Littoral 13
       (1984): 109-20.

       Claims that the texts of Lacan's seminars es-
       tablished by Jacques-Alain Miller are inaccurate,

and supports this claim with a lengthy comparison
among (1) the official text of the seminar from 16
March 1955 as established by Miller (see B13); (2)
the stenographer's transcript of that session; and
(3) the text that Allouch would propose as an alternative to Miller's. Allouch argues that
Miller's minor and, at times, major departures from
the stenographer's transcript add up to a significant theoretical distortion of Lacan's teaching.
Discussing the seminars presumably approved by
Lacan and published while he was alive, Allouch
suggests that Lacan deliberately refused to correct
Miller's mistakes in order to underscore the role
of the editor in establishing the texts. See F357.

G431.   Allouch, Jean.   "Les trois petits points du 'retour
        à . . . ." Littoral 9 (1983):   39-78.

    Analyzes the discursive structure of Lacan's
relation to Freud from the perspective of
Foucault's work, claiming that this "return" went
through three successive versions: mythic, discursive, and topological (p. 39). Allouch claims
that Lacan's notion of the "four discourses" and
his specialized use of the term "discourse" stems
from the influence of Foucault's notion of discourse as proposed in "What is an Author."

G432.   Althusser, Louis.   "La découverte du docteur
        Freud." Written in 1977 and distributed for the
        symposium on the unconscious at Tbilissi, 1979.
        Dialogue franco-soviétique sur la psychanalyse.
        Edited by Léon Chertok. Private publication,
        1984. Pp. 81-97.

    Argues that Freud never succeeded in developing a
theory of the unconscious, and claims that the
possibility of a scientific theory of the unconscious still does not exist today, despite Lacan's
effort to elaborate his great hypothesis that "the
unconscious is structured like a language." Instead of a scientific theory, Althusser says that
Lacan has produced "a fantastic philosophy of
psychoanalysis" and that he has lured many intellectuals after him because he "jouait ainsi sur
deux tableaux," speaking to philosophers as a
Master of psychoanalysis and to psychoanalysts as a
Master of philosophical knowledge. He has duped
the whole world, Althusser remarks, but he has also
duped himself.
    (Althusser also observes that Lacan's famous dic-
tum "a letter always arrives at its destination"
depends on a philosophy of destiny (destin) rather
than destination, and he proposes a materialist
version of Lacan's claim: "it happens that a let-

ter does not arrive at its destination" ("<u>il arrive
qu'une lettre n'arrive pas à destination</u>").
        For Althusser's earlier, more sympathetic reading
of Lacan, see G433. For a discussion of Althusser's relation to Lacan, see G508, G702, and G855.

G433.   Althusser, Louis. "Freud et Lacan." <u>La nouvelle
         critique</u> 161/162 (1964/65): 88-108.

        Insists on the importance of psychoanalysis for
Marxists, and claims that Lacan's work has brought
the specificity of Freud's discovery within reach
for the first time. Althusser discusses the importance of linguistics in Lacan's attempt to
establish psychoanalysis as a science, and he
claims that the most original aspect of Lacan's
work is his demonstration that the passage from the
biological to the human takes place through the
"Law of Order, the law I shall call the Law of
Culture, and that this Law of Order is confounded
in its <u>formal</u> essence with the order of language."
Althusser goes on to explain Lacan's distinction
between the symbolic and the imaginary and the
importance of the Oedipal phase to a transition
from one register to another, and he concludes with
an account of the "ideological misrecognition"
inherent in the concept of the ego.
        In a letter to the translator quoted in the
introduction to the reprinted translation in <u>Lenin
and Philosophy</u> (see below), Althusser explained how
psychoanalysis had been officially denounced as a
"reactionary ideology" by the Communist Party in
the 1950s. He warned readers that this polemical
context accounts for the particular shape of his
essay, which first appeared in the journal of the
French Communist Party. Claiming that some "corrections" were now necessary upon its translation
in 1969, Althusser went on to note that the essay
points toward a conclusion that is itself precluded
by theoretical formations of Lacan's own work: "no
theory of psycho-analysis can be produced without
basing it on historical materialism (on which the
theory of the formations of familial ideology
[i.e., the Oedipal complex] depends, in the last
instance)."
        Reprinted in Althusser, <u>Positions, 1964-1975</u>
(Paris: Editions Sociales, 1976), pp. 9-34.
Translated in <u>New Left Review</u> (1969), reprinted in
Althusser, <u>Lenin and Philosophy</u> (New York: Monthly
Review Press, 1971), pp. 189-219. Translated into
Italian in <u>Aut Aut</u> 141 (1974): 71-90. Translated
into Spanish by Muria Garreta in <u>Freud y Lacan</u>,
revised, with notes by Ramon Garcia, Cuadernos
Anagrama 5 (Barcelona: Ed. Anagrama, 1970). This
book also includes a partial translation of B24.

Translated into German by Hanns-Henning Ritter and
Herbert Nagel, Internationale Marxistische Diskus-
sion 10 (Berlin: Merve-Verlag, 1970), 41 pages.

G434.   Ames, Sanford S.   "Killer Bees: An Ontology in
         Abeyance." <u>Visible Language</u> 14, no. 3 (1980):
         241-49.

         Describes Lacan's return to Freud as a search for
         Freud's "vision of the radical complexity of being
         and its scattering in the material of language" (p.
         241), and discusses connections among <u>jouissance</u>,
         language, and ontology.

G435.   "L'an dernier, Lacan avait dissous son école."
         <u>Libération</u> 11 September 1981, p. 2.

         Briefly recounts the splits within Lacanian
         psychoanalytic associations since 1953.   See 354.

G436.   Ansaldi, J.   ["The Concept of Law in the Theology
         of Martin Luther, and in Modern French Psycho-
         Analysis" (French).] <u>Revue d'histoire et de
         philosophie religieuses</u> 63, no. 1/2 (1983):   143-
         54.

G437.   Ansaldi, J.   ["Jacques Lacan and the Question of
         Analytic Formation" (French).] <u>Etudes théolo-
         giques et réligieuses</u> 58 (1983):   577-78.

G438.   Anzieu, Didier.   "Contre [Lacan]:   une doctrine
         hérétique." <u>La quinzaine littéraire</u>, 15-31
         January 1967, pp. 14-15.

         Describes Lacan's work as the "new ideology" and
         the "new decomposition of psychoanalysis." Anzieu
         claims that psychoanalysts "founder in heresy" each
         time they depart from the specifics of psycho-
         analytic experience, which are found in the Oedipus
         complex, and embrace another model--in Lacan's
         case, that of topology and symbolic logic. Anzieu
         compares Lacan to other "dissidents" and claims
         that the leading thread of the Lacanian heresy is
         an optico-geometric illusion, the mirror stage.   In
         addition, Anzieu flatly asserts "the unconscious is
         not language" (p. 15), a misleading allusion to
         Lacan's claim that the unconscious is <u>structured
         like</u> a language. Published as part of a debate
         with G731.

G439.   Aparcio, Sol, Carmen Gallano, and Marie-Hélène
         Delanoé.   "La langue en cause: revue psych-
         analytique d'Amérique latine." <u>L'âne</u> 3 (1981):
         54.

Describes journals devoted to psychoanalysis and Lacan in Latin America, especially those centered in Buenos Aires.   Continued in L'âne 4 (1982):   p. 26, which focuses on Venezuela.

G440.   Arnoux, Daniele.   "Sur la transcription."   F357, pp. 79-84.

Argues that any effort to render Lacan's spoken word into writing conflates the roles of listening and writing into "un au(di)teur" who can only produce a critique of the seminars rather than an objective report.   Arnoux describes several exemplary difficulties in transcriptions of the recorded seminars and compares several different versions of Lacan's commentary on Plato's Symposium to suggest how a more useful text might be established that would reflect Lacan's own speech more faithfully.
Arnoux is part of a group associated with the bulletin stécriture (F405), which is devoted to producing better texts of the seminars than those now available.   Nevertheless, Arnoux admits the paradoxical situation of Lacan's work, which lies somewhere between speaking and writing (as Lacan himself described it in C71), and he concludes that any transcript of Lacan's speech will involve a significant amount of interpretation as well as transcription.   Followed by J1023.

G441.   Arrive, Michel.   "Signifiant saussurien et signifiant lacanien."   Langages 77 (1985):   105-116.

G442.   Aubert, J.   Discussion of E273.   Analytica 4 (Supplement to Ornicar? 9) (1977):   3-15.

G443.   Aubry, Jenny.   "Où les chemins divergent." Ornicar? 9 (1977):   41-73.

Describes the theoretical issues and institutional politics behind the major controversies of Lacan's career, with descriptions of the more important documents associated with each occasion.

G444.   August, Bertrand.   "The Défilement Into the Look . . . ."   Camera Obscura 2 (1977):   92-103.

Cites B22 on the instant when the regard or gaze turns into the fascinum, which Lacan describes as "the moment of the look which ends a gesture . . . the anti-life function, the anti-movement . . . where the look exercises its power directly" (B22, pp. 107ff.).

G445.   Avni, Ora.   "Ils courent, ils courent les ferret:

Mauss, Lacan et <u>Les trois mousquetaires</u>."
<u>Poétique</u> 62 (1985):   215-35.

Discusses Mauss's "<u>Essais sur le don</u>" (<u>L'année
sociologique</u> n.s. 1 [1923-24]) and C69 as they portray the moment when the object is made into a
sign, and integrates this moment into "the semantic
of the subject" (p. 216).   Translated as "The Semiotics of Transactions: Mauss, Lacan, and <u>The
Three Musketeers</u>," <u>MLN</u> 100 (1985):   728-57.

G446.   Avtonomova, N. S.   "Psikhoanaliticekaja koncepcija
         zaka lakana." [Psychoanalytical Concepts of
         Jacques Lacan.] <u>Voprosy filosofii</u> 11 (1973):
         143-50.

Praises Lacan's work as a departure from the
biological grounding of Freud's work, and claims
that Lacan's emphasis on language establishes the
social context of psychoanalysis.   For a description of this essay and other papers presented at a
symposium on Lacan's work in the Soviet Union, see
L1550 and G500.

G447.   B., R. P.   "Lacan fait le mort . . . "   F354, p. 2.

Observes that "<u>Il n'y a pas de mort sans
phrases</u>," and notes that this is especially true in
the case of such a controversial figure as Lacan.
The author reflects briefly on the importance that
death had for Lacan as a theoretical and analytic
concept, and recalls Lacan's remark to his followers, "<u>S'il arrive que je m'en aille, dites-vous
que c'est afin d'être Autre enfin</u>" ("If I should
ever leave you, say that it is in order to be Other
at last").

G***.   Backès, Catherine.   "Lacan, ou le 'porte-parole.'"
         <u>Critique</u> 249 (1968):   136-61.

Proposes a "preliminary" reading of the <u>Ecrits</u>
that will describe the central tenets of Lacan's
works, such as the ex-centricity of the subject and
the relation between truth and ethics in analytic
discourse.   For other works by this author, see
Catherine (Backès) Clément.

G448.   Baliteau, Catherine.   "La fin d'une parade miso-
         gyne: la psychanalyse lacanienne." <u>Les temps
         modernes</u> 348 (1975):   1933-53.

Claims that Lacanian psychoanalysis is the latest
avatar of western metaphysics, and that it main-
tains the essentially dualistic ethic of that metaphysics in which the moral criteria of judgment pit

an innocent father against a guilty mother.
Baliteau describes what she sees as a tendency
towards transcendence and a-historical abstraction
in Lacan's work that marks it as part of western
metaphysics, and she claims that the symbolic has
replaced the "thing-in-itself" or "the Idea," just
as the phallus has replaced the Prime Mover. Thus,
Baliteau concludes, a dualism remains at the heart
of Lacan's system in which woman is always situated
on the bad side (p. 1952). The real problem,
Baliteau says, is that so many others have accepted
the phallic referent (she names Dolto and Mannoni
as examples), and Baliteau attributes this acceptance to a "resistance to resistance" that turns
Lacan's followers into his collaborators.

G449.   Bär, E. S.   "The Language of the Unconscious
        According to Jacques Lacan." Semiotica 3 (1971):
        241-68.

        Summarizes his dissertation (I988), which focuses
        on the "semiotically interesting concepts" in
        Lacan's work, and discusses Lacan's comments on the
        Signorelli incident reported by Freud. Bär
        concludes that Lacan's linguistic model of uncon-
        scious processes needs considerable clarification
        if it is to find support in clinical experience,
        and he complains that Lacan does not consistently
        distinguish between thought and language and so
        occasionally leaves his theoretical argument vague.

G450.   Bär, Eugene.   "Understanding Lacan." Psycho-
        analysis and Contemporary Thought 3 (1974):   473-
        544.

        Focuses on the links between conscious and un-
        conscious discourses that are derived from psycho-
        analytic interpretations based on several issues in
        Lacan's work: the importance of Saussure; the
        Other; distinctions among need, desire and demand;
        the relation between metaphor and metonymy; fore-
        closure; the role of the analyst according to
        Lacan; and the problematic topic of the "cure."
        Bär claims, however, that Lacan's assertions about
        the linguistic structure of the unconscious have
        not yet been supported by clinical evidence, and he
        calls for further studies on this topic.

G451.   Barande, Ilse, and Robert Barande.   ["Jacques
        Lacan"]. Histoire de la psychanalyse en France.
        Toulouse: Edouard Privat, 1975. 181 pages.

        Surveys the major figures, movements, and issues
        in the evolution of psychoanalysis in France, and
        lists and describes the reviews, collections, and

organizations active through 1975.   The chapter on
Lacan (pp. 96-104) stresses the importance of the
mirror stage, his distinctions among the real,
imaginary, and the symbolic, and his emphasis on
the role of language in psychoanalytic experience.
The authors briefly describe critiques of Lacan by
C. Steion, A. Green, and J. Laplanche, and they
note the enduring controversy surrounding Lacan's
impact on the psychoanalytic scene in France.
Intended for general readers, much of this book
originally appeared in L'encyclopédie allemande
(Munich: Kindler).

G452.   Barrat, Robert.   "Freud est grand et Lacan est son
         prophète."   Paris-Match, 9 March 1974, pp. 3-4,
         25.

         Comments on Lacan's performance on television
         (see A3) and praises his early teaching style,
         which Barrat claims was quite different before
         Lacan's admirers and his fame led him to indulge
         his idiosyncrasies.

G453.   Bassin, F. V., and A. E. Serozija.   "Les idées de
         Jacques Lacan sauveront-elles la psychanalyse?
         Lettre ouverte à Serge Leclaire."   Revue de
         médecine psychosomatique 2 (1980):   173-89.

         Criticizes Leclaire's claim in G700 that psycho-
         analysis is the single road to man's freedom.   For
         a description of this essay and other essays that
         were presented during the conference in the Soviet
         Union at which Leclaire presented G700, see L1550
         and G500.   Bassin and Serozija also attacked
         Leclaire in G804.

G454.   Bataille, Laurence.   "D'une pratique."   F327, pp.
         7-30.

         Notes Freud's insistence that there is no "prac-
         tice" without a "theory," not even our sexual
         practices, and goes on to discuss the way Lacanian
         theory has changed his practice as a psychoanalyst.

G455.   Bauer, Jean-Pierre.   "Un itinéraire."   F327, pp.
         31-52.

         Notes the disjunction between psychoanalytic
         theory, which proposes general principles for
         analytic work, and the specific singularity of
         actual analyses, but goes on to discuss the ways
         his own techniques have been influenced by Lacan's
         teachings.

G456.   Bellasi, Pietro.   "L'Edipo depo Edipo: la perdita

e la morte nel secondo seminaro di Lacan." F307,
pp. 155-77.

G457. Benvenuto, Sergio. "Il gioco impari: a proposito
dell'epistemologia lacaniana." F307, pp. 137-54.

G458. Benvenuto, Sergio. "Note a 'Della psicosi paranoica' di Jacques Lacan." Aut-Aut 182/183
(1981): 127-36.

G459. Bertherat, Yves. "Freud avec Lacan ou la science
avec le psychanalyste." Esprit 12 (1967): 979-
1003.

G460. Besnier, Jean-Michel. "Lacan dans le siècle."
Esprit 5 (1984): 57-58.

Notes the inevitable dependence of psychoanalysis
on philosophy, especially as established by F345.

G461. Binasco, Mario. "Una questione di reale: il
bambino in psicoanalisi." F307, pp. 256-78.

G462. Bird, John. "Jacques Lacan--the French Freud?"
Radical Philosophy 30 (1982): 7-14.

Suggests that Lacan's reading of Freud is ec-
centric at best, and that what is really new in
Lacan's work is radically non-Freudian. Bird
attempts to outline basic aspects of Lacan's arguments regarding language, science, the Oedipal
complex, and the cure, and he claims that lack of
empirical data makes it difficult to evaluate
Lacan's assertions. Bird also describes Lacan's
"derealisation of Freud" as tainted by an idealism
that is also identifiable in Althusser, and he says
that Lacan "always denies the significance of
material factors and the somatic, as well as the
biological and adaptationist dimensions that were
always present in Freud's work (p. 12).
For responses to Bird see J1134 and J1115.

G463. Bishop, P. E. "Brecht, Hegel, Lacan: Brecht's
Theory of Gest and the Problem of the Subject."
Studies in Twentieth-Century Literature 10
(1986): 267-88.

G464. Blajan-Marcus, S. "Le 'bonhomme' Lacan." K1335,
pp. 11-14.

G465. Bleikasten, André. "Fathers in Faulkner." F318,
pp. 115-46.

Notes the central role that fathers play in many
of Faulkner's novels, but argues that the issue of

the father in Faulkner's fictions seldom hinges on
the father as a person or even as an archetypal
progenitor. Instead, Faulkner often evokes the
father as defined in Lacan's work: a "complex
function, both private and public, a symbolic
agency" that eludes the more traditional roles
associated with specific characters (p. 115).
Bleikasten then goes on to study the symbolic
function of the father in several of Faulkner's
more famous novels.

G466. Blévis, Jean-Jacques. "A l'impossible, chacun est
       tenu." Patio 1 (1983): 20-31.

       Notes that many analysts have denounced the ef-
       fect Lacan had on the members of his school, who
       were caught up in an "amour du Maître" that is
       really an "amour de la non-pensée." Blévis claims
       nevertheless that Lacan has opened up a new path of
       analysis for analysts in the 1970s that is espe-
       cially important in understanding the impact of the
       real in psychoanalysis (p. 23). He also observes
       that Freud's "wit" is one of the forms that Lacan
       called "la jouissance phallique," and that for
       Lacan it is the name-of-the-father that permits the
       imbrication of the worlds of the death drive and
       the sex drive, a point that makes it possible to
       understand some types of trauma which cannot be
       identified simply as sexual trauma (p. 30).

G467. Bolz, Norbert W. "Tod des Subjekts." Zeitschrift
       für Philosophische Forschung 36 (1982): 444-452.

G468. Bonato, B. ["Between Desire and Giving: A Note on
       Lacan and Levinas"]. Aut-Aut 209 (1985): 237-
       53.

G469. Bonato, Beatrice. "L'immagine, la parola, la
       morte: ipotesi di un dialogo tra Lacan e
       Heidegger" ["Imagery, the Spoken Word, and Death:
       The Hypothesis of a Dialogue Between Lacan and
       Heidegger"]. Aut-Aut 202/203 (1984): 57-85.

G470. Bonitzer, Pascal. "Le cinéma et la théorie
       lacanienne du regard." Libération, 11 September
       1981, p. 6.

       Claims that no cinematic theory today can ignore
       Lacan's theory of the gaze or look (le regard), and
       cites a number of examples of Lacanian film theory,
       such as G789, Baudry's essays in Cinétique and the
       special issue of Communications on "Cinéma et
       psychanalyse," and K1270. See F354.

G471. Bottiroli, Giovanni. "Strutturalismo e strategia

in Jacques Lacan: Un'interpretazione della
'Lettera rubata.'" F307, pp. 95-116.

G***.   Bouraux-Hartemann, Michelle. "Le mouvement de
Serge Antoinette Lacan." See F399.

G472.   Boutonier, Juliette. "A propos du 'Probléme de la
psychogénèse des névroses et des psychoses.'"
L'évolution psychiatrique (1951): 355-63.

Comments on the articles collected with C49 in
the book Problème de la psychogénèse, charac-
terizing Lacan's contribution as an essentially
phenomenological approach to the importance of
language in psychoanalysis. (Other items by this
author published under the name "Favez-Boutonier.")

G473.   Bowie, Malcolm. "Jacques Lacan." K1340, pp. 116-
63.

Describes Lacan's return to Freud as an effort to
"keep on thinking the intolerable Freudian
thought," which was the discovery of the unconscious (p. 120), and claims Lacan's work falls
somewhere between complete assent to and dissent
from Freud's texts.

G474.   Boyer, Philippe. "Le séminaire." Libération, 11
September 1981, p. 6.

Briefly describes the three stages of Lacan's
career manifested by changes in the settings and
audiences for the seminars. In the 1950s and early
1960s, the seminars focussed on technical questions
mainly of interest to psychoanalysts and psychiatrists, and they were delivered at Sainte Anne's
Hospital. In the later 1960s, Lacan split from the
Société française de psychanalyse to found the
Ecole freudienne, and he moved the seminars to the
Ecole Normale, where his audience broadened to include philosophers and, most notably, the Marxist
Louis Althusser (see G433). The years following
the 1960s through 1980 included dissension within
the Ecole freudienne, the founding of the Quatrième
Groupe, and the move to the Faculté de droit, where
Lacan began developing the mathemes and topographical knots that titillated and mystified the
Parisian intelligentsia. Boyer observes that the
early meetings were genuine seminars where others
were encouraged to speak, but the later meetings
took on an air of religious ceremony where few were
willing to interrupt the voice of the oracle in
full flight. See F354.

G475.   Brenkman, John. "The Other and the One: Psycho-

analysis, Reading, and <u>The Symposium</u>."   K1356,
pp. 396-456.

Argues that philosophical idealism depends on the
same masterful "subject supposed to know" that
Socrates tries to be in <u>The Symposium</u>, but
Alcibiades' challenge to that authority renders
such a role impossible because it undermines the
transference that is its condition of possibility.
Much of Brenkman's analysis depends on Lacan's
notion of the lack at the heart of desire, which is
discussed in detail on pp. 415-24.

G476.   Breton, Stanislas. "Jesus and Lacan."   <u>Psych-
        analystes</u> 14 (1984): p. 75 ff.

G477.   Breulet, Michel "Le médecin devant la mort."
        <u>Feuillets psychiatriques de Liège</u> 13 (1980):
        399-406.

G478.   Brisman, Susan Hawk, and Leslie Brisman.   "Lies
        Against Solitude: Symbolic, Imaginary, and
        Real." K1331, pp. 29-65.

G479.   Britton, Andrew. "The Ideology of <u>Screen</u>." <u>Movie</u>
        26 (1978/79): 2-28.

Analyzes the theoretical sources and ideological
orientation of <u>Screen</u>, focussing on the influence
of Althusser, Lacan, and Barthes. Britton attacks
the "posture or resigned religiosity of Lacanian-
ism" that tries to turn Freud into a coherent, radical theory, and he claims that what emerges from
Lacan's work is "a cunning mixture of romantic
anthropology, psychoanalytic revisionism, mysticism, self-advertisement, [and] second-hand
existentialism . . . so ostentatiously spurious as
almost to <u>invite</u> refutation" (p. 9). See especially pp. 8-18.

G480.   Broca, R. ["Freud, Marx, Zola (Lacan and
        <u>Germinal</u>)" (French).] <u>Europe: revue littéraire
        mensuelle</u> 678 (1985): 75-81.

G481.   Brousse-Delanoé, Marie-Hélène. "La psychanalyse en
        miroir." <u>Esprit</u> 62 (1982): 122-36.

Describes in detail Lacan's observations on the
function of the body in relation to the image, the
real, and language. When Lacan says there is no
sexual relation, Brousse-Delanoé argues, he means
that there is no access to the Other which does
not pass through the <u>semblant</u>, through discourse,
and that there is no other access to the body.
This is the truth that psychoanalysis can bring to

the body, Brousse-Delanoé claims: "To be man, one
gives up the harmonious corporeality of the animal
. . . for the body of disorder of the human individual, shot through with the historical arbitrariness of la langue" (p. 136).

G482.   Bruss, Neal H.   "Lacan and Literature: Imaginary
         Objects and Social Order." The Massachusetts
         Review 22, no. 1 (1981):   62-92.

         Claims that Freud does not offer a firm ground
         for reading literary works that do not deal with
         "abnormality," and argues that a definition of
         human experience based on Lacan's work would pro-
         vide a more useful point of departure for a general
         literary criticism (p. 64).   Bruss says that the
         categories of the real, the symbolic, and the
         imaginary can be applied to the analysis of lit-
         erary content but not literary stylistics, and he
         claims that Western literature depicts "a decline
         of the Symbolic, a retreat into the Imaginary,"
         which is the reverse of human maturation (p. 70).
         Bruss also offers a brief sketch of the history of
         Western literature to support that claim, and he
         concludes with the hope that Lacan's three cate-
         gories can help us face "the crisis of a prefigura-
         tive world" (p. 92).

G483.   Bruss, Neal H.   "Re-stirring the Waters, or the
         Voice that Sees the World as Patients." The
         Massachusetts Review 20 (1979):   337-54.

         Describes Lacan as Freud's "most important cur-
         rent commentator" (p. 338), but complains that the
         Norton editions of A2 and B22 do nothing to adapt
         the French texts for American readers as Wilden did
         in F420.   Bruss calls Lacan's writing "brutally
         difficult" (p. 339), but he also claims that
         Lacan's rhetoric just subjects the psychoanalysts
         in his audience to the literary experience probably
         missing from their training (p. 343).
           Bruss stresses Lacan's emphasis on the importance
         of language in Freud's work and his incorporation
         of Saussurean terms into psychoanalysis, and he
         argues that Lacan's emphasis on the role of trans-
         ference is a crucial return to Freud's own focus
         even though it may seem idiosyncratic to many
         Freudians.   Bruss also claims that Lacan's account
         of the mirror stage is at the heart of his theory
         of transference, and he directs readers to the
         importance of the symbolic in Lacan's work as well,
         offering a rudimentary synopsis of Lacan's distinc-
         tion between empty and full speech (see C58) and
         its implications for analytic practice (pp. 349-
         51).

Bruss goes on to refer to Lacan as "Freud's allegorist, his Dante," but he claims that Lacan's emphasis on "communicative development" seems to dismiss the importance of sexuality that was so central to Freud (p. 352).

G484.   Buchler, Ira.   "Orpheus and Lacan: Presence in Absence, Absence in Presence."   Semiotica, forthcoming.

G485.   Cancrini, Luigi.   "Jacques Lacan: psicoanalisi et strutturalismo."   La cultura 6 (1968):   184-220.

G486.   Carroll, David.   "For Example: Psychoanalysis and Fiction or The Conflict of Generation(s)."   Substance 21 (1978):   49-67.

Claims that Claude Simon's Le sacre du printemps (Paris, 1954) represents a simpler, more traditional Oedipal conflict than Lacan found in Poe's "The Purloined Letter" (see C69), and suggests that a comparison between these two works demonstrates a "double relation between psychoanalytic truth and literature" that undermines the usual tendency to treat either psychoanalysis or the literary text as more valuable than the other.
Carroll argues that the generational conflict in Simon's novel presents Oedipal struggles as "real" and therefore supports the Oedipal complex proposed by American ego psychology rather than Lacan's version, which considers castration a symbolic lack around which the chain of signifiers emerges.   Admitting the usefulness of Lacan's theory, Carroll nevertheless observes that Lacan's decentered subject is still a theory of the subject and carries on many traditional assumptions, such as a desire for totality and transcendence that haunts his concept of the symbolic as much as it does any imaginary notion of the ego.

G487.   Carroy-Thirard, Jacqueline.   "Charcot, Freud, Lacan."   Psychanalyse à l'université 9, no. 35 (1984):   409-28.

G488.   Casanova, Bernard.   "Psychanalyse et langue maternelle."   Langue française 54 (1982):   108-113.

Cites E251-E254 and other works by Lacan on the concept of "lalangue," and discusses the infant's earliest encounters with language at the hands of the Mother, who functions as the first incarnation of the other.

G489.   Casella, Antonio.   "Il linguaggio senza."   F307,

pp. 117-36.

G490. Casey, Edward S., and J. Melvin Woody. "Hegel,
       Heidegger, Lacan: The Dialectic of Desire."
       F403, pp. 75-112.

       Notes the importance of Hegel and Heidegger to
       Lacan's work, especially as Lacan is indebted to
       Kojève's reading of Hegel's Phenomenology, and
       argues that this philosophical influence helps
       protect Lacan from the reductionist tendency to
       treat psychoanalysis as a natural science.

G491. Castoriadis-Aulagnier, Piera, Jean-Paul Valabrega,
       and Nathalie Zaltzman. "Une néo-formation du
       lacanisme." Topique: revue freudienne 18
       (1977): Trajets analytiques.

       Denounces the creation of a "clinical section" at
       the Université de Paris VIII-Vincennes with Lacan
       as the "Scientific Director," and claims that this
       effort is what is wrong with "psychoanalysis in
       general and Lacanianism in particular" (see J1037).
       The authors reject the very notion that a univer-
       sity diploma could equip anyone to practice psycho-
       analysis, especially in two years, and they ridi-
       cule the effort to divide analysts of the Ecole
       freudienne de Paris into two classes as an attempt
       to establish Lacan's mastery over his "elect."
       (The authors are associated with the "Fourth
       Group," sometimes known as "Lacanians without
       Lacan.")

G492. Caterina, Roberto. "Il problema del ritorno a
       Freud." Nuova rivista storica 60 (1976): 648-
       52.

G493. Cerf-Bruneval, Danièle. "La place du lecteur."
       F357, pp. 87-95.

       Describes the plans of the seven people associ-
       ated with the bulletin stécriture to produce a
       "critical transcript" of Lacan's seminar on trans-
       ference, B19, and summarizes a number of attitudes
       towards the act of "transcribing" in order to dem-
       onstrate the problematic nature of the task. As do
       most of the essays in this issue of Littoral, Cerf-
       Bruneval's article repeatedly returns to the in-
       herent difficulty in converting spoken sounds into
       a graphic system and insists that any such "tran-
       scription" must be a critique as well. See L1373.
         For an important influence on the approach taken
       by the group associated with stécriture, see Jean
       Allouch, "L'écrit-lecteur," Cahiers de Fontenay 23
       (1981): Ecrit-Oral. Allouch argues that there is

something in writing that resists being reduced
simply to a double of the spoken word.

G494.   Cervantes-Léon, G., and Ch. Demoulin. "Jacques
        Lacan y la psiquiatria." Neurologia, neuro-
        cirugia, psiquiatria 23, no. 3/4 (1982): 101-
        06.

G495.   Champagne, Roland A. "The Architectural Pattern of
        a Literary Artifact: A Lacanian Reading of
        Balzac's Jesus-Christ en Flandre." Studies in
        Short Fiction 15 (1978): 49-54.

        Draws upon A3 and other works to describe the
        "non-taxonomic" concept of the unconscious sug-
        gested by Lacan's claim that the unconscious is
        structured like a language, and traces the Lacanian
        theme of a lost referent throughout Balzac's story.

G496.   Chapsal, Madeline. ["Jacques Lacan"]. Envoyez la
        petite musique . . . . Paris: Editions Grasset,
        1984.

        Describes Lacan as a surreal "fantasiste" who
        deliberately staged his public appearances to con-
        vey an impression of idiosyncratic celebrity, but
        notes his capacity for warmth and consideration in
        his personal relationship with the author.
        Chapsal's account of the Sunday afternoon gathe-
        rings at Lacan's country house at Guitrancourt il-
        luminates this side of Lacan, as do her reports of
        his fascination with gossip and his melodramatic
        affectations at restaurants. Chapsal claims to
        understand nothing of Lacan's work, and the anec-
        dotes of her impressionistic essay tend to portray
        Lacan as an intermittently charming but always
        pompous and mysterious figure whose appeal for the
        French intellectual scene was more theatrical than
        theoretical.
        Reprinted in Lire: le magazine des livres
        (December 1984): 80-86.

G497.   Chapsal, Madeleine. "La parole de Lacan."
        L'express, 25 March 1974, p. 47.

        Comments on Lacan's appearance on television (see
        A3), arguing that the event is important because
        people will get to see and hear a genuinely new
        discourse, whether or not they understand it.

G498.   Charney, Hanna. "Lacan, Don Juan, and the French
        Detective." L'esprit créateur 26, no. 2 (1986):
        15-25.

G499.   Chemla, P. "La conception du langage selon Jacques

Lacan: son importance dans la psychanalyse."
Psychologie 55 (1974):   28-33.

G***.   Cherki, Alice.   "Pour une mémoire."   See F399.

G500.   Chertok, Léon.   "Vincennes à Tbilisi ou l'art de
dialoguer."   Nouvelle critique 130 (1980):   18-
20.

Describes the conference on Lacan's work that was
held at Tbilisi, USSR, in 1979, and claims that the
Lacanians were characterized by a "political mili-
tantism" that ignored cultural differences and
seemed deliberately provocative.   Chertok says that
the behavior of the Lacanians was condemned by
other Westerners at the conference as well as by
the Russians.   For papers presented at the conference or published later in response to it, see
K1146, G446, G804, and G453.   Much of the controversy centered on a paper presented by Serge
Leclaire (G699).   For further remarks by Chertok on
this conference, see L1550.

G501.   Cixous, Hélène.   "Le rire de la méduse."   L'arc
(1975):   39-54.

Attacks the Lacanian model of the symbolic,
especially as it describes discursive positions
of the subject, and condemns Lacan's work as essentially phallocentric and so oppressive of
women's writing.   Cixous proposes the alternative
of a form of writing based on the female body, a
writing in "white ink" that will resist the symbolic categories of traditional forms of language.
"A feminine text," Cixous says, "cannot fail to be
more than subversive.   It is volcanic; as it is
written it brings about an upheaval of the old
property crust, carrier of masculine investments;
there's no other way.   There's no room for her if
she's not a he.   If she's a her-she, it's in order
to smash everything, to shatter the framework of
institutions, to blow up the law, to break up the
'truth' with laughter" (tr., p. 258).   Translated
as "The Laugh of the Medusa," Signs (Summer, 1976);
reprinted in New French Feminisms, edited by Elaine
Marks and Isabelle de Courtivron (New York:
Schocken Books, 1980, pp. 245-64.

G502.   Clain, Olivier.   "Sujet et langage, notes sur la
théorie lacanienne."   PhiZéro 10, no. 2/3 (1982):
71-123.

G503.   Clark, Michael.   "Imagining the Real: Jameson's
Use of Lacan."   New Orleans Review 11, no. 1
(1984):   67-72.

Compares Jameson's distinctions among the three "horizons" of the literary text in The Political Unconscious to Lacan's distinctions among the real, symbolic, and imaginary registers of experience, and argues that Jameson's model for the reconstruction of a text's dialogic context in the light of utopian longing historicizes Lacan's analysis of the psychic organization of individual subjectivity.

G504.   Clark, Michael. "The Lure of the Text, or Uncle Toby's Revenge." New Orleans Review 10, no. 1 (1983):   34-47.

Compares the theories of metonymy and metaphor proposed by Murray Krieger and by Lacan, focussing on the function of desire in each.

G505.   Clark, Michael. Review essay of F316 and F396. Modern Philology 83 (1985):   218-223.

Briefly sketches the development of Lacan's career and the theoretical issues involved in the various controversies associated with Lacanian psychoanalytic associations. Clark compares F316 and F396 as introductions to Lacan's work and describes F396 as a theoretical extension of Lacan's remarks about the place of death in psychoanalytic theory and training.

G506.   Clément, Catherine B. "Jacques Lacan: scénario pour un Western théorique." Magazine littéraire 127/128 (1977):   56-62.

Describes Lacan's public persona as that of a western hero out to do justice to the villains and to "restore the orphan Freud to all his rights." Reprinted in K1175, pp. 56-62.

G507.   Clément, Catherine. "Lettre à Lacan ou l'oiseau pris." F361, pp. 18-20.

Comments on the experience of attending Lacan's seminars and their curious effect, which is not so much a rigorous analysis of Freud's texts as a dramatic performance of the signifier. Clément claims that they also present the occasion for the listeners' own "formation" or Bildung.

G508.   Clément, Catherine. "Louis Althusser à l'assaut de la forteresse Lacan." Le matin, 17 March 1980, p. 35.

Describes the famous confrontation between

Althusser and Lacan during a convention that Lacan
had called after he dissolved the Ecole freudienne
de Paris to form the Cause freudienne. Clément
quotes Althusser's charge that psychoanalysts amuse
themselves with confused discourse much like a
woman sorting beans while a war is going on, and
she describes his often-cited characterization of
Lacan as a "magnificent and pitiful harlequin."
"You are cowards," Clément says Althusser told the
analysts, "fundamentally and essentially irresponsible. . . . You are the pâte à papier on which
Lacan prints what he wants." For Althusser's
comments on Lacan, see G432, G433.

G509.   Clément, Catherine.   "La mort de Jacques Lacan."
        G723, pp. 34-35.

        Describes major events in Lacan's career and a
        number of issues raised by Lacan's work, noting
        that controversy pursued him to the end of his
        life.

G510.   Clément, Catherine.   "Le réveil du Freudisme par
        Jacques Lacan."   Magazine littéraire 127/128
        (1977).

G511.   "Clochemerle chez les psychanalystes."   L'événement
        du jeudi, 25 July 1985, p. 58.

G512.   Comolli, Giampiero.   "Desiderio e bisogno: note
        critiche a Lacan e Deleuze/Guattari."   Aut-Aut
        139 (1974): 21-44.

G513.   Comolli, Giampiero.   "Padre, non vedi che brucio?
        Dall'alienazione del soggetto al campo delle
        transformazioni soggettive."   F307, pp. 3-26.

G514.   Compagnon, Antoine.   "L'analyse orpheline."   Tel
        quel 65 (1976):   41-55.

        Cites C65 on the necessity of the analyst as-
        suming the place of death in analysis ("en cadavér-
        isant sa position"), and contrasts that necessity
        to the fortified position encouraged by ego psy-
        chology, from which the patient's resistances are
        to be conquered (p. 43).   Compagnon also cites C58
        on Lacan's distinction between the time of the cure
        and the "time for understanding" ("le temps pour
        comprendre"), and he discusses in detail the com-
        plex relations among the image of the body, the
        gaze, and the objet a as diagrammed in B22,
        especially as those relations are involved in
        transference and implicated in the desire of the
        analyst (p. 49).

G515.   Contri, Giacomo. "Prémisse: Pourquoi." A4, pp.
        12-26, French translation pp. 174-85.

        Presents the collection as a means of bringing
        Lacan's work out in the open in Italy, and hopes
        that this will alleviate some of the mystery and
        obscurity that has been associated with Lacan there
        (p. 175). Contri also describes the more general
        issues raised by Lacan and his return to Freud.

G516.   Contri, Giacomo, and Sergio Finzi. "Situation de
        la psychanalyse dans le monde: l'Italie."
        Ornicar? 16 (1978):   161-64.

        Describes Lacan's influence on Italian psycho-
        analysis.

G517.   Cooper, David. "Who's Mad Anyway?" New Statesman,
        16 June 1967, pp. 844-45.

        Notes Lacan's reputation as one who has "cata-
        lysed an underground in France . . . inspired the
        Situationists at Strasbourg . . . [and] is bringing
        about a concealed but radical reorientation in
        Freudian psychiatry and psycho-analysis." Cooper
        claims that there is a divergence, however, between
        this pervasive influence and the works published in
        A2, which are marked by a "notable lack of ref-
        erence to anything that has ever happened between
        him [Lacan] and any other person." Nevertheless,
        Cooper says that Lacan succeeds in "wresting
        Freudian concepts out of their bed in biological
        analogy and expressing them in real social-
        historical terms and in Marxist terms."

G518.   Copjec, Joan. "Seduction, Sedition, and the
        Dictionary." m/f 8 (1983):   67-78.

        Discusses the topic of seduction as treated in
        F333 and in Lacanian psychoanalysis.

G519.   Copjec, Joan. "Transference: Letters and the
        Unknown Woman." October 28 (1984):   61-90.

        Stresses the importance of transference in
        Lacan's work, and provides a basic historical
        background on the general topic of transference.
        Copjec discusses K1315 and analyzes at length
        Lacan's critique of the notion of defense in C74.
        Desire must be "taken literally" in the speech of
        the patient, Copjec says, and not sought beneath
        patterns of defense. She also discusses Lacan's
        claim that "woman does not exist," arguing that it
        is a "logical" claim, not an anatomical observation
        (pp. 83-84).

G520.   Cortes, Ry. ["The Issue of the Subject and
        Discourse in the Logic of the Psychological"
        (Spanish)]. Acta psiquiatrica y psicologica de
        America Latina 29, no. 2 (1983): 96-104.

G521.   Corvez, Maurice. "Le structuralisme de Jacques
        Lacan." Revue philosophique de Louvain 66, no.
        90 (1968): 282-308.

        Notes Lacan's debt to Saussure and to Lévi-
        Strauss, whose anthropological structuralism is
        compatible with Lacan's work because they both aim
        toward "the same unconscious," which determines
        both the conduct of individuals and the life of
        societies. Corvez objects to Lacan's claim that
        all human experience is determined by language,
        however, and claims that language is only "the
        psychic translation of man's constituted reality"
        (p. 303). He concludes with remarks about the
        issue of human freedom in the "science" of psycho-
        analysis and its relation to metaphysics.
        Translated as "El estructuralismo de Jacques
        Lacan," Revista de psicologia 113 (1971): 711-41.

G522.   Corvez, Maurice. [Chapter on Lacan.] Les struc-
        turalistes. Paris: Aubier-Montaigne, 1969. 208
        pages.

G523.   Cousineau, T. J. "Descartes, Lacan, and Murphy."
        College Literature 11 (1984): 223-32.

G524.   Covello, Adele, Lucio Covello, and Gabrielle C.
        Lairy. "Les fausses correspondances: du
        monologue théorique schreberien au dialogue
        thérapeutique: II. Lacan, Freud, Schreber."
        Evolution psychiatrique 49 (1984): 1051-69.

G525.   Coward, Rosalind. "Lacan and Signification: An
        Introduction." Edinburgh '76 Magazine: Psycho-
        Analysis/Cinema/Avant-Garde, pp. 6-20.

G526.   Culler, Christopher. Review of F333 and F370.
        Lacan Study Notes 4 (1985): 13-15.

G527.   Cutler, Tony. "Lacan's Philosophical Coquetry."
        F359, pp. 90-107.

        Discusses Lacan's invocation of certain philo-
        sophical concepts in his theory of psychosis, and
        comments on the philosophical dimensions of the
        link between theory and clinical practice in
        Lacan's work.

G***.   David-Ménard, Monique. "La horde sauvage à Paris."

See F399.

G528.   David-Ménard, Monique.   "Lacanians Against Lacan."
         Translated by Brian Massumi. Social Text 6
         (1982):   86-110.

Describes the controversy surrounding Lacan's
decision to dissolve the Ecole freudienne de Paris
in 1980 (see B38), and explains the theoretical,
political, and personal stakes involved in that
controversy. David-Ménard notes the importance of
Lacan's anti-institutional arguments in his earlier
conflicts with the International Psychoanalytic
Association, but she claims that by 1969 Lacan
himself had become the "tradition" of psychoanalysis in France (p. 87). She attacks Jacques-
Alain Miller and the group associated with the
Cause freudienne for using "magic formulas" to
avoid dealing with the difficulties of analytic
theory and in particular to deny the possibility of
theoretical contradictions in Lacan's own work (pp.
98-99). David-Ménard also denounces Miller as
nothing but "a symptom of Lacan . . . a symptom of
what went awry with Lacan himself when he succeeded" (p. 108).
David-Ménard identifies the specific problem of
Lacan's success as a blurring of distinctions among
the heterogeneous levels of human experience,
specifically those of the symbolic and the political. She admits that Lacan lifted psychoanalysis
in France out of the "psychologizing rut" that had
deadened so much work in the field after World War
II, and she praises him for "manifesting the unconscious in realms where it does not usually
figure" (p. 104). Nevertheless, David-Ménard
condemns Lacan for endorsing (or at least failing
to resist) the institutionalization of the trans-
ferences that his teaching was designed to effect.
She describes the theoretical differences that led
to disagreements between Lacan and analysts such as
Françoise Dolto and Michèle Montrelay, and she recounts in details the shifting allegiances, temporary newsletters, and new groups that occurred
during the months when Lacan's "dissolution" was
overseen by the courts and debated publicly in the
press.
This is one of the most detailed and polemical
accounts of the confusing months between September
1979 (when Lacan, acting on his authority as president of the EFP, suddenly dismissed vice-president
Denis Vasse), and 27 September 1980, when a General
Assembly of the ECF was convened to complete the
formal dissolution of the school. This article is
reviewed briefly in Lacan Study Notes 1, no. 2
(1983).

G529.   Davis, Robert Con.   "Lacan and Narration: The
        Psychoanalytic Difference in Narrative Theory."
        Journal of the M[idwest] M[odern] L[anguage]
        A[ssociation] 18, no. 1 (1985):   102-05.

G530.   Davis, Robert Con.   "Lacan, Poe, and Narrative
        Repression."   F371, pp.   983-1005.

        Stresses the difference between the way repres-
        sion is treated by American ego psychology, which
        discounts its function, and by the continental
        tradition associated with Lacan, which treats
        repression as a principal figure and functional
        principle within systems of discourse.   Repression,
        Davis says, is not a single event but "an ongoing
        process of marking and suppressing differences"
        through which it "creates a textual unconscious"
        and so "makes signification and narration possible"
        (pp. 984-85).   Davis then explores the theoretical
        origins of this principle in Freud's Instincts and
        Their Vicissitudes (1915) and uses it to interpret
        Poe's "The Tell-Tale Heart."

G531.   Davis, Robert Con.   "Post-Modern Paternity: Donald
        Barthelme's The Dead Father."   Delta (Montpel-
        lier, France) 8 (1979):   127-40.

        Uses Barthelme's novel to illustrate the distinc-
        tion between the figure of a "father" in a story
        and the function of literary paternity, which
        "prohibits mere repetition and mere sequentiality"
        and appears as "the essential 'no' expressed as a
        dilemma" (p. 171).   Citing Lacan's claim that the
        symbolic father is the dead Father (p. 177), Davis
        explains how the dead father of the novel functions
        as "the archaic expression for the father as the
        source of opposition, the principle of the 'binary
        code'" that governs the symbolic and, more particu-
        larly, narrative itself.
        Reprinted in F318, pp. 169-82.

G532.   De Certeau, Michel.   "Lacan: une éthique de la
        parole."   Le débat 22 (1982):   54-69.

        Claims that the name "Lacan" designates a "rhe-
        toric of withdrawal" and a "violent gesture" of
        separation that constitute his thought (p. 21).   De
        Certeau describes what he calls the "theatrical
        art" of Lacan's public presentations, which re-
        places his bodily presence with a series of ges-
        tures that lack any inherent significance, and he
        claims that those performances raised the literary
        problem of relating voice to text or, in Lacan's
        case, analytic speech to writing (see p. 25).   The
        seminars exist somewhere between those two poles,

De Certeau says. De Certeau also notes the importance of Christian themes to Lacan's work, Lacan's
constant recourse to literary traditions, and the
founding of the Ecole freudienne de Paris on "the
ethics of the speaking subject" (p. 35).

De Certeau describes several issues raised
throughout Lacan's career, focussing on a "Christian archeology" of religious thought in Lacan's
work as he transforms religion into an "ethic of
speech [parole]." Ethics, de Certeau says, "is the
form of belief detached from an alienating imaginary where it supposed the guarantee of a real, and
thus changed into speech [la parole] which tells of
the desire instituted by this lack" (p. 67). De
Certeau also portrays L'éthique de la psychanalyse"
(B18) as derived from Freud's Moses and Monotheism
(1939) as well as Hegel's Phenomenology, and he
remarks on the politics of speech as it is manifest
in the operation of the Ecole freudienne de Paris.

Translated by Marie Rose Logan as "Lacan: An
Ethics of Speech," Representations 3 (1983): 21-
39; reprinted in De Certeau's Heterologies, pp. 47-
64.

G533. De Diéguez, Manuel. Science et nescience. Paris:
Editions Gallimard, 1970. 548 pages.

Part III, "Lacan et la psychanalyse transcen-
dentale" (pp. 253-354), situates Lacan in the
"exegetical tradition of the human sciences" (p.
263), and claims that Lacan's originality lies in
his having "placed the problem of spiritual deca-
dence of an experimental science at the heart of
psychoanalytic research" (p. 264).

G534. De Diéguez, Manuel. "Contestations philosophiques
à propos de l'ouvrage 'Les quatre concepts . . .
.'" La nouvelle revue française 248 (1973): 78-
90.

Recounts three dreams in which he discussed B22
with phantoms who tried to help him understand it.

G535. De Risio, S., A. Ciocca, and F. M. Ferro. "In toma
di struttura dell'inconscio: de Freud à Lacan"
["Structure of the Unconscious: From Freud to
Lacan"]. Riv. sper. freniatr. 31 October 1971,
pp. 872-92.

G536. De Schutter, Dirk. "A Study of Metaphor and
Metonymy in Lacan." Auslegung, A Journal of
Philosophy 10, no. 1/2 (1983): 65-74.

Investigates Lacan's use of Saussure, especially
as it involves Lacan's theory of metaphor and

metonymy and the constitution of a human subject.

G537. De Tollenaere, M. "Naar de Oorsprong van de Taal"
       ["The Origin of Language" (Dutch)]. Tijdschrift
       voor filosofie 37 (1975): 187-210.

G538. D'Agostini, Franca. "Lacan, l'immaginario e il
       problema della metafisica." F307, pp. 189-203.

G539. Dealvarez, D. E. "Jacques Lacan." Acta psiqui-
       atrica y psicologica de america latina 28 (1982):
       239-42.

G540. Dean, Carolyn. "Law and Sacrifice: Bataille,
       Lacan, and the Critique of the Subject."
       Representations 13 (1986): 42-62.

       Traces the social origins of a critique of the
       subject that is characteristic of contemporary
       literary theory and psychoanalysis in France,
       focussing on the work of Georges Bataille and
       Jacques Lacan. Dean emphasizes the importance of
       madness, criminality, and eroticism as topics of
       interest to early analysts in France, and she
       claims that these forms of "inexplicable" violence
       came to function as metaphors for the "disarticu-
       lated subjectivity" that eventually replaced the
       Cartesian Cogito. She also argues that Lacan and
       Bataille used criminality as a "metaphor of that
       which is impossible to symbolize" (p. 60).

G541. Delacampagne, Christian. "L'avenir d'un phéno-
       mène." G747, pp. 1-2.

       Notes the "Lacan phenomenon" in French intel-
       lectual life, and claims that Lacan was above all a
       "style," "un style d'homme" whose manner derived
       from traditions of oral performance and from
       literature.

G***. Delaroche, Patrick. "Signifiant lacanien et
       investissement freudien." See F399.

G542. Demangeat, Michel. "D'une scène à l'autre."
       Etudes psychothérapiques 14, no. 3 (1983): 179-
       88.

G543. Demoulin, Christian. "Pour comprendre la théorie
       psychanalytique, de Freud à Lacan." La revue
       nouvelle 76, no. 7/8 (1982): 81-92.

       Notes the importance of the "paternal imago" as
       described in C45, and observes that at the time of
       that essay Lacan had reason to see the decline of
       patriarchy as a principal cause of modern man's

psychopathological troubles. Demoulin describes
Lacan's decreasing tendency to consider the unconscious in terms of mental images by 1953 and the
consequent increase in the importance of the symbolic to his thought. Demoulin also comments on a
number of other topics in Lacan's work including
desire, the question of truth, and the identity
between the impossible and the real.

G544.   Derrida, Jacques. "Le facteur de la vérité."
        Poétique 21 (1975):   96-147.

     Claims that Lacan's essay on Poe's "The Purloined
Letter" (C69) ignores the narrative frame of the
story and assumes that there is a privileged
position--analogous to the position of the analyst
--that is outside of the story's textual indeter-
minacy. Derrida argues instead that the entire
story is caught within a network of intertextu-
ality, a scene of writing in which no truth is
possible. The letter is always divisible, Derrida
says; it never arrives at its destination, and
Dupin can never escape as Lacan claims he can
because he is caught within the trap of intersubjectivity. Derrida also condemns Lacan's reading
for its tendency to idealize the signifier and its
implicit sublimation of writing into the system of
speech, which results in an illusory "phono-
centrism."
     Reprinted in Derrida's Dissemination, and
translated in Barbara Johnson's translation of
Derrida's book (Chicago: University of Chicago
Press, 1981). Also reprinted in Derrida's Le carte
postale. G544 was first translated as "The
Purveyor of Truth" by Willis Domingo, James
Hulbert, Moshe Ron, and M.-R. L., Yale French
Studies 52 (1975): 31-113. For the first of many
comments on this exchange between Derrida and
Lacan, see G661; for a survey of the whole contro-
versy, see F374/375. Derrida comments further on
Lacan in J1040.

G545.   Dethier, Hubert. "De dood van Jacques Lacan."
        Lier en boog 5, no. 1 (1982): 66-9.

G546.   Deville, E. "Notes sur la thèse de Lacan (1932)."
        L'information psychiatrique 52 (1976):   655-58.

G547.   Dews, Peter. "The Letter and the Line." Dia-
        critics 14, no. 3 (1984): 40-49.

     Claims that the work of Jean-François Lyotard
takes place in a theoretical milieu dominated by
Lacan's notion of the unconscious as structured
like a language, and goes on to describe Lacan's

reformulation of the dream work described in
Chapter Six of Freud's The Interpretation of Dreams
(1900).   Dews emphasizes Lacan's claim that images
in dreams have no figurative function but serve as
"letters" in a kind of writing.   Lacan considered
Freud's Entstellung (distortion) as a kind of
"transposition," Dews says, somewhat similar to the
semantic instability of the "sliding of the signified under the signifier."   Dews aligns the
following terms and discusses their connections:
   Verdichtung (condensation)--selection--
      metonymy
   Verschiebung (displacement)--combination--
      metaphor.
Dews claims that Lacan's concept of metaphor and
metonymy borrows from Jakobson but is nevertheless
quite different.
   Most of Dews' remarks about Lacan involve com-
parisons to Lyotard's Discours, figure (K1255).
Lyotard objects to Lacan because Lacan participates
in a more general denigration of the visible in the
Western world, Dews claims, and he contrasts
Lyotard's notion of Freud's condensation and displacement to Lacan's.   Dews argues that Lyotard
differs from Lacan primarily in Lyotard's attribution of stasis to the intervals of linguistic systems and in his linking of the unconscious with
"the fluidity and mobility of the perceived world."
Lacan, on the other hand, equates the unconscious
with the "instability" of the symbolic.   Dews says
that Lyotard accords a special status to perception, which he associates with the primary processes of the unconscious, whereas Lacan refuses any
primacy at all in relation to the unconscious
except that of signifier (p. 47).
   Dews also claims that there is a political dimension to the difference between Lyotard and
Lacan.   For Lacan, desire is not a force and is not
the victim of externally imposed repression; but
for Lyotard, Dews says, discourse must be attacked
"in the name of its distorted and distorting
others" (p. 48).

G548.   Diamantis, Irène.   "Le roc originaire: à propos de
      la phobie."   K1297, pp. 43-52.

      Questions Lacan's use of the "Tout" and the nega-
      tion of "Pas (Tout)" in his account of sexual dif-
      ferentiation (see B31), and discusses relations
      among several different phobias as they involve the
      property of negation (p. 44).

G549.   Donnet, Jean-Luc.   "Sur l'institution psychana-
      lytique et la durée de la séance."   Nouvelle
      revue de psychanalyse 20 (1979):   241-59.

Discusses the issue of variable lengths for
psychoanalytic sessions starting with Lacan's
"short sessions," and notes the critical thrust of
Lacan's proposal against the institutionalization
of psychoanalysis and "the protocol of the cure"
(p. 243). For accompanying articles, see G565,
G668, G672, G894.

G550.   Dor, Joël. ["Do You Know How to Read Lacan?"
         (French).] Interview with F. Levy. Quinzaine
         littéraire 441 (1985): 23-24.

G551.   Doubrovsky, Serge. "Statements on Amour-propre:
         From Lacan to La Rochefoucauld." Translated by
         Stamos Metzidakis. New York Literary Forum 8/9
         (1981): 141-61.

G552.   Doumit, Eric. "Criticisme poppérien, positivisme
         logique et discours psychanalytique." Revue de
         métaphysique et de morale 86, no. 4 (1981): 514-
         44.

         Notes Lacan's claim that psychoanalysis is not a
         science although it is related to the scientific
         concept of the subject, and contrasts that claim to
         Popper's association of science with metaphysics.
         Doumit also compares Lacan's real, imaginary, and
         symbolic to Popper's "three worlds," and notes
         Lacan's refusal to orient analytic interpretation
         towards some extra-linguistic fixity. Doumit also
         notes Lacan's conclusion that interpretation does
         not have to be true or false but only "just" (C96),
         and he says that Lacan's claim about the real being
         "impossible"--the real "ne cesse pas de ne pas
         s'écrire," Lacan says--implies the exclusion of
         meaning.

G553.   Dufour, Michel. "Lacan et Althusser: une ren-
         contre et des promesses." Culture et langage.
         Edited by Jean-Claude Brodeur and Georges Leroux.
         Montréal: Hurtubise, 1973. 286 pages.

G554.   Dupuy, B. "Du côté de Zazie." F354, p. 4.

         Briefly discusses Lacan's style as a literary
         phenomenon.

G555.   Durand, Régis. "'The Captive King': The Absent
         Father in Melville's Text." F318, pp. 48-72.

         Argues that the narcissism of the child may well
         be behind most of Melville's fiction, but the
         fiction itself is "haunted by the return of the
         vanished father . . . [and] wagers its very status

and existence as fiction on the question of the
symbolic father" (p. 49).   Durand briefly sketches
the connection between discourse and the dead
father as a function of Lacan's distinction between
the symbolic father and the real father.   He also
claims that the narrative flow in many of
Melville's books is threatened, and at times
disrupted, by what he calls the "primitive," that
which has been foreclosed: the "non-symbolized" or
dead father whose power is manifest at times
through hallucinations or regressive fantasies
directly represented in the books or through "a
distortion, a perversion of the narrative vehicle"
itself (p. 53).

G556.   Durand, Régis.   "On Aphanisis: A Note on the
        Dramaturgy of the Subject in Narrative Analysis."
        F371, pp.   860-70.

        Briefly describes Lacan's concept of aphanisis
        and explores its relevance to the dissolution of
        the subject characteristic of modernist texts as
        exemplified by Thomas Pynchon's Gravity's Rainbow.

G557.   Duvivier, Yolande.   "Métaphore paternelle et
        forclusion: deux concepts clefs du lacanisme."
        Annales de l'Institut de philosophie (1978):
        157-74.

G558.   Earl, James W.   "Preface: Augustine, Freud,
        Lacan."   Thought: A Review of Culture and Idea
        61 (1986):   7-15.

        Argues that Lacan is central to an understanding
        of psychoanalysis in relation to religion.   This is
        a preface to the other essays on Lacan published in
        this issue; see G837 and G883.

G559.   Ebtinger, R., and A. Bolzinger.   "Crises, incer-
        titudes, et paradoxes de l'adolescence."   Revue
        de neuropsychiatrie infantile et d'hygiène
        mentale de l'enfance 26 (1978):   539-57.

        Cites A2 and C53 on the "assomption jubilatoire"
        of the body image by the child during the mirror-
        stage (p. 546), and claims that that moment is
        crucial to adolescent development later in life.

G560.   Eigen, M.   "The Area of Faith in Winnicott, Lacan
        and Bion."   International Journal of Psycho-
        analysis 62 (1981):   413-33.

G561.   Eros, Ferenc.   "Jacques Lacan Hamlet-
        ertelmezesehez."   Helikon: vilagirodalmi figyelo
        [Hungary] 29, no. 3/4 (1983):   363-374.

G562.   Etkin, Gustavo Ezequiel.   "The Offended Woman."
        Papers of the Freudian School of Melbourne
        (1980):   49-63.

        Discusses the place of woman in the Lacanian
        model of the Oedipus complex, especially in
        relation to the Phallus and the Other.

G563.   Evans, Martha Noel.   "Introduction to Lacan's
        Lecture: The Neurotic's Individual Myth."
        Psychoanalytic Quarterly 48 (1979):   386-404.

        Describes several key topics discussed in C60 and
        other issues related to Lacan's work, such as the
        mirror stage and the name-of-the-father, and notes
        Lacan's emphasis on the "quadrilateral," rather
        than triangular, structure of the Oedipal complex.
        Evans explains that the four-sided figure is pro-
        duced by the splitting of either parent into a real
        and a symbolic "self," and she says that Lacan
        usually confers greater power on the symbolic role.
        Normally, an "operational juncture" of the real and
        symbolic figures is achieved, but neurotics fail in
        that effort (p. 401).   In such cases, says Evans,
        when one parent splits, "the other [parent] per-
        sists as an intact sustainer of the subject" (p.
        402).

G564.   L'express, 25 September 1981.

        Notes the public interest in Lacan's death and
        claims that his prominence was due to his contro-
        versial personality and the absolute authority with
        which he manipulated his followers.

G565.   Fédida, Pierre.   "A propos du 'retour à Freud':
        nomades pensées du désert."   Nouvelle revue de
        psychanalyse 20 (1979):   103-18.

        Discusses Lacan's prominence and influence as an
        effect of a general process of transference that
        has resulted in his dominance (p. 104), but argues
        that his return to Freud has taught us to read.
        Fédida comments on several issues raised by the
        close reading of Freud's texts characteristic of
        contemporary French psychoanalysis.   For accom-
        panying articles see G549, G668, G672, and G894.

G566.   Felman, Shoshana.   "Beyond Oedipus: The Specimen
        Story of Psychoanalysis."   F371, pp.   1021-53.

        Discusses the importance of the Oedipus myth as
        the "specimen story of psychoanalysis," a "refer-
        ence narrative" that is "archetypal of the psycho-

analytic myth in that it is the story of the narrative expropriation of the story by itself, the
story or, precisely, the acknowledgement of the
misrecognition of the story by itself" (p. 1046).
Citing the scene in Oedipus at Colonous in which
Oedipus realizes that his troubles are just beginning and that his tale is essentially endless,
Felman claims that this story embodies Lacan's own
recognition that "psychoanalysis is radically about
expropriation" and about its strategic "forgetting"
of its basis in myth in favor of a "scientific"
theory.

Such an attitude misunderstands the function of
myth, Felman says, and she argues that there is a
fictive moment at the origin of any science (p.
1050).   Rather than repressing it, psychoanalysis
must relive that mythic moment of its birth and
practice a "performative acknowledgement" of the
myth and its relation to theory (p. 1046).   Felman
says that such a self-consciously performative
utilization of speech motivates Lacan's return to
Freud and explains why he remained preoccupied not
with theory itself but with the practice of psychoanalysis as a "performative encounter" (p. 1048).
Reprinted in F330.

G567.   Felman, Shoshana.   "La méprise et sa chance."
        F305, pp. 40-48.

        Comments on a number of theoretical and ethical
        implications of Lacan's emphasis on language in
        psychoanalysis.

G568.   Felman, Shoshana.   "On Reading Poetry: Reflections
        on the Limits and Possibilities of Psychoanalytic
        Approaches."   The Literary Freud: Mechanisms of
        Defense and the Poetic Will.   New Haven: Yale
        University Press, 1980.   Pp. 119-48.

        Uses Poe's story "The Purloined Letter" as an
        example to illustrate psychoanalytic approaches to
        literary analysis, focussing on Lacan's reading of
        the story (see C69).

G569.   Felman, Shoshana.   "The Originality of Jacques
        Lacan."   Poetics Today 2 (1980-81):   45-57.

        Describes Lacan's return to Freud as "a sort of
        analytic dialogue" between Lacan and Freud in which
        Freud is "returned to as the Other" who sends
        Lacan's own message back to him in an inverted
        form, and compares this kind of return to Freud's
        own discovery of a "new way of reading" in the
        discourse of hysterics.   Listening to his early
        patients, Felman says, Freud discovered the uncon-

scious--his own as well as his patients'--as a
discourse "within the discourse of the other, of
what was actively reading within himself; his
discovery, in other words, or his reading, of what
was reading--in what was being read" (p. 51). The
result was a radically new kind of reflexivity
which incorporated a passage through the Other and
so retained an absolutely asymmetrical heterogeneity within that passage that contradicts the
traditional humanistic forms of self-reflection.
      Felman describes this discovery as Freud's
"inaugural step," the "principle of originality
which has brought about the difference named psychoanalysis" (p. 49). She discusses this originality in the context of Lacan's comments on the
"Copernican revolution" brought about by Freud's
work and in relation to what she calls a new mode
of scientific knowledge in which observer and
observed revolve around each other in a decentered
ellipse.
      Reprinted in F330.

G570.   Felman, Shoshana. "Psychoanalysis and Education:
        Teaching Terminable and Interminable." Yale
        French Studies 63 (1982):   21-44.

      Emphasizes the "potential contribution of psycho-
analysis to pedagogy" as based on what she calls
the "pedagogical speech-act" of Freud's and Lacan's
work, their refusal to assume a position of mastery
and their insistance on the fundamental role of
"ignorance" or the resistance to knowledge as the
basis of their teaching. Rather than the transmission of knowledge, Felman says, psychoanalytic
teaching strives to create "a new condition of
knowledge" that will treat knowledge as a "structural dynamic" linking two subjects, each of whom--
teacher and student--must learn his knowledge from
the other.
      Felman says that knowledge is therefore a "struc-
ture of address" that functions only within a
transferential context characteristic of the analytic situation. Here, there is no subject of
absolute knowledge, no "subject supposed to know."
Teaching and learning, like analysis, must therefore be interminable to be possible at all, and
Felman calls this "the most far-reaching insight
psychoanalysis can give us into pedagogy: "the
position of the teacher is itself the position of
the one who learns, of the one who teaches nothing
other than the way he learns. . . . teaching does
not just reflect upon itself, but turns back upon
itself so as to subvert itself, and truly teaches
only insofar as it subverts itself" (pp. 37, 39).

G571.   Ferraris, Maurizio.   "Reminiscenza e ripetizione
        nel pensiero di Jacques Lacan."   F307, pp. 179-
        88.

G572.   Ferrer, Daniel.   "Hissheory ou le plaisir en trop."
        Poétique 26 (1976):   232-39.

        Cites C58 on Lacan's claim that what appears as
        redundancy in information functions as resonance in
        speech because the goal of speech is to evoke, not
        inform, and to seek the response of the Other (p.
        234).   Ferrer applies Lacan's point to an analysis
        of Finnegans Wake.

G573.   Le figaro, 21 January 1980, p. 2.   "Des enfants
        sans pére: Jacques Lacan et la dissolution de
        l'Ecole freudienne."

        Includes J1072 and J1140.

G574.   Le figaro, 11 September 1981, p. 28.

        Includes brief items on Lacan's death (J1017 and
        J1136) as well as a number of comments by public
        figures such as Minister of Culture Jack Lang,
        Gilles Deleuze, and others.

G575.   Finzi Ghisi, Virginia.   "Funzione dei residui in
        psicoanalisi: il sapere protesi del corpo."
        F307, pp. 223-42.

G576.   Fisher, David James.   "Lacan's Ambiguous Impact on
        Contemporary French Psychoanalysis."   Contem-
        porary French Civilization 6, no. 1/2 (1981-82):
        89-114.

        Describes Lacan's general prominence in French
        psychoanalysis, and notes the significance of
        Lacan's effort to "fill a key gap" in Freudian
        theory by examining "how society and law enter the
        individual" (p. 91).   Fisher compares Lacan to
        André Breton and claims they possessed very similar
        personalities and artistic sensibilities, and he
        traces elements of surrealism in Lacan's work and
        his public performances.   Fisher also praises
        Lacan's attempt to link "knowledge and liberation"
        in the political vacuum left by the split between
        the Communists and Socialists in France, noting his
        impact on the radical left after May '68.
            Fisher concludes that Lacan's departure from a
        fixed time for the analytic session and his claim
        that only the analyst can authorize himself as an
        analyst are the major points of conflict separating
        Lacanian psychoanalysis from more traditional forms
        as practiced in France and elsewhere, and he

briefly describes the controversy surrounding
Lacan's dissolution of the Ecole freudienne de
Paris in 1980.

G577.   Fisher, Eileen.   "The Discourse of the Other in Not
        I: A Confluence of Beckett and Lacan."   Theater
        [Yale University] 10, no. 3 (1979):   101-03.

        Claims that both Lacan and Beckett deny the
        existence of monologue because all speech is ad-
        dressed to an other and so is dialogic (p. 102).
        Fisher also briefly discusses the importance of
        lack and desire to both authors.

G578.   Fiumano, Marisa.   "La trasmissione di una teoria
        dell'inconscio: Il 'caso Lacan.'"   F307, pp.
        243-55.

G579.   Fleming, Keith.   "Hamlet and Oedipus Today: Jones
        and Lacan."   Hamlet Studies: An International
        Journal of Research on the Tradegie of Hamlet,
        Prince of Denmarke [New Delhi, India] 4, no 1/2
        (1982):   54-71.

        Claims that Lacan's reading of Hamlet in B17a
        needs to be supplemented by that proposed in Ernest
        Jones's Hamlet and Oedipus, but claims that Lacan
        shows us how to apply the Oedipus complex to an
        analysis of social groups broader than the family
        and including the general organization of an entire
        culture.

G580.   Flieger, Jerry Aline.   "The Purloined Punchline:
        Joke as Textual Paradigm."   F371, pp.   941-67.

        Uses Freud's Jokes and their Relation to the
        Unconscious (1905) to explore the relations among
        gender, subjectivity, and the symbolic as proposed
        by Lacan's reading of Poe's "The Purloined Letter"
        (C69).   Flieger proceeds through a series of meto-
        nymic associations that move from the intersub-
        jective dimension of subjectivity through the text
        as a "feminine" symptom to a discussion of femi-
        ninity as a specific form of subjectivity (p. 942).
        After discussing several feminist objections to
        Lacan's phallocentric concept of the symbolic,
        Flieger concludes that Freud's characterization of
        sexuality in Jokes suggests a notion of subjec-
        tivity that can accommodate both male and female
        subjects, unlike Lacan's insistence that woman is
        inevitably displaced from the symbolic.

G581.   Florenne, Yves.   "Revue des revues: Freud et ses
        docteurs."   Le monde, 13 March 1968, p. 11.

Describes a number of psychoanalytic journals, several of which are devoted to work based on Lacan's teachings.

G582. Forrester, John. "The Linguistic and the Psy-
       chotic." Times Literary Supplement, 1 October
       1982, pp. 1079-80.

Reviews B14 and briefly describes Lacan's career, claiming that his presence on the intellectual scene in France has been "perhaps the single most important influence since the Second World War." Forrester emphasizes the importance of Lacan's visit to London after the war because it was there that Lacan encountered the work of Wilfred Bion, who seemed to be leading psychoanalysis into the future (see C50). He also describes Lacan's sub- sequent troubles with the IPA and his rise in France, and claims that by the mid-1970s the au- dience for Lacan's seminars numbered almost 1,000 each week. Lacan's teaching was always ahead of his followers, Forrester says, because of its "dialectical instability"; according to Forrester, Lacan was a "didact, not a theorist." Forrester argues that the most striking thing about Lacan's psychoanalysis is his eschewal of early infantile trauma as an explanation for psychosis, and his insistence that psychoanalysts stick to what is before them: speech. (In this context, Forrester also notes Lacan's proximity to speech-act theory.)

G583. Forrester, John. "Philology and the Phallus."
       F359, pp. 45-69.

Claims that Lacan's emphasis on the importance of language in psychoanalysis was a result of his chronological reading of Freud, which started with the early works in which Freud himself emphasized language more than he did in the later works. Forrester then discusses the symbolic function of the phallus in Lacan's work and compares it to Freud's own comments on the importance of the phal- lus, and he concludes with an analysis of the sub- versive irony inherent in the work of both Lacan and Freud.

G584. Forrester, John. "Who is in Analysis with Whom?:
       Freud, Lacan, Derrida." Economy and Society 13,
       no. 2 (1984): 153-77.

Discusses issues raised by Derrida's critique of psychoanalysis in La carte postale and G544, focus- sing on the limits of analysis, the scene of writ- ing, an the role of "gossip" or "the third party" in the analytic situation. Forrester claims that

Derrida and Lacan theorize the same aporia regarding discourse and describes some theoretical
problems associated with la passe.

G585.   Fossard, André. "On purge Oedipe." Le point, 14
        January 1980, p. 58.

        Comments on Lacan's decision to "autoscissionne"
        ("self-divide") and notes that such controversies
        as that surrounding the dissolution of the Ecole
        freudienne de Paris are fairly typical of Parisian
        intellectual life.

G586.   Fougeyrollas, P.   "Lacan ou la pantomime petite-
        bourgeoise." Contre Lévi-Strauss, Lacan, et
        Althusser. Rome: Savelli, and Paris: De la
        Jonquière, 1976. Pp. 81-134.

        Criticizes the three authors for their degenera-
        tion into the obscurantism of bourgeois ideology,
        and characterizes Lacan's work as a betrayal of
        Freud, not a return.

G587.   Fouilliaron, T. "Lacan et la religion." Soins
        psychiatrique 67 (1986): 21-22. See K1335.

G588.   "La france freudienne." Le monde hebdomadiare, 25
        March 1982, p. 12.

G589.   Francion, Nicolas, Sylvie Carrouge, and Pierre
        Surin. "Almanach de la dissolution 1980-81."
        L'âne 1 (1981): 24-27.

        Traces in detail the events associated with
        Lacan's decision to dissolve the Ecole freudienne
        de Paris, and describes the formation of La Cause
        freudienne.

G590.   Francioni, M. "La psicolinguistica freudiana
        secondo Lacan: la struttura alienante della
        soggettivita e del linguaggio." Filosofia 24,
        no. 1 (1973): 35-52.

G591.   Francioni, Mario. "I significanti nell'inconscio
        secondo Lacan: la lettera e la metafora dal de-
        siderio al linguaggio." Filosofia 24 (1973):
        425-52.

G592.   Frank, Manfred. "Das 'wahre Subjekt' und sein
        Doppel: Jacques Lacans Hermeneutik." M. Frank,
        Das Sagbare und das Unsagbare: Studien zur
        neuesten französischen Hermeneutik und Text-
        theorie. Suhrkamp taschensuch wissenschaft.
        Frankfurt am Main: Suhrkamp, 1980. Pp. 114-40.

G593.   Frischer, Dominique. "Lacan au pilori." <u>Psycho-
        logie</u> 120 (1980): 26-29.

G594.   Funt, David Paul. "The Question of the Subject:
        Lacan and Psychoanalysis." <u>The Psychoanalytic
        Review</u> 60 (1973): 393-405.

        Briefly describes Benveniste's analysis of "indi-
        cators" or "shifters" and links it to Lacan's
        insistence on distinguishing between the "I" of
        discourse and the "thing" usually associated with
        it: the ego. The I usually refers to the <u>object</u>
        of discourse, Funt says, the "he" that speaks, and
        not to the ego. Funt discusses A2 more generally,
        emphasizing the circularity of discourse that Lacan
        proposes as a theoretical paradigm. He then com-
        pares that paradigm with Lacan's own style, which
        refuses to respond to the demands of the reader's
        ego for an "alter ego" that would sustain the il-
        lusion of communication (pp. 396-97). That stylis-
        tic refusal corresponds to the analyst's refusal to
        play the roles assigned to him by the patient, Funt
        says, and he describes Lacan's critique of analytic
        methods that promise to reinforce the patient's
        ego.

G595.   Gaillard, Françoise. "Au nom de la Loi: Lacan,
        Althusser et l'idéologie." <u>Sociocritique</u>.
        Edited by Claude Duchet. Papers from a col-
        loquium organized by the University of Paris-VIII
        and New York University. Paris: Fernand Nathan,
        1979. Pp. 11-24.

        Describes Lacan's theory of language as a "system
        of constraint" rather than a "primary modeling sys-
        tem," and compares it to the theory of ideology and
        the law proposed by Althusser in his essay "Ideol-
        ogy and Ideological State Apparatuses."

G596.   Galati, Dario. ["Lacan: A Coming Back to Freud?"
        (Italian).] <u>Storia e critica della psicologia</u> 1,
        no. 1 (1980): 79-91.

G597.   Gallop, Jane. "The Ghost of Lacan, the Trace of
        Language." <u>Diacritics</u> 5, no. 4 (1975): 18-24.

        Notes Mitchell's criticism of feminists who "fall
        back into biologism" in search of a "woman's psy-
        chology" (in K1274), and also her interest in the
        aspect of Freud that emphasized man's making him-
        self in culture. That is a side of Freud unknown
        to American feminists, Gallop claims. She also
        argues that Mitchell's position touches upon recent
        developments in psychoanalysis in France that are

also unknown in America, such as Lacan's rejection
of Freud's biologism.
   Gallop criticizes Mitchell for her inconsistent
use of Lacan and for mixing Lacanian topoi with un-
Lacanian explanations without marking the difference. Gallop also analyzes several instances
of this problem and then turns to C71 for a detailed description of Lacan's theory of the signifier.
   Reprinted in F333.

G598.   Gallop, Jane. "Impertinent Questions: Irigaray,
        Lacan, Sade." Sub-stance 26 (1980):   57-67.

        Discusses Irigaray's critique of Freudian phal-
        locentrism, noting that Irigaray's Freud is Lacan's
        Freud but that Lacan is curiously invisible on the
        surface of most of Irigaray's work.

G599.   Gallop, Jane. "Lacan and Literature: A Case for
        Transference." Poetics: International Review
        for the Theory of Literature 13 (1984):   301-08.

        Suggests that for Lacan psychoanalysis is a sub-
        category of literary studies, and claims that a
        Lacanian reading cannot simply look for hidden ex-
        amples of the name-of-the-father but must instead
        attend to the "literary 'dialectic'" of "something
        like" a transference between reader and text (p.
        307).
        Reprinted in F334.

G600.   Gallop, Jane. "Lacan's 'Mirror-Stage': Where to
        Begin?" Sub-stance 37/38 (1983):   118-28.

        Notes the dialectical relation in the mirror
        stage between the anticipation of coherence and a
        retrospective anxiety about the chaos that shows up
        against that anticipated coherence.
        Reprinted in F334.

G601.   Gallop, Jane. "The Ladies' Man." Diacritics 6,
        no. 4 (1976):   28-34.

        Describes the collection of articles about Lacan
        by women in F305, focussing on L1904 and the op-
        position between the "fluid," unfixed nature of the
        feminine and the fixed phallic objects constituted
        within Lacan's phallocentric system. Gallop also
        observes that Lacan's performance is itself the
        manifestation of "a prick," and she describes its
        outrageous dimension as the demonstration of desire
        without a veil.
        Reprinted in F333.

G602.   Gallop, Jane.   "Of Phallic Proportions: Lacanian
        Conceit."   Psychoanalysis and Contemporary
        Thought 4 (1981):   251-73.

G603.   Gallop, Jane.   "Phallus/Penis: Same Difference."
        Women and Literature 2 (1982):   243-51.

G604.   Gallop, Jane.   "Psychoanalysis in France."   Women
        and Literature 7, no. 1 (1979):   57-63.

        Describes the centrality of Lacan's work to the
        detailed reading of Freud that is more charac-
        teristic of psychoanalysis in France than in the
        United States.   Gallop claims that French analysts
        tend to juxtapose the most radical aspects of
        Freud's work with the more conservative, which
        results in new insights that will be crucial to
        textual studies and the analysis of sexual dif-
        ference.
           Reprinted as "Psychoanalysis and Feminism in
        France" in The Future of Difference.   Edited by
        Jardine and Eisenstein.   Boston: G. K. Hall, 1980.

G605.   Gallop, Jane.   "Reading Lacan's Ecrits."   Working
        Papers 6, Center for Twentieth Century Studies,
        Fall, 1984.

        Comments on the force of prospective and retro-
        spective orientations in language and interpreta-
        tion and in the reading of Lacan's work itself.
        Reprinted as part of F334.

G606.   Gardner, Sebastian.   "Splitting the Subject: An
        Overview of Sartre, Lacan and Derrida."   Aus-
        legung, A Journal of Philosophy 10, no. 1/2
        (1983):   57-64.

        Briefly surveys the collapse of the "classical"
        subject or the Cartesian cogito into the more con-
        temporary theories of a "split" subject such as
        proposed by Lacan, and advocates Sartre's model of
        consciousness against the ex-centric models of the
        self described by Lacan and Derrida.

G607.   Garnier, P.   "Présenter Lacan . . . "   K1335, pp.
        5-7.

G608.   Gauchet, Marcel.   "Lacan le médiateur."   L'express,
        25 September 1981, p. 29.

        Describes Lacan as an "incarnateur" of struc-
        turalism, claiming his real importance was to have
        opened up psychoanalysis to the influence of other
        fields such as linguistics and philosophy.

G609.   Gauthier, Yvon. "Langage et psychanalyse: à
        propos des Ecrits de Jacques Lacan." Dialogue 7,
        no. 4 (1969):   633-38.

        Briefly describes the role of language in Lacan's
        work, noting links between Lacan's claims and the
        work of Jakobson, Saussure, and Heidegger.

G610.   Gearhart, Suzanne. "The Scene of Psychoanalysis:
        The Unanswered Questions of Dora." Diacritics 9,
        no. 1 (1979):   114-26.

        Discusses E153 in detail, focussing on Lacan's
        analysis of transference and countertransference in
        Freud's account of the Dora case and on the rela-
        tion among transference, identification, and homo-
        sexuality that underlies Freud's analysis.
        Gearhart says that for Lacan "countertransference
        is the negative phase of a dialectical process
        which leads, practically speaking, to the positive
        transference . . . and, theoretically speaking, to
        an ultimately coherent, unified, scientific theory"
        (p. 114). Moreover, Gerhart adds that Lacan's
        reading of Freud's account "hinges on a distinction
        between an actor implicated in the scene and a
        neutral position not directly implicated in it" (p.
        116).
        Gearhart also claims that Lacan's distinction
        between the imaginary and the symbolic implicitly
        refutes feminist critiques of psychoanalysis such
        as K1220. She goes on to criticize Lacan, however,
        for excluding Freud's countertransference onto
        Dora's father from consideration, arguing that
        Lacan simply recapitulates Dora's case in terms of
        the fundamental scene of psychoanalysis described
        by Irigaray: the triad of "little girl/
        little boy/analyst" (p. 125).

G611.   George, François. "A vendre: 'Yau de poêle
        usage." Les temps modernes 411 (1980):   722-26.

        Notes that Lacan's dissolution of the Ecole
        freudienne de Paris confirms the harshest criticism
        of the Lacanian phenomenon (and so, incidently,
        helps out the sales of his own works). George
        compares Lacan to Caligula for the way he treats
        his followers and claims that Lacan grew tired of
        his school when some followers actually began to
        question him. This episode exposes the Lacanian
        school for what it always was, George says: a sect
        governed by an archaic authority (p. 724).

G612.   George, François. "Lacan ou l'effet--'Yau de
        poêle." Les temps modernes 394 (1979):   1787-
        1804.

Ridicules what he calls the "Lacan-effect," which
renders people foolish enough to follow the lead of
a charlatan such as Lacan. Failing to ingratiate
himself within the hermetic sects of Lacanians,
George claims to have discovered a secret society
devoted to the destruction of reason and signification called "La Confrèrie des Yau-de-Poêle."
George concludes with an extended critique of
Lacan's concept of the signifier, which he describes as a mass of contradictions. An extended
version of this essay was published as F335.

G613.   Gibeault, Alain.   "Symbolisme inconscient et sym-
        bolisme du langage." Revue française de psych-
        analyse 45 (1981): 139-59.

        Compares Freud's concept of the symbolic to
        Lacan's in order to contrast cultural vs. indi-
        vidual aspects of symbol formation, and argues that
        Lacan thinks of the symbolic as a fixed set of
        relations founded on the "positive conditioning" of
        the subject's access to language. On the other
        hand, Gibeault says, Freud emphasized negation as
        the basis of the symbol and therefore conceived of
        the symbolic as an endless flux.

G614.   Gilbert, R.   "Notes sur le langage, après Jacques
        Lacan." Société Alfred Binet et Théodore Simon
        551 (1976): 54-73.

G615.   Ginestet-Delbreil, Suzanne.   "L'identification par
        incorporation." K1297, pp. 75-86.

        Compares the identifications formed in trans-
        ference to the "assomption jubilatoire" of the
        image in the mirror stage (see C53), and distin-
        guishes between primary and secondary identifica-
        tions on the basis of Lacan's discussion of iden-
        tification with the father. Ginestet-Delbreil also
        comments on the Oedipal dimension of early iden-
        tifications and its relevance to the mass suicide
        of Jim Jones' Guyana cult in November 1978.

G616.   Goldberg, J.   "Notes et réflexions sur Jacques
        Lacan: le statut du sujet chez Jacques Lacan."
        Cahiers du C.E.R.M. 81 (1970).

G617.   Gorney, James E.   "The Clinical Application of
        Lacan in the Psychoanalytic Situation." Pre-
        sented at "Freud and Language: Contributions of
        Jacques Lacan--Theory and Therapy." 86th Con-
        vention of the American Psychological Associa-
        tion, Toronto, 31 August 1978. The Psychoana-
        lytic Review 69, no. 2 (1982): 241-48.

Offers a brief case history to illustrate the
application of Lacanian principles in analytic
interpretation, emphasizing the patient's passage
from "empty" to "full" speech through the recognition of his desire. Gorney's case focuses on a
fantasy of dismemberment, phonetic associations
that expose castrative fantasies of auto-mutila-
tion, and the patient's realization that he had
"relinquished" his capacity to <u>have</u> a phallus in
order to <u>become</u> a phallus for others. Gorney
claims that the case demonstrates the efficacy of
Lacan's emphasis on language as an analytic tool.
  For other papers from this conference, see G832
and G766.

G618.   Gorney, James E. "Resonance and Subjectivity: The
        Clinical Applications of Lacan." <u>Contemporary
        Psychoanalysis</u> 14 (1978): 246-73. Discussion by
        Stuart Schneiderman, pp. 274-77.

Notes the difficulty of treating seriously disturbed patients with classical psychoanalytic
technique, and cites several arguments that "the
explication and integration of unconscious material
must generally occur <u>within the therapist first</u>" if
the patient is to accomplish such an integration
himself (p. 252). Gorney argues that the limits to
classical technique can be overcome to some extent
by the therapist's awareness of his own relation
with the patient as an "other," which can be established through language that is understood as "that
fundamental structure interior to subjectivity
itself" (p. 253).
  The clinical technique Gorney describes focuses
on Lacan's concepts of "resonance" and "subjectivity" that are associated with his distinction
between the "moi" and the "je." Resonance marks
those nodes in the patient's discourse where its
vertical polyphony can emerge, Gorney says (see
C71), and he cites Ysseling's claims in G938 that
analysis proceeds through letting oneself be dominated and controlled by a word "to which one must
correspond and listen," with the analyst using his
own associations "in resonance" with the patient's
to discover what is signified at those nodal
points. Through such resonances, the analyst can
speak "evocatively" and so facilitate or enrich the
polyphony of the other's--the patient's--discourse
(see G58, pp. 62-63). The crucial task of Lacanian
analysis, Gorney says, is an effort by the analyst
"to begin to articulate to himself the authentic
language of his own being in relation to the words
spoken by that other authentic being who the
patient really is, not the patient whom the patient
presents himself to be" (p. 257).

Gorney applies this technique in his case history
of a "Miss F.," whose "ego syntonic" speech--ram-
bling, schizophrenic words that seem to soothe and
reassure her--stabilizes her ego rather than ex-
pressing genuine feeling (p. 258). Her words had
become "the permanent static of an objectified
ego," Gorney says (p. 260), and they had resulted
in the loss of her "I." The therapist's job is to
break through this empty speech, the language of
the "ossified ego" (p. 268), and hence to listen to
the language of the true self. Thus Gorney concludes, "the primary tasks of treatment . . . [are]
(1) the establishment of resonance; and (2) the
evocation and elucidation of subjective speech (p.
269)."
    In his discussion of Gorney's article, Schnei-
derman claims that Gorney's approach cannot be
truly Lacanian because he learned it from books,
and "the only way to learn the correct application
of Lacan's theories to psychoanalysis is through
supervision by a member of the Freudian School of
Paris" (p. 274). Schneiderman disagrees with
Gorney's diagnosis of Miss F. as psychotic and
schizophrenic, and argues instead that she suffers
from a grave hysteria. He also points out that
Gorney's emphasis on the analyst's articulating the
"authentic language of his own being" is contrary
to Lacan's definition of the analyst's place as
"de-being" or "desêtre," and Schneiderman says that
the discourse of the Other can in no way be considered such a thing as a "language of the self"
(pp. 276-77).

G619.   Green, André. "L'inconscient freudien et la psych-
        analyse française contemporaine." Les temps
        modernes 195 (1962): 365-79.

G620.   Green, André. "L'Objet (a) de J. Lacan, sa
        logique, et la théorie freudienne." First pre-
        sented in Lacan's seminar, 21 December 1965.
        Cahiers pour l'analyse 3 (1966): 15-37.

        Insists that the subject and the object are
        inextricably joined and that any attempt to sep-
        arate them in notions such as the "object of
        physics" is pointless. Green focuses instead on
        the constitution of the subject formed in "la
        suture," "la coupure," etc., and discusses the
        "objet a" as a limit to the incorporation of struc-
        turalism into psychoanalysis. He also discusses
        the R-schema in detail, the relation between the
        number zero and the "objet a," and the relevance of
        the "objet a" to problems of representation and
        "specularisation." Translated in F403, pp. 161-92.

G621.   Grimaud, Michel.   "Sur une métaphore métonymique
        hugolienne selon Jacques Lacan."   Littérature 29
        (1978):   98-104.

        Comments on Lacan's various remarks about Hugo's
        "Booz endormi" in A2 and compares them to other
        comments on the poem in G619 and G681.

G622.   Grisoni, Dominique.   "Politique de Lacan."   F361,
        p. 25.

        Notes that there is no written trace of Lacan's
        politics, and claims that Lacan's avoidance of
        political discourse follows the tradition in which
        "men of science" can be "neutral" and direct their
        discourse only to others in their discipline.   Such
        an attitude may have been acceptable at one time,
        Grisoni says, but it is now unthinkable,   espe-
        cially if one is Lacan.
        Grisoni does claim to find a politics implicit in
        Lacan's work, however, a "radical pessimism" that
        opts for management (la gestion) in light of the
        assumption that it is futile to try to change what
        exists.   Extrapolating from Lacan's thesis that the
        "I" does not produce the real, nor is it produced
        by the real, Grisoni concludes that for Lacan there
        is no cause, only effects; what is is, with no
        author, nor a raison d'être.   Thus, "la politique
        n'est qu'un jeu sur le réel" ("politics is only a
        play on the real").

G623.   Grossman, Marshall.   "The Subject of Narrative and
        the Rhetoric of the Self."   Papers on Language
        and Literature 18 (1982):   398-415.

        Cites several works by Lacan throughout on the
        dialectic of self and other, on the distinction
        between the subject of the énoncé and that of the
        énonciation, and in support of his own claim that
        "narrative is mimetic of the primary cognitive
        process of narrativization" (p. 412).

G624.   Gruber, Joseph.   "Das Spiegelstadium ('Stade du
        Miroir' nach Jacques Lacan) als richtungsweisende
        Entwicklungsstufe für die Identitatsfindung--
        'Normale,' 'Neurotische,' Psychotische' Entwick-
        lung"   ["The Mirror Stage . . . as a Crucial
        Stage of Development for Finding One's Identity .
        . . "].   Zeitschrift für Psychosomatische Medizin
        und Psychoanalyse 25 (1979):   342-53.

        Describes the importance of the mirror stage
        proposed by Lacan to the "normal" development of
        the child and the formation of its identity, and
        notes that neuroses and psychoses can develop from

disturbances in the mirror stage.

G625.   Gruber, Joseph.   "Zur Frage der Struktur und Psy-
chotherapie von Neurosen und Psychosen aus
Lacanscher und Mannoni'scher Sicht" ["On the
Question of Structure and Psychotherapy of
Neuroses and Psychoses by Lacan and Mannoni"].
Zeitschrift für Psychosomatische Medizin und
Psychoanalyse 24 (1978):   187-90.

Briefly describes the concepts of neurosis and
psychosis proposed in the work of Lacan and
Mannoni, focussing on their link with language, and
describes Mannoni's application of these concepts
in the psychotherapy of seriously disturbed
children.

G626.   Gunsberg, Maggie.   "The Mirror Episode in Canto XVI
of the Gerusalemme liberata."   The Italianist:
Journal of the Departments of Italian Studies,
University of Reading and University College,
Dublin 3 (1983):   30-46.

G627.   Hackett, Charles D.   "Psychoanalysis and Theology:
Jacques Lacan and Paul."   Journal of Religion and
Health 21, no. 3 (1982):   184-92.

Claims that "the hermeneutics of theology and
psychoanalysis correlate because the subject of
both is the same" (p. 185), and proceeds to explore
parallels between the understanding of the human
situation described in the work of Lacan and that
described by St. Paul. Hackett focuses on the similarity between what he calls Lacan's "construct of
the human pilgrimage in the hermeneutical circle of
psychoanalysis" and Paul's concept of sin, law,
gospel, and the Kingdom of God, and he proposes a
more tentative comparison between working through
the transference neurosis and Paul's scheme of
salvation.

G628.   Haddad, Gérad.   "Une pratique."   L'âne 3 (1981):
7.

Claims that Lacan's work is one of the greatest
achievements ever produced in France and that
future generations will consider him a Socrates.
Lacan's death closes a chapter in "parisianisme,"
Haddad says.

G629.   Hall, Gerald.   "The Logical Typing of the Symbolic,
the Imaginary, and the Real."   F421, pp. 274-77.

Claims that the three registers of experience
distinguished by Lacan are of "different logical

types" and "belong to different levels of abstraction" (p. 274).

G630.   Handwerk, Gary J.   "Irony as Intersubjectivity:
        Lacan on Psychoanalysis and Literature." Com-
        parative Criticism: A Yearbook 7 (1985):   105-
        26.

G631.   Hanzo, Thomas A.   "Paternity and the Subject in
        Bleak House."   F318, pp. 27-47.

        Argues that the domestic conditions of Bleak
        House may be read for "a metaphoric precision that
        emphasizes the structural importance of the Oedipal
        situation and the daughter's desire for the
        father's love," and claims that every novel Dickens
        wrote has incest as its theme and "reiterates the
        central failure of parental responsibility that he
        found everywhere in life" (p. 28). Hanzo also com-
        ments on the "re-creative" force of literary lan-
        guage that is understood from a Lacanian perspec-
        tive, especially as that language reproduces--for
        both the reader and the writer--the process by
        which an affective charge is pried loose from its
        original object and redirected towards other ele-
        ments, "phantasmally reproduced," on which it will
        be cathected. Thus Hanzo argues that "literary
        language has this creative power . . . the power of
        linking, through the fantasy, the unconscious and
        conscious systems" (p. 36). Through the shared
        fantasy that constitutes them as subjects, Hanzo
        concludes, readers of fiction thus "exchange among
        themselves that potential for signification that is
        the sacred fount of the phallus of the symbolic
        father" (p. 47).

G632.   Harari, Roberto. "Jacques Lacan: la vuelta de
        obligado o la vuelta de lo obligado?" ["Jacques
        Lacan: 'la vuelta de obligado' or Back Perforce
        to the Unavoidable?]" Acta psiquiatrica y psi-
        cologica de america latina 22, no. 3 (1976):
        211-24.

G633.   Harris, Adrienne E.   "The Rules of the Game:
        Discussion." Contemporary Psychoanalysis 21
        (1985):   17-26.

        Notes the resistance of North American psycho-
        analysts to hermeneutics and to Lacan's work, and
        briefly describes Lacan's theory of a decentered
        subject and of the illusory quality of stability
        associated with concepts such as Winnicott's "true
        self." Harris claims Lacan's argument is compel-
        ling but potentially frightening in a clinical
        context; discusses Lacan's distinction between the

Other and the individual who speaks; and comments
on the relations between language and gender.

G634.   Hartman, Geoffrey.   "Psychoanalysis: The French
        Connection."   Psychoanalysis and the Question of
        the Text.   Edited by Geoffrey Hartman.   Balti-
        more: Johns Hopkins University Press, 1978.

        Claims to read both Lacan and Derrida "in the
        light of what Sartre called 'la grand affaire'--the
        scandal of theological survivals in even the most
        secular thinkers."   Hartman notes, however,   that
        Lacan himself was careful to resist the hope for
        some "metalanguage" that might lead to an authen-
        ticity "beyond the eloquence of wounds or religious
        pathos or the desire for reality-mastery."   Both
        Lacan and Derrida remind us, Hartman concludes,
        "that language, like sexual difference or passion
        in general, is that in which we live and breath and
        have our being.   It cannot be subdued but remains
        part of the subtle knot that perplexes even as it
        binds together man and woman in the "scène famil-
        iale.'"
        Reprinted in K1210, pp. 96-117.

G635.   "Healing Words: Dr. Lacan's Structuralism."   Times
        Literary Supplement, 25 January 1968, pp. 73-75.

        Discusses A2 and claims that French intellectual
        life has been upset by a profound epistemological
        unrest and therefore is open to the "disquieting
        implications of psychoanalysis."   The reviewer also
        claims that Lacan's Ecrits, riding the "struc-
        turalist wave," shares with other recent works a
        drastic shift in the conception of man as the
        subject of science (p. 73).   Noting the difficulty
        of Lacan's style, the reviewer also argues that
        many of the essays collected in A2 are clear and
        vigorous despite their polemical nature.   The
        review also recounts Sartre's objections to Lacan's
        work and describes the critique of ideologies of
        freedom that pervades Lacan's work and marks its
        essentially conservative implications.

G636.   Heath, Stephen.   "Anata mo."   Screen 17, no. 4
        (1976/77):   49-66.

        Describes the function of the real as explained
        in several works by Lacan, notes its difference
        from "reality," and discusses that distinction as
        it bears on his analysis of Oshima's film Death by
        Hanging (see esp. pp. 49-56).

G637.   Heath, Stephen.   "Difference."   Screen 19, no. 3
        (1978/79):   50-112.

Discusses at length several issues in Lacan
works: his remarks on "woman" and the character of
the feminine in B31; feminist objections to Lacan's
work and to the generally phallocentric nature of
psychoanalysis; and the importance of those theoretical issues to cinematic analysis of the representation of the female form in film. Heath
criticizes B31 from a feminist perspective, attacking the "confidence of knowledge" with which Lacan
addresses the question "What does woman want?" and
proposes his own position as one of doubt and
uncertainty since he speaks as "not a woman." For
a discussion of Heath's reading, see F333.

G638.   Heath, Stephen. "Notes on Suture." Screen 18, 4
        (1977/78):   48-76.

Comments on the term "suture," which was first
introduced by Jacques-Alain Miller in G739 to name
the effect constituted by the positioning of the
subject in the symbolic order of language. Heath
offers a detailed account of the Lacanian principles behind Miller's argument and comments on
G789, where the term was first imported into film
theory. Although suture is a function of the
symbolic, Heath concludes, is it always "towards
the imaginary, the moment of junction" between the
imaginary and the symbolic at which the subject is
situated.
Heath also argues that Lacanian psychoanalysis
grounds subjectivity "in the social relations of
language as discourse" because it understands the
unconscious as "a term of subject-division in the
signifier, an action in the speaking-being." As a
result, Lacan's teaching has "a double edge": on
the one hand, discourse is the sole province of
truth; yet, on the other hand, since there is
nothing but discourse, there can be no "trans-
historical finality" either. This conclusion leads
Heath to treat Lacanian psychoanalysis as a possible ground for "a radical practice and transformation of the whole history of the subject."
Reprinted in K1211.

G639.   Hébrard, Danielle.   "Transcription et ponctuation."
        F357, pp. 99-107.

Insists on the importance of the "l'opérateur-
transcripteur" in the production of a written text
from Lacan's seminars, and demonstrates how punctuation itself necessarily structures the text in a
way unlike the oral delivery. Punctuation is interpretation, Hébrard claims, and quotes George
Sand's remark that "punctuation is more the man

than style is" (p. 105).   Even the ostensibly
neutral function of the stenographer influences the
written form of the communication, Hébrard says,
because the stenographer always "hears the text
that she will have to write" (p. 106).
In addition to commenting on the problem of
establishing a text for Lacan's seminar, Hébrard
quickly surveys the history of attitudes towards
punctuation and observes that punctuation "is a
stake in the opposition between the maximal socialization of texts . . . and the individuation of the
enunciation of an author who seeks there his style
and the very mark of his presence in the text" (p.
106).

G640.   Heim, Robert.   "Lorenzer und/oder Lacan: Das
        Subjekt zwischen Sinn und Buchstabe"   ["Lorenzer
        and/or Lacan: The Subject between Spirit and
        Letter"].   Psyche 34 (1980):   910-44.

G641.   Heinrichs, Hans-Jürgen.   "Die Schule der seelischen
        Leidenshaften: zur Psychoanalyse Jacques Lacan."
        Psyche 32 (1978):   595-632.

G642.   Hengen, Shannon.   "'your father, the thunder/your
        mother, the rain':   Lacan and Atwood."   Litera-
        ture and Psychology 32, no. 3 (1986):   36-42.

        Discusses Lacan's theory of the mirror stage in
        relation to similar themes in Atwood's work.

G643.   Hennion, C.   "Gloria, trente ans au service du
        Maître."   F354, p. 9.

        Briefly describes the many duties Lacan's secre-
        tary performed, including serving as a confidant
        for Lacan's patients.

G644.   Henry, Paul.   "On Language and the Body."   Trans-
        lated by Ben Brewster.   F359, pp. 70-74.

        Discusses the association between a system of
        language and the body that underlies Chomsky's
        work, which assumes an organic basis for linguistic
        competence.   Henry claims that Chomsky nevertheless
        relies on a dualistic distinction between language
        and the body that is quite distinct from the "cor-
        poreality of language" derived from Lacan's account
        of the nature of the signifier.

G645.   Higgins, Robert William.   "De l'actualité de la
        question religieuse en psychanalyse."   Esprit 3
        (1980):   134-36.

        Traces the religious dimension of psychoanalytic

institutions suggested by Lacan's characterization
of the International Psychoanalytic Association as
a "church" (B38a), but also explores more theoretical associations between psychoanalytic concepts such as transference and the religious concepts of faith, belief, truth, etc. Published with
G887 and L2370.

G***.   Higgins, Robert W. "Saint-Jacques-aux liens." See
        F399.

G646.   Hirsch, Elie [pseud.]. "Trés longue lettre de Elie
        Hirsch à son frère Hyacinthe, à propos de l'édi-
        tion du séminaire Les psychoses de Jacques
        Lacan." Le discours psychanalytique 7 (1983):
        35-46.

        Attacks the "official edition" of Lacan's seminar
        as a rewritten version that fails to do justice to
        a stenographic version circulated earlier. Hirsch
        recalls that Lacan used to advise people to toss
        off what they did not understand of his work be-
        cause they would come back to it later, but she
        claims that Lacan's editor seems either to have
        eliminated what he could not understand or to have
        simply rewritten it (p. 36). She also complains
        that the passages regarding clinical practice have
        been treated especially poorly, and appends a list
        of specific comparisons between the published text
        and the version circulated in typescript supposedly
        based on a stenographer's manuscript of Lacan's
        seminar. (Hirsch and "Hyacinthe" are pseudonyms
        for the anonymous author and a fictional friend, a
        format often used in this journal.)

G647.   Hobson, Irmagard W. "Goethe's Iphigenie: A
        Lacanian Reading." Goethe Yearbook: Publica-
        tions of the Goethe Society of North America 2
        (1984): 51-67.

G648.   Hogan, Patrick Colm. "Introductory Comments on
        Joyce and Lycan." The Augmented Ninth: Proce-
        edings of the Ninth International James Joyce
        Symposium. English edition by Bernard Benstock.
        Ithaca, N.Y.: Cornell University Press, forth-
        coming. German edition by Klaus Reichert.
        Frankfurt: Suhrkamp Verlag, forthcoming.

G649.   Holloway, Robin. "Jacques Lacan: Language as
        Foundational of the Unconscious." Issues in Lan-
        guage: Studies in Honor of Robert J. Di Pietro.
        Edited by Marcel Danesi. Lake Bluff, Ill.:
        Jupiter, 1981. Pp. 135-47.

G650.   Hollwitz, John. "The Performance Psychology of

Jacques Lacan." Literature in Performance: A
Journal of Literary and Performing Art 4, no. 1
(1983): 27-30.

G651. Horvat, J. A. "Freud in France." The Cambridge
       Quarterly 7, no. 4 (1977): 346-57.

       Reviews A2j and describes Lacan as the "enfant
       terrible" of Freudian psychoanalysis. Horvat
       claims that Lacan, unlike Freud, is completely
       unconcerned about making his argument clear, and he
       says that the difficulty of Lacan's writing is
       "artificial," much like Pound's in the Late Cantos
       (p. 348). Horvat argues that elliptical explana-
       tions and vague references keep Lacan's secret safe
       for the elect who attend his seminar as an
       "ashram."
       Horvat also notes Lacan's debt to Kojève's lec-
       tures on Hegel (1933-39), but he says that Lacan
       has added to Hegel the idea of "stepping into
       language." "There blows an arid wind of French
       rationalism through M. Lacan's conception of what
       language is," Horvat remarks (p. 353), and he goes
       on to claim that Lacan's reading of Freud will
       gladden the hearts of Hegelians, phenomenologists,
       and existentialists but will appear unacceptable to
       those who demand empirical evidence in support of
       theoretical claims (p. 354).
       Horvat also compares Lacan's revisions of ortho-
       dox Freudian training and the goal of therapy to
       revisionary efforts by R. D. Laing, Wilhelm Reich,
       and others, but he says that Lacan has created his
       own "establishment." Horvat concludes by con-
       trasting the obscurity of Lacan's work to the
       clearer book on Freud by Paul Ricoeur, Essai sur
       Freud, but he does admit that B22 is more acces-
       sible that Lacan's other works and advises readers
       to approach Lacan through the earlier seminars
       whenever possible.

G652. Hottois, Gilbert. "La hantise contemporaine du
       langage: essai sur la situation philosophique du
       discours lacanien." Confrontations psychia-
       triques 19 (1981): 163-88.

       Evaluates Lacan's importance from the perspective
       of linguistic philosophy.

G653. L'humanité, 11 September 1981, pp. 1, 12.

       Includes a number of items on Lacan's death by
       writers associated with this central journal of the
       French Communist Party; see J1071, J1082, J1089.
       This collection also includes brief remarks by a
       number of public figures such as Lucien Bonnafe,

Bernard Muldworf, Serge Leclaire, and others, as
well as a strange drawing of a brain with legs and
arms, wearing a black sash, with the caption "Lacan
is no more, the unconscious is in mourning" (p.
12).

G654.   Hyde, Michael J.   "Jacques Lacan's Psychoanalytic
        Theory of Speech and Language." The Quarterly
        Journal of Speech 66, no. 1 (1980):   96-108.

        Claims that the originality of Lacan's approach
        stems from his ability to "humanize" structuralist
        theory, and argues that Lacan is directing psycho-
        analysts towards an area that will be important for
        scholars studying communication (p. 96).

G655.   Ijsseling [Ysseling], S.   "Filosofie en psycho-
        analyse: Enige opmerkingen over het denken van
        M. Heidegger en J. Lacan" ["Philosophy and
        Psychoanalysis: Some Remarks on the Thought of
        M. Heidegger and J. Lacan"]. Tijdschrift voor
        filosofie 31 (1969):   261-89.

        Claims that for both Heidegger and Lacan, man
        figures in a discourse of which he is not the
        master, and that both thinkers seek the structuring
        principle of language in the "unthought" (l'im-
        pensée).

G656.   Ionescu, Cornel Mihoi.   "Heidegger 'traduit' par
        Lacan." Cahiers roumains d'études littéraires:
        revue trimestrielle de critique, d'ésthique et
        d'histoire littéraires [Romania] 1 (1983):   93-
        110.

G657.   Irigaray, Luce.   "Communications linguistique et
        speculaire." Cahiers pour l'analyse 3 (1966):
        39-55.

        Argues that "the reciprocal integration of the
        body and language from where the imaginary origi-
        nates decenters man and marks the beginning of his
        errance" (p. 39). Irigaray discusses the con-
        nection between fantasies of dismemberment and the
        desire to reinstitute the body as a place of whole-
        ness, and she claims that specular experience must
        be given a place as a possible return to (reprise)
        of the earlier integration between the body and the
        founding language of the subject (p. 45). The
        specular image is a "visualization of the signi-
        fier," Irigaray says, but it is a misleading signi-
        fier ("un signifiant trompeur") because it repre-
        sents discourse as global, totalized, and finite
        (p. 46ff.).
        Irigaray also comments on hysteria, schizo-

phrenia, and other pathological states, and concludes that the distortions of language characteristic of such states can be linked to specular
experience because specular experience "figures"
communication.

G658. Irigaray, Luce. "Cosi fan tutti." _Vel_ 2 (1975).

Comments on a number of specific remarks in B31,
focussing on Lacan's point that "There is no woman
who is not excluded by the nature of things, which
is the nature of words." Irigaray agrees with
Lacan about that and observes that psychoanalytic
theory has, indeed, described the truth about
female sexuality, though she criticizes it for
"refusing to interpret the historical determinants
of its discourse." Lacan has turned historically
specific fantasies into laws unresisted by any
reality, she asserts, and then argues that women,
in their concrete plurality, are "resistant to
discourse" and constitute a sort of "prediscursive
reality" that disrupts the order of phallocentric
language.
This essay is one of the clearest and most
pointed critiques of B31. Reprinted in K1219 and
translated there. For a discussion of this essay
see F333.

G659. Jaccard, Roland. "Salve contre Lacan." _Le monde_,
21 September 1979, pp. 19, 25.

Praises George's attack on Lacan in F335, and
describes Lacan's seminars as a meeting place for
"les curieux, gogos, jobards, et snobs"--most of
whom understand little of what is said. Jaccard
endorses George's complaint against Lacan's "intellectual terrorism," comparing Lacan's power among
his followers to that of the Ayatollah Khomeni in
Iran, and he claims that at least part of Lacan's
popularity stems from a cultural chauvinism that
wants to reclaim psychoanalysis for France. For
responses to Jaccard's attack, see J1091 and J1135.

G660. Jameson, Fredric. "Imaginary and Symbolic in
Lacan." K1356, pp. 338-95.

Argues that Freudianisms and Marxisms are both
"materialisms" because they study realms where
human consciousness is not master (p. 385), and
examines the translation of the categories of
"character" and individual experience into terms of
collective social experience. Jameson compares
this translation to a transition between Lacan's
categories of the imaginary and the symbolic, and
he discusses at length relations among these two

registers and the third that Lacan calls the real.
Jameson claims that Lacan overestimates the importance of the symbolic and that this attitude is
fundamentally ideological. Against this conservative tendency in Lacan's thought, Jameson stresses
the "tragic character" of Lacan's work and its
"dialectical possibilities." Those possibilities
are established through what Jameson calls the
"insertion of the Imaginary into the model of a
Symbolic System" (p. 381) and through Jameson's
identification of the real as "simply History
itself" (p. 384).
    For an extended commentary on this essay see
G503. Jameson elaborates his argument for the
importance of the imaginary in The Political Unconscious: Narrative as a Socially Symbolic Act
(Ithaca: Cornell University Press, 1981).

G661. Johnson, Barbara. "The Frame of Reference: Poe,
       Lacan, Derrida." K1356, pp. 457-505.

       Analyzes Lacan's reading of Poe's "The Purloined
       Letter" (C69) and Derrida's critical response
       (G544), and argues that Derrida's critique is
       misdirected. Derrida falsely attributes to Lacan a
       belief in the transcendental locus of the signi-
       fier, Johnson says; he can do that only by ig-
       noring the "frame" of Lacan's own text. Rather
       than making the signifier into the story's "truth,"
       Johnson argues, Lacan offers us an account of the
       constitutive power of the letter to situate even
       the reader within the "transferential structure of
       all reading" (p. 503).
           In fact, Johnson adds, Derrida falls into the
       very trap he describes by substituting his concept
       of dissemination for that of a transcendental
       signifier. Lacan, on the other hand, constructs a
       text that is "self-ambiguous," thus avoiding the
       assumption of any transcendent, objective place
       beyond narrative. Nevertheless, Johnson insists
       that any analysis, including psychoanalysis, simply
       re-enacts the same kind of transferential structure
       illustrated by Poe's story. "Psychoanalysis is in
       fact itself the primal scene it is seeking,"
       Johnson says. "Psychoanalysis is not itself the
       interpretation of repetition; it is the repetition
       of a trauma of interpretation" (p. 499).

G662. Jouary, J. P. ["Politics, or the Art of Taking
       One's Time: Time and Social Change in Lacan,
       Locke, and Rousseau" (French)]. La pensée 252
       (1986): 65-74.

G663. Julien, P. "Jacques Lacan, epigone de Freud."
       K1335, pp. 8-10.

G664. Julien, Philippe. "Lacan et la psychose: 1932-
       76." _Littoral_ 21 (1986): 5-26.

       Describes Lacan's remarks about psychosis
       throughout his career as an introduction to a
       collection of articles, all of which discuss psy-
       chosis from a Lacanian perspective.

G665. Julien, Philippe. "Lacan, Freud: une rencontre
       manquée." F358, pp. 17-24.

       Discusses the popular combination of Freud and
       Lacan into a "Freudo-Lacanisme," and traces some of
       its implications for psychoanalysis as a science
       that must be transmitted "to and in" scientific
       groups.

G666. Julien, Philippe. "Un psychanalyste, Jacques
       Lacan." _Etudes_ 357 (1982): 333-46.

       Describes Lacan's career and the major concepts
       of his work as they developed over the years.

G667. Juranville, Alain. Brief excerpt from F345. _L'âne_
       14 (1984): 2.

       Comments on Munch's painting _The Scream_ from a
       Lacanian perspective.

G668. Khan, M. Masud R. "D'autres parmi nous." _Nouvelle_
       revue de psychanalyse 20 (1979): 169-71.

       Cites C58 as one of several French works that
       have influenced the way Freud is used in Anglo-
       Saxon countries. For accompanying articles see
       G549, G565, G672, and G894.

G669. Kittler, Friedrica A. "Das _Phantom unseres Ichs_
       und die Literaturpsychologye: E. T. A. Hoffmann,
       Freud, Lacan." _Romantikforschung seit 1945_.
       Edited by Peter Klaus. Königstein: Hein, 1980.
       Pp. 335-56.

G670. Koolhaas, Gilberto. "The Knot of Analytic Dis-
       course." _Revista uruguaya de psicoanalisis_ 60
       (1980): 11-15.

G671. Kress-Rosen, N. "Linguistics and Anti-linguistics
       in the Work of Lacan." _Confrontation psychia-_
       triques 19 (1981): 145-62.

G672. Kristeva, Julia. "Il n'y a pas de maître à lan-
       gage." _Nouvelle revue de psychanalyse_ 20 (1979):
       119-40.

Comments on several issues raised by Lacan's claim that the unconscious is structured like a language, especially that of the role of denegation (Die Verneinung) and the concept of "lalangue" introduced in B31. Kristeva objects to the association of the bar between S and s with the concept of repression, however, and suggests that Lacan ignores the heterogeneity endemic to the persistence of "l'insymbolisable," which constitutes the condition of the speaking subject as "clivé dans une hétérogénéité inconciliable" (p. 130). For accompanying articles see G549, G565, G668, and G894.
Translated as the first part of "Within the Microcosm of 'The Talking Cure'" in F403.

G***.   Kristeva, Julia.   "Nom de mort ou de vie."   See
         F399.

G673.   Kristeva, Julia.   "Noms de lieu."   Tel quel 68
         (1976):   40-56.

Argues that Lacan's concept of the imaginary designates a space that is already organized in terms of the symbolic, and claims that human experience passes through a stage that is pre-imaginary as well, one not already marked by symbolic difference.

G674.   Kristeva, Julia.   "Le temps des femmes."   34/44:
         Cahiers de recherche de sciences des textes et
         documents 5 (1979):   5-19.

Proposes alternatives to the phallocentric model of the symbolic described by Lacan, focussing on the issues of castration and subjectivity as well as the position of woman in the symbolic order. Kristeva cites A2 and B31 on the general image of Freud as an "irritating phallocrat . . . a man who fantasized women as sub-men, castrated men."
Translated by Alice Jardine and Harry Blake as "Women's Time," Signs: Journal of Women in Culture and Society, special issue on French Feminist Theory, vol. 7, no. 1 (1981), pp. 13-35.

G675.   Kurzweil, Edith.   "Jacques Lacan: French Freud."
         Theory and Society 10 (1981):   419-38.

Emphasizes the importance of hysteria in Lacan's reading of Freud and his fusion of structural linguistics and Hegelian dialectics (p. 424). Kurzweil discusses C69 as an illustration of Lacan's style and genius, and she claims that his insistence on the centrality of language in human

experience is unquestioned even by those psychoanalysts who have split with him over other issues.
Kurzweil also notes the influence of Lacan's work
on radical political writers, despite the fact that
he generally avoids political statements.

G676. LaGuardia, Eric. "Lacan's Full and Empty Words and
Literary Discourse." Proceedings of the Sixth
Congress of the International Comparative Litera-
ture Association. Edited by Michel Cadot, et al.
Stuttgart: Bieber, 1975.

G677. Lambotte, Marie-Claude. "Interpelations . . . ."
Psychanalystes 2 (1982): p. 47ff.

G678. Landman, Claude. "Freud, Hegel et la machine." Le
discours psychanalytique 7 (1983):   65-66.

Proposes a brief reading of this lesson from
Seminar II, noting Lacan's claim that Hegel's
insistence on the future of absolute knowledge as
the end of history and as the revelation of Man by
man is nothing other than a fantasm of Mastery.

G679. Lang, Hermann. ["Repression and Splitting: Linguistic Aspects of the Split between the Neurotic
and the Psychotic" (French)]. Confrontation psychiatrique 19 (1981):   215-32.

G680. Lang, Hermann. "Zum Verhaeltnis von Struktur-
alismus, Philosophie und Psychoanalyse: Konkre-
tisiert am Phaenomen der Subjektivitaet." Tijdschrift voor filosofie 38 (1976):   559-73.

G681. Laplanche, Jean, and Serge Leclaire. "L'inconscient." L'inconscient. Colloque de Bonneval,
1960. Paris: Desclée de Brouwer, 1966.

Comments in detail on the concept of the unconscious as described by Freud and developed by later
psychoanalysts. This article proposes a Lacanian
alternative to more traditional models of the
unconscious, but it became a point of contention
between Lacan and the authors. They insist that
"the unconscious is the precondition of language"
(tr., p. 151ff.), whereas Lacan argues that language is a precondition for the unconscious.
This article was published without the discussion
in Les temps modernes 183 (1961):   81-129. Translated by Patrick Coleman in F424, pp. 118-75, with
a postscript by Laplanche, 176-78.

G682. Lapouge, Gilles. "Des tuyaux sur Lacan: pamphlet." Le point, 5 November 1979, p. 182.

Comments on F335, praising it for its healthy
skepticism but concluding that its real value may
be in getting people to read Lacan's work and to
decide for themselves whether he is the prophet or
the clown of psychoanalysis.

G683.   Larcher, D. "Linguistique et psychopathologie:
        vers une approche pragmatique." Neuropsychiatrie
        de l'enfance et de l'adolescence 29, no. 4/5
        (1981):   187-203.

Cites B12 on the symbolic function of the "je" as
it emerges in and through language (pp. 194-95).

G684.   Larmore, Charles.   "The Concept of a Constitutive
        Subject."   F359, pp. 108-31.

Briefly sketches the history of philosophical
work dealing with the question of the subject since
Kant, and discusses in detail Lacan's distinction
between the subject and the ego.   Larmore argues
that Lacan's distinction undermines the possibility
of using the subject as a stable explanatory concept from which individual motives may be understood, and he claims instead that "in the flexibility of the subject explanations comes to an end
and we face the inherent contingency and open-
endedness of experience" (p. 129).

G685.   Laroche-Parent, Madeleine.   "La femme (dite barrée)
        selon l'approche lacanienne."   Philosophiques 12,
        no. 1 (1985):   165-76.

G686.   Laurent, Eric.   "Une clinique."   L'âne 3 (1981):
        8-9.

Notes Lacan's early and constant involvement in
the clinical practice of psychoanalysis, and claims
that clinical experience was fundamental to Lacan's
return to Freud.   Laurent briefly comments on
Lacan's revisions in traditional methods of analytic practice and on Lacan's model of the discourse of analysis.   He also claims that Lacan's
practice led to a renewed ethic of psychoanalysis,
one that went beyond mastery or adaptation, and
says that Lacan developed "une clinique du sacrifice de l'être parlant à sa jouissance" (p. 9).

G687.   Lauritsen, Laurits.   "Affekt og effekt: hvad
        bliver den Freudske affekt til i Lacans psyko-
        analyse?" ["Affect and Effect: What becomes of
        Freud's Affect in the Psychoanalysis of Jacques
        Lacan?"].   Psyke and Logos 5, no. 1 (1984):   109-
        24.

G688.   Lauritsen, Laurits. "Narcissismen i Lacans psyko-
analyse" ["Narcissism in Lacan's Psychoanalysis"]. Psyke & Logos 1 (1983): 88-102.

G689.   Lavalle, Pierre. "Analyse logique." Cahiers
confrontation 15 (1986): 37-65.

Discusses the tension in Lacan's work between an
Aristotelian logic and an "intuitionniste" logic,
and traces an opposition between truth and knowledge in logic itself as invoked by Lacan's work,
especially in B31 and several essays in A2.

G690.   Lavers, Annette. "Some Aspects of Language in the
Work of Jacques Lacan." Semiotica 3 (1971):
269-79.

Discusses the influence of existentialism in
Lacan's work and his rejection of its "personalist"
emphasis on the subject. Lavers stresses Lacan's
distance from ego psychology and the consequences
of his emphasis on language as the ground of psychoanalytic practice and theory, but she concludes
that Lacan's successful "subversion of the subject"
has yielded a "glee" that is as suspicious as the
humanist complacency that preceded it. Lavers
translates a large part of E179.

G691.   Le Gaufey, Guy. "Représentation freudienne et
signifiant lacanien." F358, pp. 41-56.

Compares Freud's curiously doubled term Vorstel-
lungrepräsentanz to Lacan's concept of the signifier.

G692.   Leather, Phil. "Desire: A Structural Model of
Motivation." Human Relations 36, no. 2 (1983):
109-22.

Draws upon C86 and A2j to develop a theory of
desire for the psychology of human motivation that
will not depend on individual or instrumental
explanations but will instead explore social relationships as mediated by symbolic structures.
Leather includes a section on the "one" and the
"two" in the "logic of desire" described by Lacan
in C86, and emphasizes the derivation of the effect
of identity from repeated difference.

G693.   Leavy, Stanley A. "The Image and the Word: Further Reflections on Jacques Lacan." F403, pp. 3-
32.

Points out Lacan's emphasis on the centrality of
language to psychoanalysis and briefly describes

the implications of that emphasis for analytic
technique.   Leavy also notes the relatively minor
impact of Lacan's work on American psychoanalysis
compared to, for example, Melanie Klein's id psychology or the ego psychology associated with the
work of Heinz Hartmann and more recently Heinz
Kohut's Analysis of the Self (1971).

G694.   Leavy, Stanley A.   "The Significance of Jacques
        Lacan."   Psychoanalytic Quarterly 46, no. 2
        (1977):   201-219.

        Describes the principle linguistic functions
attributed to the unconscious by Lacan and his
emphasis on the role of the signifier.   Leavy
defends Lacan against charges of "intellectualism"
(see K1195), and he claims that Lacan simply tries
to avoid granting primacy to some feeling "behind"
language as if feelings and emotions were independent of the signifying chain.   Leavy also compares
Lévi-Strauss's analysis of the linguistic structure
of social forms to Lacan's theory of the linguistic
structure of the unconscious, and he discusses the
difference between desire and need. (pp. 211-12).
Reprinted in K1332, pp. 271-92.

G695.   Leavy, S.   "The Theme and the Word: Further Re-
        flections on Jacques Lacan."   Psychiatry and the
        Humanities 7.   Edited by Joseph Smith.   New
        Haven, Conn.:   Yale University Press, 1982.   Pp.
        271-92.

G696.   Lebovici, Serge.   "Jacques Lacan and French Psy-
        chiatry."   Psychological Medicine 13 (1983):   9-
        13.

        Briefly describes the origins and development of
psychoanalysis in France, focussing on Lacan's
influence and his controversial role as a leader of
schismatic groups.   Noting the association between
Lacanian movements and the political radicalism of
the 1960s, Lebovici claims that Lacan's prominence
on the Parisian intellectual scene was "a form of
conjunction between one man and his milieu, in
which the transmission of psychoanalysis becomes
problematical" (p. 12).
Reprinted in Salud mental 9 (1986):   2-5.

G697.   Leclaire, Serge.   "A la recherche des principes
        d'une psychothérapie des psychoses."   Evolution
        psychiatrique 1 (1958):   377-411.

        Notes the importance of intersubjective relations
to all psychoanalytic discourse, but argues that
Lacan's L-schema shows how those relations always

involve three subjects, not just two. Leclaire
also discusses the importance of Lacan's concept of
foreclosure and of several other concepts to the
study of psychoses, including the role of the
symbolic and its relation to the imaginary. See
especially pp. 398-407. This item is a continuation of L1994 and is continued in G701.

G698.   Leclaire, Serge.   "Détour."   F327, pp. 115-21.

Discusses the problems of writing, logic, and the
position of the subject in psychoanalysis in the
light of Lacan's work, arguing that Freud's approach to these issues retain their modernity a
half-century later.

G699.   Leclaire, Serge.   "Le mouvement animé par Jacques
         Lacan: psychanalyse."   Le monde, 2 October 1979,
         p. 2.

Based on Leclaire's controversial paper presented
at the Congress of Tbilisi, USSR (see G700). "What
psychoanalytic practice supports in each particular
concrete situation," Leclaire says, "is the possibility of living as a responsible, speaking being
among other responsible, speaking beings."
Leclaire goes on to comment on several issues
raised by Lacan's work, and concludes by noting the
link between many of Lacan's concepts and the
primary issues in French feminism, especially as
exemplified by the group Politique et psychanalyse.
Leclaire's remarks about the liberating potential
of psychoanalysis were interpreted as slighting
other revolutionary movements in the political
domain and generated considerable controversy at
the conference.
Appears with J1135, J1091, and J1014. For responses to Leclaire, see G453 and G804. For a
description of the conference and other papers
presented there, see G500 and L1550.

G700.   Leclaire, Serge.   "Le mouvement psychanalytique
         animé par Jacques Lacan."   Confrontations: les
         machines analytiques 3 (1980):   69-76.

Claims that psychoanalysis is the single way to
freedom for humanity. Presented at a symposium on
Lacan's work held in the Soviet Union in 1979, this
paper provoked a bitter response from some of the
Soviets. See G453 and G804. For a description of
the conference and the other papers presented
there, see L1550 and G500. Remarks by Leclaire
based on this paper were published earlier as G699.

G701.   Leclaire, Serge.   "L'obsessionel et son désir."

Evolution psychiatrique 3 (1959):   383-412.

Argues that Lacan's work on the Oedipal schema
proposed by Freud has increased its clinical utility, and discusses the importance of the Other, the
symbolic function of the phallus, and other
Lacanian themes related to the organization of the
Oedipal complex. This item is the third and last
essay in a series that includes L1994 and G697.

G702.   Lecourt, Dominique. "Lacan: psylosophe ou phil-
        analyste." Franc-Tireur, November-December 1981.

Notes the political daring of Althusser's attempt
to link Lacanian psychoanalysis to Marxism in G433,
but criticizes Althusser's "naiveté" in giving in
to the "effect of intimidation from which Lacan's
work derives a good part of its force." Lecourt
claims that the intimidating thrust of Lacan's work
stems from his success in constructing a "philosophy of psychoanalysis" that theoretically unifies
concepts Freud had borrowed from several sources.
Lacan's theory of the subject, Lecourt adds, is
actually no different from that of classical spiri-
turalism. Lacanian psychoanalysis is at bottom a
successful combination of "a materialism of the
Signifier and a spiritualism of authenticity, the
second supporting the first."
Oddly enough, Lecourt's remarks about the intimidating quality of Lacan's work and about Lacan's
effort to establish a philosophy of psychoanalysis
echo Althusser's own observations in G432. For a
bitter response to Lecourt's attack on Althusser,
see G855.

G***.   Levallois, Anne. "L'école de Lacan." See 399.

G703.   Lévy, Danièle. "L'étrange altérité de l'expéri-
        ence." F358, pp. 25-40.

Discusses Lacan's distinctions among the Four
Discourses (see E210 and E211) and their implications for the relation between analysis and
science.

G704.   Lévy, Françoise. "La lettre." Tel quel 87 (1981):
        64-73.

Discusses C69, focussing on the material characteristics of the letter in Poe's story and on
Lacan's own relation to the letter as an interpreter of the story.

G705.   Lingis, A. "The Visible and the Vision: Merleau-
        Ponty and Lacan." Journal of the British Society

for Phenomenology 15, no. 2 (1984):   155-63.

G706.   Lotringer, S.   "The 'Subject' on Trial." Semio-
         text(e) 1, no. 3 (1975):   3-8.

         Discusses Lacan's theory of the subject (pp. 4-5)
         as one of several theories of subjectivity impor-
         tant for literary theory, including extensions of
         Lacan's own work by Kristeva and Guattari.

G707.   Luhrmann, T. M.   "Popul-vuh and Lacan." Ethos 12,
         no. 4 (1984):   335-62.

         Compares the Mayan creation myth Popul vuh to
         Lacan's psychoanalytic "creation story," and empha-
         sizes the importance of chains of signification to
         each.

G708.   Lussier, André.   "Les déviations du désir: étude
         sur le fétishisme." Revue française de psych-
         analyse 47 (1983):   19-142.

         Cites C67 and describes the author's argument
         that the meaning of a symptom is to be found in
         language rather than in vague analogies to the
         visual field, and that fetishism belongs to the
         domain of the imaginary. Lussier claims that such
         a position is incomplete and argues that the fetish
         emerges on the border between anxiety and guilt,
         between the loss of a love-object in a dualistic
         relation and the lack inherent in the triangular
         relation characteristic of the subject's recogni-
         tion of the Law.

G709.   Lyotard, Jean-François.   "The Dream-Work Does Not
         Think." Translated by Mary Lydon from sections
         of K1255. Oxford Literary Review 6, no. 1
         (1983):   3-34.

         Argues that the dream work is intrinsically
         different from speech and discusses Lacan's work in
         contrast to his own reading of Freud. Lacan's
         reading of Freud's Interpretation of Dreams is more
         in keeping with the current tendency "to stuff all
         of semiology into linguistics," Lyotard says (p.
         14). Notes Lacan's debt to Jakobson for his theory
         of metaphor and metonymy, but claims they differ
         significantly, especially regarding the idea of
         condensation, or metaphor. Jakobson would have
         metaphor be the co-existence of two images simul-
         taneously, Lyotard argues, but he agrees with Lacan
         that in metaphor one term is eclipsed by another
         (p. 17). Lyotard also claims, however, that this
         blurs the line between metaphor and metonymy, and
         that Lacan is prejudiced in favor of a closed

system of language that ignores the importance of figuration argued in Freud's texts.

G710.   MacCabe, Colin.   "On Discourse."   F359, pp. 188-217.

Argues that Lacan's concept of the division of the subject in language is crucial for any theory of discourse, and that without a consideration of the subject theories of discourse tend to collapse into "a linguistic formalism or a sociological subjectivism" that is exemplified by the work of Zellig Harris and Emile Benveniste. According to MacCabe, however, the Lacanian concept of the signifier lacks a fully articulated "politics of the signifier" such as provided by the work of Michel Pêcheux (see, for example, Les vérités de la palice [1975]). MacCabe concludes with a detailed discussion of Pêcheux's work that includes comments on Althusser's use of Lacan in G433 as well as Houdebine's critique of Althusser in his review of Pêcheux's work (L1881).

G711.   MacCabe, Colin.   "Presentation: [Christian Metz's] 'The Imaginary Signifier.'"   Screen 16, no. 2 (1975):   7-13.

Describes fundamental concepts in Lacan's work that are important for understanding the essay by Metz that is translated in this issue, and claims that psychoanalysis is a necessary component of historical materialism because of its emphasis on the construction of the subject.

G712.   MacCannell, Juliet Flower.   "Oedipus Wrecks: Lacan, Stendhal, and the Narrative Form of the Real."   F371, pp. 910-40.

Observes that the role of the Oedipal complex has been drastically changed by the influence of Lacan's work, which has "historicized" the structures described by Freud and shown them to be "subject to change" (p. 913). Lacan has shown us, MacCannell says, that the primary "law of the Law" is the deflection of the psyche from its aim of satisfaction, or conscious desire (p. 933). This deflection is structured according to a simple linguistic paradigm of the third person as a term intervening between the "I" and "you" of the mother-child dyad. MacCannell suggests, however, that the dyadic couple, joined by desire, is also what Lacan considers the real (p. 916), and he therefore conceives of it as an alternative to or escape from the symbolic structures of culture.
Claiming that "History has already moved us

beyond Oedipus," MacCannell argues that it is our
responsibility to discover the possibility of a
post-Oedipal situation (p. 916). She rejects as
impossible the revolutionary goal of overthrowing
the symbolic or of returning to some pre-symbolic
condition such as Kristeva's chora, and she concludes that resistance to the symbolic "is a mat-
ter, in one's loves, of significant deletion, the
deletion of the symbolic factor" (p. 934).

G713.   Maceiras-F., Manuel.   "Lacan y su generacion en su
        memoria." Aporia 4, no. 13/14 (1981/82):   162-
        66.

G714.   Macey, David.   "Fragments of an Analysis: Lacan in
        Context." Radical Philosophy 35 (1983):   1-9.

        Notes that Lacan's early work relies more on
        Freud's "On Narcissism: An Introduction" (1914)
        than on The Interpretation of Dreams (1900), and
        claims that a major part of Lacan's theoretical
        edifice is intact long before he begins using
        theoretical linguistics in his work (p. 1). Macey
        also claims that Lacan's encounter with linguistics
        takes place through phenomenology at first, rather
        than through Saussure's theory of the sign.   In
        addition, Macey notes Lacan's contact with the
        Surrealists, the relevance of their linguistic
        practices to his own style, and the importance of
        the Surrealist cult of "convulsive beauty" and
        killer women to Lacan's interests throughout his
        career.   (For Lacan's early studies of women who
        committed violent criminal acts see especially A1
        and C42. Macey says that Lacan's later interest in
        Saint Theresa [see B31] is just another step along
        that same path.)
        Macey also offers a brief history of the resis-
        tance to psychoanalysis in France and its early
        medicalization as a branch of classical psychiatry
        (p. 4). He describes a number of specific issues
        raised by Lacan--the legal and sexual implications
        of jouissance as the possession of property rights
        as well as sexual enjoyment; the link between jouis
        and j'ouis ["come" and an archaic form of "I
        hear"]; etc.--and he concludes that whatever Lacan
        has to say about the social constitution of sexual
        identity vs. biological determinism is embedded
        within "an irreducibly phallocentric iconography of
        women" (p. 8).

G715.   Macksey, Richard.   "'Alas, Poor Yorick':   Sterne
        Thoughts." F371, pp.   1006-20.

        Describes a meeting with Lacan in which Lacan
        observed that "Tristram Shandy est le roman le plus

analytique de la littérature universelle" (p.
1007), and briefly comments on the novel as it
addresses several topics crucial to Lacan's work,
such as the issue of paternity and the "subversive
possibilities of signification, death, and sexuality."

G716.   Maggiori, Robert.   "L'homme qui a rendu célèbre la
        psychanalyse."   F354, pp. 3-4.

Summarizes several of the more controversial
aspects of Lacan's career: the obscurity of his
style, his claim that the unconscious is "structured like a language," and the tendency of his
followers to reduce his discourse to a parodic
nonsense that evokes laughter rather than thought.
Maggiori also describes Miller's account of the
development of Lacan's thought in three stages:
1953-63, when Lacan devoted the seminars of each
year to a Freudian concept and developed the field
of language as the ground of psychoanalysis; 1964-
74, following the pivotal work of B22 where Lacan
elaborated on the terms le sujet barré, l'objet a,
l'Autre, etc.; and the years since 1974, when Lacan
turned to the bases of his own discourse, the triad
of the real, symbolic, and imaginary registers, and
developed a form of "meta-theory" in which the
familiar significations of psychoanalysis gradually
withered away.
    Commenting on the notorious difficulty of Lacan's
style, Maggiori quotes Lacan's own defense in
explanation: "Je ne les ai pas écrits pour tout le
monde," Lacan said. "Il me suffit d'avoir un
public que lit. S'il ne comprend pas, patience. .
. . dans dix ans au maximum, ceux qui me lisent me
trouveront tout à fait transparent" (p. 3; see
E255). ("I have not written [my essays] for the
whole world. . . . It satisfies me to have a public
that reads. If it does not understand, wait . . .
. In ten years at most, those who read me will find
everything immediately transparent.") Maggiori
concludes by hoping for a "return to Lacan" that
will rescue his work from the excesses of
"Lacanism."

G717.   Maillet, Chantal, and Sylvie Sesé-Léger.   "Jouis-
        sance and Division."   Translated by Terese Lyons.
        Semiotext(e) 4, no. 1 (1981):   219-27.

Discusses relations between mother and daughter
as structured by the "mirror scene" and the
mother's subjection to the law of the symbolic, and
comments on two kinds of jouissance defined by
Lacan: phallic jouissance and "other jouissance."
The authors propose at least the possibility of a

feminine subject that is not entirely constituted
in terms of masculine writing and yet that would
also be free from "imprisonment in the illusion of
what is called a feminine writing."   Published with
L2145.

G718.   Malcolm, Janet.   "Therapeutic Rudeness."   New York
        Times Book Review, 3 April 1983, pp. 1, 17-18.

        Describes Schneiderman's account of his analysis
        with Lacan in F396, focussing on Schneiderman's
        defense of the short session, and suggests that
        there is a profound difference in what Lacanian and
        non-Lacanian analysts are talking about.   Malcolm
        attributes this difference to Lacan's use of philo-
        sophical traditions that non-Lacanian analysis
        ignores.   For responses to Malcolm, see F374,
        G773, and G776.

G719.   Malson, Lucien.   "Le 7e art sous l'éclairage freud-
        ien."   Le monde, 4 March 1978, p. 2.

        Briefly discusses the importance of Lacan's work
        to Metz's cinematic analysis in K1270 and to con-
        temporary film studies in general.

G720.   Mannoni, Maud.   "Le malentendu."   F305, pp. 56-61.

        Describes the revolutionary thrust of Lacan's
        work for analytic technique, and compares it to
        that of Laing and Winnicott.

G721.   Mannoni, Octave.   "A Brief Introduction to Jacques
        Lacan."   Translated by I. Ilton and A. H. Feiner.
        Contemporary Psychoanalysis 8, no. 1 (1971):   97-
        106.

        Briefly describes the state of psychoanalysis in
        France when Lacan split with the IPA in the early
        1950s; describes in more detail Lacan's theory of
        the mirror stage and his distinctions among the
        real, the imaginary, and the symbolic; and dis-
        cusses Lacan's theory of the relation between
        language and the unconscious.

G722.   ["Marx, Wallon, Lacan: The Individual in Reflec-
        tion of Others" (French)].   La pensée 243 (1985):
        40-41.

G723.   Le matin de Paris, 11 September 1981, pp. 1, 34,
        35.   "La mort de Jacques Lacan."

        Includes a brief notice of Lacan's death; re-
        actions from a number of public figures such as
        Hélène Cixous, Eric Laurent, Jack Lange, and

Antoinette Fouquet, founder of the Mouvement de
libération des femmes (MLF); a brief description of
events surrounding the dissolution of the Ecole
freudienne de Paris ("'L'affaire' Lacan: de jan-
vier 1980 à mars 1981," by Catherine Clément); and
G509.

G724.   Maugendre, Dominique. "Critique d'une 'histoire'
        de la psychoanalysis en France, ou, Lacaniens,
        encore un effort pour être psychanalystes." Les
        temps modernes 381 (1978):   1711-31.

        Describes the "scissions" that split groups
        associated with Lacan since the 1950s, and claims
        that the disputes usually derived from two kinds of
        issues: theoretical principles, and questions
        about the transmission of psychoanalysis through
        the training of new analysts. Maugendre notes the
        texts collected in F379 and concludes with sardonic
        remarks on Lacan's claim to be a "self-made man"
        (see A3). It is characteristic of self-made men,
        Maugendre says, that they build their empires and
        their fortunes on the work and exploitations of
        workers and the savage treatment of merchandise.
        One usually sees, Maugendre adds, that Lacanian's
        patients are considered as no more than "la viande
        psychanalyste," psychoanalytic meat (p. 1730).

G725.   Mayol, Pierre. "Lacan et puis après." Esprit 6
        (1982):   226-29.

        Describes Lacan's writing as a rite of initiation
        rather than a means of communication, and claims
        that psychoanalysis belongs to no single person,
        despite the tendency among Lacan's followers to
        treat him as the Master of the field.

G726.   McKenna, Ross. "Jacques Lacan: An Introduction."
        The Journal of the British Society for Phenomen-
        ology 7, no. 3 (1976):   189-97.

        Describes general tenets of Lacan's work and
        comments briefly on Lacan's place in the contem-
        porary intellectual scene in France. McKenna
        praises Lacan's attack on ego psychology and the
        notion of "communication" but also notes the dis-
        missal of six part-time lecturers from Vincennes
        for "heterodoxy." (See J1064 for an account of
        Irigaray's dismissal.)

G727.   Medina, Angel. "Heidegger, Lacan and the Bound-
        aries of Existence: Whole and Partial Subjects
        in Psychoanalysis." Man and World 18 (1985):
        389-403.

G728.   Mehlman, Jeffrey.   "The 'Floating Signifier'"   From
        Lévi-Strauss to Lacan."   F424, pp. 10-37.

        Briefly describes central premises of structural
        anthropology in the work of Lévi-Strauss, focussing
        on the importance of repression, "absence," and the
        signifier to Lévi-Strauss's method of interpreta-
        tion.   Mehlman then traces these themes in Lacan's
        work through a detailed discussion of passages from
        E211.

G729.   Mehlman, Jeffrey.   "Poe pourri: Lacan's Purloined
        Letter."   Semiotext(e) 1, no. 3 (1975):   51-68.

        Describes Lacan's reading of Poe's story, and
        comments on the inevitability of Lacan's--or any
        reader's--own repetition of the "violence, in-
        stability, and analytic fruitfulness" inherent in
        Dupin's theft of the letter.   Mehlman then proposes
        a critical analogue to Dupin's strategy for ridding
        himself of the letter that draws upon Freud's
        concept of the uncanny as he developed it in a
        reading of Hoffman's "The Sandman" (see "The Un-
        canny" [1919]).
              Reprinted in Aesthetics Today,   edited by Morris
        Philipson and Paul J. Gudel (New York: New Ameri-
        can Library, second edition, 1980), pp. 413-33.

G730.   Mehlman, Jeffrey.   "The Suture of an Allusion:
        Lacan with Léon Bloy."   Sub-stance 33/34 (1981-
        82):   99-110.

        Comments on Lacan's "inapt" allusion to Bloy's Le
        salut par les juifs (Paris: Mercure de France,
        1949) in B22, pp. 172-13, and claims that it raises
        questions about a dimension of anti-semitism in
        Lacan's return to Freud as well as about the role
        of Judaism in Freud's own writings.

G731.   Melman, Charles.   "Pour Lacan: Rétour à Freud."
        La quinzaine littéraire, 15-31 January 1967, pp.
        13-14.

        Briefly describes the field of psychoanalysis and
        situates the intervention of Lacan's work within
        it, and summarizes the central tenets of Lacan's
        arguments as represented in A2.   Published as part
        of a "debate" with G438.

G732.   Melville, Stephen.   "Psychoanalysis Demands a
        Mind."   Aesthetics Today. Edited by Morris
        Philipson and Paul Gudel.   New York: New Ameri-
        can Library, second edition, 1980.   Pp. 434-55.

        Notes a discrepancy between Lacan's "analytic

sophistication" and the "critical naiveté" of his
reading of Poe's "The Purloined Letter" (p. 453;
see C69), and describes the role of the phallus in
Lacan's distinction among demand, desire, and
need. Melville discusses Norman Holland's
eventual rejection of psychoanalytic criticism
because "psychoanalysis demands a mind" (see
Holland's "Literary Interpretation: Three phases
of Psychoanalysis" [Critical Inquiry 3, no. 2]),
and he suggests that Holland's attitude manifests
his desire for some transcendent point of stability, a true "object" of desire (p. 450).

G733. Mettayer, Arthur. "Psychanalyse et discours re-
        ligieux." Studies in Religion/Sciences religi-
        euses 8 (1979): 267-73.

        Proposes a formula for religious discourse based
        on Lacan's distinctions among the four terms in his
        four discourse, specifically as they diagram rela-
        tions between the subject and its jouissance.

G734. Miel, Jan. "Jacques Lacan and the Structure of the
        Unconscious." Yale French Studies 36/37 (1966).

        Briefly describes the split in 1953 between the
        Société psychanalytique de Paris and the Société
        française de psychanalyse, which was formed by
        Lacan, Daniel Lagache, Françoise Dolto, Juliette
        Favez-Boutonier, and Blanche Reverchon-Jouve (see
        F379). Miel also provides a sketch of Lacan's
        central premises through 1966, including a descrip-
        tion of the mirror stage and a summary of Lacan's
        argument for the primacy of linguistic analysis as
        the method for psychoanalytic inquiry. Miel claims
        that Lacan's most important contribution may well
        be his effort to establish a scientific basis for
        psychoanalytic argument that depends on the de-
        velopment of new theoretical claims through ana-
        lytic experience rather than attempting to supplant
        Freud's theoretical work with a rigidly governed
        analytic technique as the SPP had done under the
        direction of Marie Bonaparte.
            This brief article is one of the earliest intro-
        ductions to Lacan's work and is still useful,
        though it obviously relates only the most general
        aspects of his position. For a more detailed
        account of the controversial split with the SPP and
        of Lacan's theoretical arguments in general, see
        F412.
            Reprinted in Structuralism, edited by Jacques
        Ehrmann (New York: Anchor Books, 1970), pp. 94-
        101.

G735. Milan, Betty. "La transa ou l'amour deux

lalangues." META: Journal des traducteurs 27,
no. 2 (1982): 189-95.

G736.   Miller, Jacques-Alain. "D'un autre Lacan: intervention à la première Rencontre internationale du
Champ freudien--Caracas, 1980." Ornicar? 28
(1984): 49-58.

Describes what he calls "another Lacan," one who
draws out implications from the famous Lacanian
pronouncement "the unconscious is structured like a
language." Miller focuses on Lacan's approach to
what Freud considered the "impasse" that constitutes the end of analysis, which Lacan termed "the
pass." Beginning with Freud's attitude towards the
castration complex as the irreducible obstacle to
analysis, Miller comments more generally on the
role of gender identification, "Woman," and desire
as constituted in the subject's relation to the
signifying chain.
Translated by Ralph Chipman as "Another Lacan" in
Lacan Study Notes 1, no. 3 (1984): 1-3.

G737.   Miller, Jacques-Alain. "Enseignements de la presentation de malades." Ornicar? 10 (1977): 13-
24.

Comments on several remarks by Lacan regarding
specific cases including E297; contrasts Lacan's
attitude towards patients to the analyst's identification with a patient's psychosis that is
advocated by anti-psychiatry (as in the work of R.
D. Laing); and discusses Lacan's debt to Clérambault's concept of "mental automatism." Translated
in F397, pp. 42-52).

G738.   Miller, Jacques-Alain. ["Jacques Lacan"]. Encyclopédie Universalis, September 1979.

Clarifies Lacan's relation to structuralism, and
argues that "structure" is not simply a given
characteristic of symbolic systems for Lacan because he believes that structure always derives
from the Other. Miller describes Lacan's marginal
relation to most of the intellectual institutions
associated with psychoanalysis in France and notes
the more general success of Lacan's "return to
Freud," which established the possibility of
psychoanalysis on the hypothesis that the "unconscious is structured like a language."
Miller argues that the infamous difficulty of
Lacan's work stems from the contrast between a
"highly systematic thought" and the "offhand style"
in which Lacan expressed that thought, but he
insists on the continuity of Lacan's thought across

the various transformations in his career and
describes several of the concepts that mark significant stages in his development. An excerpt of
this item was reprinted as "Intraitable et puissant," La quinzaine littéraire, 1-15 October 1981,
p. 22. The whole item was translated with revisions as "Jacques Lacan: 1901-1981." Psychoanalysis and Contemporary Thought 7 (1984): 615-
28.

G739.   Miller, Jacques-Alain. "La suture (éléments de la
          logique du signifiant)." Cahiers pour l'analyse
          1 (1966): 39-51.

          Introduces the term "suture" as an inevitable
developement in the logic of the signifier, although
Lacan did not name it as such. Miller says that
"suture names the relation of the subject to the
chain of its discourse: we shall see that it
figures there as the element which is lacking, in
the form of a stand-in. For, while lacking there,
it is not purely and simply absent. Suture, by
extension, is the relation in general of the lack
to the structure of which it is an element, inas-
much as it implies the position of a taking-the-
place-of." (Miller bases much of his argument on
Frege's mathematical theories in order to determine
the logic behind the concept of identity and its
dependence on both "lack" and "repetition.")
          This essay is based on a paper delivered in
Lacan's seminar 24 February 1965; see B22. Earlier
in the seminar Lacan himself uses the term "suture"
but refers to it as "the pseudo-identification"
between "the time of terminal arrest of the gesture
and . . . the moment of seeing." Suture, Lacan
says, names "the conjunction of the imaginary and
the symbolic" (B22, pp. 117, 118). Jean-Claude
Milner follows Lacan's use of the term in G742.
          Translated by Jacqueline Rose in Screen 18, 4
(1977/78): 24-34; and reprinted in The Logic of
the Signifier, edited by Colin MacCabe (Macmillan
and Co.). For a discussion of Miller's essay and
its source in Lacanian theory see G638 and G620.
The concept of "suture" was first adopted for film
theory by Jean-Pierre Oudart in G789.

G740.   Miller, Jacques-Alain. "Table commentée des re-
          présentations graphiques." Cahiers pour l'ana-
          lyse 1/2 (1966): 171-77.

          Reproduces the graphs from A2 and Miller's com-
ments on the graphs that appeared as an appendix to
A2.

G741.   Miller, Jacques-Alain. "Théorie de la langue

(rudiment)." <u>Ornicar?</u> 1 (1975).

G742. Milner, Jean-Claude. "L'amour de la langue."
       <u>Ornicar?</u> 6 (1976).

       Follows Lacan's allusion to suture as the "junc-
       tion of the imaginary and the symbolic" (B22, p.
       118), and notes that the "subject of the enuncia-
       tion" serves as the measure for the speaking sub-
       ject and "sutures the subject within the symbolic
       order of language."

G743. Moersch, E. "Zum Befgriff des Unbewussten bei
       Jacques Lacan" ["The Concept of the Unconscious
       in Jacques Lacan"]. <u>Psyche</u> 28 (1974): 328-39.

G744. <u>Le monde</u>, 5 April 1973, pp. 20-21. "Le phénomène
       Lacan."

       Presents several observations on Lacan, some
       positive and some negative. Includes J1012, J1058,
       J1066, J1070, J1087, and J1105, J1118.

G745. <u>Le monde</u>, 11 January 1980, pp. 1, 14.

       Includes several items on the dissolution of the
       Ecole freudienne de Paris: E287b, J1043, J1073,
       J1099, and J1112. For other articles on this topic
       in <u>Le monde</u> see G746.

G746. <u>Le monde</u>, 19 January 1980, p. 2. "L'affaire
       Lacan."

       Includes several items on Lacan's decision to
       dissolve the Ecole freudienne de Paris: J1024,
       J1095, J1126. See also G745.

G747. <u>Le monde</u>, 11 September 1981, p. 2. "La mort de
       Jacques Lacan."

       Includes J1057 and J1086; accompanied by J1101
       and G541.

G748. <u>Le monde</u>, 12 September 1981, p. 25. "Après la mort
       de Jacques Lacan."

       Lists brief remarks about Lacan by many prominent
       psychoanalysts and public figures as "La théorie et
       l'influence," and includes two articles about
       Lacan's influence outside of France (J1079 and
       J1109). Also includes a brief excerpt from G738.

G749. <u>Le monde</u>, 16 September 1981, p. 2. "Avec et sans
       Lacan."

Includes J1020 and J1042.

G750. Montag, Warren. "Lacan and Feminine Sexuality."
       Quarterly of Film Studies 9 (1984): 309-17.

       Argues that recent film theory has appropriated
       certain terms and concepts from Lacan's work such
       as specularity and le regard, and claims that these
       concepts have been associated with ideas that are
       contrary to Lacan's theoretical projects. Montag
       insists that the "specular" dimension of imaginary
       relations, which has been so important to cinematic
       analysis, functioned in Lacan's account of the
       mirror stage essentially as a way of dramatizing
       his critique of American ego psychology. When
       Lacan later introduced the concept of the objet a,
       Montag says, he radically reorganized his notion of
       the imaginary to stress the impossibility of the
       specular identification with an other that had been
       at least implied by his use of the mirror scene.
         Montag also praises F333 and F370 for refusing to
       impose a "disjunctive univocity" on theoretical
       differences within Lacan's concepts of the phallus,
       and he cites G370 and K1313 as important efforts to
       distinguish Lacan's theory of the symbolic and the
       effect of the subject from culturalist theories of
       sexual difference.

G751. Montag, Warren. "Marxism and Psychoanalysis: The
       Impossible Encounter." The Minnesota Review 23
       (1984): 70-85.

       Claims that the issue of the "subject" marks the
       intersection between concepts central to psycho-
       analysis and Marxism: the unconscious and ide-
       ology. Montag rejects earlier attempts to base a
       "Freudo-Marxism" on an ego that could be adapted to
       social constraint (American ego psychology) or on
       an autonomous realm of "human nature" with in-
       stinctual needs that would form the basis of a new
       social order (Marcuse, Adorno, and the radical
       humanists of the 1960s). He cites Althusser's
       concept of the ideological "interpellation" of the
       subject as a more productive means of theorizing
       the constitution of the subject in and through the
       social order, but he notes that Althusser's inter-
       pellation ignores the "remainder" that Lacan iden-
       tified as an inevitable effect of the subject's
       place in the symbolic order. Interpellation thus
       tends to reduce the effect of the subject to a
       single, unified position entirely contained by the
       ideological order in which it is situated, and as a
       result it renders conflict invisible and resistance
       impossible.
         Montag argues, however, that Lacan's "irreducible

division of the subject of the unconscious provides
a corrective for the concept of the ideologically
constituted subject by showing that the unity of
the interpellated subject is always lacking . . . .
the subject, by definition divided against itself,
can never be entirely 'subjected' by Power or
ideology, for there is always a remainder that
escapes the process of ideological subjection and
in escaping it returns endlessly to oppose it. . . .
Struggle, resistance and opposition are not
merely possible: they are the necessary effects of
the splitting of the subject.   Hence, the production of the subject is always also the production
of an antagonism that is never obliterated or
resolved" (76-77).

This essay also contains brief remarks on a
change in Lacan's notions of language from the
structuralist model of language as a coherent order
to the concept of "lalangue," which emerged in the
late 1960s and emphasizes the equivocal disruption
of the "unicity" proposed by the earlier concept of
language.   "Lalangue," Montag says, "is that which
escapes communication, the irreducible remainder
whose return can only disrupt the transmission of
meaning.   It is precisely the constant eruption of
the equivocal in language that rules out the possibility of the self-identical subject" (p. 80).

G752.   Moran, Dermot, and Ross Skelton.   "Report on the
Dublin Workshop: Lacan, Heidegger and Psycho-
Analysis."   The Journal of the British Society
for Phenomenology 14 (1983):   219-20.

G753.   Morris, Christopher D.   "Barth and Lacan: The
World of the Moebius Strip."   Critique: Studies
in Modern Fiction 17, no. 1 (1975):   69-77.

G754.   Morris, Wesley.   "The Irrepressible Real: Jacques
Lacan and Poststructuralism."   American Criticism
in the Poststructuralist Age.   Edited by Ira
Konigsberg.   Michigan Studies in the Humanities.
Ann Arbor: University of Michigan, 1081.   Pp.
116-34.

Discusses the function of the real as a limit to
the freeplay of signification, as illustrated in
Faulkner's As I Lay Dying, and concludes that the
value of Lacan's concept of the real and its insis-
tent pressure on the symbolic is that it helps
"return poststructuralism to concrete human circumstances, to the recognition of the real, historical, even material, conditions of production,
including the production of both literary and
philosophical texts" (p. 134).

G755.   Mounin, Georges.   "Quelques traits du style de
        Jacques Lacan." Nouvelle revue française 17
        (1969): 84-92.

G756.   Moyaert, Paul.   "De grondstruktuur van de taal"
        ["The Fundamental Structure of Language"]. Tijd-
        schrift voor filosofie 44 (1982): 232-265.

G757.   Moyaert, Paul.   "De metafoor en de metonymie als
        basisstrukturen van de taal bi J. Lacan" ["Meta-
        phor and Metonymy as Fundamental Structures of
        Language According to Lacan"]. Tijdschrift voor
        filosofie 38 (1976): 436-57.

G758.   Moyaert, Paul.   "Jacques Lacan: Begeerte-taal-
        subjectiviteit." Denken in Parijs: taal en
        Lacan, Foucault, Althusser, Derrida. Edited by
        Egide Berns, Samuel Ijsseling, and Paul Moyaert.
        Alphen aan de Rijn. Brussels: Samsom Uitg,
        1979. Pp. 33-67.

G759.   Moyaert, Paul.   "Jacques Lacan: De menselijke
        begeerte en de begeerte van de Ander" ["Jacques
        Lacan: Human Desire and the Desire of the
        Other"]. Wijsgerig perspectief op maatschappij
        en wetenschap 19, no. 1 (1978/79): 11-15.

G760.   Moyaert, Paul.   "Over het ik bij Freud en Lacan"
        ["The Ego in Freud and Lacan"]. Tijdschrift voor
        filosofie 45 (1983): 388-419.

G761.   Moyaert, Paul.   "Taal en onbewuste: Freud en Lacan
        over de 'Urverdrängung.'" Algemeen nederlands
        tijdschrift voor wijsbegeerte 75 (1983): 173-91.

G762.   Moyaert, Paul.   "Wijsgerige Bedenkingen bij De
        Waelhens' 'La psychose'" ["Philosophical Reflec-
        tions on De Waelhens's Work La psychose"]. Tijd-
        schrift voor filosofie 46 (1984): 19-56.

G763.   Muller, Helene.   "Another Genesis of the Uncon-
        scious." Lacan Study Notes 5 (1985): 2-22.

        Discusses several issues raised by Hegel in the
        Phenomenology of Spirit in the light of Lacan's
        work.

G764.   Muller, John P.   "The Analogy of the Gap in Lacan's
        Ecrits: A Selection." The Psychohistory Review
        8, no. 3 (1979): 38-45.

        Discusses the theoretical function of "gaps" and
        "lacks" in Lacan's work, which Muller describes as
        the "overwhelming presence of a profound absence"
        that structures Lacan's early thought and appears

in several forms, such as the bar separating the
signifier from the signified and as distinctions
between speech and language, desire and demand, the
conscious and the unconscious, and other terms.

G765.   Muller, John P.   "Cognitive Psychology and the Ego:
        Lacanian Theory and Empirical Research."   Psy-
        choanalysis and Contemporary Thought 5 (1982):
        257-91.

        Briefly sketches Freud's concepts of the ego as
        (1) a narcissistic love object and (2) a seat of
        consciousness which establishes the subject's
        relation to reality and provides a defense against
        the id.   Muller then describes Lacan's "return to
        Freud" as an attempt to establish the primacy of
        Freud's earliest concept of the ego against the
        tendency of American ego psychology to treat
        Freud's later work on the ego as more important.
        Muller's essay is especially interesting because he
        discusses at length clinical evidence for Lacan's
        theoretical claims.

G766.   Muller, John P.   "Ego and Subject in Lacan."
        Presented at "Freud and Language: Contributions
        of Jacques Lacan--Theory and Therapy."   86th
        Convention of the American Psychological Associa-
        tion, Toronto, 31 August 1978.   The Psychoana-
        lytic Review 69, no. 2 (1982):   234-240.

        Explains Lacan's theory of the mirror-stage, and
        shows how Lacan's concept of the ego as an illusory
        image of wholeness derives from Freud's work on the
        ego after 1914.   Muller also explains how the
        Lacanian ego differs from the autonomous ego pro-
        posed by Hartmann and Erikson and he describes
        Lacan's opposition to the adaptational goals of
        American ego psychology (p. 237).
        Muller focuses on the ego's role in aggressivity,
        which is represented in fantasies of dismemberment,
        the corps morcelé that arise at moments when the
        ego is threatened by an "other."   He traces this
        idea to Kojève's account of Hegelian desire, which
        Muller describes as the desire to be the object of
        desire of an Other, and he cites Kojève's argument
        that we gain our full humanity only to the extent
        that we will risk our animal life and fight to the
        death for recognition by this Other.
        Muller outlines three ways Lacan elaborates the
        Hegelian dialectic described in the master-slave
        relationship by identifying different kinds of
        pairs proposed in Lacan's work: (1) the dyad of
        the mother and the infant, in which the infant
        desires to be the phallus, signifier of the
        mother's desire; (2) the rivalry between the infant

and his imaginary counterpart, the mirror-image or
"other"; and (3) the fight for recognition through
authoritarian mastery or obsessional slavery characteristic of clinical cases. All of these situations stem from Lacan's concept of the ego, Muller
says, which "opposes its irreducible inertia of
pretenses and méconnaissances to the concrete
problematic of the realization of the subject."
     For other papers from this conference, see G617
and G832.

G767.   Muller, John P. "Lacan's Mirror Stage." Psycho-
        analytic Inquiry 5, no. 2: 233-52.

        Comments on the general phenomenon of mirroring
        and doubling as reported by a wide range of psy-
        chologists, and uses Lacan's work on the mirror
        stage (see C53) to explain the significance of the
        phenomenon and to establish its connection to
        aggression and desire.

G768.   Muller, John P. "Language, Psychosis, and Spirit."
        Attachment and the Therapeutic Process. Edited
        by Daniel P. Schwartz, James L. Sacksteder, and
        Yoshiharu Akabane. Forthcoming.

        Discusses relations among the imaginary, sym-
        bolic, and real registers of experience as repre-
        sented in Maxine Hong Kingston's China Men and as
        an analytic perspective on the "nonpharmaceutical
        treatment of psychosis," the theme of a conference
        Muller discusses at length in the second half of
        the article. The conference brought together
        Lacanian analysts, American therapists, and medi-
        cine men from native peoples of North America, and
        Muller comments on associations among the real,
        death, and naming as evinced in "psychotic" epi-
        sodes reported from these various contexts.

G769.   Muller, John P. "Language, Psychosis, and the
        Subject in Lacan." F403, pp. 21-32.

        Focuses on the phenomenon of foreclosure in
        Lacan's theory of psychosis as presented in C80,
        and notes Lacan's reference to Winnicott to argue
        that psychosis results from the abortion of transi-
        tional phenomena in general, their failure to
        "yield toleration of separation and the significa-
        tion of absence" (p. 30).

G770.   Muller, John P. "Light and the Wisdom of the Dark:
        Aging and the Language of Desire in the Texts of
        Louise Bogan." Memory and Desire: Aging-Litera-
        ture-Psychoanalysis. Edited by K. Woodward and

Murray Schwartz.   Bloomington: Indiana University Press, 1986.   Pp. 76-96.

Traces the imagery of light throughout the poems
of Louise Bogan to argue that light is "a metonymy
of the other; light bears a relationship by way of
contiguity to the other's gaze, and the other's
gaze, in turn, suffuses the world with desire,
presenting to us the Other as desiring" (p. 77).

G771.   Muller, John P.   "The Psychoanalytic Ego in Lacan:
Its Origins and Self-Serving Functions."   Psy-
chological Perspectives on the Self, Vol. 3.
Edited by Jerry Suls and Anthony Greenwald.
Hillsdale, New Jersey: Lawrence Erlbaum Associ-
ates, 1982; rpt. 1986.   Pp. 79-106.

Presents a general overview of Lacan's theory of
the ego as an idealized image of the self that is
fundamentally "defensive and distorting," and
offers clinical evidence to support Lacan's claims
about the role of the image in the formation of the
infant's sense of self.   Muller also connects the
ego to specific psychological disturbances, concluding that "When the distorting illusion of ego
mastery is lost, depression ensues; when it is
threatened, aggressivity follows" (p. 102).

G772.   Muller, John P.   "Psychosis and Mourning In Lacan's
Hamlet."   New Literary History 12 (1980):   147-
65.

Discusses Lacan's reading of Hamlet in detail
(B17, tr. K1356), stressing the importance of
narcissistic attachment to the phallus and of
subjection to the desire of others, especially as
those themes function in the play and in Lacan's
theoretical accounts of mourning and psychosis.

G773.   Muller, John P., and William J. Richardson.   "The
Agency of the Letter . . . ."   Psychoanalysis and
Contemporary Thought 2 (1979):   347-435.

Reprinted in F374.

G774.   Muller, John P., and William J. Richardson.   "Aggressivity in Psychoanalysis."   Psychoanalysis
and Contemporary Thought 1 (1978):   503-29.

Reprinted in F374.

G775.   Muller, John P., and William J. Richardson.   "The
Function and Field of Speech . . . ."   Psychoanalysis and Contemporary Thought 2 (1979):   201-
52.

Reprinted in F374.

G776. Muller, John P., and William J. Richardson. Letter
       to the Editor. New York Times Book Review, 15
       May 1983, p. 35.

       Notes Malcolm's characterization of the short
       session as a "punitive" measure directed against
       the analysand, and claims that Malcolm misunder-
       stands Lacan's argument and distorts his difference
       from traditional Freudian method. The authors
       observe that few of Lacan's texts have been ade-
       quately translated and claim that this situation
       prevents a full understanding of his work. A
       response to G718.

G777. Muller, John P., and William J. Richardson. "The
       Mirror Stage . . . ." Psychoanalysis and Contem-
       porary Thought 1 (1978):   355-72.

       Reprinted in F374.

G778. Muller, John P., and William J. Richardson.
       "Toward Reading Lacan: Pages for a Workbook."
       Psychoanalysis and Contemporary Thought 1 (1978):
       323-372.

       Outlines the general project for a close reading
       of Lacan's Ecrits that was originally published as
       a series of articles and then as a book (F374).

G779. Muraro, L. "Maglia o uncinetto? Metafora e meto-
       nimia nella produzione simbolica." Aut-Aut
       175/176 (1980):   59-85.

G780. Mykyta, Larysa. "Lacan, Literature, and the Look:
       Woman in the Eye of Psychoanalysis." Sub-stance
       39 (1983):   49-57.

       Notes Lacan's emphasis on the symbolic dimension
       of castration, but argues that despite Lacan's
       insistence on treating the phallus as a signifier,
       his concept of the phallic function still focuses
       sexual development on a male organ because he
       justifies the primacy of the phallus by the promi-
       nent visibility of the penis in sexual copulation
       (see A2j, p. 287). Mykyta also quotes Lacan's
       remarks in B13, where he claims that "the phallus
       can be used symbolically because it can be seen . .
       . . There can be no possible symbolic use of what
       cannot be seen." Because of this emphasis on the
       visibility of the phallus/penis, Mykyta says, Lacan
       cannot resolve the problems Freud poses to fem-
       inists.
       Mykyta goes on to discuss Lacan's move from the

Freudian concept of the woman as not <u>having</u> a penis
to his ontological claim that the woman is the
"pas-toute." ("Woman does not exist," Lacan says
in B31, p. 68, and later in that same work he
observes that woman is the unconscious of man [p.
90].) She then links the importance of visibility
in Lacan's concept of male identity to his interest
in scoptophilia, and she argues that man looks at
women searching for what is hidden, for what he has
lost as it is figured in the hole/whole that is
woman. Thus Mykyta says, "the sexual triumph of
the male passes through the eye, through the con-
templation of the woman" (p. 54). (For Freud's
association of the eye with the phallus and blind-
ness with castration, see "The Uncanny" [1919].)
   Mykyta also raises the question of how woman can
speak of her sexuality in a discourse that rele-
gates her to silence, and she claims that "woman
speaks as the 'not-all' through the writing in her
body [<u>en corps</u>]" (p. 55). Man reads it, does not
understand and so translates it, and that is why
Lacan claims that desire is "interpretation itself"
(see B22, p. 176). Nevertheless, Mykyta concludes,
because woman continues to speak in the gaps of
man's speech, like the unconscious, she always
questions the conditions of power and discourse.

G781.   Nägle, Ranier. "The Provocation of Jacques Lacan:
        Attempt at a Theoretical Topography apropos a
        Book about Lacan." <u>New German Critique</u> 16
        (1979): 5-30.

        Notes the significance of Weber's <u>Ruckkher zu</u>
        <u>Freud: Jacques Lacans Ent-stellung der Psycho-</u>
        <u>analyse</u> (F418), which appeared at a time when
        Lacan's name was little more than a rumor in
        German-speaking countries, and describes early
        manifestations of Lacan's influence: a symposium
        on his work in West Berlin (6-9 April 1978; see
        F423); the founding of the Sigmund Freud Schule (a
        German equivalent of the Ecole freudienne de
        Paris); the appearance of <u>Der Wunderblock</u> (<u>The</u>
        <u>Mystic Writing Pad</u>), a psychoanalytic journal
        oriented toward Lacan; and a collection of essays
        in literary theory influenced by Lacan, K1225.
        Nägle generally recognizes the value of Lacan's
        work but notes problems in the associations between
        Freud and Marx suggested by Lacan and others. He
        reflects more generally on post-structuralism's
        purported "a-historicism" and its influence on
        Marxism, and contrasts Lacan's work with that of
        Habermas, focussing on the need to "deconstruct"
        critical theory and its reliance on the speaking
        subject. Nevertheless, Nägle insists that Habermas
        offers an approach to the public sphere of experi-

ence that is lacking in Lacan, and he situates
Weber's book at the juncture of these problems.

G782.   Nasio, Juan-David.   "The Unconscious, the Trans-
        ference, and the Psychoanalyst's Interpretation:
        A Lacanian View." Psychoanalytic Inquiry 4
        (1984): 401-411. Also in Papers of the Freudian
        School of Melbourne (1983/84): 103-16.

        Explains Lacan's theories of transference and
        interpretation, and contrasts them to those pro-
        posed by Merton Gill in Analysis of Transference
        (New York: International Universities Press,
        1983). For Gill, Nasio says, interpretation is
        rational and explanatory, whereas for Lacan it is
        an unpremeditated statement that may surprise the
        analyst himself and is important for where it
        "punctuates" the analysand's words. Nasio also
        distinguishes between imaginary and symbolic trans-
        ference and argues that "the analytic transference
        is equivalent to the unconscious" at the moment
        speech "lapses" in analysis.

G**.   Nobécourt-Granier, Solange. "Outre-mires." See
        F399.

G783.   Le nouvel observateur, 28 April 1980, pp. 44-46.
        "Les français et la psychanalyse."

        Includes J1013, J1047, J1103, J1114, J1125, and a
        general essay by Catherine David which claims that
        one cannot talk about French psychoanalysis without
        talking about Lacan. David wonders, however, if
        Lacan is a phenomenon bred and sustained by the
        sophistication of French intellectuals and re-
        stricted to that context.

G784.   Le nouvel observateur, 19 September 1981, pp. 51-
        52. "La leçon de Lacan."

        Includes an unauthorized version of E281 and
        J1046, J1124, and J1133.

G785.   Nowak, Virginie. "Lacan: le jongleur." Paris-
        Match, 25 September 1981, p. 79.

        Comments on the phenomenon of Lacan's popularity
        and his controversial influence in France, and
        briefly describes his major works.

G786.   Olrik, Hilde. "Oeil lésé, corps morcelé: ré-
        flexions à propos de L'oeuvre d'Emile Zola."
        Revue romane 11 (1976): 334-57.

        Discusses Zola's use of images of dismembered

bodies and its relation to death as described in
B22, and argues that woman's body appears in
L'oeuvre only as a corps morcelé, around which
fantasms of origin develop.

G787.   Olsen, Ole. A.   "Signifiant-begrebet hos Lacan."
Subjekt of tekst: bidrag til semiotikkens teori.
Edited by Nils L. Knudsen, Ole A. Olsen, and Erik
Svejgaard. Nordisk Sommeruniversitets skrift-
serie 5. Kongerslev: GMT, 1974. Pp. 57-125.

G788.   O'Neill, John.   "The Specular Body: Merleau-Ponty
and Lacan on Infant Self and Other." Synthese 66
(1986):   201-17.

G789.   Oudart, Jean-Pierre.   "La suture." Cahiers du
cinéma 211 (1969):   36-39, and 212 (1969):   50-
55.

Discusses the relation between the cinematic
subject, as determined by the énoncé of a film, and
the position of the spectator in relation to the
filmic image. "Suture represents the closure of
the cinematic énoncé in conformity with the relationship sustained with it by its subject . . . the
spectator." Oudart argues that our first response
to the cinematic image is pleasure with the image
itself, but we quickly move on to view the image as
constituted within the "frame" of cinematic dis-
course--i.e., a discourse produced by and for a
viewing eye that is invisible or absent. This is
the moment at which the image comes to function as
a signifier, Oudart says, and hence the moment at
which the viewer is "sutured" into the signifying
order as its subject.
Oudart's argument derives from Miller's original
proposal of the term "suture" in G739, and together
with Miller's essay Oudart's article became very
influential among writers associated with the
journal Screen.
Translated by Kari Hanet as "Cinema and Suture"
in Screen 18, no. 4 (1977/78):   35-47, where it
appeared with G739 and G638. For a comment on
Oudart's importance, see K1211, where his connection with Metz is explored. Oudart continued to
elaborate on his theory of suture in a series of
articles in Cahiers du cinéma between 1969 and
1971.

G790.   Pankow, Gisela.   "Zum Problem des Spiegelbilder-
lebnisses in der Nevrose und in der Psychose."
Confina psychiatrica 3 (1960):   36-56.

G791.   Parain-Vial, Jeanne.   "La structuralisme de Lacan."
Parain-Vial, Analyses structurales et idéologies

structuralistes. Paris: Privat, 1969. Pp. 139-
53.

Argues that Lacan's use of the idea of structure
is more philosophical than scientific, and compares
Lacan's reading of Freud to Althusser's reading of
Marx as two aspirations toward "science." Parain-
Vial also comments briefly on mathematical for-
malism and the status of truth in Lacan's work.

G792.   Pasternac, Marcelo. "Aspects de l'édition des
        Ecrits de Lacan en espagnol." Translated by Nora
        Pasternac. F357, pp. 63-76.

Describes the confusion surrounding the translation and publication of the Ecrits in Spanish
(which he compares to the story of Rashomon), and
discusses specific problems with the translations.
This essay offers a valuable analysis of the concrete issues involved in the dissemination of
Lacan's work through the ordinary channels of
publication, as well as providing detailed information about the Spanish editions of the Ecrits.

G793.   Patterson, David. "Dostoevsky's Dvoinik per
        Lacan's Parole." Essays in Literature 10, no. 2
        (1983): 299-307.

Describes the relation between Self and Word
established in C58, and claims that Lacan enables
us to trace in Dostoevsky's Goliadkin a madness
that is "generated by the loss of the Word" and
that cannot be reduced to a strictly social phenomenon (p. 300).

G794.   Paull, Gayle. "A Case for Topology." Papers of
        the Freudian School of Melbourne (1982): 69-84.

Discusses several of Lacan's schemata to investigate the analyst's reconstruction of the patient's
past through traces that emerge in analytic speech.

G795.   Pavan, Luigi. "Considerations on the Importance of
        Linguistics in Some Psychoanalytical Orienta-
        tions, in Particular in the Work of Jacques
        Lacan." Rivista di psichiatria 5, no. 2 (1970):
        81-96.

G796.   Peraldi, François. "Pas sans Lacan." F327, pp.
        53-80.

Discusses the influence of Lacan's work on his
thinking at the moment of the pass, the passage
from his analysis to his practice, and traces the
practical results of that influence through the

example of a case history.

G797.   Perrella, Ettore.   "Tempo e transfert."   F307, pp.
        292-300.

G798.   Petitjean, Gerard.   "Les grands prêtres de l'uni-
        versité française."   Le nouvel observateur, 7
        April 1975, pp. 52-57.

        Reports on his visits to the public lectures of
        intellectual superstars in Paris, and comments on
        the bizarre behavior he witnessed at Lacan's semi-
        nars.   He also notes Foucault's observation that it
        is almost impossible to find one's way in Lacan's
        "langage ésotérique," and claims that Lacan's real
        trick is the ability to make the listener believe,
        at any given instant, that he and he alone has
        understood what Lacan has just said.

G799.   Peyrol, Georges.   "Sous Lacan."   La situation
        actuelle sur le front de la philosophie.   Paris:
        François Maspero, 1977.   Pp. 53-82.

        Discusses the place of dialectic in Lacan's work
        and comments on the concept of rebellion as pro-
        posed in Guy Lardreau and Christian Jambet, L'ange:
        ontologie de la révolution (Paris: Grasset, 1976).
        See K1291.

G800.   Pichon, Edouard.   "La famille devant M. Lacan."
        Revue française de psychanalyse 11, no. 1 (1939):
        107-35.

        Describes C45 and C46, and objects to Lacan's use
        of excessively arcane terms, his penchant for
        catachresis, and his invocation of foreign words
        and usages (especially those borrowed from German
        philosophers).   Nevertheless, Pichon recognizes the
        general importance and originality of Lacan's
        theory of the mirror stage and his emphasis on the
        social dimension of psychic development, and
        Pichon's detailed analysis of Lacan's theoretical
        innovations establishes connections between Lacan's
        work and that of other French psychologists whom
        Lacan seldom, if ever, cites as his sources.
        Pichon's specific criticisms of Lacan's "bizarre
        vocabulary" are especially interesting because they
        show the precise points at which Lacan was begin-
        ning to reject not only many of the practices of
        conventional psychiatry and psychology but also the
        very discourse in which those disciplines repre-
        sented human experience.   (See, for example,
        Pichon's objection to Lacan's claim that Freud
        "imagined" the Oedipal complex. Although Pichon
        considers Lacan's verb a gratuitous departure from

the usual observation that Freud "discovered" the
complex, in fact the word marks Lacan's crucial
departure from the positivistic concept of psychoanalysis as a science dealing with objective
facts.)
    This is the first extended analysis of Lacan's
early work and provides a clear and accurate account of the conceptual differences between Lacan
and the psychological community of Paris in the
1930s.

G801.   Pirard, Regnier.   "Si l'inconscient est structuré
        comme un langage. . ." Revue philosophique de
        Louvain 77, no. 36 (1979):   528-68.

        Notes the tremendous influence of Lacan's claim
        that the unconscious is structured like a language,
        and explores its origins in Lacan's linguistic
        sources and how he adapted them to psychoanalysis.
        Pirard claims that C71 serves as an "epistemo-
        logical break" in Lacan's work because it clearly
        establishes the primacy of the signifier, but
        Pirard says that two questions remain: what phi-
        losophy of language is implied by Lacan's work, and
        does the rhetoric of unconscious formations exhaust
        the "nature" of the unconscious itself? He con-
        cludes that the unconscious is structured more like
        a langue in Saussure's sense, and that it is the
        job of psychoanalysis to "disarticulate" the forma-
        tions of the unconscious so that Lacan's signi-
        fiers--"'atomes' inconscient"--can enter into more
        supple and satisfying combinations.

G802.   Pontalis, Jean-Bertrand.   "A travers les revues:
        Psychanalyse et sciences de l'homme [La psych-
        analyse 3]." Bulletin de psychologie 11 (1958):
        297-303.

        Notes the influence of structural linguistics and
        the anthropological theories of Claude Lévi-Strauss
        on the work of Lacan and others represented in this
        issue of La psychanalyse. Pontalis claims that
        Lacan describes the unconscious as a language in
        which unities are reduced to differential elements
        combined in a closed order, and, commenting on C71,
        he notes Lacan's emphasis on the "materiality" of
        the signifier and on the independence of the signi-
        fier over the signified. Pontalis refers to meta-
        phor in Lacan's work as the function that "allows
        truth to be understood between the lines."

G803.   Pontalis, J.-B.   "Freud aujourd'hui." Les temps
        modernes 124 (1956):   1666-80; 125 (1956):   1890-
        1902; 126 (1956):   174-86.

Surveys the prominent issues in contemporary
French psychoanalysis, and in no. 126 argues that
the dominance of the Oedipal complex in traditional
psychoanalysis has changed now to include three
different themes: pre-verbal structures, object
relations, and the manifestation of transference
and counter-transference. Pontalis claims that
Lacan has influenced this shift in emphasis by
stressing the importance of the maternal imago and
of the phallus to our understanding of the Oedipus
complex, and by arguing that neuroses manifest "the
absurd aspects of a disconcerted symbolization" (p.
182).

G804.   Prangisvili, A. S., A. E. Serozija, and F. V.
         Bassin. "Bezpocvennyje pritiazanija psikhoana-
         liza." ["The Baseless Pretensions of Psychoana-
         lysis"]. Literaturnaja gazeta, 21 May 1980, p.
         3.

         Condemns the political claims made for psycho-
         analysis by Leclaire in G700, but admits that
         psychoanalysis may possess definite therapeutic
         benefits. For a description of this essay and
         other papers presented at a symposium on Lacan's
         work that was held in the Soviet Union in 1979, see
         L1550 and G500. Bassin and Serozija attacked
         Lacan's work again in G453. See also G700.

G805.   Prasse, Jutta. "Freud, Lacan e una questione di
         realismo." F307, pp. 205-22.

G806.   Puche Nararro, Rebeca. "Lacan: Language and
         Unconscious." Revista latinoamericana de psi-
         cologia 3, no. 2 (1971): 167-81.

G807.   Rabant, Christiane. "La bête chanteuse." F305,
         pp. 15-20.

         Compares Lacan's work to that of Marguerite
         Duras, especially on the topic of femininity and
         the Oedipal complex in relation to Duras' character
         Lol V. Stein.

G808.   Rabaté, Jean-Michel. "A Clown's Inquest into
         Paternity: Fathers, Dead or Alive, in Ulysses
         and Finnegans Wake." F318, pp. 73-114.

         Discusses the issue of fatherhood that is raised
         in Joyce's novels according to three different
         aspects of the father's function defined in Lacan's
         claims that (1) the father is not an individual but
         a function; (2) the father is not a person but "the
         focal point where castration can be brought to bear
         on the structure of desire"; and (3) the father "is

not a 'problem,' but a nexus of unresolved enigmas,
all founded on the mysterious efficacy of a Name,
which in itself remains a riddling cipher."
Rabaté claims that Joyce rejects the father's
role in simple designation for a more subtle problematic of the function of paternity, and he claims
that Joyce's texts dramatize the substitutive chain
derived from the death or absence of the father.
(For a clinical study of the father as a "riddling
cipher" and its effects on the subject's perception
of identity, see L2349.

G809.   Racevskis, Karlis. "The Imaginary, the Symbolic,
        and the Real: Nexus for the Authorial Subject."
        <u>Generative Literature and Generative Art: New
        Essays</u>. Edited by David Leach. New York: N. B.
        Frederiction, 1983.

        Summarizes Lacan's thought as useful for literary
        interpretation that treats the artist as a "nexus"
        in a "network of cultural artifacts" rather than as
        an autonomous creative agent (pp. 35-37).

G810.   Radzinski, A. "Lacan/Saussure: les contours
        théoriques d'une rencontre." <u>Langages</u> 77 (1985):
        117-24.

G811.   Ragland-Sullivan, Ellie. "Counting from 0 to 6:
        Lacan and the Imaginary Other." <u>University of
        Wisconsin Working Papers</u> 7, University of Wiscon-
        sin Center for Twentieth Century Studies, Fall,
        1984.

        Describes what she calls an "Imaginary text" that
        links between "Symbolic pre-suppositions and uncon-
        scious knowledge" as proposed by Lacan, and claims
        that there are "six pivotal unconscious numbers"
        which are "real, universal, and natural" and are
        found "in the domain of Imaginary realism" (p. 25).

G812.   Ragland-Sullivan, Ellie. "Explicating Jacques
        Lacan: An Overview." <u>University of Hartford
        Studies in Literature</u> 11, no. 2 (1979): 140-56.

        Describes several major concepts in Lacan's work,
        and suggests that Lacan is important for literary
        criticism because he has radically altered our
        understanding of man's relation to the word.
        Ragland-Sullivan also claims that Lacan's theories
        "offer to bridge the gap between the human mind and
        emotions and their expression in words" (p. 154),
        and says that his emphasis on the role of language
        in human experience can serve as a link between
        phenomenology and psychology. She concludes that
        Lacan can provide critics with the basis for an

intersubjective interaction between critic and text
that will replace the autonomous text proposed by
formalist structuralism (pp. 154-55).

G813.   Ragland-Sullivan, Ellie.   "Jacques Lacan: Feminism
        and the Problem of Gender Identity."   Sub-stance
        36 (1982):   6-20.

        Claims that Lacan's thought provides a key for
        understanding "the socialization and symbolization
        processes which have shaped woman's specificity
        through the ages" (p. 7), and rejects the effort of
        utopian feminisms to go "beyond the phallus," as
        Lacan ironically suggests they do in B31.   Ragland-
        Sullivan claims that even separatist feminist
        groups will be phallocentric because all groups
        evolve their own phallocratic structures and be-
        cause a need for recognition and power is inherent
        in the structure of the human subject (p. 19).   She
        does suggest, however, that "differentiations" can
        be made more equitably than they are now.

G814.   Ragland-Sullivan, Ellie.   "Jacques Lacan, Literary
        Theory, and The Maids of Jean Genet."   K1282, pp.
        100-19.

        Describes Lacan's account of the formation of the
        subject, focussing on the importance of the mirror
        stage and the disruption of imaginary identity
        through castration and the phallus.   Ragland-
        Sullivan comments at length on the function of
        language in Lacan's concept of the unconscious and
        in the subject's relation to the real, to the ego,
        and to his or her desire.   She then analyzes at
        length Genet's The Maids as a dramatization of what
        happens when the Oedipus complex is distorted be-
        cause of a failure in the function of language and
        the law.   See G818.

G815.   Ragland-Sullivan, Ellie.   "Lacan, Language and
        Literary Criticism."   The Literary Review 24, no.
        4 (1981):   562-77.

        Claims that the major importance of F412 is to
        encourage Anglo-American critics to take Lacan's
        work seriously and to pursue his emphasis on lan-
        guage as a far more powerful and pervasive in-
        fluence in human experience than is usually sus-
        pected.   She describes basic tenets of Lacan's
        "bridge between language and psyche," including the
        role of the signifier and of the phallus, and
        claims that Lacan's thought is a "natural ally of
        literary criticism" because of the priority he
        accords to language.   Ragland-Sullivan warns,
        however, that the literary critic should not be a

psychoanalyst looking for some fixed meaning in the author's life. Rather, in a Lacanian criticism, text and reader "would merge indissolubly in a synthesis much like creation itself" (p. 577).

G816.   Ragland-Sullivan, Ellie. "The Magnetism Between Reader and Text: Prolegomena to a Lacanian Poetics." Poetics 13 (1984): 381-406.

Claims that Lacan suggests that "literature operates a magnetic pull on the reader because it is an allegory of the psyche's fundamental structure" (p. 381), and that literary texts organize themselves around the structural axes of Desire and Law, much like personality and culture do (p. 404).

G817.   Ragland-Sullivan, Ellie. "The Psychoanalysis of Aging in Oscar Wilde's Picture of Dorian Gray: A Lacanian View." Edited by Kathleen Woodward and Murray Schwarz. Aging, Literature, and Psycho-analysis. Bloomington, Indiana: University of Indiana Press, 1985.

G818.   Ragland-Sullivan, Ellie. "The Psychology of Narcissism in Jean Genet's The Maids." Gradiva 2, no. 1 (1979): 19-40.

Cites A1 and several other works that use the Lacanian view of narcissism to elucidate the deep dramatic structure of The Maids (p. 20). See G814.

G819.   Rajchman, John. "Lacan and the Ethics of Modernity." Representations 15 (1986): 42-56.

Follows the "ethical status of the unconscious" in Lacan's reading of Kant's distinction between morality and ethics.

G820.   Rapaport, Herman. "Lacan Disbarred: Translation as ellipsis." Diacritics 6, no. 4 (1976): 57-60.

Notes the absence of the bar between the picture of a tree and the word "tree" and between the bathroom doors and "Ladies" and "Gentlemen" in Jan Miel's translation of C71 and in Jane Gallop's discussion of that diagram in G597. Rapaport suggests that the failure to "translate" the bar from the French text implies a serious form of misreading, and he notes that Lacan insisted on the bar to emphasize the difference between the syntagmatic chain of signifiers and an "undecidable" beneath it. Rapaport calls this "the imperative of difference" and says that it is not the arché of some prior signified but rather a force, a "pul-

sion" or "glissement."   Signifiers and signifieds
are absolutely discontinuous, Rapaport argues.
They are not joined in some dialectic or hierarchy,
and the bar represents that discontinuity.   The bar
is also the place of the subject, Rapaport concludes, and marks its dislocation.   Hence the
subject is not situated in terms of what Gallop
calls the "sovereignty of the signifier," though
Rapaport admits the importance of such a claim for
the feminist reading of Lacan Gallop is proposing.
(Rapaport also cites F348 to describe the bar as a
Moebius strip.)

G821.   Rapaport, Herman.   "Living On: Lacan and Freud."
       New Orleans Review 9, no. 1 (1982):   89-100.

       Notes Lacan's emphasis on a Socratic teaching
       style that eschewed writing for the more "psycho-
       analytic" relations constituted within spoken
       discourse, and claims that one cannot read the
       Ecrits without a prior knowledge, passed along by
       word-of-mouth, of what one is reading.   Rapaport
       stresses the theoretical importance of Lacan's
       refusal to become the center of a worshipful cult
       and of his apparently spontaneous "interventions"
       in social and political events (p. 91), and he
       suggests a similarity between Lacan's actions in
       such situations and his mode of intervention in
       analysis.   Nevertheless, as Rapaport points out,
       there are some at least potentially repressive
       implications in Lacan's interest in crime as a
       social intervention (see C42) and in his disturbing
       consonance with certain attitudes of the National
       Socialists.

G822.   Reboul, Jean.   "Jacques Lacan et les fondements de
       la psychanalyse."   Critique 187 (1962):   1056-67.

       Stresses the importance of emptiness and death in
       Lacan's account of language, but concludes that
       between the alienated ego and the ex-centric "I"
       lies language, or symbolization in its most pro-
       found essence.   Reboul describes that essence as
       "the work [travail] of meaning [sens]--meaning of
       its history [histoire] and the meaning of its
       desire--which is the work of truth and the ac-
       complishment of being" (p. 1066).

G823.   Reeves, A. C.   "Lacan's World."   Heythrop Journal
       20, no. 1 (1979):   65-71.

       Criticizes Lacan for focussing only on those
       parts of Freud that stress the importance of lan-
       guage and ignoring the rest, even though he claims
       to be teaching the "whole" Freud.   Reeves also says

Lacan lacks any historical perspective on the
development of Freud's thought, and that he has
translated Freud's theory of psychic determinism
into his own theory of linguistic determinism. He
does, however, briefly praise F392 and F420 as good
introductions to Lacan's difficult writing.

G824.   Regnault, François. "Un enseignement." L'âne 3
        (1981): 6.

        Comments briefly on "the place of death" and its
relation to university discourse, to science, and
to truth. Regnault claims that Lacan occupies the
place of death as the Other of the matheme, and
says that Lacan founded his ethic on the truth of a
phrase from Nicomacheus: "the analysis of an
aporia is a discovery" or, in Lacanian terms,
"analyser le noeud, ça, c'est une travaille." This
essay was written for the opening session of the
Département de psychanalyse, Université de Paris-
VIII, Vincennes, 29 October 1981.

G825.   Rella, Franco. "Corpo e linguaggio: nota sulla
        filosofia di Lacan." F307, pp. 71-93.

G826.   Rella, Franco. "Il divano di Santa Teresa." Aut-
        Aut 148 (1975): 135-46.

G827.   Rendon, Mario. "Structuralism in Psychoanalysis."
        American Journal of Psychoanalysis 39 (1979):
        343-51.

        Briefly describes Lacan's contributions to psy-
choanalysis and his opposition to ego psychology,
and argues that Lacan's major contribution may well
be his demonstration that Freud's theory of the
unconscious was "vitiated by his ideological background, namely the positivism and the individualism
of the nineteenth century" with its stress on the
monadic individual.

G828.   Ribettes, Jean-Michel. "Réel-Lacan." Infini 3
        (1983): 87-106.

        Relates Lacan's account of the difficulty posed
by the real to speech and meaning (p. 89), and
describes in detail the function of the real as
proposed in Lacan's later work, especially the
seminars from 1973-76.

G829.   Richard, Claude. "Destin, Design, Dasein: Lacan,
        Derrida and 'The Purloined Letter.'" Iowa Review
        12, no. 4 (1981): 1-11.

G830.   Richardson, William J.   "Lacan and Anti-
        Philosophy." Continental Philosophy. Edited by
        Hugh Silverman. London: Routledge and Kegan
        Paul, 1986.

        Traces the implications of Lacan's allusions to
        continental philosophers (primarily Heidegger) and
        discusses their relevance to Lacan's understanding
        of the signifying chain, desire, and other topics
        grounded in psychoanalytic experience. For a more
        extended treatment of this topic, see F345.

G831.   Richardson, William J.   "Lacan and the Subject of
        Psychoanalysis." F403, pp. 51-74.

        Discusses the relation between the speaking
        subject and the subject of psychoanalytic inquiry,
        the unconscious, as proposed in Lacan's theory of
        an "ex-centric" subject.

G832.   Richardson, William J.   "Lacan's View of Language
        and Being." Presented at "Freud and Language:
        Contributions of Jacques Lacan--Theory and
        Therapy." 86th Convention of the American
        Psychological Association, Toronto, 31 August
        1978. The Psychoanalytic Review 69, no. 2
        (1982): 229-233.

        Claims that C53 marks the culmination of Lacan's
        thought before his encounter with the work of Lévi-
        Strauss, which offered him a new way to approach
        the social component of personality by explaining
        it in linguistic terms. Richardson also describes
        the importance of Saussure's work to Lacan and
        notes Lacan's emphasis on the parallel between the
        linguistic functions of metonymy and metaphor and
        Freud's concepts of displacement and condensation.
        For other papers from this conference, see G766
        and G617.

G833.   Richardson, William.   "The Mirror Inside: The
        Problem of the Self." Review of Existential Psy-
        chology and Psychiatry 16 no. 1/2/3 (1978-79):
        95-112.

        Describes Lacan's concept of the ego as it
        evolved from his earliest work on the "personality"
        and its relation with the social milieu (see A1) to
        the function of the mirror stage presented in C53.
        Richardson then stresses the importance of Lacan's
        later concept of an ex-centric subject and its
        relation with language, especially in comparison
        with Heidegger's association among Dasein, Logos,
        and a de-centered self. (All of these theoretical
        issues are raised in the context of a case of a

twenty-year-old man suffering from depression.)
For more comments on the parallels between
Heidegger and Lacan, see G835.

G834.   Richardson, William J.   "Phenomenology and Psycho-
         analysis." Journal of Phenomenological Psy-
         chology 11, no. 2 (1980):   1-20.

         Cites several items by Lacan in an overview of
         his work that describes Lacan's debt to Heidegger
         for his theory of language, and that stresses the
         centrality of language to what Lacan claims is the
         "deepest nature of man," especially as language
         determines the subject's relation to the Other.

G835.   Richardson, William J.   "Piaget, Lacan, and Lan-
         guage."   K1327, pp. 144-63; discussion 163-70.

         Compares Piaget's and Lacan's theories of the
         child's initial access to language, arguing that
         Piaget is more concerned with language as a sym-
         bolic function that comes to pass within every
         individual, whereas Lacan is more interested in
         symbolic behavior as part of the social order.
         Richardson also compares Piaget's "epistemic sub-
         ject" to Lacan's theory of an ex-centric subject
         (p. 155), and he proposes an ontological analysis
         of what each means by "structure" that would take
         into account Heidegger's concept of Dasein to
         establish a link between Being and logos (see
         G833).

G836.   Richardson, William J.   "Psychoanalysis and the
         Being-question." F403, pp. 139-59.

         Assesses Heidegger's influence on Lacan's work,
         insisting that there is a necessary connection
         between philosophy and psychoanalysis.

G837.   Richardson, William J.   "Psychoanalysis and the
         God-Question." Thought: A Review of Culture and
         Idea 61 (1986):   68-83.

         Emphasizes the religious dimension of Lacan's
         category of the real, and proposes a Lacanian
         analysis of Sebastian Flyte in Brideshead Revisi-
         ted. Reprinted in Fordham University Quarterly.
         For other essays on Lacan published in this issue,
         see G558 and G883.

G838.   Ricon, L. ["Some Considerations About Transference
         in Psychosis" (Spanish)]. Acta psiquiatrica y
         psicologica de America Latina 30, no. 2 (1984):
         105-111.

G839.   Rodriquez, J.   "L'inconscient structure comme un
        langage: le point de vue linguistique."   In-
        formation psychiatrique 58 (1982):   1275-88.

G840.   Roelens, R.   "Problèmes de structure et de dé-
        centrement du sujet dans l'oeuvre de Jacques
        Lacan."   Evolution psychiatrique 33 (1968):   469-
        500.

        Discusses Lacan's account of the subject on two
        levels: (1) the imaginary, with its topics of the
        image, identification, and the mirror; and (2) the
        symbolic, with its topics of the primacy of the
        signifier and the problematic topology of the
        id/ça.   Roelens claims that Lacan's attempt to
        answer the question "Who is speaking" with the ex-
        centricity of the subject may introduce a meta-
        physical distortion into an otherwise profound and
        provocative critique.

G841.   Roffe, R.   "Manuel Puig del kitsch a Lacan."
        Hispania: A Journal Devoted to the Interests of
        the Teaching of Spanish and Portuguese 68 (1985):
        674-75.

G842.   Romano, Bruno.   "Disiderio, riconoscimento e dirit-
        to secondo J. Lacan: linee par una discussione."
        Revista internazionale di filosofia del dritto 61
        (1984):   95-126.

G843.   Romet, Gilles.   "Un démon pensant."   F359, pp. 10-
        11.

        Argues that Lacan's literary references play a
        unique role in his texts and are crucial to the
        development of his argument, and concludes that
        "les Ecrits sont le rassemblement d'écrits en quoi
        puissent venir s'inscrire tous les écrits" (p. 11).

G844.   Roquefort, D.   ["Romans 7.7 According to Jacques
        Lacan" (French)].   Etudes théologiques et religi-
        euses 61 (1986):   343-52.

G845.   Rose, Jacqueline.   "The Imaginary."   F359, pp. 132-
        61.

        Describes how Lacan's concept of the imaginary
        has been adopted by film theory (especially in the
        work of Christian Metz [see K1270]), and points out
        several problems in the use of this concept to
        account for some aspects of the cinematic spec-
        tator's experience.   Based on a paper first pre-
        sented in 1975.   See also J1123.

G846.   Rosolato, Guy. "Le symbolique." La psychanalyse 5
        (1959):   225-33.

G847.   Ross, Andrew. "The Eternal Varieties." Diacritics
        13, no. 4 (1983): 2-11.

        Cites Lacan's claim that "there is no sexual
        relation" (see B31) as indicative of the dissymetry
        between sexual categories and of Lacan's emphasis
        on the androcentric nature of the symbolic in B13.
        Ross briefly discusses the concept of feminine
        jouissance, and he describes Lacan's argument that
        woman is a "not-all" that is "useless" in the
        economy of the symbolic (pp. 7-8). The epistemo-
        logical failure represented by woman is the very
        cornerstone of the symbolic, Ross says, and there-
        fore the female represents the difficulty of con-
        structing sexual identity and the impossibility of
        any sort of "equality" in the ordinary sense. This
        last point suggests Ross's critical reading of the
        book under review here, F370.

G848.   Rosset, Clement. "Propos d'outre-monde." La
        nouvelle revue française 305 (1978):   79-85; 306
        (1978):   89-95; 307 (1978):   83-89; and 308
        (1978):   121-25.

        Comments on the metaphysical dimension of Lacan's
        work and traces its links to more traditional forms
        of the issues as they appear in philosophy, the-
        ology, and literature. Based on a reading of B13.

G849.   Rotmiler de Zentner, Maria Ines. "The Identifica-
        tion and the Ideal." Papers of the Freudian
        School of Melbourne (1981):   103-118.

        Distinguishes between the intersubjective charac-
        ter of identification and the psychological il-
        lusion of identity.

G850.   Rouanet, Marc. "Lacan et Freud: expérience d'un
        savoir et division du sujet." F361, pp. 12-13.

        Describes Lacan's theory of a split or divided
        subject and argues that it moves psychoanalysis
        toward the human sciences more than Freud's work
        may warrant in itself.

G851.   Roudinesco, Elisabeth. "L'action d'une métaphore:
        remarques à propos de la théorie du signifiant
        chez Jacques Lacan." La pensée 162 (1972):   54-
        73.

        Explains the centrality of language to Lacanian
        psychoanalysis, and argues that the symbolic char-

acter of the dream described by Freud was not a "symbolic" of representation but a "travail" of meaning, a deformation and transcription that is an effect of metaphor and, hence, the basis for Lacan's interest in metaphor. Roudinesco also discusses Lacan's use of Saussure, emphasizing the irreducible difference between the synchrony of signifiers and the diachrony of signified and comparing it to the difference between manifest and latent dream content in Freud.

Reprinted in Un discours au réel (Paris: Mame, 1973).

G852.   Roudinesco, Elisabeth. "Cogito et science du réel, ou l'assèchement du Zuyderzée." F305, pp. 62-72.

Describes the division between truth and knowledge proposed by Lacan, and claims that it helps situate the fantasm of a creative Ego as well as a subject whose "decentering" by linguists introduces the element of Cartesian doubt into Freud's discovery.

G853.   Roudinesco, Elisabeth. "Crise actuelle de la théorie et de l'institutions analytiques." K1196, pp. 165-77.

Briefly describes the introduction of psychoanalysis in France, and then discusses in detail the issues at stake in Lacan's dissolution of the Ecole freudienne de Paris in 1980. Roudinesco concludes with a sketch of some current psychoanalytic organizations and the reviews associated with them.

G854.   Roudinesco, Elisabeth. "Jacques Lacan: linguistique et linguisterie (linguysterie) (à suivre)." Cahiers de poétique comparée 2, no. 1 (1975): 35-44.

G855.   Roudinesco, Elisabeth. "Madame Soleil entre Althusser et Lacan." Franc-Tireur (January 1982).

Criticizes Dominique Lecourt's attack on Althusser (G702) for falling under Lacan's spell. Roudinesco rejects Lecourt's assertion that Althusser had been intimidated or hypnotized by Lacan's personality and claims instead that Althusser identified with the theoretical solitude of both Lacan and Freud, with their isolation from a supportive intellectual community and with their gradual alienation even from many of their own followers. At the time Althusser finished G433, Roudinesco says, Lacan had just left Ste. Anne,

suspended his seminar, and had no place to speak.
Fernand Braudel subsequently invited him to continue the seminars at l'Ecole pratique des hautes
études, and with Althusser's help Lacan finally got
a room where he continued the seminars on 15 January 1964. For Althusser's own remarks about
Lacan, see G432 and G433.

G856. Rousseau-Dujardin, Jacqueline. "Du temps, qu'en-
       tends-je?" F305, pp. 31-39.

       Notes the recent attacks on psychoanalysis in
       texts such as K1170, and contrasts the place of
       sexuality in Freud's discovery to Lacan's emphasis
       on the signifier.

G857. Roussel, Jean. "Introduction to Jacques Lacan."
       New Left Review 51 (September-October 1968): 63-
       77.

       Describes several concepts central to Lacan's
       work, including Lacan's theories of the ego, his
       distinctions among the real, imaginary, and sym-
       bolic registers, and his emphasis on language.
       Roussel also stresses the importance of Lacan's
       analytic strategies, such as (1) his insistence on
       reactivating primordial ego images of the patient
       through the analyst's impersonality, and (2) his
       effort to help the patient re-establish the con-
       tinuity of his conscious speech.
       Followed by the 1968 translation of C53.

G858. Rovatti, Pier Aldo. "Per un uso di Lacan: nota su
       potere e sapere." F307, pp. 59-70.

G859. Ruegg, Maria. "Metaphor and Metonymy: the Logic
       of Structuralist Rhetoric." Glyph 6 (1980):
       141-57.

       Discusses the use of metaphor and metonymy by
       Jakobson and Lacan, and argues that the irony of
       Lacan's rhetoric rests on a rhetoric of mastery
       that offers the illusion of open-ended poetic play
       which is in fact rigidly controlled. Ruegg at-
       tributes the seductive power of the text in psycho-
       analytic criticism to a "metaphysical security"
       guaranteed by the guise of a "clinically proven"
       scientific truth, and she claims that that security
       is simply another form of epistemological mastery.

G860. Ruhs, A. "Die Schrift der Seele: Einfuhrung in
       die Psychoanalyse nach Jacques Lacan" ["The
       Writings of the Soul: Introduction to Psycho-
       analysis According to Jacques Lacan"]. Psyche 34
       (1980): 885-909.

G861.   Runte, A. ["The Gender of Angels: The Theory of
        Transsexualism in the School of Lacan" (German)].
        Psyche-Zeitschrift für psychoanalyse und ihre
        anwendungen 39 (1985):   930-62.

G862.   Rupolo, Hector.   "Psychoanalysis: A Nodal
        Writing."   Papers of the Freudian School of Mel-
        bourne (1983/84):   117-53.

        Discusses the role of writing in the transmission
        of psychoanalysis as conceived within a Lacanian
        topology.

G863.   Safouan, Moustapha.   "De la structure en psycho-
        analyse: contribution à une théorie de manque."
        K1178, pp. 239-98.

        Describes the role of structure in psychoanalysis
        as proposed by Lacan in his seminars from 1958-63,
        focussing on Lacan's theory of the unconscious and
        castration.   Safouan argues that the Oedipal com-
        plex is neither a myth nor a drama that determines
        everyone's experience, but a structure that orders
        desire to the extent that it constitutes an effect
        of the relation between the human being and lan-
        guage.

G864.   Safouan, Moustafa [Moustapha].   ["Feminine Sexu-
        ality in Psychoanalytic Doctrine" (French)].
        Scilicet 5 (1975):   91-104.

        Briefly discusses the young girl's Oedipal di-
        lemma, which involves not only a separation from
        the mother but also a redirection of desire towards
        an object of the other sex, the father.   Safouan
        focuses that dilemma on the question of the demand
        addressed to the mother by the girl, and he dis-
        tinguishes between the demand that is spoken and
        "Demand," which resists articulation and consists
        in the fading of the subject described in C80.
        Translated by Jacqueline Rose in F370, pp. 123-
        36.

G865.   Safouan, Moustapha.   "Seminars of the Freudian
        School of Melbourne" Papers of the Freudian
        School of Melbourne (1981):   83-116.

        Seminar I--"On Symbolism":   discusses Jones' dis-
        tinction between symbol and metaphor and explores
        the role of metaphor and interpretation in
        psychoanalysis.
        Seminar II--"On Jokes":   focuses on jokes as they
        involve metaphor, metonymy, and the "retroactive
        passing of meaning."

G866.   Safouan, Moustapha. "Seminars of the Freudian
        School of Melbourne." Papers of the Freudian
        School of Melbourne (1982):   125-94.

        Seminar I--"Transference and Acting-Out"
        Seminar II--"On Plato's Symposium"
        Seminar III--The Place of the Analyst in the Trans-
        ference"
        Seminar IV--"Topographic Point of View of the
        Unconscious"

G867.   Salgas, J. P. ["The Unconscious in the Courtroom
        (Publishing Lacan's Seminaires)" (French)].
        Quinzaine littéraire 454 (1986):   7.

G868.   Salma, Alain-Gerard. "Lacan: pinacle à Milan." Le
        point, 18 February 1980, p. 122.

        Claims that Lacanian psychoanalysts resemble
        readers confronting a text more than doctors con-
        fronting a patient, and that Lacanian psychoanaly-
        sis owes more to literature and philosophy than to
        medicine. Salma is commenting more generally about
        the conference at Milan, where William Burroughs
        appeared with Lacan.

G869.   Samuel, Laurent. "La psychanalyse en France vue
        par une Américaine." Psychologie 149 (1982):
        48-49.

G870.   Sasaki, Takatsugu. "Lettre du Japon." L'âne 17
        (1984):   8-9.

        Discusses Lacan's remarks about Japanese and its
        relation to the possibility of practicing psycho-
        analysis in Japanese (see D106).

G871.   Sasaki, Takatsugu. "Mettre la psychananlyse en
        japonais." L'âne 26 (1986):   8-9.

G872.   Schleifer, Ronald. "The Space and Dialogue of
        Desire: Lacan, Greimas, and Narrative
        Temporality." F371, pp.   871-90.

        Claims that the central question of narrative is
        "how does theme or structure manifest itself in
        time" (p. 872), and suggests that the answer lies
        in the interaction between two different discourses
        defined by Lacan in C65: the "metaphoric nonsense"
        of truth and the "metonymic 'fable'" of the desk
        that "speaks" for him as he for it. Identifying
        these discourses with the imaginary and the sym-
        bolic respectively, Schleifer claims that narrative
        represents temporality as it realizes desire "os-

cillating" between the two registers, as it does
between need and demand (p. 884). This oscillation
is marked in the text by "hesitation," Schleifer
claims, which is "the space of desire, the dialogue
of one discourse and another" (p. 885).

G873.   Schmidt, Patrice. "De la psychose paranoïaque dans
        ses rapports avec Salvador Dali." Dali [a cata-
        log for an exhibit at Pompidou Center], 1979-80
        (second edition). Pp. 262-66.

        Claims that Lacan's early work on paranoia is
        endebted to long conversations he had with Dali.
        Marcey (G714) doubts this and claims a simple
        parallel between their work, whereas Pierre (L2233)
        claims that Dali owed much more to Freud than to
        Lacan.
        Another version of this essay was printed as
        "Dali et Lacan dans leurs rapports à la psychose
        paranoïaque" in Art et désordre, edited by Anne
        Tronche (Paris: Aubier Montaigne, 1980).

G874.   Schneider, Monique. "L'ordre symbolique, la dé-
        voration et l'infanticide." Etudes freudiennes
        15/16 (1979): 203-18.

        Comments on Lacan's revisions to Freud's Oedipal
        model of psychic development, especially those
        bearing on the role of the father and the mother.

G***.   Schneider, Monique. "Transcendance du symbolique:
        un platonisme décapité." See F399.

G875.   Schneiderman, Stuart. "Afloat with Jacques Lacan."
        Diacritics 1, no. 2 (1971): 27-34.

        Describes Lacan's concept of the Other and of the
        unconscious as it is manifest in the subject's
        relation to language, focussing on the intersubjec-
        tive dimension of discourse as a "symbolic exchange
        in which each participant gains recognition" (p.
        33). Schneiderman orients his account of Lacan's
        work towards the ontological and historical issues
        of man's being that are raised by Heidegger. Lacan
        understands the Other as the locus of language and
        "the ground for the interactions that form the
        reality of human life," Schneiderman says, and that
        notion undercuts the metaphysics of presence by
        situating the subject within the paradox of absence
        and presence that constitutes the text.

G876.   Schneiderman, Stuart. "Lacan et la littérature."
        Tel quel 84 (1980): 39-47.

        Describes Lacan's reading of Freud as a "dé-

tournement de textes" accomplished through two
gestures that Schneiderman terms "literature" and
"erasure" ("rature").

G877.   Schneiderman, Stuart. "Mon analyse avec Lacan."
         Psychologie 102 (1978):   30-36.

G878.   Schneiderman, Stuart. "The Most Controversial
         Freudian Since Freud." Psychology Today 11
         (1978):   50-59.

    Briefly recounts Lacan's career and his most
controversial innovations in analytic technique,
focussing on the short session and the controversy
it caused with the International Psychoanalytic
Association. Schneiderman also describes Lacan's
behavior during analytic sessions and suggests that
American analysts might revive the status of their
profession by learning from the Lacanians. This
essay offers a clear and concrete introduction to
the clinical dimension of Lacan's work for a general audience.

G879.   Schopf, Alfred. "Das Begehren und die Sprache:
         Zur Genese des Subjekts bei Jacques Lacan" ["De-
         sire and Language: The Development of the Sub-
         ject in the Works of Jacques Lacan"]. Philoso-
         phische Rundschau 30, no. 1/2 (1983):   30-43.

G880.   Schwab, Gabriele. "Projektion und Dezentrierung
         des Subjekts" ["Projection and the Decentering of
         the Subject"]. In Gabriele Schwab, Samuel
         Becketts Endspiel mit der Subjectivität.
         Stuttgart: J. B. Metzler, 1981. Pp. 54-63.

G881.   Schwab, Gabriele. "The Subject Genesis: The
         Imaginary and the Poetical Language." Diogènes
         115 (1981):   55-80.

    Observes that Lacan's claim that the unconscious
is structured like a language implies a "dialo-
gicity" such as Bakhtin described (though one
distinctly internal to the subject) and an "alien
speech" that is "produced as much by the self as by
the symbolic order" (p. 454). The formation of
this ex-centric subject thus involves the "capacity
of imagining a thing that does not exist," and
Schwab argues that such a capacity demonstrates the
implication of imaginary functions in the genesis
of the subject itself. She then goes on to discuss
those functions as conceived by Lacan and D. W.
Winnicott, and suggests applications for a theory
of poetic language.
    This essay was revised by the author and re-
translated as "Genesis of the Subject, Imaginary

Functions, and Poetic Language." <u>New Literary</u>
<u>History</u> 15 (1983/84): 453-74.

G882. Sciacchitano, Antonello. "A tempo e a luogo: note
       sulla struttura del simbolico." F307, pp. 301-
       29.

G883. Scott, Charles E. "The Pathology of the Father's
       Rule: Lacan and the Symbolic Order." <u>Thought:</u>
       <u>A Review of Culture and Idea</u> 61 (1986): 118-30.

       Argues that the masculine image of the Father's
       Rule, which represents our relation to language in
       Lacan's work, appears inadequate in the light of a
       critique informed by the work of Derrida and
       Heidegger. For other essays on Lacan published in
       this issue see G837 and G558.

G884. Scott, Charles E. "The Unconscious and Lacan."
       <u>Man and World</u> 17, no. 2 (1984): 197-211.

       Reviews F374 and claims that the authors have not
       tried to mediate between Lacan's language and the
       reader, but that they have simply cleared the way
       for Lacan's style to "take over and have its ef-
       fect" (p. 198). Scott points out in Lacan's style
       a "strange combination of structuralist rigor and a
       disturbing de-centering language of resonance,
       innuendo, irony, and dissonance" (p. 206), but he
       also argues that Lacan offers a clearer and more
       articulate methodology than most structuralist
       studies (p. 199).
       Scott says that the difficulty of Lacan's style
       may well be just a "growing pain" in a language
       that is struggling to be true to a shifting, un-
       tamed, and inexpressible core, but he also criti-
       cizes Lacan for failing to escape from the western
       metaphysical tradition. Lacan's emphasis on the
       rule-structure of language, Scott concludes, simply
       constitutes a metaphor for the usual "essences" of
       metaphysics, and it still holds out the promise
       that intelligence can be the key to understanding
       "our crazy world" (p. 208). Scott also says that
       Lacan's concept of desire is just one more metaphor
       of "depth," and that his theory of the phallus as a
       primary signifier fails to challenge the imagery of
       male egocentricism in Freud.

G885. Scrutton, Roger. "Incantations of the Self."
       <u>Times Literary Supplement</u>, 11 August 1978, p.
       909.

       Describes Lacan's style as "choked, bombastic,
       and arcane," and says that his writings read like a
       parody of French intellectual manners. Scrutton

refers to Lacan as a mind pursued by delusion and
grandeur and suggests that Lacan's publications
must be conceived as satires. He also dismisses
F392 as worthless. For replies see J1060, J1078,
J1081, J1088, and J1098.

G886.   Sédat, Jacques. "L'analyse amatricide: réflexions
         sur le transfert, la théorie, et l'institution en
         psychanalyse." Esprit 13 (1978):   113-21.

Notes the controversy that K1315 created when it
appeared, and argues that one's concept of transference inevitably determines one's relation to the
theory of psychoanalysis and the role of its institutions. Sédat claims that the importance of
transference to the theoretical and institutional
dimensions of psychoanalysis also suggests that the
patient remains central to its practice, and he
says that any concept of transference that legiti-
mizes the subjection of the patient to the analyst
"en personne" leads to a sacralization of theory
and to the incorporation of theory as a single
person, whether Freud or Lacan.
Sédat thus concludes that it is necessary to
return to the experience of analysis itself and to
the type of transference it makes possible in order
to perceive the true stakes of these issues. The
true analytic institution for each analyst, Sédat
claims, is that of the couch and the exchange that
takes place between analyst and analysand.

G***.   Sédat, Jacques. "L'état maniaque de la théorie."
         See F399.

G887.   Sédat, Jacques. "Théorie et pratique." Esprit 3
         (1980):   139-51.

Comments on the relation between theory and
practice in psychoanalysis in general but especially as implied by the distinctions between the
A.E. and the A.M.E. within the Ecole freudienne.
Sédat discusses at length the "analyse mathématique" derived from Lacan's mathemes as an example
of the "taste for formalization" characteristic of
the Ecole freudienne de Paris and of Jacques-Alain
Miller's work in particular, and he claims that
this "flight into theoretical activism derives from
an incapacity for giving full significance to
interior reality, from a disavowal of psychic
reality" (p. 151). Published with L2370 and G645.

G888.   Shullenberger, William. "Lacan and the Play of
         Desire in Poetry." Massachusetts Studies in Eng-
         lish 7, no. 1 (1978):   33-40.

Describes Lacan's theory of desire and argues
that poetry is a "repetition-compulsion of this
primal catastrophe described by Lacan" in which
language returns to "its genesis in loss" (p. 35).

G889.   Sichère, Bernard. "Lacan: éthique de l'amour
contre éthique de la jouissance." Infini 3
(1983): 78-86.

Discusses Lacan remarks about sainthood and the
"angel's smile" from B31, especially regarding
jouissance and its importance in Bataille's work.
Sichère emphasizes jouissance as a force against
ordinary subjectivity, which is constituted and
constrained by the symbolic, and he contrasts
jouissance to love, another form of relation that
eludes differentiation. Throughout the essay,
Sichère also explores the importance of these
concepts to an ethic that would resist the isolation of symbolic definition. (This item is an
excerpt from F401.)

G890.   Sichler, Liliane. "Lacan gourou." L'express, 26
January 1980, pp. 59-60.

Comments on the dissolution of the Ecole freudienne de Paris, noting that many of its members
intended to "murder a father"--Lacan--who had no
intention of letting that happen. Sichler goes on
to mock Lacan's role as the Master and the excessive adoration directed towards him by his followers.

G891.   Siebers, Tobin. "The Ethical Unconscious." Psychoanalytic Review 73 (1986): 309-30.

Discusses the connection between ethics and
psychoanalysis as elaborated in Lacan's work, and
comments on the limits of Lacan's understanding of
their association.

G892.   Silverman, Kaja. "Lost Objects and Mistaken Subjects." Wide Angle 7, no. 1/2 (1985).

G***.   Silverman, Kaja. "The Subject." K1328, pp. 126-
93.

Describes psychoanalytic models of the subject
proposed by Freud and Lacan, and notes Lacan's
extension of the Freudian model to consolidate "the
theoretical interconnections between subject,
signifier, and cultural order" (p. 151). Silverman
claims that Lacan's theory of the subject "reads
like a classic narrative" that moves from birth
through "the territorialization of the body" to the

Oedipal stage, and much of this chapter is devoted
to what Silverman identifies as four stages of that
narrative: birth, the imaginary, signification,
and the symbolic.

G893.   Skelton, Ross. "Lacan and the Rational Ego."
        Irish Philosophical Journal 2 (1985): 53-66.

G894.   Smirnoff, Victor N. "De Vienne à Paris: Sur les
        origines d'une psychanalyse 'à la française.'"
        Nouvelle revue de psychanalyse 20 (1979): 13-58.

        Traces the history of psychoanalysis in France,
        focussing on Lacan's prominence as a major force in
        making psychoanalysis a dominant form of intel-
        lectual discourse in France today (see esp. pp. 39-
        58). Smirnoff also comments on Pichon's response
        to Lacan (see G800) as an example of the early
        resistance to the "German" quality of psycho-
        analysis. For accompanying articles see G549,
        G565, G668, and G672.

G895.   Soler, Colette. "Lacan et la butée freudienne."
        L'âne 5 (1982): 9.

        Briefly describes Lacan's concepts of the symptom
        and the objet a and notes their implications for
        clinical practice.

G896.   Soler, Colette. "Le pari de Jacques Lacan." L'âne
        4 (1982): 11.

        Wonders whether or not there is a Lacanian psy-
        choanalysis, and comments on the varieties of
        Lacanian psychoanalysts from different countries.
        Soler notes Lacan's admonition to do as he does,
        not to imitate him ("Faites comme moi, ne m'imitez
        pas"), and argues that Lacan's work is primarily a
        return to Freud.

G897.   Soler, Colette. "Sur la passe." L'âne 5 (1982):
        10.

        Describes the pass and its dialectical relation
        to more traditional methods of certifying analysts,
        and claims that the pass does not offer less con-
        trol over the formation of new analysts but "more"
        ("plus") in the sense of "plus-fondé." Soler also
        says that the pass is derived from the practice of
        psychoanalysis and its incidence in the real. See
        C88 the proposal of la passe.)

G898.   Sollers, Philippe. "Hommage à Lacan." F361, p. 9.

        Describes his impressions upon hearing Lacan for

the first time, and comments on the style of
Lacan's speech.

G899. Sorel, P. "Pour quoi "lacanien"? Et surtout!
       Comment?" Soins psychiatrique 67 (1986): 17-18.
       See K1335.

G900. Souza, Remy de. "Una 'chave' para Lacan?" Revista
       brasileira de filosofia 28 (1978): 80-82.

G901. Speziale-Bagliacca, Roberto. "Lacan
       l'ineludibile." Nuova corrente: rivista di let-
       teratura 82/83 (1980): 97-129.

G902. "stécriture: à la recherche d'une méthode." F357,
       pp. 96-97.

       Observes the inevitable paradox in the aim of
       rendering a text of Lacan's seminar on transference
       "readable but . . . with a minimum of correction"
       (p. 96). Much of this brief note is given over to
       explaining the editorial symbols used in the text
       of the seminar that was composed by the group
       associated with the bulletin stécriture, but the
       authors also remark on the significance of editing
       the text as a group rather than trying to propose a
       single person to fulfill the role of "author" in
       Lacan's place. "A mourning for Lacan-author is at
       the beginning of the work of retranscription," they
       observe, and they reformulate the paradox of ren-
       dering Lacan's speech into writing as the task of
       "rendering the text readable but . . . also the
       operations effected on the text from the begin-
       ning," starting with the stenographer who recorded
       it.
           On the origin of "stécriture" as a term, see B22,
       p. 23. The authors here clearly intend the word
       to emphasize the curious status of the written
       transcript, which exists somewhere between
       writing ("écriture") and a shorthand report
       ("sténographe").

G903. Stewart, David W. "Jacques Lacan and the Language
       of the Unconscious." Bulletin of the Menninger
       Clinic 47, no. 1 (1983): 53-69.

       Describes basic tenets of Lacan's work, focussing
       on the unconscious and its relation to language as
       a gap in conscious discourse.

G904. Stewart, D. W. "Lacan's Linguistic Unconscious and
       the Language of Desire." Psychoanalytic Review
       73 (1986): 17-29.

G905. Stewart, David W. "The Linguistic Unconscious of

Jacques Lacan." _American Journal of Psycho-_
Analysis 45 (1985):   348-59.

G906.   Stewart, D. W. "The Symptom as Metaphor in Lacan's
Theory of the Unconscious." _Hillside Journal of_
Clinical Psychiatry 8 (1986):   75-88.

G907.   Straub, Kristina. "Psychoanalytic Relation and
Feminist Praxis in _Reading Lacan_." _Literature_
and Psychology 32, no. 4 (1986):   68-72.

Comments generally on F334.

G908.   Svejgaard, Erik. "Om driftsbegrebet hos Lacan."
Subjekt of tekst: bidrag til semiotikkens teori.
Edited by Nils L. Knudsen, Ole A. Olsen, and Erik
Svejgaard. Nordisk Sommeruniversitets skrift-
serie 5. Kongerslev: GMT, 1974. Pp. 126-66.

G909.   Szafran, A. W. "Propos sur les concepts du langage
et de l'inconscient chez Lacan et la tradition
esotérique." _Acta psychiatrica belgica_ 73
(1973):   484-96.

Describes a striking similarity between the
Jewish mystic concepts of God and Man, Lacan's
attitude towards Freud's texts, verbal expression
in general, and the unconscious. Szafran claims
that Lacan's unconscious language is equivalent to
the "inside world" described by Kabbalists, and
compares Lacan's practice of free association and
"unconscious formation" to the Kabbalists' "science
of combination."

G910.   Tabouret-Keller, Andrée. "'La conscience détrou-
née': de Freud à Lacan." _La pensée_ 229 (1982):
27-37.

Notes the uproar surrounding Lacan's death, and
claims that the importance of Freud as well as of
Lacan may be overestimated at the moment (p. 27).
Tabouret-Keller attempts to give a brief account of
why Marxists might be interested in psychoanalysis
and especially in Lacan's reading of Freud, and he
describes Lacan's effort to construct what Lacan
called a "materialist definition of the phenomenon
of consciousness" (see B12, Chap. iv).

G911.   Tabouret-Keller, Andrée. "De l'autre côté du
miroir: la contrée humaine." _La pensée_ 243
(1985):   89-96.

Discusses the importance of the general idea of
the imaginary to psychoanalysis, especially as it
has been formulated by Lacan to emphasize inter-

dependence as a fundamental factor in human experience.   Tabouret-Keller also notes the links
between language and the foundation of the ego in
the imaginary, and claims that "human reality" is
situated at the intersection of the imaginary and
the foundation of the subject in the symbolic.

G912.   Taillandier, Gérôme.   "Quelques problèmes de
l'établissement du séminaire de J. Lacan."   F357,
pp. 121-26.

Offers a descriptive summary of all the transcripts from Lacan's seminars, their sources, and
their relations to each other.   Unfortunately,
Taillandier refuses to identify his sources beyond
cryptic sets of initials, but his description of
extant texts from each seminar and of their various
origins helps clarify the difficulty involved in
establishing any single text as the authoritative
version of Lacan's oral presentations.

G913.   Thom, Martin.   "The Unconscious Structured Like a
Language."   <u>Journal of the Anthropology Society
of Oxford</u> 6, no. 2, and <u>Economy and Society</u> 5
(1976):   434-69.

Comments on Freud's understanding of the relation
between manifest dream content and latent dream-
thoughts from the perspective of Lacan's theory of
metaphor and metonymy and his claim that the unconscious is structured like a language.   Thom
describes Lacan's use of structural linguistics and
his debt to Saussure and Jakobson specifically, and
he criticizes the universal application of what
Lévi-Strauss defines as the "Symbolic Order."
This paper follows G681 quite closely, but a
second section, added when the paper was revised
and published again in F359, pp. 1-44, critiques
the reading of Lacan proposed by G681 and stresses
the interaction between primal repression and the
child's capture by the imaginary.   This new section
also insists on distinctions among the real, symbolic, and imaginary aspects of familial relations.

G914.   Thom, Martin.   "Verneinung, Verwerfung, Ausstos-
sung: A Problem in the Interpretation of Freud."
F359, pp. 162-87.

Comments on Freud's "Die Verneinung" by comparing
various English and French translations, focussing
on Lacan's own claim that <u>Verneinung</u> is best translated as "<u>dénégation</u>" and on the implications of
that translation for Lacan's theory of psychosis.

G915.   Toscani, Claudio. "Giuliano Gramigna, o la scrit-
         tura come fine (lettura lacaniana de il testo del
         racconto." Forum Italicum 11 (1977):   164-83.

G916.   Toupence, William F.   "The Way of the Subject:
         Jacques Lacan's Use of Chuang Tzu's Butterfly
         Dream." Tamkang Review 11 (1981):   249-65.

         Comments on Lacan's use of Tzu's dream in B31 to
         clarify certain aspects of Freud's theory of
         dreams, and argues that in Tzu's work as well as
         Lacan's, dreams undermine a secure sense of sub-
         jectivity by introducing an "otherness" into the
         subject's sense of self. Hence, the dream also
         subverts the possibility of an objectified ego.

G917.   Turkle, Sherry.   "Contemporary French Psycho-
         analysis: I.   The History of the French
         Psychoanalytic Movement." Human Context 7
         (1975):   333-42;   Part II in Human Context 7,
         no. 3 (1975).

         Early version of F412.

G918.   Turkle, Sherry.   "Mon oncle de Marienbad": Socio-
         biology Comes to the Land of the Structuralists."
         Contemporary French Civilization 6, no. 1/2
         (1982):   67-87.

         Claims that much social theory in France has
         situated itself within a Lacanian space since 1968,
         and argues that Lacan's notion of a "social-
         linguistic construction of the self" has informed
         contemporary understandings of the way the in-
         dividual is connected to society. Turkle compares
         Lacan's work to that of the Frankfurt school be-
         cause of their common interest in the social di-
         mensions of individual experience, and she dis-
         cusses Lacan's impact on feminist debates and on
         the work of the New Philosophers.
         Turkle describes Lacan's early associations with
         the political left in France through the late
         1960s, but claims that Lévy's book K1253 aligned
         Lacan with the new right wing movements. She con-
         cludes by arguing that psychoanalysis inevitably
         introduces a humanist tendency into structuralism
         that works like a trojan horse (see F412 and G919),
         and that the current fashion for blending psycho-
         analysis with sociobiology has taken a decidedly
         un-Lacanian turn toward a sympathy for strength-
         ening the ego. We may be subject to pressures of
         biological programming, the sociobiologists say,
         but we can understand and transcend them through
         mastery of the self and environment. Turkle sug-
         gests that this attitude is analogous to the ego-

psychologist's desire for the ego to conquer the
id.

G919.   Turkle, Sherry. "The New Philosophy and the Agony
        of Structuralism: Enter the Trojan Horse."
        Chicago Review 32, no. 3 (1981): 11-28.

        Claims that Lacan's work made possible a bridge
        between psychoanalysis and radical social thought
        because it focussed on the individual's entry into
        social processes (see L2090). This shift in focus
        undermined the thrust of many theories of social
        engineering and even of the Frankfurt school's
        notion that society has an "influence" on the in-
        dividual; for Lacan, the individual is not auton-
        omous from society in the first place. Instead,
        Turkle says, for Lacan society "comes to dwell
        within him or her" and "we become social with the
        appropriation of language."
        Turkle describes the way radicals extrapolated a
        "political naturalism" out of Lacan's work after
        May '68, citing K1170 as a prime example of such
        applications, and she says that they also under-
        stood Lacan's notion of psychoanalysis as the
        "reconstitution of associative chains of significa-
        tion" to imply the possibility of following those
        chains out of the symbolic and back to Eden. This
        escape from the phallocentric symbolic to some
        primitive imaginary state assumed a parallel be-
        tween social protest and the psychoanalytic cure,
        Turkle says, and it tended to treat both protest
        and psychoanalysis as "a liberating ritual whose
        goal is to trace a way back to a truthful idiom"
        (p. 17). Lacan, Turkle argues, would see such an
        "escape" as psychotic and is more pessimistic
        because he lacks a theory for any sort of change at
        all.
        Turkle claims that psychoanalysis was the "trojan
        horse" of French structuralism because it focussed
        on the psychology of the individual even as it con-
        stituted that individual structurally, and because
        any psychoanalysis, even Lacan's explicitly anti-
        humanist work, inevitably opens the way to ego-
        psychology and so always threatens to slip back
        into a traditional humanism. (Most of Turkle's
        remarks focus on a comparison between Lacan's work
        and Levi's Barbarism with a Human Face, K1253.)
        For a similar argument, see G918.

G920.   Tytell, Pamela. "Lacan et l'anglais tel qu'on le
        parle." F361, pp. 14-18.

        Recounts her own experience as an American read-
        ing Lacan's text in French and in English and then
        undergoing separate analyses in both languages.

Tytell claims that the analytic experience helps
resolve many of the difficulties of Lacan's written
texts and that the written texts join the experience of analysis in "the common terrain of lan-
guage--the truth" (p. 18).

G921.   Tytell, Pamela. "Lacune aux U.S.A." F305, pp. 79-
82.

Describes the slow introduction of Lacan's work
in the United States.

G922.   Ver Eecke, Wilfried. "Hegel as Lacan's Source for
Necessity in Psychoanalytic Theory." F403, pp.
113-38.

Claims that Lacan's effort to establish a scientific basis for psychoanalysis rests on his claims
for the necessity of phenomenon central to the discipline, and argues that those claims are based on
a Hegelian framework rather than psychoanalytic
experience. Ver Eecke compares Lacan's mirror
stage to Hegel's discussion of the master-slave
relationship and Lacan's theory of aggressivity to
Hegel's "Law of the Heart."

G923.   Ver Eecke, Wilfried. "The Look the Body and the
Other." Dialogues in Phenomenology. Edited by
Don Ihde and Richard M. Zaner. Selected Studies
in Phenomenology and Existential Philosophy 5.
The Hague: Nyhoff, 1975. Pp. 224-46.

G924.   Vergote, Antoine. "De 'l'autre scène' de Freud à
'l'autre' de Lacan." Qu'est ce que l'homme?
Hommage à A. De Waelhens. Brussels: Faculté
universitaires Saint-Louis, 1982, pp. 683-709.

Compares the theories of the unconscious proposed
by Lacan and Freud, and argues that their difference may be traced in Lacan's proposition that
the unconscious is structured like a language.
"Language" and "structured" are ascendent in
Lacan's thought, Vergote says, while Freud may be
read as stressing the "like" and the disjunction
that that adverb opens up. Translated by Thomas
Acklin and Beryl Schlossman as "From Freud's 'Other
Scene' to Lacan's 'Other,'" F403, pp. 193-221

G925.   Verstraten, P. "L'homme du plaisir chez Hegel et
l'homme du désir chez Lacan." Revue de l'Université de Bruxelles 3/4 (1976): 351-94.

G926.   Viderman, Serge. "L'institution comme résistance à
l'analyse." K1196, pp. 113-20.

Comments on the role of the analyst as indicated by Lacan's phrase "le sujet supposé savoir."

G927.   Vigano, Carlo.   "Il soggetto della conoscenze paranoica: sugli 'antecendenti' dell'insegnamento di J. Lacan."   F307, pp. 279-91.

G928.   Weyergans, François.   "Voyage en Lacanie."   Le point, 23 February 1981, p. 122.

Discusses F316, noting Clément's account of Lacan's attitude towards his patients.

G929.   Wieland, J. H.   "De psychoanalyse van Jacques Lacan" ["The Psychoanalysis of Jacques Lacan"]. Tijdschrift voor filosofie 36 (1974):   483-520.

G930.   Wilden, Anthony.   "Freud, Signorelli, and Lacan: The Repression of the Signifier."   American Imago 23, no. 4 (1966):   332-66.

Discusses the relation between the subject and language as described by Lacan, and explains the absence of Signorelli's name recounted by Freud in The Psychopathology of Everyday Life (1901) as the suppression of one signifier by another.   Wilden also comments on Freud's "address to the Other" and the existence of a "double subject" suggested by the L-schema.   Translated into French as "Freud, Signorelli, and Lacan: Repression of the Signifier," Revue de psychologie et des sciences de l'éducation 8 (1973):   427-65.

G931.   Wilden, Anthony.   "Jacques Lacan's Structuralism: Libido as Language."   Psychology Today 5, no. 12 (1972):   40-42.

G***.   Wilden, Anthony.   "Lacan and the Discourse of the Other."   F420, pp. 159-311.

This item is described at F420.

G932.   Wilden, Anthony.   "On Lacan: Psychoanalysis, Language, and Communication."   Contemporary Psychoanalysis 9 (1973):   445-70.

G933.   Will, David.   Letter in response to L2201.   Screen 22, no. 3 (1981):   107-09.

Claims that contributors to Screen such as Pagaczkowska have split Lacan's work into the "good Lacan" and the "bad Lacan," and that they have elevated the "good Lacan" to the status of an ego ideal whose remarks are accepted without any reservations at all.   Will also criticizes Lacan's own

"incorrect appropriation of the clinical phenomenon
of fetishism . . . as a metaphor for the global
structure of subjectivity" (p. 109).

G934.   Wollheim, Richard.   "The Cabinet of Dr. Lacan."
        New York Review of Books 25 January 1979, pp. 36-
        45.

Claims that Lacan's work lacks the explanatory
force of Freud's because (1) he assigns no place to
"maturation" and so fails to consider the connection between mental experience and the body; (2)
he is vague about the internal structure of the
psyche; and (3) he "depreciates the contribution of
[clinical] experience to psychoanalytic explanation" (p. 44).
Wollheim discusses Lacan's work as one of several
contemporary efforts to compensate for Freud's
failure to provide a coherent account of cognitive
development or of symbolism, and he claims that
Lacan's effort is less successful than those of the
New York school of ego psychology and the "English
School" of Karl Abraham and Melanie Klien because
he does not offer concrete evidence for his theoretical claims.   Wollheim also argues that Lacan
emphasizes several points--specifically, the centrality of symbolism in cognitive development--
that others have already established with more
substantial clinical support, and he objects that
Lacan's excessive emphasis on the importance of
speech in the analytic situation has led to extreme
variations in technique such as the short session
(p. 38).
Most of Wollheim's article is devoted to a description of Lacan's work as "layered like a cake"
with five distinct levels or foci: (1) drives, or
the affective side of the subject's life; (2) the
conative side of the infant's life, which is related to need and described by Wollheim as the
"effortful side of life through which drives get
realized"; (3) the formation of the unconscious, or
repression; (4) distinctions among need, demand,
and desire; and (5) man's psychosexual development
through language, the phallus, and the name-of-the-
father.   Wollheim singles out Lacan's concept of
the phallus as particularly problematic, and concludes that "Lacan's ideas and Lacan's style, yoked
in an indissoluble union, represent an invasive
tyranny.   And it is by a hideous irony that this
tyranny should find its recruits among groups that
have nothing in common except the sense that they
lack a theory worthy of their cause or calling:
feminists, cinéastes, professors of literature" (p.
45).
For responses to this article, see J1052 and

J1129.   For Wollheim's response to these comments, see J1138.

G935.   Wordsworth, Ann.   "Derrida and Criticism."   Oxford Literary Review 3, no. 2 (1978):   47-52.

Cites B31 on the non-humanistic link between desire and the constitution of the subject in the symbolic, and on the gaze as the basis for a "Möbian topology of art/psychoanalysis" (p. 51). Wordsworth compares these Lacanian topics to the "aestheticizing psychoanalysis" proposed by Derrida's work on Freud.

G936.   Wordsworth, Ann.   "Lacanalysis: Lacan for Critics."   The Oxford Literary Review 2, no. 3 (1977):   7-8.

G937.   Yañez, Cortez R.   "La figura del deseo en la fonomenologia del espiritu de Hegel y la psicologia. Aporte para la explicitation del deseo en las teorias de Freud y Lacan" ["The Representation of Desire in Plato's Dialogues and in Psychology: A Contribution to the Explanation of Desire in the Theories of Freud and Lacan"].   Acta psiquiatrica y psicologica de america latina 24, no. 4 (1978):   271-78.

G938.   Ysseling, Samuel.   "Structuralism and Psychoanalysis in the Work of Jacques Lacan."   International Philosophical Quarterly 10, no. 1 (1970):   102-117.

Identifies three kinds of problems in considering Lacan's work from a structuralist perspective: (1) the difficulty of his style, in which the associative nature of Lacan's argument may carry out a psychoanalysis in itself and so functions properly only in a psychoanalytic situation; (2) the ambiguous effect of talking about psychoanalysis under any conditions, which tends to turn it into either philosophy or science, two fields that Lacan has questioned; and (3) the difficulty of labelling Lacan a structuralist at all, despite his claim in 1968 that "Le Lacanisme, c'est le structuralisme de la stricte observance" (p. 104).
Ysseling also notes more generally that Lacan and structuralism share an emphasis on "transindividual discourse," and that Lacan insisted that the only medium of psychoanalysis is the patient's words, not a general inquiry into truth or meaning.   He briefly sketches Lacan's account of analytic discourse, the role of the analyst, and the goal of psychoanalysis, which Ysseling describes as being "opposed to every humanistic, culturalistic, and

psychological interpretation of Freud" (p. 117),
and he quotes Serge Leclaire's claim that, at the
end of analysis, "the patient will not know any
better who he is, but only to what he is subjected
[assujeter], of what 'cipher' he is the respondent
[de quel 'chiffre' il est le répondant]."

G939.   Zampino de Vincenti, A. Francesca. "La critica
         freudiana dell'associazionismo e la ristrut-
         turazione del rapporto verita/realta nella rilet-
         tura di Jacques Lacan" ["The Freudian Criticism
         of Associationism and the Restructurization of
         the Relation Truth/Reality in the Interpretation
         of Jacques Lacan"]. Storia e critica della
         psicologia 3, no. 1 (1982): 63-77.

G940.   Zenoni, Alfredo. "Métaphore et métonymie dans la
         théorie de Lacan." Cahiers internationaux de
         symbolisme [Belgium] 31/32 (1976): 187-98.
         Translated in Enclitic 5 (1981): 5-18.

G941.   Zentner, Oscar. "The Death of Lacan." Papers of
         the Freudian School of Melbourne (1981): 9-13.

         Briefly comments on C96 and on the effect of
         Lacan's death on those who follow or "accompany the
         Lacanian teaching."

G942.   Zentner, Oscar. "From the Verneinung of Freud to
         the Verwerfung of Lacan." Papers of the Freudian
         School of Melbourne (1983/84): 9-30.

         Discusses the functions of negation and fore-
         closure, especially as they relate to the I and to
         the position of the subject in the order of signi-
         fiers.

G943.   Zentner, Oscar. "A Note on Letter 52 and on the
         Ethics of Psychoanalysis: the Dissolution of
         L'Ecole Freudienne de Paris " Papers of the
         Freudian School of Melbourne (1979): 1-5.

         Translates B38 in support of his claim that "the
         psychoanalytic act is always an ACT OF ETHICS," and
         to underscore his sympathy with the Lacanian pro-
         ject. Zentner, an analyst of the Freudian School
         of Buenos Aires, founded the Freudian School of
         Melbourne in 1977 along with Maria-Inès Rotmiler de
         Zentner and a small group of local clinicians. The
         School offers two weekly seminars, one on Freud and
         the other on Lacan, and sponsors an annual "Homage
         to Freud." The papers from the annual meeting are
         collected with other documents from the seminars
         and published annually. Most of the items pub-
         lished in this journal deal with Lacan, at least

indirectly; selected items are cited in Section G.
For a list of citations from this journal, see the
journal index.

G944.   Zentner, Oscar.   "The Woman and the Real as a
        Paradigm of Psychosis."   Papers of the Freudian
        School of Melbourne (1979):   73-92.

        Comments on the concept of femininity as proposed
        by Freud and Lacan, especially in reference to C69.

G945.   Zizek, Slavoj.   "La phénoménolgie, science du
        fantasme."   L'âne 24 (1986):   23.

G***.   Zrehen, Richard.   "Tous les chemins."   See F399.

Section H

Reviews of Primary Works

De la psychose paranoïaque dans ses rapports avec la
        personalité (A1)

H946.   Giraud, P.   Annales médico-psychologiques 1, no. 1
        (January 1933).

        Briefly describes A1 and notes several problems
        with Lacan's argument: (1)   Although Lacan claims
        that the personality "joue sur des mécanismes de
        nature organique," i.e., that it "organizes" these
        mechanisms, Lacan fails to explain the relation
        between the psychic structure of the personality
        and our experience of organic sensations.   (2)
        Lacan also fails to define the origin of the per-
        sonality, other than to note its developmental
        character and a vague "psychogenic" relation to the
        external world.   (3)   Lacan neglects to consider
        carefully the possible influence of a paranoiac
        "constitution" and so cannot explain why one in-
        dividual may respond to a given situation by be-
        coming paranoid and another may respond "normally."
        Lacking such an explanation, Giraud says that
        Lacan must conclude that paranoiacs will simply be
        people who were raised poorly between the age of
        two or three years.
        Giraud ends with a complaint against the "artis-
        tic" and philosophical quality of Lacan's style,
        which became a major issue among readers within the
        psychiatric community even before Lacan adopted the
        cryptic, paronomastic style of his post-war writ-
        ings.   See G800.

H947.   Kremer-Marietti, Angèle.   Les études philosophique
        2 (1980):   240-42.

        Claims that the central point of A1 is the inter-
        section of psychoanalysis and psychiatry that

Lacan effected there, and notes Lacan's discussion
of Schreber's memoirs in B14 and A2, where he
explains that the drama of madness is situated in
the relation of man to the signifier. Kremer-
Marietti also reviews Paul Duquenne's translation
of Schreber's writings, Mémoires d'un névropathe
(Paris: Editions du Seuil, 1975).

Ecrits (A2)

H948.   Pollock, George H.   American Journal of Psychiatry
          135 (1978):   517.

          Notes the potential utility of the essays trans-
        lated in A2j, but claims that the book is too
        amorphous without a more systematic exposition of
        Lacan's theory.

H949.   Chessick, Richard D.   "Critique: Some Unusual
          Books Published in 1978." American Journal of
          Psychotherapy 33 (1979):   312-15.

          Describes B22 and A2 as an "incredibly obscure
        hodge-podge" that reflects the more opaque existen-
        tial philosophy written in France.

H950.   Booklist, 1 November 1977, pp. 439-40.

          Notes that Lacan's essays reformulate and rein-
        terpret some classic themes of psychoanalysis,
        especially those of the significance of the phal-
        lus, aggression, language, and the unconscious.

H951.   Choice 14 (1978):   1711.

          Notes the difficulty of Lacan's style, briefly
        describes the essays collected in A2j, and suggests
        F420 as a good introduction to Lacan's thought.

H952.   Kennedy, Deveraux.   "Lacan Against Man." Con-
          temporary Sociology 10, no. 1 (1981):   46-49.

          Briefly describes Lacan's emphasis on metaphor
        and metonymy as the two poles of language, and
        summarizes Lacan's account of the child's entry
        into culture and its implications for the "being"
        of the subject. Kennedy also reviews B22 and F392.

H953.   Backés[-Clément], Catherine. "Lacan, ou le 'porte-
          parole.'" Critique 249 (1968):   136-61.

          Emphasizes the spoken character of Lacan's
        "Ecrits" and discusses several issues raised in

that book, including the ex-centricity of the subject and the role of truth and ethics in psychoanalytic discourse.

H954.   King, Richard. Georgia Review 32 (1978):   926-30.

Claims that Lacan's attacks on ego-psychology are
an implicit political critique of the American way
of life, and criticizes them for their "national
and political chauvinism" and "vulgar Ideologie-
kritik" (p. 926). King argues that Lacan's account
of the unconscious is nothing like Freud's, and he
denies any link between metonymy and desire.
Nevertheless, King does praise Lacan's formulation
of the imaginary and the symbolic, and he claims
that Lacan's notions of the paranoic ego and of the
centrality of desire have an "Adlerian" quality.
King also reviews K1237 and praises its relative
clarity.

H955.   Ragland-Sullivan, Ellie. Gradiva 2, no. 1 (1979):
58-63.

Emphasizes the centrality of clinical practice to
Lacan's work, but argues that he does offer "a new
philosophy of man and a new theory of discourse"
with implications far beyond the clinical context
of psychoanalysis. Ragland-Sullivan also claims
that Lacan is especially important to literary
criticism because he has reopened questions about
our ideas of truth, knowledge, and language, and
radically reoriented the role of intentionality in
interpretation at the level of both the conscious
and the unconscious.

H956.   Kris, Anton. Journal of the American Psychoanalytic Association 28 (1980):   223-24.

Complains about Lacan's dogmatic and unsupported
assertions and about his "undisciplined theoretical
exposition" (p. 224), though Kris admits that there
may be some utility in applying linguistics to
psychoanalysis.

H957.   Heaton, J. M. Journal of the British Society for
Phenomenology 9, no. 3 (1978):   204-05.

Briefly recounts Lacan's version of the Oedipal
conflict and notes that Lacan situates the father
as central to man's access to culture, an approach
quite different from the tendency among Anglo-
American psychoanalysts to emphasize the importance
of the mother (p. 205). Heaton says that Lacan's
work is a significant advance on Freud but claims
to agree with Piaget that Lacan's work needs to be

"decentered" (see K1292). Also reviews A2.

H958.   Kuczkowski, Richard. <u>Library Journal</u> 15 October
        1977, p. 2168.

        Notes the importance of Lacan's work but warns
        readers about the difficulty of his writing even in
        this "serviceable" translation.

H959.   Morton, John. <u>Mankind</u> 13, no. 3 (1982):   264-65.

        Affirms the value of Lacan's project but decries
        the needless difficulty of his style, and praises
        K1340 as a useful access to difficult writers.

H960.   Lacroix, Jean. "Les <u>Ecrits</u> de Lacan ou retour à
        Freud." "<u>Le monde</u>, 24 December 1966, p. 11.

        Describes A2 as a "treatise on the omnipresence
        of human discourse" and as a work that is "dif-
        ficult, often irritating, always passionate."
        Lacroix also notes that 5,000 copies were sold in
        the first three days of publication.

H961.   Schneiderman, Stuart. <u>New Republic</u>, 12 November
        1977, p. 34.

        Comments on the surprising silence surrounding
        Lacan's work in the international psychoanalytic
        community after his "excommunication," and insists
        on the importance of such historical controversies
        to a reading of Lacan's work. Schneiderman admits
        the difficulty of Lacan's style, but he attributes
        it to Lacan's attempt to restore the importance of
        language in the determination of psychical symptoms
        according to Freud's methods. He goes on to stress
        Lacan's emphasis on the analyst's own desire and on
        the effect of his speech in interventions, and
        notes Lacan's rejection of ego-psychology and the
        corollary practice of strengthening the patient's
        ego.

H962.   Thom, Martin. "Return to Freud." <u>New Society</u>, 7
        July 1977, p. 35.

        Praises A2j for its insistence on returning
        psychoanalysis to a close study of Freud's texts
        and for the focus on language as an order which
        binds us all. Thom notes Lacan's rejection of the
        Ego as a "Captain of the Soul" and his association
        of the ego with a Hegelian "other," and he claims
        that Lacan's emphasis on language as a preexistent
        structure enables a feminist critique of psycho-
        analysis because it presents sexual distinctions as
        culturally determined.

H963.   Leavy, S. New York Times Book Review, 2 October
        1977, pp. 10, 38-39.

        Praises Lacan's introduction of Saussurean lin-
        guistics into psychoanalysis and claims that
        biology and neurology were always inappropriate
        bases for a scientific explanation of the uncon-
        scious. Leavy briefly describes Lacan's emphasis
        on the "otherness" of self, the difficulties of his
        style, and his polemical attacks on established
        analytic practice, and he argues for the general
        importance of Lacan's contribution.

H964.   Kurzweil, Edith. "Structuralist Psychoanalysis."
        Partisan Review 45, no. 4 (1978): 642-46.

        Contrasts Lacan's "legitimation" of psychoanaly-
        sis with linguistics to American psychoanalysts'
        use of biology (p. 643), and says that although the
        id, or "ça," talks for Lacan, Freud believed that
        it was irrational and tended to "act out" rather
        than speak. Kurzweil attributes some of Lacan's
        impact to his audacity and exhibitionism, but she
        also suggests that his emphasis on the pleasure of
        analysis may allow American Freudians to see that
        their distance and restraint is counter-productive
        to analysis (p. 646).

H965.   Leavy, Stanley. Psychoanalytic Quarterly 46
        (1977): 311-17.

        Argues for the importance of Lacan's work, but
        regrets his style and its "free-associative" flow
        because it drives readers away. Leavy concludes
        that the real value of Lacan's work will emerge
        only as it can be expressed in more rational
        language.

H966.   Psychology Today 11, no. 7 (1977): 162.

        Describes A2j as a "radical restatement of Freud"
        based on linguistic theories.

H967.   Barham, Peter. "Sanctuaries of the Text."
        Sociology 13, no. 1 (1979): 111-15.

        Describes A2 as one among other structuralist
        works such as Foucault's Discipline and Punish, and
        claims that Lacan can urge sociologists to pay
        closer attention to social fortifications and the
        life that goes on within them.

H968.   Ragland-Sullivan, Ellie. "Jacques Lacan: Ecrits."
        Sub-stance 21 (1978): 166-73.

Comments on the difficulty of Lacan's style and
on his relevance for literary criticism, and
briefly describes several concepts central to his
work: the structure of the ego in relation to
narcissism, psychosis, and neurosis; the signifying
chain; and the Oedipal complex.

H969.   Turkle, Sherry.   Theory and Society 9 (1980):   655-
61.

Notes that the American controversy over Lacan's
teaching has just begun to reflect the uproar in
France, and claims that this translation of Ecrits
won't help new readers very much.   Turkle goes on
to describe Lacan's work, focussing on (1) the
mirror stage as a reaction against ego-psychology;
(2) Lacan's resistance to conventional psychoanalytic associations and their institutional
hierarchies; and (3) Lacan's use of the symbolic as
a bridge between psychoanalysis and politics.

The Language of the Self (F420)

H***.   Choice 5 (1969):   1509.

Describes Lacan as a "heretical French psychoanalyst" whose style is "aphoristic, cryptic,
orphic, and dense."

H970.   Paul, Louis.   Etc. A Review of General Semantics
27, no. 2 (1970):   239-41.

Declares Lacan an anachronism because "we have
gone past Freud" (p. 239), and complains that the
patient's "Word" is too narrow a concept to serve
as the focus for psychoanalysis.

Les complexes familiaux (A6)

H971.   Soler, Colette.   L'âne 19 (1984):   25-26.

Describes several issues discussed in A6 and
their place in Lacan's later work, and concludes
that for Lacan the complexes were certainly
familial whereas neurosis remained strictly "individual" and "contingent."   "The subject is no
more innocent of his complex in 1938 that he will
be of his phantasm later," Soler says (p. 26).

H972.   Calame, Alain. La nouvelle revue française 381
        (1984): 101-03.

        Describes A6 as the missing link between A1 and
        A2, and notes that its style is typical of Lacan,
        yet accessible. Calame says that A6 shows the
        beginning of Lacan's interest in the mirror stage
        and other key concepts in his later work.

H973.   Gordon, Clive. "Family Complexes Within the Devel-
        opment of the Individual: An Analysis of One
        Psychological Function." Times Literary Supple-
        ment, 13 July 1984, p. 779.

        Notes Lacan's insistence on a fundamental split
        within the infant's sense of itself as a result of
        the mirror stage, and summarizes Lacan's argument
        that any analysis attempting to integrate such
        imaginative productions by putting them under the
        control of a unifying ego simply sustains the lie
        of unity. Gordon also describes Lacan's account of
        the family pathology behind neurosis and psychosis,
        both of which are structured according to a rejec-
        tion that is coupled with an affirmation of unity.

Seminar I (B12)

H***.   Blomeyer, R. Analytische Psychologie 16, no. 1
        (1985): 79-80. See H979.

Seminar II (B13)

H***.   Blomeyer, R. Analytische Psychologie 16, no. 1
        (1985): 79-80. See H979.

H974.   Benoist, Alain de. "Le triomphe de l'abracadabra."
        Le figaro, 8 January 1978, p. 25.

        Denounces Lacan's work as impenetrable nonsense,
        the obscurity of which appeals to superficial minds
        and which is "unfalsifiable" only because it makes
        no verifiable claims.

H975.   Delacampagne, Christian. "Le moi selon Lacan et
        Freud." Le monde, 7 April 1978, p. 17.

        Argues that the seminars are destined to become
        one of the great monuments in analytic literature--
        and in literature in general--and claims that this
        volume confirms the historical importance of the
        "phénomène Lacan." Delacampagne also comments at

some length on the way Lacan has turned several of
Freud's concepts to his own use.

Seminar III (B14)

H976. Scarpetta, Guy. "Vous avez dit Lacan . . . ." Le
       nouvel observateur, 13 March 1982, p. 58.

       Claims that, despite all of the controversy,
Lacan remains a formidable force for rigor, culture, and lucidity whose influence has just begun
to be measured.

H977. Calame, Alain. La nouvelle revue française 351
       (1982): 132-34.

       Characterizes B14 as a giant detective novel, and
briefly describes Lacan's analysis of Schreber's
case, emphasizing (1) Lacan's rejection of a "pre-
history" to psychosis, (2) the function of the
Oedipus complex as described by Lacan, and (3) the
importance of paranoia as a common ground for
psychoanalysis and psychiatry.

Seminar XI (B22)

H978. Tourney, Garfield. American Journal of Psychiatry
       136 (1979): 1000-01.

       Claims that Lacan "has a fetish for the ambig-
uous" that plays on the French penchant for "the
cult of the unintelligible." Tourney briefly
describes the controversies surrounding many moments of Lacan's career, and notes Lacan's debts
to Heidegger, phenomenology, and structuralism.
For a response to Tourney's charges, see J1049.

H***. Chessick, Richard D. "Critique: Some Unusual
       Books Published in 1978." American Journal of
       Psychotherapy 33 (1979): 312-15. See H949.

H979. Blomeyer, R. Analytische psychologie 16, no. 1
       (1985): 79-80.

       Also reviews B12 and B13.

H980. Booklist, 15 July 1978, p. 170.

       Claims that Lacan probes the links between
psychoanalysis, religion, and science, and praises
B22b as a summary statement of Lacan's position.

H981.   Fordham, Michael.   British Journal of Psychiatry
        136 (1980):   405.

        Warns readers of the difficulty of this book and
        notes Lacan's frequent attacks on other forms of
        psychoanalysis.

H982.   Choice 15 (1978):   1131.

        Notes the difficulty of Lacan's style but praises
        Sheridan's translation and claims that it is help-
        ful in dealing with an "enigmatic" body of work.

H983.   Margolin, Jean-Claude.   Les études philosophiques 4
        (1975):   497-98.

        Claims that Lacan's interest in the gaze ("le
        regard") raises important questions and that this
        book will revive interest in Freudian
        psychoanalysis.

H***.   Heaton, J. M.   Journal of the British Society for
        Phenomenology 9, no. 3 (1978):   204-05.   See
        H957.

H984.   Gross, Elizabeth.   Language, Sexuality and Sub-
        version.   Edited by Paul Foss and Meaghan Morris.
        Working Papers Collection.   Darlington,
        Australia: Feral Publications, 1978.

        Notes the difficulty of the text, describes its
        major points, and notes three objections to Lacan's
        work: (1) his concept of the unconscious remains
        ontological, despite his effort to conceive it in
        terms of the signifier; (2) he is unable to escape
        the phallocentric orientation of psychoanalysis,
        despite his more sophisticated understanding of the
        function of the phallus as a symbol; and (3) more
        generally, his work has grown into the same
        "bureaucratic dogmatism and political conservatism"
        for which he condemns the International Psycho-
        analytic Association.

H985.   Clare, Anthony.   "French Guru."   New Society, 1
        December 1977, pp. 535-36.

        Claims that it is much easier to figure out what
        Lacan opposes than what he proposes, especially in
        terms of his rejection of Truth as an external
        reality toward which analysis is oriented.   Clare
        describes B22 as unintelligible, and applies to
        Lacan what Sir Peter Medawar once said of De
        Chardin when he referred to his style as "that
        tipsy, euphoric prose-poetry which is one of the

more tiresome manifestations of the French spirit."

H986. De Diéguez, Manuel. <u>La nouvelle revue française</u>
       248 (1973):   78-90.

    Describes three dreams he had upon considering
    B22 for the first time, in which some of Lacan's
    claims are quoted briefly as parts of an oneiric
    dialogue and usually horrify the author's dream-
    persona.

H987. Leavy, Stanley A. <u>Psychoanalytic Quarterly</u> 49
       (1980):   526-29.

    Claims that the seminar is unified by Lacan's
    constant recourse to the psychoanalytic situation,
    in which the unconscious is invoked as "a gap
    speaking between the conscious elements of the
    analytic discourse" (p. 527). Leavy claims that
    Lacan's emphasis on transference also grounds the
    unconscious in the presence of the analyst and so
    reveals the unconscious to be transpersonal and
    dialectical, a dimension of experience peculiar to
    speaking animals.

·Section I

Dissertations

1988.   Bär, Eugene Silas.   "The Language of the Uncon-
        scious According to Jacques Lacan."   Ph.D.
        Dissertation, Yale University, 1971.   218 pages.

        Describes Lacan's work as "predominantly semio-
        tic," and discusses Lacan's treatment of the
        symptom as "a polysemous linguistic element."   Bär
        also studies several cases that illustrate "the
        linguistic irruptions of the unconscious" and so
        demonstrate "the heteronomy of the preconscious-
        conscious subject," and he claims that Lacan's
        approach has an advantage over other forms of
        psychoanalytic interpretation because, for Lacan,
        the analyst's guesses about unconscious "inten-
        tions" are guided by "mechanisms" based on the
        "empirical evidence of linguistic behavior."
        Nevertheless, Bär argues that Lacan's concepts
        need considerable clarification if they are to be
        measured against clinical facts.   For articles
        based on this dissertation, see G449 and G450.

1989.   Claridge, Laura P.   "Discourse of Desire: The
        Paradox of Romantic Poetry."   Ph.D. Disserta-
        tion, University of Maryland, 1985.   364 pages.

        Studies various texts by Wordsworth, Shelley,
        and Byron, focussing on "individual poetic myths"
        as they derive from "a Lacanian collusion of
        death, desire and language."

1990.   Glogowski, James Edward.   "The Oedipus Tyrannos of
        Freud and Lacan: Clinical Reflections of Lit-
        erary Structure."   Ph.D. Dissertation,   State
        University of New York at Buffalo, 1985.   186
        pages.

        Describes psychoanalysis as doubly-endebted to
        Sophocles' play and to the clinic, and studies the

play "as a paradigm for clinical interventions."
Glogowski concludes that Freud reached a "tragic
proposition" through his understanding of
Sophocles' work: "the subject is always finally a
subject of a contradiction, to the extent that it
is subject to death . . . [i.e., to] the discourse
of the Other." Lacan offers an "essential theoretical elaboration" of this fundamental proposition, Glogowski says, because he shows how <u>Oedipus
Tyrannos</u> "reveals the basic way in which a subject
comes to be positioned" in a dialectic with the
signifier. Thus through Lacan's work the tragic
origin of psychoanalysis--the subject's relation
to death--comes to be mapped on the <u>topos</u> of the
signifier.

I991. Grant, Rena Jane. "From Clarissa to Lady
        Chatterley: Character in the British Novel."
        Ph.D. Dissertation, Yale University, 1985. 189
        pages.

        Discusses the social context of several novels
        and argues that the "intentional structure" of
        those novels derives from their social bases.
        Grant's method of analysis draws on Lacan's work,
        though she claims to "resituate" psychoanalysis in
        terms of "marxist concepts of the ideological
        production of the subject."

I992. Hill, Melvyn A. "The Concept of the Ego and the
        Schools of Psychoanalysis." Ph.D. Dissertation,
        York University (Canada), 1981.

        Traces the development of the concept of the ego
        in Freud's writings, and explores the subsequent
        development of an "ego-psychology" in the light of
        Lacan's criticism that such an emphasis on the ego
        is evidence of psychoanalysis turning away from
        Freud's work.

I993. Holloway, Gregory Robin. "Psychoanalysis as
        Linguistic Analysis: An Examination of the
        Theories of Habermas and Lacan." Ph.D. Dis-
        sertation, University of Toronto, 1978.

        Argues that it is plausible to treat psycho-
        analysis as a form of linguistic analysis and
        theory rather than as a subdivision of biology,
        and that psychoanalysis may be useful for philo-
        sophical anthropology and educational theory.
        Holloway compares many aspects of Lacan's work to
        issues and themes in the work of Habermas, focus-
        sing on Lacan's distinctions among the real,
        symbolic, and imaginary registers, his theory of
        the signifier, and "Lacan's notion of the ego as

the locus of communicative distortions." A concluding chapter discusses Edelson's application
of Chomsky's linguistics to psychoanalysis (see
K1181) in the light of Lacan's use of Saussure and
of Habermas's explicit rejection of Chomsky's
theories.

I994. Jalbert, Ronald Gaston. "Lacan's Concept of
       Desire in the Mirror Phase and Its Implications
       for Psychoanalytically-oriented Psychotherapy."
       Ph.D. Dissertation, University of Pittsburgh,
       1983. 375 pages.

       Compares Lacan's theory of the mirror stage to
       Hegel's theory of desire, and discusses at length
       therapeutic applications of several aspects of
       Lacan's work. Jalbert especially emphasizes the
       clinical implications of a distinction between
       "imaginary mirroring," within which the "pro-
       jected" ideals of the client's desire appear in
       "embodied" form, and "symbolic mirroring," whereby
       the "objects" of the client's desire are "intro-
       jected" by being named and so are capable of
       leading to the recognition of desire.
          Most of this dissertation is based on A2 and B22
       and uses Ricoeur's "hermeneutical methodology" as
       a point of departure.

I995. Jardine, Alice Ann. "Gynesis: Configurations of
       Woman in the Contemporary Imagination--American
       Feminist Readings/French Texts of Modernity."
       Ph.D. Dissertation, Columbia University, 1982.

I996. McCorkle, James Donald Bruland. "Gaze, Memory,
       and Discourse: Self-Reflexivity in Recent
       American Poetry." Ph.D. Dissertation,
       University of Iowa, 1984. 336 pages.

       Uses Lacan's concepts of the full word, the
       mirror-stage, and the gaze to examine self-
       reflexivity in the work of several poets: Bishop,
       Ashbery, Merwin, and Wright. In these works,
       McCorkle claims, "through the recognition of the
       other the self emerges as an-other."

I997. Morgan, Veronica. "Reading Hart Crane by
       Metonymy." Ph.D. Dissertation, University of
       Michigan, 1986. 212 pages.

       Investigates the role of metonymy in Crane's
       poetry, using Lacan's distinction between metaphor
       and metonymy as her point of departure and focus-
       sing on the link between desire, metonymy, and
       subjectivity as theorized by Lacan and illustrated
       by Crane.

I998.   Presnell, Michael. "Sign, Image, and Desire:
        Semiotic Phenomenology and the Film Image."
        Ph.D. Dissertation, Southern Illinois University
        at Carbondale, 1983.   229 pages.

        Examines Metz's treatment of the film image as a
        sign (see K1270), claiming that it vacillates
        between "subjectivism and reductionistic material-
        ism."   Presnell proposes as a corrective a concept
        of "critical desire" based in part on Lacan's
        notion of desire and its relation to the produc-
        tion of meaning.

I999.   Ruegg, Maria Ruth.   "Mimetology: Philosophy
        and/or Literature in the Platonic and
        Aristotelian Texts."   Ph.D. Dissertation, Yale
        University, 1976.

        Explores the Greek origins of distinctions
        between philosophical and literary discourse, and
        traces the emergence of a theoretical approach in
        contemporary work such as Lacan's that does not
        depend on that distinction: "mimetology."   Pp.
        47-60 are devoted to a discussion of Lacan's
        distinction between metaphor and metonymy and his
        analysis of their interaction in relation to the
        individual's position as subject in and to the
        symbolic order of language.

I1000. Siegert, Mark Barry.   "The Phenomenological
        Experience of Metaphor in Psychotherapy."   Ph.D.
        Dissertation, University of Tennessee, 1984.
        159 pages.

        Studies transcripts of several therapy sessions
        in which metaphors were produced by the patient or
        the therapist, and interviews the therapists to
        determine the "internal experience" at the moment
        of metaphor in hopes of defining the phenomeno-
        logical context of metaphor-production in
        analysis.

I1001. Stenslie, Craig Eliott.   "The Contribution of Otto
        Rank's Psychology to the Critical Understanding
        of the Psychoanalytic Concept of Narcissism."
        Ph.D. Dissertation, Pennsylvania State
        University, 1984.   484 pages.

        Compares contemporary theories of narcissism
        proposed by Kohut, Kernberg, and Grunberger to
        theories proposed by Freud, Rank, and Lacan,
        focussing on the issue of individuals as "con-
        sciously acting subjects."   Lacan's reading of
        Freud is studied as especially important to our

understanding of the relation between narcissism
and theories of "drives" and to an accurate evalu-
ation of ego psychology.

I1002.   Stewart, David Wilson. "Topology of the
         Imaginary: the Origin and Structure of the
         Lacanian Unconscious." Ph.D. Dissertation,
         University of Tennessee, 1981. 159 pages.

         Explores Lacan's claim that the unconscious is
         structured like a language, emphasizing the theo-
         retical origins of the claim in studies of lan-
         guage acquisition and pursuing its implications
         through two clinical examples. The second section
         of the dissertation studies Lacan's developmental
         theory and compares it to several theories of
         primal repression, and Stewart then discusses the
         structure of the unconscious using Lacan's dis-
         tinctions among the real, the symbolic, and the
         imaginary as his point of departure. He concludes
         by proposing his own theory of development that
         links the unconscious to different stages of
         negation through a structural model that he claims
         is consistent with Lacan's later work.

I1003.   Turkle, Sherry. "Psychoanalysis and Society: The
         Emergence of French Freud." Ph.D. Dissertation,
         Harvard University, 1976.

         Published as F412.

I1004.   Tytell, Pamela Van. "The French Psychoanalytic
         Culture: French Psychoanalysts and their
         Relationship to the Literary Text." Ph.D.
         Dissertation, Columbia University, 1979. 481
         pages.

         Explores the reciprocal influence between
         psychoanalysis and literature in France, arguing
         that "the relationship of the psychoanalyst's ear
         to the analysand's discourse" determines a speci-
         fic "écoute." This special form of listening and
         what is heard as a result leads to a particular
         way of understanding the signifier, Tytell says,
         and that understanding has influenced the reading
         and writing of literary texts. Tytell studies
         psychoanalytic readings of various literary texts,
         and she discusses Lacan's use of Poe's "The Pur-
         loined Letter" as an illustration of this theory
         of the signifier (see C69). Chapter Five is
         devoted to an extended study of Lacan's literary
         contributions to French psychoanalysis, including
         occasional allusions to his more extended readings
         of literary texts.

I1005.   Vink, Donald James.   "Freud and Spenser: A Dream
         Poetic: An Isomorphic Comparison of Freud's _The
         Interpretation of Dreams_ and Spenser's _The
         Faerie Queene_" Emphasizing Books II and VI."
         Ph.D. Dissertation, Tulane University, 1985.
         506 pages.

         Uses Lacan as one of several sources to es-
         tablish the role of language in psychoanalysis
         and to draw correlations between "Freudian dream-
         structures" and literary structures.   Vink claims
         these correlations produce an "oneiropoetic" which
         can then be applied to Spenser's texts.

I1006.   Wilden, Anthony G.   "Jacques Lacan and the
         Language of the Self: The Function of Language
         in Psychoanalysis."   Ph.D. Dissertation, Johns
         Hopkins University, 1968.   Published as F420.

Section J

Miscellaneous Secondary Works

J1007. Ambrosi, Jean. "Lacan, un talmudiste moderne."
        Psychologie 140 (1981): 8-9.

        Brief obituary.

J1008. Anzieu, Didier. Discussion of C57 and C58. La
        psychanalyse 1 (1956): 228-31.

        Criticizes Lacan's claim that language is every-
        thing in analysis and his emphasis on the con-
        stitutive power of language in our experience of
        reality. Anzieu also notes Lacan's debt to the
        poetic tradition stemming from Nerval, Rimbaud,
        and the surrealists, and adds that Lacan's ex-
        clusive dependence on language as the foundation
        of analytic experience is no different, methodo-
        logically, from behaviorists such as Watson or
        Pavlov who try to derive all human behavior from
        one fixed idea. See F386.

J1009. "L'appel aux vrais fidèles." Le monde, 15 March
        1980, p. 34.

        Prints Lacan's letter of 10 March 1980 (E290),
        Delenda Est, and notes another request by the
        Secretary General of the Ecole freudienne de
        Paris, Eric Laurent, for support against those
        resisting Lacan's decision to abolish the school.
        See J1127.

J1010. Aubert, Jacques. "Entretien avec Jacques Aubert."
        L'âne 6 (1982): p. 5ff.

        Published with C95, refers in passing to
        Aubert's comment in Lacan's seminar on Joyce.

J1011. "L'avenir d'un phénomène." Le monde hebdomadaire,
        10 September 1981, p. 8.

Obituary.

J1012.   Axelos, Kostas.   "Et la pensée?"   G744, p. 21.

Claims that Lacan is trapped by the notions of
reality and truth, and that Lacan is a "epigone
full of savage geniality and Parisian narcissism"
who takes refuge in obscurity.

J1013.   Beller, Isi.   "L'Ecole est finie . . . ."   G783,
pp. 44-45.

Describes the very public controversies among
French psychoanalysts since the dissolution of the
Ecole freudienne de Paris, and argues that Lacan's
emphasis on the obstacles to totalizing knowledge
and on the difference between the ego and the
other can never be reduced to a matheme.   That is
why psychoanalysis is stronger than Lacanian
theory, Beller says, and he goes on to condemn
Lacan's role as a "Master."

J1014.   Benoit, Guy.   Response to G597.   Le monde, 2
October 1979, p. 2.

Praises Lacan for his psychoanalytic practice
and technique, and insists that we should not lay
the excesses of his followers at his feet.   Appears with G699, J1091 and J1135.

J1015.   Besnier, J. M.   ["On Lacan, A Chapter in the
History of Philosophy (and On a Recent book
About Him by A. Juranville [F345])" (French)].
Esprit 5 (1984):   57-58.

J1016.   Bonaparte, Marie, et al.   Responses to C54.   Revue
française de psychanalyse 15, no. 1 (1951):   62-
84.

Raises a number of issues related to the interaction of psychoanalysis and criminology, especially regarding psychoanalytic contributions to
our understanding of the relationship between
pathological psychological states and the actual
commission of a criminal act.   For Lacan's response to these responses, see E152.   For his
own, earlier interest in "le passage à l'acte,"
see E140.

J1017.   Bonilauri, Bernard.   "Le mépris de la thérapeu-
tique."   G574, p. 28.

Briefly comments on Lacan's controversial reception by other psychoanalysts, and notes his wide-

spread influence in many fields.

J1018.   Castoriadis-Aulagnier, Piera, et al.   Letter of
         withdrawal from the Ecole freudienne de Paris,
         26 January 1969.   Scilicet 2/3 (1970):   51.

         Announces the intention of several members to
         withdraw from the EFP following its vote to accept
         la passe and other proposals set forth in C88.

J1019.   Cherbuliez, Theodore.   Review of F329.

         Describes F329 and complains that Fages's fidel-
         ity to Lacan's own discourse obscures its limits
         and ambiguities.

J1020.   Chiland, Colette.   "Anatomie d'un succès conquis
         par la parole."   G749, p. 2.

         Claims that Lacan's teaching and practice was "a
         perversion of psychoanalysis by seduction, the
         manipulation of transference," and dismisses him
         as not only a shaman but a sophist as well, an
         "intellectual terrorist."   Chiland observes that
         what is really "lacking" in Lacan's work is any
         interest in the patient.

J1021.   Chiland, Colette.   "Qui osera dire que l'empereur
         est nu?"   Le monde, 9 February 1980, p. 2.

         Claims that we must ask whether Lacan's work is
         genius or simply mystification, and says that most
         of his famous proclamations are "pauvres de pen-
         sée" when translated into ordinary French.   Such
         playing with words does not auger well for the
         future of psychoanalysis in France, Chiland says,
         because it threatens to swallow up those who are
         working hard and actually caring for others.

J1022.   Choice 15 (1978):   468.

         Briefly reviews F392 and claims that both the
         book and Lacan's work in general are "undecod-
         able."

J1023.   Chollet, Monique.   Comment on G440.   F357, pp. 84-
         85.

         Briefly describes her own efforts to establish a
         reliable text of Lacan's seminar on "identifica-
         tion" (B20) that would be based on several tape
         recordings, notes, and other sources, and argues
         that it is important to "try to recreate in
         writing the climate of the seminar" as she found
         it when she attended.   Chollet warns readers to be

careful about considering any of the circulating
typescripts of the seminars as definitive
versions. See F358.

J1024. Clavreul, Jean. "L'église freudienne de Paris."
        G746, p. 2.

        Claims that the Ecole freudienne de Paris has
        become a church with its own ritual masses--white
        and black--as well as its own inquisitors and
        sorcerers, and argues that Lacan's work has been
        treated as a "revealed Truth" that cannot be
        questioned but only repeated.

J1025. Clément, Catherine. "'L'affaire Lacan' devient
        judiciaire." Le matin de Paris, 18 January
        1980, p. 32.

        Describes the legal issues involved in the
        challenge to Lacan's right to dissolve the Ecole
        freudienne de Paris.

J1026. Clément, Catherine. "L'affaire Lacan (suite):
        deux communiques et un pamphlet." Le matin de
        Paris, 29 January 1980, p. 22.

        Briefly describes the legal supervision of the
        Ecole freudienne de Paris during its dissolution,
        and comments on F353.

J1027. Clément, Catherine. "Ecole freudienne: victoire
        de Lacan." Le matin de Paris, 29 April 1980, p.
        24.

        Briefly comments on the meeting of the Ecole
        freudienne de Paris under Mme. Zécri, and notes
        the dossier of items on Lacan in Le nouvel ob-
        servateur for this week.

J1028. Clément, Catherine. "Ephémérides III." L'âne 3
        (1981): 24-25.

        Briefly comments on the treatment of Lacan's
        death in the press.

J1029. Clément, Catherine. "Le forum convoque par Lacan
        s'ouvre demain." Le matin de Paris, 27 March
        1981, p. 30.

        Reports remarks by Serge Leclaire and Colette
        Soler at a forum on the Ecole freudienne de Paris.
        Leclaire warns the analysts not to forget analysis
        itself while occupied with the various duties
        associated with the university and publishing, and
        Soler claims that the central issue at stake is

Lacan's relation to the institution of psychoanalysis.

J1030. Clément, Catherine. "Le forum de Lacan: un week-
        end serein." Le matin de Paris, 31 March 1981,
        p. 26.

        Briefly describes the forum called to debate the
        future of the Ecole freudienne de Paris.

J1031. Clément, Catherine. "Lacan dissout son école pour
        en fonder une nouvelle." Le matin de Paris, 10
        January 1980, p. 29.

        Notes the obvious fatigue that has marked
        Lacan's latest public appearances, and describes
        his decision to dissolve the Ecole freudienne de
        Paris in the face of dissension despite his dubi-
        ous legal authority for such a gesture. Clément
        also suggests that psychoanalysis seems to need a
        new kind of organization, neither school nor
        association.

J1032. Clément, Catherine. "Naissance, vie et mort du
        mythe Lacan." Le matin de Paris, 12 February
        1980, p. 14.

        Describes Lacan's gradual evolution into
        "Lacan," and argues that his public phenomenon was
        the creation of the same people who now condemn
        him for his mythic persona. Clément admits,
        however, that Lacan eventually came to enjoy this
        role himself.

J1033. Clément, Catherine. "Les psychanalystes de
        l'Ecole aux prises avec le droit." Le matin de
        Paris, 18 March 1980, p. 23.

        Describes the first meeting of the Ecole freud-
        ienne de Paris under its new administrateur de
        justice, Mme. Zécri. Clément notes that the
        specific votes dealt with technical aspects of the
        statutes of associations but were in fact votes
        for or against Lacan, and she reports the vote
        tallies for various issues.

J1034. Clément, Catherine. "Rebondissements dans l'af-
        faire Lacan." Le matin de Paris, 5 January
        1981, p. 23.

        Describes the dissension that has already arisen
        within the Ecole de la Cause freudienne a few
        months since its beginning, and attributes it
        largely to Lacan's increasingly fragile health and
        the effort by some members of the group to seize

the occasion to move the association in new directions contrary to Lacan's wishes. Clément questions the authenticity of several documents issued
under Lacan's name, and claims that this latest
controversy is just part of the continuing
troubled history of psychoanalysis in France since
1953.

J1035.   Clément, Catherine. "Scission officielle dans
         l'école de Lacan." Le matin de Paris, 29
         January 1981, p. 23.

         Notes the new, "official" dissension in the
         Ecole de la Cause freudienne, marked by the defec-
         tion of 21 members including Octave and Maud
         Mannoni, Jean Clavreul, and Claude Dumézil, and
         accuses the leadership of the ECF of violating
         "l'éthique analytique" by setting up a hierarchy
         of submission within the ECF. According to
         Clément, the ECF has split along rather tradi-
         tional lines, with the medical doctors lining up
         against Jacques-Alain Miller and other academic
         analysts.

J1036.   Clément, Catherine. ["The Virginal, Amorous,
         Mystic Ecstasies of Fragile Bellini and
         Donizetti Heroines, With Particular Considera-
         tion of Elvira, Amina, and Lucia" (French)].
         Avant Scène-Opera 96 (1987):   86-89.

J1037.   "Creation de la section clinique." Issued by the
         Departement de la psychanalyse, Champ Freudien,
         Université de Paris-VIII, Vincennes, October
         1976. Jacques Lacan, Directeur scientifique.

         Announces the start of a program leading to the
         "Diplôme de clinique psychanalytique" that can be
         completed in two years. Reprinted in G491.

J1038.   Dadoun, Roger. "Jacques Lacan: 1901-81." La
         quinzaine littéraire, 1-15 October 1981, p. 22.

         Brief reflections on the impact of Lacan's
         death, tracing his influence on the intellectual
         scene in Paris.

J1039.   David, Catherine. "La loi du Seigneur." Le
         nouvel observateur, 21 January 1980, p. 41.

         Attributes the extraordinary strife over the
         dissolution of the Ecole freudienne de Paris to a
         nearly absurd fidelity to Lacan exhibited among
         some members of the EFP, and suggests that it is
         surprising to see Lacan so interested in solid-
         ifying his intuitions in "revealed truths," given

the skeptical attitude toward truth proclaimed in his teachings.

J1040. David, Catherine. "Tempête chez les lacaniens." Le nouvel observateur, 16 February 1981, p. 48.

Notes the continuing dissension among Lacanians following the dissolution of the Ecole freudienne de Paris, and claims that this controversy resembles the struggle for power that usually follows the death of a strong leader, even though Lacan is still alive.

J1041. Derrida, Jacques. Interview with Jean-Louis Houdebine and Guy Scarpetta. Promesse 30/31 (1971).

Argues that his concept of dissemination resists the effect of subjectivity, subjection, and the other characteristics of what Lacan calls the symbolic. Ecriture "escapes and disorganizes" the symbolic without falling under the categories of the imaginary or the real, Derrida says, and he insists on a radical distinction between the "effective violence" of écriture and Lacan's notion of castration, which functions as a "signified or a transcendental signifier" or, more simply, as "truth."
In an extended note to this section of the interview as reprinted in Positions, Derrida further specifies his objections to Lacan's work. While observing that Lacan's problematic may be necessary within the field of psychoanalysis, Derrida says that Lacan's use of Hegel and Heidegger is quite dated and results in a logocentric faith in the "truth" as a fundamental support of discourse (p. 117).
This note includes brief remarks on C69 that Derrida later developed into G544. (Derrida first mentioned Lacan in print in a note to L1617 when it was reprinted in Ecriture et la différence, p. 282.) This interview was reprinted in Positions (Paris: Editions de Minuit, 1972), pp. 51-126 (esp. 107-20), and translated as part of the English edition of that book.

J1042. Didier-Weill, Alain. "L'éthique analytique." G749, p. 2.

Stresses the importance of relations among the real, symbolic, and imaginary registers, and claims that Lacan's understanding of the real orients an "analytic ethic."

J1043. "La dissolution de l'Ecole freudienne: une marée

de protestations." G745, p. 14.

Claims that the conflict surrounding the Ecole freudienne de Paris really focuses on Lacan himself; compares it to Lacan's split with the Société française de psychanalyse in 1953; and briefly describes Lacan's current associations with journals and universities where his work is taught and discussed.

J1044. Dolto, Françoise. Discussion of C57 and C58. F386, pp. 222-28.

Complains that Lacan seems to ignore the hypothesis of affective maturation, and claims that women have a special insight into this topic because of their natural predisposition to nurturing infants. Dolto goes on to argue that language does not constitute the intersubjective relation of mother and infant but that there is a "gift of presence" that ties the two together beyond language. For a related argument on the mother-child relation and its importance for Lacanian theories of language, see Kristeva's articles on motherhood in K1229.

J1045. Dolto, Françoise. "Françoise Dolto défend Lacan." Lire: le magazine des livres (December 1984): 86-87.

Briefly recounts her professional relationship with Lacan and claims to have been interested in his work but to have learned little from it. Dolto observes that Lacan was "very masculine in his writing and his thoughts, and feminine in his behavior," and claims that the essential thing to remember about him was his "immense passion for Freud."

J1046. Dolto, Françoise. "Lacanian? Ca ne veut rien dire." G784, p. 52.

Praises Lacan for opening the field of psychoanalysis through his extensive clinical experience, and claims that, despite its difficulty, his theoretical work has clarified a great deal of clinical work, including her own.

J1047. Doubrovsky, Serge. "Un parapluie sur un divan." Le nouvel observateur, 28 April 1980, p. 46.

Notes the literary dimension of Lacan's work, concluding that in Lacan, "the writer cannibalizes the psychoanalyst. Chased from lacanian theory, the ego returns at a gallop in lacanian writing."

J1048. Easthope, Antony. "Lacan. A Reply to Ree."
Radical Philosophy 25 (1980): 26-27.

Complains that L2273 confuses Lacan's integration of Freud and Saussure, and suggests that
Lacan's claim that the subject exists in language
is not incompatible with historical materialism.

J1049. Emery, Edward J. "On Reading Lacan: Fundamental
Concepts." American Journal of Psychiatry 137
(1980): 1281-82.

Defends Lacan's work against the criticism
levied by Tourney in H978, and claims that more
obscure passages in Lacan's seminar are "examples
of free associative cognitions" similar to the
fabric of dreams. "Lacan should be read like . .
. a good joke," Emery says, and he asserts that
Lacan's writing testifies to the essentially
"ambiguous and provisional" nature of all human
expression (p. 1281).

J1050. Enthoven, Jean-Paul. "Pour un ultime hommage au
camarade Lacan." Le nouvel observateur, 29
October 1979, p. 86.

Comments at length on F335 and on the nearly
mythic status of Lacan's place in contemporary
French culture.

J1051. Favez-Boutonier, Juliette. Letter to Lacan read
at the first congress of the Société française
de psychanalyse, 26 September 1953. F386, pp.
211-13.

Professes her general agreement with the major
points of C58, but objects to Lacan's identification of the symbolic with language. Favez-
Boutonier suggests that the symbolic extends
beyond language to other forms of behavior, and
claims that Lacan's further identification of the
symbol with the "murder of the thing" is unjust to
the imaginary and ignores a "desire to bring-into-
being" ("un désir de faire-être, de continuer ou
de multiplier la chose, dans la création du symbole" [p. 213]). Favez-Boutonier also refers to
C58 as the "manifesto" of the SFP, an epithet
that it still carries today.

J1052. Fleischmann, Fritz. Response to G934. New York
Review of Books, 5 April 1979, p. 45.

Expresses surprise that feminists would find
Lacan's work useful and requests examples of such

applications, which Wollheim provides in J1138.

J1053. Francion, Nicolas. "Traductions de Lacan."
        Ornicar? 30 (1984): 166-67.

    Lists publishers of Lacan's works in transla-
    tion, and briefly describes the titles published
    as of 1984 and forthcoming.

J1054. Gallop, Jane. Review of F316. Sub-stance 32
        (1981): 77-88.

    Discusses Clément's remark that her attachment
    to Lacan and his work parallels romantic love, and
    describes her analysis of that sentiment in terms
    of transference (see B31).

J1055. Gasquéres, Anne. "Discussion." (K1297), pp.
        136-37.

    Briefly comments on Lacan's distinction among
    real, imaginary, and symbolic fathers, and on the
    obstacle posed by the role of the master in
    institutional discourse.

J1056. Granoff, Wladimir. Discussion of C57 and C58.
        F386, pp. 221-22.

    Briefly argues for the importance of the object
    in analytic technique, as opposed to Lacan's
    emphasis on the intersubjective relation between
    the analyst and the patient.

J1057. Green, André. "Une figure messianique." G747, p.
        2.

    Claims that Lacan is "a sacred monster of the
    cultural scene," but that above all else, Lacan
    was "a voice." Green also notes Lacan's aspira-
    tion toward a rigorous mathematization of Freud's
    thought but concludes that his major influence
    was, unfortunately, expended on a school of fol-
    lowers less intelligent and imaginative than he
    who turned his work into an irresponsible analytic
    technique and who encouraged his groundless specu-
    lations in the seminars.

J1058. Held, René-R. "Un practicien: 'Et si l'incon-
        scient n'etait pas structuré.'" G744, p. 21.

    Questions the validity of Lacan's claim that the
    unconscious is structured like a language, and
    expresses skepticism about the value of the
    mathemes and graphs that pervade Lacan's work
    after A2. Held also comments on Lacan's work with

Clérambault, noting the influence of Clérambault's concept of "l'automatisme mentale" on Lacan's argument that the unconscious (or id) speaks, "Ca parle."

J1059.   Hesnard, Angelo.   Letter to Lacan, end of May, 1953.   F379, p. 81.

Professes his support for Lacan's position and asks him for his vote in the controversy surrounding Nacht's attempt to employ his own statutes for the training institute of the Société psychanalytique de Paris.   For related documents, see F379 and F412.

J1060.   Higgins, John.   Reply to G885.   Times Literary Supplement, 1 September 1978, p. 972.

Attacks G885 for several misconceptions about Freud's understanding of the connection between an individual's experience in childhood and then later as an adult, and defends what Scrutton described as Lacan's "fundamentalism." Higgins denies that Lacan worships Freud as a master, and argues that Lacan's return to Freud is, instead, a legitimate concern with rigor that is essential to any practitioner of psychoanalysis.   Other replies to Scrutton are listed in the note to G885.

J1061.   Hyppolite, Jean.   Discussion of C70.   Bulletin de la Société française de philosophie 51, no. 2 (1957):   100-01.

Praises Lacan for going beyond the traditional, excessively positivistic readings of Freud, but wonders what a sign might be without the "final intention of meaning" once the signifier has been split off from the signified as Lacan describes.

J1062.   International Journal of Psycho-Analysis 35 (1954):   276-78; and 37 (1956):   122.

Reports on deliberations and discussions regarding the split within the Société psychanalytique de Paris.   See F379.   Reprinted in October 40 (1987):   72-75.

J1063.   International Journal of Psychol-Analysis 45, pts. 2-3 (1964):   468, 481.

Reports on the SFP's general compliance with the Edinburgh Requirements, but notes that Lacan is still training analysts, has failed to comply with the Requirements, and has "hindered" the work of the Advisory Committee.   The IPA demands that

Lacan be dropped from the list of training analysts by 31 October 1963 and warns that failure
to do so will jeopardize official recognition of
the SFP.
    Reprinted in <u>October</u> 40 (A11/B12).

J1064. Irigaray, Luce. ["Question IV"]. K1219, tr. pp.
        167-69.

    Describes her teaching plans for the year in
answer to a question addressed to her by the
Department of Psychoanalysis at the University of
Paris, Vincennes, before it was restructured along
Lacanian lines in 1974. Through an analysis of
<u>Antigone</u>, Irigaray plans to explore the subjection
of women as one of the "constituent necessities of
rationality" that is still causing a problem in
the present, and to explore the way philosophical
language has determined the status of the feminine
"within discursive systematicity, <u>so that psychoanalytic interpretation will not fall back into
the norms of philosophical discursivity</u>." She
notes that a committee appointed by Lacan refused
to accept this proposal and that she was suspended
from teaching at Vincennes. Translated in <u>This
Sex Which Is Not One</u> (K1219), pp. 167-69.

J1065. Jaccard, Roland. "Les héritiers de Freud." <u>Le
        monde dimanche</u>, 1 June 1980, p. xvi.

    Surveys major movements in psychoanalysis since
Freud, focussing on three major currents: the
English school of Melanie Klein, the Chicago
school, and the Ecole freudienne de Paris.
Jaccard also notes the feminist critique of
phallocentricism in psychoanalysis and the increasing tendency to apply psychoanalytic concepts
to social and political phenomena.

J1066. Jaccard, Roland. Introduction to G744. <u>Le monde</u>,
        5 April 1973, p. 20.

    Briefly notes Lacan's tremendous influence on
contemporary French psychoanalysis, and comments
on the broader public appeal of Lacan's work as
part of the structuralist movement associated with
Foucault, Althusser, and others.

J1067. Jaccard, Roland. "Lacan, Pop Star." <u>Le monde</u>, 6
        February 1981, p. 15, 19.

    Claims that Clement's representation of Lacan in
F316 irritates him at times but is generally
convincing in its portrayal of Lacan's importance
to psychoanalysis and its account of the seductive

character of Lacan's teaching.   Jaccard agrees
that the mathemes are nonsense and observes that
Lacan's discourse owes more to the rhythms of myth
than to mathematics.

J1068.   Jaccard, Roland.   "Lettres à Lacan; polémique."
         Le monde, 1 February 1980, p. 15.

         Wryly comments on a pamphlet of letters os-
         tensibly addressed to Lacan by "lacanophobes et
         habiles pasticheurs de surcroît" that was pur-
         portedly received under mysterious conditions at
         Editions Solin.   See F353.

J1069.   Jaccard, Roland.   "La psychanalyse désenchanté:
         écoles."   Le monde dimanche, 20 January 1980, p.
         xvi.

         Comments on the controversy surrounding Lacan's
         decision to dissolve the Ecole freudienne de Paris
         as the latest in a long line of controversies in
         French psychoanalysis, and concludes that one
         cause for this history of disturbances is the fact
         that French psychoanalysts have simply been re-
         peating the same old truisms since Freud's death.

J1070.   Jarry, André.   "Saussure 'détourné.'"   G744, p.
         21.

         Praises F348 for showing how Lacan has distorted
         Saussure's understanding of the signifier.

J1071.   Jouary, Jean-Paul.   "La théorie et la passion."
         G653, pp. 1, 12.

         Notes Lacan's influence in all the human sci-
         ences, even at the level of writing styles, and
         notes that now, with the absence of Lacan's per-
         son, the "réelle positivité" of his work may
         emerge.

J1072.   Julia, Jacques.   "De l'idolatrie à la haine."
         G573, p. 2.

         Notes the controversy surrounding the dissolu-
         tion of the Ecole freudienne de Paris; discusses
         Lacan's problematic relation to the school and
         within the institutional structure of psycho-
         analysis in general; and claims that Lacan has
         come to identify too much with Freud as the
         Master.   As a result, Julia says, Lacan's latest
         demands for loyalty are a "return to himself" that
         wages an "intellectual terrorism" within the ECF
         itself.

J1073. Kajman, Michel. "Cygnifiant?" G746, p. 14.

Comments briefly on Lacan's unilateral decision
to dissolve the Ecole freudienne de Paris, referring to Lacan as "L'ayatollah Can."

J1074. Lacan Study Group. Letter. New Left Review 97
(1976).

J1075. Lagache, Daniel. Discussion of C70. Bulletin de
la Société française de philosophie 51, no. 2
(1957): 86-87.

Claims that Lacan's effort to interpret Freud's
theory of the death-instinct and the repetition
compulsion in terms of a mathematical or logical
formalism distorts the "naturalist realism" that
underlies Freud's argument, and observes that the
most unique aspect of Lacan's own position is his
emphasis on the transcendent dimension of language.

J1076. Lagache, Daniel. Introduction to C57. F386, pp.
199-201.

Notes the controversy surrounding the formation
of the Société française de Psychanalyse (see
F379) and thanks the Italian Society of Psychoanalysis for hosting the first congress of the
SFP.

J1077. Lagache, Daniel. Discussion of C57 and C58.
F386, pp. 211-21.

Notes Lacan's critique of the role of objectivi-
zation in psychoanalysis and his emphasis on the
instrumental role of speech (la parole) in the
intersubjective relation that constitutes the
analytic experience. Lagache generally agrees
with Lacan's arguments, but accuses him of over-
simplifying the notion of "two-bodies psychology"
that Lacan criticizes in the work of Michael
Balint. Lagache also agrees with Lacan's insistence on a flexible length for the analytic session, but adds that there are other ways of modi-
fying this rule without adopting Lacan's technique
of the "short session."

J1078. Larissy, Edward. Reply to G885. Times Literary
Supplement, 25 August 1978, p. 953.

Attacks Scrutton for ignoring Lacan's most basic
claims, and argues that Scrutton even scrambled
Saussure's distinction between signifiers and
signifieds. Larissy suggests that Scrutton's

essay may be a parody of the English reviewing style. Other replies are listed in the note to G885.

J1079. Le Rider, Jacques. "En Allemagne, à l'ombre du 'dernier' Heidegger." G748, p. 25.

Notes the French psychoanalysis was virtually unknown in Germany before 1973, when the first translation of A2 appeared along with F349. Le Rider claims that Lacan's popularity in Germany was also related to the more general interest in structuralism and that his greatest influence has been felt in the human sciences.

J1080. Leavy, Stanley A. Review of F374. Psychoanalytic Quarterly 53, no. 4 (1984): 582-585.

Praises the authors' willingness to report their bafflement at more obscure passages, and describes their effort as similar to the exegetical analysis most often applied to the Bible.

J1081. Lecercle, Ann, and Jacques Lecercle. Reply to G885. Times Literary Supplement, 25 August 1978, p. 953.

Describes Scrutton's essay as "a bad case of Podsnappery" and as infused with a tone of hysteria. Members of the Department of English at the University of Paris, Nanterre, the authors claim to write as linguists in support of Lacan's insights into the way language works. Other replies are listed in G885.

J1082. Léonardini, Jean-Pierre. "Il ne s'efface pas." G653, p. 12.

Briefly describes Lacan's career and comments on the difficulty of his writing.

J1083. Lévi-Strauss, Claude. "Entretien avec L'âne sur l'homme." L'âne 20 (1985): 27-30.

Notes that Lacan had much closer relations with structural linguistics and Jakobson's phonology than Lévi-Strauss himself ever did, and says that Lacan consequently had a much greater need to detach himself from those movements later. Lévi-Strauss recalls attending the first session of B22 but remembers paying more attention to the concrete ethnographic situation of the meeting than to what Lacan said. What most impressed him, Lévi-Strauss adds, was "cette espèce de rayonnement," the great power over the listeners that

Lacan possessed, and he describes it as similar to a shaman's power. He also remembers feeling odd that he did not understand much of what Lacan said, even though the crowd around him seemed to follow Lacan's words closely.

J1084. Lipiansky, Patricia. "L'inquiétude du analysés." Le monde, 9 February 1980, p. 2.

Suggests that Lacan himself needs to see a psychiatrist or an analyst, and that the controversy surrounding this "mandarin au verbe haut" is causing great consternation among those currently undergoing analysis.

J1085. Mamou, Yves, ed. "L'émoi-et-moi-chez le psych-analystes de l'ex-Ecole." F354, p. 7.

A collection of brief remarks on Lacan's death, including statements by Françoise Dolto, Michèle Montrelay, Serge Leclaire and others.

J1086. Mannoni, Octave. "De longs et difficiles chemins." G747, p. 2.

Briefly describes several major contributions of Lacan's career, and expresses confidence that Lacan's innovations in analytic technique will have a long future.

J1087. Mannoni, Octave. "La question fondamentale." G744, p. 20.

Describes Lacan's style of speaking, insisting that the seminars are themselves embodiments of this spoken style rather than writing, and notes that Lacan's allusive gestures are often misunderstood. Mannoni claims that this misunderstanding is a major source of what has been vehemently criticized as obscurity in Lacan's work.

J1088. Mannoni, Octave. Reply to G885. Times Literary Supplement, 25 August 1978, p. 953.

Denies ever engaging in any "single combat" with Lacan as Scruton suggested, and criticizes Scrutton's remarks about Lacan, Freud, and Hegel. Other replies are listed in G885.

J1089. Marchais, Georges. G653, p. 12.

Admires Lacan's tremendous influence on a whole age of intellectuals.

J1090. Melman, Charles. Open letter to Jacques Lacan, 7

December 1980.   F324, pp. 28-34.

Complains bitterly about various machinations surrounding the formation of the Cause freudienne and the use of Lacan's name as a "fetish" by several groups struggling to inherit Lacan's place on the psychoanalytic scene.

J1091.   Mendel, G.   Response to G659.   Le monde, 2 October 1979, p.   2.

Praises Lacan's resistance to normative psychology in the 1950s, but claims that Lacan has become the grand Priest of a sort of esoteric religion and deserves to be ridiculed by works such as F335.   Appears with G700 and J1135.

J1092.   Merleau-Ponty, Maurice.   Discussion of C70. Bulletin de la Société française de philosophie 51, no. 2 (1957):   98-99.

Admits that Lacan has convinced him that contemporary psychoanalysis has little connection to what Freud actually wrote, but objects that Freud did not really think of language and the philosophical function of speech in the way Lacan claims.   Nevertheless, Merleau-Ponty says, that is all the more reason philosophers should follow Lacan's return to Freud.

J1093.   Metz, Christian.   "Ce qui m'importe chez Lacan ce sont les directions qu'il a ouvertes . . . ." Le monde, 4 March 1978, p. 2.

Comments on his use of several concepts proposed by Lacan, including the mirror stage; defends the clarity of Lacan's discourse; but denies that he is either a disciple of Lacan or a Lacanian.

J1094.   Milhau, Jacques.   "Sur la connaissance-reflet: dialectique et métaphore."   La pensée 237 (1984):   74-90.

Cites Lacan, Derrida, and others as part of a new movement away from "idealist intellectualism," which treats language and metaphor in terms of "meaning," and towards a more properly materialist conception of language that is compatible with Marxism.

J1095.   Miller, Jacques-Alain.   "L'avenir d'un symptôme." G746, p. 2.

Comments on the issues behind Lacan's decision to dissolve the Ecole freudienne de Paris.

J1096. Miller, Jacques-Alain. "Intraitable et puissant."
        La quinzaine littéraire, 1-15 October 1981, p.
        22.

        Briefly comments on Lacan's career and his
        marginal status on the French intellectual scene
        until the 1960s, and observes that even then Lacan
        never occupied the usual positions of prestige.
        This item is based on an excerpt from G738.

J1097. Miller, Jacques-Alain. "Pour Jacques-Alain
        Miller." Le matin de Paris, 10 January 1980, p.
        29.

        Comments briefly on the dissolution of the Ecole
        freudienne de Paris, and claims that Lacan's
        decision is just another strategy to resist his
        becoming the "Other of the Other," which is no
        more than a trompe-l'oeil. Miller observes that
        "psychoanalysis is a social practice" since it
        begins with two people, "à deux." But he goes on
        to add that psychoanalysis also stops there at the
        pair, and that means it is impossible for analysts
        to base broader social organizations among them-
        selves on their practice.

J1098. Mitchell, Juliet, and Jacqueline Rose. "Feminine
        Sexuality: Interview 1982." m/f 8 (1983): 3-
        16.

        Comments on F370.

J1099. Mitchell, Sollace. Reply to G885. Times Literary
        Supplement, 22 September 1978, p. 1055.

        Claims that Scrutton is a philosopher ill-
        equipped to handle work primarily directed to the
        practice of psychoanalysis, and criticizes him for
        dismissing Lacan without considering his most
        fundamental tenets about language and the subject.

J1100. Le monde, 9 January 1980, p. 48.

        Brief notice of Lacan's decision to dissolve the
        Ecole freudienne de Paris. See G745 and G746.

J1101. Le monde, 15 March 1980, p. 34. "La nouvelle
        école de M. Jacques Lacan . . . ."

        Announces that a representative of the French
        judiciary, Simone Rozès, has appointed a Mme.
        Zécri to oversee the debates about the dissolution
        of the Ecole freudienne de Paris.

J1102.   Le monde, 11 September 1981, p. 1.

Announces Lacan's death on 9 September 1981
following an operation for an abdominal tumor on 2
September.   See G747.

J1103.   Moscovici, Serge.   "Le mythe de Colombey."   Le
nouvel observateur, 28 April 1980, p. 45.

Comments on the ideological dimension of Lacan's
prominence and influence, and suggests that
Lacan's authoritative power in psychoanalysis
parallels DeGaulle's position in post-war France.
See G783.

J1104.   "Motion d'ordre."   13 October 1963.   L'excommunication. Supplement to Ornicar? 8 (1977):   p.
87.

Removes Lacan from the list of training analysts
for the Société française de psychanalyse.   This
motion was instigated by Wladimir Granoff and
signed by Juliette Favez-Boutonier, Daniel
Lagache, and George Favez.   The motion was proposed at the urging of the International Psychoanalytic Association, which had agreed to recognize the SFP only if Lacan were prohibited from
training analysts.   When this motion was ratified
on 19 November 1963, Serge Leclaire and François
Perrier, the president and vice-president of the
Society, announced their resignation, and the next
day Lacan announced that his seminar at Saint
Anne's Hospital would be terminated immediately.
For Lacan's announcement, see E172.   Other
related documents are published in F380.   For an
account of this controversy in English, see F412,
p. 115.

J1105.   Mounin, Georges.   "Un linguiste: 'Du sense des
mots.'"   G744, p. 21.

Criticizes Lacan for a deceptive and inexact use
of linguistic terms such as the phoneme, and
claims that Lacan's use of such terms as synchrony
and diachrony is "purely decorative."   Mounin also
suggests that Lacan's psychoanalysis is closer to
semiology than linguistics.

J1106.   Muller, John P.   Review of F333.   Psychoanalytic
Quarterly 53, no. 4 (1984):   588-594.

Praises the book generally but regrets Gallop's
failure to consider relations between desire and
aggression fully enough.

J1107.   Muller, John P. Review of F397. Psychoanalytic
         Quarterly 51 (1982): 461-465.

         Describes the various clinical papers, focus-
         sing on the treatment of psychosis, but notes that
         these brief reports do not meet the need for a
         more extended case history that would exemplify
         Lacanian clinical practice more clearly.

J1108.   Mulliken, Richard. Review of F397. The Psycho-
         analytic Review 69, no. 2 (1982): 314-16.

         Praises Lacanian psychoanalysts for carefully
         listening to their patients and so allowing the
         "psychic reality" of the individual to emerge,
         rather than submerging it beneath abstractions
         such as "phase" and "defense." Mulliken notes
         that Lacanians seem to arrive at conclusions
         similar to other kinds of analysts despite their
         highly original premises. He also observes that
         Lacan's methods seem to work best with patients
         who suffer from highly organized paranoia and/or
         literate neuroses, and claims that this condition
         suggests a limit in Lacan's theoretical framework.
         Against the usual accusation of impenetrable
         obscurity, Mulliken remarks that Lacan's style is
         highly rhetorical but precise, and he says that it
         may provide a useful corrective to the excessive
         abstraction characteristic of psychoanalysts
         trying to mimic the natural sciences.

J1109.   Nobécourt, Jacques. "Les expéditions d'Italie."
         G748, p. 25.

         Briefly describes Lacan's appearances at con-
         ferences in Italy and notes the conflict between
         La Cause freudienne in Rome, which is associated
         with Muriel Drazien, and the several Lacanian
         groups in Milan. See A4 and F307.

J1110.   Nobécourt, Jacques. "Nouvelles dissensions parmi
         les disciples du Docteur Lacan." Le monde, 31
         January 1981, p. 35.

         Describes the long and continuing history of
         dissent among psychoanalysts associated with
         Lacan.

J1111.   Nobécourt, Jacques. "La psychanalyse lacanienne
         remanie ses méthodes de travail." Le monde, 6
         January 1981, p. 11.

         Describes the various groups with which people
         have aligned themselves in the year since the

dissolution of the Ecole freudienne de Paris.

J1112. Nobécourt, Jacques. "Tout 'retour à Freud' est
        inconfortable: Lacan disperse les siens." G746,
        pp. 1, 14.

        Briefly describes the controversies within the
        Ecole freudienne de Paris that led to Lacan's
        decision to dissolve the school, and claims that
        those conflicts resemble the stages through which
        Freud's own followers passed. Nobécourt also
        traces the legal issues involved in Lacan's ges-
        ture and concludes that the whole controversy
        tests the "frontiers of liberty" within psycho-
        analysis.

J1113. [Brief Announcement]. Ornicar? 3 (1975): 111.

        Describes the course of study for a new degree
        offered by the Université de Paris VIII-Vincennes:
        the "Doctorat du Champ freudien." Also includes
        the call for course proposals by those who want to
        teach in the newly reorganized department to be
        submitted to a committee presided over by Lacan.
        For an example of the controversial effect of this
        policy, see J1064.

J1114. Ozouf, Mona. "Sondage: 65% des français re-
        fuseraient une psychanalyse, même gratuité."
        G783, pp. 42-43.

        Reports findings from a survey that generally
        suggest the French public is not as interested in
        psychoanalysis as it might seem, and that 80% of
        those polled had never even heard of Lacan.

J1115. Pepeli, Hara. "A Lacanian Psychoanalyst's Comment
        on John Bird." Radical Philosophy 34 (1983):
        46-47.

        Responds to G462 and attempts to correct several
        misconceptions regarding Bird's account of Lacan's
        theory of the symbolic and the signifier, and
        describes Lacan's attack on the training analysis
        ("analyse didactique") in B31. For other re-
        sponses to Bird's critique, see G462.

J1116. Phillips, James. Review of F319. American
        Journal of Psychiatry 137 (1980): 141.

        Describes de Waelhens's attempt to use Lacan's
        work to bridge the gap between contemporary phe-
        nomenology and classical psychoanalysis, but
        warns that de Waelhens assumes a foreknowledge of
        Lacan's work. Phillips also notes the relevance

of K1307 to issues raised by Lacan and de
Waelhens.

J1117.   Pivot, Bernard.   "I LIKE LACAN."   Le figaro littéraire, 29 December 1966, p. 2.

Pictures a button bearing this phrase as a
slogan that Pivot says is fitting "pour femmes du
monde."

J1118.   Poirot-Delpech, Bertrand.   "En d'autres termes."
G744, p. 20.

Proposes to translate various comments by Lacan
into "les mots du Monde sinon ceux de tout le
monde."

J1119.   Portalier, Raymond.   "Voyage chez les lacaniens:
l'amphi, le noeud borroméen, et le maître." Le
matin de Paris, 11 February 1980, p. 12.

Reports on his first visit to a seminar and the
"rite lacanien" that he found there, and comments
on the strange behavior of the audience, who hung
on Lacan's every word.

J1120.   Porter, Dennis.   "Un changement aux USA."
Interview. L'âne 23 (1985):   8-9.

Comments on the reception of Lacan's work in the
United States by philosophers, literary critics,
and analysts, and describes the interest surrounding a conference on Lacan's work at the University
of Massachusetts, Lacan's Legacy--Lessons of the
Transference.

J1121.   Pulver, Terry.   Review of F374. Journal of Phenomenological Psychology 17, no. 1 (1986):   106-
110.

J1122.   La quinzaine littéraire. 1-15 October 1981, p.
21.

Full page quotation from Lacan presented by his
publisher, Le Seuil, on the occasion of Lacan's
death: "Je dis toujours la vérité: pas toute,
parce que toute la dire, on n'y arrive pas . . .
les mots y manquent. C'est même par cet impossible que la vérité tient au réel."

J1123.   Rapaport, Herman.   Review of F359. Language in
Society 12, no. 2 (1983):   256-62.

Criticizes the essays in F359 as positivistic
reductions of Lacan's work that ignore the "slip-

page of the signifier," and singles out G845 and
G913 for their amateurish failure to distinguish
between Freud's own claims and what Lacan does
with them. Rapaport observes that such a failure
is characteristic of most of the essays in the
book.

J1124. Roudinesco, Elisabeth. "Avec Clérambault, Kojève,
et Breton." G784, p. 52.

Claims that Lacan's contact with the three
figures of her title marked his entry into psychoanalysis from psychiatry. (Roudinesco also notes
that Clérambault never liked Lacan very much,
considered him to have "l'esprit faux," and barred
his path to the agrégation for his degree.

J1125. Roudinesco, Elisabeth. "Une histoire en quatre
scissions." Le nouvel observateur. G783, p.
46.

Recounts the controversies that marked Lacan's
career in 1953, 1964, 1969 (the departure of the
Quatrième Groupe from the Ecole freudienne de
Paris), and 1980.

J1126. Roustang, François. "Peut-être: l'affaire
Lacan." G746, p. 2.

Claims that Lacan does not have the authority to
dissolve the Ecole freudienne de Paris on his own,
and concludes that the psychoanalytic experience
cannot survive beyond a minimal hypothesis:
"plusieurs hommes, plusieurs chemins, plusieurs
paroles."

J1127. S., JO. "L'école freudienne en référe; après les
décisions de Dr. Jacques Lacan." Le monde, 23
January 1980, p. 18.

Describes the appeal by several members of the
Ecole freudienne de Paris to Mme. Simone Rozès,
Président du tribunal de Paris, asking her to
appoint a provisional administrator for the EFP
who could convoke a general assembly of the Ecole
to vote on Lacan's decision to dissolve it.
Lawyers for the groups appealing to Rozès were
Claude Crinon and Daniel Soulez-Larivière. Lacan
was represented by Roland Dumas, who argued that a
mere 4 per cent of the six hundred members were
complaining and that their resistance was an
attack on Lacan himself rather than on any legal
principle. Rozès later appointed a Mme. Zécri to
oversee the Ecole; see J1009.

J1128.   Sasaki, Takatsugu. "L'autre japonais." L'âne 4
          (1982): 50.

          Briefly comments on the difficulty of translat-
          ing Lacan's work into Japanese, and illustrates
          the problem by discussing relations between the
          terms for "the Other" and "the other."

J1129.   Schneiderman, Stuart. Response to G934. New York
          Review of Books, 5 April 1978, p. 45.

          Accuses Wollheim of a systematic reading of
          Lacan that tends to collapse psychoanalysis into a
          branch of philosophy and that simply misrepresents
          other aspects of Lacan's work. For Wollheim's
          response, see J1138.

J1130.   Sédat, Jacques. "Le label lacanien." Le monde, 9
          February 1980, p. 2.

          Distinguishes between "Lacanians" who have
          simply related to the person of Lacan through
          transference, and more properly "lacanian" ana-
          lysts whose work is directed towards issues Lacan
          has discussed in his texts and seminars. Sédat
          claims that Lacan dissolved the Ecole freudienne
          de Paris just to get away from the first group
          after they had become an obstacle to the second.

J1131.   Shands, Harley. Abstract of F420. Semiotica 3
          (1971): 280-87.

          Claims that the most remarkable aspect of F420
          is that Wilden has taken it upon himself to be
          such a devoted disciple, but argues that Lacan is
          more generally useful because he underscores the
          centrality of language to human experience despite
          his impenetrable style.

J1132.   Soler, Colette. "Lacan, y est-tu?" Le nouvel
          observateur, 9 March 1981, p. 50.

          Notes the increasing mystery surrounding Lacan's
          withdrawal from public teaching and writing, and
          claims that the real problem continues to be the
          need to choose among several different varieties
          of clinical practice: that of Freud and the more
          contemporary varieties inspired by Lacan. Such a
          necessity requires that psychoanalysts renounce
          literature and the ethic of silence, Soler says,
          and that they submit their practice to the test of
          reason.

J1133.   Sollers, Philippe. "Le gai savoir d'un jésuite
          zen." G784, p. 51.

Reflects on Lacan's mysterious presence, but claims that finally, in the end, Lacan spoke only to be understood.

J1134.   Squire, Corinne. "For Lacan." Radical Philosophy 31 (1982): 43-44.

Responds to G462 and notes that most of Bird's criticisms come back to the charge of Lacan's style being too difficult. Squire describes that as an irrelevant complaint and notes what she calls Lacan's own defense that "resemblance of the unconscious to language must intrude into linguistic explanations" (p. 43). She also claims that Lacan is not just repeating Freud but that he has radically changed psychoanalysis by "writing structuralist linguistics into it," and she attributes most of Bird's misperceptions to his failure to recognize the centrality of language to Lacan's thought.

J1135.   Stein, M. Conrad. Response to G659. Le monde, 2 October 1979, p. 2.

Claims that Lacan has been responsible for generating a legitimate reading of Freud's texts, whatever his excesses. Appears with G699 and J1091.

J1136.   This, Bernard, and Claude This. "Cet étonnant penseur." G574, p. 28.

Praises Lacan's effort to establish a more rigorous discourse for psychoanalysis.

J1137.   Times (London), 11 September 1981, p. 7.

Brief notice of Lacan's death.

J1138.   Wollheim, Richard. Response to responses to G934. New York Review of Books, 5 April 1979, pp. 45-46.

Defends G934 against Schneiderman's criticism (see J1129), and responds to Fleischmann's question (J1052) by explaining that "Lacanian feminism" originally grew out of the French group Psychanalyse et Politique, the anti-anti-psychoanalysis section of Mouvement de la libération des Femmes, which began in 1968. Wollheim also notes the influence of Lacanian ideas on American filmmakers and artists and on much of the work published in the journals m/f, Ideology and Consciousness, and Camera Obscura, all of which are marked by a feminist orientation.

J1139. Woronoff, Denis. "Un peu d'irrespect." Le monde,
        9 February 1980, p. 2.

        Briefly comments on the phenomenon of disrespect
        manifest in the resistance to Lacan even in a time
        when intellectuals are revered.

J1140. Zarifan, Edouard. "Le dernier scandale." G573,
        p. 2.

        Briefly describes Lacan's career and the most
        general theoretical propositions of his work, and
        claims that however uncertain the future, Lacan
        will continue to surprise us.

For Product Safety Concerns and Information please contact our EU
representative GPSR@taylorandfrancis.com
Taylor & Francis Verlag GmbH, Kaufingerstraße 24, 80331 München, Germany